Treffpunkt Deutsch, Seventh Edition

Make language practice fun with Duolingo for Pearson!

More than 150 million people have used **Duolingo's** simple, game-like interface to help them learn a language.

Now Pearson has partnered with **Duolingo** to bring our market-leading content to their award-winning, simple, and fun mobile language-learning app.

Pair **Duolingo** for Pearson with *Treffpunkt Deutsch* and your students will have access to exclusive digital content that is aligned to the textbook and designed to help higher education language learners succeed in the classroom and beyond.

Key benefits

Duolingo for Pearson content helps educators and learners achieve their goals through a learning experience that is:

Relevant

Pearson created exclusive content for Duolingo to accompany our textbooks, so the work that students complete in Duolingo for Pearson aligns with what they're learning and practicing in the classroom. Its variety of activity types provide opportunities for effective contextualized practice.

Simple

Intuitive, bite-sized lessons look and feel like games, to keep students engaged. Finely tuned algorithms evaluate learner responses and tailor the content through spaced repetition. And the app lets instructors track student progress toward specific milestones.

Mobile

Duolingo for Pearson lets students learn and practice on their mobile devices whenever they find the time and wherever inspiration strikes. This mobility, together with push notifications to remind students to practice, encourages consistent daily practice.

Fun

Duolingo for Pearson uses elements of gamification—point scoring and social competition with others—to keep students engaged and moving forward as they acquire new language skills.

Treffpunkt Deutsch

Grundstufe

SEVENTH EDITION

Margaret Gonglewski
The George Washington University

Beverly Moser
Appalachian State University

Cornelius Partsch
Western Washington University

E. Rosemarie Widmaier

Fritz T. Widmaier

Pearson

330 Hudson Street, New York, NY 10013

Executive Editor of Courseware Portfolio Management: Amber Chow
Editor in Chief: Carolyn Merrill
Director of Market Development: Helen Richardson Greenlea
Senior Field Marketing Manager: Mellissa Yokell
World Languages Consultants: Yesha Brill, Doug Brauer, Raúl J. Vázquez López
Product Development Manager: Bridget Funiciello
Managing Editor: Harold Swearingen
Program Manager: Ana Piquinela

Development Editor: Barbara Lasoff
Senior Digital Media Manager: Amy Gibbons
Producer, Production & Digital Studio for MyLab German: Amanda Albert Podeszedlik
Cover Designer: Jill Ort
Cover Photo: sborisov/123RF
Interior Designer: Lumina Datamatics, Inc.
Composition: Lumina Datamatics, Inc.
Printer/Binder: LSC Communications, Willard
Cover Printer: Phoenix Color/Hagerstown
This book was set in 9.5/13 Palatino Lt Pro.

Cataloging-in-Publication data is on file with the Library of Congress.

Printed in the United States of America
16 2023

Student Edition:
ISBN 10: 0-134-79712-4
ISBN 13: 978-0-134-79712-0

Annotated Instructor Edition:
ISBN 10: 0-134-81382-0
ISBN 13: 978-0-134-81382-0

A la Carte Edition:
ISBN 10: 0-134-81392-8
ISBN 13: 978-0-134-81392-9

Brief Contents

Preface   xvi

EK Erste Kontakte   2

1 Jahraus, jahrein   20

2 Freunde   52

3 Familie   84

4 Alltagsleben   114

5 Freizeit – Ferienzeit   148

6 Ein Blick zurück   178

7 Feste und Feiertage   210

8 Wohnen   242

9 Ich und meine Umwelt   272

10 Lust auf Lesen   300

11 Geschichte und Gegenwart   330

12 So ist das Leben   356

Anhang   A-1

Expressions for the Classroom   A-2

German Grammatical Terms   A-3

Useful Word Sets   A-4 – A-10

Grammatical Tables   A-11

Principal Parts of Irregular and Mixed Verbs   A-17

German-English Vocabulary   A-20

Index   A-51

Credits   A-56

Scope and Sequence

Preface

Kapitel	Lernziele	Kultur

Erste Kontakte 2	E.1 Greet someone appropriately in German 4
	E.2 Say how you are doing 4
	E.3 Identify formal and informal ways to say *you* in German 5
	E.4 Discover the countries where German is spoken 7
	E.5 Spell German words and abbreviations 9
	E.6 Recognize sounds and letters different from those in English 10
	E.7 Use German numbers and letters for daily tasks 12
	E.8 Identify words you already know in German 16
	E.9 Learn vocabulary for greeting people and asking for basic information 18
		Kultur 1
		• A first look at the German-speaking cultures 7
		  • Landschaft: Sächsische Schweiz
		  • Politik: Aydan Özoğuz
		  • Windenergie
		  • Innovation
		  • Moderne Musik
		  • Sport: Roger Federer
		  • Autoindustrie: VW
		
		Kultur 2
		• German in English / English in German 16

1
Jahraus, jahrein 20
	1.1 Describe the geography and climate of the German-speaking countries 23
	1.2 Learn vocabulary to talk about the weather and to state your nationality and country 25
	1.3 Distinguish between **ei** and **ie** in German 27
	1.4 Identify people and things using German nouns 28
	1.5 Ask and respond to simple questions 31
	1.6 Compare and contrast university life in the U.S. and the German-speaking countries 36
	1.7 Talk about people and things using pronouns 38
	1.8 Express states and actions 39
	1.9 Understand authentic video of German speakers introducing themselves 43
	1.10 Learn vocabulary to talk about the days of the week, the months, and the seasons; say where you're going 45
		Kultur 1
		• Welcome to countries where German is spoken 23
		  • Landscapes
		  • Climate
		
		Kultur 2
		• Studying at the university 36
		  • Going to college
		  • The Bologna Process
		  • The international campus
		  • Affordable education
		  • Taking classes

2
Freunde 52
	2.1 Compare and contrast sports involvement in Germany and North America 55
	2.2 Learn vocabulary to talk about friends, sports, and hobbies 57
	2.3 Distinguish between long and short **a, e, i, o,** and **u** 59
	2.4 Use the verb **haben** to express ownership 61
	2.5 Express likes, dislikes, and preferences 62
	2.6 State the time 63
	2.7 Compare and contrast online practices in Germany and North America 69
	2.8 Identify the subject in a sentence 70
	2.9 Describe people, places, and things—nominative case 72
	2.10 Understand authentic video of German speakers introducing their friends 78
	2.11 Learn vocabulary to talk about daily activities, clothing, and studying at the university 80
		Kultur 1
		• Sports and clubs in the German-speaking countries 55
		  • Sports at universities
		  • The club system
		  • Two contrasting examples
		  • Fußball: King of sports in Germany
		
		Kultur 2
		• Social media use in Germany 69
		  • What's popular?
		  • The generation gap
		  • Digital natives
		  • Privacy concerns

Sprache im Kontext	Strukturen im Kontext	Wörter: Aussprache, Bedeutung, Form

Hallo!
• Semesterticket 3
• Beim Studentenwerk 3
• Im Hörsaal 5
• Im Konferenzsaal 6
	• Greetings 4
	• **Wie geht's?** 4
	• *You:* **du, ihr,** and **Sie** 5
		• The German alphabet 9
		• Sounds and letters different from English: **ä, ö, ü, ß, ch, v, w, z** 10
		• Numbers in German 12
		  • The numbers from 0 to 1000
		  • Telephone numbers
		  • E-mail and Web addresses
		  • Postal addresses
		
		Wortschatz 18

Vorschau
• Eine Wetterkarte 21
• Semesterbeginn 22
 	
Video-Treff
• Das bin ich 43
 	
Alles zusammen
• Drei Promi-Profile 49
  • Schritt 1:
    Zum Lesen
  • Schritt 2:
    Zum Schreiben
  • Schritt 3:
    Zum Präsentieren
	Kommunikation und Formen 1
	• Nouns 28
	  • Nouns: gender and definite articles
	  • Plural forms: definite articles and nouns
	  • The indefinite articles **ein** and **kein**
	• Word order 31
	  • Position of the verb in yes/no questions
	  • Position of the verb in information questions
	  • Position of the verb in statements
	  • Position of **nicht**
	  • Expressions of time and place
	
	Kommunikation und Formen 2
	• Personal pronouns 38
	• Verbs in the present tense 39
	  • The present tense of **sein**
	  • The verb: infinitive and present tense
		Zur Aussprache
		• German **ei** and **ie** 27
		
		Wortschatz 1 25
		
		Wortschatz 2 45
		• **Wörter unter der Lupe** 47
		  • Cognates
		  • Why German and English are similar: The Angles and Saxons
		
		Sprachnotiz
		• Verb forms in English and German 31
		• The present tense to express future time 42
		• **lernen** vs. **studieren** 47

Vorschau
• Uni-Sport 53
• Freunde – zwei Perspektiven 54
 	
Video-Treff
• Freundschaften 78
 	
Alles zusammen
• Freunde 82
  • Schritt 1:
    Zum Lesen
  • Schritt 2:
    Zum Schreiben
  • Schritt 3:
    Zum Präsentieren
	Kommunikation und Formen 1
	• The present tense of **haben** 61
	• Verb + **gern** or **lieber** 62
	  • Verb + **gern**
	  • Verb + **lieber**
	• Telling Time 63
	  • **Wie spät ist es?**
	  • Official time: the 24-hour clock
	  • Expressions of time referring to parts of the day
	  • More on expressions of time
	
	Kommunikation und Formen 2
	• The nominative case 70
	  • The subject
	  • Articles (*the* and *a*) in the nominative case
	  • The question words **wer** and **was**
	• Articles and adjectives in the nominative case 72
	  • **Der**-words in the nominative case
	  • Nominative endings of adjectives after **der**-words
	  • **Ein**-words in the nominative case: **ein, kein,** and the possessive adjectives
	  • Nominative endings of adjectives after **ein**-words
	  • Nominative endings of unpreceded adjectives
		Zur Aussprache
		• The vowels **a, e, i, o,** and **u** 59
		
		Wortschatz 1 57
		
		Wortschatz 2 80
		• **Wörter unter der Lupe** 81
		  • More on cognates
		
		Sprachnotiz
		• **gern haben** 63
		• Five minutes before and after the half hour 67
		• Omission of the indefinite article 72
		• The subject completion 77

Kapitel	Lernziele	Kultur
3 Familie 84	3.1 Recognize Austria's role in the world, past and present 87 3.2 Learn vocabulary to talk about family 90 3.3 Recognize and pronounce two-vowel sounds 92 3.4 Identify important building blocks of a sentence 93 3.5 Say the things you need or want to buy with accusative forms of *the* and *a* 93 3.6 Retell the life story of an important historical person, using key dates 98 3.7 Describe people, places, and things (accusative case) 100 3.8 Say that you do not have, know, or understand something 102 3.9 Talk about your everyday life using verbs like eating, reading, running, and sleeping 102 3.10 Listen for some details about real people's families 107 3.11 Learn vocabulary to describe people and to talk about what they do 109	**Kultur 1** • Österreich 87 • A rich and diverse history • Austria today • Cultural richness and natural beauty in winter and summer • Music, art, and architecture • Film and literature **Kultur 2** • Mozart: Das musikalische Wunderkind Österreichs 98 • Ein Wunderkind • Erstes Konzert in Wien • Musikalische Sensation in Europa • Arbeit im Orchester und als Komponist • Hochzeit mit Constanze Weber • Mozarts Tod
4 Alltagsleben 114	4.1 Describe Swiss contributions to the international community 118 4.2 Learn vocabulary to talk about food and eating habits 120 4.3 Distinguish between long and short **ä, ö,** and **ü** 121 4.4 Talk about what you can do, have to do, and want to do 122 4.5 Say what you are allowed to do, supposed to do, and what you like/dislike 124 4.6 Build vocabulary by adding prefixes to verbs 126 4.7 Explore a prominent Swiss company with worldwide exports 132 4.8 Express commands or requests and give advice 134 4.9 Create longer sentences with connectors 138 4.10 Understand authentic video of German speakers talking about their typical day 140 4.11 Learn vocabulary to talk about travel and everyday activities 143	**Kultur 1** • Die Schweiz 118 • Diverse cultures, rugged terrain • Ingenuity in industry, Swiss style • Diversity of people and languages • Alpine landscapes + Bustling cities = Diverse Swiss lifestyles • Mileposts in Swiss history **Kultur 2** • Schweizer Innovation: Die Firma Victorinox 132 • Karl Elsener, Schweizer Messerschmied • Das Schweizer Offiziersmesser und die Firma Victorinox • Export in alle Länder: Schweizer Innovation
5 Freizeit – Ferienzeit 148	5.1 Investigate ways of traveling in the German-speaking countries 151 5.2 Learn vocabulary to talk about travel and geography 153 5.3 Recognize and practice the two ways of pronouncing **ch** in German 155 5.4 Talk about people or things without naming them explicitly 156 5.5 State when you are doing something, where you are, and how you get there 158 5.6 Make comparisons 160 5.7 Compare vacationing choices of Germans 164 5.8 Use complex sentence structure 165 5.9 Talk about what and whom you know 168 5.10 Talk about events in the past 168 5.11 Understand authentic video of German speakers talking about their vacations 171 5.12 Learn vocabulary to talk about travel and useful everyday objects 173	**Kultur 1** • Affordable travel 151 • By car, bus, or plane • By train • Affordable accommodations **Kultur 2** • Reisezeit 164 • Vacationing in Germany • Infografik: Die beliebtesten Reiseziele

Sprache im Kontext	Strukturen im Kontext	Wörter: Aussprache, Bedeutung, Form

Vorschau
• Tante Bettinas Mercedes: Ein Familienauto? 85
• Zwei Verwandte sprechen über Tante Bettina 85
 	
Video-Treff
• Meine Familie 107
 	
Alles zusammen
• Meine Familie – mein Stammbaum 112
  • Schritt 1: Zum Lesen
  • Schritt 2: Zum Sprechen
  • Schritt 3: Zum Präsentieren
	Kommunikation und Formen 1
	• Sentence construction 93
	  • The direct object
	• Articles in the accusative case 93
	  • The interrogative pronoun **wen**
	  • **Der**-words in the accusative case
	  • **Ein**-words in the accusative case
	
	Kommunikation und Formen 2
	• More on the accusative case 100
	  • Accusative endings of adjectives preceded by **der**-words
	  • Accusative endings of adjectives preceded by **ein**-words
	  • Accusative endings of unpreceded adjectives
	• More on the position of **nicht** 102
	• Verbs with stem-vowel changes 102
	  • Verbs with stem-vowel changes in the present tense
	  • Verbs with stem-vowel change from **e → i** or **ie**
	  • Verbs with stem-vowel change from **a → ä** or **au → äu**
		Zur Aussprache
		• The dipthongs 92
		
		Wortschatz 1 90
		
		Wortschatz 2 109
		• **Wörter unter der Lupe** 111
		  • More cognates
		
		Sprachnotiz
		• Expressing *favorite* 86
		• Expressing time with the accusative case 97
		• The expression **es gibt** 104

Vorschau
• Wie und warum frühstückt man? 115
• Frühstücksrezept: Schweizer Birchermüsli 116
 	
Video-Treff
• Ein typischer Tag 140
 	
Alles zusammen
• Konkrete Poesie 146
  • Schritt 1: Zum Lesen
  • Schritt 2: Zum Sprechen
  • Schritt 3: Zum Schreiben
	Kommunikation und Formen 1
	• The modal verbs **können, müssen,** and **wollen** 122
	• The modals **dürfen, sollen,** and **mögen** 124
	  • **Möchte** versus **mögen**
	  • Omitting the main verb after modal verbs
	  • Position of **nicht** in sentences with modal verbs
	• Separable-prefix verbs 126
	  • Meaning of separable-prefix verbs
	  • Position of the separable prefix
	  • Position of separable-prefix verbs with modals
	  • Verb-noun and verb-verb combinations
	
	Kommunikation und Formen 2
	• Commands (Imperatives) 134
	  • The **Sie**-imperative
	  • The **ihr**-imperative
	  • The **du**-imperative
	• Word order 138
	  • Position of the verb in independent and dependent clauses
		Zur Aussprache
		• The vowels **ä, ö,** and **ü** 121
		
		Wortschatz 1 120
		
		Wortschatz 2 143
		• **Wörter unter der Lupe** 145
		  • **Denn** versus **dann**
		
		Sprachnotiz
		• The pronoun **man** 116
		• More about separable prefixes 127
		• Position of **nicht** with separable-prefix verbs 129
		• Flavoring particles and **bitte** in imperative sentences 135
		• Word order when the dependent clause comes first 139

Vorschau
• Am Grundlsee 149
 	
Video-Treff
• Ferienzeit 170
 	
Alles zusammen
• Ein Besuch in Leipzig 176
  • Schritt 1: Zum Hören und Sehen
  • Schritt 2: Zum Sprechen
  • Schritt 3: Zum Präsentieren
	Kommunikation und Formen 1
	• Personal pronouns in the accusative case 156
	• Accusative prepositions 158
	• The comparative and superlative 160
	  • The comparative
	  • The superlative
	
	Kommunikation und Formen 2
	• Word order 165
	  • Object clauses introduced by **dass**
	  • Information questions as object clauses
	  • Yes/no questions as object clauses
	• The verb **wissen** 168
	• The simple past of **sein, haben,** and the modal verbs 168
	  • The simple past of **sein**
	  • The simple past of **haben**
	  • The simple past of modal verbs
		Zur Aussprache
		• German **ch** 155
		
		Wortschatz 1 153
		
		Wortschatz 2 173
		• **Wörter unter der Lupe** 175
		  • Predicting gender: the suffixes -or, -ent, -er, -in, -ur, -ment, -(i)um, -chen, -lein
		
		Sprachnotiz
		• Accusative prepositions in contractions 158
		• Adjectives in the comparative and superlative before a noun 163
		• **Wissen** versus **kennen** 168

Kapitel	Lernziele	Kultur

6
 	
Ein Blick zurück 178
	6.1 Understand the history of German immigration to North America 182
	6.2 Learn vocabulary to talk about your heritage 184
	6.3 Form the German **l** sound 185
	6.4 Talk about events in the past 186
	6.5 Present a profile of a recent immigrant to Germany 195
	6.6 Talk more about events in the past 197
	6.7 Rank people and things 201
	6.8 State the date 202
	6.9 Understand authentic video of German speakers talking about their first job 203
	6.10 Learn vocabulary to talk about more everyday activities 205
		Kultur 1
		• German roots in North America 182
		  • German-speaking immigrants in the New World
		  • Bedeutende Deutsch-Amerikaner im 19. Jahrhundert
		
		Kultur 2
		• Explore how migration is impacting the German-speaking countries 195
		  • Krieg und Migration – Wo ist mein Zuhause?
		  • Das Wirtschaftswunder – Deutschland braucht Arbeiter!
		  • Perestroika – Der Ostblock fällt!
		  • Weg vom Krieg – Wir wollen leben!
		  • Menschen mit Migrationshintergrund

7
 	
Feste und Feiertage 210
	7.1 Recognize key holidays and festivals celebrated in the German-speaking countries 213
	7.2 Learn vocabulary to talk about holidays and gifts 216
	7.3 Distinguish the German **r** sound from the English **r** 218
	7.4 Indicate the person *to whom* or *for whom* something is done 218
	7.5 Use expressions that require the dative case 223
	7.6 Identify cultural practices for celebrating birthdays, giving presents, and congratulating people 226
	7.7 Use various expressions for time, manner, and place with dative prepositions 227
	7.8 Describe people, places, and things 234
	7.9 Understand authentic video of German speakers talking about getting gifts 235
	7.10 Learn vocabulary to talk about parties, presents, and everyday items 237
		Kultur 1
		• Feste und Feiertage 213
		  • The Christmas season
		  • In the New Year
		  • Muslim holidays
		  • Easter holidays
		  • Secular holidays
		  • Regional, local, and seasonal festivals
		
		Kultur 2
		• Parties and presents 226
		  • Geburtstag feiern!
		  • Geburtstagsgeschenke
		  • Einladung zum Essen
		  • Glückwünsche

8
 	
Wohnen 242
	8.1 Compare student housing options and amenities in North America and the German-speaking countries 245
	8.2 Learn vocabulary to talk about where and how you live 247
	8.3 Recognize and pronounce various sounds spelled with **s** in German 249
	8.4 Distinguish between **wohin** and **wo** in questions and answers 250
	8.5 Use two-way prepositions to distinguish between *movement toward a destination* and *being at a fixed location* 251
	8.6 Describe moving things from one place to another 253
	8.7 Describe where something is located 254
	8.8 Identify important characteristics and accomplishments of the Bauhaus School 256
	8.9 Say when something occurs 258
	8.10 Create more complex sentences using infinitive phrases 259
	8.11 Indicate possession or relationships 262
	8.12 Understand authentic video of German speakers talking about their living situation 265
	8.13 Learn vocabulary to talk about everyday things at home and in town 268
		Kultur 1
		• Student housing 245
		  • Privat wohnen
		  • Im Studentenheim
		  • Nachhaltig leben
		
		Kultur 2
		• Das Bauhaus: Visionäre Kunsthochschule 256
		  • Der Beginn des Bauhauses
		  • Klare geometrische Linien
		  • Das Bauhaus zieht nach Dessau
		  • Das Ende des Bauhauses
		  • Der Einfluss des Bauhauses
		  • Das Bauhaus nach 100 Jahren

Sprache im Kontext	Strukturen im Kontext	Wörter: Aussprache, Bedeutung, Form

Vorschau
• Ein deutscher Auswanderer 179
• Eine Einwanderin 180
 	
Video-Treff
• Mein erster Job 203
 	
Alles zusammen
• Ein interessantes Experiment 208
  • Schritt 1: Zum Lesen
  • Schritt 2: Zum Spielen
  • Schritt 3: Zum Schreiben
	Kommunikation und Formen 1
	• The present perfect tense 186
	  • The past participle of regular verbs
	  • Position of auxiliary verb and past participle
	  • Position of auxiliary verb and past participle in a dependent clause
	  • Position of **nicht** in sentences in the perfect tense
	  • Irregular verbs in the perfect tense
	  • The verb **sein** as auxiliary in the perfect tense
	
	Kommunikation und Formen 2
	• More on the past 197
	  • The past participle of verbs with separable prefixes
	  • The past participle of verbs with inseparable prefixes
	  • The past participle of mixed verbs
	• Ordinal numbers 201
	• Dates 202
		Zur Aussprache
		• German l 185
		
		Wortschatz 1 184
		
		Wortschatz 2 205
		• **Wörter unter der Lupe** 206
		  • Predicting gender: the suffix **-ung**
		  • Giving language color: expressions using names of parts of the body
		
		Sprachnotiz
		• The perfect tense of **sein** and **haben** 193

Vorschau
• Eine Geburtstagskarte 211
 	
Video-Treff
• Mein bestes Geschenk 235
 	
Alles zusammen
• Herzlichen Glückwunsch! 240
  • Schritt 1: Zum Lesen
  • Schritt 2: Zum Sprechen
  • Schritt 3: Zum Schreiben
	Kommunikation und Formen 1
	• The dative case 218
	  • The dative case: the indirect object
	  • The interrogative pronoun in the dative case: **wem**
	  • Personal pronouns in the dative case
	• More on the dative case 223
	  • Dative verbs
	  • The dative case with adjectives
	  • The dative case in idiomatic expressions
	
	Kommunikation und Formen 2
	• The dative prepositions 227
	  • Contractions
	  • **Nach** versus **zu**
	  • **Aus** versus **von**
	  • The preposition **seit**
	• Dative endings of preceded adjectives 234
	  • Dative endings of unpreceded adjectives
		Zur Aussprache
		• German r 218
		
		Wortschatz 1 216
		
		Wortschatz 2 237
		• **Wörter unter der Lupe** 238
		  • Predicting gender: infinitives used as nouns
		  • Giving language color: expressions using food vocabulary
		
		Sprachnotiz
		• Word order: sequence of objects 223
		• Word order: time/manner/place 228
		• **Wo, woher,** and **wohin** and the dative prepositions 230
		• **Derselbe, dasselbe, dieselbe** 238

Vorschau
• Mitbewohner gesucht! 243
• Wo Studenten wohnen 244
 	
Video-Treff
• Mein Zuhause 266
 	
Alles zusammen
• Das ist mein Zuhause 271
  • Schritt 1: Zum Hören und Sehen
  • Schritt 2: Zum Sprechen
  • Schritt 3: Zum Präsentieren
	Kommunikation und Formen 1
	• **Wohin** and **wo:** a review 250
	• Two-way prepositions 251
	• The verbs **stellen, legen,** and **hängen** 253
	• The verbs **stehen, liegen,** and **hängen** 254
	  • German **an, auf, in,** and English *to*
	
	Kommunikation und Formen 2
	• The two-way prepositions **an, in, vor,** and **zwischen** in time phrases 258
	• Word order 259
	  • Infinitive phrases
	  • Infinitive phrases introduced by **um**
	• The genitive case 262
	  • The interrogative pronoun **wessen**
	  • Genitive endings of preceded adjectives
		Zur Aussprache
		• German s-sounds when appearing as **st** and **sp** 249
		
		Wortschatz 1 247
		
		Wortschatz 2 268
		• **Wörter unter der Lupe** 270
		  • Compound nouns
		  • Giving language color: expressions using house and furniture vocabulary
		
		Sprachnotiz
		• Using **von** + dative instead of the genitive 265

xi

Kapitel	Lernziele	Kultur

9
 	
Ich und meine Umwelt 272
	9.1 Explore the variety of food in the German-speaking countries and learn eating customs 275
	9.2 Learn vocabulary to talk about food and eating out 277
	9.3 Distinguish between the pronunciation of German **s** and **z** 278
	9.4 Talk about actions one does to or for oneself 279
	9.5 Use idiomatic reflexive verbs 285
	9.6 Discuss ways people in German-speaking countries lead healthy, sustainable lifestyles 287
	9.7 Use relative clauses to describe people, places, and things 288
	9.8 Understand authentic video of German speakers talking about what they like to eat and drink 292
	9.9 Learn vocabulary to talk about your daily life and sustainable lifestyles 295
		Kultur 1
		• Im Gasthaus 275
		  • Was ist „deutsches" Essen?
		  • Die internationale Gastronomie
		  • Schnellrestaurants
		  • Im Gasthaus
		  • Wie man isst
		
		Kultur 2
		• Nachhaltig leben! 287
		  • Ein Leben ohne Auto?
		  • Einplanen, reduzieren, wiederverwerten
		  • Und die Mülltrennung!

10
 	
Lust auf Lesen 300
	10.1 Identify several German contributions to communication technology 303
	10.2 Learn words to talk about current media and technology 305
	10.3 Distinguish between German **f, v,** and **w** sounds 307
	10.4 Narrate past events 308
	10.5 Distinguish between three ways to say **when** in German 314
	10.6 Read and understand an authentic German fairy tale from the Brothers Grimm 316
	10.7 Create detailed descriptions of people, places, and things 318
	10.8 Use adjectives to describe people, places, and things 320
	10.9 Understand authentic video of Germans talking about what they like to read 323
	10.10 Learn vocabulary used in classic fairy tales and other types of writing 325
		Kultur 1
		• Kommunikation und neue Technologien 303
		  • 1450: Die Erfindung des Buchdrucks
		  • 1534: Die Entwicklung einer Sprache, die alle verstehen
		  • 1650: Veröffentlichung der ersten Tageszeitung
		  • 1810: Sammlung deutscher Geschichten und Wörter
		
		Kultur 2
		• Ein Märchen der Brüder Grimm: *Der Hase und der Igel* 316

11
 	
Geschichte und Gegenwart 330
	11.1 Identify key features of the Berlin Wall before and after it fell 332
	11.2 Learn vocabulary to talk about the Berlin Wall, past and present 334
	11.3 Pronounce **pf** and **kn** in German 336
	11.4 Describe processes using the passive voice 337
	11.5 Describe people, places, and things using past participles 339
	11.6 Identify and order important dates in German history since 1918 341
	11.7 Expand the meaning of verbs with prepositions 343
	11.8 Ask questions using prepositions: **wo**-compounds 346
	11.9 Make statements using prepositions: **da**-compounds 347
	11.10 Understand authentic video of German speakers talking about their experiences in the former East Germany (GDR) 349
	11.11 Learn vocabulary to talk about German history and people's reactions to it 351
		Kultur 1
		• Die Berliner Mauer 332
		  • 1949 und der Kalte Krieg: Warum baute man die Mauer?
		  • 1961–1975: Erst Stacheldraht, dann Beton
		  • Bis 1989: Der Todesstreifen. An der Mauer Schießbefehl!
		  • Die Mauer heute: Was bleibt?
		
		Kultur 2
		• Kleine deutsche Chronik: 1918 bis heute 341

Sprache im Kontext	Strukturen im Kontext	Wörter: Aussprache, Bedeutung, Form

Vorschau
- Im Restaurant 273

Video-Treff
- Was ich gern esse und trinke 292

Alles zusammen
- Leben Sie umweltfreundlich? 298
  - Schritt 1: Zum Lesen
  - Schritt 2: Zum Sprechen
  - Schritt 3: Zum Kreieren

Kommunikation und Formen 1
- Reflexive pronouns 279
  - Reflexive pronouns in the accusative case
  - Reflexive pronouns in the dative case
  - Reflexive pronouns used to express **each other**
- Reflexive verbs 285

Kommunikation und Formen 2
- Relative Clauses 288
  - Relative clauses and relative pronouns in English
  - Relative clauses and relative pronouns in German: Subject forms
  - Relative clauses and relative pronouns: Object and indirect object forms

Zur Aussprache
- Pronouncing German **s** and **z** 278

Wortschatz 1 277

Wortschatz 2 295
- **Wörter unter der Lupe** 297
  - Predicting gender: agent nouns

Sprachnotiz
- The relative pronoun in the genitive case 292

Vorschau
- Historische Figuren 301

Video-Treff
- Meine Lieblingslektüre 323

Alles zusammen
- Nun eine Sage 328
  - Schritt 1: Zum Lesen und Sprechen
  - Schritt 2: Zum Schreiben
  - Schritt 3: Zum Sprechen

Kommunikation und Formen 1
- The simple past tense 308
  - The simple past of regular verbs
  - The simple past of irregular verbs
  - The simple past of mixed verbs
- **Wann, als,** and **wenn** 314

Kommunikation und Formen 2
- The relative pronoun as object of a preposition 318
- A review of adjective endings 320
  - Adjectives preceded by **der**-words
  - Adjectives preceded by **ein**-words
  - Unpreceded adjectives

Zur Aussprache
- German **f, v,** and **w** 307

Wortschatz 1 305

Wortschatz 2 325
- **Wörter unter der Lupe** 326
  - Words as chameleons: **als**
  - Giving language color: expressions using names of animals

Sprachnotiz
- Principal parts of verbs 311
- The simple past of separable-prefix verbs 312
- German **n**-nouns 321

Vorschau
- Extrablatt: Berliner Morgenpost 331

Video-Treff
- So war's in der DDR 349

Alles zusammen
- Zeitreise per Fahrrad (auf dem Mauerweg): ein Video 354
  - Schritt 1: Zum Ansehen
  - Schritt 2: Zum Schreiben
  - Schritt 3: Zum Präsentieren

Kommunikation und Formen 1
- The passive voice 337
  - Distinguishing between active and passive voice
  - Use of the passive voice in present tense
  - Use of the passive voice in the past tense
- Describing people, places, and things 339
  - The past participle used as an adjective

Kommunikation und Formen 2
- Special verb-preposition combinations 343
- Asking questions about things or ideas using **wo**-compounds 346
  - **Wo**-compounds as question words
- Use **da**-compounds to refer to things and ideas already mentioned 347
  - **Da**-compounds

Zur Aussprache
- The consonant clusters **pf** and **kn** 336

Wortschatz 1 334

Wortschatz 2 351
- **Wörter unter der Lupe** 352
  - Words as chameleons: **gleich**
  - Predicting gender: the suffixes **-heit** and **-keit**

Sprachnotiz
- Using **eigentlich** and **überhaupt** to intensify expressions 335
- Using **von** to indicate the agent in a passive sentence 339

Kapitel	Lernziele	Kultur

12
 	
So ist das Leben 356
	12.1 Discuss the status of women in Germany 359
	12.2 Learn vocabulary to talk about future work, hopes, and dreams 362
	12.3 Learn to pronounce glottal stops in German 364
	12.4 Talk about contrary-to-fact situations 364
	12.5 Express wishes and polite requests 368
	12.6 Make polite requests 369
	12.7 Explore opportunities for civic engagement using German 370
	12.8 Talk about how things might have been 372
	12.9 Use common genitive prepositions 374
	12.10 Understand authentic video about how to spend a windfall fortune 376
	12.11 Learn vocabulary used to apply for volunteer or work opportunities 378
		Kultur 1
		• Frauen im 21. Jahrhundert 359
		  • Die Verfassungen
		  • Frauen zwischen Beruf und Familie
		  • Frauen in der Politik
		
		Kultur 2
		• Freiwilligendienst in Deutschland und Europa 370
		  • Was ist Freiwilligendienst?
		  • Welche Bereiche gibt es beim Freiwilligendienst?
		  • Kann man auch im Ausland dienen?
		  • Wollt ihr mehr über den Freiwilligendienst lernen?

Anhang A-1

- Expressions for the Classroom A-2
  - What you might say or ask A-2
  - What your instructor might say or ask A-2

- German Grammatical Terms A-3

- Useful Word Sets A-4
  - Studienfächer A-4
  - Jobs und Berufe A-4
  - Hobbys und Sport A-5
  - Musikinstrumente A-6
  - Kleidungsstücke A-6
  - Accessoires A-7
  - Essen und Trinken A-7
  - Länder A-8
  - Sprachen A-9
  - Persönliche Merkmale A-9
  - Freundliche Ausdrücke A-10

- Grammatical Tables A-11

- Principal Parts of Irregular and Mixed Verbs A-17

- German-English Vocabulary A-20

- Index A-51

- Credits A-56

Sprache im Kontext	Strukturen im Kontext	Wörter: Aussprache, Bedeutung, Form

Vorschau
- Annett Louisan: „Eve" (ein Lied) 357

Video-Treff
- Wenn ich im Lotto gewinnen würde, … 376

Alles zusammen
- Mein Lebenslauf 380
  - Schritt 1: Zum Lesen
  - Schritt 2: Zum Schreiben
  - Schritt 3: Zum Sprechen

Kommunikation und Formen 1
- The subjunctive in contrary-to-fact situations 364
  - Present-time subjunctive
  - **Würde** + infinitive
- The subjunctive in wishes and polite requests 368
- The subjunctive in polite questions 369

Kommunikation und Formen 2
- The subjunctive in contrary-to-fact situations in the past 372
  - Past-time subjunctive
  - **Haben** and **sein** in past-time subjunctive
- Expressing cause, opposition, alternatives, and simultaneity 374
  - Genitive prepositions

Zur Aussprache
- The glottal stop 364

Wortschatz 1 362

Wortschatz 2 378
- **Wörter unter der Lupe** 379
  - The adjective suffix -**los**
  - The adjective suffix -**bar**

Sprachnotiz
- The future tense 364
- **Kommen** and **gehen** in present-time subjunctive 369

Preface

We are pleased to present you with the seventh edition of *Treffpunkt Deutsch*, an introductory program with a student-centered, communicative approach to teaching German. Since its first edition, *Treffpunkt Deutsch* has enabled students to use the language actively and successfully. The title *Treffpunkt* reflects a major objective of the program: to transform the classroom into a **Treffpunkt**, a *meeting place*, where students get to know one another, as well as the German-speaking countries, by using German.

We are indebted to our loyal following of instructors and students from the previous six editions. The changes to the seventh edition stem from valuable feedback they provided and from the authors' commitment to provide an up-to-date view of the German-speaking world that engages students in every chapter.

What's New in the Seventh Edition?

- **Streamlined, shorter** *Vorschau* **sections** orient students more quickly to each chapter theme. Many *Vorschau* sections are based on texts from daily life (e.g., tweets, a recipe for a favorite Swiss breakfast, a menu from a popular student restaurant).

- **Two (rather than one)** *Kultur* **sections per chapter** intensify *Treffpunkt's* integration of culture. Now, both full-length sections have activities that encourage greater reflection on cultural products, practices, and perspectives of the German-speaking world. Topics include:
  - studying in Germany (e.g., the affordability of university study, the new Bachelor curriculum);
  - the use of social media and other technologies among students;
  - affordable travel and accommodations, especially for students;
  - recent migration to Germany, featuring an oral history of a new citizen with a migration background;
  - unique festivals that span the German-speaking countries;
  - green living, leading a sustainable lifestyle;
  - service-learning opportunities for young people in Germany and Europe;
  - simple résumé writing for students ready to take the next step of studying or working abroad.

- The pronunciation section *Zur Aussprache* **now appears early in each chapter,** as suggested by our readers.

- *Wortschatz* sections contain *Treffpunkt's* popular practice of new vocabulary. **New picture-based activities in** *Wörter im Kontext* entice students to explore the meaning of new vocabulary and phrases via realia.

- *Alles zusammen,* **a new, final section of the chapter,** provides thematically connected, hands-on tasks that show students what they can already do with the language. This three-part modified Integrated Performance Assessment is shorter and more engaging than the earlier *Zusammenschau* section. Students read a text or watch an authentic video, talk about this with a partner or group, and present their new "take" on the topic, orally or in writing. Some tasks involve online research (e.g., research a prominent newcomer to Germany); others encourage students to use simple media (eg., make a video tour of where you live). These activities help students synthesize and appreciate the progress they are making as they learn to communicate in German.

- Also new, easy-to-find **student notes** alert students to interesting aspects of German (*Ach so!*), point out easy-to-confuse elements (*Achtung!*) and offer helpful learning tips (*Lerntipp!*)

- **New Integrated Performance Assessments (IPAs)** and *Can-Do Statements* in **MyLab German**™. Driven by research and shaped by experts from the field, **four full-fledged Integrated Performance Assessments** and *NCSSFL-ACTFL Can-Do Statements* help instructors assess learners' progress towards performance goals. As students progress through the course, instructors can assign IPA tasks to complete online every three chapters. Each IPA is based on authentic materials and focuses on real-life contexts that students find engaging and meaningful. After each IPA, students complete a self-assessment based on the *Can-Do Statements*. This helps students track their own progress towards proficiency goals. Both features are available online in **MyLab German**™ after every three chapters.

Hallmark Features of *Treffpunkt Deutsch*

Treffpunkt Deutsch builds students' ability to communicate in German in many ways: to listen to and understand spoken German and read short texts, to interact with others in brief interchanges (including with native speakers), and to write simple texts that convey an individual point of view.

- In **speaking and writing activities,** students are guided from contextualized, form-focused exercises to more open-ended activities in which they express individual preferences and viewpoints. Speaking and writing tasks synthesize material, add depth to chapter content, and provide opportunities to communicate in real-life contexts.

- **Listening practice** is provided via *Video-Treff*. Short video segments put students face-to-face with real speakers from the target culture, adding both visual and cultural interest to listening comprehension activities.

- **Reading practice** encourages students to negotiate meaning in German in realia (charts/graphs, ads, etc.) and informational texts, as well as short literary excerpts, poems, and fairy tales. These varied genres respond to multiple learning styles and interests and expose students to a broad range of models in German.

- **Vocabulary development** is crucial to this communication-focused program. *Treffpunkt Deutsch* provides two vocabulary lists in each chapter, organized according to parts of speech. Within these sections, words are grouped semantically. The lists are followed by exercises (*Wörter im Kontext*) that reinforce the new lexical items and support growing communication abilities even at the very beginning level.

- **Engagement with culture** is a cornerstone of *Treffpunkt Deutsch*. The program highlights significant events and accomplishments as well as the daily life of those living in the German-speaking countries today. Two in-depth *Kultur* sections per chapter provide insights into the ways our cultures are similar yet different, and examine differences between German, Austrian, and Swiss cultures.

- **Pronunciation practice** is linked with vocabulary learning in the *Zur Aussprache* section towards the start of each chapter. The fun activities help students develop strong pronunciation skills that enhance their ability to communicate effectively. Direct comparisons to English help students build on what they know.

The process-oriented, student-centered approach in *Treffpunkt Deutsch* is aligned with the 2015 *World Readiness Standards for Language Learning*, which have guided our work. The three modes of communication (interpretive, interpersonal, presentational) provide a framework for activities throughout *Treffpunkt Deutsch*, starting with each realia-based *Vorschau* section. Through varied authentic materials, students encounter the cultures of the German-speaking countries and learn to communicate in meaningful, real-life contexts. They are encouraged to draw cross-cultural comparisons and to connect their study of German language and culture with other disciplines and experiences. Opportunities for students to interact with German-speaking communities, for example via activities involving online research, connect students virtually with the countries where German is spoken.

Organization of *Treffpunkt Deutsch*

Treffpunkt Deutsch consists of an introduction (*Erste Kontakte*) and twelve full-length chapters. *Erste Kontakte* is the warm-up for the course. Each chapter follows a consistent structure with **eight** main sections:

- **Vorschau.** Each chapter opens with engaging realia (such as a poster or an ad) to introduce vocabulary and structures connected to the chapter theme in natural, idiomatic German. Follow-up activities check comprehension and encourage immediate use of new vocabulary and forms.

- **Kultur 1** and **2.** These sections present a cultural reading or authentic text on the chapter theme with an activity where students engage with the topic. The transition to German for **Kultur** sections starts in the secound **Kultur** section of Chapter 3. By Chapter 9, all **Kultur** sections are presented entirely in German.

- **Wortschatz 1** and **2.** Chapter vocabulary appears in two lists containing useful, high-frequency words related to the chapter theme. The lists are followed by *Wörter im Kontext* exercises that encourage students to use the new words in a variety of contexts. **Wortschatz 2** concludes with the *Wörter unter der Lupe* section, which takes a closer look at words by discussing cognates, words that change their meaning in different contexts, word families, compound words, suffixes that signal gender, and idiomatic expressions.

- **Zur Aussprache** provides engaging audio-based pronunciation activities.

- **Kommunikation und Formen 1** and **2.** Clear, concise grammar explanations focus on basic structures essential to communication. Exercises for pairs and group work, often based on photos or drawings, move from guided, contextualized practice to open-ended, personalized activities.

- **Video-Treff.** The *Treffpunkt Deutsch* video presents dynamic, on-the-scene interviews with young Germans. The video provides visual context to support comprehension of unscripted language. This offers a direct window into German-speaking cultures at a level manageable to introductory students.

- **Sprachnotizen.** These brief notes call students' attention to idiomatic features of colloquial German as well as less important grammar points helpful in students' developing knowledge of German.

- **Alles zusammen.** In this final section of the chapter, students integrate their language skills to interpret a text or video, investigate some aspect of the text or text's topic on their own, and create and present a response to the topic, orally or in writing.

Other Program Components
Student Resources

Student Activities Manual (SAM). The Student Activities Manual provides meaningful and communicative writing, listening, and speaking practice, incorporating the vocabulary and structures introduced in each chapter and offering additional skill-building activities. The SAM is available in electronic format via **MyLab German™**.

Answer Key for the Student Activities Manual. This Answer Key is available for optional inclusion in course packages; it includes answers for all discrete and short-answer exercises in the SAM.

Audio for the Student Activities Manual. Students and instructors have access to the audio recordings for the SAM on **MyLab German™**.

Treffpunkt Deutsch Video. The well-loved video for *Treffpunkt*, featuring unscripted interviews with young native speakers in the places where they live, work, and play, can be accessed on **MyLab German™**.

Audio for the Text. All audio materials from the text, including materials from the *Vorschau, Wortschatz, Zur Aussprache*, and *Alles zusammen* sections, are available on **MyLab German™**.

Instructor Resources

Annotated Instructor's Edition (AIE). Extensive marginal notes make the AIE an indispensible resource for the novice and experienced instructor alike. They offer warm-up activities, cultural information, answer keys, and suggestions for using and expanding activities and materials in the textbook. Instructor's annotations also include the scripts for listening sections for ease in teaching.

Instructor's Resource Manual (IRM). The IRM provides *Treffpunkt Deutsch* instructors with an extensive array of resources, including sample syllabi for one-, two-, and three-term course sequences, along with numerous sample lesson plans. The IRM is available in downloadable format via the **Instructor's Resource Center** and **MyLab German™**.

Testing Program. A flexible testing program allows instructors to customize tests by selecting the modules they wish to use or by changing individual items. This complete testing program, available in a downloadable electronic format via the **Instructor's Resource Center** and **MyLab German™**, includes quizzes, chapter tests, and comprehensive examinations that test listening, reading, and writing skills as well as cultural knowledge.

Audio for the Testing Program. All listening tests are recorded for the instructor's use in a classroom or laboratory setting on **MyLab German™**.

Online Resources

Instructor's Resource Center (IRC). The IRC can be found at http://www.pearsonhighered.com and provides password-protected instructor access to the Instructor's Resource Manual and Testing Program, available in a downloadable format.

MyLab German™. Part of the world's leading collection of online homework, tutorial, and assessment products, Pearson's **MyLab Languages** program is designed with a single purpose in mind: to improve the results of all higher education students, one student at a time.

Revolutionary and evolutionary: Created by and for language instructors and learners, and based on years of research and data collection from over one million users, **MyLab German™** brings together a wide array of language learning tools and resources in one convenient, easily navigable site. The *Treffpunkt Deutsch* **MyLab German™** course includes an interactive version of the student text, an online *Student Activities Manual*, and all audio and video materials. *Vocabulary and Grammar tutorials, English Grammar Readiness checks*, and practice tests can be personalized by the instructor to meet the unique needs of individual students. Instructors can use the system to, among many other things, create assignments, set grading parameters, review and create student synchronous video and asynchronous audio activities, and provide feedback on student work. For more information, visit us at www.pearson.com/mylab/languages.

Acknowledgments

We would like to express our gratitude to the many instructors and coordinators who took time from their busy schedules to assist us with comments and suggestions over the course of the development of all seven editions of *Treffpunkt Deutsch*.

Rita Abercrombie, *Baylor University*
Tim Altanero, *Austin Community College*
Keith Anderson, *St. Olaf College*
Reinhard Andress, *St. Louis University*
William Anthony, *Northwestern University*
John Austin, *Georgia State University*
Linda Austin, *Glendale Community College*
Thomas Bacon, *Texas Tech University*
Linda Daves Baldwin, *Washington College*
Katharina Barbe, *Northern Illinois University*
Gamin Bartle, *University of Alabama*
Gary Bartlett, *Normandale Community College*
Claudia A. Becker, *Loyola University*
Christel Bell, *University of Alabama*
Helga Bister-Broosen, *University of North Carolina*
John M. Brawner, *University of California, Irvine*
Brigitte Breitenbücher, *Elgin Community College*
Johannes Bruestle, *Grossmont College*
Joan Keck Campbell, *Dartmouth College*
Belinda Carstens-Wickham, *Southern Illinois University*
Heidi Crabbs, *Fullerton College*
Rudolph Debernitz, *Golden West College*
Sharon M. DiFino, *University of Florida*
Thomas John DiNapoli, *Louisiana State University*
Christopher Dolmetsch, *Marshall University*
Randall Donaldson, *Loyola University Maryland*
Esther Enns-Connolly, *University of Calgary*
Nikolaus Euba, *University of California, Berkeley*
Sigrid Fertig, *SUNY Buffalo*
Judith Fogle, *Pasadena City College*
Catherine C. Fraser, *Indiana University, Bloomington*
Rachel Freudenburg, *Boston College*
Juergen Froehlich, *Pomona College*
Harold P. Fry, *Kent State University*
Henry Fullenwider, *University of Kansas*
Johnathan Gajdos, *Monterey Peninsula College*
Anna Glapa-Grossklag, *College of the Canyons*
Andrea Golato, *University of Illinois at Urbana-Champaign*
Peter Gölz, *University of Victoria*
Anne-Katrin Gramberg, *Auburn University*
Christian Hallstein, *Carnegie Mellon University*
Barbara Harding, *Georgetown University*
Beverly Harris-Schenz, *University of Pittsburgh*
Frauke A. Harvey, *Baylor University*
Elizabeth Hasler, *Xavier University*
Gisela Hoecherl-Alden, *University of Maine*
Robert G. Hoeing, *SUNY Buffalo*

Bradley A. Holtman, *Mansfield University*
Deborah L. Horzen, *University of Central Florida*
Carrie N. Jackson, *Pennsylvania State University*
Charles James, *University of Wisconsin, Madison*
William Keel, *University of Kansas*
George Koenig, *SUNY Oswego*
Richard Alan Korb, *Columbia University*
Arndt A. Krüger, *Trent University*
John A. Lalande II, *University of Illinois, Chicago*
Alan H. Lareau, *University of Wisconsin, Oshkosh*
Martina Lindseth, *University of Wisconsin-Eau Claire*
Dr. Richard March, *Northern Virginia Community College*
Betty Mason, *Valencia Community College*
Dennis R. McCormick, *University of Montana*
Laura McGee, *Western Kentucky University*
Robert Mollenauer, *University of Texas*
Juan Carlos Morales, *Miami Palmetto Sr. High School*
Kamakshi P. Murti, *Middlebury College*
Eva Margareta Norling, *Bellevue College*
Margaret Peischl, *Virginia Commonwealth University*
Manfred Prokop, *University of Alberta*
Robert C. Reimer, *University of North Carolina, Charlotte*
Richard C. Reinholdt, *Orange Coast College*
Michael D. Richardson, *Ithaca College*
Veronica Richel, *University of Vermont*
Roger Russi, *Middlebury College*
Gerd Schneider, *Syracuse University*
Tracy Shepherd, *Lone Star College –North Harris*
Ruth Sondermann, *Boston College*
Carolyn Wolf Spanier, *Mt. San Antonio College*
Bruce H. Spencer, *University of Iowa*
Christine Spreizer, *Queens College CUNY*
Thomas Stefaniuk, *Florida Gulf Coast University*
Gerhard Strasser, *Pennsylvania State University*
Michael L. Thompson, *University of Pennsylvania*
Suzanne Toliver, *University of Cincinnati*
Walter Tschacher, *Chapman University*
Hulya Unlu, *Pennsylvania State University*
Helga Van Iten, *Iowa State University*
Janet Van Valkenburg, *University of Michigan*
Wilfried Voge, *University of California, Los Angeles*
Morris Vos, *Western Illinois University*
Elizabeth I. Wade, *University of Wisconsin, Oshkosh*
Susan Wansink, *Virginia Wesleyan College*
William Garrett Welch, *West Texas A&M University*
Hendrik H. Winterstein, *University of Houston*
Margrit V. Zinggeler, *Eastern Michigan University.*

We thank Pearson Education for its seventh edition of *Treffpunkt Deutsch*. We are grateful to our faithful Barbara Lasoff, our Developmental Editor, who shepherded this edition through a tight schedule and still kept her patience and helpful attitude. Thanks also go to Karen Hohner for her careful copyediting of the manuscript and to Harriet Dishman for her coordinating of many aspects of the revision, including the Integrated Performance Assessments. Enormous thanks to Ohlinger Publishing Services' Carolyn Merrill, Editor-in-Chief, and Harold Swearingen, Managing Editor, for their work on this project. Our heartfelt appreciation goes to Ana Piquinela of Ohlinger Publishing for her take-charge attitude and hard work when it really counted, and for her "equal-opportunity harassment" when useful in order to nudge us through tight deadlines. Her always cheerful, ever helpful attitude (and encouragement with jars of chocolate hazelnut spread) were gifts we noticed and appreciated. We thank Jennifer Feltri-George for her contributions as Program Manager.

We also thank Pearson's Amber Chow, Executive Editor of Courseware Portfolio Management, for her leadership, and Amanda Albert Podeszedlik, Producer, Production & Digital Studio for **MyLab German**™, for her work in the development of this book's **MyLab German**™.

Katie Ostler, Project Manager, and Katy Gabel, Senior Project Manager, at Lumina Datamatics Inc., have our thanks for diligently managing the turnover of all materials, helping to keep us organized. We also thank Lumina Datamatics Inc. for the new interior design of this edition. We thank the marketing and sales team for their enthusiasm in promoting the book!

The seventh edition of *Treffpunkt Deutsch* benefits greatly from the new ancillary materials developed by talented colleagues: Our thanks go to Sandra Alfers for her work on the Student Activities Manual and to Juan Carlos Morales for developing the engaging Integrated Performance Assessments, brand-new to this edition. Thanks, five times (!) to Patricia Lanners-Kaminski, for letting us feature her in Chapter 6, for voice-recording and editing her "story," and for completing major updates to the Student Activities Manual, the Testing Program, and the Instructors Resource Manual. A special thanks also goes to Jane Pittman, who has been involved from the beginning with *Video-Treff*, for giving this edition's work a terrific update.

We are indebted to our family members, friends, and colleagues who provided photos and art for this edition. In particular, we give a big shout out to Beth Lewis for the many beautiful graphics she did for this edition, along with Bess Gonglewski, Emily Sieg, and Rich Robin for their help creating art items. For their eagerness to provide requested photos and other realia from Europe, we thank especially Andrew Dexter, Alice Gonglewski, Julia Harris, and Silvia Weko. And to Karin Baumgartner, thanks for her voice recordings in Chapter 4 which feature her native Switzerland.

Finally, we gratefully dedicate *Treffpunkt Deutsch* to our students and fellow German teachers and also to our families. Their unconditional support for us made our work on this edition possible, and their enthusiasm for the final product made this work enjoyable, too.

About the Authors

Margaret Gonglewski

Margaret Gonglewski is Associate Professor of German and International Affairs at the George Washington University in Washington, DC, where she directs the German language program. She earned her PhD from Georgetown University. She has published articles on topics such as effective uses of technology in language teaching and learning, business language teaching methodology, and critical issues in materials selection and creation. From 2004 to 2008, she served as the first Director of the George Washington University Language Center, initiating innovative programming as well as support and recognition for language faculty. She has been awarded numerous grants for developing materials to assist faculty in teaching business language and culture, and she is currently Business Language Program Coordinator for the university's Center for International Business Education and Research, funded by a grant from the U.S. Department of Education. She has received university awards for innovation in teaching and for excellence in undergraduate advising.

Beverly Moser

Beverly Moser is Professor of German at Appalachian State University in Boone, North Carolina. She received her PhD from Georgetown University, where her dissertation received the Emma Marie Birkmaier award from ACTFL and the Modern Language Journal for its contribution to foreign language education. A specialist in reading and writing pedagogy for German as a foreign language, she publishes teaching materials that develop students' literacy skills. Her most recent work adapts authentic youth literature for the college classroom. Dr. Moser served as Principal and Co-Principal Investigator on three grants funded by the U.S. Department of Education for projects directed at improving the quality and scope of foreign language teaching in the K–12 or college setting, on strengthening interdisciplinary connections for all foreign languages, and on teacher development. She has served as the Director of a large-scale German program, helping graduate students through their first few semesters teaching college-level German, and she regularly conducts methodology workshops for pre-collegiate and postsecondary instructors of German, French, Spanish, and English as a Second Language.

Cornelius Partsch

Cornelius Partsch is a native of Landstuhl and grew up in the nearby Saarland in southwestern Germany. He is Professor of German at Western Washington University in Bellingham, Washington. In 2013, the German Section at Western Washington was recognized as a National Center of Excellence by the American Association of Teachers of German (AATG). He received his PhD from Brown University. He previously taught German at Hamilton College, Colby College, Smith College, and Mount Holyoke College, as well as at the German summer schools at the University of Rhode Island, Middlebury College, and Portland State University. Dr. Partsch is the author of *Schräge Töne. Jazz und Unterhaltungsmusik in der Kultur der Weimarer Republik* (Stuttgart: J. B. Metzler) and has published articles on various aspects of 20th- and 21st-century German popular culture. His interest in language pedagogy lies in curriculum design, assessment, and the teaching of culture using film, music, and fiction. He served as a teacher/trainer in the Goethe Institute's trainer network for the western United States from 2007–2011 and is currently *Ortslektor* for the German Academic Exchange Service (DAAD).

Erste Kontakte

Studenten in Wien

Learning Objectives

E.1 Greet someone appropriately in German

E.2 Say how you are doing

E.3 Identify formal and informal ways to say *you* in German

E.4 Discover the countries where German is spoken

E.5 Spell German words and abbreviations

E.6 Recognize sounds and letters different from those in English

E.7 Use German numbers and letters for daily tasks

E.8 Identify words you already know in German

E.9 Learn vocabulary for greeting people and asking for basic information

E.1 Hallo!

Semesterticket

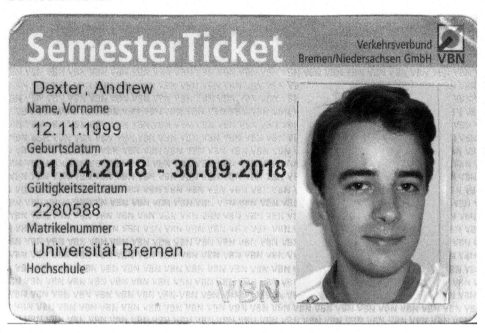

Semesters at German universities usually run from mid-October to mid-February **(Wintersemester)** and from mid-April through mid-July **(Sommersemester).**

E-1 Semesterticket. Look at this public transportation pass from an exchange student living in Germany. What can you learn about him by looking carefully at his pass?

1. The student's name is: _____
2. He's studying at: _____
3. His ticket is valid for the months of: _____
4. His birthday is: _____

The Semesterticket costs about $80 for six months and lets students get around town practically for free.

))) Beim Studentenwerk

*Christian Lohner and Asha Singh meet at the student center at the **Humboldt-Universität** in Berlin. Listen to their conversation.*

____ Hallo, ich heiße Christian, Christian Lohner.

____ Und ich bin Asha Singh. Woher kommst du, Christian?

____ Ich komme aus Hamburg. Und du, woher bist du?

____ Ich bin aus Mumbai.

E-2 Wir lernen einander kennen. *(Getting to know each other.)* Walk around the classroom and get to know as many classmates as possible. In the German-speaking countries, people often shake hands when greeting each other.

Student 1: Hallo, ich heiße _____.
           Wie heißt du?

Student 2: Ich heiße _____.

Student 1: Ich komme aus _____.
           Woher bist du?

Student 2: Ich bin aus _____.
           (Ich bin auch° aus _____.)   *too*

Greetings

E.1 Greet someone appropriately in German

In the German-speaking countries, there are various ways of saying hello and good-bye. In North America it is customary for people to shake hands when they first meet each other. In the German-speaking countries, people often shake hands whenever they meet or say good-bye.

> Young German speakers commonly use the English "Hi" as an informal greeting.

	FORMAL	LESS FORMAL	
GREETINGS	Guten Tag!	Tag!	*Hello!*
	Guten Morgen!	Morgen!	*Good morning!*
	Guten Abend!	'n Abend!	*Good evening!*
		Hallo!	
		Grüß dich!*	*Hello! Hi!*
FAREWELLS	Auf Wiedersehen!	Wiedersehen!	*Good-bye!*
		Tschüss!	
		Ciao!	*Bye! So long!*
	Gute Nacht!		*Good night!*

*Use for greeting just one person.

Some regional variations for informal greetings (*Hello!* or *Hi!*): **Grüß Gott!** (*Southern German*), **Moin!** (*Northern German*), **Grüezi!** (*Swiss*), **Servus!** (*Austrian*).

E-3 Grußformeln. Identify the most appropriate greeting or farewell for each situation.

1. One morning, you run into your German professor on campus.
2. At an evening concert, you meet two exchange students from Austria.
3. At an evening lecture, you are introduced to a visiting scholar from Berlin.
4. At a German Club event one afternoon, you say hello to a German student you know from a class.
5. After an afternoon class, you say good-bye to fellow students from your German course.

a. Servus!
b. Tschüss!
c. Grüß dich!
d. Guten Abend!
e. Guten Morgen!

Wie geht's?

E.2 Say how you are doing

E-4 Wie geht's? Looking at the scale, decide how you would respond to this question today. Then ask a few classmates the question **Wie geht's?** to find out how they're doing.

))) Im Hörsaal

Ali knows Martin and Claudia, but he hasn't met Claudia's roommate Stephanie yet. Listen as Claudia introduces them after class in the lecture hall.

MARTIN: *(to Claudia and Stephanie)* Hallo, ihr zwei! Wie geht's?
CLAUDIA: Super. Du, Ali, das ist Stephanie, meine Mitbewohnerin.
ALI: Grüß dich, Stephanie.
STEPHANIE: Hallo, Ali.
MARTIN: Geht ihr jetzt° auch in die Mensa°?
CLAUDIA: Nein, noch nicht.
MARTIN: Na, dann tschüss, ihr zwei.
STEPHANIE: Ciao!

now / university cafeteria

E-5 Grüß dich! Walk up to two classmates and greet one by name and ask how she/he is. She/He will answer your question and then introduce the other classmate to you. Then continue finding new classmates to introduce each other to.

S1: Grüß dich, _____, wie geht's?

S2: Super. Du, _____ (name of S1), das ist _____ (name of S3).

S1: *(to S3)* Grüß dich, _____.

S1: Woher kommst du, _____?

S1: Ich komme aus _____.

S3: *(to S1)* Hallo, _____.

S3: Ich bin aus _____. Und du?

> Try varying your greeting and your response to the question **Wie geht's?**

You: *du, ihr,* and *Sie*

E.3 Identify formal and informal ways to say *you* in German

German has more than one way of saying *you*. The familiar **du** is used to address family members, close friends, children, and teenagers up to about age sixteen. It is also used among students, even if they are not close friends. The plural form of **du** is **ihr.**

The formal **Sie** is used for addressing adults who are not close friends. **Sie** is always capitalized and does not change in the plural.

	Singular	Plural
FAMILIAR	du	ihr
FORMAL	Sie	Sie

E-6 Du, ihr oder Sie? Indicate how you would address the following people in a German-speaking setting.

	du	ihr	Sie
1. your professor	_____	_____	_____
2. your roommate	_____	_____	_____
3. your roommate's parents	_____	_____	_____
4. two classmates	_____	_____	_____
5. a doctor	_____	_____	_____
6. your friend's dog	_____	_____	_____
7. a salesperson in a clothing store	_____	_____	_____
8. a kindergarten class	_____	_____	_____

> If you are unsure about which form of address to use, it is better to err on the side of caution and use **Sie.**

))) Im Konferenzsaal

Ms. Ziegler and Mr. O'Brien are business associates who have frequently corresponded, but are meeting for the first time at a conference.

— Entschuldigung, mein Name ist O'Brien. Sind Sie Frau Ziegler aus Göttingen?
— Ja. – Ach, Herr O'Brien aus Dublin! Guten Tag! Wie geht es Ihnen?
— Danke, gut.

E-7 Guten Tag! You are meeting a business associate with whom you have been corresponding. Introduce yourself, using your last name. Address your partner with **Frau** or **Herr** and don't forget to shake hands.

S1: Entschuldigung, mein Name ist _____ *(your last name)*. Sind Sie Frau/Herr _____ aus _____ ?

S2: Ja. – Ach, Frau/Herr _____ aus _____ ! Guten Tag! Wie geht es Ihnen?

S1: Danke, gut.

E-8 Formell oder informell? Listen to the short conversations and choose **formell** or **informell** to indicate how the speakers are addressing each other.

1. _____ formell   _____ informell
2. _____ formell   _____ informell
3. _____ formell   _____ informell
4. _____ formell   _____ informell
5. _____ formell   _____ informell

E.2 Kultur 1

A first look at the German-speaking cultures

E.4 Discover the countries where German is spoken

Studying German involves not only becoming proficient in the language but also acquiring cultural literacy—learning about the various peoples, practices, products, and perspectives of the German-speaking countries. An integral part of your learning will be to reflect on the similarities and the differences between your own, familiar culture and another culture, which may be unfamiliar and full of surprises. Here is a first look at the cultural variety of the German-speaking countries.

In the German-speaking countries, wind energy is valued as an alternative to fossil fuels because it is plentiful, renewable, clean, and produces no greenhouse gas emissions during operation. Large-scale wind farms, such as this one in the Tauern mountain range in the Austrian state of Styria (**Steiermark**), can also be found offshore in the North and Baltic Seas. At an elevation of 6,234 feet, the Tauern Wind Park is the highest in Europe.

> Germany ranks among the top solar and wind energy producers worldwide.

1. Windenergie

2. Aydan Özoğuz

In 2013, Özoğuz became a member of Chancellor Merkel's cabinet, as Federal Government Commissioner for Migration, Refugees, and Integration, entrusted with the complicated task of enabling the successful integration of immigrants—often fleeing from violence and deprivation in their home countries. Özoğuz is the daughter of Turkish immigrants who came to Hamburg via the guest worker program in 1958. She started her political career in Hamburg's **SPD** (**Sozialdemokratische Partei Deutschlands**) and has been a Member of the **Bundestag** for that party since 2009.

Switzerland in Germany? This national park gets its name from its alpine look. A unique blend of craggy sandstone formations, deep ravines, pristine streams, and primeval forests make it a favorite destination for climbers, hikers, and bikers. The Elbe river winds its way through this dramatic landscape, known as Saxon Switzerland.

3. Sächsische Schweiz

For the 2006 Soccer World Cup (**Fußball-Weltmeisterschaft**), this giant sculpture of soccer shoes was placed in front of Berlin's central train station to commemorate an influential idea the family of Adi Dassler had in 1953: screw-in studs. Some believe that this innovation helped the West German team accomplish a miracle by defeating heavily favored Hungary in the 1954 World Cup Final in Berne, Switzerland. Can you guess which company was the first to mass-produce this type of shoe?

4. Land der Ideen

Techno, Rave, and House are hugely popular in the German-speaking countries. The Love Parade was a popular electronic dance music festival that originated in West Berlin in 1989 and took place in Berlin and other German cities until 2010. To this day, large spin-off festivals such as The Street Parade in Zürich are taking place in many other European cities. Back in Berlin, the Berghain nightclub, housed in a former power plant, has become a world-famous destination for techno fans.

5. Im Technoclub

The "Swiss Maestro" is, according to some, the greatest tennis player of all time. He has held the number one position in the world rankings for a record 237 consecutive weeks and won more Grand Slam singles titles than any other male player, as well as an Olympic Gold Medal in doubles with his compatriot Stanislas Wawrinka. Federer, a native of Basel, is the first living individual to be honored on a Swiss stamp. Federer is fluent in English, French, German, and Swiss German (**Schwyzerdütsch**).

6. Roger Federer

In the **Autostadt** in Wolfsburg there are two of these glass silos, high-tech storage facilities for new Volkswagens. When purchasing a car, a customer may opt to travel to the **Autostadt** to pick it up. There, customers can watch how a robotic arm plucks each new car out of the silo compartment and moves it onto an automatic elevator. The car is then transported through a tunnel to the customer service center without having been driven a single yard, and with the odometer showing "0." Volkswagen is the main sponsor of the professional soccer team VfL Wolfsburg, which plays its home games at Volkswagen Arena.

7. Volkswagen in Wolfsburg

E-9 Was ist das? Each German term below relates to one of the themes of this **Kultur** section. Match each word to the number of the appropriate **Kultur** reading.

Windpark ____

Tanzrhythmus ____

Fußballschuh ____

Politik ____

Vorhand ____

Sandstein ____

Autosilo ____

E.3 Letters and numbers in German

The German alphabet: Letters and their sounds

E.5 Spell German words and abbreviations

The name of almost every letter in the German alphabet contains the sound represented by that letter. Learning the alphabet is therefore useful not only for spelling, but also for your pronunciation. Listen and repeat the sounds that you hear, as closely as you can.

))) **E-10** Hören Sie gut zu und wiederholen Sie. *(Listen carefully and repeat.)*

a	ah	**g**	geh	**m**	emm	**s**	ess	**y**	üppsilon
b	beh	**h**	hah	**n**	enn	**t**	teh	**z**	tsett
c	tseh	**i**	ee	**o**	oh	**u**	oo		
d	deh	**j**	yott	**p**	peh	**v**	fow		
e	eh	**k**	kah	**q**	coo	**w**	veh		
f	eff	**l**	ell	**r**	airr	**x**	iks		

E-11 Wie schreibt man das? *(How do you spell that?)* Your instructor will spell six German last names. Find the beginning of the name and fill in the rest according to what you hear. Search for the names online to find out their first names and learn what they are famous for!

Di_____   Ko_____
Fa_____   Ei_____
Lu_____   Me_____

E-12 Abkürzungen. Your instructor will read the names below. For each name, identify the appropriate abbreviation and spell it aloud.

Bundesrepublik Deutschland
Vereinigte Staaten von Amerika
Bayerische Motorenwerke
Volkswagen
Allgemeiner Deutscher Automobilclub
Deutsches Jugendherbergswerk
Christlich-Demokratische Union
Europäische Union
Sozialdemokratische Partei Deutschlands

EU   USA   BRD   CDU   VW

DJH   ADAC   BMW   SPD

🔊 Zur Aussprache

Sounds and letters different from those in English

E.6 Recognize sounds and letters different from those in English

Some sounds and letters that are quite different from those found in English are presented here. Listen carefully and imitate the sounds you hear.

The umlauted vowels ä, ö, and ü

The sound represented by the letter **ä** is close to the sound represented by the letter *e* in English *let*.

short *ä*		long *ä*	
Bäcker	Gärtner	Käse	Universität

The sound represented by the letter **ö** has no equivalent in English. To produce this sound, pucker your lips as if to whistle, hold them in this position, and say *eh*.

short *ö*		long *ö*	
zwölf	Göttingen	schön	hören

The sound represented by the letter **ü** also has no equivalent in English. To produce this sound, pucker your lips as if to whistle, hold them in this position, and say *ee*.

short *ü*		long *ü*	
fünf	Tschüss!	grün	Grüß dich!

The *Eszett*

The letter **ß**, which is called **Eszett,** is pronounced like an *s*.

heiß	heißen	dreißig

German *ch*

After **a, o,** and **u,** the sound represented by **ch** resembles a gentle gargling.

acht	noch	auch

After **i** and **e,** the sound represented by **ch** is pronounced like a loudly whispered *h* in *huge*.

ich	nicht	sechzehn

The suffix **-ig** is pronounced as if it were spelled **-ich.**

windig	zwanzig	dreißig

German *v*

The sound represented by the letter **v** is generally pronounced like English *f*.

vier   viel   Volkswagen

German *w*

The sound represented by the letter **w** is always pronounced like English *v*.

woher   Wie geht's?   Wiedersehen!

 Willkommen in Deutschland

German *z*

The sound represented by the letter **z** is pronounced like English *ts* in *hits*.

zwei   zehn   zwanzig

E-13 **Was ist das auf Englisch?** Choose a city name from the box, spell it in German for your partner, then ask what it is in English. Locate each city on a map.

Speakers of German saying the alphabet do not include the three umlauted vowels (**ä, ö, ü**) or the **Eszett (ß)**. They do not use the term **a-, o-,** or **u-Umlaut** when spelling. To spell the word **Käse** they would say **kah-ä-ess-eh**.

Athen   Rom

Genf   MÜNCHEN

Zürich   Brüssel

Nürnberg   WIEN

Köln

Numbers in German

E.7 Use German numbers and letters for daily tasks

The numbers from 0 to 1000

0	null						
1	eins	11	elf	21	ein**und**zwanzig	30	drei**ß**ig
2	zwei	12	zwölf	22	zweiundzwanzig	40	vierzig
3	drei	13	dreizehn	23	dreiundzwanzig	50	fünfzig
4	vier	14	vierzehn	24	vierundzwanzig	60	sechzig
5	fünf	15	fünfzehn	25	fünfundzwanzig	70	siebzig
6	sechs	16	**sech**zehn	26	sechsundzwanzig	80	achtzig
7	sieben	17	siebzehn	27	sieb**en**undzwanzig	90	neunzig
8	acht	18	achtzehn	28	achtundzwanzig		
9	neun	19	neunzehn	29	neunundzwanzig		
10	zehn	20	zwanzig				

100	(ein)hundert	200	zweihundert	1000	(ein)tausend
101	(ein)hunderteins	300	dreihundert	2000	zweitausend
102	(ein)hundertzwei	400	vierhundert	3000	dreitausend

and so on usw. und so weiter°

Note the following:

1. The **-s** in **eins** is dropped in combination with **zwanzig, dreißig,** etc.: **einundzwanzig, einunddreißig,** etc.

2. The numbers from the twenties through the nineties are "turned around": **vierundzwanzig** (four and twenty), **achtundsechzig** (eight and sixty), etc.

3. **Dreißig** is the only one of the tens that ends in **-ßig** instead of **-zig.**

4. The final **-s** in **sechs** is dropped in **sechzehn** and **sechzig.**

5. The **-en** of **sieben** is dropped in **siebzehn** and **siebzig.**

E-14 Wie viel kostet das? Find out what each item at this stand at the flea market costs.

1. Wie viel kostet die Gitarre? Die Gitarre kostet _____ Euro.
2. Wie viel kostet die Lampe? Die Lampe kostet _____ Euro.
3. Wie viel kostet der Fußball? Der Fußball kostet _____ Euro.
4. Wie viel kostet der Teddybär? Der Teddybär kostet _____ Euro.
5. Wie viel kostet das Sweatshirt? Das Sweatshirt kostet _____ Euro.

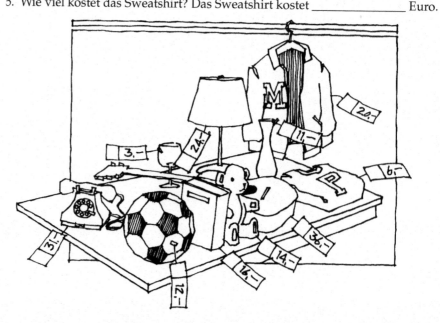

E-15 Mathematik.

▶ 2 + 2

S1: Was ist zwei plus zwei?   **S2:** Zwei plus zwei ist vier.

▶ 4 − 2

S1: Wie viel ist vier minus zwei?   **S2:** Vier minus zwei ist zwei.

1. 2 + 1	3. 5 + 0	5. 9 + 6	7. 10 + 1	9. 15 − 3
2. 4 − 3	4. 8 − 6	6. 7 − 5	8. 6 − 2	10. 11 + 8

Telephone numbers

Most German telephone numbers are written as pairs of digits. The telephone number **25 13 84** can be said either as individual numbers **"zwei, fünf, eins, drei, acht, vier,"** or in pairs **"fünfundzwanzig, dreizehn, vierundachtzig."** The area code is called **die Vorwahl.**

E-16 Was ist die Telefonnummer? Which number would you need to call to do the following in Hamburg? Read the number aloud when you find it.

1. Fix your computer
2. Get a language partner
3. Order a pizza
4. Report a theft
5. Make an appointment for a haircut
6. Find a yoga class

a. Ristorante Roma 17 53 81
b. Fitnessstudio 12 10 39
c. Tech-Spezialist 15 03 76
d. LinguaGruppe 91 40 67
e. HaarPort 21 05 18
f. Polizei 112

E-17 Telefonnummern. To start a German study group with some classmates, you need their telephone numbers. Listen as the following students say their telephone numbers. Write their numbers next to their names. Then exchange phone numbers with two of your classmates.

1. Heather: _____
2. Mark: _____
3. Sara: _____

4. Jason: _____
5. _____
6. _____

E-mail and Web addresses

German speakers typically use English when saying the @ sign in e-mail addresses. The English term *dot* is used for the period in e-mail and Web addresses, although it is also common to hear **Punkt.** All other words and numbers are simply spoken as words, unless it is necessary to clarify spelling.

Written: claudia.berger1@yahoo.de
Spoken: **Claudia Punkt Berger eins at yahoo Punkt deh eh**

Other common symbols in e-mail and Web addresses are - **(Strich)** and / **(Querstrich)**.

E-18 Was ist die Webadresse? Do a Web search to find the Web address for the following organizations. Spell out the URLs that you find. Note especially the Web address suffixes for each of the four German-speaking countries.

Universität Heidelberg

Austrian newspaper *Kurier*

Lindt & Sprüngli Schweiz

Liechtenstein national tourist board

E-19 Eine WhatsApp an Stephanie. Read Ali's text message to Stephanie on the display of his **Handy** and then mark the correct answers to the questions below.

1. Where will Stephanie find Ali at 10 a.m.?

   a. in lecture hall 9   b. in lecture hall 12   c. in the cafeteria

2. Where will Stephanie find Ali at 12 noon?

   a. in lecture hall 9   b. in lecture hall 10   c. in the cafeteria

3. When did Ali send this text message to Stephanie?

   a. at 8 a.m.   b. at night   c. in the afternoon

> Hi S, ich bin um 10 in Hörsaal 9. Um 12 gehe ich in die Mensa. Gute N8! 21:48 ✓✓
>
> Super! 21:48

Postal addresses

Looking at this envelope, you can see that in the German-speaking countries, letters are addressed a bit differently than in North America. The house number follows the name of the street (e.g., **Lindenstraße 29**). The postal code **(die Postleitzahl)** precedes the name of the city.

E-20 Ein Brief von Mutter. Peter has just received a letter from his mother.

1. Peters Familienname ist _____.
2. Peters Hausnummer ist _____.
3. Die Hausnummer von Peters Mutter ist _____.
4. Peters Postleitzahl ist _____.
5. Die Postleitzahl von Peters Mutter ist _____.
6. Ein Brief von Berlin nach München kostet _____ Cent.

Ackermann
Alleestraße 10
10827 Berlin

0,70 €

Peter Ackermann
Zürner Straße 16
81679 München

E-21 Mein Semesterticket. Now you can fill out the form to apply for your own Semesterticket.

Antragsformular Semesterticket

Familienname: _____   Vorname: _____

E-Mail-Adresse: _____

Vorwahl: _____   Telefon: _____

Straße und
Hausnummer: _____

Postleitzahl: _____   Ort: _____

[ZURÜCK]   [WEITER]

E-22 Wir lernen einander besser kennen. Find out your partner's last name, e-mail and postal addresses, and telephone number.

S1: Was ist dein Familienname?
Wie bitte?° Wie schreibt man das?
Was ist deine E-Mail-Adresse?
Was ist deine Adresse?
Was ist deine Telefonnummer?

S2: Mein Familienname ist ….
…
Meine E-Mail-Adresse ist …
Meine Adresse ist …
Meine Telefonnummer ist ….

Pardon?

E-23 Eine Jugendherberge. For young people traveling in Europe, youth hostels are a popular and inexpensive place to stay. Find out more about this one by reading the Web site excerpt and answering the questions.

1. The **Seebad** in **Ostseebad** means *seaside resort.* Look at the map of **Deutschland Bundesländer,** find the **Ostsee,** and give the English equivalent.

2. What is the name of the street this hostel is located on?

3. What is the overall rating for this youth hostel? In what area do guests rate them particularly highly?

4. Do a Web search for **Ostseebad Sellin Jugendherberge** to explore another well-known seaside youth hostel.

Jugendherberge Ostseebad Highlights:
• 3 km Sandstrand mit Wanderweg
• Wind- und Kitesurfen
• Paddeln und Beachvolleyball

Sandstraße 106
24217 Schönberg / Ostsee
Tel: +49 4344 5892
ostseebad1@jugendherberge.de

4,5 / 5 Sehr gut
basiert auf 392 Bewertungen
Kategorien:

Service ★ ★ ★ ★ ★ **4,7**

Gastronomie ★ ★ ★ ★ ★ **4,5**

Sport & Unterh. ★ ★ ★ ★ ★ **4,3**

E.4 Kultur 2

German in English / English in German

E.8 Identify words you already know in German

Of the many words you will encounter as you learn German, some will already be familiar to you. This is because languages borrow words from one another. Some German words used in English are specific to the jargon of a particular field, such as *doppelgänger* in psychology, or *leitmotif* in music. Others have become so commonplace that their German origin has been largely forgotten, such as *kitsch* and *hamburger*.

Ach so!
In English, borrowed words from German follow English rules for capitalization, but German rules for spelling. In their original German spelling, all these words would be capitalized because they are nouns.

E-24 Deutsch in Englisch. By matching appropriately in each of the two sets below, you can reconstruct some German words commonly used in English.

1. kinder-   a. kraut
2. wunder-   b. garten
3. knack-   c. geist
4. polter-   d. kind
5. glocken-   e. wurst
6. sauer-   f. land
7. hinter-   g. lust
8. wander-   h. spiel

Similarly, German borrows many words from English. Many of these borrowed words reveal the particular influence English has on areas like advertising, business, fashion, fast food, and pop culture. They include nouns like **das Marketing, das Meeting, der Blazer, der Softdrink,** and **der DJ;** adjectives like **cool, hip,** and **fit;** and verbs like **lunchen, stylen,** and **rappen.**

Chicken-Mix-Menü
verschiedene Chicken-Snacks
mit 2 Dips,
Pommes Frites
und 0,3 l Getränk
5,50 €

German has also adopted many English words for technology. Verbs like **downloaden, chatten,** and **googeln** have become a regular part of the language, and nouns like **die Homepage** and **die E-Mail** are far more common than their German equivalents **die Einstiegsseite** and **die elektronische Post**.

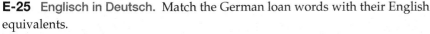

Although these borrowed words take on German grammatical forms like gender or verb endings (*das* **Meeting, wir lunch***en*), they usually have the same meaning as in English. However, some English words used in German have a rather unexpected meaning for speakers of English.

E-25 Englisch in Deutsch. Match the German loan words with their English equivalents.

1. der Smoking
2. der Oldtimer
3. der Shootingstar
4. das Set
5. der Dressman
6. das Handy
7. das Notebook
8. der Beamer

a. suddenly successful person
b. male model
c. laptop
d. cell phone
e. place mat
f. vintage car
g. LCD projector
h. tuxedo

Mehr Englisch in Deutsch
Additional English words used in German with unexpected meanings to English speakers: **der Neckholder:** halter top; **das Shooting:** filming; **der Talkmaster:** talk show host; **der Cutter:** film editor; **das Peeling:** exfoliation.

⟩⟩ E.5 Wortschatz

Wichtige Vokabeln

Wichtige Vokabeln: Be sure to learn the numbers presented earlier.

E.9 Learn vocabulary for greeting people and asking for basic information

Informelle Situationen

Morgen!	Good morning!
Tag!	Hello!
'n Abend!	Good evening!
Grüß dich!	Hi! *(to greet one person)*
Hallo!	Hi!
Tschüss! ⎫ **Ciao!** ⎭	Bye!
Wie heißt du?	What's your name?
Ich heiße …	My name is …
Ich bin …	I'm …
Woher kommst (bist) du?	Where are you from?
Ich komme (bin) aus …	I'm from …
Wie geht's?	How are you?
Danke, gut.	Fine, thanks.

Formelle Situationen

Guten Morgen!	Good morning!
Guten Tag!	Hello!
Guten Abend!	Good evening!
Auf Wiedersehen!	Good-bye!
Wie heißen Sie?	What is your name?
Ich heiße … ⎫ **Mein Name ist …** ⎭	My name is …
Woher kommen (sind) Sie?	Where are you from?
Wie geht es Ihnen?	How are you?
Frau	Mrs., Ms.
Herr	Mr.

Nützliche Phrasen *(Useful Phrases)*

Was ist …	What is …
Wie viel ist …	How much is …
Das ist …	This/That is …
Wie bitte?	Pardon?
Wie schreibt man das?	How do you write (spell) that?
Was ist das auf Englisch?	What is that in English?
Wie viel kostet das?	How much does this cost?
Entschuldigung!	Excuse me!
Danke!	Thanks!
Bitte.	You're welcome.

Hallo
ich heiße
Günther

Lerntipp!
In this course you'll want to communicate in German with your instructor and classmates as much as possible. In the *Anhang* you'll find some useful classroom expressions to help you do this.

Das Gegenteil *(The Opposite)*

ja ≠ nein	yes ≠ no
gut ≠ schlecht	good ≠ bad
super, fantastisch ≠ miserabel	super, fantastic ≠ miserable

Wörter im Kontext

E-26 Formell oder informell? How could you greet the following people at the times given?

	Your professor	Your fellow students
9 a.m.	_____	_____
3 p.m.	_____	_____
7 p.m.	_____	_____

E-27 Wie viel ist das? Match each problem with its correct solution.

1. Wie viel ist zwei plus fünf?
2. Was ist elf minus eins?
3. Wie viel ist dreizehn plus vier?
4. Was ist siebzig minus zehn?

a. Das ist zehn.
b. Das ist sechzig.
c. Das ist sieben.
d. Das ist siebzehn.

E-28 Fragen und Antworten.

1. Wie heißt du?
2. Woher kommst du?
3. Was ist deine Adresse?
4. Was ist „excuse me" auf Deutsch?
5. Was ist deine Telefonnummer?
6. Wie geht's?

a. Entschuldigung.
b. 3 14 89.
c. Gut!
d. Aus Stuttgart.
e. Herderstraße 16.
f. Johanna.

E-29 Was passt wo? *(What goes where?)* Complete with the appropriate word or expression.

Wie geht's	Name	Nein	Entschuldigung
Wie geht es Ihnen	Super	Wie bitte	

1. MARTIN: Grüß dich, Claudia. _____?
   CLAUDIA: _____.
2. PETER: _____, bist du Asha Singh?
   YVONNE: _____, ich bin Yvonne Harris.
3. HERR PEERY: Guten Tag. Mein _____ ist Peery.
   FRAU BORG: _____? Wie heißen Sie?
   HERR PEERY: Ich bin Frank Peery.
   FRAU BORG: Oh, Herr Peery aus Iowa! _____?
   HERR PEERY: Danke, gut.

Was ist „Sonnenschein" auf Englisch?

Kapitel 1
Jahraus, jahrein

Studenten in der Universitätsstadt Tübingen

Learning Objectives

1.1 Describe the geography and climate of the German-speaking countries

1.2 Learn vocabulary to talk about the weather and to state your nationality and country

1.3 Distinguish between *ei* and *ie* in German

1.4 Identify people and things using German nouns

1.5 Ask and respond to simple questions

1.6 Compare and contrast university life in the U.S. and the German-speaking countries

1.7 Talk about people and things using pronouns

1.8 Express states and actions

1.9 Understand authentic video of German speakers introducing themselves

1.10 Learn vocabulary to talk about the days of the week, the months, and the seasons, and to say where you're going

1.1 Vorschau

Eine Wetterkarte

1-1 Wie ist das Wetter? Which day and date is this weather report for? Match each city with the most appropriate weather description based on the information on the weather map.

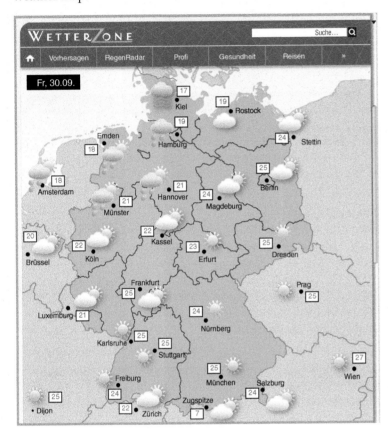

In Stuttgart …	ist es sehr windig.
In Rostock …	ist es kalt.
In Kiel …	ist es sonnig und der Himmel ist blau!
In Wien …	regnet es.
Auf der Zugspitze …	scheint die Sonne gar nicht.
In Hamburg …	zeigt das Thermometer 27 Grad.

 1-2 Was passt zusammen? *(What goes together?)* Working with a partner, find the sentences that describe each illustration.

Heute ist es gar nicht schön.

Heute ist es schön.

Die Sonne scheint.

Es regnet.

Der Himmel ist grau.

Der Himmel ist blau.

Es ist windig.

Es ist windstill.

Was für ein Sauwetter!

Was für ein Superwetter!

1-3 Celsius und Fahrenheit. When traveling in Europe, it is helpful to be familiar with the Celsius scale. With a partner, work on converting Celsius to Fahrenheit.

approximately

S1: Was ist zwanzig Grad Celsius in Fahrenheit?

S2: Zwanzig Grad Celsius ist etwa° achtundsechzig Grad Fahrenheit.

Grad Celsius

Grad Fahrenheit

Semesterbeginn

| Suche... 🔍 | Einleitung | Profil | Finde Freunde |

Stephanie @ichbinStephB · 30. Sep
Viel zu tun heute: Zuerst gehe ich zum Auslandsamt, dann gehe ich in die Mensa. Heute Nachmittag kaufe ich meine Bücher. #Uni #Studentenleben

↩ ↻ ♥ 1 ...

Stephanie @ichbinStephB · 30. Sep
Und wann beginnen endlich die Vorlesungen?? Erst morgen. 😊 Typisch #Ersti, oder? 😊 #Semesterbeginn

↩ ↻ ♥ 1 ...

> The term **Ersti** derives from **Erstsemester** and refers, either endearingly or condescendingly, to students who are in their first semester at school.

1-4 Was macht Stephanie? Read Stephanie's tweets and then put the following actions in the order that she plans to do them.

_____ Stephanie geht in die Vorlesung.   _____ Stephanie geht in die Buchhandlung.

_____ Stephanie geht in die Mensa.   _____ Stephanie geht zum Auslandsamt.

> Ach so!
> Mensa = Cafeteria

1-5 Drei kleine Gespräche. With a partner, unscramble the exchanges in the following three mini-conversations by numbering appropriately. Then role-play the conversations for your classmates.

S1:

great

_____ Toll°! Gehst du heute schwimmen?

_____ Na, dann bis später.

_1_ Wie ist das Wetter?

S2:

_____ Ja, klar!

_____ Sehr schön! Das Thermometer zeigt fast dreißig Grad.

_____ Ciao!

S1:

_____ Was für ein Sauwetter!

_1_ Regnet es noch?

_____ Nein, noch nicht.

S2:

_____ Ja, und das Thermometer zeigt fünf Grad.

_____ Gehst du jetzt in die Vorlesung?

_____ Na, dann tschüss!

S1:

_1_ Hallo!

_____ Und wann kaufst du deine Bücher?

_____ Was machst du jetzt?

S2:

_____ Das mache ich heute Nachmittag.

_____ Ich gehe in die Vorlesung.

_____ Grüß dich!

1.2 Kultur 1

Welcome to countries where German is spoken

1.1 Describe the geography and climate of the German-speaking countries

Located in the center of Europe, the German-speaking countries together are only about two-thirds the size of Texas. And yet, the topography and climate of **Deutschland, Österreich, die Schweiz**, and **Liechtenstein** are enormously varied.

1-6 With a partner, take turns reading aloud about the German-speaking regions and finding the places mentioned on maps of Germany, Austria, Switzerland, and Liechtenstein.

Landscapes

It is about a day's journey from the coastlines of the **Nordsee** and the **Ostsee** to the peaks of the German, Swiss, and Austrian **Alpen** in the south. The Lowlands of Northern Germany extend from the Dutch border in the west to the border of Poland in the east. Just south of the **Lüneburger Heide,** where you can hike through thousands of acres of purple heather, the Lowlands give way to the mountain ranges of Central Germany, such as the **Harz** mountains and the **Thüringer Wald.** To the west you find the fabled **Rhein**. Following it south, you pass by a number of important cities like **Düsseldorf, Köln,** and **Wiesbaden** until you reach the densely forested mountains of the **Schwarzwald.** From its highest point, the **Feldberg** (4898 feet), you can see the snow-covered peaks of the Swiss **Alpen** to the south. The highest Swiss peak, the **Dufourspitze,** rises to a height of 15,203 feet. Most Swiss citizens live in **Mittelland,** a hilly plateau wedged between the Jura Mountains and the **Alpen.**

Am Rhein

Schloss Vaduz: Hier residiert der Fürst von Liechtenstein.

Situated on the banks of the **Rhein** and nestled in the **Alpen** between Austria and Switzerland lies the principality of **Liechtenstein** (capital: **Vaduz**). With an area of only 62 square miles (15.6 miles long and 3.75 miles wide), it is the smallest of the German-speaking countries. The 37,000 inhabitants of Liechtenstein enjoy a high standard of living, due in part to the country's status as a tax haven.

It also takes about a day to drive from **Freiburg,** at the western edge of Southern Germany, to the eastern border of Austria. You can follow the **Donau,** as it flows through a succession of significant towns like **Regensburg** and **Linz,** until you reach **Wien,** the capital of Austria.

Hallstatt in Oberösterreich

Climate

The German-speaking countries show considerable climatic variation. In the north, the weather is influenced by the cool air currents coming off the **Nordsee** and the **Ostsee.** The summers are only moderately warm and the winters are mild, but often stormy and very wet.

An der Ostsee ist es oft sehr windig.

In den Schweizer Alpen

On the beaches of the North Sea and the Baltic Sea there is often a cool onshore wind. **Strandkörbe** (literally: *beach baskets*) can be rented as shelter from the wind.

In the central region, between the Northern Lowlands and the **Alpen** in the south, the summers are usually much warmer and the winters much colder than in the north. The highest summer temperatures occur in the protected valleys of the **Rhein** and **Mosel** rivers, providing perfect growing conditions for the thousands of acres of vineyards that produce the famous white wines of Germany.

To the south, the climate of the Swiss and Austrian **Alpen** is characterized by high precipitation, shorter summers, and longer winters. But even in these small countries, the variation in climate from one area to the next is quite striking. In Switzerland, which is about half the size of the state of Maine, the climate is so varied that you can go windsurfing and skiing in a single summer's day!

1-7 Ein bisschen Geografie. First supply the two missing letters in each geographical name, then identify the appropriate category for each. Can you give the English names as well?

	Region or Country	City	River or Sea
1. Alp_____	_____	_____	_____
2. S_____warzwald	_____	_____	_____
3. W_____n	_____	_____	_____
4. Schw_____z	_____	_____	_____
5. N_____dsee	_____	_____	_____
6. Liechtenst_____n	_____	_____	_____
7. Osts_____	_____	_____	_____
8. Mos_____	_____	_____	_____
9. _____terreich	_____	_____	_____
10. Don_____	_____	_____	_____

)) 1.3 Wortschatz 1

Wichtige Vokabeln

1.2 Learn vocabulary to talk about the weather and to state your nationality and country

There are two vocabulary lists per chapter. Organized according to parts of speech, items are also grouped alphabetically by theme wherever possible.

Nomen *(Nouns)*

der Himmel	sky; heaven
die Sonne	sun
das Wetter	weather
das Auslandsamt	foreign student office
das Buch, die Bücher	book
die Karte, die Karten	map
die Mensa	university cafeteria
die Vorlesung, die Vorlesungen	lecture; class

Mensa am Park
Mensa • Cafeteria • InfoTake
Nur für Studierende und Angehörige der Hochschulen

Verben

beginnen	to begin	regnen	to rain
gehen	to go	scheinen	to shine
kaufen	to buy	schreiben	to write
kommen	to come	studieren	to study; to major in
machen	to do; to make	zeigen	to show

Andere Wörter *(Other words)*

auch	also	nicht	not
dann	then	noch	still
ein bisschen	a bit; a little	noch nicht	not yet
ein paar	a few	nur	only
fast	almost	oft	often
gar nicht	not at all	schön	nice; beautiful
heute	today	viel	much; a lot
heute Nachmittag	this afternoon	windig	windy
jetzt	now	zuerst	first
morgen	tomorrow		

Ausdrücke *(Expressions)*

Bis später!	See you later!
Klar!	Of course!
Toll!	Super!
Das Thermometer zeigt zehn Grad.	The thermometer reads (shows) ten degrees.
Die Vorlesungen beginnen erst morgen.	(The) lectures don't begin until tomorrow.

Das Gegenteil

bitte ≠ danke	please ≠ thank you
heiß ≠ kalt	hot ≠ cold

Lerntipp!
Some helpful strategies for learning vocabulary include writing out words, quizzing a partner, and creating your own sentences. You should also listen to and repeat aloud the recorded vocabulary items.

Die Farben

blau		blue	rosarot		pink
braun		brown	rot		red
gelb		yellow	schwarz		black
grau		gray	violett		purple
grün		green	weiß		white

The names of most countries are neuter and are not normally preceded by an article (e.g., **England**, **Dänemark**). When the name of a country is masculine, feminine, or plural, the article must be used (e.g., **der Libanon, die Türkei, die USA**).

Leicht zu verstehen (Easy to understand)

das Semester, die Semester   die Studentin, die Studentinnen
der Student, die Studenten   die Universität, die Universitäten (die Uni, die Unis)

Ländernamen

die Bundesrepublik Deutschland (die BRD)	the Federal Republic of Germany (the FRG)
Österreich	Austria
die Schweiz	Switzerland
die Vereinigten Staaten (die USA)	the United States (the U.S.)
Kanada	Canada

Die Nationalität

Er ist Deutscher.	He's a German.
Sie ist Deutsche.	She's a German.
Er ist Österreicher.	He's an Austrian.
Sie ist Österreicherin.	She's an Austrian.
Er ist Schweizer.	He's Swiss.
Sie ist Schweizerin.	She's Swiss.
Er ist Amerikaner.	He's an American.
Sie ist Amerikanerin.	She's an American.
Er ist Kanadier.	He's a Canadian.
Sie ist Kanadierin.	She's a Canadian.

Signs similar to the one depicted here can be found at border points of the European Union member countries (28 as of 2017).

Wörter im Kontext

 **1-8 Fragen und Antworten.** Choose the appropriate response to your partner's questions or statements.

S1:	S2:
1. Woher kommst du?	a. Biologie und Chemie.
2. Was studierst du?	b. Ich auch nicht.
3. Beginnen die Vorlesungen heute?	c. Nicht viel.
4. Gehst du in die Mensa?	d. Nein, erst morgen.
5. Was machst du heute Nachmittag?	e. Aus Österreich.
6. Ich gehe nicht oft in die Disco.	f. Nein, noch nicht.

1-9 Fragen und Antworten. Choose the appropriate response to your partner's questions.

S1:	S2:
1. Wie ist das Wetter?	a. Ja, fast dreißig Grad.
2. Regnet es noch?	b. Nur zehn Grad.
3. Was zeigt das Thermometer?	c. Nein, jetzt scheint die Sonne.
4. Ist es heiß?	d. Gar nicht schön.
5. Was machst du morgen?	e. Nein, ich komme erst morgen.
6. Kommst du heute?	f. Zuerst schreibe ich ein paar E-Mails und dann gehe ich schwimmen.

1-10 Was sind die Farben?

1. Schokolade ist _____.
2. Gras ist _____.
3. Milch ist _____.
4. Butter ist _____.
5. Ein Zebra ist _____ und _____.
6. Blut ist _____.
7. Die Sonne scheint und der Himmel ist _____.
8. Der Himmel ist _____ und es regnet.

1-11 Die Nationalität, bitte!

1. Frau Bürgli ist aus Zürich. Sie ist _____.
2. Herr Karlhuber kommt aus Salzburg. Er ist _____.
3. Frau Kröger ist aus Hamburg. Sie ist _____.
4. Herr Chang ist aus San Francisco. Er ist _____.
5. Frau Thomson kommt aus Vancouver. Sie ist _____.

1.4 Zur Aussprache

German *ei* and *ie*

1.3 **Distinguish between *ei* and *ie* in German**

))) **1-12** Hören Sie gut zu und wiederholen Sie!

Wein	Wien	sein	Sie
dein	die	bei	Bier

Distinguish between **ei** and **ie** by reading the following sentences aloud.

1. Wie viel ist drei und vier? Drei und vier ist sieben.

2. Wie heißen Sie? Ich heiße Ziegler.

3. Das ist nicht mein Bier.°

4. Die Schweiz ist eine Demokratie.

5. Dieter und Melanie reisen in die Schweiz.

colloquial for: *That's not my problem!*

))) **1-13** **Ist das *ei* or *ie*?** The words in the word pairs you hear are written with either **ei** or **ie.** Fill in the blanks with **ei** or **ie** as appropriate. Don't be concerned if you don't know the meaning of some of the words. You will find out their meaning in later chapters.

1. W____n   W____n   4. fr____   fr____ren   7. n____n   n____
2. w____der w____ter   5. k____n   K____l   8. dr____   v____r
3. r____sen   r____sig   6. z____hen z____gen   9. Theor____ Poliz____

🗱 **1-14** **Wie sagt man das?** Take a look at the following phrases found on signs in the German-speaking countries. With a partner, say them out loud, focusing on your pronunciation of German **ei** and **ie.** Can you figure out their meaning?

1.5 Kommunikation und Formen 1

Nouns

1.4 Identify people and things using German nouns

Nouns: gender and definite articles

Nouns are the words used to name people and things. In English all nouns have the definite article *the*. In German every noun has *grammatical gender*. Nouns that are masculine have the definite article **der,** nouns that are neuter have the definite article **das,** and nouns that are feminine have the definite article **die.**

Masculine	Neuter	Feminine
der	das	die
the	*the*	*the*

Although nouns referring to males are usually masculine (*der* **Mann,** *der* **Vater**) and nouns referring to females are usually feminine (*die* **Frau,** *die* **Mutter**), the gender of German nouns is not always logical.

<table>
<tr><td>**der** Himmel</td><td>**das** Wetter</td><td>**die** Sonne</td></tr>
<tr><td>**der** Computer</td><td>**das** Buch</td><td>**die** Vorlesung</td></tr>
</table>

You should learn each noun with its definite article as *one unit.*

1-15 Wer ist das? Identify the members of the Ziegler family.

1. Das ist …
2. Das ist …
3. Das ist …
4. Das ist …

die Mutter	der Vater	die Tochter	der Sohn

1-16 Verwandte Wörter. *(Related words.)* The names of the objects below are very close in form and meaning to their English equivalents. With a partner, read the names of the objects listed in the box, find each one in the illustration, and read the corresponding number.

S1: Der Computer ist Nummer vierzehn. Und der Fußball?
…

S2: Der Fußball ist Nummer siebzehn. Und der Hammer?
…

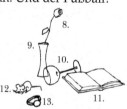
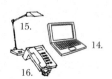

Masculine	Neuter	Feminine
der Computer	das Auto	die Bluse
der Fußball	das Boot	die Jacke
der Hammer	das Bett	die Karotte
der Mond	das Buch	die Maus
der Ring	das Weinglas	die Lampe
der Schuh	das Haus	die Rose
der Teekessel	das Telefon	die Vase

Plural forms: definite articles and nouns

All three definite articles **(der, das, die)** have the same plural form: **die.**

Singular	Plural
der ⎫	
das ⎬	die
die ⎭	

Although a few English nouns have irregular plural forms (e.g., woman, wom*e*n; child, child*ren*; mouse, m*ice*), most English nouns form the plural by adding *-s* or *-es* (e.g., student, students; class, class*es*).

The table below shows the five basic plural forms for German nouns. The column *dictionary entry* shows how nouns are presented in vocabulary lists with the abbreviated plural forms. The column *you should learn* shows how a German noun must be learned, i.e., with its definite article and its plural form.

	Abbreviation of plural form	Dictionary entry	You should learn
1	**-**	der Finger, **-**	der Finger, die Finger
	∴	die Mutter, **∴**	die Mutter, die M**ü**tter
2	**-e**	der Freund, **-e**	der Freund, die Freund**e**
	∴e	die Maus, **∴e**	die Maus, die M**äu**se*
3	**-er**	das Kind, **-er**	das Kind, die Kind**er**
	∴er	das Buch, **∴er**	das Buch, die B**ü**ch**er**
4	**-n**	die Karte, **-n**	die Karte, die Karte**n**
	-en	die Vorlesung, **-en**	die Vorlesung, die Vorlesung**en**
	-nen	die Freundin, **-nen**	die Freundin, die Freundin**nen****
5	**-s**	das Auto, **-s**	das Auto, die Auto**s**

* In the diphthong (vowel combination) **au,** it is always the **a** that receives the umlaut in the plural.

** All nouns with the plural ending **-nen** are derived from masculine nouns, e.g., **der Student, die Student*in*, die Student*innen*.**

1-17 Was sind die Farben? The nouns beneath the illustrations are listed as you would find them in a dictionary. Using the plural forms, say what colors the objects or animals are.

S1: Die Tennisbälle sind gelb. Und die Schuhe?
…

S2: Die Schuhe sind braun. Und die Äpfel?
…

1.
der Tennisball, ∴e

2.
der Schuh, -e

3.
der Apfel, ∴

4.
der Pullover, -

5.
das Auto, -s

6.
das Haus, ∴er

7.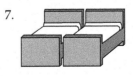
das Bett, -en

8.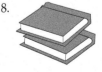
das Buch, ∴er

9.
die Banane, -n

10.
die Blume, -n

11.
die Katze, -n

12.
die Maus, ∴e

The indefinite articles *ein* and *kein*

The forms of the indefinite article (*a, an*) are **ein** (masculine and neuter) and **eine** (feminine). Just like *a* and *an*, **ein** and **eine** have no plural form.

Das ist **ein** Buch über die EU und hier ist **eine** Europakarte.

*This is **a** book about the EU and here is **a** map of Europe.*

	Masculine	Neuter	Feminine
DEFINITE	**der** Student	**das** Buch	**die** Studentin
INDEFINITE	**ein** Student	**ein** Buch	**eine** Studentin

If the numeral *one* (**eins**) precedes a noun, German uses the indefinite article instead.

Jen hat heute nur **eine** Vorlesung.

*Jen has only **one** lecture today.*

The negative forms of the indefinite article (*not a, not any, not, no*) are **kein** (masculine and neuter) and **keine** (feminine). Note that **kein** does have a plural form: **keine.**

Das ist **kein** Restaurant, das ist eine Mensa.

*That's **not a** restaurant, that's a cafeteria.*

Das sind **keine** Amerikaner, das sind Kanadier.

Those aren't Americans, they're Canadians.

1-18 Was für dumme Fragen! Correct your partner.

▶ Glas (n)

S1: Ist das ein Glas?

S2: Nein, das ist kein Glas. Das ist eine Vase.

▶ Lilien (pl)

S1: Sind das Lilien?

S2: Nein, das sind keine Lilien. Das sind Tulpen.

1. Mikroskop (n)

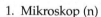

2. Tennisball (m)

3. Jacke (f)

4. Biergläser (pl)

5. Sweatshirt (n)

6. Mäuse (pl)

| Pullover (m) | Ratten (pl) | Fußball (m) | Teleskop (n) | Bluse (f) | Weingläser (pl) |

Word order

1.5 Ask and respond to simple questions

Position of the verb in yes/no questions

In yes/no questions the verb is always the *first element*.

Regnet es noch?   *Is* it still **raining?**
Scheint die Sonne heute?   *Is* the sun **shining** *today?*

1	2
verb	rest of question

1-19 Wie ist das Wetter? Compose yes/no questions and then answer them, providing the correct information according to the illustration.

► ist / blau / der Himmel

S1: Ist der Himmel blau?   **S2:** Nein, der Himmel ist grau.

1. es / regnet
2. heiß / ist / es
3. windig / es / ist
4. zehn Grad / zeigt / das Thermometer

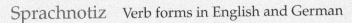

Sprachnotiz   Verb forms in English and German

The three forms of the English present tense have only one equivalent in German, i.e., forms like *it is raining* and *it does rain* do not exist in German.

it rains
it is raining ⎫ **es regnet**
it does rain ⎭

In Hamburg it rains very often.   *In Hamburg* **regnet** *es sehr oft.*
It's **raining** *today.*   *Es* **regnet** *heute.*
How often **does** *it* **rain** *in Hamburg?*   *Wie oft* **regnet** *es in Hamburg?*

Position of the verb in information questions

In information questions the verb immediately follows a question word or phrase.

Wie **ist** das Wetter heute?   *How* **is** *the weather today?*
Was **zeigt** das Thermometer?   *What* **does** *the thermometer* **read?**
Wie kalt **ist** es heute?   *How cold* **is** *it today?*

1	2	3
question word or phrase	verb	rest of question
Was	**machst**	**du heute?**

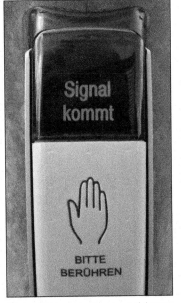

Signal kommt: How would you say this in English?

Be careful to distinguish between **wo** (*where*) and **wer** (*who*). Don't let the similarities with English confuse you!

In German all question words begin with the letter **w** (pronounced like English *v*).

wann?	*when?*	**wie viel?**	*how much?*
warum?	*why?*	**wie viele?**	*how many?*
was?	*what?*	**wo?**	*where? (in what place?)*
wer?	*who?*	**woher?**	*where … from? (from what place?)*
wie?	*how?*	**wohin?**	*where? (to what place?)*

Note that German uses three words for the word *where*, according to whether it means *in what place, from what place,* or *to what place.*

Wo ist Graz?	***Where** is Graz?*
Woher ist Martin?	***Where** is Martin **from**?*
Wohin gehst du heute Abend?	***Where** are you going tonight?*

1-20 Fragen und Antworten. Choose the appropriate response to your partner's questions.

S1:

1. Wann beginnt der Winter?
2. Was kostet die Winterjacke?
3. Warum gehst du nicht schwimmen?
4. Was macht ihr heute Abend?

5. Woher kommt Stephanie?
6. Wo ist Chicago?
7. Wer ist Stephanie?
8. Wohin geht Stephanie?

9. Wann ist die Party?
10. Wie alt ist Karl?
11. Wie viele Studenten studieren hier?
12. Wie viel Grad Celsius ist 32 Grad Fahrenheit?

S2:

a. Ich finde es zu kalt.
b. Hundert Euro.
c. Im Dezember.
d. Wir gehen ins Kino.

e. In die Mensa.
f. In Illinois.
g. Aus Chicago.
h. Sie ist Studentin.

i. Null Grad.
j. Zweitausend.
k. Im Sommer.
l. Er ist 18.

1-21 So viele Fragen! Introduce the following questions with a question word. Your partner should know the answers.

▶ _____ kommt Heidi Klum?

S1: Woher kommt Heidi Klum?   **S2:** Heidi Klum kommt aus Deutschland.

1. _____ ist das Wetter heute?
2. _____ beginnt der Sommer, im Juni oder im Juli?
3. _____ ist Innsbruck, in Deutschland oder in Österreich?
4. _____ kommt Justin Trudeau, aus England oder aus Kanada?
5. _____ singt besser, Adele oder Beyoncé?
6. _____ Meter hat ein Kilometer?
7. _____ ist einunddreißig plus sechs?
8. _____ sind im Winter so viele Deutsche in Florida?

Position of the verb in statements

In English statements the verb usually follows the subject. This holds true whether the statement begins with the subject or with another element (e.g., an expression of time or place).

| | *The thermometer* | *reads* | *only ten degrees.* |
| *Today* | *the thermometer* | *reads* | *only ten degrees.* |

In German statements the verb is *always the second element*. If the statement begins with an element other than the subject, the subject follows the verb.

1	2	3	
subject	verb	rest of statement	
Das Thermometer	**zeigt**	nur zehn Grad.	

1	2	3	4
other element	verb	subject	rest of statement
Heute	**zeigt**	**das Thermometer**	nur zehn Grad.

1-22 Schönes Wetter. Read the following sentences, beginning each one with the expression of place or time given in parentheses.

1. Das Wetter ist heute sehr schön. (in München)
2. Das Thermometer zeigt fast dreißig Grad. (im Moment)
3. Stephanie hat keine Vorlesungen. (heute Nachmittag)
4. Sie geht mit Claudia, Ali und Martin schwimmen. (später)

Heute ist das Wetter in München sehr schön.

Ja, nein, and the conjunctions in the table below do not count as elements in a sentence.

und	*and*	**aber**	*but*
oder	*or*	**denn**	*because*

Ist das Wetter schön?	*Is the weather nice?*
Ja, die Sonne **scheint**	*Yes, the sun is shining*
und der Himmel **ist** blau,	*and the sky is blue,*
aber es **ist** sehr windig.	*but it's very windy.*

1-23 Und, oder, denn, aber?

1. Regnet es _____ scheint die Sonne?
2. Der Himmel ist grau, _____ es regnet nicht.
3. Ich gehe heute nicht schwimmen, _____ es ist kalt _____ es regnet.
4. Fünfzehn Grad ist nicht sehr warm, _____ es ist auch nicht sehr kalt.
5. Der Himmel ist blau, _____ es regnet nicht mehr.

1-24 Wie ist das Wetter heute? Answer your partner's questions according to the illustration. Begin each answer with **heute.**

S1: Ist der Himmel heute grau oder blau?   **S2:** Heute ist der Himmel blau.

1. Ist es heute kalt oder heiß?
2. Zeigt das Thermometer heute zwanzig Grad oder dreißig Grad?
3. Ist es heute windig oder windstill?
4. Scheint die Sonne heute oder regnet es?

Position of *nicht*

You have already learned that you use **kein/keine** to negate a noun preceded by **ein/eine** or a noun without an article.

Ist das ein Restaurant oder eine Kneipe?	Das ist **kein** Restaurant und auch **keine** Kneipe. Das ist ein Bistro.
Hast du morgen Vorlesungen?	Nein, morgen habe ich **keine** Vorlesungen.

When you want to negate any other words or expressions, you use **nicht** and place it directly in front of those words or expressions.

Es ist **nicht kalt.**	Ich gehe **nicht in die Disco.**
Es ist **nicht sehr** windig.	Ich gehe **nicht oft** in die Disco.
	Ich gehe **nicht mit Bernd** in die Disco.

When you don't want to negate a particular word or expression, you place **nicht** at the end of the sentence.

Claudia kommt heute Abend **nicht.**
Martin kommt auch **nicht.**
Heute scheint die Sonne **nicht.**

1-25 Was für dumme Fragen! Your partner doesn't seem to be very knowledgeable. Use **nicht** to answer her/his questions.

S1: Ist fünf plus sechs zwölf?   **S2:** Nein, fünf plus sechs ist nicht zwölf.

1. Regnet es in Israel viel?   Nein, in Israel _____.
2. Beginnt der Winter im Januar?   Nein, der Winter _____.
3. Ist der Winter in Italien sehr kalt? Nein, in Italien _____.
4. Donnert und blitzt es° am Nordpol?   Nein, am Nordpol _____.
5. Regnet es am Südpol?   Nein, am Südpol _____.
6. Schneit es oft in Houston?   Nein, es schneit _____.

donnert und blitzt es: is it thundering and lightning

1-26 Was zeigt die Wetterkarte? (a) Listen to two short weather reports and identify the cities.

1. Wo ist das? Das ist _____.
2. Wo ist das? Das ist _____.

(b) Now choose another city on the map and compose a weather report for it. Read your report to a classmate, who will guess which city you are describing. The phrases below will help you write your report.

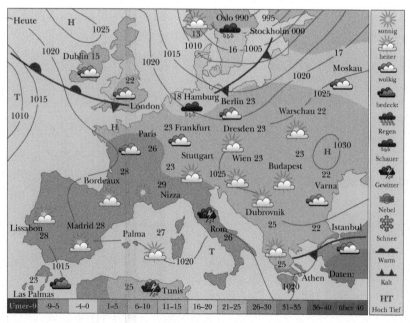

es regnet in Strömen	*it's pouring*
es donnert und blitzt	*it's thundering and lightning*
es ist heiter	*it's mostly sunny*
es ist bedeckt	*it's cloudy (overcast)*
es ist wolkig	*it's partly cloudy*
es ist schwül	*it's humid*

Expressions of time and place

In German, expressions of time precede expressions of place. In English it is the reverse.

	Time	Place
Gehst du	**jetzt**	**in die Bibliothek?**
Nein, ich gehe	**jetzt**	**in die Kneipe.**

	Place	Time
Are you going	**to the library**	**now?**
No, I'm going	**to the pub**	**now.**

GERMAN: **time**   before   **place**

 1-27 Wohin gehst du jetzt? Your partner isn't going where you expect. Use the expressions of place from the box below.

▶ jetzt

S1: Gehst du jetzt in die Bibliothek?   **S2:** Nein, ich gehe jetzt nicht in die Bibliothek. Ich gehe in die Vorlesung.

1. jetzt

2. heute Abend

3. später

4. morgen Abend

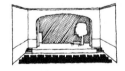 

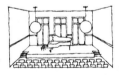

ins Theater	in die Mensa	in die Kneipe	ins Bett
in die Disco	in die Bibliothek	ins Konzert	in die Vorlesung

1-28 Was machst du heute Abend? Ask your classmates where they are going tonight, and respond to their questions.

S1: Hallo, _____. Wohin gehst du heute Abend?

S1: Ich gehe …

S2: Ich gehe heute Abend … Und du? Wohin gehst du?

Additional places you might be going: **ins Sportzentrum, ins Café, auf eine Party, nach Hause** *(home).*

1.6 Kultur 2

Studying at the university

1.6 Compare and contrast university life in the U.S. and the German-speaking countries

Going to college

In Germany a smaller percentage of the population than in North America attends the **Universität** or **Hochschule,** but those who do are more likely than their North American counterparts to complete a master's degree. In order to be considered for admission, students must successfully complete the **Abitur,** a series of exams given in the last year of a **Gymnasium,** a college preparatory high school, or pass other kinds of aptitude and entrance examinations.

> The Bologna reforms carry important implications for foreign students interested in studying in Germany, since they will greatly increase their study abroad choices for destination and curriculum and also help them transfer credits to their home institutions.

The Bologna Process

The university system in Germany, as in most other countries in Europe, has been undergoing a major reform. Universities are changing from older, nationally specific degrees and curricula to a **Bachelor-** and **Master**-degree system, which is to ensure the comparability in the standards and quality of higher education qualifications across Europe. As of now, well over 80 percent of programs already lead to a Bachelor or Master. A Bachelor's degree is expected to require 6–8 semesters of study and a Master's degree an additional 2–4. This so-called Bologna Process is to be completed by 2020.

The international campus

More than 10 percent of students at German universities are international students, showing that Germany is one of the most attractive destinations for students from around the world. The **Akademische Auslandsamt** is the office on campus where international students can go to receive help in all matters related to their stay. German students, too, have many opportunities to study in other countries, for example through the European Union's Erasmus program, a generously funded student exchange program. Most German students opt for study abroad in Spain, France, and Great Britain.

Affordable education

Although the number of private universities has been increasing in recent years, most students still attend public universities, which are much less expensive in Germany than in North America. In the fall of 2014, the last of the federal states decided to do away with tuition, and even before that tuition fees were minimal. Mandatory fees exist to finance student government and the **Studentenwerk** *(student affairs),* but these generally do not exceed 200 euros per semester. In many universities, the **Studentenwerk** is in charge of running the **Mensa** and other smaller cafeterias and pubs on campus, as well as student housing, support services for international students, a variety of counseling services, cultural programming, and even childcare. Another benefit students obtain through the mandatory fee is the **Semesterticket,** a low-cost pass valid on public transportation in the area where they study.

Eine Mensa in Bremen

Taking classes

Students choose their area of study right away and take courses in that field from the beginning; there are no general education requirements. The Bachelor curriculum is divided into a series of **Module** *(thematic units),* which consist of several interrelated courses. Courses are concluded with presentations, term papers, or exams, from which an average grade is calculated for a particular **Modul.** The grading system uses numbers rather than letters: An A is a **1 (eine Eins),** a B is a **2 (eine Zwei),** etc. A student's academic history is recorded in the **Studienbuch** (often electronic), similar to the North American transcript. Students generally complete a Bachelor degree by writing a thesis during their last semester.

Ich bin noch im ersten Semester.

In the German-speaking countries, university students receive much less guidance than in North America. They often select their courses without the help of an advisor. Classes often meet just once per week, and no attendance is taken, but many students find a group of students with common academic interests during their first year. Students' schedules are flexible as is the number of semesters they spend at the university. For this reason, students talk about where they are in their studies according to semesters (e.g., **Ich bin im vierten Semester**), instead of saying "sophomore."

1-29 Das Studienbuch. Read the excerpt from a typical German transcript and indicate what the student's major might be, and the particular focus within the field of study. What are the three different modules that are listed? How was this student's work being assessed at the end of the semester? How did this particular student do in her classes?

Modul	Art°	Titel	Wochenstunden°	Note	
Einführungsmodul: Neuzeit	Vorlesung mit Examen	Neuzeit	2	2.0	*type / hours per week*
Aufbaumodul: Neuzeitliche Geschichte	Seminar mit Hausarbeit	Neuzeit - Historiografische Perspektiven	2	1.7	
Wahlmodul: Geschichte des 20. Jahrhunderts	Vorlesung	Deutsche Außenpolitik in der Weimarer Republik	2	ohne° Note	*without*

1-30 Zum Diskutieren. Identify three aspects of university study in Germany described here that are different when compared to your own institution of higher learning. What three aspects are similar? What piece of information do you find most surprising?

1.7 Kommunikation und Formen 2

Personal pronouns

1.7 Talk about people and things using pronouns

When you want to talk about people without repeating their names, you use personal pronouns. The personal pronouns are categorized under three "persons."

1st person:	I / we *(to talk about oneself)*
2nd person:	you / you *(pl)* *(to talk <u>to</u> a second party)*
3rd person:	he, it, she / they *(to talk <u>about</u> a third party)*

What facility does this sign point to?

	Singular			Plural	
1ST PERSON	**ich**	*I*		**wir**	*we*
2ND PERSON	**du**	*you (familiar)*		**ihr**	*you (familiar)*
	Sie	*you (formal)*		**Sie**	*you (formal)*
3RD PERSON	**er**	*he, it*			
	es	*it*		**sie**	*they*
	sie	*she, it*			

As you have already learned, German nouns are either masculine, neuter, or feminine. The pronouns in the 3rd person singular **(er, es, sie)** are chosen according to the principle of *grammatical gender*, i.e., **er** for all nouns with the article **der, es** for all nouns with the article **das,** and **sie** for all nouns with the article **die.**

Ist **der** Student intelligent?	Ja, **er** ist sehr intelligent.
Ist **der** Film lang?	Ja, **er** ist sehr lang.

big

Ist **das** Thermometer kaputt?	Ja, **es** ist kaputt.
Ist **das** Studentenheim groß°?	Ja, **es** ist sehr groß.

Ist **die** Professorin fair?	Ja, **sie** ist sehr fair.
Ist **die** Vorlesung interessant?	Ja, **sie** ist sehr interessant.

In the 3rd person plural, the personal pronoun for all three genders is **sie** *(they).*

Sind **die** Studenten intelligent?	Ja, **sie** sind sehr intelligent.
Sind **die** Vorlesungen gut?	Ja, **sie** sind sehr gut.

Singular	Plural
der → er	
das → es	die → sie
die → sie	

1-31 Wie ist die Uni? With your partner, take turns asking each other about your university. Be sure to use the appropriate pronoun for each noun. Note that with plural nouns, the verb is **sind**.

S1: Ist die Uni gut?   S2: Ja, sie ist sehr gut.
S1: Sind die Vorlesungen voll? S2: Nein, sie sind nicht sehr voll.

Ist die Uni gut?   Sind die Studenten intelligent?
Ist der Campus groß?   Ist die Bibliothek groß?
Ist das Sportzentrum gut?   Sind die Studentenheime modern?
Ist das Footballteam gut?   Ist die Mensa gut?
Sind die Professoren fair?   Sind die Computer alle up to date?

Ein rollendes Café

1-32 Welche Farbe hat Lisas Bluse? Your instructor will ask you the colors of your classmates' clothes. Sometimes you may want to add **hell** or **dunkel** to the basic color, e.g., **hellblau** (light blue), **dunkelblau** (dark blue).

LEHRER(IN): Welche Farbe hat   STUDENT(IN): Sie ist rot.
            Lisas Bluse?

1. die Jacke

2. der Pullover

3. die Bluse

4. das Hemd

5. die Hose

6. der Rock

7. das Sweatshirt

8. die Jeans

9. die Baseballkappe

10. die Schuhe

Verbs in the present tense

1.8 Express states and actions

The present tense of *sein*

The present-tense forms of **sein** (*to be*) are as frequently used and as irregular as their English counterparts. Be sure to learn them well.

Singular			Plural		
ich	bin	*I am*	wir	sind	*we are*
du	bist	*you are*	ihr	seid	*you are*
er/es/sie	ist	*he/it/she is*	sie	sind	*they are*
	Sie sind	*you are*			

Because the **Sie**-form is both singular and plural, it's generally placed at the bottom of a chart between the singular and plural forms.

1-33 Kleine Gespräche. In groups of three, take on the roles of the people below. Read the conversations, supplying the correct forms of **sein.**

1. LUKAS: Hier ist ein Foto von Stephanie und Ali.
    Sie _____ gute Freunde.

    JULIA: Wie alt _____ Stephanie?

    LUKAS: Sie _____ neunzehn.

    ERGEM: Und wie alt _____ Ali?

    LUKAS: Er _____ einundzwanzig.

    Ali   Stephanie
    21 J.   19 J.

2. FRAU ERB: Wie alt _____ du, Brigitte?

    BRIGITTE: Ich _____ fünf.

    FRAU ERB: Und du, Holger, wie alt _____ du?

    HOLGER: Ich _____ drei.

    FRAU ERB: Und woher _____ ihr zwei?

    BRIGITTE: Wir _____ aus Stuttgart.

    Holger Brigitte

3. REPORTER: _____ Sie Amerikaner, Herr Smith?

    HERR SMITH: Nein, ich _____ Kanadier.

    REPORTER: Und Sie, Frau Jones, _____ Sie auch Kanadierin?

    FRAU JONES: Nein, ich _____ Amerikanerin.

    Frau Jones

    Herr Smith

1-34 Wie bist du? Fom the words shown below, choose the ones that describe you best right now. You can modify each one by adding **sehr** or **nicht sehr.** Then find out about your partner!

S1: Bist du sportlich?

S2: Ja, ich bin sehr sportlich. Bist du auch sportlich?

S1: Nein, ich bin nicht sehr sportlich.

S2: Ich bin nicht konservativ. Und du?

organisiert	optimistisch	konservativ	populär
fantasievoll	extrovertiert	progressiv	mysteriös
humorvoll	sportlich	respektvoll	talentiert

The verb: infinitive and present tense

The infinitive: In English the infinitive form of the verb is usually signaled by *to: to ask, to answer, to travel, to do*. German infinitives consist of a *verb stem* plus the ending **-en** or **-n.**

Infinitive	Stem	Ending
spielen *(to play)*	**spiel**	-en
arbeiten *(to work)*	**arbeit**	-en
reisen *(to travel)*	**reis**	-en
tun *(to do)*	**tu**	-n

The present tense: In English only the 3rd person singular has an ending in the present tense: he asks, she answers, she does, it works. In German *all* the forms of the present tense have endings. These endings are attached to the verb stem.

Singular		Plural	
ich	spiel**e**	wir	spiel**en**
du	spiel**st**	ihr	spiel**t**
er/es/sie	spiel**t**	sie	spiel**en**
	Sie	spiel**en**	

1-35 Semesterbeginn. On their way to the cafeteria, Claudia and Martin meet Ali and Carlo. Supply the appropriate verb endings.

    ALI: Grüß dich, Claudia! Tag, Martin! Das ist mein Freund Carlo aus Italien.

CLAUDIA: Tag, Carlo. Woher in Italien komm _____ du?

  CARLO: Ich komm _____ aus Rom. Und ihr, woher komm _____ ihr?

CLAUDIA: Ich bin aus Hamburg und Martin komm_____ aus Mannheim.

 MARTIN: Was studier_____ du, Carlo?

  CARLO: Ich studier_____ Linguistik.

CLAUDIA: Was mach_____ ihr jetzt? Geh _____ ihr auch in die Mensa?

    ALI: Nein, wir kauf _____ jetzt unsere° Bücher, denn morgen beginn _____   *our*
             die Vorlesungen.

If a verb stem ends in **-t** or **-d** (**antwort-en, arbeit-en, find-en**) or in certain consonant combinations like the **gn** in **regnen**, an **-e-** is inserted before the personal endings **-st** and **-t** (**du arbeit*e*st, er find*e*t, es regn*e*t**).

Singular		Plural	
ich	arbeit**e**	wir	arbeit**en**
du	arbeit**est**	ihr	arbeit**et**
er/es/sie	arbeit**et**	sie	arbeit**en**
		Sie	arbeit**en**

If a verb stem ends in **-s, -ß,** or **-z,** the personal ending in the 2nd person singular is only a **-t** (not an **-st**): **du reis*t*, du heiß*t*, du sitz*t*.**

Singular		Plural	
ich	reis**e**	wir	reis**en**
du	rei**st**	ihr	reis**t**
er/es/sie	reis**t**	sie	reis**en**
		Sie	reis**en**

Verbs with the infinitive ending **-n** (as opposed to **-en**) also have the ending **-n** in the 1st and 3rd person plural and in the **Sie**-form: **wir tu*n*, sie tu*n*, Sie tu*n*.**

1-36 Morgen. Select the appropriate verb to complete the conversation.

 ROBERT: Hi Sarah. Was [machst, machen] du morgen?

  SARAH: Hi Robert, mein Vater und ich [arbeite, arbeiten] morgen im Garten.

 ROBERT: Ich [glaubt, glaube]°, ihr [arbeiten, arbeitet] zu viel!   *think; believe*

  SARAH: Und du, du [sitzt, sitze] auf dem Sofa und [tun, tust] nichts°!   *nothing*

 ROBERT: Falsch! Ich [fliegt, fliege] morgen nach Finnland. Bei Lufthansa [kostet, kosten] das Ticket im Moment nur 79 Euro!

1-37 Kleine Gespräche. Complete the following conversations with the correct forms of the verbs. Then role-play each short scene with a partner.

Beim Rockfest

 SABINE: Ich heiß_____ Sabine. Wie heiß_____ du?

 THOMAS: Thomas. Wie find_____ du die Band?

 SABINE: Die Band spiel_____ sehr gut. Sag mal, tanz_____ du?

 THOMAS: Klar! Komm, wir tanz_____.

Im Winter

FRAU ZIEGLER: Tag, Frau Berg. Das _____ ja kalt! (sein)

 FRAU BERG: Ja, das Thermometer _____ minus zehn! (zeigen)

FRAU ZIEGLER: Wann _____ Sie nach Spanien, Ende Dezember? (reisen)

 FRAU BERG: Nein, wir _____ erst im Januar, da° _____ es nicht so viel.   *then*
            (fliegen, kosten)

Sprachnotiz The present tense to express future time

German uses the present tense to express future time more frequently than English. However, the context must show that one is referring to the future.

Nächstes Jahr **fliege** ich nach Leipzig.   *Next year I'm flying to Leipzig.*
Next year I'll be flying to Leipzig.

Was **machst** du dort?   *What will you be doing there?*
What are you going to do there?

Ich **arbeite** bei DHL.   *I'll be working for DHL.*
I'm going to be working for DHL.

The international courier firm DHL is a subsidiary of Deutsche Post DHL Group. In 2008 the company moved its European hub from Brussels to Leipzig, creating about 10,000 new jobs in the area. DHL stands for the first letter of the last names of Adrian Dalsey, Larry Hillblom, and Robert Lynn, the American founders of the company.

1-38 Sibylle und Marc. Write sentences using the elements given.

1. kommen / Sibylle und Marc / aus Dresden
2. Sibylle / Politik / Marc / und / Biologie / studieren
3. am Wochenende / arbeiten / Marc / in Potsdam
4. fliegen / die zwei / im Sommer / nach Spanien

1-39 Morgen. Read the following list of activities. In the column **Ich**, indicate **ja, nein**, or **vielleicht** (*maybe*) for each activity. Then ask your partner yes/no questions (**Gehst du morgen joggen?** etc.) and mark down the responses in the third column.

Morgen	Ich	Meine Partnerin / Mein Partner
Ich gehe joggen.	_____	_____
Ich reise nach Europa.	_____	_____
Ich arbeite bei Starbucks.	_____	_____
Ich lerne die Deutsch-Vokabeln.	_____	_____
Ich tue nichts.	_____	_____
Ich gehe in die Bibliothek.	_____	_____
Ich spiele Computerspiele.	_____	_____
Ich gehe ins Sportzentrum.	_____	_____
Ich lerne Swing tanzen.	_____	_____
Ich spiele Fußball.	_____	_____
Ich kaufe neue Schuhe.	_____	_____

1.8 Video-Treff

Das bin ich

1.9 **Understand authentic video of German speakers introducing themselves**

In the *Treffpunkt Deutsch* video, you will get to know some Germans—where they live, study, work, and have fun. Each of the 12 segments contains clips from informal, unscripted interviews with native speakers on topics relating to the chapter theme. In this segment the interviewees introduce themselves.

1-40 **Was ist das auf Englisch?** Find the English equivalents for the German words in boldface.

1. Ich **arbeite als** Radiomoderator.	a. live
2. Das **buchstabiert sich** S-o-w-a-d-e.	b. at the
3. Homburg ist **eine Kleinstadt** nahe der französischen Grenze.	c. work as
	d. was born
4. Nicolai **ist bald** drei Jahre alt.	e. is spelled
5. Brandenburg ist **im Osten von Deutschland.**	f. will soon be
6. Ich studiere **an der** Humboldt-Universität.	g. a small town
7. Ich studiere hier **Germanistik** und Sport.	h. German Studies
8. Ich **bin** in Mainz **geboren.**	i. in Eastern Germany
9. Ich **lebe** in Berlin und arbeite auch hier.	

> Always complete the **Was ist das auf Englisch?** exercise *before* watching the video in every chapter. This pre-viewing activity introduces you to some words and expressions you'll encounter in the video.

Before you watch the video, read through the exercises below. This will give you some additional information and let you know what you should be watching and listening for.

Look for visual cues in the video for more information about the speakers and what they're saying. Watch the entire video first, then watch again and pause and replay as needed to complete the tasks. Keep in mind that you don't need to understand every single word!

1-41 **Was passt?** Choose the appropriate information to complete the sentences below.

1. Stefan Kuhlmann ist _____ und Radiomoderator in Berlin.
   ☐ Student ☐ DJ

2. Ursula Klein-Turak ist 36 und kommt aus _____.
   ☐ Homburg ☐ Leipzig

3. Thomas Scheier ist Student und ist _____ Jahre alt.
   ☐ 24 ☐ 23

4. Thomas studiert in Berlin _____.
   ☐ Finanzwirtschaft ☐ Volkswirtschaft

5. Maiga Reitzenstein studiert an der _____ in Berlin.
   ☐ Humboldt-Universität ☐ Freien Universität

6. Maiga Reitzenstein ist aus Göttingen und studiert _____.
   ☐ Englisch und Japanisch ☐ Englisch und Spanisch

7. _____ Brieger ist 35 Jahre alt und ist aus Bocholt.
   ☐ Christoph ☐ Christina

8. _____ Brieger ist 37 Jahre alt und kommt aus Mainz.
   ☐ Christoph ☐ Christina

9. Nicolai Brieger ist fast drei Jahre alt und kommt aus _____.
   ☐ Wiesbaden ☐ Mainz

1-42 Richtig oder falsch? Decide whether the following statements are **richtig** or **falsch.** If the statement is **falsch,** provide a corrected version.

	RICHTIG	FALSCH
1. André Sowade kommt aus Ostdeutschland.	☐	☐
2. André ist 21 Jahre alt.	☐	☐
3. Anja Peter ist 23 und ist aus Brandenburg im Osten von Deutschland.	☐	☐
4. Susann arbeitet in Dresden, aber sie kommt aus Berlin.	☐	☐
5. Karen studiert Politik, Philosophie und Kunstgeschichte.	☐	☐
6. Stefan Meister ist 31.	☐	☐
7. Stefan Meister ist Student.	☐	☐
8. Anja Szustak kommt aus Leipzig und studiert auch dort.	☐	☐
9. Der Löwe ist das Symbol von Berlin.	☐	☐

Der Löwe als Stadtsymbol

1.9 Wortschatz 2

Wichtige Vokabeln

1.10 Learn vocabulary to talk about the days of the week, the months, and the seasons; say where you're going

Nomen

der Tag, -e	day	der Freund, -e	friend; boyfriend
die Woche, -n	week	die Freundin, -nen	friend; girlfriend
der Monat, -e	month	der Lehrer, -	(*male*) teacher
das Jahr, -e	year	die Lehrerin, -nen	(*female*) teacher
die Jahreszeit, -en	season	der Mitbewohner, -	(*male*) roommate
der Frühling	spring	die Mitbewohnerin, -nen	(*female*) roommate
der Sommer	summer		
der Herbst	fall, autumn		
der Winter	winter		

In German the same word is used for a friend and for someone to whom one is romantically attached.

Verben

arbeiten	to work
finden	to find
fliegen	to fly
glauben	to believe; to think
kosten	to cost
lernen	to learn; to study (*e.g., for a test*)
reisen	to travel
sitzen	to sit
spielen	to play
stehen	to stand
tanzen	to dance
tun	to do

Konjunktionen

und	and	aber	but
oder	or	denn	because

Fragewörter

wann?	when?	wie viel?	how much?
warum?	why?	wie viele?	how many?
was?	what?	wo?	where? (*in what place?*)
wer?	who?	woher?	where … from? (*from what place?*)
wie?	how?	wohin?	where? (*to what place?*)

Andere Wörter

besonders	particularly, especially	sportlich	athletic
interessant	interesting	vielleicht	maybe
nichts	nothing	von … bis	from … to
sehr	very	zusammen	together

Ausdrücke

am Montag	on Monday	nach Claudias Vorlesung	after Claudia's lecture
Ende Januar	at the end of January	nach Florida	to Florida
im Januar	in January	Claudia kommt auch nicht.	Claudia isn't coming either.
im Winter	in the winter		

Das Gegenteil

die Frage, -n ≠ die Antwort, -en	question ≠ answer	hier ≠ dort	here ≠ there
fragen ≠ antworten	to ask ≠ to answer	richtig ≠ falsch	true ≠ false
hell ≠ dunkel	light ≠ dark	viel ≠ wenig	much ≠ little

Wohin gehst du?

in die Bibliothek	to the library	ins Bett	to bed
in die Disco	to the disco	ins Kino	to the movies
in die Kneipe	to the bar/pub	ins Konzert	to a concert
in die Mensa	to the cafeteria	ins Theater	to the theater
in die Vorlesung	to the lecture		

> Like the months and the seasons, the days of the week are masculine.

Die Wochentage

der Montag
der Dienstag
der Mittwoch
der Donnerstag
der Freitag
der Samstag
der Sonntag

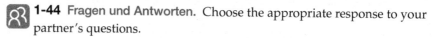

Die Monate

der Januar	der April	der Juli	der Oktober
der Februar	der Mai	der August	der November
der März	der Juni	der September	der Dezember

Wörter im Kontext

1-43 Konjunktionen, bitte!

1. Claudia _____ Stephanie studieren in München.
2. Kommt Martin aus Berlin _____ aus Mannheim?
3. Ist es kalt? Ja, _____ nicht sehr.
4. Heute kaufe ich meine Bücher, _____ morgen beginnen die Vorlesungen.

1-44 Fragen und Antworten. Choose the appropriate response to your partner's questions.

S1:

1. Wann reisen Sie nach Italien, Frau Erb?
2. Wohin fliegen viele Deutsche im Winter?
3. Wie lange seid ihr in Berlin?
4. Wie heißt Claudias Mitbewohnerin?
5. Spielt ihr heute Eishockey?
6. Was tust du heute Abend?

S2:

a. Nach Florida.
b. Ja, nach Alis Vorlesung.
c. Nichts.
d. Von Freitag bis Sonntag.
e. Im Herbst.
f. Stephanie.

1-45 Fragen und Antworten. Choose the appropriate response to your partner's questions.

S1:

1. Wie viele Monate hat ein Jahr?
2. Wie viel kosten Alis Bücher?
3. Wie viele Tage hat eine Woche?
4. Wo arbeitet Frau Berger?
5. Was macht ihr heute Abend?
6. Wie tanzt Stephanie?

S2:

a. Hundertfünfzig Euro.
b. Im Supermarkt.
c. Zwölf.
d. Sehr gut.
e. Sieben.
f. Ich glaube, wir gehen in die Bibliothek und lernen.

Sprachnotiz lernen vs. studieren

Both verbs can mean *to study*, but with different connotations.

Thomas **studiert** Germanistik.   *Thomas is studying German language and*
                                     literature (as a major).

Andrea **lernt** für das Quiz.   *Andrea is studying for the quiz.*

Lernen also means *to learn*, as in English.

Andrea **lernt** Deutsch.   *Andrea is learning German* (learning the
                             language, taking a language course).

1-46 **Was passt nicht?** In each group, identify the word that doesn't fit.

1. der Tag	die Woche	2. interessant	lernen	3. sitzen	reisen
der Monat	das Jahr	sportlich	gut	nichts	kosten
die Kneipe		dunkel		tun	

1-47 **Gegenteile.**

1. Der Tag ist _____ und die Nacht ist _____.

2. Der Professor _____ und der Student _____.

3. Fünfhundert Euro sind _____ und fünf Euro sind _____.

4. Ein „A" ist _____ und ein „F" ist _____.

1-48 **Ergänzen Sie!**

1. Heute ist Montag und morgen ist _____.

2. Gestern war° Samstag und heute ist _____.   *was*

3. Heute ist Donnerstag und gestern war _____.

4. Heute ist Sonntag und morgen ist _____.

5. Gestern war Donnerstag und morgen ist _____.

Fischverkauf
Öffnungszeiten

Sommer 1.5. – 31.10.

Montag	:	9.00 - 18.00 Uhr
Dienstag	:	**Ruhetag**
Mittwoch	:	9.00 - 18.00 Uhr
Donnerstag	:	9.00 - 18.00 Uhr
Freitag	:	9.00 - 18.00 Uhr
Samstag	:	9.00 - 18.00 Uhr
Sonntag	:	11.00 - 18.00 Uhr

Was ist ein Ruhetag?

Wörter unter der Lupe
Cognates

In *Erste Kontakte* and this chapter you have seen that German and English are closely related languages. Many words are so close in sound and spelling to their English equivalents that you can easily guess their meanings. Words in different languages that are identical or similar in form and meaning are called *cognates*.

Some words are identical or almost identical in form, but different in meaning. These are sometimes called "false friends": **arm** (*poor*), **also** (*so*), **fast** (*almost*), **bekommen** (*to receive*).

Why German and English are similar: The Angles and Saxons

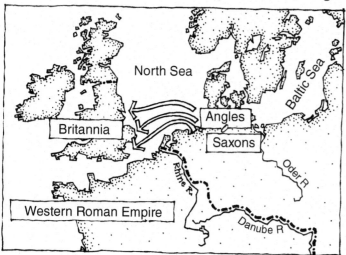

North Sea

Baltic Sea

Angles

Saxons

Britannia

Rhine R.

Oder R.

Western Roman Empire

Danube R

Many of the similarities between English and German can be traced back 1600 years to the time when the Angles and Saxons, Germanic tribes from what is today northern Germany, invaded Britain and settled there. Around CE 200 the Roman Empire encompassed not only the countries around the Mediterranean, but also present-day Austria, Switzerland, Southern Germany, France, and most of the British Isles. Beginning about the fourth century CE shiploads of Angle and Saxon warriors crossed the North Sea to England and attacked the increasingly vulnerable defenses of the Roman Empire. When the Romans finally retreated from Britain in the fifth century, the Angles and Saxons remained and settled the country. It was the Germanic languages of these tribes that became the foundation for present-day English.

1-49 Leicht zu verstehen. Give the English cognates of the following sets of German words.

1. *Family:* die Mutter, der Vater, der Sohn, die Tochter, der Bruder, die Schwester
2. *Parts of the body:* das Haar, die Nase, die Lippe, die Schulter, der Arm, der Ellbogen, die Hand, der Finger, der Fingernagel, das Knie, der Fuß
3. *Descriptive words:* jung, alt, neu, hart, lang, laut, voll, frisch, sauer, dumm, gut, reich
4. *Animals:* der Fisch, die Ratte, die Maus, die Katze, der Hund, die Laus, der Wurm, der Fuchs, der Bulle, die Kuh
5. *Food and drink:* die Butter, das Brot, der Käse, der Apfel, das Salz, der Pfeffer, das Wasser, das Bier, der Wein, die Milch

1-50 Wie heißt das Restaurant? In the German-speaking countries, many restaurants and hotels have ornate wrought-iron signs. Look at the sampling below and match them with the names in the box.

1.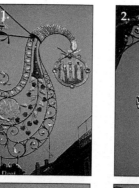
2.
3.
4.
5.
6.
7.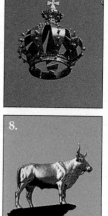
8.

The Norman invasion of Britain in 1066 brought further changes to the English language. French became the language of the ruling class, and evidence of this can be seen in examples like the following: It was the lower-class farmer who raised *swine, cows, and sheep,* all words of Germanic origin (in modern German **Schwein, Kuh, Schaf**). However, when the meat of these animals was served to the nobility, it was called *pork, beef,* and *mutton* (French **porc, bœuf, mouton**).

der Ochse	die Krone	die Sonne	das Lamm
der Schwan	das Kreuz	das Einhorn	die drei Könige

1.10 Alles zusammen

Drei Promi-Profile°

celebrity profiles

This popular German format shows basic information about a famous person. In this *Alles zusammen* section, you'll read three **Promi-Profile,** write your own **Profil,** and record a self-introduction using some of the features you've learned about here.

> Now try out your German step by step *(Schritt für Schritt)*. Look for cognates and see how much you can already understand.

Promi-Profil

Christoph Waltz

Der österreichische Film-Promi ist auch in Hollywood beliebt – 2010 und 2013 gewinnt er Oscars (Inglourious Basterds, Django Unchained). In Europa und Amerika liebt man Waltz und seine Filme.

BEKANNT ALS	**Christoph Waltz**
VORNAME	**Christoph**
NAME	**Waltz**
GEBURTSTAG	**4. Oktober 1956**
ALTER	**62 Jahre**
GEBURTSORT	**Wien / Österreich**
GRÖSSE	**1,70 m**
STERNZEICHEN	**Waage**

Promi-Profil

Alexandra Popp

Den Titel „Fußballerin des Jahres" bekommt sie schon mit 23 Jahren. Die Deutsche Meisterschaft und vieles mehr gewinnt die Sportlerin jahrein, jahraus.

BEKANNT ALS	**Alexandra Popp**
VORNAME	**Alexandra**
NAME	**Popp**
GEBURTSTAG	**6. April 1991**
ALTER	**27 Jahre**
GEBURTSORT	**Witten / Deutschland**
GRÖSSE	**1,74 m**
STERNZEICHEN	**Widder**

Promi-Profil

Ana ist eine Tennis-Legende. Sie hat einen French Open Titel aus dem Jahr 2008. Klasse ist auch ihr neues Leben mit Ehemann Bastian Schweinsteiger!

Ana Ivanovic

BEKANNT ALS	**Ana Ivanovic**
VORNAME	**Ana**
NAME	**Ivanovic**
GEBURTSTAG	**11. Juni 1987**
ALTER	**31 Jahre**
GEBURTSORT	**Belgrad / Jugoslawien**
GRÖSSE	**1,84 m**
STERNZEICHEN	**Zwillinge**
EHEMANN:	**Profi-Fußballer Bastian Schweinsteiger**

BEFREUNDET MIT

Schritt 1: Zum Lesen

1-51 Lesen Sie die drei Promi-Profile.

1-52 Wer bin ich? Now match each statement to the star that it describes.

Christoph Waltz	Alexandra Popp	Ana Ivanovic

1. Ich bin Sportlerin und spiele professionell Fußball.
2. Ich komme nicht aus Deutschland, und auch nicht aus Österreich.
3. Ich komme aus Wien und arbeite als Schauspieler.
4. Ich habe für *Inglourious Basterds* einen Oscar gewonnen!
5. Mein Mann ist Fußballspieler.
6. Ich bin im April geboren.
7. Ich bin über 1,80 Meter groß.
8. Ich habe blonde Haare.

> Do a German web search for *Christoph Waltz* to keep up with his latest work and awards.

Schritt 2: Zum Schreiben

1-53 Ihr Promi-Profil. Now write a **Promi-Profil** about yourself, using the form below.

Promi-Profil

Mein Foto hier!

BEKANNT ALS _____

VORNAME _____

NAME _____

GEBURTSTAG _____

ALTER _____

GEBURTSORT _____

GRÖSSE _____

STERNZEICHEN _____

Wassermann
21. Januar - 19. Februar

Fische
20. Februar - 20. März

Widder
21. März - 20. April

Stier
21. April - 20. Mai

Zwillinge
21. Mai - 21. Juni

Krebs
22. Juni - 22. Juli

Löwe
23. Juli - 23. August

Jungfrau
24. August - 23. September

Waage
24. September - 23. Oktober

Skorpion
24. Oktober - 22 November

Schütze
23. November - 21. Dezember

Steinbock
22. Dezember - 20. Januar

Schritt 3: Zum Präsentieren

1-54. Das bin ich! Present your profile to the class. Be sure to focus on your pronunciation.

Congratulations! You've just read three German texts, written a German **Profil**, and introduced yourself to your teacher and classmates in German!

Kapitel 2
Freunde

Beste Freundinnen

Learning Objectives

2.1 Compare and contrast sports involvement in Germany and North America

2.2 Learn vocabulary to talk about friends, sports, and hobbies

2.3 Distinguish between long and short *a, e, i, o,* and *u*

2.4 Use the verb **haben** to express ownership

2.5 Express likes, dislikes, and preferences

2.6 State the time

2.7 Compare and contrast online practices in Germany and North America

2.8 Identify the subject in a sentence

2.9 Describe people, places, and things—nominative case

2.10 Understand authentic video of German speakers introducing their friends

2.11 Learn vocabulary to talk about daily activities, clothing, and studying at the university

2.1 Vorschau

Uni-Sport

Just as in North America, universities in the German-speaking countries hold
a variety of sports events for students throughout the year. Check out this flyer
advertising a sports-related event, and glean the information you need to respond to
the questions below.

2-1 Was ist das auf Deutsch? Look for German equivalents in the flyer for the
following: *tournament, drinks, running, entry/admission, information, 1:00.*

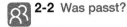 **2-2 Was passt?**

1. Wann ist das Fest?
   a. Im Sommer.
   b. Im Winter.
2. Wo ist das Fest?
   a. In Basel.
   b. Im Uni-Sportzentrum.

3. Wie viel kostet ein Ticket zum Turnier?
   a. 12 Euro.
   b. Nichts.

4. Wie groß sind die Teams für Beachvolleyball?
   a. Nicht mehr als sechs Personen.
   b. Nicht mehr als zwei Personen.

5. Wann endet das Programm?
   a. Um Mitternacht.
   b. Um 15 Uhr.

Freunde – zwei Perspektiven

))) Listen to the two different descriptions of Alexander.

Nina Ziegler sagt: Das ist mein Freund Alexander. Er ist groß und schlank und hat ein tolles Motorrad. Alex hat viele Hobbys: er spielt sehr gut Basketball und Eishockey, und er schwimmt gern. Übrigens spielt Alex ganz toll Gitarre (er hat eine Band!). Er studiert Politik und bekommt immer gute Noten.

Robert Ziegler sagt: Ich finde Alexander doof. Er telefoniert oft stundenlang mit Nina und abends ist er oft bis zehn oder elf bei uns und spielt seine blöde Gitarre. Was findet meine Schwester denn so toll an Alex? Ich finde nur sein Motorrad toll!

2-3 Anders gesagt. With a partner, read *Freunde* again and find equivalents for the following statements.

➤ Alexander ist sehr musikalisch. = Alexander spielt ganz toll Gitarre.

1. Alexander ist sehr sportlich.

2. Alex ist auch sehr intelligent.

3. Ich finde Alexander gar nicht toll.

4. Alex ist abends oft bis 22 oder 23 Uhr bei Zieglers.

5. Nina und Alexander telefonieren viel miteinander.

The flavoring particle **denn** is frequently added to questions. It may express curiosity and interest, but it can also indicate irritation. It doesn't change the basic meaning of the question. **Denn** usually follows the subject of the question.

))) **2-4 Richtig oder falsch?** You will hear the two descriptions of Alexander. Indicate whether the statements about the descriptions are **richtig** or **falsch**.

	Richtig	Falsch
1.	_____	_____
2.	_____	_____
3.	_____	_____

2-5 Meine beste Freundin/Mein bester Freund. Answer your partner's questions about your best friend. You will find additional vocabulary to describe personal characteristics and personality traits under **Persönliche Merkmale** in the *Anhang* on p. A-9.

S1: Wie heißt deine beste Freundin/ dein bester Freund? **S2:** Sie/Er heißt …

S1: Wie alt ist sie/er? **S2:** Sie/Er ist …

S1: Wie ist sie/er? **S2:** Sie/Er ist …

nice	groß	sehr nett°	(nicht) sehr praktisch
short	klein°	sehr intelligent	(nicht) sehr sportlich
	schlank	immer optimistisch	(nicht) sehr musikalisch
plump	mollig°	sehr kreativ	

2.2 Kultur 1

Sports and clubs in the German-speaking countries

2.1 Compare and contrast sports involvement in Germany and North America

Sports at universities

Students and staff at German universities can become involved in sports in numerous ways. **Hochschulsport**, as in North America, has two purposes: to offer facilities and instruction for both non-competitive and competitive sports. **Breitensport** focuses on bringing people of various backgrounds together to improve their fitness and to have fun doing sports. In this area, students may participate in intramural competitions. **Leistungssport** involves training hard and competing in national and international sporting events. Competitions between universities do not have the same economic and cultural significance as Division I collegiate competition in the United States.

The club system

The same dual purpose of organized sports also characterizes sports culture outside of the universities. Most sports activity in Germany takes place in a **Verein** or **Klub**. In 2015, there were over 90,000 sports clubs in Germany, with nearly 23 million members. **Vereine** rely on membership fees, corporate sponsorship, and a great deal of help from volunteers, both in management positions and for maintenance, events, and competitions. Only the top levels of clubs, e.g., professional teams such as the world-renowned **Fußball-Club Bayern München**, which has been a dominant force in the **1. Bundesliga** (highest professional league) for some time, are organized as corporations.

> 35% of German men and 23% of German women are members in a **Sportverein**.

König Ludwig Lauf in Oberammergau (Bayern)

Two contrasting examples

The **1. FC Kaiserslautern (FCK)** was founded in 1900, currently has 18,500 members, and is a well-known soccer club in a mid-size town in **Rheinland-Pfalz**. The professional soccer team is currently in the **2. Bundesliga**. As is typical for clubs of this stature, the club has soccer teams for all ages and is hoping that some of the under-17 players it is training today will some day play at the professional level.

> This annual cross-country skiing race in southern Bavaria is organized by the **König Ludwig Lauf Verein** and is a good example of an event that includes both **Leistungssport** and **Breitensport**.

Over time, the **FCK** has added divisions for other sports, such as basketball, boxing, handball, field hockey, track and field, running, and triathlon. Such variety is typical for many of the larger sport clubs in Germany.

On the other side of the spectrum stands a club like the **Harzer Tischtennisclub 2009 Wernigerode (HTTC 09)**. This club is located in a small town in **Sachsen-Anhalt** and was founded in 2009, originally with 44 members. The HTTC 09 homepage proudly announces that number has now doubled and its various teams have been reaching new levels of achievement by moving up into higher divisions. In table tennis, as in all other competitive sports in Germany, a promotion and relegation system is in place. Teams that finish at the top of the division are promoted up to the next level **(Aufstieg)**. If things do not go well during the next season they will be relegated down to the lower level again **(Abstieg)**.

> **Vereine** are also for non-sporting activities, like music or theater groups, writing circles, nature clubs, etc.

2-6 Vereine. Explore the variety of German club culture in sports and beyond by doing a Web search of the word **Vereine** and a German city of your choice. Write down two **Sportvereine** focused on sports that you can recognize in German, as well as one other **Verein** that intrigues you. Which one(s) would you want to be a part of? How do these clubs compare to those in your hometown? Share your findings with your class.

Fußball: King of sports in Germany

Fußball is so much a part of Germany's sports culture that it's hard to imagine it hasn't always been that way. Before World War II, Germany had only a lackluster national team, especially compared to its successful competitors in Austria, Hungary, and England. It was not until 1954, when the West German national team won its first World Cup in Bern, Switzerland, that **Fußball** really came into its own.

Today **Fußball** is a multimillion-euro business. Top **Fußballspieler** enjoy celebrity status and earn large salaries. Many players from other countries play in the professional leagues in Germany. On soccer season weekends, about 300,000 fans flock to the stadiums to cheer on their favorite teams in the **Bundesliga.** With 6 to 7 million viewers, televised games pull in huge advertising revenues. While not as lucrative as men's soccer, professional women's soccer holds its own: The German national team won two World tournaments as well as four Olympic medals,

> Organized sports are similar in the other German-speaking countries. In Austria and Switzerland, soccer is the most popular sport to play and to watch, but winter sports rank higher in popularity than in Germany.

including a gold at the Rio de Janeiro Olympic games in 2016.

Fußball is more than just a spectator sport in Germany. Germans of all ages play the game. Just about every town has an amateur soccer team and each team belongs to the **Deutscher Fußball-Bund.** With 25,000 clubs and 6.9 million members, this umbrella organization is the largest sporting association in the country.

Jubelnde Fußballfans in Berlin

2-7 Fußball. Get to know the professional soccer leagues and the relegation system in Germany by visiting the official Web site of the **Bundesliga.** Choose a team, find its roster, and write down how many foreign players are on the team and where they are from. Are there any Americans or Canadians playing in the **Bundesliga** today?

⟨⟩ 2.3 Wortschatz 1

Wichtige Vokabeln

2.2 Learn vocabulary to talk about friends, sports, and hobbies

Nomen

der Fußballspieler, -	
die Fußballspielerin, -nen	soccer player
die Liga, Ligen *(pl)*	league
der Verein, -e	club
das Handy, -s	cell phone
das Motorrad, ̈er	motorcycle
die Note, -n	grade

Verben

bekommen	to get; to receive
haben	to have
sagen	to say
telefonieren (mit)	to talk on the phone (with)
trinken	to drink

Andere Wörter

bis	until
blöd	
doof	stupid
immer	always
miteinander	with each other; together
nett	nice
übrigens	by the way

Ausdrücke

bei uns	at our house
bei Zieglers	at the Zieglers
Ich koche gern.	I like to cook.

Das Gegenteil

groß ≠ klein	big; tall ≠ little, small; short
intelligent ≠ dumm	intelligent ≠ stupid; dumb
schlank ≠ mollig	slim ≠ plump

Zeit

die Zeit, -en	time
die Minute, -n	minute
die Sekunde, -n	second
die Stunde, -n	hour
stundenlang	for hours
die Uhr, -en	clock; watch
zehn Uhr	ten o'clock
um zehn Uhr	at ten o'clock

> **die Minute, die Sekunde, die Stunde:** Remember that most nouns that end in **-e** are feminine.

Getränke

das Getränk, -e	beverage, drink
das Bier	beer
die Cola	cola
der Kaffee	coffee
die Milch	milk
der Tee	tea
das Wasser	water
der Wein	wine

Sport

Sport machen	to do sports
Fitnesstraining machen	to work out
Basketball spielen	to play basketball
Eishockey spielen	to play hockey
Fußball spielen	to play soccer
Golf spielen	to play golf
Tennis spielen	to play tennis
joggen gehen	to go jogging
schwimmen gehen	to go swimming
snowboarden gehen	to go snowboarding
wandern gehen	to go hiking

More sports and hobbies are listed in the *Anhang* on p. A-5.

Andere Hobbys

bloggen	to blog
fotografieren	to photograph, take pictures
Gitarre spielen	to play the guitar
Klavier spielen	to play the piano
kochen	to cook
singen	to sing

Hobby: Loan words like **Hobby** and **Baby** form the plural simply by adding **-s.**

Leicht zu verstehen

die Band, -s
das Hobby, -s
der Klub, -s
die Perspektive, -n
der Softdrink, -s
kreativ
modern
musikalisch
praktisch

Both **Klub** and **Club** are acceptable.

Wörter im Kontext

2-8 Was passt wo? Complete the sentences with the correct form of the appropriate verb.

kochen / haben / telefonieren / bekommen / sagen

1. Heute Nachmittag _____ wir keine Vorlesungen.
2. Mein Freund _____ immer gute Noten.
3. Robert _____, er findet Alexanders Motorrad toll.
4. Warum _____ du immer so lang, Nina?
5. Was _____ wir heute Abend: Spaghetti oder Risotto?

2-9 Was passt wo? One of the words in the list is to be used twice.

Zeit / stundenlang / Uhr / Stunde / Sekunden

1. Nina telefoniert oft _____ mit Alexander.
2. Für Alexander hat Nina immer _____.
3. Alexander ist abends oft bis elf _____ bei Zieglers.
4. Eine Rolex ist eine sehr gute _____.
5. Eine _____ hat sechzig Minuten und eine Minute hat sechzig _____.

2-10 Was für Getränke passen hier?

1. In _____, in _____ und in _____ ist Koffein.
2. Babys trinken _____.
3. In _____ und in _____ ist Alkohol.
4. In allen Getränken ist sehr viel _____.

2-11 Was passt wo? Some of the words in the list are to be used twice.

mollig / schlank / groß / klein / intelligent

1. Elefanten sind _____ und Mäuse sind _____.
2. Fotomodelle sind sehr _____ und sehr schick.
3. Balletttänzerinnen sind nicht _____, sondern schlank.
4. Basketballspieler sind oft sehr _____.
5. Jockeys sind _____.
6. Delfine und Schimpansen sind sehr _____.

2-12 Getrennte Wörter. Reconstruct the cognates below by matching the parts appropriately.

1. mo- _____   a. -tisch
2. fotogra- _____   b. -kalisch
3. intelli- _____   c. -dern
4. kre- _____   d. -nieren
5. prak- _____   e. -ativ
6. telefo- _____   f. -fieren
7. musi- _____   g. -gent

2.4 Zur Aussprache

In English the spelling of a word does not always indicate how it is pronounced (e.g., pl*ough*, thr*ough*, thor*ough*, en*ough*). English pronunciation is also a poor indicator of spelling (e.g., b*e*, s*ee*, bel*ie*ve, rec*ei*ve). In German, spelling and pronunciation are much more consistent. Once you have mastered a few basic principles, you should have no trouble pronouncing and spelling new words.

The vowels *a*, *e*, *i*, *o*, and *u*

2.3 Distinguish between long and short *a*, *e*, *i*, *o*, and *u*

In a stressed syllable, each of these five vowels is either long or short. Listen carefully to the pronunciation of the following words and sentences and at the same time note the spelling. You will see that certain letter combinations indicate quite reliably whether a vowel in a stressed syllable is long or short.

Always long

- A doubled vowel: H**aa**r, T**ee**, B**oo**t.
- A vowel followed by an **h**: J**a**hr, g**e**ht, S**o**hn, **U**hr.
- An **i** followed by an **e**: B**ie**r, s**ie**ben.
- A vowel followed by one consonant plus another vowel: N**a**se, wen**i**g, K**i**no, Th**o**mas, Min**u**te.
- A vowel followed by an **ß**: gr**o**ß, Str**a**ße, F**u**ßball.

Always short

- A vowel followed by a doubled consonant: M**a**nn, W**e**tter, L**i**ppe, S**o**mmer, S**u**ppe.

Usually short

- A vowel followed by two or more consonants: L**a**nd, M**e**nsa, tr**i**nken, T**o**chter, St**u**nde.

 2-13 Hören Sie gut zu und wiederholen Sie!

a (lang)	a (kurz)
Haar, lahm, Lama	hart, Lampe, Lamm
Mein Name ist Beate Mahler.	Tanja tanzt gern Tango.
Mein Vater ist aus Saalfeld.	Walter tanzt lieber Walzer.

e (lang)	e (kurz)
Tee, gehen, leben	Teddybär, gestern, lernen
Peter geht im Regen segeln.	Ein Student hat selten° Geld.

seldom

i (lang)	i (kurz)
Liebe, Miete, Kino	Lippe, Mitte, Kinder
Dieter liebt Lisa.	Fischers Fritz fischt frische Fische.

o (lang)	o (kurz)
doof, Sohn, Ton	Donner, Sonne, toll
Warum ist Thomas so doof?	Am Sonntag kommt Onkel Otto.

u (lang)	u (kurz)
Stuhl, Schule, super	Stunde, Schulter, Suppe
Utes Pudel frisst° nur Nudeln.	In Ulm, und um Ulm, und um Ulm herum.

eats (feeds on)

 2-14 Lang oder kurz? Listen to the *stressed* vowel in each of the words you hear. Repeat the word after the speaker, and select the corresponding designation.

1. _____ a kurz _____ a lang   9. _____ i kurz _____ i lang
2. _____ a kurz _____ a lang   10. _____ o kurz _____ o lang
3. _____ a kurz _____ a lang   11. _____ o kurz _____ o lang
4. _____ e kurz _____ e lang   12. _____ o kurz _____ o lang
5. _____ e kurz _____ e lang   13. _____ u kurz _____ u lang
6. _____ e kurz _____ e lang   14. _____ u kurz _____ u lang
7. _____ i kurz _____ i lang   15. _____ u kurz _____ u lang
8. _____ i kurz _____ i lang

Peter geht im Regen segeln.

2.5 Kommunikation und Formen 1

The present tense of *haben*

2.4 Use the verb *haben* to express ownership

Like English *to have*, the verb **haben** has many functions. For example, it is used to show ownership or possession of something.

Zieglers **haben** ein schönes Haus.	*The Zieglers have a beautiful house.*
Hast du ein Motorrad, Robert?	*Do you have a motorcycle, Robert?*
Ich **habe** braune Augen.	*I have brown eyes.*
Eine Minute **hat** sechzig Sekunden.	*A minute has sixty seconds.*
Wie viele Vorlesungen **habt** ihr heute?	*How many lectures do you have today?*
Heute **haben** wir viel Zeit.	*Today we have a lot of time.*

Singular		Plural	
ich	habe	wir	haben
du	**hast**	ihr	habt
er/es/sie	**hat**	sie	haben
	Sie haben		

Note that the **b** of the verb stem is dropped in the 2nd and 3rd person singular.

2-15 Was passt zusammen?

1. Alexander _____
2. Zieglers _____
3. Du _____
4. Ich _____
5. Ihr _____

a. habe sehr gute Professoren.
b. hast so schöne, braune Augen, Claudia.
c. habt ein schönes, großes Zimmer°.   *room*
d. hat ein tolles Motorrad.
e. haben viele Freunde.

2-16 Fragen und Antworten. Supply the appropriate forms of **haben**.

S1:

1. _____ du heute Abend Zeit?
2. _____ Claudia blaue Augen?
3. _____ Peters Eltern ein Haus?
4. _____ ihr heute viele Vorlesungen?
5. _____ Sie ein Auto, Herr Berger?
6. Wie viele Stunden _____ ein Tag?
7. Wie viele Kinder _____ Herr und Frau Obama?
8. _____ Robert eine Freundin?
9. Wie viel Geld _____ ihr noch?
10. Was _____ du jetzt, Politik oder Deutsch?

S2:

Nein, heute Abend _____ ich keine Zeit.
Nein, sie _____ braune Augen.
Ja, sie _____ ein sehr schönes Haus.
Nein, heute _____ wir nur zwei Vorlesungen.
Nein, aber ich _____ ein Motorrad.
Ein Tag _____ vierundzwanzig Stunden.
Sie _____ zwei Kinder.

Nein, er _____ keine Freundin.
Wir _____ nur noch fünfzig Euro.
Zuerst _____ ich Deutsch und dann Politik.

Verb + *gern* or *lieber*

2.5 Express likes, dislikes, and preferences

Verb + *gern*

In German the most common way of saying that you like to do something is to use a verb with **gern**. To say that you don't like to do something, you can use a verb with **nicht gern**.

Tom kocht **gern**.	*Tom **likes to** cook.*
Helga spielt **gern** Klavier.	*Helga **likes to** play the piano.*
Nina geht **gern** tanzen.	*Nina **likes to** go dancing.*
Robert lernt **nicht gern**.	*Robert **doesn't like** studying.*

2-17 Was für Musik hörst du gern? Find out from two classmates what they like to listen to. You can also ask about specific singers, bands, or composers, as in the example below.

S1: Was für Musik hörst du gern?   **S2:** Ich höre gern Hip-Hop.

S1: Cool! Hörst du gern Kanye West?   **S2:** Klar! Und du, was für Musik hörst du gern?

Jazz	Pop	Rock	Country und Western	Heavy Metal
Klassische Musik	Reggae	Hip-Hop	Techno	Soulmusik

2-18 Was für Sport machen diese Leute gern? Take turns asking your partner what each person here likes—or doesn't like—to do, according to the information in the chart. Use the verbs from the box below.

S1: Was macht Anna gern?   **S2:** Sie geht gern schwimmen.

	swim	tennis	snowboard	basketball	soccer	hiking
Anna	👍					
Peter		👍			👍	
Moritz				👍		
Maria			👍			👍
Lena		👍			👍	

Tennis spielen	Fußball spielen	Basketball spielen
snowboarden gehen	wandern gehen	schwimmen gehen

2-19 Was für Sport machst du gern? Interview your partner about what sports she or he likes to do.

S1: Was für Sport machst du gern?   **S2:** Ich gehe (spiele) gern …

You will find additional vocabulary for **Hobbys und Sport** in the *Anhang* on p. A-5.

Sprachnotiz   gern haben

Gern haben is used to express fondness for someone.

STEFAN: Liebst du Maria?   *Are you in love with Maria?*
LUKAS: Nein, aber ich **habe** sie sehr **gern.**   *No, but I like her a lot.*

Verb + *lieber*

To express a preference, German uses a verb plus **lieber.**

Was spielst du **lieber,** Karten   *What do you **prefer to** play, cards*
   oder Scrabble?   *or Scrabble?*
Ich spiele **lieber** Scrabble.   *I **prefer to** play Scrabble.*

 2-20 Das mache ich gern. Working with a partner, tell each other what you like or don't like to do. Follow the model. You will find additional vocabulary in the *Anhang* on pages A-7 and A-5 under **Essen und Trinken** and **Hobbys und Sport.**

▶ spielen: Golf / Tennis / Fußball / …

S1: Ich spiele gern Golf.   **S2:** Ich auch. / Ich nicht, ich spiele lieber Tennis.

1. gehen: ins Konzert / ins Theater / ins Museum / …
2. gehen: schwimmen / snowboarden / tanzen / …
3. spielen: Billard / Darts / Videospiele / …
4. trinken: Kaffee / Tee / Cola / …
5. hören: Rock / Jazz / Mozart / …
6. trinken: Wein / Bier / Wasser / …

Telling time

2.6 State the time

Wie spät ist es?

In colloquial German, telling time is similar to our system. You can answer the question **Wie spät ist es?** *(What time is it?)* with or without the word **Uhr** *(o'clock):*

Es ist zwei Uhr. (Es ist zwei.)   *It's two o'clock. (It's two.)*

To ask for the time, you can say either **Wie spät ist es?** or **Wie viel Uhr ist es?**

To indicate minutes *past* the hour, use **nach**; to indicate minutes *before* the hour, use **vor.** You can use **Viertel** to refer to quarter past or to the hour. German expresses 30 minutes past the hour as half way towards the coming hour.

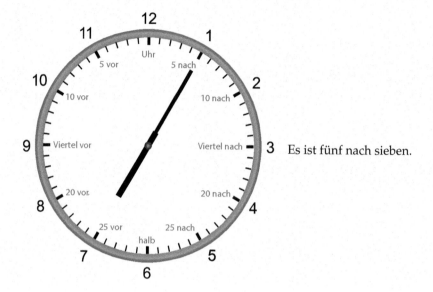

Es ist fünf nach sieben.

2-21 Wie spät ist es? Respond to your partner's questions.

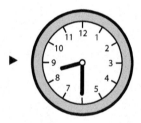

S1: Wie spät ist es? **S2:** Es ist halb neun.

1. 2. 3. 4. 5.

6. 7. 8. 9. 10.

Official time: the 24-hour clock

Another way to tell time in German counts the day from 0 to 24 hours and is used for things such as train schedules, public announcements, and TV program listings. Because speakers of German see and hear this way of telling time every day, it is common to use the official forms in everyday speech as well.

Clock face	Digital	Written	Spoken
(clock showing 1:00)	13:00	13.00 Uhr	dreizehn Uhr
(clock showing 1:05)	13:05	13.05 Uhr	dreizehn Uhr fünf
(clock showing 1:30)	13:30	13.30 Uhr	dreizehn Uhr dreißig
(clock showing 1:50)	13:50	13.50 Uhr	dreizehn Uhr fünfzig

> Note the different position of **Uhr** in writing (**13.30 *Uhr***) and speaking (**dreizehn *Uhr* dreißig**).

2-22 Wie viel Uhr ist es? Respond to your partner's questions using official time.

► 15:10

S1: Wie viel Uhr ist es?   **S2:** Es ist fünfzehn Uhr zehn.

1. 6:55   2. 17:20   3. 20:15   4. 22:39   5. 2:41

))) **2-23 Wann kommt der Bus?** Your friend takes the bus regularly and knows the bus schedule in front of the dorm by heart. Listen to his statements and write the exact time he gives you for each destination.

1. Zum Studentenwerk: Um _____

2. Zum Stadtzentrum: Um _____

3. Zum Supermarkt: Um _____

4. Zur Stadtbibliothek: Um _____

5. Zum Stadtpark: Um _____

movie theater   6. Zum Odeon°: Um _____

2-24 Wann ist das? Use North American equivalents to answer the questions about events in this small town in the German state of Baden-Württemberg.

Heute in Schorndorf

Samstag, 1. Februar:

Vereine / Organisationen

Jugendmusikschule: Instrumentendemonstration , 14 bis 16 Uhr, Gottlieb-Daimler-Realschule im Schulzentrum Grauhalde.
Vogel- und Aquarienverein: Hauptversammlung, 20 Uhr, Vereinsheim.
Radfahrverein „Wanderer": Mountainbiker-Treff 14 Uhr, Gmünder Straße 49.

Kultur

Manufaktur: Flamenco-Workshop, 12 bis 15.30 Uhr; Schwof mit Musik aus den 70ern, ab 22 Uhr; Bilderwand – Neue Arbeiten von Gui Ripper, Foyer, 1. Stock.

1. When does the mountain bike club meet?

2. When does a demonstration of musical instruments take place?

3. When is the workshop on flamenco?

4. What time does the bird and aquarium club meeting start?

Expressions of time referring to parts of the day

German has no equivalents for the terms *a.m.* and *p.m.* In colloquial German, you use the following adverbs of time to refer to the parts of a day. Note that these adverbs of time end in **-s**.

vormittags	*in the morning*	**abends**	*in the evening*
nachmittags	*in the afternoon*	**nachts**	*at night*

2-25 Um wie viel Uhr ist das? Take turns asking your partner when specific TV shows start, giving the colloquial time along with the adverb telling the time of day.

S1: Um wie viel Uhr ist eine Talkshow?   **S2:** Um Viertel nach zehn abends.

TV Heute - LiveStream im Internet		
BR	10.05	Pinguin, Löwe & Co. Geschichten aus dem Zoo
DMAX	13.15	D Motor Bike, *Doku*
ZDF	14.00	Fußball: WM der Frauen. Vorrunde: Japan – Mexiko, *Fußball*
ARD	15.05	Verbotene Liebe, *Daily Soap*
ARTE	16.45	Metropolen der Welt: Hongkong, Dokureihe
RTL	18.30	CSI: Cyber, #Digitalmord, *Krimiserie* (USA 2016)
WDR	20.00	Tagesschau, *Nachrichten*
SAT.1	21.20	The Voice of Germany (D 2016)
SWR/SR	22.15	Nachtcafé, *Talk*
PRO7	23.45	Stromberg, Die Konferenz, *Comedyserie*

1. Um wie viel Uhr beginnt ein Fußballspiel?
2. Um wie viel Uhr beginnt eine Sendung über Elefanten, Giraffen und große Katzen?
3. Um wie viel Uhr ist eine deutsche Komödie?
4. Um wie viel Uhr kommt die Sendung über Motorräder?
5. Um wie viel Uhr beginnt eine Musiksendung?
6. Um wie viel Uhr beginnt eine amerikanische Serie?

Sprachnotiz   Five minutes before and after the *half* hour

In colloquial German, the five minutes before and after the half hour are often spoken as follows:

 Es ist fünf vor halb zwei.   Es ist fünf nach halb neun.

They can also be spoken as **ein Uhr fünfundzwanzig** and **acht Uhr fünfunddreißig**.

More on expressions of time

You just learned that adverbs like **nachmittags** and **abends** refer to parts of the day. You can also use them to express that something happens *repeatedly* or *regularly*.

Ich habe **nachmittags** Vorlesungen und **abends** gehe ich oft in die Bibliothek.   *I have classes in the afternoon and in the evening I often go to the library.*

You can use this same approach with days of the week, e.g., **freitags** (*on Fridays, every Friday*).

Ich habe **montags** viel zu tun.   *I have a lot to do on Mondays.*

Alex hat **mittwochs** von 10 bis 12 Biologie.   *Alex has biology every Wednesday from 10 to 12.*

You can get even more specific by putting days and parts of the day together: **freitagabends, montagvormittags.**

2-26 Leons Stundenplan. Find out about Leon's weekly schedule.

S1: Wann hat Leon Zoologie?   **S2:** Montags von 8 bis 10.

	Mo	Di	Mi	Do	Fr
8.00	Zoologie			Arbeit	Spanisch
9.00	Zoologie		Mikrobiologie	Arbeit	Spanisch
10.00		Botanikseminar	Mikrobiologie	Arbeit	
11.00		Botanikseminar		Arbeit	
12.00					Matheübung
13.00		Arbeit	Mathematik für Biologen		Matheübung
14.00		Arbeit	Mathematik für Biologen		
15.00	Genetik	Arbeit			
16.00	Genetik	Arbeit		Botanikübung	
17.00				Botanikübung	
18.00		Yoga Sporthalle 1		Basketball Sporthalle 1	Filmklub
19.00		Yoga Sporthalle 1		Basketball Sporthalle 1	Filmklub

1. Wann hat er Mikrobiologie?
2. Wann lernt er Spanisch?
3. Wann hat er eine Übung?
4. Wann arbeitet Leon?
5. Wann geht er ins Kino?
6. Wann macht er Sport?
7. Wann hat er ein Seminar?

You can find a list of **Studienfächer** in the *Anhang* on p. A-4.

2-27 Was machst du heute? Find out your partner's schedule for today. Fill out a blank schedule as you get answers to your questions, following the examples below. Once your schedules are complete, see if there's a time during the day when you can meet to study German together!

S1:

Was hast du vormittags?

Und dann? Was hast du um 10?

Was für Vorlesungen hast du nachmittags?

habe frei: *am free*   Was hast du von 2 bis 4? …

S2:

Von 9 bis 10 habe ich …

Von 10 bis 12 arbeite ich.

Von 1 bis 2 habe ich Geografie und von 4 bis 5 habe ich Politik.

Von 2 bis 4 habe ich frei°.

2-28 Wann…? Find out more about your partner's schedule by asking the questions below.

usually

1. Wann gehst du normalerweise° in die Mensa?
2. Wann lernst du?
3. Um wie viel Uhr gehst du normalerweise ins Bett?
4. Was machst du gern samstagabends?

2.6 Kultur 2

Social media use in Germany

2.7 Compare and contrast online practices in Germany and North America

What's popular?

Germans are active users of a wide variety of increasingly blended and integrated social media options, which include microblogs, photo communities, instant messaging, and social networking. While Facebook is by far the most popular choice, millions of Germans also use Twitter, XING, LinkedIn, google+, YouTube, Pinterest, Instagram, Snapchat, WhatsApp, and studiVZ **(Studentenverzeichnis),** as well as its relative meinVZ. XING, a professional network service similar to LinkedIn, is the most successful networking site of German origin. Founded in 2003 in Hamburg, it has been growing steadily, with almost all its users living in the German-speaking countries.

The generation gap

85 percent of adults use the Internet, 78 percent own a smartphone. As is the case in nearly every country in the world, younger Germans (aged 18-34) are much more likely to be Internet and smartphone users compared with those ages 35 and older. This difference is even more pronounced in the use of **soziale Netzwerke** or **soziale Medien**, resulting in a relatively low overall use of social media in Germany (50 percent) when compared with many other countries, as for example the United States (71 percent). In fact, Germany has been called a country of **Social-Media-Muffel** (*grumps*).

Digital natives

Among those aged 12-25, the digital world is nearly ubiquitous. 99 percent of all young Germans have access to the Internet and spend about 18 hours a week online. For most teenagers, the smartphone ranks as the most important item they own. They only rarely use their phones to make phone calls, but instead to participate in a variety of social networking sites and instant messaging services. Most young Germans are online for three reasons: entertainment, information, and interaction. They are becoming increasingly active users, generating content themselves through blogging, reviewing, uploading, commenting, and sharing. Many believe that they are missing out if they are not logged on and view participation in the digital world as a social activity. For them, being online has become a permanent way of being, although they do not want to be known as Internet addicts or **Dauerdaddler** (*someone constantly playing games*).

Immer am Handy

Ein Selfie in Bonn

Privacy concerns

Young Germans are online, but also skeptical of the big corporations whose platforms and products they use. More than 80 percent do not trust these corporations, convinced that they are using the data they collect for profit, and view them as behemoths out to control the Internet. Many users are concerned about privacy and shy away from posting intimate details about themselves, afraid that their footprint will be on the Web **für immer**. Of equal concern is the issue of **Cyber-Mobbing** (*cyber-bullying/hate speech*) in its various forms. For these reasons, Germans tend to be in favor of their government exercising stronger control over corporations like Google and Facebook and protecting users' rights and privacy.

2-29 Soziale Medien. Sign in to your own social networking service, sharing community, or instant messaging account and switch the language from English to German. What are the German equivalents of the familiar functions, site categories, actions, and comments? Create a brief dictionary of online terminology containing about 10 items. Look for commonly used terms such as *like, nudge, register, message, share*, etc.

2.7 Kommunikation und Formen 2

The nominative case

2.8 Identify the subject in a sentence

The subject

A simple sentence consists of a noun or pronoun *subject* and a *predicate*. The subject is the person, place, or thing that the sentence is about. The predicate consists of a verb or a verb plus other parts of speech.

The boldfaced words in the following examples are the subjects of the verbs.

Subject	Predicate	
	VERB	OTHER PARTS OF SPEECH
Nina	tanzt	gern.
Nina und Alexander	gehen	oft in die Disco.
Sie	tanzen	dort oft bis zwölf Uhr nachts.

Remember that in German the subject does not always have to be the first element. If it is not first, it must immediately follow the verb.

Other parts of speech	Verb	Subject	Other parts of speech
Freitagabends	gehen	**Nina und Alexander**	in die Disco.
Dort	tanzen	**sie**	oft bis zwölf Uhr.

2-30 Alexander. Find the subjects.

Nina sagt:

1. Alex ist abends oft bei uns.

2. Er tanzt gern und kocht auch gern und gut.

3. Abends lernen wir zusammen.

Robert sagt:

1. Ninas Freund ist viel zu oft bei uns.

2. Von morgens bis abends spielt er seine blöde Gitarre.

3. Ich finde sein Motorrad toll.

Alexander sagt:

1. Ich mache gern Sport.

2. Samstagnachmittags gehen Nina und ich joggen.

3. Dann spielen wir Videospiele.

Articles (*the* and *a*) in the nominative case

As you progress through this text, you will learn that German grammar assigns every noun or pronoun in a sentence to one of four cases. These cases signal the function of the noun or pronoun in the sentence.

In the following examples, the forms of the definite or indefinite articles show that the nouns are in the *nominative case*, which indicates that they are the subjects.

Der Pulli kostet nur 20 Euro.   *The sweater costs only 20 euros.*

Normalerweise kostet **ein** Pulli viel mehr.   *Usually a sweater costs much more.*

	Masculine	Neuter	Feminine	Plural
NOMINATIVE	der ein }Pulli kein	das ein }Hemd kein	die eine }Jacke keine	die — }Schuhe keine

Remember:

- Like *a* and *an* in English, **ein** and **eine** have no plural forms.
- **Kein** and **keine** do have a plural form.

2-31 Ich kaufe gern Kleider.

▶ Mantel (m)

S1: Wie viel kostet der Mantel°?

S2: Der Mantel kostet 490 Euro.

1. Rock (m)
2. Bluse (f)
3. Kleid (n)
4. Schuhe (pl)
5. Sweatshirt (n)
6. Gürtel° (m)
7. Socken (pl)
8. Jacke (f)

coat

belt

Karstadt is a large German department store chain whose headquarters are in Essen. The first store opened in Wismar in 1881. As of July 2016, the company owned 114 stores in Germany and employed about 16,500 people.

The question words *wer* and *was*

The nominative forms of the question words are **wer** and **was**.

Wer ist Mark Zuckerberg?	*Who is Mark Zuckerberg?*
Was ist Facebook?	*What is Facebook?*

	Question words	
	PERSONS	THINGS OR IDEAS
NOMINATIVE	wer?	was?

2-32 Wer oder was? Complete each question with **wer** or **was**. Your partner responds appropriately from the choices given.

1. _____ ist Red Bull?   Ein Land.
2. _____ ist *Rolling Stone*?   Komponisten.
3. _____ ist Hillary Clinton?   Ein Getränk.
4. _____ ist Afrika?   Autorin.
5. _____ ist Mexiko?   Ein Kontinent.
6. _____ sind Chopin und Tschaikowski?   Ein Magazin.
7. _____ sind Moskitos?   Politikerin.
8. _____ ist J. K. Rowling?   Insekten.

Sprachnotiz   Omission of the indefinite article

When stating someone's membership in a specific group (e.g., nationality, place of residence, occupation, or religious affiliation), German does not use the indefinite article.

Ashley ist **Amerikanerin.**	*Ashley is **an** American.*
Ich bin **Berliner.**	*I am **a** Berliner.*
Kurt ist **Koch.**	*Kurt is **a** cook.*

Articles and adjectives in the nominative case

2.9 Describe people, places, and things—nominative case

Der-words in the nominative case

The endings of words like **dieser** (*this*), **jeder** (*each, every*), and **welcher** (*which*) correspond closely to the forms of the definite article. For this reason these words, along with the definite article, are called **der**-words.

Welches T-Shirt kaufst du?	**Which** *T-shirt are you buying?*
Ich glaube, ich kaufe **dieses** blaue T-Shirt hier.	*I think I will buy **this** blue T-shirt here.*
Jedes T-Shirt kostet heute nur 7,90 Euro.	**Each** *T-shirt is only 7.90 euros today.*

	Masculine	Neuter	Feminine	Plural
NOMINATIVE	dies**er** Wein	dies**es** Bier	dies**e** Milch	dies**e** Getränke
	(d**er**)	(d**as**)	(d**ie**)	(d**ie**)

2-33 *Dies-, jed- oder welch-?* Choose the appropriate **der-**words to complete each conversation.

1. SAM: Ist dieses / welches Buch gut?

   GINA: Ja, aber nicht jedes / welches Buch von Hemingway finde ich gut.
2. FRAU BENZ: Dieses / Jedes kalte Wetter ist gar nicht schön.

   FRAU HAAG: Ja, aber jeder / welcher Winter ist hier so kalt.

2-34 *Viele Fragen!* Supply the correct endings on the **der-**word **welch-** in each question.

1. Welch_____ Magazin (n) ist so interessant wie der *Stern*?
2. Welch_____ Oper (f) ist von Mozart, *Don Giovanni* oder *Carmen*?
3. Welch_____ Wein (m) ist besser, der Beaujolais oder der Chianti?
4. Welch_____ Zeitung (f) ist das, die *Frankfurter Allgemeine* oder die *Süddeutsche*?
5. Welch_____ Bücher (pl) findest du gut?

Nominative endings of adjectives after *der-*words

An adjective takes an ending when it comes directly before the noun it describes.

Die braun**en** Schuhe kosten nur 50 Euro.   *The brown shoes cost only 50 euros.*

	Masculine	Neuter	Feminine	Plural
NOMINATIVE	der rot**e** Pulli	das blau**e** Hemd	die weiß**e** Jacke	die braun**en** Schuhe
	dieser rot**e** Pulli	dieses blau**e** Hemd	diese weiß**e** Jacke	diese braun**en** Schuhe

In the nominative, these same endings occur after *all* **der-**words, e.g., **der** rote Pulli, **dieser** rote Pulli, **jeder** rote Pulli, **welcher** braune Pulli.

2-35 **Was ist das auf Englisch?** For each of the items pictured, identify the gender of the subject and then try your hand at providing an English translation.

1.

2.

3.

Ernest
Hemingway

Der alte Mann und das Meer

4.

5.

Das große
Kochbuch für
Babys & Kleinkinder

Peek & Cloppenburg is a large clothing store chain. Founded in Germany in 1900, it has about 14,000 employees throughout Europe.

2-36 Bei Peek & Cloppenburg. Supply the missing adjective endings.

1. **S1:** Wie viel kosten diese hübsch____ Blusen?

   S2: Die rot ____ Bluse kostet 40 Euro und die weiß____ Bluse kostet 35 Euro.

2. **S1:** Wie viel kosten diese schick____ Pullis?

   S2: Der weiß____ Pulli kostet 35 Euro und der rot____ Pulli kostet 60 Euro.

3. **S1:** Wie viel kosten diese toll____ Sweatshirts?

   S2: Das blau____ Sweatshirt kostet 20 Euro und das rot____ Sweatshirt kostet 30 Euro.

4. **S1:** Wie viel kosten diese cool____ Jacken?

   S2: Die schwarz____ Jacke kostet 110 Euro und die weiß____ Jacke kostet 115 Euro.

Ein-words in the nominative case: *ein, kein,* and the possessive adjectives

Both **ein** and **kein** belong to a group of words called **ein**-words. Also included in this group are the possessive adjectives, which are used to indicate possession or relationships, e.g., *my* book, *my* friend. The chart below shows the personal pronouns with their corresponding possessive adjectives.

Singular				Plural			
PERSONAL PRONOUN		POSSESSIVE ADJECTIVE		PERSONAL PRONOUN		POSSESSIVE ADJECTIVE	
ich	*I*	**mein**	*my*	**wir**	*we*	**unser**	*our*
du	*you*	**dein**	*your*	**ihr**	*you*	**euer**	*your*
Sie	*you*	**Ihr**	*your*	**Sie**	*you*	**Ihr**	*your*
er	*he, it*	**sein**	*his, its*				
es	*it*	**sein**	*its*	**sie**	*they*	**ihr**	*their*
sie	*she, it*	**ihr**	*her, its*				

> Note that like the formal **Sie**, the formal **Ihr** is always capitalized.

The possessive adjectives take the same endings as **ein** and **kein.**

Wo leben **deine** besten Freundinnen jetzt, Kirsten?	*Where do **your** best friends live now, Kirsten?*
Meine Freundin Maria lebt in Hamburg, und **meine** Freundin Anna und **ihr** Mann leben in Düsseldorf.	***My** friend Maria lives in Hamburg and **my** friend Anna and **her** husband live in Düsseldorf.*
Wie alt sind **Ihre** Kinder, Frau Ziegler?	*How old are **your** children, Ms. Ziegler?*
Unsere Tochter ist sechzehn und **unser** Sohn ist vierzehn.	***Our** daughter is sixteen and **our** son is fourteen.*

In the following chart the possessive adjective **unser** is used as an example to show the nominative forms of all possessive adjectives.

	Masculine	Neuter	Feminine	Plural
NOMINATIVE	ein Freund	ein Auto	eine Freundin	—
	unser Freund	**unser** Auto	**unsere** Freundin	**unsere** Kinder

When an ending is added to **euer,** the **e** before the **r** is dropped.

Ist **eure** Mensa gut?	*Is **your** dining hall good?*

2-37 Leon. Supply the appropriate forms of **mein.**

Ich heiße Leon, bin zwanzig Jahre alt und studiere hier in Leipzig Genetik. _____ Eltern leben auch hier in Leipzig. _____ Vater ist Polizist und _____ Mutter ist Lehrerin. _____ Bruder Stefan ist siebzehn und geht noch in die Schule. _____ Schwester Melanie ist zweiundzwanzig und studiert in Hamburg Biochemie. _____ Freundinnen heißen Helga und Tina und sie studieren auch hier in Leipzig.

2-38 Ein kleines Gespräch. Supply the appropriate forms of **ihr, Ihr,** and **unser.**

FRAU BENN: Wie alt sind _____ Kinder jetzt, Herr Haag?

HERR HAAG: _____ Tochter ist sechsundzwanzig und _____ Söhne sind einundzwanzig und siebzehn.

FRAU BENN: Und wo lebt _____ Tochter?

HERR HAAG: Laura und _____ Mann leben in Hannover.

FRAU BENN: Und _____ Söhne?

HERR HAAG: Lukas studiert in Münster und _____ Sohn Daniel ist noch hier bei uns.

2-39 Wie ist eure Uni? Imagine that you and your partner are studying at different universities. Find out about your partner's school by completing the questions and responses with the appropriate forms of **euer** and **unser.**

S1:	S2:
1. Wie alt ist _____ Uni (f)?	_____ Uni ist fast 200 Jahre alt.
2. Ist _____ Campus (m) groß?	Nein, _____ Campus ist nicht sehr groß.
Wie sind _____ Vorlesungen (pl)?	_____ Vorlesungen sind sehr interessant.
4. Ist _____ Bibliothek (f) gut?	Ja, _____ Bibliothek ist sehr gut.
5. Sind _____ Professoren (pl) freundlich?	Ja, _____ Professoren sind fast alle freundlich.
6. Wie ist _____ Mensa?	_____ Mensa ist gut, aber ein bisschen zu teuer°.
7. Sind _____ Studentenheime (pl) schön?	Ja, _____ Studentenheime sind sehr modern und sehr schön.
8. Wie gut ist _____ Footballteam (n)?	_____ Footballteam ist echt spitze°.

expensive (for item 6)
really great (for item 8)

2-40 Unsere Uni. Gather in groups of four or five. One student plays a reporter who is interested in finding out more about your university or college. The reporter can use the questions in the previous activity as a model. Take turns responding to the reporter's questions.

Nominative endings of adjectives after *ein*-words

	Masculine	Neuter	Feminine	Plural
NOMINATIVE	ein rot**er** Pulli	ein blau**es** Hemd	eine weiß**e** Jacke	keine braun**en** Schuhe

In the chart above, you see that the **ein**-word has no ending in the masculine and neuter. In these two instances, the adjective itself shows the gender and case of the noun by taking the appropriate **der**-word ending: dies**er** Pulli, **ein** rot**er** Pulli; dieses Hemd, **ein** blau**es** Hemd.

Dein rot**er** Pullover ist echt toll.	*Your red sweater is really fabulous.*
Ja, und er war nur halb so teuer wie mein neu**es** blau**es** Hemd.	*Yes, and it was only half as expensive as my new blue shirt.*

2-41 Wir spielen Trivial Pursuit. Take turns asking a partner who or what the items in each category are.

S1: Wer ist Neymar?	S2: Neymar ist ein brasilianischer Fußballspieler.
S2: Was ist Chianti?	S1: Chianti ist ein italienischer Rotwein.

Leute (Wer?)		Getränke (Was?)		Geografie (Was?)	
Neymar	englische Sängerin	Chianti	irisches Bier	Angola	italienischer Vulkan
Margaret Atwood	deutsche Modedesignerin	Jägermeister	italienischer Rotwein	Linz	russischer Fluss
Adele	amerikanischer Filmstar	Darjeeling	amerikanischer Softdrink	die Wolga	deutsches Bundesland
Tom Hanks	kanadische Autorin	Mist Twist	deutscher Likör	Brandenburg	österreichische Stadt
Jil Sander	brasilianischer Fußballspieler	Guinness	indischer Tee	der Vesuv	afrikanisches Land

2-42 Komplimente. Look at what your classmates are wearing and compliment them on a specific article of clothing.

Lisa, dein roter Rock ist sehr schick.

David, deine schwarze Jacke ist echt cool.

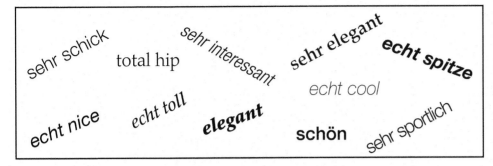

Sprachnotiz   The subject completion

Sometimes the predicate contains a noun that further describes what the subject is or what the subject is called. This noun is called a *subject completion*.

The boldfaced words in the following examples are subject completions. The verbs **heißt** and **ist** function like equal signs, i.e., they show that the subject and the subject completion are one and the same person or thing. Thus, like the subject, they are in the nominative case.

Ninas Freund heißt **Alexander.** (Ninas Freund = **Alexander**)

Er ist **ein toller Tänzer.** (Er = **ein toller Tänzer**)

Nominative endings of unpreceded adjectives

	Masculine	Neuter	Feminine	Plural
NOMINATIVE	gut**er** Wein	gut**es** Bier	gut**e** Salami	gut**e** Oliven

Adjectives that are not preceded by a **der**-word or an **ein**-word show the gender, number, and case of the noun by taking the appropriate **der**-word ending.

Warum ist dies**er** Kaffee so teuer?   *Why is this coffee so expensive?*
Gut**er** Kaffee ist immer teuer.   *Good coffee is always expensive.*

 2-43 Herr Ziegler im Feinkostgeschäft°.

gourmet foods store

▶   dieser Kaffee

S1: Warum ist dieser Kaffee so teuer?   **S2:** Guter Kaffee ist immer teuer.

1. diese Salami
2. dieses Brot°
3. diese Pistazien (pl)
4. dieser Tee
5. dieser Wein
6. diese Oliven (pl)
7. dieses Olivenöl
8. diese Schokolade

bread

Mediterrane Feinkost

TÄGLICH

• frisches Brot
• frischer Salat
• feine Salami
• eingelegte Oliven
• eingelegte Fische
kalte Getränke

2.8 Video-Treff

Freundschaften

2.10 Understand authentic video of German speakers introducing their friends

In this video segment Anja Szustak, André, Susann, Thomas, Karen, and Stefan Kuhlmann will introduce good friends. Be sure to complete the **Was ist das auf Englisch?** exercise before watching the video.

2-44 Was ist das auf Englisch?

1. Wir haben ein **gemeinsames** Hobby, und das ist Schwimmen.
2. Wir kochen nicht so **häufig** zusammen.
3. Wir **kennen uns** seit zwei Jahren.
4. Wir **sind** zusammen zur Schule **gegangen.**
5. Wir wohnen zusammen in einer **Wohngemeinschaft** in Kreuzberg.
6. Er arbeitet als **Veranstaltungstechniker.**
7. Meine Freundin ist sehr offen und **natürlich.**
8. Er ist jetzt **zirka** sechs Jahre alt.
9. Meine Freundin und ich sind beide sehr **verliebt.**

a. approximately
b. often
c. natural
d. went
e. common
f. event technician
g. have known each other
h. in love
i. shared housing

Before you watch the video, read through the exercises below. This will give you some additional information and let you know what you should be watching and listening for. Then watch the video and complete the exercises.

2-45 Wer sagt das? The following statements fit what Anja, André, or Susann said about their friends. Identify the person who best matches each statement.

	Anja	André	Susann
1. Meine Freundin und ich gehen gern schwimmen.	☐	☐	☐
2. Meine Freundin heißt Ines.	☐	☐	☐
3. Meine Freundin studiert in Dresden Medizin.	☐	☐	☐
4. Meine Freundin heißt Charlotte oder „Charlie".	☐	☐	☐
5. Meine Freundin und ich gehen gern ins Kino oder tanzen.	☐	☐	☐
6. Meine beste Freundin heißt Kristina.	☐	☐	☐
7. Meine Freundin und ich gehen oft zusammen joggen.	☐	☐	☐
8. Meine Freundin fotografiert sehr gern.	☐	☐	☐
9. Meine Freundin arbeitet in Berlin.	☐	☐	☐
10. Meine Freundin und ich hören beide gern Sinatra.	☐	☐	☐

2-46 Richtig oder falsch? Decide whether the following statements about Thomas, Karen, and Stefan Kuhlmann's friends are **richtig** or **falsch**. If the statement is **falsch**, provide a correct version.

	RICHTIG	FALSCH
1. Thomas: Meine Freundin ist Deutsche und kommt aus Frankfurt.	☐	☐
2. Thomas: Meine Freundin heißt Elisabeth.	☐	☐
3. Thomas: Meine Freundin ist sehr offen und natürlich.	☐	☐
4. Karen: Öcsi ist 20 Jahre alt.	☐	☐
5. Karen: Öcsi und ich sind schon vier Jahre zusammen.	☐	☐
6. Karen: Mein Freund arbeitet nicht.	☐	☐
7. Karen: Chirac ist ein großer weißer Hund.	☐	☐
8. Karen: Chirac ist etwa sechs Jahre alt.	☐	☐
9. Stefan Kuhlmann: Meine Freundin heißt Barbara.	☐	☐
10. Stefan Kuhlmann: Meine Freundin ist 22 Jahre „jung".	☐	☐

2.9 Wortschatz 2

Wichtige Vokabeln

2.11 Learn vocabulary to talk about daily activities, clothing, and studying at the university

Nomen

die Frau, -en	woman, wife
der Mann, -̈er	man, husband
die Arbeit	work
die Freundschaft, -en	friendship
das Geld	money
die Sendung, -en	TV show
das Wochenende, -n	weekend
das Haus, -̈er	house
das Land, -̈er	country
die Leute *(pl)*	people
die Stadt, -̈e	city; town
die Straße, -n	street
das Zimmer, -	room

Universitätsleben

das Fach, -̈er / **das Studienfach, -̈er**	field of study; subject
das Studentenheim, -e	student residence, dormitory
der Stundenplan, -̈e	schedule, timetable
die Übung, -en	lab; discussion section
an der Uni	at the university
zur Uni	to the university

Kleidungsstücke

das Kleidungsstück, -e	article of clothing
der Anzug, -̈e	*(men's)* suit
die Bluse, -n	blouse
der Gürtel, -	belt
das Hemd, -en	shirt
die Hose, -n	pants
die Jacke, -n	jacket
die Jeans *(pl)*	jeans
das Kleid, -er	dress
die Kleider *(pl)*	clothes
der Mantel, -̈	coat
der Pulli, -s	light sweater
der Pullover, -	sweater
der Rock, -̈e	skirt
der Schuh, -e	shoe
die Shorts *(pl)*	shorts
die Socke, -n	sock
der Stiefel, -	boot
das Sweatshirt, -s	sweatshirt
das T-Shirt, -s	T-shirt

Verben

bedeuten	to mean
besuchen	to visit
hören	to hear
leben	to live *(in a country or city)*
wohnen	to live *(in a building or on a street)*

Andere Wörter

bald	soon
beide	both; two
freundlich	friendly
gemeinsam	common
hübsch	pretty
natürlich	natural (*also:* of course)
schick	chic
schon	already
wieder	again

Ausdrücke

Um wie viel Uhr …?	(At) what time …?
Wie spät ist es? / **Wie viel Uhr ist es?**	What time is it?
zu Ende sein	to be over
echt spitze	really great
so … wie	as … as
Heute ist es (nicht) so kalt wie gestern.	Today it's (not) as cold as yesterday.

Das Gegenteil

dick ≠ dünn	thick; fat ≠ thin; skinny
lang ≠ kurz	long ≠ short
teuer ≠ billig	expensive ≠ cheap
immer ≠ nie	always ≠ never

Leicht zu verstehen

der Euro	**die Olive, -n**
der Film, -e	**das Olivenöl**
der Job, -s	**die Salami**
das Konzert, -e	**die Schokolade**
das Magazin, -e	**cool**
das Museum, Museen	**elegant**
die Oper, -n	**hip**

Wörter im Kontext

2-47 Was passt nicht?

1. das Hemd	2. die Jeans	3. die Jacke	4. die Schuhe
die Hose	der Rock	der Gürtel	der Pullover
die Bluse	die Hose	der Mantel	das Sweatshirt
der Pullover	die Socken	das Kleid	das Hemd

2-48 *Leben* oder *wohnen?*

1. Stephanie und Claudia _____ beide im Studentenheim.
2. Stephanies Eltern _____ in Chicago.
3. Maria ist aus Salzburg, aber sie _____ jetzt in Wien und _____ dort bei ihrer Großmutter.

> **Leben and wohnen: Leben** is usually used in reference to the country or city of residence. **Wohnen** is used in reference to a building, street, or family (e.g., **Michael lebt in Berlin und wohnt in der Crellestraße**).

2-49 Was ist die richtige Reihenfolge? What's the proper sequence? Number the following items from largest to smallest (1 to 4).

_____ das Haus   _____ die Stadt   _____ das Land   _____ die Straße

2-50 Was passt wo?

dick ≠ dünn / immer ≠ nie / lang ≠ kurz / billig ≠ teuer

1. Im Winter sind die Tage _____ und die Nächte _____.
2. Silber ist nicht _____, aber es ist nicht so _____ wie Gold.
3. Sweatshirts sind _____ und T-Shirts sind _____.
4. Warum hörst du _____ nur Rock und _____ Mozart oder Beethoven?

Wörter unter der Lupe: More on cognates

In *Kapitel 1* you saw that you often don't need a dictionary to understand cognates. If you know the "code," you will be able to add many German words to your vocabulary simply by recognizing the patterns they follow. You should have no trouble guessing the meaning of the German words in each category below. Words followed by (*v*) are the infinitive forms of verbs.

> When trying to guess the English meanings of cognates, it often helps to say the German words out loud.

- German **f** or **ff** is English *p*

der A**ff**e	das Schi**ff**
schar**f**	hel**f**en (*v*)
die Har**f**e	o**ff**en
rei**f**	ho**ff**en (*v*)

- German **d, t,** or **tt** is English *th*

das Ba**d**	der Bru**d**er
danken (*v*)	der Va**t**er
das **D**ing	die Mu**tt**er
dick	die Fe**d**er
dünn	das Le**d**er
tausend	das We**tt**er

- German **b** is English *v* or *f*

ha**b**en (*v*)	das Kal**b**
das Gra**b**	une**b**en
hal**b**	das Fie**b**er

2-51 Was ist das auf Englisch? Read each item aloud and then craft a suitable English translation.

2.10 Alles zusammen

Freunde

Mein Uni-Profil

Suche 🔍

Meine Freunde (1,478)

Meine Gruppen (27)

Meine Uni-Kurse (4)

Meine Fotoalben (75)

Kalender

Spiele

Live-Video

Chatten

Flirten

Meine Favoriten:
   Musik im Netz
   Tier-Videos

Mein Lebensmotto:
Das Leben ist besser
im Pyjama.

Allgemeine Infos

Name: Claudia Berger
Geschlecht: weiblich
Geburtstag: 25.08.1999
Geburtsort: Hamburg

Studium

Hochschule: LMU München (seit 2017)
Studienfach: Chemie

Kontaktinfos

E-Mail-Adresse: claudia.berger1@yahoo.de
Mobiltelefon: privat

Persönliches

Freund/Freundin: single im Moment
Politische Richtung: liberal
Interessen: Segeln, Windsurfen, Tanzen
Lieblingsmusik: Rock, Rap
Lieblingsfilme: Wonder Woman, Philadelphia Story, Metropolis
Lieblingsbuch: Binge Living: Callcenter-Monologe

Arbeit

Firma: BioChem-Zentrum München
Tätigkeiten: Labor-Assistentin

2-52 Wer ist Claudia Berger? Mark the appropriate responses.

Claudia ist …

☐ Studentin in München. ☐ politisch konservativ.

☐ gar nicht sportlich. ☐ aus Hamburg.

Claudia hat …

☐ lange, blonde Haare. ☐ keine Arbeit.

☐ 75 Fotos. ☐ amerikanische Filme gern.

2-53 Claudias Leben. Complete the description below based on the information from Claudia's **Mein Uni-Profil** page.

1. Studium: Sie kommt aus _____ und studiert _____ an der Ludwig-Maximilians-Universität (LMU) in _____.

2. Sport: Sie geht gern _____.

3. Arbeit: Claudia arbeitet bei _____ als _____.

4. Musik: Am liebsten hört Claudia gern _____und _____.

Schritt 2: Zum Schreiben

2-54 Das ist meine beste Freundin/mein bester Freund. Now write a profile of your best friend. Use the questions here to guide your writing. Be sure to include a picture of her/him.

- Wie heißt deine beste Freundin/dein bester Freund?
- Wie alt ist sie/er?
- Woher kommt sie/er, und wo lebt sie/er jetzt?
- Was studiert sie/er?
- Arbeitet sie/er?
- Wie ist sie/er?
- Was für Sport macht sie/er gern?
- Was für Musik hört sie/er gern?
- Was macht ihr gern zusammen?

Activity 2-54: Refer to the *Anhang* for word lists that will help you respond to the questions.

Schritt 3: Zum Präsentieren

2-55 Das ist meine beste Freundin/mein bester Freund. Now record a presentation about your best friend. Follow one of the models below, substituting the information about your friend where necessary. Be sure to focus on your pronunciation.

> ▶ Mein bester Freund heißt Josh. Er ist 18 Jahre alt. Er kommt aus Florida aber er lebt jetzt in New York. Er ist sehr intelligent und studiert Mathematik. Wir gehen gern zusammen ins Kino.

> ▶ Meine beste Freundin heißt Maddy. Sie ist 21 Jahre alt. Sie kommt aus Toronto und sie lebt jetzt in Toronto. Sie ist sehr sportlich. Im Sommer spielt sie gern Beachvolleyball, und im Winter geht sie gern snowboarden.

Kapitel 3
Familie

Eine österreichische Familie im Sommer

Learning Objectives

3.1 Recognize Austria's role in the world, past and present

3.2 Learn vocabulary to talk about family

3.3 Recognize and pronounce two-vowel sounds

3.4 Identify important building blocks of a sentence

3.5 Say the things you need or want to buy with accusative forms of *the* and *a*

3.6 Retell the life story of an important historical person, using key dates

3.7 Describe people, places, and things (accusative case)

3.8 Say that you do not have, know, or understand something

3.9 Talk about your everyday life using verbs like eating, reading, running, and sleeping

3.10 Listen for some details about real people's families

3.11 Learn vocabulary to describe people and to talk about what they do

3.1 Vorschau

Der Mercedes-Benz SLS AMG

Tante Bettinas Mercedes: Ein Familienauto?

3-1 Cockpit? Flügel? Was für ein Auto! Der Mercedes-Benz SLS AMG. German engineering is valued worldwide. Look at the photo of the car and select the appropriate completions to describe this amazing automobile.

1. Der Mercedes-Benz SLS AMG ist ein Auto …	a. für Familien.
2. Der SLS AMG ist aber kein Auto …	b. mit Cockpit.
	c. auf der Straße.
3. Der SLS AMG ist …	d. ein Flugzeug für die Straße.
4. Das Auto hat zwei …	e. sportliche Flügel.
5. Das Auto fliegt …	

◗)) Zwei Verwandte sprechen über Tante Bettina
Listen to the two different descriptions of Bettina Ziegler.

Oma Ziegler sagt: Das ist meine Tochter Bettina. Sie ist nicht verheiratet und hat keine Kinder, aber sie ist eine sehr gute Physiotherapeutin. Bettina kauft gern teure Kleider, sie hat einen viel zu teuren Wagen und sie fährt auch oft zu schnell. Und warum reist Bettina denn immer so viel?

Nina sagt: Tante Bettina ist meine Lieblingstante. Sie hat ein echt tolles Leben: viel Geld, schicke Kleider, und ein rotes Sportcoupé. Sie macht auch gern große Reisen, zum Beispiel nach Nordamerika, denn sie spricht sehr gut Spanisch.

Bettina Ziegler in Mexiko

◗)) 3-2 Richtig oder falsch? Based on the two descriptions of Bettina Ziegler, indicate whether the statements you hear about her are **richtig** or **falsch**.

	Richtig	Falsch		Richtig	Falsch
1.	_____	_____	3.	_____	_____
2.	_____	_____	4.	_____	_____

3-3 Anders gesagt. With a partner, read *Zwei Verwandte* again, and find equivalents for the following statements.

▶ Oma Ziegler ist Bettinas Mutter. = Oma Ziegler sagt: Das ist meine Tochter Bettina.

1. Bettina hat keinen Mann.
2. Bettinas Kleider kosten viel Geld.
3. Bettina reist oft nach Nordamerika.
4. Bettina hat einen sehr sportlichen Wagen.

3-4 Eine Familie. The following well-known children's rhyme describes one family. Read the poem. Then study the family tree and answer the questions.

Der Vater, der heißt Daniel,
der kleine Sohn heißt Michael,
die Mutter heißt Regine,
die Tochter heißt Rosine,
der Bruder, der heißt Christian,
der Onkel heißt Sebastian,

male cousin

know

die Schwester heißt Johanna,
die Tante heißt Susanna,
der Vetter°, der heißt Benjamin,
die Kusine, die heißt Katharin,
die Oma heißt Ottilie –
jetzt kennst° du die Familie.

Ein Stammbaum

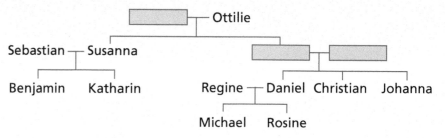

1. Wie heißen Johannas Brüder?
2. Wie heißen Susannas Kinder?
3. Wie heißt Michaels Schwester?
4. Wie heißen Daniels Geschwister°?
5. Wie heißen Katharins Vettern?

6. Wie heißt Ottilies Tochter?
7. Wie heißt Benjamins Kusine?
8. Wie heißt Rosines Tante?
9. Wie heißt Johannas Großmutter?
10. Wie heißen Katharins Eltern?

siblings

BUNT
IST MEINE
LIEBLINGSFARBE.

WALTER GROPIUS

Sprachnotiz Expressing *favorite*

The noun **Liebling** means *darling* or *favorite*. With the addition of an **-s (Lieblings-)**, you can create many nouns to express favorite people or things.

Tante Bettina ist meine **Lieblings**tante.
Was ist dein **Lieblings**auto?

*Aunt Bettina is my **favorite** aunt.*
*What's your **favorite** car?*

Note that in compound words like these, the last word always determines the gender:

der Film ➔ der Lieblings**film**   die Musik ➔ die Lieblings**musik**

3-5 Lieblingsdinge. What are your partner's favorite things or activities? Write the information in the spaces provided and report your findings to the class.

S1: Was ist dein Lieblings_____?

Lieblingssport (m) _____

Lieblingsfilm (m) _____

Lieblingsband (f) _____

Lieblingsshow (f) _____

S2: Mein Lieblings_____ ist …

Lieblingsauto (n) _____

Lieblingsbuch (n) _____

Lieblingsgetränk (n) _____

Lieblingsvorlesung (f) _____

3.2 Kultur 1

Österreich

3.1 Recognize Austria's role in the world, past and present

A rich and diverse history

Members of the Habsburg family ruled in **Österreich** nearly continuously between 1279 and 1918. The last phase of monarchical rule lasted from 1867 to 1918 and ended with a defeat in World War I. Until that time, the Austrian capital **Wien** (*Vienna*) was the political center of the vast multinational Austro-Hungarian Empire, which included not only Austrians and Hungarians, but also many Slavic peoples. After World War I, the German-speaking part of the empire became the Republic of Austria, while the areas making up most of the territory of the former Habsburg empire became sovereign nation states. In 1938, Austria was annexed, not entirely against its will, by Nazi Germany. When Vienna fell to the Allies at the end of World War II, the city and Austria as a whole were occupied by the Allies to oversee the post-war transition. The last Allied occupation troops left in 1955, and the country again became an independent, democratic state. Austria's national holiday is October 26, the date when Austria declared its "permanent neutrality" by an act of parliament in 1955. For this reason, the country is not a member of NATO.

The map from 1914 shows how this once vast empire extended much farther to the east and encompassed multiple cultures and language groups. This can still be observed today in the linguistic diversity of Austria. In the south, the federal states of **Kärnten** (*Carinthia*) and **Steiermark** (*Styria*) are home to a significant Slovene-speaking minority while in the easternmost state of **Burgenland** there are significant Hungarian- and Croatian-speaking minorities.

Österreich-Ungarn, 1914

Das Österreichische Parlament in Wien

Austria today

In 1995, Austria became a member of the **EU (Europäische Union)** and in 2002 it adopted the **Euro** as its currency. Today, Vienna easily rivals Geneva as a center for international conferences and headquarters for international organizations such as the Organization of Petroleum Exporting Countries (OPEC) and the International Atomic Energy Agency (IAEA), which promotes the peaceful, non-military use of nuclear energy and was awarded the Nobel Peace Prize for its work in 2005. Austria now plays an active role in the peacekeeping efforts of the United Nations. The country's current population is around 8.7 million, about 10 percent of whom are foreigners, primarily from Turkey and the former Yugoslavia.

Cultural richness and natural beauty in winter and summer

Austria is home to nine UNESCO World Heritage Sites, among them the historic centers of the cities of Vienna, Salzburg, and Graz. This unique combination of cultural centers and beautiful alpine landscapes attracts over 25 million visitors annually. With 3500 lifts for ski and snowboard enthusiasts, Austria is also a leader in alpine ski technology. The city of Kitzbühel hosts frequent World Cup ski events, and Innsbruck, a city in the state of **Tirol** (*Tyrol*), has hosted two Winter Olympics. In the summer, thousands of kilometers of trails attract hikers, mountain bikers, and climbers.

Innsbruck (Tirol)

Die Hundertwasserkirche in Bärnbach (Steiermark)

Music, art, and architecture

"Austria" is virtually synonymous with "music." It has been home to many famous composers. Haydn, Mozart, Schubert, Mahler, Johann Strauß, and Arnold Schoenberg were born in Austria. Beethoven, though born in Germany, lived and worked in Vienna until his death. Today, Vienna's glittering opera houses, theaters, and concert halls continue to be world-class. The annual summertime **Festspiele** in Salzburg and in Bregenz (featuring opera, drama, and concerts) are known worldwide, while the **Donauinselfest** in Vienna is Europe's largest free open-air music festival featuring popular music on numerous stages on an island in the Danube.

Early twentieth-century Austrian artists are also world-renowned. The painter Gustav Klimt contributed to the **Jugendstil** (*art nouveau*) movement, which in turn influenced the Austrian artist and architect Friedensreich Hundertwasser. In addition to creating richly colorful paintings and prints, Hundertwasser, an avid environmentalist, designed buildings that defied more traditional approaches to architecture.

Film and literature

With actresses such as Hedy Lamarr, Maria Schell, and Romy Schneider, and actors such as Peter Lorre, Christoph Waltz, and Arnold Schwarzenegger, as well as directors like G. W. Pabst (*Joyless Street*, starring Greta Garbo), Fritz Lang (*Scarlet Street*, starring Edward G. Robinson), and Billy Wilder (*Some Like It Hot*, starring Marilyn Monroe), Austrians and Austrian emigrants have made their mark in the world of cinema. In Austria, Michael Haneke directed the award-winning film **Die Klavierspielerin** (*The Piano Teacher*), based on a novel by Austrian writer Elfriede Jelinek, who won the Nobel Prize for Literature in 2004. Jelinek's highly controversial work is sharply critical of many aspects of contemporary society. Stefan Ruzowitzky's **Die Fälscher** (*The Counterfeiters*) won the 2007 Oscar for Best Foreign Language Film, and Haneke's **Amour** won in 2012, while his **Das weiße Band** (*The White Ribbon*) received two nominations for the 2009 Academy Awards. In 2010 and in 2013, Christoph Waltz won Oscars for his supporting roles in *Inglourious Basterds* and in *Django Unchained*.

Jugendstil in Wien

3-6 Snow & Spaß. As you've seen, Austria has plenty of natural beauty and outdoor entertainment, summer and winter. Read the following ad for a popular winter ski location, and mark all correct responses according to the text.

1. Bei Snow & Spaß kann man
   ☐ nachts Ski laufen   ☐ Skilaufen lernen   ☐ Skihütten finden

2. Erwachsene heißt auf Englisch
   ☐ children   ☐ youth   ☐ grown-ups

3. Eine Tageskarte für einen 16-jährigen kostet
   ☐ 25 Euro   ☐ 18 Euro   ☐ 36 Euro

4. Die Schneemännchen-Tageskarte für 12 Euro ist für:
   ☐ Teenager   ☐ Schulkinder   ☐ sehr junge Kinder

Snow & Spaß in Österreich

Optimales Skivergnügen für die Familien!

Mit 10 Liften (1 Vierersessellift, 8 Schlepplifte, 1 Übungslift) ist **Snow & Spaß** ein attraktives Skigebiet für die ganze Familie.

✶ Skischule ✶ Skikindergarten
✶ Skiverleih ✶ Skihütten
✶ Snowpark ✶ Beleuchtete Pisten

TAGESKARTEN

	1/2 Tag	Tag
Kinder*	€ 18,00	€ 25,00
Jugendliche	€ 25,00	€ 36,00
Erwachsene	€ 32,00	€ 51,00

*auch Schneemännchen-Tageskarte
(für Kinder unter 6 Jahren) 12,00

Betriebszeiten:
Mo. bis So. von 09.00 bis 22.00 Uhr

))) 3.3 Wortschatz 1

Wichtige Vokabeln

3.2 Learn vocabulary to talk about family

Nomen

das Ding, -e	thing
das Leben, -	life
der Liebling, -e	darling; favorite
die Reise, -n	trip

Die Familie

die Familie, -n	family
der/die Verwandte, -n	relative
die Eltern (*pl*)	parents
die Mutter, ¨	mother
die Stiefmutter, ¨	stepmother
der Vater, ¨	father
der Stiefvater, ¨	stepfather
das Kind, -er	child
das Einzelkind, -er	only child
die Tochter, ¨	daughter
der Sohn, ¨e	son
die Schwester, -n	sister
der Bruder, ¨	brother
die Geschwister (*pl*)	sisters and brothers, siblings
die Großeltern (*pl*)	grandparents
die Großmutter, ¨	grandmother
die Oma, -s	grandma
der Großvater, ¨	grandfather
der Opa, -s	grandpa
der Enkel, -	grandson; grandchild
die Enkelin, -nen	granddaughter
die Tante, -n	aunt
der Onkel, -	uncle
die Kusine, -n	(*female*) cousin
der Vetter, -n	(*male*) cousin
die Nichte, -n	niece
der Neffe, -n	nephew
das Haustier, -e	pet
der Hund, -e	dog
die Katze, -n	cat

Fahrzeuge

das Fahrzeug, -e	vehicle
das Auto, -s ⎫	
der Wagen, - ⎭	car
der Bus, -se	bus
das Fahrrad, ¨er	bicycle
das Rad, ¨er	bike; wheel
das Motorrad, ¨er	motorcycle
der Zug, ¨e	train
das Flugzeug, -e	airplane
der Flügel, -	wing

Verben

kennen	to know; to be acquainted with
lachen	to laugh
verstehen	to understand

Ausdrücke

viel zu schnell	much too fast
Was ist dein Lieblingsbuch?	What's your favorite book?

Das Gegenteil

freundlich ≠ unfreundlich	friendly ≠ unfriendly
interessant ≠ langweilig	interesting ≠ boring
schnell ≠ langsam	fast ≠ slow(ly)
verheiratet ≠ ledig	married ≠ single
verheiratet ≠ geschieden	married ≠ divorced
oft ≠ selten	often ≠ seldom
optimistisch ≠ pessimistisch	optimistic ≠ pessimistic

Leicht zu verstehen

der Partner, -	**das Problem, -e**
die Partnerin, -nen	**die Show, -s**

Wörter im Kontext

3-7 Die Familie. What are the male or female counterparts?

1. die Kusine
2. die Schwester
3. die Großmutter
4. der Onkel
5. der Opa
6. der Vater
7. die Tochter
8. die Enkelin
9. der Neffe
10. der Partner

3-8 Was passt zusammen? See how many new compound words you can understand by looking at the words below and matching appropriately. Note the word **Zeug** in several word combinations; what does it seem to mean?

1. Stiefvater
2. Haustier
3. Hausschuhe
4. Halbbruder
5. Flugzeug
6. Schreibzeug
7. Bettzeug
8. Spielzeug

a. half brother
b. airplane
c. slippers
d. writing implement (pen, pencil, etc.)
e. stepfather
f. sheets, bedclothes
g. toy, plaything
h. pet

3-9 Was passt wo?

Zug / Fahrräder / Flugzeug / Motorräder / Wagen

1. Der Mercedes-Benz SLS AMG ist ein sehr guter und sehr teurer _____.
2. _____ und _____ haben nur zwei Räder.
3. Ein Bus ist nicht so lang wie ein _____.
4. Mit dem _____ fliegt man schnell nach Deutschland.

3-10 Was passt wo?

interessant / langweilig / schnell / langsam / optimistisch / pessimistisch

1. Daniel ist immer sehr _____ und hat oft Depressionen.
2. Laura lacht gern und ist immer _____.
3. _____, bitte! Ich verstehe noch nicht so gut Deutsch.
4. Fahrräder fahren nicht so _____ wie Motorräder.
5. FRANK: Ist das Buch _____?
   UWE: Nein, ich finde es sehr _____.

3.4 Zur Aussprache

The diphthongs

3.3 Recognize and pronounce two-vowel sounds

A diphthong is a combination of two vowel sounds. There are three diphthongs in German.

 3-11 Hören Sie gut zu und wiederholen Sie!

The diphthong **ei** (also spelled **ey, ai, ay**) is pronounced like the *i* in *mine*.

eins	zwei	drei
Herr Meyer	Herr Sailer	Herr Bayer

ei: Remember this sound by saying *Einstein*.

Heike Bayer und Heinz Frey heiraten am zweiten Mai.

The diphthong **au** is pronounced like the *ou* in *house*.

brauchen	laufen	kaufen
blau	braun	grau

The word **blau** can also mean *drunk*.

Paul, du bist zu laut. Ich glaube, du bist blau.
Brautkleid bleibt Brautkleid und Blaukraut bleibt Blaukraut.

The diphthong **eu** (also spelled **äu**) is pronounced like the *oy* in *boy*.

heute	teuer	neu
Häuser	Mäuse	Verkäufer

—Wer ist Frau Bäuerles neuer Freund?
—Ein Verkäufer aus Bayreuth.

3-12 Berühmte Musik. Pronounce the composers' names and the titles of their famous works, played again and again in orchestra halls all over the world.

3.5 Kommunikation und Formen 1

Sentence construction

3.4 Identify important building blocks of a sentence

The direct object

You already know that a simple sentence consists of a *subject* and a *predicate* and that the predicate is whatever is said about the subject. The predicate consists of a verb and often other parts of speech as well.

One of the "other parts of speech" is often a noun or pronoun that is the target of what is expressed by the verb (such as the people or things that get *visited, met* or *worn* in the examples below). This noun or pronoun is called the *direct object*. The boldfaced words in the following examples are the direct objects.

Subject	Predicate	
	VERB	DIRECT OBJECTS AND OTHER PARTS OF SPEECH
Aunt Bettina	visits	**exotic countries** on vacation.
She	meets	**interesting people** there.
She	wears	**expensive clothes** all the time.

3-13 Onkel Alfred. Robert Ziegler and his father are talking about another family relative, the rich but boring Uncle Alfred. Find the subjects and direct objects.

SUBJECT		DIRECT OBJECT
Mein Bruder Alfred	verdient°	viel Geld.
Er	liest°	langweilige Bücher.

earns

reads

> **Ach so!**
> Note how the fourth sentence in this exercise starts with the direct object, which gives the direct object more emphasis.

Herr Ziegler sagt:
1. Kennen Sie meinen Bruder Alfred?
2. Er trinkt teure Weine.
3. Er kauft auch teure Anzüge.
4. Seinen großen Mercedes finde ich toll.

Robert sagt:
5. Onkel Alfred hat keine Familie und keine Freunde.
6. Er liest nur langweilige Bücher!
7. Er macht keinen Sport und auch keine Reisen.
8. Ich finde meinen Onkel doof und sein Leben stinklangweilig.

> **stinklangweilig:** In colloquial German, **stink-** is often prefixed to adjectives, e.g., **stinknormal, stinkteuer.** The English equivalent is *very,* or, more informally, *totally, freaking,* etc.

Articles in the accusative case

3.5 Say the things you need or want to buy with accusative forms of *the* and *a*

The masculine forms of both the definite article **(der)** and the indefinite article **(ein)** change depending on whether they are part of the subject or the direct object.

Subject forms	Direct object forms
Der Mantel ist schön.	Ich kaufe **den** Mantel.
Ein Mantel ist teuer.	Ich brauche° **einen** Mantel.

need

The neuter and feminine forms of the definite article **(das, die)** and of the indefinite article **(ein, eine)** remain unchanged, regardless of whether they are part of the subject or the direct object.

Das Sweatshirt ist schön.　　　Ich kaufe **das** Sweatshirt.
Ein Sweatshirt ist teuer.　　　Ich brauche **ein** Sweatshirt.

Die Jacke ist schön.　　　Ich kaufe **die** Jacke.
Eine Jacke ist teuer.　　　Ich brauche **eine** Jacke.

The plural form of the definite article **(die)** also remains unchanged.

Die Schuhe sind schön.   Ich kaufe **die** Schuhe.

You already know that subjects and subject completions are in the *nominative case*. Direct objects are in the *accusative case*.

> nominative case = subject and subject completion
> accusative case = direct object

	Masculine	Neuter	Feminine	Plural
NOMINATIVE	der ein } Mantel kein	das ein } T-Shirt kein	die eine } Jacke keine	die — } Schuhe keine
ACCUSATIVE	d**en** ein**en** } Mantel kein**en**	das ein } T-Shirt kein	die eine } Jacke keine	die — } Schuhe keine

Note that the only accusative forms that differ from the nominative are the masculine (d**en**, ein**en**, and kein**en**). All other accusative forms are the same as nominative.

Motorrad: The word itself is neuter, but when it is referred to by a brand name, it is always feminine (e.g., **die Honda, die Harley, die BMW**). Car brands are always masculine.

3-14 Was hast du alles? Ask each other questions about some of the items below, as in the examples.

S1: Hast du einen Wagen?   **S2:** Ja, ich habe einen Wagen.
S2: Hast du ein Motorrad?   **S1:** Nein, ich habe kein Motorrad.

Verwandte	Fahrzeuge	Technik	Haustiere
einen Bruder	ein Fahrrad	ein Handy	eine Katze
eine Schwester	einen Mercedes	eine Digitalkamera	einen Hund
einen Enkel	ein Flugzeug	einen Server	einen Goldfisch

3-15 Bei H&M.

S1: Brauchst du einen Pullover?   **S2:** Ja, ich brauche einen Pullover.
                                                   Nein, ich brauche keinen Pullover.

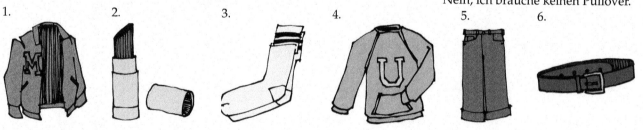

1.   2.   3.   4.   5.   6.

Jacke (f)		Lippenstift (m)		Jeans (pl)
Socken (pl)		Sweatshirt (n)		Gürtel (m)

3-16 Was für Klamotten brauchst du und wo kaufst du sie? Respond to your classmates' questions according to the model. Practice with several different clothing items from the previous exercise or from the list in the *Anhang* on p. A-6.

S1: Was für Klamotten brauchst du? S2: Ich brauche eine Jacke.
S1: Und wo kaufst du die Jacke? S2: Ich kaufe die Jacke bei Gap.
S2: Was für Klamotten brauchst du? S3: Ich brauche …

> **Klamotten:** This is an informal expression originally used to describe shabby clothes. It is commonly used among young people instead of **Kleider**.

The interrogative pronoun *wen*

Many speakers of American English don't make a distinction between *who* and *whom* and use *who* as the only interrogative pronoun (question word) for people. But in German the interrogative pronoun for a person changes depending on its case. If it is *nominative* (the subject), it is **wer;** if it is *accusative* (the object), it is **wen.**

Nominative

Wer arbeitet als Physiotherapeutin? *Who works as a physical therapist?*
Wer ist Ninas Lieblingstante? *Who is Nina's favorite aunt?*

Accusative

Wen besucht Nina dieses Wochenende? *Whom is Nina visiting this weekend?*
Wen findet Robert langweilig? *Whom does Robert find boring?*

Interrogative pronouns for people	
NOMINATIVE	wer?
ACCUSATIVE	w**en**?

3-17 Was machst du? S1 completes the questions with **wer** or **wen.** S2 selects the correct response from the options in the second column.

S1:
1. _____ besuchst du am Wochenende?
   _____ ist das? Birgit?
2. _____ ist dein Deutschlehrer?
   Und _____ hast du für Physik?
3. _____ ist dein Lieblingsautor?
   Und _____ liest Ali gern?

S2:
Nein, sie heißt Maria Braun.
Eine gute Freundin.
Den alten Professor Seidlmeyer.
Er heißt Rothermundt.
Er liest Crichton auch gern.
Das ist Michael Crichton.

Der-words in the accusative case

In the accusative case, as in the nominative, the endings of words like **dieser** (*this*), **jeder** (*each, every*), and **welcher** (*which*) correspond closely to the forms of the definite article (**der**).

Ich verstehe **diesen** Text nicht. *I don't understand **this** text.*
Ich finde **jeden** Satz schwer! *I find **every** sentence hard!*

> **Lerntipp!**
> The other **der**-words you have learned (**jeder, welcher**) take the same endings as **dieser** in this chart. The only accusative form that differs from the nominative is **diesen** (**jeden, welchen**).

	Masculine	Neuter	Feminine	Plural
NOMINATIVE	dieser	dieses	diese	diese
ACCUSATIVE	diesen	dieses	diese	diese

3-18 Das alte Familienfoto. Take a look at this old family photo. Supply the appropriate nominative or accusative endings to complete the conversation about it below.

SABINE: Dies___ alte Foto (n) zeigt meine ganze Familie.

NINA: Wer ist denn dies___ blonde Frau da?

guy SABINE: Das ist meine Mutter! Und kennst du dies___ Typ° (m)?

NINA: Ist dies___ Typ dein Vater?

SABINE: Nein, das ist mein Vetter. Dies___ große Mann hier ist mein Vater.

NINA: Und wer hat dies___ schwarzen Hund?

SABINE: Das ist Tante Susannes alter Hund, Bärli.

Das ist meine Familie.

3-19 Meine Familie. Bring a family photo to class. Discuss your photo with a partner, and take turns asking who individual people are. Here are some phrases that will help. You can also use the previous activity as a guide.

S1:	S2:
Wer ist **dieser** große Mann da? Dein Onkel?	Nein, das ist mein Vater.
Wie heißt **dieses** kleine Kind? Ist das dein Neffe?	Nein, das ist mein …
Wie heißt **diese** elegante Frau? Ist das deine Mutter?	Das ist meine …
Wer sind **diese** zwei Kinder?	Das sind meine zwei …

Ein-words in the accusative case

You already know that the **ein-**words are **ein, kein,** and the possessive adjectives, and that all **ein-**words take the same endings. The chart below reviews the possessive adjectives.

Possessive adjectives			
mein	*my*	**unser**	*our*
dein	*your*	**euer**	*your*
sein	*his, its*	**ihr**	*their*
ihr	*her, its*		
		Ihr	*your*

Remember that just like the formal **Sie,** the formal **Ihr** is always capitalized.

Warum verkaufen Sie **Ihren** Wagen, Herr Ziegler?

*Why are you selling **your** car, Mr. Ziegler?*

In the chart below, **mein** shows the nominative and accusative endings of *all* possessive adjectives.

	Masculine	Neuter	Feminine	Plural
NOMINATIVE	mein Freund	mein Auto	meine Freundin	meine Eltern
ACCUSATIVE	mein**en** Freund	mein Auto	meine Freundin	meine Eltern

> **Lerntipp!**
> The only accusative form that differs from the nominative is masculine accusative (**meinen, deinen, seinen, ihren, unseren,** etc.).

Remember that when an ending is added to **euer** (*your*), the **e** before the **r** is dropped: **eure, euren.**

Warum verkauft ihr **euren** Wagen?

*Why are you selling **your** car?*

3-20 Warum denn? Why are these people selling the things mentioned? **S1** completes the questions with the proper forms of **dein, euer,** or **Ihr. S2** selects the appropriate response from the options in the second column.

S1:
1. Warum verkaufen Sie _____ Kamera (f)?
2. Warum verkauft ihr _____ Fahrräder (pl)?
3. Warum verkaufst du _____ Saxofon (n)?
4. Warum verkaufen Sie _____ Wagen (m)?
5. Warum verkauft ihr _____ Haus (n)?

S2:
Ich spiele viel lieber Gitarre.
Es ist viel zu klein für uns.
Ich nehme jetzt immer den Bus.
Wir haben jetzt einen Wagen.
Ich fotografiere jetzt mit meinem Handy.

Sprachnotiz   Expressing time with the accusative case

To express definite points of time, German often uses time phrases in the accusative case.

Ich fliege **diesen Freitag** nach Salzburg.   *I'm flying to Salzburg this Friday.*

The accusative case is also used to express a duration of time *(for a month, for a week).* Note that German does not use a preposition like *for* as we sometimes do in English.

Ich bleibe **eine Woche** dort.   *I'll stay there (for) a week.*

Jedes Jahr ein neues Smartphone

3-21 Besuche dieses Wochenende. **S1** asks the question using the appropriate form of **machen. S2** answers by completing the phrase directly opposite with the correct form of the missing possessive adjective (**sein, ihr,** or **unser**).

▶ Was _____ Maggie dieses Wochenende?   Sie besucht _____ Schwester in Paris.

S1: Was macht Maggie dieses Wochenende?

S2: Sie besucht ihre Schwester in Paris.

1. Was _____ Nina diesen Samstag?

   Sie besucht _____ Lieblingstante.

2. Was _____ Robert?

   Er besucht _____ langweiligen Onkel Alfred.

3. Was _____ Oma Ziegler?

   Sie besucht _____ Sohn Klaus.

4. Was _____ Alexander diesen Samstag?

   Er besucht _____ Freundin Nina.

5. Was _____ Herr und Frau Ziegler?

   Sie besuchen _____ Freunde in Heidelberg.

6. Was _____ Bergers?

   Sie besuchen _____ Tochter Claudia in Berlin.

7. Was _____ ihr dieses Wochenende?

   Wir besuchen _____ Großeltern.

3-22 Besuche bei Freunden und Verwandten. Ask whom your partner is planning to visit at the times below. **S2** can use family vocabulary from *Wortschatz 1* as a guide.

S1: Wen besuchst du im Dezember?

S2: Ich besuche meine Oma (f)/meinen Opa (m) …

S2: Und du? Wen besuchst du an Thanksgiving?

dieses Wochenende	jeden Sommer	nächstes Jahr

3.6 Kultur 2

Mozart: Das musikalische Wunderkind Österreichs

3.6 Retell the life story of an important historical person, using key dates

3-23 Wolfgang Amadeus Mozart. What do you associate with Mozart? Mark all that apply.

ein berühmter Komponist:
a famous composer

☐ klassische Musik   ☐ ein berühmter Komponist°   ☐ Mozartkugeln

☐ eine musikalische Familie   ☐ ein Wunderkind   ☐ Klaviermusik

3-24 Was ist das auf Englisch? Match the bold word in the left column with its definition in the right column.

1. Der Konzertmeister in einem Orchester spielt **ausgezeichnet** Violine.
2. Ein guter **Geschäftsmann** verdient sehr gut.
3. Maria Theresia war die **Kaiserin** von Österreich.
4. In der katholischen Kirche in Salzburg gibt es einen **Erzbischof.**
5. Mozart macht eine musikalische **Tournee,** als er noch sehr jung ist.
6. Eine populäre Mozart-Oper heißt *Die Hochzeit des Figaro.*
7. Der 35-jährige Mozart wird in Wien sehr **krank.**
8. Im Dezember 1791 ist der junge Mozart schon **tot.**
9. Über 200 Jahre nach seinem **Tod** hört und spielt man immer noch die Musik dieses Wunderkinds.
10. Klassische Musik ist Musik, die nie **stirbt**!

  a. sick
  b. tour
  c. dead
  d. excellent(ly)
  e. businessman
  f. death
  g. marriage
  h. empress
  i. archbishop
  j. dies

Ein Wunderkind

Am 27. Januar 1756 kommt Wolfgang Amadeus Mozart in diesem Haus in der Getreidegasse in Salzburg auf die Welt. Sein Vater, Leopold Mozart, ist Violinist im Orchester des Erzbischofs und auch Musiklehrer und Komponist. Das kleine Wunderkind Wolfgang schreibt schon mit vier Jahren seine ersten Kompositionen. Mozarts Schwester Nannerl ist eine ausgezeichnete Pianistin.

Erstes Konzert in Wien

Im Jahre 1762 reist die ganze Familie nach Wien. Dort spielen die beiden Wunderkinder – Nannerl ist jetzt elf und Wolfgang sechs – für die Kaiserin Maria Theresia. Die Kinder bekommen schöne Kleider und verdienen viel Geld.

Musikalische Sensation in Europa

Mozarts Vater Leopold ist nicht nur ein guter Musiker, sondern auch ein guter Geschäftsmann. Er organisiert für seine Kinder eine große Tournee. Von 1763 bis 1767 – fast vier Jahre lang – reisen die Mozarts Tausende von Kilometern durch Deutschland, Belgien, Frankreich, England und Holland und geben Hunderte von Konzerten. Im Jahre 1769 reist der jetzt 13-jährige Wolfgang mit seinem Vater nach Italien. Fünfzehn Monate lang ist der junge Pianist und Komponist auch dort die große Sensation.

Arbeit im Orchester und als Komponist

1772 ist Wolfgang wieder in Salzburg und wird sechzehn Jahre alt. Aber jetzt ist er kein Wunderkind und keine Sensation mehr, sondern nur ein ganz normaler Musiker im Orchester des Erzbischofs.

Hochzeit mit Constanze Weber

1781 geht Mozart mit 25 Jahren wieder nach Wien und verdient dort als Pianist und Komponist wieder ganz gut. 1782 heiratet er die Wienerin Constanze Weber. Er lebt mit seiner Frau wie ein König und braucht immer mehr Geld. Mozart arbeitet Tag und Nacht und verdient jedes Jahr mehr.

Mozarts Tod

Im Jahr 1791, seinem letzten Lebensjahr, schreibt Mozart zwei Opern, ein Klavierkonzert, ein Klarinettenkonzert, ein Quintett und eine Kantate und arbeitet an einem Requiem. Aber im November 1791 wird er sehr krank und kann nicht mehr arbeiten. Am fünften Dezember ist Mozart tot. Er stirbt sehr jung: Er ist erst fünfunddreißig Jahre alt.

Familie Mozart: Schwester Nannerl, Wolfgang, und Leopold

This famous painting by Johann Nepomuk della Croce shows Wolfgang and his sister Nannerl at the harpsichord and father Leopold with his violin. The mother, who died before the portrait was painted, is included by means of the painting on the wall. Leopold and his wife Anna had seven children, but only two survived past infancy.

Arbeit mit dem Text

3-25 Biografische Information. What took place in the following years of Mozart's life? Complete the timeline by matching each year with the appropriate events under "Biografische Informationen"!

- Reise nach Italien – Mozart ist die große Sensation!
- Konzert vor der Kaiserin Maria Theresia
- Mozarts Tod
- Mozarts Geburt
- Hochzeit mit Constanze Weber
- Lange Tournee durch Europa
- Arbeit als Pianist und Komponist in Wien
- Orchesterposten beim Erzbischof in Salzburg

Achtung!

When saying dates in German, **-hundert**- must be expressed, e.g., **1772: siebzehn***hundert* **zweiundsiebzig.**

Jahr	Mozart ist	Biografische Informationen
1756	—	
1762	6 J.	
1763–7	7–11 J.	
1769	13 J.	
1772	16 J.	
1781	25 J.	
1782	26 J.	
1791	35 J.	

3-26 Wie findest du Mozarts Musik? Listen as your instructor plays a few of Mozart's well-known works. Use phrases below to respond to the music, saying how you like it.

    Mozarts Musik finde ich …

echt schön	O.K.	nicht so toll
super	nicht schlecht	langweilig
besser als …	interessant	nicht so gut

3-27 Moderne Musik in Österreich. Explore today's music scene in Austria by doing a Web search using the terms **Österreich** and a current style of music that you like, such as **Rock, Hip-Hop, Jazz, Indie,** etc. Share your findings in a small group by using some of the following phrases:

    Meine Lieblingsmusik ist …   **Hier ist ein Song von …**   **Wie findet ihr das?**

3.7 Kommunikation und Formen 2

More on the accusative case

3.7 Describe people, places, and things (accusative case)

Accusative endings of adjectives preceded by *der*-words

	Masculine	Neuter	Feminine	Plural
NOMINATIVE	der neue Computer	das teure Handy	die neue Maus	die tollen Kopfhörer
ACCUSATIVE	den neuen Computer	das teure Handy	die neue Maus	die tollen Kopfhörer

- Note that the adjective endings are identical in both cases, except for the masculine accusative singular.
- In the masculine accusative singular, the adjective ending is **-en.**
- Adjectives that end in **-er** or **-el** drop the e when they take an ending (**teu**er: den teu**ren** Computer; dunk**el**: das dunk**le** Handy)

CHRISTA: Welch**en** Computer kaufst du, **den** teuren oder **den** billigen?

ANNA: Ich glaube, ich kaufe **den** billigen.

Which computer are you going to buy, the expensive one or the cheap one?
I think I'm going to buy the cheap one.

3-28 Bei Saturn. You and your partner are shopping at Saturn, an electronics superstore. Complete the dialogues by supplying the missing adjective endings according to the example. Note that both speakers are practicing accusative endings.

▶ Welchen Computer; hell oder dunkel

S1: Welchen Computer kaufst du, den hellen oder den dunklen?

S2: Ich glaube, ich kaufe den dunklen Computer.

1. Welches Handy: weiß oder schwarz
2. Welchen Tabletcomputer: dünn oder dick
3. Welche Smartwatch: blau oder schwarz
4. Welchen e-Bookreader: teuer oder billig
5. Welche Kopfhörer: groß oder klein

> Large-scale warehouses for electronics are as popular in Germany as they are in North America. Saturn is the go-to place for everything electronic in almost every German city.

Accusative endings of adjectives preceded by *ein*-words

	Masculine	Neuter	Feminine	Plural
NOMINATIVE	ein neuer Computer	ein teures Handy	eine neue Maus	meine tollen Kopfhörer
ACCUSATIVE	einen neuen Computer	ein teures Handy	eine neue Maus	meine tollen Kopfhörer

- Just as you saw with the adjective endings following **der**-words, the adjective endings following **ein**-words are identical in both cases, except for the masculine accusative singular.
- In the masculine accusative singular, the adjective always ends in **-n.**
- Remember that wherever the **ein**-word has no ending (nominative masculine and neuter, and accusative neuter), the ending that shows gender goes on the adjective instead: Das ist ein neu**er** Drucker. Ich kaufe ein teu**res** Notebook.

Möchten Sie ein**en** preisgünstigen Drucker?
Ja, ich möchte ein**en** preisgünstigen kleinen.

Would you like an inexpensive printer?
Yes, I'd like an inexpensive small one.

3-29 Im Elektronikgeschäft. Now you're ready to talk to the salesperson at Saturn about what products to buy. **S1** is the salesperson and **S2** expresses a preference.

▶ der Fernseher: groß oder klein

S1: Möchten Sie einen großen oder einen kleinen Fernseher?

S2: Ich möchte einen großen Fernseher.

1. der Monitor: groß oder klein
2. das Notebook: schwer oder leicht
3. die Smartwatch: blau oder violett
4. das Computerspiel: deutsch oder amerikanisch
5. das Fitnessarmband: schwarz oder rot

 3-30 Was hast du im Rucksack? Check out what tech and other items your classmates have with them. Use one or more adjectives as you reveal what you have.

S1: Hast du eine Smartwatch?

S2: Ja, ich habe eine neue schwarze Smartwatch.

> **Lerntipp!**
> It's easy to talk about feminine objects—just add an **-e** to the end of each adjective!

| Handy (n) | Smartwatch (f) | USB-Stick (m) |

| Handy-Cover (n) | Computer (m) | Sonnenbrille (f) |

| Stift (m) | Fitnessarmband (n) |

Accusative endings of unpreceded adjectives

	Masculine	**Neuter**	**Feminine**	**Plural**
NOMINATIVE	guter Kaffee	gutes Bier	gute Schokolade	gute Oliven
ACCUSATIVE	gut**en** Kaffee	gutes Bier	gute Schokolade	gute Oliven

- In the masculine accusative singular, the ending of an unpreceded adjective is **-en.**
- The other accusative endings are identical to those in the nominative.

| KELLNER°: Möchten Sie lieber schottisch**en** oder kanadisch**en** Lachs? | *Would you rather have Scottish or Canadian salmon?* | server |
| GAST°: Heute esse ich mal kanadisch**en** Lachs. | *Today I'm going to eat Canadian salmon for a change.* | guest |

 3-31 Studentenessen. From the items below, choose two things you eat and drink each week, and choose at least one adjective to give more detail about each item. Then compare this list with your partner's.

S1: Was isst du und trinkst du jede Woche?

S2: Ich esse jede Woche … und … . Ich trinke … und auch … .

Essen	**Getränke**
Salat (m): gesund, grün	Softdrinks (pl): kalt, kalorienfrei
Sushi (n): frisch, kalt	Kaffee (m): heiß, stark
Pizza (f): heiß, billig, lecker	Smoothies (pl): gesund, kalt
Schokolade (f): gut, dunkel	Bier (n): kalt, deutsch

More on the position of *nicht*

3.8 Say that you do not have, know, or understand something

Nicht usually follows the direct object.

> Mein Freund kennt den Film *Good Bye, Lenin!* **nicht.**
> Warum verstehen meine Eltern meine Probleme **nicht?**
> Ich glaube, ich kaufe den Computer **nicht.**

Remember that nouns preceded by the indefinite article **ein** or nouns without an article are negated with **kein.**

> Ein VW Jetta ist **kein** SUV!
> Ich habe **keinen** SUV!

> Do a Web search to research two of these Austrian items that you don't know and report what you find to the class!

3-32 Was kennst du, und was kennst du nicht? Find out how much your partner knows about Austrian people, places, and things!

1. Kennst du die österreichische Firma Swarowski?
2. Kennst du den österreichischen Entrepreneur Dietrich Mateschitz?
3. Kennst du den österreichischen Koch Wolfgang Puck?
4. Kennst du die österreichische Spezialität Kaiserschmarrn?
5. Kennst du den österreichischen Filmemacher Michael Haneke?
6. Kennst du den österreichischen Film *Ich seh Ich seh*?
7. Kennst du das *Requiem* von Mozart?
8. Kennst du die österreichische Nationalhymne?
9. Kennst du Sachertorte?

Eine österreichische Spezialität

Verbs with stem-vowel changes

3.9 Talk about your everyday life using verbs like eating, reading, running, and sleeping

Verbs with stem-vowel changes in the present tense

Some German verbs have a stem-vowel change that occurs only in the **du**-form and in the **er/es/sie**-form of the present tense.

e → i		e → ie		a → ä		au → äu	
sprechen		lesen		fahren		laufen	
ich	spreche	ich	lese	ich	fahre	ich	laufe
du	sprichst	du	**lie**st	du	f**ä**hrst	du	l**äu**fst
er/es/sie	spricht	er/es/sie	**lie**st	er/es/sie	f**ä**hrt	er/es/sie	l**äu**ft
wir	sprechen	wir	lesen	wir	fahren	wir	laufen
ihr	sprecht	ihr	lest	ihr	fahrt	ihr	lauft
sie/Sie	sprechen	sie/Sie	lesen	sie/Sie	fahren	sie/Sie	laufen

In dictionaries, verbs that have vowel changes in the present tense ("irregular verbs")
are usually listed as follows:

sprechen (spricht)	*to speak*
fahren (fährt)	*to drive*

Verbs with stem-vowel change from *e → i* or *ie*

e → i				
essen	*to eat*	ich esse	du **isst**	er **isst**
geben	*to give*	ich gebe	du **gibst**	er **gibt**
nehmen	*to take*	ich nehme	du **nimmst**	er **nimmt**
sprechen	*to speak*	ich spreche	du **sprichst**	er **spricht**
sterben	*to die*	ich sterbe	du **stirbst**	er **stirbt**
werden	*to become; to get; to be*	ich werde	du **wirst**	er **wird**
e → ie				
lesen	*to read*	ich lese	du **liest**	er **liest**
sehen	*to see*	ich sehe	du **siehst**	er **sieht**

3-33 Ein bisschen etwas über dich. Complete each question with the correct form
of the verb given. Then answer the question truthfully! Then ask another student
these questions to see how similar or different you are!

▶ **essen:** Was ___isst___ du lieber, Pizza oder Spaghetti?
Meine Antwort: _____

1. **nehmen:** _____ du den Bus zur Uni?
Meine Antwort: _____

2. **sprechen:** Wie viele Sprachen _____ du?
Meine Antwort: _____

3. **werden:** Wie alt _____ du nächstes Jahr?
Meine Antwort: _____

4. **lesen:** _____ du jeden Morgen die Zeitung°?   *newspaper*
Meine Antwort: _____

5. **sehen:** _____ du gern Horrorfilme?
Meine Antwort: _____

6. **geben:** _____ du dieses Wochenende auf eine Party?
Meine Antwort: _____

Two common expressions using **es gibt** are **Was gibt's?** (*What's up?*) and **Was gibt's Neues?** (*What's new?*)

Sprachnotiz   The expression *es gibt*

German conveys *there is* or *there are* using the expression **es gibt** (from the verb **geben**). Note that **es gibt** always has an accusative object.

Es gibt viele McDonald's in Hamburg.   *There are many McDonald's in Hamburg.*
Wo **gibt es** hier einen schönen Park?   *Where is there a nice park around here?*

3-34 Was für eine Touristenattraktion gibt es in …? Match the locations with the appropriate attractions.

1. In San Francisco gibt es   a. den Fudschijama
2. In Arizona gibt es   b. die Pyramiden
3. In Japan gibt es   c. den Eiffelturm
4. In Wyoming gibt es   d. die Golden-Gate-Brücke
5. In Ägypten gibt es   e. den Taj Mahal
6. In Paris gibt es   f. den Yellowstone Nationalpark
7. In Indien gibt es   g. den Grand Canyon

3-35 Bei uns gibt es … Select from the list below three attractions in your hometown. Consider what adjectives you could use to describe each attraction. Then present your list to the class.

Ich komme aus ….   Dort gibt es   ein**en** klein**en** Zoo (m).

ein berühmt**es** Theater (n).

☐ Sportstadion (n)   ☐ Pizzeria (f)   ☐ Monument (n)
☐ Museum (n)   ☐ Brauhaus (n)   ☐ Mall (f)
☐ Konzerthalle (f)   ☐ Restaurant (n)   ☐ Club (m)
☐ Sinfonieorchester (n) ☐ …

Verbs with stem-vowel change from *a → ä* or *au → äu*

a → ä				
backen	*to bake*	ich backe	du **bäckst**	er **bäckt**
fahren	*to drive*	ich fahre	du **fährst**	er **fährt**
halten	*to hold; to stop; to keep*	ich halte	du **hältst**	er **hält**
lassen	*to let; to leave*	ich lasse	du **lässt**	er **lässt**
schlafen	*to sleep*	ich schlafe	du **schläfst**	er **schläft**
tragen	*to wear*	ich trage	du **trägst**	er **trägt**
waschen	*to wash*	ich wasche	du **wäschst**	er **wäscht**
au → äu				
laufen	*to run*	ich laufe	du **läufst**	er **läuft**

3-36 Kurze Konversationen. Complete each conversation with the correct forms of the verb given.

1. **backen:** MARKUS: Oma, was _____ du?

   OMA: Ich _____ eine Torte!

2. **fahren:** MELISSA: Was für einen Wagen _____ deine Eltern?

   JAN: Meine Mutter _____ einen Prius und mein Vater _____ einen Jeep.

3. **halten:** HERR HEINS: Entschuldigung, wo _____ hier der Bus?

   HERR POWITZ: Der Bus _____ hier direkt vor McDonald's.

4. **lassen:** BRAD: Wann _____ ihr die Katze ins Haus?

   LAURA: Wir _____ die Katze abends ins Haus.

5. **schlafen:** LISA: Wie lange _____ du am Sonntagmorgen?

   JULIA: Ich _____ normalerweise bis halb zwölf.

6. **tragen:** MAX: Was _____ du heute Abend zur Party?

   ANNA: Ich _____ blaue Jeans und ein weißes T-Shirt.

7. **waschen:** JOHANNES: Wie oft _____ ihr euer Auto?

   LAURA: Wir _____ es jede Woche.

8. **laufen:** FRANK: _____ du gern die hundert Meter?

   ALEX: Nein, aber meine Freundin _____ die hundert Meter sehr schnell.

3-37 Was machen diese Leute?

S1: Was macht Tanja?   **S2:** Sie läuft Ski.

► … Ski.

1. Was macht Helga?

… ein Bad.

2. Was macht Günter?

… alles doppelt.

3. Was macht Ralf?

… sein Motorrad.

4. Was macht Herr Lukasik?

… seinen Wagen.

5. Was macht Frau Schneider?

… ein Buch.

6. Was macht Tina?

… einen Apfel.

7. Was macht Charlyce?

… mit Bernd.

8. Was macht Monika?

…

3-38 **Was bedeutet das?** Each item below uses one of the new verbs you just learned. Identify the verbs and try to figure out the meanings based on the context, the visuals, or other words.

3-39 **Wer ist das?** Working in small groups, take turns describing the style and color of a classmate's clothing and hair. The rest of your group will guess who is being described. Use the descriptive adjectives below and be sure to attach the correct endings in the accusative.

Kleider

S1: Sie trägt ein**e** schwarz**e** Hose (f), ein toll**es**, dunkelgrün**es** T-Shirt (n) und ein**e** schwarz**e** Brille° (f).

glasses

- lang, kurz, groß, klein
- elegant, schick, schön, toll, hübsch
- blau, grün, rosarot, schwarz, hellblau, dunkelrot

straight / curly / wavy

- lang, kurz, glatt°, lockig°, wellig°
- blond, brünett, rot, schwarz

Haare

S2: Sie hat lang**e**, blond**e**, wunderschön**e** Haare.

Sie/Er trägt	einen	_____en, _____en Pullover (Rock, Mantel, Gürtel)
	ein	_____es, _____es Polohemd (T-Shirt, Sweatshirt, Kleid)
	eine	_____e, _____e Hose (Jogginghose, Jacke, Bluse)
		_____e, _____e Jeans (Shorts, Leggings, Schuhe, Stiefel, Sandalen)

3-40　Was machen alle gern?　After reading through what Matt and Alexa like to eat, read, watch, etc., provide the information about yourself.

	Matt	**Alexa**	**Ich**
essen	Döner, Pommes, Nutella	Nudeln, Wurst, Gummibärchen	
lesen	Comics, Online-Zeitungen	Science-Fiction, Magazine, Blogs	
sehen	Katzenvideos und Musikvideos auf YouTube	Horrorfilme, Dokufilme, Sportreportagen	
sprechen	Englisch und ein bisschen Deutsch	Deutsch, Spanisch und Französisch	
fahren	einen alten Jeep	ein gutes Mountainbike	
tragen	Bermudashorts, Sandalen	Jeans, T-Shirts	

3-41　Ein kurzes Interview.　Find out your partner's responses by asking the questions below.

- Was isst du gern?
- Was liest du gern?
- Was für Filme siehst du gern?
- Welche Sprachen sprichst du?
- Was für einen Wagen fährst du?
- Was für Kleider trägst du gern?

3.8　Video-Treff

Meine Familie

3.10　Listen for some details about real people's families

Maiga, Stefan Meister, Anja Peter, Thomas, André, and Karen are talking about their families. Be sure to complete the **Was ist das auf Englisch?** exercise before watching the video.

Mein Vater hat ein Segelboot.

3-42　Was ist das auf Englisch?

1. Meine Eltern leben seit drei Jahren **getrennt.**
2. Mein Bruder geht in **die 11. Klasse.**
3. Mein Vater hat ein **Segelboot.**
4. Ich habe eine **supersüße** Nichte.
5. Meine Eltern haben ein schönes Haus **in einer tollen Gegend.**
6. Sie wohnen jetzt **außerhalb von** Berlin.
7. Meine Schwester **macht** ihre Klamotten **selber.**
8. Ich habe zwei Halbgeschwister; wir haben alle drei **unterschiedliche** Mütter.
9. Ich habe eine **ältere** Schwester.

a. sailboat
b. in a great area
c. different
d. makes … herself
e. eleventh grade
f. separated
g. older
h. outside of
i. very sweet

3-43 Was ist die richtige Antwort? Choose the appropriate answer to the following questions about the families of Maiga, Stefan, and Anja.

Maiga

1. Maigas Mutter heißt ☐ Bettina. ☐ Regina.
2. Maigas Eltern wohnen in ☐ Göttingen. ☐ Berlin.
3. Maigas Bruder Philipp ist ☐ Schüler. ☐ Student.
4. Ihr Bruder Philipp spielt gern ☐ Fußball. ☐ Gitarre.

Stefan

5. Stefans Vater heißt ☐ Hans-Jürgen. ☐ Karl-Heinz.
6. Sein Vater ist … von Beruf. ☐ Lehrer. ☐ Kaufmann.
7. Als Hobby geht Stefans Vater gern ☐ segeln. ☐ angeln.
8. Stefan hat ☐ eine Schwester. ☐ einen Bruder.

Anja

9. Anja hat ☐ keine Geschwister. ☐ einen Bruder.
10. Ihre Eltern haben ☐ eine schöne Wohnung. ☐ ein schönes Haus.

3-44 Wer sagt das? Select the name of the person who matches the statement best.

	Thomas	André	Karen
1. Mein Vater heißt Wolfgang.	☐	☐	☐
2. Meine Mutter und mein Vater sind 51 Jahre alt.	☐	☐	☐
3. Mein Vater ist Manager von Beruf.	☐	☐	☐
4. Meine Schwester kauft sehr gern Schuhe.	☐	☐	☐
5. Mein Bruder studiert Theologie und Germanistik.	☐	☐	☐
6. Meine Eltern wohnen nicht weit von Berlin.	☐	☐	☐
7. Ich habe zwei Halbgeschwister.	☐	☐	☐
8. Meine Eltern sind geschieden.	☐	☐	☐
9. Meine Mutter ist Lehrerin.	☐	☐	☐

))) 3.9 Wortschatz 2

Wichtige Vokabeln

3.11 Learn vocabulary to describe people and to talk about what they do

Nomen

der Familienname, -n	last name
der Vorname, -n	first name
das Geschäft, -e	store; business
der Geschäftsmann, ¨er	businessman
die Geschäftsfrau, -en	businesswoman
das Kleidergeschäft, -e	clothing store
die Klamotten (*pl*)	clothes
das Kaufhaus, ¨er	department store
der Verkäufer, -	sales clerk
die Verkäuferin, -nen	
die Hochzeit, -en	wedding
der Tod	death
die Sonnenbrille, -n	sunglasses
die Sprache, -n	language
die Zeitung, -en	newspaper

Verben

brauchen	to need
heiraten	to marry
verdienen	to earn
backen (bäckt)	to bake
fahren (fährt)	to drive
halten (hält)	to hold; to stop; to keep
lassen (lässt)	to let; to leave
laufen (läuft)	to run
schlafen (schläft)	to sleep
tragen (trägt)	to wear
waschen (wäscht)	to wash
essen (isst)	to eat
geben (gibt)	to give
lesen (liest)	to read
nehmen (nimmt)	to take
sehen (sieht)	to see
sprechen (spricht)	to speak
sterben (stirbt)	to die
werden (wird)	to become; to get; to be

Andere Wörter

ausgezeichnet	excellent
laut	loud
offen	open
preisgünstig	inexpensive
berühmt	famous
tot	dead
wunderbar	wonderful
wunderschön	very beautiful
blond	blonde
brünett	brunette
glatt	straight (*of hair*)
lockig	curly
gestern	yesterday
mehr	more
immer mehr	more and more

In German, eyeglasses and sunglasses are singular: **die Brille, die Sonnenbrille.** You would only use the plural when referring to more than one pair.

Ausdrücke

es gibt (+ *acc*)	there is, there are
die ganze Famlie	the whole family
nächstes Jahr	next year
Er arbeitet nicht mehr.	He's not working any more.
Sie sind nicht mehr verheiratet.	They're no longer married.
Sie wird zwanzig.	She's turning twenty.
Was sind Sie von Beruf?	What is your occupation?
nicht X, sondern Y	not X, but rather Y

Das Gegenteil

kaufen ≠ verkaufen	to buy ≠ to sell
erst ≠ letzt	first ≠ last
krank ≠ gesund	sick ≠ healthy
neu ≠ alt	new ≠ old
alles ≠ nichts	all ≠ nothing

Leicht zu verstehen

der Horrorfilm, -e	das Orchester, -
das Interview, -s	die Person, -en
die Kamera, -s	der Preis, -e
die Klasse, -n	die Sandale, -n
der Komponist, -en	die Sensation, -en
das Mountainbike, -s	die Tournee, -n

Wörter im Kontext

3-45 Jennifers Familie. Jennifer's parents are American but have German ties. Soon they will visit their daughter who is studying abroad. Complete with words from the list.

nimmt / wird / von Beruf / nächste / gibt es / bekommt / offen

1. Jennifers Vater und ihr Bruder Kurt sind beide Koch _____.
2. Im Restaurant von Jennifers Eltern _____ oft deutsche Spezialitäten.

nobody, no one

3. Montags ist das Restaurant nicht _____, denn montags isst fast niemand° im Restaurant.
4. Übermorgen fliegt Jennifers Mutter nach Deutschland, denn Jennifer _____ _____ Woche einundzwanzig.
5. Ihr Flugzeug landet auf dem Hamburger Flughafen, und von dort _____ sie dann den Zug nach Kiel.
6. Jennifer _____ von ihren Eltern dreihundert Euro zum Geburtstag.

3-46 Was passt zusammen? For each sentence in the first column, find the most appropriate statement in the second column and complete it with the correct form of a suitable verb from the following list.

essen / tragen / schlafen / waschen / sehen / fahren

1. Er ist Polizist.
2. Sie ist Studentin.
3. Er ist ein Gourmet.
4. Das ist ein Bär.
5. Das ist eine Katze.
6. Er ist Hausmann.

a. Er kocht und bäckt und _____.
b. Er _____ fast den ganzen Winter.
c. Er _____ eine Uniform.
d. Sie _____ jeden Morgen zur Uni.
e. Er _____ gern Kaviar.
f. Sie _____ auch bei Nacht sehr gut.

3-47 Anders gesagt. Decide which two sentences in each group have approximately the same meaning.

1. a. Maria ist Verkäuferin.
   b. Maria kauft Klamotten.
   c. Maria verkauft Klamotten.
2. a. Wie viel Geld verdienst du?
   b. Wie viel Geld bekommst du?
   c. Wie viel Geld brauchst du?
3. a. Tom spricht viele Sprachen.
   b. Toms Muttersprache ist Englisch.
   c. Toms Englisch ist ausgezeichnet.
4. a. Tom und Maria heiraten morgen.
   b. Maria wird morgen Toms Frau.
   c. Maria und Tom sind geschieden.

_upe

More cognates

In *Kapitel 2* you saw that it is often quite simple to decode the English meanings of certain cognates. Below is another list with the "code" that will help you figure out the English meanings. In some cases it helps to say the German words out loud. Words followed by *(v)* are verbs in their infinitive form.

- German **s**, **ss**, or **ß** is English *t* or *tt*

das Wasser	rasseln *(v)*	vergessen *(v)*	der Fuß	der Kessel
hassen *(v)*	besser	beißen *(v)*	die Nuss	was

- German **z** or **tz** is English *t* or *tt*

setzen *(v)*	die Katze	grunzen *(v)*	zehn
sitzen *(v)*	die Minze	die Warze	zwölf
der Sitz	das Salz	zu	die Zunge
glitzern *(v)*	das Netz		

- German **pf** is English *p* or *pp*

der Apfel	der Pfennig	das Pfund	der Pfad (**d** → *th!*)
der Krampf	die Pflanze (**z** → *t!*)	der Pfeffer (**f** → *p!*)	die Pfeife (**f** → *p!*)
die Pfanne	der Pfosten		

Salz und Pfeffer

3.10 Alles zusammen

Meine Familie – mein Stammbaum

Schritt 1: Zum Lesen

3-48 Machen Sie das Kreuzworträtsel zur Familie Mozart!

Ein großes Talent aus Salzburg

Ach so!

If you need help with some answers, re-read section *3.6 Kultur 2* in this chapter.

Waagerecht →

3. Der Name von Mozarts Vater ist …
8. Mozart und Nannerl spielen …
10. Als Kind ist Mozart ein kleines musikalisches …
11. Mozart trifft Constanze Weber in …
12. In diesem Monat stirbt Mozart.

Senkrecht ↓

1. Mozarts Vater spielt …
2. Der Vorname von Mozarts Frau ist …
4. Im Jahr 1791 schreibt Mozart zwei …
5. Mozarts zweiter Name ist …
6. Mozarts Schwester heißt …
7. Mozart ist … Jahre alt, als er seine erste Komposition schreibt.
9. Mozart stirbt sehr …

Schritt 2: Zum Sprechen

3-49 Familie Mozarts Stammbaum. Geben Sie mit einer Partnerin/einem Partner die richtigen Informationen zu Mozarts Familie!

S1: Was ist Mozarts Vater von Beruf? …
S2: Was für ein Instrument spielt Mozarts Schwester? …

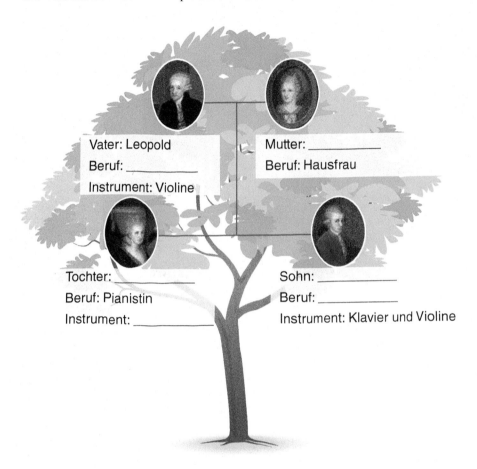

Vater: Leopold
Beruf: _____
Instrument: Violine

Mutter: _____
Beruf: Hausfrau

Tochter: _____
Beruf: Pianistin
Instrument: _____

Sohn: _____
Beruf: _____
Instrument: Klavier und Violine

Schritt 3: Zum Präsentieren

3-50 Mein eigener Familienstammbaum. Wer ist in Ihrem Familienstammbaum? Schreiben Sie die Namen und drei Fakten zu jeder Person auf. Dann präsentieren Sie den Stammbaum mit Phrasen aus dem Kasten.

> Ich habe eine kleine / große / mittelgroße Familie.
> Meine Eltern sind verheiratet / getrennt / geschieden.
> Ich habe einen Stiefvater / eine Stiefmutter.

> Mein Vater / Meine Mutter / Meine Schwester heißt …
> Er/Sie ist … Jahre alt.
> Er/Sie ist … von Beruf.
> Er/Sie studiert an …
> Er/Sie geht noch in die Schule.
> Er/Sie spielt gern …

Use the same format as Mozart's **Stammbaum**, but change, rearrange, or add to it to fit your particular family. If you'd prefer to present on a ficticious family, that's fine, too.

You can talk about musical instruments, games, and most sports using the catch-all **spielt gern** … .

The verb **studieren** is only used for college-level study. What phrase in the word bank corresponds to *is still in (grade) school?*

Kapitel 4
Alltagsleben

Obst- und Gemüsemarkt in Biel, Schweiz

Learning Objectives

4.1 Describe Swiss contributions to the international community

4.2 Learn vocabulary to talk about food and eating habits

4.3 Distinguish between long and short *ä*, *ö*, and *ü*

4.4 Talk about what you can do, have to do, and want to do

4.5 Say what you are allowed to do, supposed to do, and what you like/dislike

4.6 Build vocabulary by adding prefixes to verbs

4.7 Explore a prominent Swiss company with worldwide exports

4.8 Express commands or requests and give advice

4.9 Create longer sentences with connectors

4.10 Understand authentic video of German speakers talking about their typical day

4.11 Learn vocabulary to talk about travel and everyday activities

4.1 Vorschau

Wie und warum frühstückt man?

4-1 Frühstücksgewohnheiten. Read some results from a recent survey about breakfast habits in Germany. What's your must-have breakfast beverage? Would you give similar reasons for why you eat (or don't eat) breakfast?

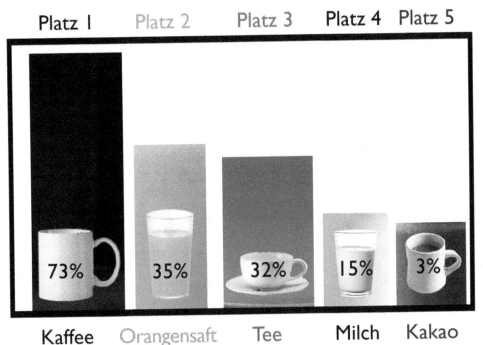

Lieblingsgetränke zum Frühstück
Welches Getränk gewinnt?

Platz 1	Platz 2	Platz 3	Platz 4	Platz 5
73%	35%	32%	15%	3%
Kaffee	Orangensaft	Tee	Milch	Kakao

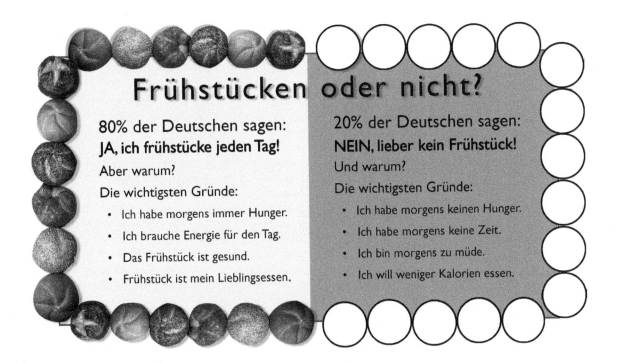

Frühstücken oder nicht?

80% der Deutschen sagen:
JA, ich frühstücke jeden Tag!

Aber warum?

Die wichtigsten Gründe:
- Ich habe morgens immer Hunger.
- Ich brauche Energie für den Tag.
- Das Frühstück ist gesund.
- Frühstück ist mein Lieblingsessen.

20% der Deutschen sagen:
NEIN, lieber kein Frühstück!

Und warum?

Die wichtigsten Gründe:
- Ich habe morgens keinen Hunger.
- Ich habe morgens keine Zeit.
- Ich bin morgens zu müde.
- Ich will weniger Kalorien essen.

4-2 Frühstück in Deutschland. Warum frühstückt man? Und was trinkt man zum Frühstück? Respond to the following.

1. Warum frühstückt man in Deutschland?

☐ Man ist hungrig.   ☐ Man braucht Energie.

☐ Man isst gern Nutella.   ☐ Das Frühstück schmeckt gut.

☐ Das Frühstück ist gesund.

2. Die meisten Deutschen trinken zum Frühstück …

☐ Tee   ☐ Kaffee   ☐ Kakao

3. Nicht so viele trinken zum Frühstück …

☐ Tee   ☐ Saft   ☐ Kakao

Sprachnotiz   The pronoun *man*

The pronoun **man** is used to make generalizations and is the equivalent of *one, you, they,* or *people*. The word **man** (not capitalized) is always singular.

Wie sagt **man** das auf Deutsch?   *How does one (do you) say that in German?*

In Deutschland isst **man** oft Wurst und Käse zum Frühstück.   *In Germany they (people) often eat cold cuts and cheese for breakfast.*

))) Frühstücksrezept: Schweizer Birchermüsli

Listen to the demonstration of how to make traditional Swiss Birchermüsli.

Wie macht man ein Birchermüsli nach originalem Schweizer Rezept? In einer Schüssel mischt man:

- 150 g Haferflocken
- 300 ml Milch
- 60 ml Apfelsaft
- und 3 Esslöffel Zitronensaft zusammen.

Diese Mischung stellt man über Nacht in den Kühlschrank.

Am nächsten Morgen mischt man Folgendes hinzu:

- einen Apfel, gerieben
- 2 Esslöffel Honig
- 400 g Joghurt
- 2-3 Esslöffel gehackte Nüsse

Für besonders knuspriges Müsli kann man Kürbiskerne daraufstreuen.

4-3 Richtig oder falsch? You will hear three statements about how to make traditional Swiss Birchermüsli. Indicate whether the statements are **richtig** or **falsch.**

	Richtig	Falsch		Richtig	Falsch		Richtig	Falsch
1.	_____	_____	2.	_____	_____	3.	_____	_____

4-4 Was isst und trinkst du zum Frühstück? Working with a partner, interview each other about your breakfast habits. Take notes so you can report your findings to the class.

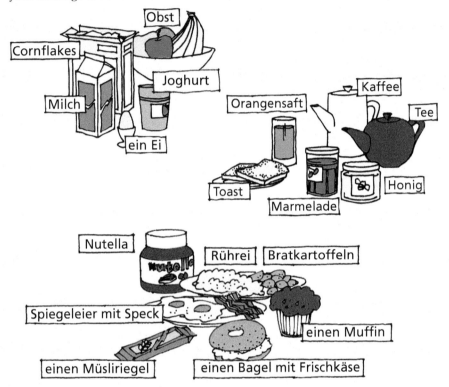

S1:

Was isst du zum Frühstück?

Und was trinkst du dazu?

Und am Wochenende? Was isst du dann?

S2:

Am liebsten esse ich …

Und ich trinke dazu …

Am Wochenende esse ich meistens° …   *usually*

> More breakfast foods are listed in the *Anhang* on p. A-7!

4-5 Unsere Frühstücksgewohnheiten. Report to the class on the breakfast habits of your partner. Here are some phrases to get you started.

S: An Wochentagen isst [*Name*] … Und sie/er trinkt …

Aber am Wochenende isst sie/er … Und sie/er trinkt …

Ein Frühstückstisch in Deutschland

4.2 Kultur 1

Die Schweiz

4.1 Describe Swiss contributions to the international community

Männlichen, Blick zum Jungfraujoch

Diverse cultures, rugged terrain

Die Schweiz is a country of four distinct cultures and many diverse regions. About 70 percent of the country has a rugged Alpine landscape. The topography led to the development of many isolated areas, each of which developed autonomously, giving rise to the 26 **Kantone** that later came together to form the **Schweizerische Eidgenossenschaft** (*Swiss Confederation*) we know today.

Ingenuity in industry, Swiss style

Though Switzerland has limited natural resources, it enjoys one of the highest standards of living in the world. Persistence and ingenuity have allowed the Swiss to develop many prosperous industries in this tiny country. Today, Swiss cheeses, milk chocolate, and baby foods are known internationally through brand names like Lindt and Nestlé. The Swiss are leaders in chemicals, high-fashion textiles, banking, and insurance. Switzerland also holds a niche in small- and large-scale precision products, producing everything from the smallest watches to enormous diesel engines. The Swiss are also famous for their achievements in civil engineering, enabling them to provide infrastructure in Switzerland's rugged terrain. Roads, viaducts, water management, and tunnels such as the awe-inspiring Gotthard Base Tunnel are examples of Swiss ingenuity needed in the **Schweizer Alpen.**

Der Gotthard-Basistunnel

The Gotthard Base Tunnel, at 57 km (35.5 miles) in length, is the world's longest and deepest rail tunnel. It took 17 years to build.

Diversity of people and languages

Switzerland has four official languages **(Deutsch, Französisch, Italienisch,** and **Rätoromanisch).** Its population is largely multilingual. Of the country's 8.4 million, 64 percent speak German, 23 percent speak French, 8 percent speak Italian, and about 0.5 percent speak Romansch.

Alpine landscapes + Bustling cities = Diverse Swiss lifestyles

The natural beauty and recreational opportunities of this mountainous country and its modern cities rich in cultural arts are the basis for Switzerland's flourishing tourist trade. **Genf** *(Geneva)* has long been the headquarters for many international organizations and a neutral site for dialogue between nations with opposing ideologies. The Swiss finance center of **Zürich**, the human rights and peace-keeping organizations of Genf, and the country's capital, **Bern**, all are parts of the Swiss mosaic.

Zürich, Finanzzentrum der Schweiz

Mileposts in Swiss history

1291	Cantons of **Schwyz, Uri** and **Unterwalden** unite against Habsburg oppressors, forming Confoederatio Helvetica **(CH),** the start of today's Switzerland.
1523	The Reformation begins in Switzerland, led by Huldrych Zwingli, a Zurich priest. A period of religious conflict begins.
1815	Switzerland declares itself politically neutral, becoming a safe space for dialogue between countries with opposing ideologies.
1859	Swiss citizen Henry Dunant witnesses bloody battle of Solferino (Italy), riveted by the suffering of thousands of soldiers left on battlefield to die. He organizes help for wounded soldiers on both sides, regardless of their nationalities.
1863	Dunant brings horrors of war to world's attention in his book *Erinnerung an Solferino* (A Memory of Solferino). He appeals to humanity to take care of soldiers who have risked everything for war.
1864	Dunant joins four others in Geneva to found what becomes **das Internationale Komitee vom Roten Kreuz.** Sixteen states send representatives to Geneva, where the **Genfer Konvention** (Geneva Convention) is signed. It protects soldiers by declaring the absolute neutrality of medical workers in times of war.
1901	Dunant receives first-ever Nobel Prize for Peace for his life's work to prevent senseless suffering in war and handle its aftermath. He shares prize with French peacemaker Frédéric Passy.
1949	The **Genfer Konvention** is expanded after World War II to handle problems of displaced people, among other things.
2018	The International Red Cross continues to provide help for people worldwide. The **Genfer Konvention** is a living document that outlines the rights of all people affected by war.

4-6 Ein Blick ins Netz. In pairs or small groups, explore on the Internet what has evolved because of the ground-breaking work of Switzerland's Henry Dunant in 1863.

1. **Research.** Use the main key word plus the specific keyword(s) for your chosen task: "International Committee of the Red Cross" + one additional keyword, such as: where, conflict, war, Red Crescent

2. **Reflect and present.** Use graphics, pictures, or diagrams to prepare a one-page visual (in English) reflecting what you learned in your research. Present this information to your small group using your one-page visual.

)) 4.3 Wortschatz 1

Wichtige Vokabeln

4.2 Learn vocabulary to talk about food and eating habits

Nomen

das Frühstück	breakfast
zum Frühstück	for breakfast
das Brot, belegte	bread,
Brote *(pl)*	(open-faced) sandwiches
das Brötchen, -	roll
das Ei, -er	egg
die Frucht ̈e	fruit
die Haferflocken *(pl)*	oats (oatmeal)
der Honig	honey
der Joghurt	yogurt
der Käse	cheese
die Marmelade	jam
das Müsli	muesli
der Müsliriegel, -	granola bar
die Nuss, ̈e	nut
der Orangensaft	orange juice
das Rezept, -e	recipe
der Zucker	sugar
der Becher, -	cup; container
ein Becher Joghurt	a container of yogurt
das Glas, ̈er	glass
ein Glas Orangensaft	a glass of orange juice
die Scheibe, -n	slice
eine Scheibe Brot	a slice of bread
die Schüssel, -n	bowl
eine Schüssel Müsli	a bowl of muesli
die Tasse, -n	cup
eine Tasse Kaffee	a cup of coffee
das Mittagessen	noon meal; lunch
zum Mittagessen	for lunch
das Abendessen	evening meal
zum Abendessen	for supper; for dinner

> The smaller, evening meal of bread, cheese, and cold cuts is sometimes called **das Abendbrot.**

das Fleisch *(sing)*	meat
das Gemüse *(sing)*	vegetables
die Kartoffel, -n	potato
die Pommes frites *(pl)* }	French fries
die Pommes *(pl)*	
die Wurst, ̈e	sausage; cold cuts

der Nachtisch	dessert
zum Nachtisch	for dessert
das Eis	ice cream; ice
das Obst *(sing)*	fruit
der Nachmittagskaffee	afternoon coffee
zum Nachmittagskaffee	for afternoon coffee
der Kuchen, -	cake
die Torte, -n	layer cake
das Stück, -e	piece
ein Stück Torte	a piece of layer cake

Verben

frühstücken	to have breakfast
mischen	to mix
schmecken	to taste; to taste good

Andere Wörter

fertig	finished; ready
genau	exact(ly); carefully
meistens	most of the time, usually
normalerweise	normally, usually

Ausdrücke

Wie sagt man	How does one (do you) say
das auf Deutsch?	that in German?
Bist du heute Abend	Will you be (at) home
zu Hause?	tonight?
Gehst du nach Hause?	Are you going home?
Ich habe Hunger.	I'm hungry.
Ich habe Durst.	I'm thirsty.
Wann isst du zu Mittag	When do you have lunch
(zu Abend)?	(supper)?
Guten Appetit!	Enjoy the meal!

Das Gegenteil

einfach ≠ kompliziert	simple ≠ complicated
früh ≠ spät	early ≠ late
manchmal ≠ oft	sometimes ≠ often

Leicht zu verstehen

die Energie	der Fisch, -e
der Hunger	die Nudel, -n
der Bagel, -s	die Orange, -n
die Banane, -n	der Salat, -e
die Butter	der Toast

Fitness Frühstück
Früchtemüsli mit Joghurt, Milch,
Honig und frischen Früchten dazu
ein frischer Orangensaft 0,2l

Wörter im Kontext

4-7 Was passt nicht?

1. das Fleisch	2. die Nudel	3. der Becher	4. die Torte
der Orangensaft	der Nachtisch	das Glas	das Eis
der Käse	die Kartoffel	die Scheibe	der Kuchen
die Wurst	das Brötchen	die Tasse	das Rezept

> **Fleisch, Gemüse,** and **Obst** are always singular. **Wurst** is singular when it refers to cold cuts. The word **Frucht** refers to pieces of fruit, so it can also appear in the plural as **Früchte.**

4-8 *Nach Hause* oder *zu Hause?*

Zieglers fahren nach Hause

Zieglers sind zu Hause

1. Isst du heute im Restaurant oder _____ ?
2. Wann kommt Stephanie _____ ?
3. Ich gehe jetzt _____ .
4. Ich muss um sieben _____ sein.
5. Wohnt dein kleiner Bruder noch _____ ?

> Don't let the fact that **zu** is a cognate of *to* confuse you here: *zu* Hause means *at home.* Use *nach* Hause to say that you're going *to* (your) home.

4-9 Was passt wo?

zum Mittagessen / zum Frühstück / zum Nachtisch / manchmal

1. _____ esse ich Brötchen oder eine Schüssel Müsli.
_____ esse ich Fleisch und Gemüse.
_____ esse ich Obst oder italienisches Eis.
Am Wochenende esse ich _____ ein warmes Frühstück.

Joghurt / Pommes frites / Käse / Chips / Butter

2. _____, _____ und _____ macht man aus Milch.
_____ und _____ macht man aus Kartoffeln.

eine Scheibe / eine Tasse / einen Becher / ein Glas / ein Stück

3. Zum Frühstück trinke ich normalerweise _____ kalten Orangensaft und _____ schwarzen Kaffee und esse _____ Toast dazu. Zum Nachmittagskaffee esse ich _____ Torte und abends esse ich zum Nachtisch oft _____ Fruchtjoghurt.

Hast du Hunger und Durst?

4.4 Zur Aussprache

The vowels *ä, ö,* and *ü*

4.3 Distinguish between long and short *ä, ö,* and *ü*

The vowels **a, o,** and **u** can be umlauted: **ä, ö,** and **ü**. These umlauted vowels can be long or short. Listen carefully and you will hear the difference between **a, o, u** and their umlauted equivalents.

))) **4-10** Hören Sie gut zu und wiederholen Sie!

a (lang)	ä (lang)	a (kurz)	ä (kurz)
Glas	Gläser	alt	älter
Rad	Räder	kalt	kälter
Vater	Väter	lang	länger

o (lang)	ö (lang)	o (kurz)	ö (kurz)
Brot	Brötchen	oft	öfter
Sohn	Söhne	Tochter	Töchter
groß	größer	Wort	Wörter

If you have trouble producing the sound **ö,** pucker your lips as if to whistle, hold them in this position, and say *eh*.

u (lang)	ü (lang)	u (kurz)	ü (kurz)
Buch	Bücher	Mutter	Mütter
Bruder	Brüder	jung	jünger
Fuß	Füße	dumm	dümmer

If you have trouble producing the sound **ü,** pucker your lips as if to whistle, hold them in this position, and say *ee*.

))) **4-11** **Zum Wiederholen.** Read and practice each of these tongue twisters, taking care to make distinctions between long and short vowels with umlauts.

1. Bäcker Käfer bäckt gern Käsekuchen.
2. Frau Böckmanns schöne Töchter spielen Flöte.
3. Jürgen Künder isst schon zum Frühstück Gemüse.

))) **4-12** **Ein bisschen Schwyzerdütsch.** You will hear three sayings, first in Swiss German, and then in standard German. What is one main difference in pronunciation?

1. Es git nüt Bessers als gueti Fründe, usser gueti Fründe mit Schoggi.
2. Frage chostet nüt.
3. Uf alte Pfannä lehrt me choche.

4.5 Kommunikation und Formen 1

The modal verbs *können*, *müssen*, and *wollen*

4.4 Talk about what you can do, have to do, and want to do

Verbs like the English *can, must,* and *want to* are called modal verbs. They modify the meaning of other verbs (*I **can study** now, I **must study** now, I **want to study** now*).

In German there are six modal verbs. When you use a modal verb, the main verb is placed at the end of the sentence. Notice how German word order tucks all other information neatly in before the main verb, which completes the thought.

modal verb   main verb

Ich **kann** heute Abend **lernen.**	*I can study tonight.*
Ich **muss** wieder allein **lernen.**	*I must study again by myself.*
Ich **will** später mit Julia **lernen.**	*I want to study later with Julia.*

Brötchen: The **ö** and the suffix **-chen** signal that this is the diminutive form of **Brot** (compare English **pig** and **piglet**). The diminutive forms of nouns with **a, o, u** and **au** add an umlaut. What are the diminutive forms of **Haus, Bett, Hund,** and **Sohn?**

Below are the present-tense forms of **können** (*to be able to, to know how to, can*), **müssen** (*to have to, must*), and **wollen** (*to want to*).

können		müssen		wollen	
ich	kann	ich	muss	ich	will
du	kannst	du	musst	du	willst
er/es/sie	kann	er/es/sie	muss	er/es/sie	will
wir	können	wir	müssen	wir	wollen
ihr	könnt	ihr	müsst	ihr	wollt
sie/Sie	können	sie/Sie	müssen	sie/Sie	wollen

Note:
- These modals have a stem-vowel change in the **ich-, du-,** and **er/es/sie-**forms. None of the singular forms of modals takes an umlaut.
- Modals have no endings in the **ich-** form and the **er/es/sie-** form, and these two forms are identical.

4-13 Wer kann was besonders gut?

1. Tante Bettina _____ ziemlich gut Spanisch.
2. Nina und Alexander _____ sehr gut Klavier spielen.
3. Alexander _____ ausgezeichnet Basketball spielen.
4. Ich _____ Gedichte° schreiben.   *poems*

LEHRER/IN: Und Sie? Was können Sie besonders gut?
STUDENT/IN: Ich _____ ziemlich gut (sehr gut, ausgezeichnet) …

4-14 Was müssen Zieglers alles tun?

1. Herr und Frau Ziegler _____ beide arbeiten und Geld verdienen.
2. Robert _____ jeden Abend seine Hausaufgaben machen und jedes Wochenende sein Zimmer aufräumen.
3. Herr Ziegler _____ jeden Morgen das Frühstück machen und jeden Samstag das Haus putzen°.   *clean*
4. Frau Ziegler _____ jeden Abend kochen und jeden Samstag einkaufen°.   *go shopping*

LEHRER/IN: Und Sie? Was müssen Sie alles tun?
STUDENT/IN: Ich _____ …

4-15 Was wollen Nina, Robert und Alexander werden?

1. Nina _____ Journalistin werden.
2. Robert _____ Fußballprofi werden.
3. Alexander _____ Ingenieur werden.

LEHRER/IN: Und Sie? Was wollen Sie werden?
STUDENT/IN: Ich _____ …
LEHRER/IN: Und warum wollen Sie … werden?
STUDENT/IN: Ich finde diesen Beruf sehr interessant.
               Ich arbeite gern mit Kindern / mit alten Leuten / mit Tieren / …
               Ich kann sehr gut schreiben / fotografieren / …
               Ich will viel Geld verdienen.

> **Achtung!**
> German **will** doesn't mean English *will*, as in "*I will do X.*" It means "*I want to do X*"!

The modals *dürfen, sollen,* and *mögen*

4.5 Say what you are allowed to do, supposed to do, and what you like/dislike

Below are the present-tense forms of **dürfen** (*to be allowed to, to be permitted to, may*), **sollen** (*to be supposed to, should*), and **mögen** (*to like*).

Ich darf hier nicht hinein !

Signs like these are common in Germany, because people sometimes bring their dogs on short shopping trips in town.

dürfen		sollen		mögen	
ich	darf	ich	soll	ich	mag
du	darfst	du	sollst	du	magst
er/es/sie	darf	er/es/sie	soll	er/es/sie	mag
wir	dürfen	wir	sollen	wir	mögen
ihr	dürft	ihr	sollt	ihr	mögt
sie/Sie	dürfen	sie/Sie	sollen	sie/Sie	mögen

Note:

- **Sollen** is the only modal that does not have a stem-vowel change in the **ich-, du-,** and **er/es/sie-** forms.
- Like the other modals you have learned, the **ich-** and **er/es/sie-**forms are identical and have no endings.
- **Mögen** is usually used without an infinitive.

Remember, if you want to say you like *to do* something, use **gern** rather than a modal:
Ich spiele gern Tennis.
Ich trinke gern Kaffee.

Ich **mag** Stephanie.	*I **like** Stephanie.*
Warum **mögt** ihr kein Gemüse?	*Why **don't** you **like** vegetables?*

The legal driving age in the German-speaking countries is 18.

4-16 Was dürfen Maiers alles nicht tun?

1. Herr und Frau Maier _____ keinen Kaffee trinken.
2. Ihre Tochter Hannah ist erst sechzehn und _____ noch nicht Auto fahren.
3. Ihr Sohn Georg ist vierzehn und _____ nicht nach Mitternacht nach Hause kommen.

LEHRER/IN: Und Sie? Was dürfen Sie alles nicht tun?
STUDENT/IN: Ich _____ nicht …

4-17 Was sollen Maiers nächsten Samstag alles tun?

1. Frau Maier und Hannah _____ nächsten Samstag Oma Maier besuchen.
2. Georg _____ nächsten Samstag seine Hausaufgaben für Montag machen.
3. Herr Maier _____ nächsten Samstag die Waschmaschine reparieren.

LEHRER/IN: Und Sie? Was sollen Sie nächsten Samstag alles tun?
STUDENT/IN: Ich _____ nächsten Samstag …

4-18 Was mögen Maiers alles?

1. Herr Maier _____ Joghurt mit Früchten.
2. Die beiden Teenager _____ Toast mit Nutella.
3. Fleisch _____ Frau Maier besonders gern.

4-19 **Was magst du und was magst du nicht?** You and your partner ask each other what you especially like to eat and what you don't like at all. You will find additional food items under **Essen und Trinken** in the *Anhang* on p. A-7.

S1: Was magst du besonders gern?	**S2:** … mag ich besonders gern.
Was magst du gar nicht?	… mag ich gar nicht.

Möchte versus *mögen*

Although the modal **möchte** is derived from **mögen,** it is not used to express what one likes or dislikes, but what one *would like* to have or to do. **Ich möchte** is therefore a more polite way of saying **ich will. Möchte** is used when making requests and ordering food.

Ich **mag** Käsekuchen.   *I **like** cheesecake.*
Ich **möchte** ein Stück Käsekuchen.   *I **would like** a piece of cheesecake.*

It would be impolite to say:

Ich **will** ein Stück Käsekuchen.   *I **want** a piece of cheesecake.*

Singular		Plural	
ich	möchte	wir	möchten
du	möchtest	ihr	möchtet
er/es/sie	möchte	sie	möchten
	Sie	möchten	

4-20 Wer möchte was?

1. Frau Maier _____ nach Kanada fahren.
2. Herr Maier _____ einen Porsche.
3. Georg _____ ein neues Mountainbike.
4. Hannah und Monika _____ ein Jahr in Amerika studieren.

LEHRER/IN: Und Sie? Was möchten Sie?
STUDENT/IN: Ich _____ …

Omitting the main verb after modal verbs

If the meaning of a sentence containing a modal is clear without an infinitive, the infinitive is often omitted.

Ich muss jetzt nach Hause (gehen).   *I have to **go** home now.*

4-21 Welcher Infinitiv passt?

trinken / gehen / essen / fliegen / sprechen / haben

1. Wir müssen jetzt in die Vorlesung.
2. Können deine Eltern Türkisch?
3. Möchten Sie ein Stück Kuchen?
4. Warum dürfen wir denn nicht auf die Party?
5. Kannst du schon ein bisschen Deutsch?
6. Möchtet ihr lieber Kaffee oder Tee zum Frühstück?
7. Heute Abend muss ich zum Supermarkt.
8. Warum willst du denn nicht ins Kino?
9. Wollt ihr nächsten Sommer nach Australien?
10. Wann soll deine kleine Schwester heute ins Bett?

> German speakers use the verb **können** to say that they can speak a language. The verb **sprechen** is left out.

Position of *nicht* in sentences with modal verbs

You know how to negate a particular word or expression with **nicht:** Put **nicht** directly before it. The same rule applies in sentences with modal verbs.

Ich will **nicht jede Woche** so viel arbeiten.   *I don't want to work so much every week.*

However, when you want to negate the sentence as a whole, **nicht** comes directly before the main verb. This makes **nicht** the second to last word in the sentence:

Professor Raab kann heute **nicht** kommen.   *Professor Raab can't come today.*
Toll! Dann muss ich seinen Artikel **nicht** lesen.   *Great! Then I don't have to read his article.*

4-22 Immer negativ. Respond to your partner's question by negating the sentence as a whole.

S1: Kannst du kochen?   **S2:** Nein, ich kann nicht kochen.

1. Kann dein Professor backen?   Nein, er kann …
2. Sollen wir das Mittagessen machen?   Nein, ihr sollt …
3. Möchtest du dieses Buch lesen?   Nein, ich will …
4. Können deine Eltern surfen?   Nein, sie können …
5. Kann deine Professorin   Nein, sie kann …
   snowboarden?
6. Willst du mein Referat lesen?   Nein, ich will …

4-23 Immer negativ. Now switch roles and respond to your partner's question by negating the word or expression in bold.

S1: Kannst du **gut** kochen?   **S2:** Nein, ich kann nicht gut kochen.

1. Kann dein Professor **gut**   Nein, er kann …
   Schwyzerdütsch sprechen?
2. Sollen wir **diesen Artikel** lesen?   Nein, ihr sollt …
3. Willst du **den ganzen Abend** zu   Nein, ich will …
   Hause bleiben?
4. Müsst ihr **alle** Vokabeln lernen?   Nein, wir müssen …
5. Kann deine Professorin **gut** singen? Nein, sie kann …
6. Darfst du **jedes Wochenende** auf   Nein, ich darf …
   Partys?

4-24 Mal ganz ehrlich. *(Let's be honest.)* Ask your partner what she/he is not so good at. Report your findings to the class.

S1: Was kannst du nicht so gut?   **S2:** Ich kann nicht so gut …
                                          Ich kann gar nicht gut …

Separable-prefix verbs

4.5 Build vocabulary by adding prefixes to verbs

Meaning of separable-prefix verbs

In English the meaning of certain verbs is modified or changed when you add a preposition or an adverb after the verb. In German the same effect is achieved by adding a prefix to the verb. In pronunciation, the stress always falls on the separable prefix.

*to go **out***	**aus**gehen	*to try **out***	**aus**probieren
*to go **away***	**weg**gehen	*to clean **up***	**auf**räumen
*to come **back***	**zurück**kommen	*to stand **up***	
*to come **home***	**heim**kommen	*to get **up***	**auf**stehen
*to try **on***	**an**probieren		

Separable-prefix verbs are not always similar to their English equivalents.

abfahren	*to depart, to leave*	**ein**laden	*to invite*
ankommen	*to arrive*	**ein**schlafen	*to fall asleep*
anfangen	*to begin, to start*	**fern**sehen	*to watch TV*
aufhören	*to end, to stop*	**herum**hängen	*to hang out*
anhören	*to listen to*		
anrufen	*to call (on the phone)*		

> The verb **herumhängen** (*to hang out*) is a casual expression and usually gets shortened to **rumhängen**.

Sprachnotiz   More about separable prefixes

By combining prefixes with verbs, German creates a host of new verbs. In each set below, look at the first example and its English equivalent. Then figure out the meaning of the other verbs.

mitkommen *(to come along)*: mitbringen, mitnehmen, mitlesen, mitsingen

weggehen *(to go away)*: wegfahren, wegsehen, weglaufen, wegnehmen

weiterlesen *(to continue reading)*: weiterarbeiten, weiteressen, weiterfahren

zurückrufen *(to call back)*: zurückbringen, zurückfahren, zurückgeben

Die kleine Schwester fährt mit.

Hier läuft der Vater mit!

Position of the separable prefix

In the infinitive form, the prefix is attached to the front of the verb (**aus**gehen, **heim**kommen, etc.). In the present tense, the prefix is separated from the verb and placed at the end of the sentence.

Ich **gehe** jetzt **aus**.   *I'm going out now.*
Ich **komme** sehr spät **heim**.   *I'm coming home very late.*

4-25 Was bringst du mit? In a group of four, choose one of the situations below. Brainstorm a list of all the things you'd need or want to take along. Remember to use the accusative case for each thing you need.

- Wir machen ein Picknick.
- Wir machen eine Party.
- Wir fahren im Winter nach Europa.

S1: Was bringst du mit?
S2: Ich bringe ... mit.

4-26 Was machst du heute Nachmittag? Use one of the verbs in the boxes below to respond to your partner's questions.

▶ du heute Nachmittag

mein neues Album anhören

S1: Was machst du heute Nachmittag?

S2: Da höre ich mein neues Album an.

> Since each answer starts with the word **da** instead of the subject, the verb will be next, followed by the subject.

1. du am Samstagmorgen

2. du am Samstagabend

3. du morgen Abend

4. ihr am Sonntagabend

fernsehen	mit Claudia ausgehen
erst um elf aufstehen	mein Zimmer aufräumen

5. du heute Abend

6. ihr bei Karstadt

> The **Bodensee** (Lake Constance) borders Switzerland, Austria and Germany, and is a popular tourist destination. The English name refers to the German lakeside town of **Konstanz**.

7. du am Bodensee

8. ihr am Freitagabend

rumhängen	mein Surfbrett ausprobieren
meine Eltern anrufen	ein paar Kleider anprobieren

Position of separable-prefix verbs with modals

When used with a modal, the separable-prefix verb appears as an infinitive at the end of the sentence, just like other verbs.

Du **musst** jetzt **aufstehen.**	*You have to get up now.*
Du **musst** jetzt **essen.**	*You have to eat now.*

4-27 Kleine Gespräche.

▶ aufstehen

Warum _____ du denn so früh _____?

anrufen

Ich will meine Kusine in Deutschland _____.

S1: Warum stehst du denn
so früh auf?

S2: Ich will meine Kusine in
Deutschland anrufen.

1. ausgehen

_____ du heute Abend mit

uns _____?

aufräumen

Nein, ich muss endlich mal° mein

Zimmer _____.

endlich mal: *finally*

2. anhören

Möchtest du das neue Album von

Coldplay _____?

ausprobieren

Nein, ich möchte lieber deine

neuen Spiele _____.

3. vorhaben

Was _____ du heute

_____?

anprobieren

Ich will bei Karstadt Kleider

_____.

4. anrufen

Kann ich Claudia abends um elf

noch _____?

fernsehen

Klar! Sie _____ jeden Abend

bis nach Mitternacht _____.

5. heimgehen

Können wir jetzt endlich

_____?

aufhören

Nein, erst muss der

Regen _____.

Sprachnotiz Position of *nicht* with separable-prefix verbs

When you want to negate a separable-prefix verb, **nicht** is the second-to-last element.

Ich gehe heute **nicht** aus.
Ich will heute **nicht** ausgehen.

*I'm **not** going out today.*
*I **don't** want to go out today.*

4-28 Was bedeuten diese Schilder°? Match each sign with its intended meaning.

sign

traffic signs

Verkehrszeichen°		**Andere Schilder**	
1.	2.	7.	8.
3.	4.	9.	10.
5.	6.	11.	12.

The red border around a round German sign usually indicates that something is restricted or prohibited.

The preferred term to refer to people with disabilities is **Menschen mit Behinderung**. On city buses, for example, there is priority seating for the elderly and others with limited mobility to make it easier for them to get around independently.

- Hier darf man nicht über 60 fahren.
- Diese Straße hört bald auf.
- Hier fängt die Autobahn an.
- Man soll hier parken.
- Hier muss man langsam fahren, weil Kinder hier spielen.
- Hier darf man nicht rauchen°.

- Hier kann man schwimmen.
- Hier darf man nur nach rechts fahren.
- Hier kann man campen.
- Essen darf man hier nicht.
- Hier darf man seine Freunde nicht anrufen.
- Diesen Sitzplatz soll man für Menschen mit Behinderung frei halten.

to smoke

4-29 Ich will mein Leben ändern. Tell your classmates about three things you want to change in your life.

Ich will nicht mehr so viel (so oft, so spät, so lange) …		Ich will mehr …
fernsehen	in die Kneipe gehen	Wasser trinken
schlafen	Bier trinken	Gemüse und Obst essen
aufstehen	Junkfood essen	lernen
ausgehen	Kaffee trinken	Sport machen
rauchen	ins Bett gehen	…
…	…	

4-30 Was machst du den ganzen Tag? Ask your partner about a typical day. Practice using **meistens** to say *most of the time.*

S1:
Wann stehst du morgens auf?
Wann fangen deine Vorlesungen an?

Wann kommst du heim?
Gehst du abends oft aus?

seldom

S2:
Ich _____ meistens um … _____.
Meine Vorlesungen _____ meistens um … _____.
Ich _____ meistens um … _____.
Ja, ich _____ abends oft _____.
Nein, ich _____ abends nur sehr selten° _____.

Verb-noun and verb-verb combinations

Some verbs are so closely associated with a noun or another verb that they function like separable-prefix verbs. With nouns this happens most frequently with the verbs **spielen, laufen,** and **fahren.**

Im Sommer **fährt** David fast jeden Tag **Rad.**   *In the summer David goes cycling almost every day.*
Im Winter **läuft** er fast jedes Wochenende **Ski.**   *In the winter he skis almost every weekend.*

With verbs this happens most frequently with the verb **gehen.**

Er **geht** jeden Abend **joggen.**   *He goes jogging every evening.*

If a modal is used, both parts of these verb-noun or verb-verb combinations appear at the end of the sentence. They work together as one element, like separable-prefix verbs, but they are written as separate words.

Ich **will** im Sommer **Rad fahren.**   *I want to go biking in the summer.*
Ich **kann** in der Schweiz **Ski laufen.**   *I can ski in Switzerland.*
Ich möchte die **Schweiz kennenlernen.**   *I'd like to get to know Switzerland.*

Again, when **nicht** is used to negate the verb, it is the second-to-last element. If there is a modal, as in the second sentence below, the **nicht** precedes the entire combination.

Claudia geht heute **nicht spazieren.**   *Claudia isn't going for a walk today.*
Sie will auch **nicht Tennis spielen.**   *She also doesn't want to play tennis.*

4-31 Was Tanja, Dieter und Laura können oder nicht können. Look at the second column of the table to determine what Tanja does well or doesn't do. Then do the same for Dieter and Laura. Finally, add information about yourself and tell the class what you can and can't do!

	TANJA	**DIETER**	**LAURA**	**ICH**
Skateboard fahren	sehr gut	nicht	sehr gut	
Gitarre spielen	nicht	sehr gut	sehr gut	
Ski laufen	sehr gut	sehr gut	nicht sehr gut	

1. Tanja fährt … und sie läuft auch …, aber sie kann …
2. Dieter spielt … und er läuft auch …, aber er kann …
3. Laura fährt … und sie spielt auch …, aber sie kann …
4. Ich fahre … und ich spiele … . Ich kann …

4-32 Verben im Kontext. Many verbs for traveling have separable prefixes. Read the following description of a train trip and match the verbs for train travel with their English equivalents from the list below.

Zuerst **steigen** wir in Dortmund in den ICE 517 **ein**.
Wir **fahren** um 10:37 **ab**.
In Mannheim **steigen** wir **um.**
Dort **fährt** der ICE 279 um 13:36 **ab**.
Wir kommen dann um 15:34 in Basel **an**.

to arrive	to depart
to change trains	to board the train

4-33 Eine Reise in die Schweiz! Below are some cities fast trains stop in between Dortmund in Germany and Basel in Switzerland. Which city would you choose for some sightseeing on the way to Switzerland? And which connecting train would you use after a three-hour excursion is over? Use your favorite search engine with the key word "Deutsche Bahn" and select "Deutsch" for this activity.

> Not all train tickets allow you to get on and off trains as you like; however, many rail passes do.

Köln   **Bonn**   **Karlsruhe**   **Freiburg**

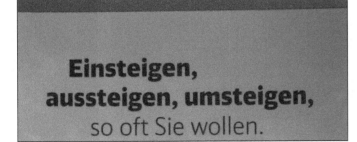

Einsteigen, aussteigen, umsteigen, so oft Sie wollen.

4-34 Unsere Reise nach Basel. Now present the trip planned in **4-33** above to another group of two, using the sentence starters below. Be sure to say where you'll stop, what you'll see, and when you'll leave for Basel, in addition to when the train will finally arrive in Switzerland.

Wir wollen auf der Reise in … kurz aussteigen.
In … sehen wir … an.
Um … steigen wir wieder in den Zug ein. Wir fahren nach Basel weiter
    und kommen um … an.

> Remember to use the accusative case when you talk about what you're going to see in the city where you stop.

4.6 Kultur 2

Schweizer Innovation: Die Firma Victorinox

4.7 Explore a prominent Swiss company with worldwide exports

4-35 The Swiss Army Knife.

1. Do you own a **Taschenmesser** such as an original Swiss Army Knife?
2. Do you know the name of the company that manufactures this and other Swiss products?
3. How many products pictured on this page have you seen before?

4-36 Was ist das auf Englisch? Get ready to read about the Elsener family business by learning a few specialized words.

1. Ein **Messerschmied** macht Messer aus Metal.
2. Ein Messerschmied arbeitet in einer **Werkstatt.**
3. Wenn viele Messerschmiede zusammen arbeiten wollen, **gründen** sie einen **Messerschmiedverband.**
4. Karl Elsener möchte um 1890 Messer für **Soldaten** produzieren.
5. Später **entwickelt** Karl Elsener das Schweizer „Offiziersmesser".
6. Moderne Taschenmesser macht man aus **rostfreiem Stahl**.
7. 1945 ist der **Zweite Weltkrieg** zu Ende und die Taschenmesser werden populär.
8. Die Firma Victorinox ist heute noch sehr **erfolgreich**.
9. Victorinox Produkte sind heute in vielen Ländern **bekannt**.
10. 2008 bekommt die Firma Victorinox einen wichtigen Preis für **Nachhaltigkeit**.

a. stainless steel
b. develops
c. soldiers
d. successful
e. found … knifesmiths' association
f. Second World War
g. knifesmith
h. well-known
i. workshop
j. sustainability

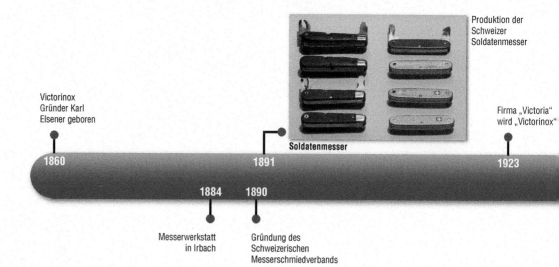

Produktion der Schweizer Soldatenmesser

Soldatenmesser

Victorinox Gründer Karl Elsener geboren

Firma „Victoria" wird „Victorinox"

1860

1891

1923

1884

1890

Messerwerkstatt in Irbach

Gründung des Schweizerischen Messerschmiedverbands

Schweizer Innovation: Die Firma Victorinox

Karl Elsener, Schweizer Messerschmied

Im Jahre 1884 eröffnet Karl Elsener in Irbach im Kanton Schwyz eine kleine Messerwerkstatt. Es gibt in der Schweiz noch keine industrielle Massenproduktion, und die Schweizer Armee kauft für ihre Soldaten Taschenmesser in Deutschland. Aber Elsener will die „Soldatenmesser" in der Schweiz produzieren. Deshalb[1] gründet er mit fünfundzwanzig Kollegen den Schweizerischen Messerschmiedverband. Schon 1891 beginnt die Produktion des Schweizer Soldatenmessers.

Das Schweizer Offiziersmesser und die Firma *Victorinox*

Mit der Zeit produziert Elsener noch schönere[2] Messer, auch elegante „Offiziersmesser", die die Offiziere selber bezahlen müssen. Diese Messer sind so schön, dass auch andere die Messer kaufen wollen. Bald aber kommen billige Imitationen aus Deutschland. 1909 darf Elsener sein Offiziersmesser mit dem Schweizer Kreuz schützen[3]. In diesem Jahr stirbt[4] auch seine Mutter Victoria, und er nennt seine Firma „Victoria". 1923 sind die Messer dann aus dem rostfreien Stahl *Inox* und Elseners Firma heißt „Victorinox".

Export in alle Länder: Schweizer Innovation

Elseners Messer werden nach dem Zweiten Weltkrieg bei den vielen amerikanischen Soldaten in Deutschland bekannt. So beginnt der Export in viele andere Länder.

Im Jahre 2008 bekommt die schweizer Firma den Preis der schweizerischen Umweltstiftung. Dieser Preis zeigt, dass Victorinox die Nachhaltigkeit als wichtiges Prinzip hält.

Heute produziert Victorinox täglich 34 000 Taschenmesser und exportiert Messer und weitere Victorinox-Produkte in über hundert Länder. Heute leitet Carl Elsener IV. die Firma seiner Familie. Man findet auch in amerikanischen Kleinstädten die innovativen Schweizer Produkte von Victorinox: Rucksäcke, Wasserflaschen und das superdünne „Swissbit Schweizer-Offiziersmesser mit Memory Stick".

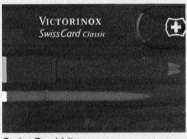

SwissCard Lite

[1]*because of this*   [2]**noch schönere:** *even more beautiful*   [3]*protect (against imitation)*   [4]*dies*

Modernes Offiziersmesser: großer Export ins Ausland beginnt, zuerst nach Amerika und in PX Stores weltweit

Carl Elsener IV. Geschäftsführer von Victorinox

1945

2000   **2008**   **2014**

Produktion von dem Victorinox-USB Stick beginnt

Preis der Schweizerischen Umweltstiftung

Victorinox feiert 130. Jubiläum

4-37 Wer oder was ist das? Match the following items from the story of the Swiss Army Knife appropriately.

1. Victoria Elsener
2. Soldatenmesser
3. Inox
4. Carl Elsener IV.
5. Schweizer Kreuz

a. Taschenmesser für Schweizer Soldaten
b. Schweizer Nationalsymbol
c. Karl Elseners Mutter
d. rostfreier Stahl
e. jetziger Direktor von Victorinox

4-38 Das Schweizer Offiziersmesser. Respond briefly with information from the text.

1. Warum heißt die Firma heute „Victorinox"?
2. Warum ist die Firma heute noch so erfolgreich?
3. Was für Produkte exportiert Victorinox weltweit?
4. Haben Sie ein Victorinox-Taschenmesser oder ein anderes Produkt von Victorinox?

4-39 Ein Blick ins Netz. Learn more about the Victorinox Company on its Web site. Be sure to switch the language to German before reading! Search: Victorinox Schweiz + Produkte. Select one item that you would like to buy. Prepare a one-page visual of "your" product and its key features and use this to present to your partner or small group. Consider the following: Why did you choose that particular item? What would you use it for?

Mein Lieblingsprodukt von Victorinox ist … Ich finde es schön, denn …
Ich kaufe bei Victorinox … Das Produkt ist toll, denn …

4.7 Kommunikation und Formen 2

Commands (Imperatives)

4.8 Express commands or requests and give advice

You can use the imperative form of a verb to express a command, make a request, or give advice. Since English has only one form of address *(you)*, it has only one imperative form. German has three forms of address (**Sie, ihr,** and **du**), and so it has three imperative forms. In written German, imperative sentences often end with an exclamation mark.

Kommen Sie! **Kommt!** **Komm!**	*Come!*

The *Sie*-imperative
The **Sie**-imperative is the infinitive of the verb followed directly by **Sie.**

Wiederholen Sie bitte, was ich sage!   *Please repeat what I say.*

The prefix of a separable verb appears at the end of the imperative sentence.

Hören Sie bitte gut **zu!**   *Please listen carefully.*

Again, verb-noun and verb-verb combinations function like separable-prefix verbs.

Spielen Sie doch mit uns **Volleyball!**   *Play volleyball with us.*
Gehen Sie nicht allein **schwimmen!**   *Don't go swimming alone.*

The verb **sein** is slightly irregular in the **Sie**-imperative.

Seien Sie doch nicht so nervös!   *Don't be so nervous.*

Sprachnotiz   Flavoring particles and *bitte* in imperative sentences

Imperative sentences frequently contain the flavoring particles **doch** and/or **mal.** Depending on your tone of voice they can help to express either well-meant advice or strong irritation.

Gehen Sie **doch mal** zum Arzt.   *You should really go to the doctor.*
Lassen Sie mich **doch** in Ruhe!   *Why don't you leave me alone!*

The addition of **bitte** to an imperative sentence can transform it into a request, but it can also intensify a command.

Rufen Sie mich **bitte** morgen an.   *Please call me tomorrow.*
Machen Sie **bitte,** was ich sage!   *Please do as I say!*

4-40 Frau Ziegler geht zum Arzt. Match Frau Ziegler's problem at the left with the appropriate suggestion from her doctor at the right.

1. Ich bin immer so müde°.
2. Ich kann nicht gut schlafen.
3. Ich bin zu dick.
4. Ich habe so viel Stress bei der Arbeit!
5. Vormittags habe ich keine Energie.

a. Dann trinken Sie nicht so viel Kaffee!   *tired*
b. Dann gehen Sie früh ins Bett!
c. Dann machen Sie doch mal Yoga!
d. Dann gehen Sie doch mal ins Fitnessstudio!
e. Dann essen Sie mal ein gesundes Frühstück!

4-41 In Professor Kühls Deutschkurs.

1. _____ _____ bitte ein bisschen lauter! (sprechen)
2. Kevin, _____ _____ bitte das Wort! (wiederholen°)   *repeat*
3. _____ _____ diese Vokabeln bitte _____! (auf·schreiben)
4. Andrea, _____ _____ bitte _____! (an·fangen)
5. Monika, _____ _____ bitte so nett und _____ _____ _____! (sein / weiter·lesen)
6. _____ _____ jetzt bitte gut _____! (zu·hören)
7. _____ _____ die Übung 12 bitte schriftlich°! (machen)   *in writing*

> **auf·schreiben,** etc.: The raised dot indicates a separable-prefix verb.

The *ihr*-imperative

The **ihr**-imperative is the **ihr**-form of the verb without the pronoun.

Kommt, Kinder! Wir gehen schwimmen.   *Come on, children! We're going swimming.*
Nehmt eure Badeanzüge **mit!**   *Take your bathing suits along.*
Seid doch bitte nicht so laut!   *Please don't be so noisy.*

4-42 Ein Picknick. You and your friends are going on a picnic. Your mother gives last-minute instructions.

1. _____ mich bitte _____, wenn ihr dort seid! (an·rufen)
2. _____ doch das Frisbee _____! (mit·nehmen)
3. _____ auch eure Badeanzüge _____! (ein·packen)
4. _____ bitte die Sonnencreme nicht! (vergessen)
5. _____ auch ein paar schöne Fotos! (machen)
6. _____ genug° Brote _____! (ein·packen)   *enough*
7. _____ bitte nicht zu schnell! (fahren)
8. _____ bitte viel Wasser! (trinken)
9. _____ bitte vor neun wieder zurück! (sein)
10. _____ doch endlich _____! (ab·fahren)

The *du*-imperative

The **du**-imperative is simply the stem of the verb.

Notice that verbs that have a stem vowel change from **a** to **ä** do *not* use the changed stem in the **du**-imperative.

Lass mich in Ruhe!	*Stop bothering me!*
Komm nicht wieder so spät **heim!**	*Don't come home so late again!*
Sei doch nicht immer so unordentlich, Peter!	*Don't always be so sloppy, Peter!*

Verbs that have a stem-vowel change from **e** to **i** or **ie** in the 2nd and 3rd person singular of the present tense (e.g., **ich lese, du l*ie*st, er l*ie*st**) use the changed stem in the **du**-imperative.

Nimm doch nicht so viel Fleisch, Robert!	*Don't take so much meat, Robert!*
Iss nicht wieder den ganzen Kuchen!	*Don't eat all the cake again!*

Verbs with stems ending in **-d** or **-t** add an **-e** in the **du**-imperative.

Rede doch nicht so viel!	*Don't talk so much.*
Antworte bitte so bald wie möglich!	*Please answer as soon as possible.*

4-43 Mach bitte, was ich sage! You and your partner are siblings. One tries to lord it over the other, but it isn't working.

▶ _____ doch endlich _____! (auf·stehen)

_____ still und _____ mich schlafen! (sein, lassen)

S1: Steh doch endlich auf!

S2: Sei still und lass mich schlafen!

1. _____ doch endlich mal deine Cornflakes! (essen)

   _____ still und _____ deinen Kaffee! (sein, trinken)

2. _____ doch nicht immer hier _____! (rum·hängen)

   _____ mich in Ruhe und _____ deine Hausaufgaben! (lassen, machen)

3. _____ bitte gleich hier _____! (auf·räumen)

   _____ still und _____ dein Referat fertig! (sein, schreiben)

4. _____ deinen Freund doch nicht schon wieder _____! (an·rufen)

   _____ mich in Ruhe und _____ doch auf dein Zimmer! (lassen, gehen)

5. _____ bitte nur ein Stück Kuchen! (nehmen)

   _____ still und _____ dein Buch! (sein, lesen)

6. _____ bitte gleich meinen Wagen! (waschen)   *yourself*

   _____ deinen Wagen doch selbst°! (waschen)

4-44 Du nervst mich! Using the suggestions below, tell your roommate or a family member to stop doing things that get on your nerves.

▶ doch nicht so schnell fahren

S: Fahr doch nicht so schnell!

doch nicht so langsam fahren

snore   doch nicht so laut schnarchen°

doch nicht immer nur Junkfood essen

doch nicht immer so lange telefonieren

doch nicht so schnell essen

vor dem Fernseher: *in front of the TV*   doch nicht immer so viel reden

doch nicht so schnell / langsam sprechen

doch nicht immer nur deine doofen Comics lesen

doch nicht immer nur vor dem Fernseher° sitzen

4-45 Was soll man hier tun? Just like in English, German imperative forms are common in advertising. In each of the items below, identify the imperative form and give a basic translation in English.

> Until recently, **Halloween** was known to Germans only through American movies. Today it is not uncommon to see children wearing costumes and knocking on doors calling **Süßes oder Saures!**

> In pedestrian-oriented German cities where young children walk to school alone, jaywalking and crossing streets against the lights is strongly discouraged. One way people keep children safe are reminders like these about following the signals at crosswalks

Word Order

4.9 Create longer sentences with connectors

Position of the verb in independent and dependent clauses

You already know four of the following conjunctions. The final one (**nicht … sondern**) is new.

und	*and*	**aber**	*but*
denn	*because, for*	**nicht … sondern …**	*not … but rather …*
oder	*or*		

These conjunctions are called coordinating conjunctions. They connect independent clauses, i.e., clauses that can stand alone as complete sentences. Coordinating conjunctions do not affect the position of the verb.

Independent clause	Conjunction	Independent clause
Bernd hat endlich ein Zimmer	**und**	es kostet nur 150 Euro im Monat.
Es ist nur ein kleines Zimmer,	**aber**	es ist groß genug für Bernd.
Bernd geht **nicht** zu Fuß zur Uni,	**sondern**	er nimmt den Bus.

- The conjunctions **aber** and **sondern** are always preceded by a comma.
- The clause preceding **sondern** states what is *not* happening. The clause following **sondern** states what is happening *instead*.

4-46 Bernd hat ein Problem. Make Bernd's story read more smoothly. Using the appropriate coordinating conjunctions, connect the sentences in the left column with those directly opposite in the right column.

1. Ich habe endlich ein Zimmer!	Es kostet nur 150 Euro im Monat!
2. Das Zimmer ist sehr schön.	Von hier zur Uni ist es sehr weit°.
3. Ich muss mit dem Bus fahren	Zu Fuß ist es zu weit.
4. Soll ich jetzt dieses Zimmer nehmen?	Soll ich ein anderes Zimmer suchen?

far

The following conjunctions are called subordinating conjunctions:

bevor	*before*	**weil**	*because*
obwohl	*although; even though*	**wenn**	*if; when*

> Some students call subordinating conjunctions "verb kickers" because they "kick" the verb to the end of the clause!

Subordinating conjunctions introduce dependent clauses, i.e., clauses that cannot stand alone and make sense only in connection with an independent clause. Subordinating conjunctions affect the position of the verb: the verb stands at the end of the clause. A dependent clause is *always* separated from the independent clause by a comma.

Independent clause	Dependent clause
Bernd möchte das Zimmer,	**weil** es schön und preisgünstig **ist.**
Er möchte das Zimmer,	**obwohl** es von dort zur Uni sehr weit **ist.**

In clauses introduced by a subordinating conjunction, modal verbs appear at the end of the clause and separable-prefix verbs are no longer separated.

Independent clause	Dependent clause
Bernd möchte das Zimmer,	**weil** er von dort zur Uni laufen **kann.**
Er muss ein Zimmer finden,	**bevor** das Semester **anfängt.**

4-47 Interview: Wohin gehst du, wenn ...? Take turns asking a question and choosing an appropriate response from the right-hand column.

S1: Wohin gehst du, wenn du Hunger hast?   **S2:** In die Mensa.

1. wenn du Hunger hast?   In die Disco.
2. wenn du neue Klamotten brauchst?   Auf den Markt.
3. wenn du ein interessantes Buch lesen   In die Bibliothek.
   möchtest?   In mein Lieblingsrestaurant.
4. wenn du tanzen möchtest?   Zu Gap.
5. wenn du frisches Gemüse möchtest?

6. wenn du eine Tasse Kaffee trinken willst?   Ins Bett.
7. wenn du ein Taschenmesser brauchst?   Zu IKEA.
8. wenn du eine neue Digitalkamera suchst?   Zu Best Buy.
9. wenn du ein neues Sofa kaufen möchtest?   Zu Starbucks.
10. wenn du müde bist?   Zu Target.

4-48 Frühstück oder keines? Use the sentence completions below to make variations that describe your habits about eating breakfast. Make sure you choose completions that make sense! Compare your habits with your partner's.

Ich esse Frühstück, wenn ...
Ich frühstücke nicht, wenn ...
Ich muss frühstücken, bevor ...
Ich kann nicht frühstücken, weil ...

...ich viel Zeit habe.   ...ich am Wochenende nicht arbeiten muss.

...ich keine Vorlesungen habe.

                    ...meine Vorlesungen anfangen.

...ich um 9 in die Vorlesung muss.

                              ...ich Kaffee trinke.

...ich spät aufstehe.   ...ich lernen muss.

Sprachnotiz   Word order when the dependent clause comes first

If the dependent clause comes at the beginning of the sentence, the entire clause serves as the first element. It is followed by a comma and then the conjugated verb of the independent clause. The conjugated verbs of both clauses thus appear side by side, separated by a comma.

Bevor ich **frühstücke, sehe** ich eine halbe Stunde fern.
Wenn du fit bleiben **willst, musst** du Sport machen.

4-49 Warum lernst du Deutsch? Consider one or two reasons why you're studying German, and share them with others in your class. Use some options from the box below, or write your own.

▶ Ich lerne Deutsch, weil Deutsch eine coole Sprache ist. Und du?

☐ Deutsch ist eine coole Sprache.
☐ Ich liebe lange deutsche Wörter.
☐ Ich möchte deutsche Popmusik verstehen.
☐ Ich mag deutsches Bier.
☐ Ich will in Österreich studieren.
☐ Ich will später mal in Europa arbeiten.
☐ Ich will Deutsch als Hauptfach studieren.
☐ Ich habe deutschsprachige Verwandte.
☐ Meine Eltern/Großeltern sprechen Deutsch.
☐ Mein Freund/Meine Freundin kommt aus Deutschland.
☐ Ich liebe deutsche Filme (oder Literatur).
☐ Ich studiere Philosophie (oder Geschichte).
☐ Ich habe Freunde in dieser Klasse.

4.8 Video-Treff

Ein typischer Tag

4.10 Understand authentic video of German speakers talking about their typical day.

Christina Brieger, Ursula, André, Maiga, and Stefan Kuhlmann talk about their daily routines. Be sure to complete the **Was ist das auf Englisch?** exercise before watching the video.

4-50 Was ist das auf Englisch?

1. Ich **bringe** dann die Wohnung **in Ordnung.**
2. Ich habe eine Vorlesung in **Sinologie** und lerne chinesische Aussprache.
3. Ich esse **entweder** ein Brot von zu Hause **oder** ich gehe in die Mensa.
4. Wenn ich **großen Hunger habe,** dann gehe ich in die Mensa.
5. Ich gehe um eins oder zwei ins Bett. Ich bin **ein Nachtmensch.**
6. Ein typischer Tag fängt **ohne** Frühstück an, weil ich nicht gern frühstücke.
7. Danach fahre ich mit dem Fahrrad in die Uni, meistens **etwas knapp.**

a. either . . . or
b. without
c. a night person
d. Chinese Studies
e. just barely in time
f. am really hungry
g. tidy up

4-51 Was passt? Choose the appropriate information to complete these sentences about Christina Brieger, Ursula, and André.

1. Christina steht morgens gegen _____ auf.
   ☐ sechs Uhr   ☐ sieben Uhr

2. Manchmal essen Christina und Nicolai _____ zum Frühstück.
   ☐ Schokomüsli mit Joghurt   ☐ Toast mit Marmelade

3. _____ bringt Nicolai zum Kindergarten.
   ☐ Christoph   ☐ Christina

4. Christina arbeitet _____.
   ☐ im Büro   ☐ zu Hause

5. Ursula steht meistens um _____ auf.
   ☐ 7.30   ☐ 8.30

6. Dann geht sie _____ im Park joggen.
   ☐ 30 Minuten   ☐ 15 Minuten

7. Ursula arbeitet _____.
   ☐ zu Hause   ☐ im Büro

8. André steht im Semester immer _____ auf.
   ☐ früh   ☐ spät

9. Wenn André frühstückt, _____.
   ☐ sieht er oft fern   ☐ liest er oft Zeitung

10. Wenn er nachmittags frei hat, _____.
    ☐ lernt er zu Hause   ☐ geht er in die Bibliothek

4-52 Richtig oder falsch? Decide whether the following statements about Maiga and Stefan Kuhlmann are **richtig** or **falsch**. If the statement is **falsch**, provide a correct version.

	RICHTIG	FALSCH
1. Wenn Maiga eine Vorlesung hat, steht sie so gegen halb neun oder neun Uhr auf.	☐	☐
2. Zum Frühstück isst sie nichts, weil sie keinen Hunger hat.	☐	☐
3. Maiga nimmt den Bus zur Uni.	☐	☐
4. Maiga bringt ihr Mittagessen oft zur Uni mit.	☐	☐
5. Maiga ist bis 16 Uhr an der Uni.	☐	☐
6. Stefan isst immer ein großes Frühstück.	☐	☐
7. Stefan trinkt morgens eine Tasse Tee.	☐	☐
8. Stefan hört morgens Musik.	☐	☐
9. Abends sieht Stefan oft fern, oder er geht ins Kino.	☐	☐
10. Stefan geht meistens früh ins Bett.	☐	☐

Ich gehe heute Nachmittag joggen.

)))4.9 Wortschatz 2

Wichtige Vokabeln

4.11 Learn vocabulary to talk about travel and everyday activities

Nomen

die Autobahn, -en	freeway
der Bahnhof, ⸚e	train station
der Fahrplan, ⸚e	train or bus schedule

> **Autobahn, Bahnhof:** The literal meaning of **Bahn** is *path* or *track*. By itself, **die Bahn** is now used to refer to the whole German railway system.

die Hausaufgabe, -n	homework (assignment)
das Referat, -e	(oral) report; paper
das Seminar, -e	seminar course

> A **Referat** is usually presented orally in a **Seminar** and then handed in in written form for final grading.

der Fernseher, -	television set
vor dem Fernseher	in front of the TV
das Messer, -	knife
die Tasche, -n	pocket; bag
das Taschenmesser, -	pocket knife

Verben

bleiben	to stay, to remain
rauchen	to smoke
reden	to talk, to speak
vergessen (vergisst)	to forget
ab·fahren (fährt ab)	to leave, to depart
an·halten (hält an)	to stop
an·fangen (fängt an)	to start
an·hören	to listen to
an·kommen	to arrive
an·probieren	to try on (*as in clothes*)
an·rufen	to call (*on the phone*)
auf·passen	to pay attention
auf·räumen	to straighten up, clean up
auf·wachen	to wake up

> **ab·fahren**, etc.: The raised dot indicates that these are separable-prefix verbs.

aus·gehen	to go out
aus·probieren	to try out
aus·steigen	to get off (*train, bus, etc.*)
durch·lesen (liest durch)	to read through
ein·laden (lädt ein)	to invite
ein·schlafen (schläft ein)	to fall asleep
ein·steigen	to board, get on (*train, bus, etc.*)
fern·sehen (sieht fern)	to watch TV
heim·kommen	to come home
mit·kommen	to come along
um·steigen	to change (*trains*)
vor·haben	to plan, to have planned
weg·fahren (fährt weg)	to drive away
weiter·fahren (fährt weiter)	to continue driving; to continue traveling
weiter·lesen (liest weiter)	to continue reading
zurück·kommen	to come back
kennen·lernen	to get to know
Rad fahren (fährt Rad)	to ride a bike, to go cycling
spazieren gehen	to go for a walk

Konjunktionen

bevor	before
obwohl	although, even though
weil	because
wenn	if; when (*whenever*)

Andere Wörter

bekannt	well-known
deshalb	therefore; that's why
endlich	finally, at last
erfolgreich	successful(ly)
genug	enough
gleich	right away
schriftlich	in writing; written
selbst	myself, yourself, herself, etc.
sondern	(*but*) … instead, but rather

Ausdrücke

nach Mitternacht	after midnight
zu Fuß gehen	to walk
Lass mich in Ruhe!	Stop bothering me!

Das Gegenteil

an·fangen (fängt an) ≠ auf·hören	to start ≠ to stop
der Anfang, ¨e ≠ das Ende, -n	beginning ≠ end
gesund ≠ ungesund	healthy ≠ unhealthy
möglich ≠ unmöglich	possible ≠ impossible
oft ≠ selten	often ≠ seldom, rarely
ordentlich ≠ unordentlich	neat, tidy ≠ messy, sloppy
rechts ≠ links	right, to the right ≠ left, to the left
zuerst ≠ zuletzt	first ≠ last

Leicht zu verstehen

der Alkohol
die Firma, Firmen
das Foto, -s
die Innovation, -en
der Stress
die Zigarette, -n
Yoga machen
innovativ
typisch
nervös

Wörter im Kontext

4-53 Welches Präfix passt hier?

weg / auf / ein / vor / heim

1. Wachst du immer so früh _____?
2. Wann fährst du morgens _____ und wann kommst du abends _____?
3. Was hast du heute Nachmittag _____?
4. Schläfst du in Professor Altmanns Vorlesung auch immer _____?

fern / an / mit / weiter / aus / ab

5. Heute Abend gehen wir alle _____. Kommst du _____?
6. Siehst du immer so viel _____?
7. Warum hörst du denn auf, Matthias? Lies doch _____.
8. Wann fährt euer Zug in Frankfurt _____ und wann kommt er in Hannover _____?

4-54 Was macht hier Sinn? Imagine you are taking a trip from Berne, Switzerland, to Berlin. Put the sentences in the most sensible order. The first one is completed for you.

1. Ich komme sechs Stunden später in Berlin an. _____
2. Ich steige in der Schweiz in den Zug ein. __1__
3. Der Zug fährt von Bern ab. _____
4. Ich fahre bis Mannheim, denn ich muss in Mannheim umsteigen. _____
5. Bald kommt in Mannheim der nächste Zug. _____
6. Dieser Zug fährt ab. _____

4-55 Was passt wo?

bekannt / in Ruhe / endlich / genug / zu Fuß / innovativ

1. Die Firma Victorinox ist für ihre Innovation _____.
2. Die Schweizer Taschenmesser sind besonders _____.
3. Hast du noch _____ Geld?
4. Warum kannst du mich denn nicht endlich _____ lassen?
5. Nehmt ihr den Bus oder geht ihr _____?
6. Ich nehme den Bus, wenn er _____ kommt!

Der Bus kommt gleich.

4-56 Gegenteile.

selten / ungesund / möglich / rechts / oft / links / gesund / unmöglich

1. Sport machen ist _____. Rauchen ist _____.
2. In Finnland schneit es _____. In Sizilien schneit es nur sehr _____.
3. In England fährt man _____. In Nordamerika fährt man _____.
4. Ich fahre so schnell wie _____, aber ich kann _____ in zehn Minuten zu Hause sein.

Wörter unter der Lupe

Denn **versus** dann

The words **denn** and **dann** occur very frequently in German. Because these words are so similar in sound and appearance and because **denn** has two very different meanings, they deserve a closer look.

- The flavoring particle **denn** occurs only in questions. It expresses curiosity and interest, and sometimes irritation.

  Wann stehst du **denn** endlich auf?   *When are you finally going to get up?*

- The coordinating conjunction **denn** introduces a clause that states the reason for something. Its English equivalents are *because* and *for*.

  Ich esse jeden Tag Frühstück, **denn** ich habe morgens immer Hunger!

- The adverb **dann** is an equivalent of English *then*. It expresses that a certain thing or action follows another thing or action.

  Zuerst koche ich Kaffee und **dann** esse ich ein Brötchen mit Butter und Käse.

4-57 *Denn or dann?*

1. HEIKE: Was schreibst du _____ da?
    SYLVIA: Einen Brief an meine Eltern.
    HEIKE: Und _____? Was machst du _____?
    SYLVIA: _____ rufe ich Holger an, _____ wir wollen heute Abend zusammen ins Kino gehen.
2. SONJA: Wann rufst du _____ endlich deine Eltern an?
    LAURA: Erst heute Abend, _____ _____ sind sie bestimmt° zu Hause.   *definitely*

4.10 Alles zusammen

Konkrete Poesie

Schritt 1: Zum Lesen

4-58 Eugen Gomringer Gedichte. Die folgenden drei Gedichte findet man in Gomringers *worte sind schatten* (1969). Können Sie zu **jedem** Gedicht das Thema identifizieren?

schweigen	schweigen	schweigen
schweigen	schweigen	schweigen
schweigen		schweigen
schweigen	schweigen	schweigen
schweigen	schweigen	schweigen

Gomringer uses repetition and word placement to create images that speak beyond the content (**Inhalt**). What purpose might the open (or closed) spaces in the poems have? Does repetition (**Wiederholung**) affect the meaning? What form or figure (**Form, Figur**) is created, and how might we interpret this?

das erste grün

das erste grün
das erste rot
das erste gelb
das erste weiss
das erste grün

Mensch is the German word for person, as in *human being*. It focuses on the human dimensions of being a person.

mensch hcsnem mensch hcsnem
hcsnem mensch hcsnem mensch
yɔsuǝɯ ɥɔsuǝɯ ɥɔsuǝɯ ɥɔsuǝɯ
ɥɔsuǝɯ ɥɔsuǝɯ ɥɔsuǝɯ ɥɔsuǝɯ

Wer ist Eugen Gomringer?

Born in 1925 (in Bolivia) as the son of a Bolivian mother and a Swiss father, Eugen Gomringer has been revered as the founder of **Konkrete Poesie** from the 1950s until today. His concrete poetry fuses words and meanings on the printed page to create new and changing understandings of familiar ideas. Gomringer explores, among other things, the way the concrete form allows for a sense of dialogue in his poems. Perhaps best known for his work **Schweigen**, Gomringer has continued to write and read poetry, even beyond his 90th birthday. He writes in German, Swiss German, Spanish, French, and English. Gomringer directs ikkp, **institut für konstruktive kunst und konkrete poesie**, in Rehau (Franconia), Germany. His daughter, Nora-Eugenia, is also an active poet.

Schritt 2: Zum Sprechen

 **4-59 Mein Lieblingsgedicht.** Wie finden Sie Gomringers Gedichte? Diskutieren Sie mit einem Partner über Ihr Lieblingsgedicht. Sagen Sie auch, warum!

- Mein Lieblingsgedicht ist …, weil es so … ist.
- Die Form von … ist …
- Die Wiederholung von … finde ich …
- Und den Inhalt finde ich …

innovativ	simpel	vielseitig	interessant	verrückt	cool
spielerisch	unkonventionell	komplex	modern	komisch	traurig

Schritt 3: Zum Schreiben

4-60 **Schreiben Sie nun ein Gedicht im Stil von Gomringer.** Hier sind ein paar Ideen für Themen, aber seien Sie kreativ!

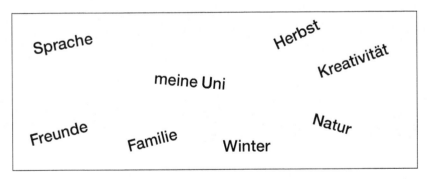

Consider the suggested topics here or use your own ideas. Enjoy making new meaning through repetition and the interaction between words and the form they create. If you like the looks of Gomringer's **kleinschreibung**, incorporate that, too!

Kapitel 5
Freizeit – Ferienzeit

Kajaker auf der Müritz-Elde-Wasserstraße

Learning Objectives

5.1 Investigate ways of traveling in the German-speaking countries

5.2 Learn vocabulary to talk about travel and geography

5.3 Recognize and practice the two ways of pronouncing *ch*

5.4 Talk about people or things without naming them explicitly

5.5 State when you are doing something, where you are, and how you get there

5.6 Make comparisons

5.7 Compare vacationing choices of Germans

5.8 Use complex sentence structure

5.9 Talk about what and whom you know

5.10 Talk about events in the past

5.11 Understand authentic video of German speakers talking about their vacations.

5.12 Learn vocabulary to talk about travel and useful everyday objects

5.1 Vorschau

Am Grundlsee

The hotel advertised below is situated on a hill at the head of the Grundlsee, an alpine lake in the Ausseerland region in the Austrian state of **Steiermark** *(Styria)*. The region offers visitors spectacular natural beauty and a wide range of sport and leisure activities throughout the year. Take a look at this ad for a special package deal when the **Narzissen** *(daffodils)* are in bloom and respond to the questions below.

> The **Ausseerland** region is part of Austria's lake-dotted **Salzkammergut.** The **Grundlsee** is approximately 80 kilometers (50 miles) southeast of Salzburg.

Narzissenblüte im Ausseerland–4 Nächte

Buchungszeitraum: 30.04.2017–25.05.2017

Preis: € 259 pro Person/Aufenthalt im Doppelzimmer

Leistungen Narzissenblüte:

- 4 Übernachtungen im Doppelzimmer
  Donnerstag–Sonntag oder Sonntag–Donnerstag

- täglich Frühstücksbüffet in unserem Restaurant

- Verwöhnpaket in Ihrem Zimmer bei der Anreise
  (1 Flasche Sekt, feinste Schokoladen)

- Gemütliche Wanderung durch blühende Wiesen zu
  den schönsten Plätzen des Ausseerlandes

- Freie Nutzung des Wellness-Bereichs

- 1 Aroma-Massage (30 min. pro Person),
  im Wert von € 35,00

Preis: € 259,00 pro Person im Doppelzimmer
Einzelzimmerzuschlag: € 50,00
Ortstaxe: € 1,50 pro Person/Nacht

> Direkt anfragen

> Dieses Angebot buchen

5-1 Was ist das auf Englisch? Find the following words in the ad and choose the meaning that best fits the context.

1. Übernachtung
2. Sekt
3. Wellness-Bereich
4. Zuschlag
5. Nutzung
6. Verwöhnpaket

a. surcharge
b. spa
c. sparkling wine
d. overnight stay
e. "Let us spoil you" package
f. use

Der Grundlsee in Österreich

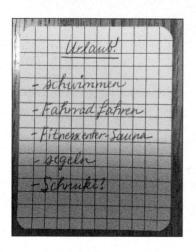

5-2 Was verstehen Sie?

1. Die Narzissen blühen am Grundlsee normalerweise im Monat ____.
   a. März
   b. Mai
2. In einem Doppelzimmer ist Platz für ____.
   a. eine Person
   b. zwei Personen
3. Das Paket „Narzissenblüte" kostet für zwei Personen ____ für vier Tage.
   a. 518 Euro
   b. 396 Euro
4. Wenn man allein reist, kostet das Paket „Narzissenblüte" ____ für vier Tage.
   a. 259 Euro
   b. 309 Euro
5. Welche Leistung ist im Paket „Narzissenblüte" *nicht* inklusive? ____
   a. Frühstück im Restaurant
   b. eine gemütliche Bootsfahrt
   c. eine Wanderung durch die Wiesen
   d. eine Flasche Sekt

5-3 Campen im Erzgebirge. Welcher Campingplatz ist optimal?

Lisa und Ralf haben bald Urlaub und wollen campen gehen. Sie wollen jeden Tag baden und möchten auch ein paar kleine Radtouren machen. Ralf möchte gern einen Campinglatz mit Fitnesscenter und Sauna. Lisas Lieblingssport ist Segeln. Lisa und Ralf sind auch passionierte Angler. Sie möchten auch natürlich ihren Hund Schnuki mitnehmen.

Was ist der ideale Campingplatz für Lisa und Ralf? _____

	Bademöglichkeit	W-Lan	Supermarkt	Fahrradverleih	Bootsverleih	Tiere erlaubt	Gaststätte	Surfen/Segeln	Minigolf	Waschmaschine	Fitnesscenter	Sauna	Duschen	Kinderspielplatz	Angeln	Barrierefrei
Altenberg	●	●	●	●		●	●	●	●		●	●	●	●	●	
Freiberg	●	●	●		●		●				●	●	●			●
Lindenau	●	●		●		●							●	●		
Malter	●			●	●	●		●			●	●	●		●	

Legende:

- 🏞 Bademöglichkeit
- 📶 W-Lan
- 🛒 Supermarkt
- 🚲 Fahrradverleih
- ⛵ Bootsverleih
- 🐕 Tiere erlaubt
- 🍽 Gaststätte
- ⛵ Surfen/Segeln
- ⛳ Minigolf
- 🧺 Waschmaschine
- 🏋 Fitnesscenter
- Sauna
- 🚿 Duschen
- Kinderspielplatz
- 🎣 Angeln
- ♿ Barrierefrei

5.2 Kultur 1

Affordable travel

5.1 Investigate ways of traveling in the German-speaking countries

By car, bus, or plane

There are still a few stretches of **Autobahn** where the only limit to how fast you can go is the engine of your car. Yet the high cost of gasoline has been putting the brakes on this legendary enjoyment of speed somewhat: Because Germans are paying about $5/gallon, many drive at or below the recommended speed of **130 Stundenkilometer** (81 mph) on highways. Others use a **Mitfahrzentrale** (*ride-sharing agency*) to find groups of people traveling the same route and willing to share the cost of gas.

Die Autobahn: Hier darf man sehr schnell fahren!

Going by **Fernbus** (*long-distance coach*) has become popular with budget-conscious travelers, resulting in even more competition for railways and airlines. A bus ticket from Hamburg to Frankfurt (a seven-hour ride) can cost as little as 20 euros. Flying the same route with a **Billigflieger** (*no frills airline*) like Eurowings can cost just 60 euros and takes just over one hour. Travelers who have flexible travel dates or are prepared to book last-minute can enjoy unbelievably low prices for bus or air travel to many European destinations.

> Major **Fluggesellschaften** (*airlines*) offering service to and from North America are Lufthansa, Austrian Airlines, Swiss, and Eurowings.

> For North American students, a popular way to explore Europe is with the Eurail Pass, which provides unlimited travel for a specified duration through 28 European countries.

By train

In the German-speaking countries, train transportation is a vital part of life. The railway systems are renowned for their fast and efficient passenger service, and companies in industrial regions of Germany and mountainous Austria and Switzerland depend on trains to transport raw materials and finished products. The fastest passenger trains of the **Deutsche Bahn (DB)** are the **ICEs** (*Intercity Express trains*), which connect major German cities to each other and to other cities in Europe at speeds of up to **330 Stundenkilometer** (about 205 mph). These trains have restaurant cars, onboard audio entertainment programs, comfortable workspaces, with improved mobile phone reception and wireless internet **(W-Lan)**, as well as **Ruhewagen**, designated zones where talking on cell phones is discouraged.

After arriving at the **Bahnhof** (*train station*), passengers can explore cities on a bike rented from **DB**, or use the extensive public transportation options. The **DB** is also a full-service travel operator, offering packages including hotel accommodations, rental cars, and event tickets. These factors and the dense network of rail lines in Europe make trains a viable and convenient alternative to traveling by car.

Hier darf man nicht telefonieren und nicht laut sprechen.

Der Glacier Express fährt in die Schweizer Alpen.

Both Austria and Switzerland have built an extensive mountain rail system in addition to the city-to-city routes of the **Österreichische Bundesbahn (ÖBB)** and the **Schweizerische Bundesbahn (SBB)**. Apart from connecting millions of skiers to alpine slopes, train companies offer scenic trips such as the Swiss **Glacier Express,** a day-long ride that traverses 291 bridges, 91 tunnels, and navigates the 2033-meter-high (6670 feet) Oberalp Pass. All train companies offer a great variety of tickets, tailored to the needs of individuals, groups, commuters, or for specific age groups, regions, weekends, or seasons. For example, a group of five people can purchase a **Schönes-Wochenende-Ticket** for unlimited weekend travel across Germany for just 56 euros.

Affordable accommodations

A network of about 700 **Jugendherbergen** *(youth hostels)* in Germany, Austria, and Switzerland provides reasonably priced, clean overnight accommodations and meals. Accommodations are often dorm-like but much cheaper than a room in a hotel, and some **Jugendherbergen** are housed in interesting old buildings such as medieval castles or monasteries. In Germany, the hostels are operated by the **Deutsches Jugendherbergswerk (DJH)**, a not-for-profit **Verein** *(registered association)* with about 2 million members who pay a low annual fee (between 7 and 22 euros) for the right to use the hostel network and for additional benefits such as travel insurance. In addition to a range of outdoor activities, many hostels offer cultural and educational events for individual travelers or

Die Jugendherberge Burg Altena in Nordrhein-Westfalen

groups, making them a popular choice for the organizers of school trips. If you're planning to travel while studying abroad in Germany, **Jugendherbergen** are a good place to get to know other young people from all over the world.

5-4 Wie reist man am besten? Plan a trip for this weekend from **Köln** *(Cologne)* to **Leipzig**. Research online to compare your options for bus, rail, ride-share, and air travel. Use search terms such as "**Fernbus**," "**Deutsche Bahn**," and "**Mitfahrgelegenheit**" to locate the corresponding sites. For air travel, try one of the airlines mentioned (Lufthansa, Air Berlin, or Eurowings). Be sure to select "**Deutsch**" on the sites you visit! Which method of travel is the most affordable and which is most appealing to you?

Strecke: von Köln nach Leipzig   **Datum:**

	Kosten / Ticketpreis in Euro	Reisedauer (in Stunden, Minuten)
Fernbus		
Bahn		+ Umsteigen in _____
Mitfahrgelegenheit		
Flugzeug		+ Mit _____ *(Airline)*

))) 5.3 Wortschatz 1

Wichtige Vokabeln

5.2 Learn vocabulary to talk about travel and geography

Nomen

die Freizeit	free time
die Ferien *(pl)*	vacation *(generally of students)*
der Urlaub	vacation *(generally of people in the workforce)*
der Aufenthalt, -e	stay *(in a hotel, city, etc.)*
das Angebot, -e	offer
die Bademöglichkeit, -en	(place to go) swimming; swimming facility
der Campingplatz, ¨e	campground; campsite
der Fahrradverleih, -e	bike rental
der Fernbus, -se	long-distance coach, bus
die Jugendherberge, -n	youth hostel
die Mitfahrgelegenheit, -en	ride-sharing opportunity
das Paket, -e	package; package deal (offer)
der Platz, ¨e	place; space, room
der Baum, ¨e	tree
der Berg, -e	mountain
das Dorf, ¨er	village
das Feld, -er	field
der Fluss, ¨e	river
das Gebirge, -	mountain range
die Insel, -n	island
die Landschaft, -en	landscape
der See, -n	lake
der Strand, ¨e	beach
der Wald, ¨er	woods; forest
die Flasche, -n	bottle
der Sekt	sparkling wine
eine Flasche Sekt	a bottle of sparkling wine

Verben

angeln	to fish
baden	to swim; to bathe
blühen	to blossom; to flourish
buchen	to book *(travel)*
fließen	to flow
übernachten	to stay overnight
wissen (weiß)	to know

Andere Wörter

barrierefrei	wheelchair accessible
frei	free
gemütlich	cozy; comfortable

Ausdrücke

Anfang Juli	(at) the beginning of July
Ende Juli	(at) the end of July
Mitte Juli	(in) mid-July
eine Reise machen	to go on a trip, to take a trip
Ferien (Urlaub) machen	to go on vacation
Wo machst du am liebsten Ferien?	Where's your favorite vacation spot?
vierzehn Tage	two weeks

Das Gegenteil

alt ≠ jung	old ≠ young
erlaubt ≠ verboten	permitted ≠ prohibited
weit ≠ nah	far ≠ near

Möglichkeit actually means *possibility* or *opportunity*. What are the literal meanings of **Bademöglichkeit, Einkaufsmöglichkeit, Kochmöglichkeit, Parkmöglichkeit,** and **Schlafmöglichkeit?** What do you think their English equivalents might be?

Leicht zu verstehen

die Broschüre, -n	campen
das Campen	ideal
das Hotel, -s	passioniert
der Plan, ¨e	
die Sauna, -s	
der Supermarkt, ¨e	

Wörter im Kontext

5-5 Was passt zusammen?

1. Hotelzimmer	a. angelt man.
2. Pläne	b. bucht man.
3. Fische	c. trinkt man.
4. Sekt	d. macht man.
5. Wenn man Freizeit hat,	e. blühen die Narzissen.
6. Wenn man baden gehen möchte,	f. wird die Reise nicht so teuer.
7. Wenn man an einen See fährt,	g. muss man einen Strand suchen.
8. Wenn man eine Mitfahrgelegenheit findet,	h. muss man nicht arbeiten.
9. Wenn es Frühling ist,	i. kann man angeln.

5-6 Was passt zusammen?

1. Lisa und Ralf machen immer dann Urlaub,	a. weil sie gern campen und weil Tiere auf den Campingplätzen erlaubt sind.
2. Sie reisen oft ins Erzgebirge,	b. buchen Lisa und Ralf ein Zimmer in einer Jugendherberge.
3. Wenn es keinen Platz auf dem Campingplatz gibt,	c. weil sie passionierte Angler sind.
4. Lisa und Ralf fahren immer an einen See,	d. gehen sie zum Fahrradverleih.
5. Wenn sie eine Radtour machen wollen und kein Rad haben,	e. wenn es schönes Wetter gibt.

5-7 Was ist das?

1. die Alpen	a. eine Insel	5. Superior	e. ein Dorf
2. Sherwood	b. ein Gebirge	6. eine Tanne	f. ein Berg
3. Jamaika	c. ein Fluss	7. Smallville	g. ein See
4. die Elbe	d. ein Wald	8. Matterhorn	h. ein Baum

Die Elbe fließt durch Dresden.

5.4 Zur Aussprache

German *ch*

5.3 Recognize and practice the two ways of pronouncing *ch* **in German**

German **ch** is one of the few consonant sounds that has no equivalent in English.

))) **5-8** Hören Sie gut zu und wiederholen Sie!

- **ch** after **a, o, u**, and **au**
  When **ch** follows the vowels **a, o, u**, or **au**, it resembles the sound of a gentle gargling.

  Frau Ba**ch** kommt Punkt a**ch**t.

  Am Wo**ch**enende ko**ch**t immer meine To**ch**ter.

  Warum su**ch**st du denn das Ko**ch**bu**ch**?

  Ich will versu**ch**en°, einen Ku**ch**en zu backen.   *try*

  Hat Herr Rau**ch** au**ch** so einen Bierbau**ch**° wie Herr Strau**ch**?   *beer belly*

- **ch** after all other vowels and after consonants
  The sound of **ch** after all other vowels (including the umlauted vowels) and after consonants is similar to the sound of a loudly whispered *h* in *huge* or *Hugh*.

  Mi**ch**aels Kät**zch**en mö**ch**te ein Teller**ch**en° Mil**ch**.   *little dish*

  The ending **-ig** is pronounced as if it were spelled **-ich**, unless it is followed by a vowel.

  Es ist sonn**ig**, aber sehr wind**ig**.

- The two types of **ch** sounds are often found in the singular and plural forms of the same noun.

die Na**ch**t	die Nä**ch**te	das Bu**ch**	die Bü**ch**er
die To**ch**ter	die Tö**ch**ter	der Bierbau**ch**	die Bierbäu**ch**e

- The combination **-chs** is pronounced like English *x*.

  das Wa**chs**   se**chs**   der O**chs**e   der Fu**chs**

> Once you pronounce the words **Wachs, Ochse,** and **Fuchs** appropriately you should be able to guess their English meanings!

5-9 **Das deutsche *ch*.** Pronounce the words and phrases on the German signs pictured. Be sure to focus on your pronunciation of the German **ch** sounds.

5.5 Kommunikation und Formen 1

Personal pronouns in the accusative case

5.4 Talk about people or things without naming them explicitly

In English the object forms of the personal pronouns are often different from the subject forms, e.g., *I love **him** and he loves **me** too.*

    The same is true in German, where the accusative (object) forms of the personal pronouns are often different from the nominative (subject) forms.

Ich liebe **ihn** und er liebt **mich** auch.	*I love **him** and he loves **me** too.*

Remember that *things* also have gender in German and that this is reflected in the pronoun forms.

Warum liest du **den Roman** nicht fertig?	*Why don't you finish reading **the novel**?*
Ich finde **ihn** langweilig.	*I find **it** boring.*

Sie wollen Sommer?
WiR HABEN iHN!
www.REISEinfos.de

Personal pronouns							
Singular				**Plural**			
NOMINATIVE		ACCUSATIVE		NOMINATIVE		ACCUSATIVE	
ich	*I*	**mich**	*me*	**wir**	*we*	**uns**	*us*
du	*you*	**dich**	*you*	**ihr**	*you*	**euch**	*you*
er	*he, it*	**ihn**	*him, it*				
es	*it*	**es**	*it*	**sie**	*they*	**sie**	*them*
sie	*she, it*	**sie**	*her, it*				
Sie	*you*	**Sie**	*you*	**Sie**	*you*	**Sie**	*you*

5-10 Reisepläne. You and your partner are making plans for a trip. Respond to your partner's questions using the appropriate pronouns.

S1: Kennst du den Grundlsee?   **S2:** Ja, ich kenne ihn.

1. Kennst du den Campingplatz? (die Jugendherberge, den Strand, das Schloss)
2. Nehmen wir den Hund mit? (die Wanderschuhe, die Fahrräder, den Kajak)
3. Hast du die Kreditkarten? (den Fahrplan, die Kamera, das Handy)
4. Buchen wir jetzt das Doppelzimmer in dem schicken Hotel? (das Paket „Narzissenblüte", die Bootsfahrt auf dem See, das Ticket für das Sektfrühstück)

5-11 *Lieben* und *mögen*. Supply the appropriate personal pronouns.

1. Philipp loves Vanessa but, although she is fond of him, Vanessa doesn't love Philipp.

   PHILIPP: Ich liebe dich, Vanessa, liebst du _____ auch?
   VANESSA: Ich mag _____, Philipp, aber ich liebe _____ nicht.

2. Sarah quizzes Philipp about his feelings for Vanessa.

   SARAH: Liebst du Vanessa?
   PHILIPP: Ja, ich liebe _____, ich liebe _____ sehr.
   SARAH: Und Vanessa? Liebt sie _____ auch?
   PHILIPP: Sie sagt, sie mag _____, aber sie liebt _____ nicht.

3. Sarah quizzes Vanessa about her feelings for Philipp.

SARAH: Liebst du Philipp?
VANESSA: Ich mag _____, aber ich liebe _____ nicht.
SARAH: Und Philipp? Liebt er _____?
VANESSA: Er sagt, er liebt _____ sehr.

 5-12 Wie findest du Davids Pullover? Look at your fellow students. How do you like their clothes, hairdos, beards, glasses, jewelry?

S1: Wie findest du Davids Pullover?   **S2:** Ich finde ihn echt spitze.
S2: Wie findest du …?   **S3:** Ich finde …
      …

der Pulli	sehr schön	
der Pullover	sehr elegant	
das Sweatshirt	echt spitze	
das T-Shirt	sehr schick	
das Hemd	echt toll	
die Jeans	sehr hübsch	
die Hose	ziemlich° cool	*kind of (colloq.)*
der Rock	sehr geschmackvoll°	*tasteful*
die Schuhe	gar nicht schlecht	

die Frisur

der Ohrring, -e

das Armband, ¨er

die Tätowierung, -en

der Ring, -e

die Halskette, -n

die Brille

der Nasenstecker, -

der Haarschnitt

der Bart

der Schnurbart

die Baseballkappe, -n

Accusative prepositions

5.5 State when you are doing something, where you are, and how you get there

A preposition is a word that combines with a noun or pronoun to form a phrase.

For whom are you printing out this brochure, *for Kevin* or *for me?*

The noun or pronoun in the prepositional phrase is called the object of the preposition. After the following German prepositions, the noun or pronoun object appears in the accusative case.

durch	through	Nächsten Sommer möchte ich mit dir **durch die Schweiz** reisen.
für	for	**Für wen** druckst du diese Broschüre aus, **für mich?**
gegen	against	Ja, hast du etwas **gegen meine Idee?**
	around (with time)	Nein, ich möchte die Reise mit dir planen. Hast du morgen **gegen neun** Zeit?
ohne	without	Ja, aber mach bitte keine Pläne **ohne mich!**
um	around	Das nächste Reisebüro ist gleich **um die Ecke°.**
	at (with time)	Das Reisebüro öffnet morgen **um acht.**

corner

Sprachnotiz   Accusative prepositions in contractions

In colloquial German the prepositions **durch, für,** and **um** are often contracted with the article **das: durchs, fürs, ums.**

Wir laufen **durchs** Hotel.	*We're walking through the hotel.*
In deutschen Hotels muss man **fürs** Frühstück nicht extra bezahlen.	*In German hotels you don't have to pay extra for breakfast.*
Ums Parkhotel stehen viele alte Bäume.	*Around the Park Hotel there are many old trees.*

SCHIFFSFAHRT ca. 1 Stunde
durchs alte und neue Berlin
Fahrzeiten täglich: 11.00 / 11.30 / 12.30 und 13.00 Uhr

5-13 Ich reise nie ohne … What would you never travel without? Check off some items in the list below and add some of your own. Tell your classmates one item that is important to you and then call on another student. Follow the example.

S1: Ich reise nie ohne ein gutes
Buch. Und du, David?

S2: Ich reise nie ohne …

☐ mein Handy
☐ meine Kopfhörer
☐ meine ATM-Karte
☐ meine Kreditkarten
☐ eine warme Jacke
☐ meinen Kindle
☐ _____

☐ meinen Pass
☐ meine elektrische Zahnbürste°   *toothbrush*
☐ meinen Regenschirm°   *umbrella*
☐ meine Wasserflasche
☐ meinen Studentenausweis°   *student I.D.*
☐ meine Medikamente
☐ _____

5-14 Ein voller Koffer. Your partner has returned from a trip to Europe with a suitcase full of gifts. Take turns asking your partner for whom she/he intended the gifts.

▶   dieses Poster   Für mein__ Schwester

S1: Für wen ist dieses Poster von Berlin?   **S2:** Für meine Schwester.

> **Achtung!**
> Remember that only masculine
> nouns change in the accusative:
> **der → den; ein → einen.**

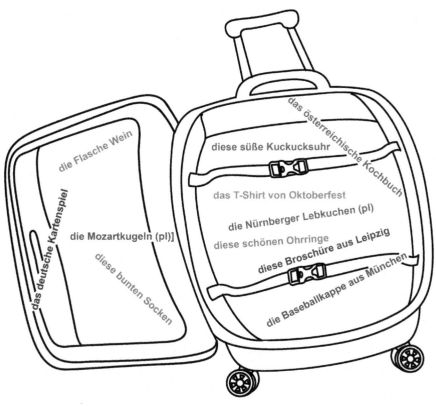

Für wen?

Für mein__ Freund
Für mein__ Freundin
Für mein__ Schwester
Für mein__ Bruder
Für mein__ Eltern

Für mein__ Professorin
Für mein__ Professor
Für mein__ Großeltern
Für mein__ besten Freunde
Für mich!

5-15 Durch, für, gegen, ohne, um? Supply the appropriate prepositions.

1. Bist du _____ oder _____ diese Politikerin?
2. Hier ist ein Brief _____ dich.
3. Heute müsst ihr mal _____ mich angeln gehen.
4. Gibt es immer noch die Pizzeria _____ die nächste Ecke?
5. Trinkst du deinen Kaffee immer _____ Milch und Zucker?
6. _____ dich mache ich diese Radtour nicht.
7. Spielt die deutsche Nationalmannschaft morgen _____ die Schweizer?
8. Fährt der Zug nach München _____ 17.35 Uhr oder _____ 18.35 Uhr?

on the dot   9. _____ sieben ist nicht Punkt° sieben. Es ist ein bisschen vor oder nach sieben.
10. Komm, wir laufen ein bisschen _____ den Park.

Vielen Dank
für Ihren
Besuch!

The comparative and superlative

5.6 Make comparisons

The comparative

You can compare characteristics and qualities by using the comparative forms of adjectives and adverbs. In contrast to English, German has only one way of forming the comparative: by adding **-er** to the adjective or adverb, e.g., **klein*er*, schnell*er*, schön*er*, gemütlich*er*.** Note that the German equivalent of *than* is **als.**

Vom Hotel ist es ein bisschen **weiter** zum See **als** vom Campingplatz.	*From the hotel it's a bit **farther** to the lake **than** from the campground.*
Lisa und Ralf finden den Campingplatz **interessanter als** ein Hotel.	*Lisa and Ralf find the campground **more interesting than** a hotel.*

Most German one-syllable adjectives or adverbs with the vowels **a, o,** or **u** are umlauted in the comparative.

a → ä	o → ö	u → ü
nah – näher	oft – öfter	jung – jünger
warm – wärmer	groß – größer	kurz – kürzer

Die Sommerferien sind viel **länger als** die Weihnachtsferien.	*Summer vacation is much **longer than** Christmas vacation.*
Unsere Nachbarn machen **öfter** Urlaub **als** wir.	*Our neighbors go on vacation **more often than** we do.*

5-16 Wie alt und wie groß bist du? Walk around the classroom and find out the age and height of your classmates. Use the scale to convert feet and inches to metric measure.

S1: Wie alt bist du?	**S2:** Ich bin …

S1: Dann bist du | so alt wie ich.
älter als ich.
jünger als ich.

S1: Und wie groß bist du?	**S2:** Ich bin …

S1: Dann bist du | so groß wie ich.
größer als ich.
kleiner als ich.

Adjectives that end in **-er** or **-el** drop the **e** in the comparative.

teuer – **teurer**　　　　　　　　dunkel – **dunkler**

Ein gutes Hotel ist **komfortabler als**　　*A good hotel is **more comfortable***
　eine Jugendherberge.　　　　　　*　**than** a youth hostel.*

As in English, a few adjectives and adverbs have irregular comparative forms.

gut – **besser**　　　　　　hoch° – **höher**　　　　　　　*high*
viel – **mehr**　　　　　　gern – **lieber**

Ich übernachte **lieber** in Jugendherbergen　*I would **rather** stay in youth hostels*
　als in Hotels.　　　　　　　　　　　*　**than** in hotels.*
In Österreich sind die Berge **höher als**　*In Austria the mountains are **higher than***
　in Deutschland.　　　　　　　　　　　*　in Germany.*

> Remember how heights are read: **1,68 = eins achtundsechzig (ein Meter und achtundsechzig Zentimeter).** Note that a comma is used where English would use a decimal point.

5-17 Komparativformen in Schildern und Sprüchen. Identify the adjectives shown in the comparative form in the images below and provide your best English translation. Which adjective is not shown as a comparative?

Mehr Service.
Mehr Vorteile.
Mehr Bonus.

* **Bis zu 5% Bonus bei jedem Einkauf**

* **Exklusive Specials und Preisvorteile**

ich bekomme immer alles was ich will, früher oder später :D

5-18 Was ist höher, größer, besser? Take turns responding to the questions below. Do you and your partner have the same opinions in the second set?

> S1: Welcher Berg ist höher, der Matterhorn oder die Zugspitze?
> S2: Der Matterhorn ist höher als die Zugspitze.

1. Welche Berge sind höher, die Smokies oder die Rockies?
2. Wer verdient mehr, ein Rockstar oder ein Bundespräsident?
3. Wo ist das Wetter schöner, in England oder in Italien?

4. Wer spielt besser, die Phillies oder die Cubs?
5. Wer spielt besser Tennis, Serena Williams oder Venus Williams?
6. Wo machst du lieber Urlaub, in Europa oder Amerika?

The **Matterhorn** (Switzerland) is 14,692 feet: the **Zugspitze** (Germany) is 9,718 feet.

5-19 Vergleiche. Make comparisons using the given adjectives. In the second set, share your opinions with a partner. Be sure to alternate roles with your partner.

> ▶ S1: Leipzig / New York / klein   S2: Leipzig ist kleiner als New York.

1. Madrid / Hamburg / warm
2. ein Becher Joghurt / eine Flasche Sekt / billig
3. ein Jaguar / eine Maus / schnell
4. ein Flug in der ersten Klasse / ein Flug in Economy / teuer
5. zehn Euro / zehn Dollar / viel

6. deutsches Bier / italienisches Bier / gut
7. Baseball / Basketball / interessant
8. in den Bergen leben / an der Küste leben / schön
9. campen / im Hotel übernachten / gemütlich°   *cozy*
10. der Audi A3 / der Volkswagen Tiguan / cool

The superlative

You can indicate the greatest level of a quality or a characteristic in relation to others by using the superlative forms of adjectives and adverbs. Unless the superlative precedes a noun (see below), you form it by using the pattern **am _____sten** (e.g., **am** billig**sten**).

Ein Flugticket ist billig, ein Bahnticket ist billiger, aber ein Fernbusticket ist **am billigsten.**	*An airline ticket is cheap, a train ticket is cheaper, but a long-distance bus ticket is **the cheapest.***

If the adjective or adverb ends in **-d, -t,** an **s**-sound, or a vowel, you add an **e** before the **st** (e.g., **am leichtesten, am heißesten, am neuesten**). In contrast to English, German uses the pattern **am _____(e)sten** with all adverbs and adjectives, regardless of their length (e.g., **am interessantesten**).

Evas Referat war interessant, Davids Referat war noch interessanter, aber Lauras Referat war **am interessantesten.**	*Eva's report was interesting, David's report was even more interesting, but Laura's report was **the most interesting**.*

Ach so!
German uses the ending **-(e)st** to form the superlative of all adjectives and adverbs, no matter how long the word is!

Most one-syllable adjectives or adverbs with the stem vowels **a, o,** or **u** are umlauted in the superlative, just as they are in the comparative (e.g., **am k**ä**ltesten, am w**ä**rmsten, am j**ü**ngsten**).

Im Juli und im August ist es hier **am wärmsten.**

*In July and in August it's **warmest** here.*

A few adjectives and adverbs have irregular superlative forms.

Irregular superlative forms		
gut	besser	**am besten**
viel	mehr	**am meisten**
groß	größer	**am größten**
gern	lieber	**am liebsten**
hoch	höher	**am höchsten**
nah	näher	**am nächsten**

5-20 Ein paar persönliche Fragen. Using the superlative forms of the words provided, ask each other the following questions. Keep track of the two most interesting answers so you can share these with another pair of students.

1. Was für Musik findest du am _____? (schön)
2. Welche Sprache sprichst du am _____? (gut)
3. Welche Sprache sprichst du am _____? (gern)
4. Welches Fach findest du am _____? (interessant)
5. Für welches Fach musst du am _____ lernen? (viel)
6. Was machst du am _____ im Urlaub? (gern)
7. Was für einen Wagen findest du am _____? (cool)
8. Was für Filme findest du am _____? (interessant)

Was Österreicher in ihrem Urlaub am liebsten tun

Sprachnotiz Adjectives in the comparative and superlative before a noun

When adjectives in the comparative or superlative precede a noun, they require an adjective ending.

Laura hat eine schöner**e** Wohnung als ich, aber ich habe das cooler**e** Auto!
Ich habe die best**en** Eltern in der Welt!

Laura has a nicer apartment than I do, but I have the cooler car!
I have the best parents in the world!

5.6 Kultur 2

Reisezeit

After World War II, **Südtirol** became an autonomous Italian province with three official languages. Of a population of 511,000, 62% speak German, 23% speak Italian, and 4% speak Ladin, a Rhaeto-Romance dialect much like the one spoken in Switzerland.

5.7 Compare vacationing choices of Germans

For many Germans, **Ferienzeit** means it's **Reisezeit**, because Germans are world travelers. Most travel internationally rather than within Germany. In their travels, they frequently choose countries that offer sunshine and warmth—something often hard to find during the long winter months in central and northern Europe. High on this list are **Spanien** and **die Türkei**, but also **die USA**, with sunny Florida and California among the top states visited by Germans.

Italien is among the most popular destinations for German travelers, not only because of the warm temperatures, ancient and modern cultures, and delicious food, but also because it is relatively close to Germany. The drive from **Frankfurt** to **Mailand** *(Milan)* takes a mere seven hours. The country even boasts a German-speaking region: the northern Italian province of **Südtirol** (**Alto Adige** in Italian), located in the **Alpen.**

With its spectacular mountains and its valleys of orchards and vineyards, **Südtirol** is a mecca for tourists. In fact, **Tourismus** employs over half of the work force. Of the 6.5 million tourists who visit annually, about half come from Germany.

Vacationing in Germany

About one in every four Germans opts to vacation *within* Germany rather than travel abroad. The most popular **Reiseziel** *(travel destination)* in Germany—both for Germans and for international tourists visiting Germany—is **Bayern** *(Bavaria).*

München, the capital of **Bayern,** is one of Germany's major cultural centers. It boasts over 60 theaters and six orchestras. The most famous of its many art museums include the **Alte Pinakothek,** the **Neue Pinakothek,** and the **Pinakothek der Moderne,** where you can view great artists' works from Albrecht Dürer to Andy

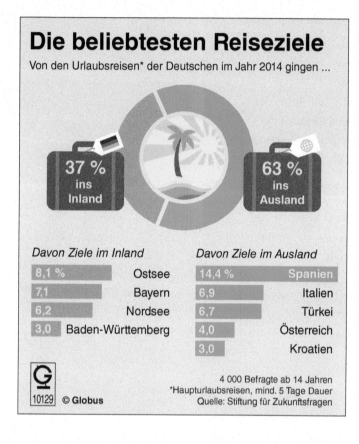

Die beliebtesten Reiseziele

Von den Urlaubsreisen* der Deutschen im Jahr 2014 gingen ...

37 % ins Inland

63 % ins Ausland

Davon Ziele im Inland		Davon Ziele im Ausland	
8,1 %	Ostsee	14,4 %	Spanien
7,1	Bayern	6,9	Italien
6,2	Nordsee	6,7	Türkei
3,0	Baden-Württemberg	4,0	Österreich
		3,0	Kroatien

4 000 Befragte ab 14 Jahren
*Haupturlaubsreisen, mind. 5 Tage Dauer
Quelle: Stiftung für Zukunftsfragen

10129 © **Globus**

Weinberge in Südtirol

Surfen am Eisbach

Warhol. **München** has the largest technical museum in the world, the **Deutsches Museum,** which is so large that viewing all the exhibits requires a ten-mile walk.

The **Englischer Garten,** an enormous park in the heart of the city, is a favorite playground for tourists as well as students of the adjacent **Ludwig-Maximilians-Universität.** Visitors spend their time strolling, cycling, sunbathing, swimming or even surfing in the chilly waters of the **Eisbach,** in water that flows from the glaciers in the Alps south of the city.

The end of September marks the beginning of **München**'s 16-day **Oktoberfest,** the world's largest **Volksfest,** first held in 1810 to celebrate the wedding of King Ludwig I von Bayern and his bride Therese von Sachsen-Hildburghausen. Each year it attracts about six million visitors, who, aside from consuming local **Bier,** also enjoy carnival rides, parades, and performances.

Das Oktoberfest in München

5-21 Eine Umfrage. Now that you've learned about where Germans like to vacation, find out about your classmates' preferences. Fill in the questionnaire with the information you collect. Then report your results to the class.

| As a high-tech center, **München** is also the home of **BMW (Bayerische Motorenwerke).** At BMW World, visitors can admire the latest cars and motorcycles and take a tour of the nearby BMW factory. |

S1: Wann machst du am liebsten Ferien?   **S2:** Ich mache am liebsten im Winter Ferien.

Wo machst du am liebsten Ferien?   Ich mache am liebsten in Colorado Ferien.

Warum bist du so gern dort?   Weil ich gern Ski laufe.

PERSON	WANN?	WO?	WARUM?
Lisa	im Winter	in Colorado	Weil sie gern Ski läuft.

5.7 Kommunikation und Formen 2

Word order

5.8 Use complex sentence structure

Object clauses introduced by *dass*

Sometimes the object of a verb is not a noun or a pronoun, but a clause. When you introduce an object clause with the conjunction **dass** *(that),* the clause becomes a dependent clause, so the conjugated verb moves to the end of the clause. Separable-prefix verbs (like **zurückkommen** below) come back together at the end.

Like **weil** and **wenn,** this new conjunction **dass** will always send the verb to the end!

Verb	*dass*-clause (ends with conjugated verb)	
Ich hoffe°,	**dass** ihr immer schönes Wetter **habt.**	*hope*
Ich hoffe,	**dass** ihr dort viel wandern **könnt.**	
Ich hoffe,	**dass** ihr total fit **zurückkommt.**	

Remember that **doch** and **mal** are often used when giving advice.

Danke, dass du hier nicht rauchst.

Achtung!
You know **die Karte** to mean *map* but it can also mean *ticket.*

5-22 Meine überkritischen Eltern. Using clauses with **dass,** talk about your parents' criticisms. Your partner responds with advice.

▶ Ich kann nicht gut kochen.   suchen / doch mal ein paar Kochtipps im Internet.

S1: Meine Eltern denken, dass ich nicht gut kochen kann.   **S2:** Dann such doch mal ein paar Kochtipps im Internet.

1. Ich schlafe nicht genug.   gehen / doch mal früher ins Bett
2. Ich bin zu nervös.   trinken / doch weniger Kaffee
3. Meine Noten sind schlecht.   sitzen / doch mal länger in der Bibliothek
4. Ich sitze zu viel am Computer.   gehen / doch mal ins Fitnesscenter

Information questions as object clauses

You can introduce information questions with phrases like **Weißt du, …** or **Entschuldigung, wissen Sie, …** The information questions then become object clauses. These object clauses are dependent clauses, so the conjugated verb moves to the end of the clause. Separable-prefix verbs (like **anfangen**) come back together at the end.

Information question	Introductory phrase + object clause	
Wie viel Uhr **ist** es?	Weißt du,	wie viel Uhr es **ist?**
Wann **fängt** das Konzert **an?**	Weißt du,	wann das Konzert **anfängt?**
Wo **kann** man Karten bekommen?	Weißt du,	wo man Karten bekommen **kann?**

5-23 Ratschläge geben. Tell your classmates about something you do that annoys your family or friends. See if your classmates can give you some good advice on how to change.

S1: Meine Eltern sagen, dass ich zu viel fernsehe.   **S2:** Dann lies doch mal ein gutes Buch.

S3: Dann mach doch ein bisschen mehr Sport.

S4: Mein Mitbewohner sagt, dass ich …   **S5:** …

- spiele zu oft Videospiele
- putze das Badezimmer nicht
- trinke am Wochenende zu viel Bier
- räume mein Zimmer nicht auf
- esse zu oft Junkfood
- …

5-24 Höfliche Fragen. You are a stranger in town. Politely ask for directions and information.

▶ Wie komme ich zum Fußballstadion?   nehmen / am besten ein Taxi

S1: Entschuldigung, wissen Sie, wie ich zum Fußballstadion komme?   **S2:** Nehmen Sie am besten ein Taxi.

1. Wo kann man hier billig übernachten?   gehen / am besten in die Jugendherberge
2. Wie komme ich zur Jugendherberge?   nehmen / am besten die S-Bahn
3. Wo kann man hier gut und billig essen?   gehen / am besten ins Ristorante Napoli
4. Wann fängt das Fußballspiel an?   fragen / am besten den Kellner°
5. Wie komme ich zum Bahnhof?   nehmen / am besten die Buslinie 10

server

Yes/no questions as object clauses

You can also introduce a yes/no question with phrases like **Weißt du, …** or **Könnten Sie mir bitte sagen, …** When a yes/no question is the object of an introductory phrase, it begins with the conjunction **ob** *(whether)*, and you must put the conjugated verb at the end of the clause.

Yes/no question	Introductory phrase + object clause	
Ist Claudia zu Hause?	Weißt du,	**ob** Claudia zu Hause **ist?**
Hat sie heute Abend etwas **vor?**	Weißt du,	**ob** sie heute Abend etwas **vorhat?**
Möchte sie mit uns ausgehen?	Weißt du,	**ob** sie mit uns ausgehen **möchte?**

 5-25 Höfliche Fragen in München.

▶ Fährt dieser Bus zum Bahnhof?

Nein, er fährt zum …

S1: Wissen Sie, ob dieser Bus zum Bahnhof fährt?

S2: Nein, er fährt zum Englischen Garten.

> The **Englischer Garten** in Munich was designed by an Englishman, Sir Benjamin Rumford, and officially opened in 1789.

1. Fährt dieser Bus zum Flughafen?

Nein, er fährt zum …

2. Ist das die Alte Pinakothek?

Nein, das ist …

3. Beginnt das Konzert um 20 Uhr?

Nein, ich glaube, es beginnt …

4. Ist das das Deutsche Museum?

Nein, das ist …

5. Fährt dieser Zug nach Hamburg?

Nein, das ist der Intercity …

The verb *wissen*

5.9 Talk about what and whom you know

The present tense of **wissen** (*to know*) is irregular in the singular.

Singular		Plural	
ich	**weiß**	wir	wissen
du	**weißt**	ihr	wisst
er/es/sie	**weiß**	sie	wissen
	Sie wissen		

The meaning difference between **wissen** and **kennen** is mirrored in many other languages, such as French (*savoir* and *connaître*) and Spanish (*saber* and *conocer*). Do you know another language that differentiates between two forms of *to know?*

As you have already seen, the object of the verb **wissen** can be a dependent clause. It can also be a pronoun like **das, es, alles,** or **nichts.**

Weißt du, **ob wir morgen eine Klausur schreiben?**
*Do you know **whether we have a test tomorrow?***
Nein, **das** weiß ich nicht.
*No, I don't know **(that).***

5-26 Wer weiß das? Supply the appropriate forms of **wissen.**

1. KURT: _____ deine Eltern, dass du so schlechte Noten hast?
   GÜNTER: Meine Mutter _____ es, aber mein Vater _____ es noch nicht.

2. TOURISTIN: Entschuldigung, _____ Sie, wohin dieser Bus fährt?
   TOURIST: Nein, das _____ ich leider° auch nicht.

   unfortunately

3. BERND: _____ ihr, wo Peter ist?
   MARTIN: Nein, das _____ wir auch nicht.
   CLAUDIA: Frag doch Stephanie! Sie _____ es bestimmt°.

   definitely

4. FRAU KOHL: Warum _____ du denn nicht, wie man Sauerkraut kocht?
   HERR KOHL: Ich kann doch nicht alles _____.

Sprachnotiz   *Wissen* versus *kennen*

Whereas **wissen** means *to know something as a fact*, **kennen** means *to know* in the sense of *to be acquainted with someone* or *to be familiar with something*. **Kennen** is always followed by a direct object. It cannot be followed by an object clause.

Kennst du Günters neue Freundin?
*Do you **know** Günter's new girlfriend?*
Ja, ich **kenne** sie sehr gut.
*Yes, I **know** her very well.*
Weißt du, wie alt sie ist?
*Do you **know** how old she is?*
Nein, das **weiß** ich nicht.
*No, that I don't **know**.*

The simple past of *sein, haben,* and the modal verbs

5.10 Talk about events in the past

When writing or speaking about events that occurred in the past, speakers of German generally use the simple past tense with common verbs such as **sein, haben,** and the modal verbs (**dürfen, können, mögen, müssen, sollen, wollen**).

Warum **warst** du gestern Abend nicht auf Lisas Party?
*Why **weren't** you at Lisa's party last night?*
Ich **hatte** keine Zeit. Ich **musste** für eine Klausur lernen.
*I **had** no time. I **had to** study for a test.*

The simple past of *sein*

The simple past stem of **sein** is **war.** Note that there are no personal endings in the 1st and 3rd person singular.

Singular		Plural	
ich	war	wir	waren
du	warst	ihr	wart
er/es/sie	war	sie	waren
	Sie waren		

5-27 Kleine Gespräche. Use the simple past of **sein** in the following mini-conversations. **S2** answers with the appropriate phrase from the box below.

▶   Wo _____ ihr gestern Abend?   im Kino

_____ der Film gut?   Nein, _____ viel zu sentimental.

S1: Wo wart ihr gestern Abend?   **S2:** Wir waren im Kino.
S1: War der Film gut?   **S2:** Nein, er war viel zu sentimental.

1. Wo _____ ihr letztes
   Wochenende?

   _____ das Wasser warm?   Nein, _____ noch ziemlich kalt.

2. Wo _____ Sie letzten Sommer?

   _____ es heiß?   Ja, _____ sehr heiß.

3. Wo _____ du am
   Sonntagnachmittag?

   _____ es interessant?   Ja, _____ sehr interessant.

4. Wo _____ ihr am
   Samstagnachmittag?

   _____ das Bier gut?   Ja, _____ sehr gut.

5. Wo _____ du am
   Sonntagabend?

   _____ der Solist gut?   Ja, _____ ganz fabelhaft.

im Biergarten	im Konzert	im Deutschen Museum
am Strand	in Italien	

The simple past of *haben*

The simple past stem of **haben** is **hatt-**.

> You know these verb endings already: They are the same as for the verb **möchten!**

Singular		Plural	
ich	hatte	wir	hatten
du	hattest	ihr	hattet
er/es/sie	hatte	sie	hatten
	Sie hatten		

5-28 Warum denn? Find sensible answers to each question from the responses at the right. Be sure to switch roles after each question.

S1: Warum …

- warst du im Deutschunterricht so müde?
- warst du letzten Sommer nicht in Europa?
- hattest du keine Zeit zum Frühstücken?
- warst du gestern Abend nicht im Kino?

S2: Ich …

- hatte einen Sommerjob.
- war bis Mitternacht in der Bibliothek.
- hatte keine Lust auf Horrorfilme.
- hatte um 8 Uhr eine Vorlesung.
- hatte kein Geld.

S1: Warum …

- wart ihr mit dem Deutschklub nicht im Theater?
- wart ihr heute nicht in der Mensa?
- wart ihr so lange in der Bibliothek?
- wart ihr am Wochenende nicht zu Hause?

S2: Wir …

- hatten heute eine Klausur.
- waren in New York.
- waren bei McDonald's.
- hatten keine Lust.
- waren im Schwimmbad.

The simple past of modal verbs

You form the simple past of modal verbs by adding the past tense marker **-t-** to the verb stem and then adding the personal endings. When a modal has an umlaut in the infinitive form, you drop the umlaut in the simple past. Note that the **g** of **mögen** becomes **ch**.

> **Achtung!**
> Modal verbs have no umlauts in the past tense!

dürfen	können	mögen	müssen	sollen	wollen
ich d**u**r**fte**	ich k**onnte**	ich m**ochte**	ich m**usste**	ich s**ollte**	ich w**ollte**

> **Good news!** The endings for modal verbs in the simple past tense are the same as those for the simple past tense of **haben.**

In the simple past, all modals follow the pattern shown in the table below.

Singular		Plural	
ich	konnt**e**	wir	konnt**en**
du	konnt**est**	ihr	konnt**et**
er/es/sie	konnt**e**	sie	konnt**en**
	Sie konnt**en**		

5-29 **Meine Reise nach München.** Have you seen Munich yet? Do you know anyone who has been to Bavaria? Practice modal verbs in the past tense to talk about a trip, real or imagined.

1. Ich _____ schon immer nach Deutschland reisen. (wollen)
2. Ich _____ zuerst viel Geld sparen°. (müssen)   *to save*
3. Zum Glück _____ ich direkt nach München fliegen. (können)
4. Marienplatz _____ ich sehr – das Glockenspiel war toll! (mögen)
5. Ich _____ im Eisbach surfen, aber ich _____ nicht.
   Das Wasser war einfach zu kalt! (wollen, können)
6. Ich _____ Weißwürste sehr und das Bier war auch ganz
   toll. (mögen)

Das Glockenspiel in München

> The **Marienplatz** is Munich's central square that features the famous **Glockenspiel** in the tower of the New City Hall. **Weißwürste** are a Bavarian specialty made from veal and spices.

5-30 **Freizeit – Ferienzeit.** Now it's your turn to tell a real travel story from the last few years. Use the simple format of 5-29 above as a guide, and tell a partner about your own trip to a favorite destination.

5-31 **Weißt du das noch?** Ask each other about childhood memories and make note of your partner's responses. Then report your findings to the class. You will find vocabulary to describe **Jobs und Berufe** and **Essen und Trinken** in the *Anhang* on pages A-4 and A-7.

S1:

1. Was wolltest du als Kind werden?
2. Was durftest du als Kind nicht?
3. Was konntest du als Kind besser als andere Kinder?
4. Was mochtest du als Kind nicht essen?
5. Musstest du das dann trotzdem° essen?

S2:

Ich wollte … werden.
Ich durfte nicht …
Ich konnte besser …

Ich mochte kein__ …

Ja, das musste ich. / Nein, das musste ich nicht.

anyway

5.8 Video-Treff

Ferienzeit

5.11 Understand authentic video of German speakers talking about their vacations.

Christoph and Christina Brieger, Stefan Meister, André, and Stefan Kuhlmann talk about their vacation preferences. Be sure to complete the **Was ist das auf Englisch?** exercise before watching the video.

5-32 **Was ist das auf Englisch?**

1. Wir machen **zweimal** im Jahr Urlaub   a. Mediterranean Sea
2. Wir fahren **ans Meer** und sind viel am Strand. b. know
3. Englisch ist die Fremdsprache, die ich am besten c. in the world
   beherrsche.
4. Man kann im **Mittelmeer** schwimmen.   d. rental car
5. Das war unser **Mietwagen:** der Ford Ka.   e. fell in love
6. Ich **habe mich** in die Frau und in das Land   f. to the ocean
   verliebt.
7. Australien ist das schönste Land **der Welt.**   g. twice

5-33 Richtig oder falsch? Decide whether the following statements about the Briegers and Stefan Meister are **richtig** or **falsch**. If the statement is **falsch**, provide a correct version.

	RICHTIG	FALSCH
1. Christoph und Christina machen im Sommer und im Winter Urlaub.	☐	☐
2. Im Sommer fahren sie am liebsten nach Holland.	☐	☐
3. Im Winter fahren sie gern in den schweizerischen Bergen Ski.	☐	☐
4. Im Urlaub geht Christina gern tauchen.	☐	☐
5. Stefan Meister fährt am liebsten nach Amerika, Neuseeland und Australien, weil es für ihn dort sehr billig ist.	☐	☐
6. Stefan sagt, er kann gut Spanisch.	☐	☐
7. Stefan macht Urlaub, wenn es warm ist und wenn man nur ein T-Shirt tragen kann.	☐	☐
8. Stefan zeigt Fotos vom Wassersport in Australien.	☐	☐

5-34 Wer ist das? The following statements fit what André or Stefan Kuhlmann said about vacation preferences. Identify the person who best matches each statement.

	André	**Stefan Kuhlmann**
1. Er macht gern Ferien, wenn es sehr warm ist.	☐	☐
2. Er glaubt, „Oz" ist das schönste Land der Welt.	☐	☐
3. Er findet die spanische Kultur sehr schön.	☐	☐
4. Er macht nicht sehr oft Urlaub.	☐	☐
5. Er war mit seiner Freundin letztes Jahr in Andalusia.	☐	☐
6. Er sagt, man kann in der Sierra Nevada im Sommer Ski laufen.	☐	☐
7. In Australien hatte er eine Freundin.	☐	☐

))) 5.9 Wortschatz 2

Wichtige Vokabeln

5.12 Learn vocabulary to talk about travel and useful everyday objects

Nomen

die Hauptstadt, ¨e	capital city
die Karte, -n	ticket; map
der Pass, ¨e	passport
das Reisebüro, -s	travel agency
der Studentenausweis, -e	student ID
die Welt, -en	world
die Kunst, ¨e	art
der Roman, -e	novel
der Arzt, ¨e die Ärztin, -nen }	physician; doctor
der Chef, -s die Chefin, -nen }	boss
die Jugend (sing)	youth
der Mensch, -en	human being; person; (pl) people
der Bart, ¨e	beard
der Schnurrbart, ¨e	mustache
die Frisur, -en	hair style; hairdo
der Haarschnitt, -e	haircut
die Brille, -n	(eye)glasses
die Kontaktlinse, -n	contact lens

> **Achtung!**
> **Brille** is used in the plural only when it refers to more than one pair of glasses.

das Armband, ¨er	bracelet
die Halskette, -n	necklace
der Nasenstecker, -	nose stud
der Ohrring, -e	earring
die Tätowierung, -en	tatoo
die Klausur, -en	test
das Quiz, -	quiz
die Ecke, -n	corner
die Pflanze, -n	plant
die Zimmerpflanze, -n	house plant

---

geschmacklos: Many words form their opposites in meaning by adding the suffix **-voll** or **-los.** What are the English equivalents of the following sets of opposites: **liebevoll ≠ lieblos; humorvoll ≠ humorlos; taktvoll ≠ taktlos; respektvoll ≠ respektlos?**

Verben

an·schauen	to look at
ein·kaufen	to shop
hoffen	to hope
lieben	to love

Andere Wörter

bestimmt	definite(ly); for sure
hoch	high
leider	unfortunately
natürlich	of course
trotzdem	anyway; nevertheless

Ausdrücke

als Kind	as a child
am Strand	at the beach
um die Ecke	around the corner
ziemlich cool	kind of cool (colloquial)

Das Gegenteil

der Junge, -n ≠ das Mädchen, -	boy ≠ girl
altmodisch ≠ modern	old-fashioned ≠ modern
arm ≠ reich	poor ≠ rich
geschmackvoll ≠ geschmacklos	tasteful ≠ tasteless
etwas ≠ nichts	something ≠ nothing
mit ≠ ohne	with ≠ without

Leicht zu verstehen

das Argument, -e	die Literatur, -en
die ATM-Karte, -n	die Maschine, -n
die Baseballkappe, -n	das Museum, Museen
das Experiment, -e	der Ring, -e
der Kalender, -	der Tourist, -en
das Kompliment, -e	die Touristin, -nen
die Kreditkarte, -n	fantastisch
der Kurs, -e	sentimental

> **Museum, Museen:** Remember that nouns that end in **-um** are almost always neuter, and many form the plural this way. What are the singular forms for **Alben, Zentren, Daten?**

Das Mercedes-Benz Museum in Stuttgart

Wörter im Kontext

5-35 Was passt zusammen?

1. Wenn man schöne tolle Autos anschauen möchte,
2. Wenn man sehr teure Ohrringe kaufen will,
3. Wenn man eine ATM-Karte braucht,
4. Wenn man krank ist,
5. Wenn man eine Reise planen will,

6. Wenn man einen guten Roman finden will,
7. Wenn man billig übernachten will,
8. Wenn man eine Brille oder Kontaktlinsen braucht,

a. geht man zum Reisebüro.
b. geht man in die Jugendherberge.
c. geht man zum Optiker.
d. geht man zum Juwelier.
e. geht man ins Mercedes-Benz Museum.
f. geht man zum Arzt.
g. geht man zur Bank.
h. geht man in die Bibliothek.

5-36 Was passt zusammen?

1. Wenn ich kein Geld habe,
2. Wenn ich meinen Chef nicht mag,
3. Wenn ich eine Klausur habe,
4. Wenn ich in München das Glockenspiel sehen will,
5. Wenn ich eine Klausur nicht schreiben kann,
6. Wenn ich für eine Konzertkarte weniger bezahlen will,

a. muss ich leider einen neuen Job finden.
b. kann ich nicht einkaufen gehen.
c. brauche ich einen Studentenausweis.
d. muss ich mit meinem Professor sprechen.
e. muss ich viel lernen.
f. gehe ich zum Marienplatz.

5-37 Was passt zusammen? Match appropriately in each set.

1. die ATM-Karte	a. die Galerie	4. der Pass	d. die Weltreise
2. der Kalender	b. das Geld	5. der Kurs	e. der Roman
3. die Kunst	c. das Jahr	6. die Literatur	f. die Klausur

5-38 Kleine Gespräche.

Brille / als Kind / Museum / Strand / Touristen / Ziemlich

1. STEFAN: Wo warst du oft im Sommer _____ _____?
   HORST: Am _____ in Florida.
2. ANNA: Wie findest du meine neue _____?
   JULIA: _____ cool!
3. MARIA: Was machen diese _____ hier in Leipzig?
   LUKAS: Sie gehen oft ins _____.

Wörter unter der Lupe

Predicting gender

The gender of many German nouns is indicated by their suffixes. Here are some examples.

- Nouns with the suffixes **-or** and **-ent** are masculine.

  der Profess**or**   **der** Stud**ent**

- Nouns with the suffix **-er** that are derived from verbs are always masculine. These nouns can refer to people as well as things.

  arbeiten   **der** Arbeit**er**   fernsehen   **der** Fernseh**er**

  Suffix -er: English also derives many so-called agent nouns from verbs. As in German, they do not always refer to people: *to work/worker; to serve/server; to wash/ washer; to dry/dryer.*

- Nouns with the suffix **-in** added to a masculine noun are feminine.

  die Professor**in**   **die** Arbeiter**in**

- Nouns with the suffix **-ur** are almost always feminine.

  die Temperat**ur**   **die** Klaus**ur**

  Note: **das Abitur** is an exception.

- Nouns with the suffix **-ment** are almost always neuter.

  das Instru**ment**   **das** Experi**ment**   **das** Argu**ment**

- Nouns with the suffix **-(i)um** are almost always neuter.

  das For**um**   **das** Gymnas**ium**

- Nouns with the diminutive suffixes **-chen** and **-lein** are always neuter. These two suffixes (compare English *-kin* in mani*kin* and lamb*kin,* or *-let* in star*let*, book*let*, and pig*let*) can be affixed to virtually every German noun to express smallness. This also explains why both **Mädchen** *(girl)* and **Fräulein** *(Miss; young lady)* are neuter. The vowels **a, o, u,** and the diphthong **au** are umlauted when a diminutive suffix is added to the noun. Remember that with the diphthong **au** it is the **a** that is umlauted.

die Stadt	**das** Städt**chen**	**der** Bruder	**das** Brüder**lein**
die Tochter	**das** Töchter**lein**	**das** Haus	**das** Häus**chen**

5-39 *Der, das* oder *die*? Say the following nouns with their definite articles. If a noun has a corresponding feminine form, give that form and the corresponding article as well.

1. Präsident	8. Assistent	15. Dokument	22. Medium
2. Element	9. Fahrer	16. Agent	23. Lautsprecher
3. Mäuschen	10. Kompliment	17. Autor	24. Literatur
4. Motor	11. Fischlein	18. Individuum	
5. Verkäufer	12. Mentor	19. Projektor	
6. Aquarium	13. Kätzchen	20. Patient	
7. Frisur	14. Besucher	21. Ornament	

5.10 Alles zusammen

Ein Besuch in Leipzig

In *5.2 Kultur 1* you planned your travel to Leipzig. Now you can plan what to do while you're there! You'll hear an introduction to the city and get some ideas for what to see. Then, you'll plan out a visit with a partner and share this with others in your class.

Schritt 1: Zum Hören und Sehen

))) **5-40** Leipzig für Touristen. Lernen Sie die schöne Stadt Leipzig durch die Präsentation kennen. Welche Schlüsselwörter aus der Liste hören Sie?

1. Das ist Leipzig!	2. Bach in Leipzig	3. Der Leipziger Zoo	4. Das „Völki"	5. Das Kaffeemuseum
☐ Hallo	☐ Denkmal	☐ Attraktion	☐ Prinz	☐ Maschinen
☐ Willkommen	☐ Komponisten	☐ Indien	☐ Truppen	☐ Tee
☐ Reisetipps	☐ Tradition	☐ Pflanzen	☐ Museum	☐ Kuchen

1. Das ist Leipzig!

3. Der Leipziger Zoo

2. Bach in Leipzig

4. Das Völkerschlachtdenkmal

5. Das Kaffeemuseum

Schritt 2: Zum Sprechen

5-41 Eine Touristenattraktion in Leipzig. Jetzt wissen Sie vom Hörtext, was man in Leipzig sehen kann! Welche von diesen Attraktionen möchten Sie und Ihre Partnerin oder Ihr Partner nächsten Samstag zusammen in Leipzig besuchen? Finden Sie folgende Infos zu dieser Attraktion im Internet:

Attraktion: _____

Öffnungszeiten am Samstag: _____

Kosten (Tickets usw.): _____

Was kann man dort sehen? _____

_____

Was möchten Sie dort machen? _____

_____

> **Ach so!**
> Reduced prices for students are often listed as **Studentenermäßigung** or just **ermäßigt**.

Schritt 3: Zum Präsentieren

5-42 Unser Besuch in Leipzig. Präsentieren Sie kurz Ihre Leipziger Attraktion! Zeigen Sie auch die Webseite oder ein paar schöne Fotos.

Hier sind ein paar nützliche Sätze:

Wir möchten … besuchen. Das finden wir am interessantesten, weil …
Wir wollen … Stunden dort bleiben. Es kostet …
Hier sieht man / Auf dem Foto sieht man …
Wenn wir dort sind, möchten wir … und …

Kapitel 6
Ein Blick zurück

1924: Einwandererkinder auf Ellis Island

Learning Objectives

6.1 Understand the history of German immigration to North America

6.2 Learn vocabulary to talk about your heritage

6.3 Form the German *l* sound

6.4 Talk about events in the past

6.5 Present a profile of a recent immigrant to Germany

6.6 Talk more about events in the past

6.7 Rank people and things

6.8 State the date

6.9 Understand authentic video of German speakers talking about their first job

6.10 Learn vocabulary to talk about more everyday activities

6.1 Vorschau

Ein deutscher Auswanderer

Herr Keilhaus Pass

6-1 Wer war Hans Keilhau? Read over the information in Hans Keilhau's passport.

1. Herr Keilhau heißt mit Vornamen …
   - ☐ Johannes.
   - ☐ Schlosser.

2. Keilhau ist am … geboren.
   - ☐ 27. Juni 1930
   - ☐ 6. November 1902

3. Werdau (Sachsen) ist Keilhaus …
   - ☐ Geburtsort.
   - ☐ Wohnort.

4. Keilhaus Haar war …
   - ☐ blond.
   - ☐ dunkelbraun.

5. Keilhau hatte …
   - ☐ blaue Augen.
   - ☐ braune Augen.

6. Sein Gesicht war …
   - ☐ rund.
   - ☐ oval.

7. Herr Keilhau war …
   - ☐ ledig.
   - ☐ verheiratet.

8. Er hatte …
   - ☐ zwei Kinder.
   - ☐ keine Kinder.

Passports always indicate a person's **Geburtsort** (place of birth). In American passports, the **Wohnort** (place of residence) is written in by hand. Why do you think this is so?

In the U.S., a driver's license is the most typical form of ID in most places, yet this is not typical worldwide. In German-speaking countries, either the **Personalausweis** or the **Pass** is used when handling official transactions, such as opening a bank account or registering a new place of residence.

))) **Eine Einwanderin**

Hier erzählt Patricia Lanners-Kaminski ihre Familiengeschichte.

Danzig is the German word for Gdansk, a city in Poland that was part of the Third Reich until the end of World War II.

The U.S. is one of the few countries in the world that grants citizenship based solely on the fact that a child is born on American soil. While there are pathways to becoming a citizen in the German-speaking countries, the process can be a long and complicated one.

After World War II, West German citizenship was extended to ethnic Germans, many of whom lived in Eastern Bloc countries that didn't allow these groups to leave until restrictions were loosened in the late 1980s. Because Patricia Lanners-Kaminski's family had German heritage on her father's side, they were able to obtain a German passport quickly.

Patricia Lanners-Kaminski, 2018. Deutsche? Polin? Amerikanerin?

Meine Vorfahren kommen alle aus Osteuropa. Meine Großeltern mütterlicherseits sind aus Polen und der Ukraine – da gibt es ein bisschen Mischmasch. Meine Vorfahren väterlicherseits kommen aus Danzig.

Meine Oma mütterlicherseits ist 1978 alleine nach Amerika ausgewandert, nach Chicago. Mein Opa ist nicht mitgekommen, weil er damals krank war. Sie musste arbeiten und das Geld nach Polen schicken.

Meine Mutter war 23 und hat meine Oma dort besucht. Als meine Mutter in die USA gegangen ist, war sie schwanger mit mir. Ich bin da in Chicago geboren und habe deshalb den amerikanischen Pass bekommen.

Ich habe zwei Jahre in den USA gelebt. Mein Vater war in der polnischen Armee, das heißt, er konnte nicht in die USA kommen. Nach zwei Jahren sind meine Mutter und ich nach Polen zurückgezogen, zu meinem Vater. Dort haben meine Eltern ein Haus gekauft und wollten in Polen ihr Leben aufbauen.

Aber nach zwei Jahren haben sie 1989 dann entschieden, nach Deutschland auszuwandern. Ich war damals vier Jahre alt. Ich habe einen deutschen Pass bekommen, ging in Rheinland-Pfalz in die Schule, und studierte später auch in Rheinland-Pfalz an der Universität Trier.

))) **6-2 Richtig oder falsch?** You will hear some statements about Patricia Lanners-Kaminski's immigration story. Indicate whether the statements are **richtig** or **falsch**.

	RICHTIG	FALSCH
1.	☐	☐
2.	☐	☐
3.	☐	☐
4.	☐	☐

6-3 Meine Familiengeschichte. Draw a simple family tree with the names of your parents and grandparents on both sides. Include your **Urgroßeltern** (*great-grandparents*) if you want. Write names and where each person comes from.

6-4 Woher sind deine Vorfahren? Working with a partner, find out about each other's ancestors by asking the questions below. You can use any of the useful phrases provided in your responses!

1. Wo sind deine Eltern geboren?

   Meine Eltern sind gebürtige° Amerikaner / Europäer / Afrikaner / …   *by birth*

   Meine Mutter / Mein Vater kommt aus Südamerika / aus Europa / …

2. Woher kommen deine Großeltern mütterlicherseits? Und väterlicherseits?

   Da gibt es ein bisschen Mischmasch.

3. Woher waren deine Urgroßeltern mütterlicherseits? Und väterlicherseits?

   Mein Urgroßvater mütterlicherseits war aus Asien, aber meine Urgroßmutter mütterlicherseits war …

4. Wo bist du geboren? Und deine Geschwister?

   Ich bin in Asien (in Nordamerika / in Australien, …) geboren. Mein Bruder ist …

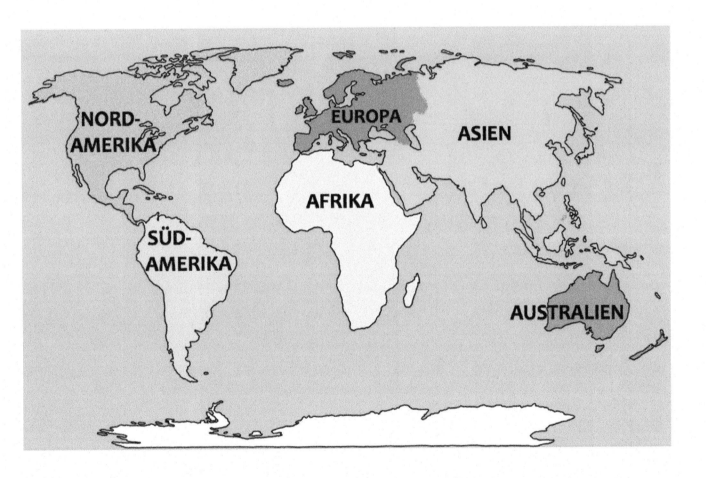

6.2 Kultur 1

German roots in North America

6.1 Understand the history of German immigration to North America

German-speaking immigrants in the New World

> **German-American Day** is celebrated on October 6 in many cities across the U.S. This date coincides with the landing of the Concordia in Pennsylvania.

1600s: 13 families from **Krefeld** in Northern Germany crossed the ocean on the Concordia (the "German Mayflower") at the invitation of William Penn, the Quaker founder of Pennsylvania. They sought freedom from religious prosecution and founded Germantown. Following them was a wave of German-speaking immigrants, including Amish, Mennonites, and others seeking new freedoms in North America. Today, hundreds of towns are named after the German, Swiss, or Austrian birthplaces of their founders. There are 26 Berlins, countless Frankforts, Bern(e)s, Hanovers, Hamburgs, and Viennas.

1700s: German-speaking immigrants soon left their mark on all areas of society. They brought German expertise with the printing press to the New World, and by the mid 1700s, most cities in the American colonies had at least one German newspaper. When the Declaration of Independence was signed on July 4, 1776, the German press broke the story first. Just two days later, on July 6, 1776, a German translation of this important document had already appeared on the streets of Philadelphia!

Eine Erklärung im Kongress 1776

Ein wichtiger Satz für Amerikaner

6-5 Ein wichtiges amerikanisches Dokument — auf Deutsch! Find this famous passage of the *Declaration of Independence* in the second German excerpt above: "We hold these Truths to be self-evident, that all men are created equal, that they are endowed by their Creator with certain unalienable Rights, that among these are Life, Liberty, and the Pursuit of Happiness." Hint: Look for **Wir** as the starting point!

1800s: European life in the 1800s was fraught with political turmoil, persecution, and economic hardship. Unemployment, land seizures, and the failed liberal revolution in Germany in 1848 drove many from the German-speaking regions to seek a better life in North America. This was helped by advances in technology, as the steamship had made crossing the Atlantic much safer and faster than before. In the 1800s, more than 5 million people left Germany to make a new life in North America. They came from what is now Germany, but also from eastern regions, such as Romania and present-day Poland.

Bedeutende Deutsch-Amerikaner im 19. Jahrhundert

- **Levi Strauss,** born Löb Strauß, left Bavaria in 1847 and eventually settled in California, where he and a partner patented and produced riveted blue jeans.

- **Margarethe Meyer-Schurz** founded the first Kindergarten in the United States (in Wisconsin) in 1854, modeled after early childhood education in her native Hamburg.

- **John Roebling,** born Johann August Röbling, a civil engineer who left Prussia in 1831, designed the world-famous Brooklyn Bridge, a wire-rope structure that spans the East River between Brooklyn and Manhattan.

> By 1889, immigration to America was at its peak, with over 1.4 million German-speaking immigrants becoming permanent residents in one decade alone. Soon, quotas would be established to limit migration from Europe.

1900s: The twentieth century saw far fewer immigrants from German-speaking countries. After World War I, quotas were established, and anti-German sentiment drove many Americans to underplay their German heritage. Many who immigrated in the 1930s fled Hitler's totalitarian and anti-Semitic regime. Their emigration was an immeasurable loss to Germany and Austria. From 1933 to 1938, approximately 130,000 German and Austrian Jews came to North America. After World War II, over 800,000 refugees from former German territories in Eastern Europe and other disillusioned Germans crossed the Atlantic.

Roeblings weltbekannte Brücke

2000s: Migration and the rich diversity it allows continue to shape the face of all countries in North America.
By 2015, 13.1 percent of the United States population was foreign-born, though Europe is no longer a prominent source of new inhabitants. And in Canada, the latest census (2011) revealed that every fifth resident of Canada was born abroad. As Canadian Prime Minister Justin Trudeau shared in a Tweet in January 2017: "Diversity is our strength."

6-6 Deutsch-Amerikaner. Wer hat welchen Beruf?

1. Albert Einstein
2. Arnold Schwarzenegger
3. Heidi Klum
4. Arnold Schoenberg
5. Thomas Mann
6. Marlene Dietrich
7. John Jacob Bausch und Henry Lomb
8. Wernher von Braun

a. Komponist
b. Raketeningenieur
c. Politiker
d. Fotomodell
e. Filmstar
f. Physiker
g. Autor
h. Optiker und Unternehmer

> According to the U.S. Census 2010, the cities with the highest numbers of German speakers are New York, Chicago, Los Angeles, and Washington, D.C.

> **Achtung!**
> A couple have more than one profession.

🔊 6.3 Wortschatz 1

Wichtige Vokabeln

6.2 Learn vocabulary to talk about your heritage

Nomen

der Geburtsort, -e	place of birth
der Wohnort, -e	place of residence
die Geschichte, -n	history; story
das Land, ¨er	country; state
der Pass, ¨e	passport
die Einwanderung	immigration
der Auswanderer, -	emigrant
die Auswanderin, -nen	
der Einwanderer, -	immigrant
die Einwanderin, -nen	
der Mensch, -en	person; human being
die Urgroßeltern *(pl)*	great-grandparents
die Urgroßmutter, ¨	great-grandmother
der Urgroßvater, ¨	great-grandfather
die Vorfahren *(pl)*	ancestors
gebürtige Amerikaner *(pl)*	native-born Americans
der Ingenieur, -e	engineer
die Ingenieurin, -nen	
der Politiker, -	politician
die Politikerin, -nen	
der Unternehmer, -	entrepreneur
die Unternehmerin, -nen	
das Leben	life
ein neues Leben	a new life
die Erklärung, -en	declaration; explanation
die Freiheit	freedom, liberty
das Recht, -e	right
die Unabhängigkeit	independence
die Unabhängig-keitserklärung	the Declaration of Independence

Der Körper

der Fuß, ¨e	foot
die Hand, ¨e	hand
der Arm, -e	arm
der Finger, -	finger
das Haar, -e	hair
das Gesicht, -er	face
das Auge, -n	eye
die Nase, -n	nose
der Mund, ¨er	mouth

Die Kontinente

Afrika	Africa
Asien	Asia
Australien	Australia
Europa	Europe
Nordamerika	North America
Südamerika	South America

Verben

aus·wandern	to emigrate; to leave a country
ein·wandern	to immigrate; to move to a country
erklären	to declare; to explain
erzählen	to tell
schicken	to send
ziehen	to move; to change residence
zurück·ziehen	to move back

> German speakers commonly say **alleine,** as Patricia did in her **Familiengeschichte.**

Andere Wörter

allein	alone
bedeutend	important, prominent
gleich	equal
schwanger	pregnant
wichtig	important
das heißt	that means; that is

Ausdrücke

Wo bist du geboren?	Where were you born?
Ich bin in Polen geboren.	I was born in Poland.
Meine Tante ist nach Chicago gezogen.	My aunt moved to Chicago.
ein (neues) Leben aufbauen	to build a (new) life

Das Gegenteil

abhängig ≠ unabhängig	dependent ≠ independent
väterlicherseits ≠ mütterlicherseits	paternal ≠ maternal

Leicht zu verstehen

der Emigrant, -en	**der Mischmasch**
die Emigrantin, -nen	**oval**
der Immigrant, -en	
die Immigrantin, -nen	

Wörter im Kontext

6-7 Meine Vorfahren.

ausgewandert / Vorfahren / väterlicherseits / gebürtige Amerikaner

Meine Familiengeschichte beginnt in Österreich. Meine _____
mütterlicherseits kommen aus Innsbruck. Sie sind um 1900 nach Amerika
_____. Meine Großeltern _____ waren auch aus
Österreich. Aber mein Vater, mein Bruder, meine Mutter, meine Schwester und ich
sind _____. Wir mussten Deutsch in der Schule lernen.

6-8 Was passt wo?

Urgroßeltern / Geburtsort / Wohnort / Emigrant / Emigrantin

1. Wenn ich in ein anderes Land auswandere, bin ich ein _____ oder eine
   _____.
2. Die Großeltern von meinen Eltern sind meine _____.
3. Wenn ich in Boston geboren bin, dann ist Boston mein _____.
4. Wenn ich in Hamburg lebe und wohne, dann ist diese Stadt mein _____.

6-9 Was ist das?

a. Das ist sein schwarzbraunes _____.

b. Das ist seine _____.

c. Das sind seine braunen _____.

d. Das ist sein _____.

e. Das ist sein ovales _____.

6-10 Was steht in dem Dokument vom 4. Juli 1776?

Unabhängigkeitserklärung / gleich / Freiheit / Menschen / entscheiden /
abhängig / unabhängig

1. Die amerikanische _____ ist ein wichtiges Dokument
   aus Philadelphia.
2. Nun sind die Amerikaner politisch nicht mehr von England
   _____. Sie sind _____!
3. Alle _____ haben im neuen Land bestimmte Rechte.
4. Alle haben das Recht auf _____, das heißt, jeder ist und lebt frei.
5. Das Recht auf Leben heißt, jeder darf über sein Leben _____.
6. Die Rechte von allen Menschen in Amerika sind _____.

6.4 Zur Aussprache
German *l*

6.3 Form the German *l* sound

In English the sound represented by the letter *l* varies according to the vowels and
consonants surrounding it. (Compare the *l* sound in *leaf* and *feel*.) In German the
sound represented by the letter **l** never varies and is very close to the *l* in English *leaf*.
Try to maintain the sound quality of the *l* in *leaf* throughout the exercise below.

))) 6-11 Hören Sie gut zu und wiederholen Sie!

Lilo lernt Latein°.

Latein ist manchmal langweilig.

Lilo lernt Philipp kennen.

Philipp hilft° Lilo Latein lernen.

Philipp bleibt lange bei Lilo.

Lilo lernt viel.

Lilo lernt Philipp lieben.

Latin

helps

> **Professionelle Nachhilfe
> für alle Klassen:**
> ✓ Englisch
> ✓ Latein
> ✓ Biologie
> und viele andere!
> Anmeldung: schulnachhilfe.de

6.5 Kommunikation und Formen 1

The present perfect tense

6.4 Talk about events in the past

To talk about past events in conversational situations, you use the perfect tense in German. In English we generally use the simple past for this purpose.

Was **hast** du gestern **gemacht?**	*What **did** you **do** yesterday?*
Ich **habe** mit Ali Tennis **gespielt.**	*I **played** tennis with Ali.*

The perfect tense consists of an auxiliary verb (usually **haben**) that takes personal endings and a past participle that remains unchanged.

Singular		Plural	
ich	habe gespielt	wir	haben gespielt
du	hast gespielt	ihr	habt gespielt
er/es/sie	hat gespielt	sie	haben gespielt
	Sie haben gespielt		

Depending on the context, the German perfect tense can correspond to any of the following English verb forms.

ich habe gespielt
I played
I have played
I have been playing
I was playing
I did play

The past participle of regular verbs

Most German verbs form the past participle by adding the prefix **ge-** and the ending **-t** or **-et** to the verb stem. The ending **-et** is used if the verb stem ends in **-d, -t,** or certain consonant combinations.

	Prefix	Verb stem	Ending	Past participle
lernen	ge	lern	t	= gelernt
arbeiten	ge	arbeit	et	= gearbeitet
baden	ge	bad	et	= gebadet
regnen	ge	regn	et	= geregnet

Past participles of verbs ending in **-ieren** do not have the prefix **ge-**.

	Prefix	Verb stem	Ending	Past Participle
reparieren	–	reparier	t	= repariert

The perfect tense is sometimes referred to as the present perfect tense or the conversational past.

The auxiliary verb is sometimes called the helping verb.

Most English verbs form the past participle in a similar way: by adding -ed to the verb stem: learned, worked, bathed, rained.

FAHRRAD-
PARKPLATZ
VON
6.00 - 22.00
GEÖFFNET

Position of auxiliary verb and past participle

The auxiliary verb takes the regular position of the verb and the past participle stands
at the end of the sentence.

Subject	Auxiliary verb	Rest of sentence	Past participle
Ich	**habe**	für das Quiz	**gelernt.**

The order of the subject and the auxiliary verb must change if you put something else
first to emphasize it, or if you ask a question:

Am Nachmittag **habe** ich **gearbeitet**.   *In the afternoon I **worked**.*

Was **hast** du gestern **gemacht**?   *What **did** you **do** yesterday?*

Hast du auch **gearbeitet**?   *Did you **work**, too?*

Nein, ich **habe** Klavier **geübt**.   *No, I **practiced** the piano.*

 6-11 Was haben Ali und Frank gestern gemacht?

S1: Was hat Ali gestern gemacht?   **S2:** Am Vormittag hat er Klavier geübt.
                                        Am Nachmittag hat er …

	Ali	**Frank**
am Vormittag		
am Nachmittag		
am Abend		

für ein Quiz gelernt	Fußball gespielt
Klavier geübt	seinen Koffer gepackt
sein Fahrrad repariert	im Garten gearbeitet

6-12 Was hast du gestern gemacht? Use a few of the following expressions to
tell each other some of the things you did yesterday.

Gestern habe ich …

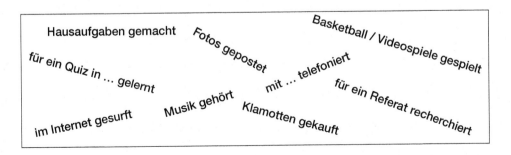

Hausaufgaben gemacht   Fotos gepostet   Basketball / Videospiele gespielt

für ein Quiz in … gelernt   mit … telefoniert

im Internet gesurft   Musik gehört   Klamotten gekauft   für ein Referat recherchiert

Position of auxiliary verb and past participle in a dependent clause

In a dependent clause, the auxiliary verb stands at the end of the clause, and the past participle precedes it.

Heute bin ich müde, **weil** ich gestern
gearbeitet habe.

I'm tired today, **because** *I* **worked**
yesterday.

Position of *nicht* in sentences in the perfect tense

> The rules you already learned about the position of **nicht** still apply.

In the present perfect tense, **nicht** is placed directly before the past participle, unless a particular word or expression is negated.

Warum **hast** du deine Hausaufgaben
nicht gemacht?

Why **didn't** *you* **do** *your homework?*

 6-13 Warum hast du das nicht gemacht?

deinen Koffer packen

mit Monika telefonieren

S1: Warum hast du deinen Koffer nicht gepackt?

S2: Weil ich mit Monika telefoniert habe.

> Since the majority of German verbs are regular, you can easily figure out the past participle forms of most verbs, even if they are unfamiliar to you.

1.

2.

3.

Tennis spielen	frühstücken	den Hund füttern
mit Freunden Karten spielen	für dein Referat recherchieren	Gitarre üben

Irregular verbs in the perfect tense

Irregular verbs are a small but frequently used group of verbs. The past participles of these verbs end in **-en.** The verb stem often undergoes a vowel change and sometimes consonant changes as well.

	Prefix	Verb stem	Ending	Past participle
finden	ge	f**u**nd	en	= gefunden
nehmen	ge	n**omm**	en	= genommen
schlafen	ge	schlaf	en	= geschlafen

Here are several verbs that are familiar to you, together with how they appear in the present perfect (past) tense. Additional past participle forms are listed in the *Anhang* on pp. A-17–A-19.

Infinitive	Auxiliary	Past participle
backen	ich **habe** …	**gebacken**
schlafen	ich **habe** …	**geschlafen**
waschen	ich **habe** …	**gewaschen**
essen	ich **habe** …	**gegessen**
lesen	ich **habe** …	**gelesen**
sehen	ich **habe** …	**gesehen**
finden	ich **habe** …	**gefunden**
singen	ich **habe** …	**gesungen**
trinken	ich **habe** …	**getrunken**
nehmen	ich **habe** …	**genommen**
sprechen	ich **habe** …	**gesprochen**
schreiben	ich **habe** …	**geschrieben**
sitzen	ich **habe** …	**gesessen**
stehen	ich **habe** …	**gestanden**

Lerntipp!
Get a head start memorizing past-tense verb forms by grouping the easiest set of irregular verbs together. This first group of verbs has a past-tense stem identical to the infinitive.

This second group of verbs requires more practice, but you will notice patterns. Try writing them out and underlining the stem change in another color.

6-14 Was haben Julia und Ayse gestern gemacht?

S1: Was hat Julia gestern gemacht?

S1: Und am Nachmittag?

S2: Am Vormittag hat sie ein Bad genommen.

S2: Am Nachmittag hat sie …

	Julia	**Ayse**
am Vormittag		
am Nachmittag		
am Abend		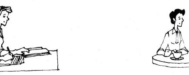

mit Professor Berg sprechen	ein Referat schreiben
ein Bad nehmen	mit Ali Kaffee trinken
die Zeitung lesen	einen Kuchen backen

6-15 **Ein langer Tag.** Work in groups of three and recall many activities from your long day. After **S1** asks the question, **S2** and **S3** answer according to the pictures. Be sure to switch roles after each set!

S1: Was habt ihr heute gemacht?

S2: Ich habe die Zeitung gelesen.

S3: Ich habe vor dem Fernseher gesessen.

1.

2.

3.

ein gutes Buch lesen	ein bisschen schlafen	ein Stück Kuchen essen
mit Professor Berg sprechen	meinen Wagen waschen	ein Referat schreiben
vor dem Fernseher sitzen	die Zeitung lesen	

6-16 **Was Eva gestern alles gemacht hat.** Listen to what Eva did yesterday. Then take turns retelling the story with a partner. Begin the sentences as indicated and use the verbs provided.

1. Um halb sieben hat Eva noch im Bett gelegen und geschlafen.
2. Um … (nehmen)
3. Um … (trinken, lesen)
4. Dann … (gießen°)
5. Später … (schreiben)
6. Um … (sprechen)
7. Um … (essen)
8. Am Nachmittag … (die Wäsche waschen)
9. Danach … (eine Pizza backen)
10. Später … (sitzen)
11. Und am Abend … (singen)

to water plants

6-17 **Ein paar persönliche Fragen.** Respond to your partner's questions, using the perfect tense. Add one or two questions of your own.

- Bis wann hast du heute Morgen geschlafen?
- Was hast du zum Frühstück (zum Mittagessen) gegessen und getrunken?
- Welche interessanten Bücher hast du in letzter Zeit° gelesen?
- Was hast du in letzter Zeit im Fernsehen gesehen?
- Wie viele Klausuren hast du letzte Woche geschrieben? …

in letzter Zeit: *recently*

The verb *sein* as auxiliary in the perfect tense

In English you always use the verb *to have* as the auxiliary in the perfect tense. In German you usually use **haben,** but for verbs that express a change of location or a change of condition, you use **sein.** These verbs can be regular or irregular.

Singular		Plural	
ich	bin gekommen	wir	sind gekommen
du	bist gekommen	ihr	seid gekommen
er/es/sie	ist gekommen	sie	sind gekommen
	Sie sind gekommen		

Change of location:

Ist Eva ins Kino **gegangen?**	*Has Eva gone to the movies?*

Some common verbs that express a change of location:

fahren	**ist ... gefahren**	kommen	**ist ... gekommen**
fliegen	**ist ... geflogen**	reisen	**ist ... gereist**
gehen	**ist ... gegangen**	wandern	**ist ... gewandert**

Change of condition:

Opa Ziegler **ist** plötzlich sehr krank **geworden** und **gestorben.**	*Grandpa Ziegler suddenly **became** very ill and **died.***
Wann **ist** das **passiert?**	*When **did** that **happen?***

Some common verbs that express a change of condition:

werden	**ist ... geworden**	*to become*
sterben	**ist ... gestorben**	*to die*
passieren	**ist ... passiert**	*to happen*

Be careful! Two very common verbs use **sein** as an auxiliary; however, they are a special group, since they express neither a change of location nor a change of condition:

bleiben	**ist ... geblieben**	*to stay; to remain*
sein	**ist ... gewesen**	*to be*

Warum **ist** Sylvia zu Hause **geblieben?**	*Why **did** Sylvia **stay** home?*
Wo **bist** du **gewesen,** Sylvia?	*Where **have** you **been,** Sylvia?*

Here are more common verbs you've learned that need **sein** as an auxiliary:

bleiben	**ist ... geblieben**	kommen	**ist ... gekommen**
fahren	**ist ... gefahren**	sein	**ist ... gewesen**
fliegen	**ist ... geflogen**	sterben	**ist ... gestorben**
gehen	**ist ... gegangen**	werden	**ist ... geworden**

Lerntipp!

You've already learned the past participles of many irregular verbs. Try to remember this set as a group, since all of them use **sein** in the perfect tense. Be sure to write out **ist** each time you are practicing these verb forms.

6-18 Opa Ziegler ist gestorben. Brigitte Ziegler calls her friend Beverly and tells her why she and Klaus can't come for dinner tonight. Supply the appropriate perfect forms.

ist … geworden / ist … passiert / ist … gefahren / ist … gestorben / ist … gekommen

BRIGITTE: Du Beverly, wir können leider nicht zum Abendessen kommen. Klaus musste ganz schnell zu seinen Eltern nach Hamburg.
BEVERLY: Was _____ denn _____?
BRIGITTE: Opa Ziegler _____ plötzlich° sehr krank _____.　　*suddenly*
BEVERLY: Ist er im Krankenhaus?
BRIGITTE: Ja, und dort _____ er heute Morgen um zehn _____.
BEVERLY: Hoffentlich° _____ Klaus nicht zu spät _____.　　*hopefully*
BRIGITTE: Nein. Er _____ vom Bahnhof direkt ins Krankenhaus _____ und konnte noch ein paar Worte mit Opa sprechen.

Sprachnotiz　　The perfect tense of *sein* and *haben*

In Austria, Southern Germany, and Switzerland, the perfect tense of **sein** and **haben** is used quite frequently in conversational situations.

Wo **bist** du gestern **gewesen?**　　*Where **were** you yesterday?*
Wie viele Vorlesungen **hast** du gestern **gehabt?**　　*How many classes **did** you **have** yesterday?*

But remember that most speakers of German use the simple past of these verbs.

Wo **warst** du gestern?　　*Where **were** you yesterday?*
Wie viele Vorlesungen **hattest** du gestern?　　*How many classes **did** you **have** yesterday?*

6-19 Ein Austauschsemester in Deutschland. Jennifer and Rob are talking about Rob's study abroad last year. Supply the needed forms of **haben** or **sein** in their conversation.

JENNIFER: Wann _____ du nach Deutschland geflogen? Konntest du direkt fliegen?
ROB: Ich _____ mit einem Freund nach Deutschland gereist. Wir _____ direkt von New York nach Frankfurt geflogen und _____ mit dem Fernbus weiter nach Trier gefahren.
JENNIFER: Wie _____ ihr die Stadt gefunden?
ROB: Oh, Trier ist ganz schön! Wir _____ zuerst in einer Jugendherberge übernachtet. Und Mitte Oktober _____ die Vorlesungen angefangen. Mein Freund _____ an seine Uni nach Freiburg gefahren. Und ich _____ dann mein Zimmer im Wohnheim bekommen.
JENNIFER: Was _____ ihr zu Weihnachten gemacht?
ROB: Wir _____ eine Woche Urlaub gemacht, und das war schön! Wir _____ einen BMW gemietet und _____ nach München gefahren. Dort _____ wir in einem preiswerten Hotel gewohnt und _____ in München auch Neujahr gefeiert.
JENNIFER: _____ du deine Familie nicht vermisst°?　　*missed*
ROB: Doch, ein bisschen. Aber wir _____ oft per Skype telefoniert.

> Rob's semester abroad kept him in Europe over the winter holidays, since the German **Wintersemester** lasts from mid-October to mid-February.

6-20 Aris Wochenende. The weekend is over, but Ari is starting back to class exhausted. What went wrong? Switch off with a partner.

▶ bis Mitternacht vor dem Computer sitzen

Ari hat bis Mitternacht vor dem Computer gesessen.

- zu viel Junkfood essen
- am Freitag sehr viel Bier trinken
- am Sonntag bis Mitternacht lesen
- nicht genug schlafen

- lange in der Bibliothek sitzen
- spät ins Bett gehen
- sehr viel Kaffee trinken
- am Samstag lang Fußball spielen

6-21 Meine letzte Reise. Respond to your partner's questions using the perfect tense.

Wann hast du deine letzte Reise gemacht?
Wohin bist du gereist? Bist du geflogen oder gefahren?
Wie lang bist du geblieben? Was hast du dort gemacht?
Was hast du dort gesehen? Was hast du am interessantesten gefunden?

hard

6-22 „Claudias Mittwoch" oder „Das Studentenleben ist schwer°!" As you hear what Claudia did on Wednesday, number each picture to show the order in which everything took place. Number one has been completed for you.

ᴜ.ᴜ Kultur 2

Explore how migration is impacting the German-speaking countries

6.5 Present a profile of a recent immigrant to Germany

While many **Einwanderer** have come to Germany for a wide variety of reasons over the past 75 years, there are four larger groups with similar backgrounds and reasons for leaving their homes and coming to Germany.

Krieg und Migration — Wo ist mein Zuhause?
When: At the end of World War II, into the 1950s

From where: Displaced Persons (DPs) from Eastern Europe, ethnic Germans residing within the old borders of the Reich, evacuees from heavily bombed German cities.

1945: DPs am Anhalter Bahnhof in Berlin

World War II forced migrants and transitory populations into cramped German territory, now occupied by Allied forces. This included about 3 million DPs, 12 million ethnic Germans, primarily from Eastern Europe, and 10 million Germans evacuated from German cities due to Allied bombings in the final stages of the war. The repopulation, repatriation, and/or integration of this great number of homeless people lasted well into the 1950s.

The Geneva Convention was updated in 1949 to add protections for the thousands of people displaced by World War II. For the first time, rights for civilian populations affected by war, and not just the soldiers and the wounded, were spelled out. These revisions also identified the postwar responsibilities of occupying forces.

Das Wirtschaftswunder — Deutschland braucht Arbeiter!
When: After World War II, guest worker programs from 1955 to 1973

From where: Italy, Yugoslavia, Greece, Spain, Portugal, Tunisia, Morocco, Turkey

1973: Gastarbeiter im Volkswagen-Werk Salzgitter

Postwar West Germany recruited **Gastarbeiter** from these countries to bolster the workforce during a time of huge economic growth. In the 1970s, many decided to make their home in Germany, and their families made the move to join them. This meant that the children of this generation grew up knowing Germany, its language and culture, as their **Heimat** (*homeland*).

The term **Gastarbeiter**, although very common, has long been controversial. Critics find it ironic, since you would not put your guests to work, and euphemistic, since guest workers were a socially marginalized group—and often the victims of discrimination. Proponents point to the fact that neither the German government nor the foreign workers originally planned for long-term stays.

1989: Die Grenze zwischen Ungarn und Österreich ist offen!

Perestroika — Der Ostblock fällt!
When: Late 1980s through the 1990s

From where: Poland, Hungary, Czechoslovakia, Romania

The fall of the Berlin Wall and the Eastern Bloc in Europe brought still more refugees to Germany, seeking freedom and economic prosperity after years of oppression, hardship, and controls by the **Sowjetunion.**

Weg vom Krieg — Wir wollen leben!

When: From the 1990s to the present

From where: Former Yugoslavia, Iraq, Afghanistan, Syria, Somalia

To escape their war-torn countries, many thousand **Flüchtlinge** *(refugees)* make the long, risky journey to Germany and Austria to seek **Asyl** *(asylum)*. If successful, they can start a new life free of persecution in Europe.

2015: Syrische Flüchtlinge am Münchner Hauptbahnhof

Menschen mit Migrationshintergrund

Name: Cem Özdemir

Geburtsjahr: 1965

Geburtsort: Bad Urach

Vorfahren: aus der Türkei

Wohnort jetzt: Berlin

Beruf: Politiker (Die Grünen)

Name: Ace Tee (Tarin Wilda)

Geburtsjahr: 1993

Geburtsort: Berlin

Vorfahren: aus Ghana

Wohnort jetzt: Hamburg

Beruf: Hairstylistin und Sängerin

Research Cem Özdemir and Ace Tee online to find more photos, YouTube or music videos, and interesting facts about them, their families, and their work. Be sure to bring an up-to-date picture for your presentation.

6-23 Kurze Präsentation. From the immigrants pictured here, choose one that interests you and prepare a short presentation to the class about him or her. Use the presentation below about Patricia Lanners-Kaminski, whom you met in the *Vorschau*, as a model for your presentation.

Patricia Lanners-Kaminski ist eine junge Frau mit Migrationshintergrund. Sie ist 33 Jahre alt. Sie ist in Chicago geboren, aber ihre Vorfahren kommen aus Polen. Patricia und ihre Familie sind 1989 nach Deutschland eingewandert. Patricia lebt schon 28 Jahre in Deutschland. Sie hat in Trier studiert.

6.7 Kommunikation und Formen 2

More on the past

6.6 Talk more about events in the past

The past participle of verbs with separable prefixes
To form the past participle of separable-prefix verbs, you simply attach the prefix to the past participle of the base verb. Separable-prefix verbs can be regular or irregular.

Regular verbs		Irregular verbs	
INFINITIVE	PERFECT TENSE	INFINITIVE	PERFECT TENSE
anhören	hat **... angehört**	fernsehen	hat **... ferngesehen**
abreisen°	ist **... abgereist**	mitsingen	hat **... mitgesungen**
anprobieren	hat **... anprobiert**	aufstehen	ist **... aufgestanden**

to depart

Remember:

- Verbs that express a change of location or condition use **sein** as an auxiliary.
- Past participles of regular verbs ending in **-ieren** do not add **ge-** to the verb stem.

 6-24 Was habt ihr letzte Woche gemacht?

▶   am Samstagnachmittag   bei H&M Klamotten anprobiert

S1: Was habt ihr am Samstag gemacht?   **S2:** Wir haben bei H&M Klamotten anprobiert.

1. am Sonntagvormittag

2. am Sonntagnachmittag

3. am Sonntagabend

4. am Montag früh

5. am Dienstagabend

6. am Freitagabend

alle zusammen ausgegangen	unser Zimmer aufgeräumt	zu Hause rumgehangen
Bilder von Rembrandt angeschaut	im Studentenchor mitgesungen	bis Mitternacht ferngesehen

Ach so!
The colloquial expression **rumhängen** *(to hang out)* forms its past tense with **haben.**

6-25 Was hast du nun *wirklich* gemacht? Think back over your last week and select three activities that you did. Add another two that aren't on the list (and choose interesting ones!). Then compare your last week's activities with your partner's.

S1: Was hast du nun wirklich letzte Woche gemacht?

S2: Letzte Woche habe ich … / Letzte Woche bin ich …

☐ mit Freunden rumgehangen
☐ einen Tag sehr spät aufgestanden
☐ mit meinem Freund/meiner Freundin ausgegangen
☐ zweimal im Kino gewesen
☐ meine Wohnung aufgeräumt
☐ Videospiele gespielt
☐ *Game of Thrones* angeschaut
☐ viel zu viel ferngesehen

☐ _____

☐ _____

The past participle of verbs with inseparable prefixes

Many regular and irregular verbs have inseparable prefixes. The three most common inseparable prefixes are **be-**, **er-**, and **ver-**. The past participles of verbs with inseparable prefixes do not add **ge-**. Whereas separable prefixes are *stressed* in pronunciation, inseparable prefixes are *unstressed*.

Regular verbs		Irregular verbs	
INFINITIVE	PERFECT TENSE	INFINITIVE	PERFECT TENSE
besuchen	hat … **besucht**	bekommen	hat … **bekommen**
erzählen	hat … **erzählt**	erfinden°	hat … **erfunden**
verkaufen	hat … **verkauft**	verstehen	hat … **verstanden**

to invent

6-26 Kleine Gespräche. Complete the mini-dialogues with the perfect tense of the verbs given in parentheses.

1. STEFAN: _____ Professor Kluge die Relativitätstheorie gut _____? (erklären)

   MATTHIAS: Ja, aber ich _____ trotzdem nicht alles _____. (verstehen)

2. MICHAEL: _____ du letzten Sommer gut _____? (verdienen)

　　VERONIKA: Ja, meine Chefin _____ mich sehr gut _____.
　　　　　　　(bezahlen)

3. FRAU FELL: Was? Sie _____ Ihr Auto _____? (verkaufen)

　　FRAU HOLZ: Ja, das stimmt. Ich _____ fast 20 000 Euro dafür _____.
　　　　　　　(bekommen)

4. KATHRIN: Was _____ dein Freund von seinem Urlaub _____?
　　　　　　(erzählen)

　　SYLVIA: Nichts, ich glaube er _____ schon viel _____.
　　　　　　(vergessen)

5. HORST: _____ du in Berlin deine Kusine Sophia _____?
　　　　　(besuchen)

　　INGRID: Ich _____ es _____. Aber sie war nie zu Hause.　　　　*to try*
　　　　　(versuchen°)

The past participle of mixed verbs

There is a small group of verbs that have characteristics of regular *and* irregular verbs.
The past participle of these mixed verbs has a stem change like an irregular verb and
ends in **-t** like a regular verb. Be sure to learn these common verbs.

Infinitive	Perfect tense	English infinitive
bringen	hat … **gebracht**	*to bring*
denken	hat … **gedacht**	*to think*
kennen	hat … **gekannt**	*to know (be acquainted with)*
nennen	hat … **genannt**	*to name, to call*
rennen	ist … **gerannt**	*to run*
wissen	hat … **gewusst**	*to know (a fact)*

6-27 Kleine Gespräche. Complete the mini-dialogues with the auxiliaries and
appropriate past participles.

gedacht / gewusst / genannt / gekannt / weggerannt / gebracht

1. HOLGER: Warum _____ Paul denn plötzlich _____? (wegrennen)
　　KARL: Weil du ihn einen Esel _____ _____. (nennen)

2. KATHRIN: Warum _____ du Tina Blumen _____? (bringen)
　　MAX: Ich _____ _____, sie hat heute Geburtstag°. (denken)　　*birthday*

3. HERR KRUG: _____ Sie Frau Merck gut _____? (kennen)
　　FRAU FELL: Ja, aber ich _____ nicht _____, dass sie gerade nach Kanada
　　　　　　　ausgewandert ist. (wissen)

Blumen zum Geburtstag

6-28 Hat Tina Geburtstag? Complete the paragraph with the past participle of the verbs given in parentheses.

Ich habe Tina schon im Gymnasium gut _____ (kennen) und ich habe Tina oft Blumen zum Geburtstag _____ (bringen). Heute Morgen habe ich meinen Kalender angeschaut und gesehen, dass heute der zehnte April ist. „Mann," habe ich _____ (denken), „das ist doch Tinas Geburtstag!" Ich bin schnell zum nächsten Blumengeschäft _____ (rennen) und habe frische Tulpen gekauft. Tina hat mich zuerst nur mit offenem Mund angeschaut. Dann hat sie gelacht, die Tulpen „wunderschön" _____ (nennen) und gesagt: „Lieber Max, den Tag hast du richtig _____ (wissen), aber der Monat ist falsch. Mein Geburtstag ist nicht am zehnten April, sondern am zehnten Mai."

6-29 Mein letzter Sommerjob. Find three classmates who had a summer job last year. Find out what they did and how much they earned. Use the phrases below to ask and respond to the questions, and use your classmates' responses to complete the chart. Then report your findings to the class.

Hattest du letzten Sommer einen Job?	Ja, ich hatte einen guten / interessanten / langweiligen Job.
Wo hast du gearbeitet?	Ich habe bei … gearbeitet.
Wie viel hast du verdient?	Ich habe … Dollar pro Stunde verdient.

Name	Job	hat pro Stunde … verdient

Ordinal numbers

6.7 Rank people and things

Ordinal numbers indicate the position of people and things in a sequence (e.g., the first, the second).

Der **erste** Zug fährt um sieben.	*The **first** train leaves at seven.*
Dann nehme ich lieber den **zweiten** Zug.	*Then I'd rather take the **second** train.*

For the numbers 1 through 19, you form the ordinal numbers by adding **-t-** and an adjective ending to the cardinal number. The few irregular forms are indicated below in boldface.

der **erste**	der elfte
der zweite	der zwölfte
der **dritte**	der dreizehnte
der vierte	der vierzehnte
der fünfte	der fünfzehnte
der sechste	der sechzehnte
der **siebte**	der siebzehnte
der **achte**	der achtzehnte
der neunte	der neunzehnte
der zehnte	

> The examples here use the masculine **der,** but the gender must change when the subject is feminine, neuter or plural: **die erste Frau, das erste Kind, die ersten Immigranten.**

From the number 20 on, you form the ordinal numbers by adding **-st-** and an adjective ending to the cardinal number.

der zwanzigste	der dreißigste
der einundzwanzigste	etc.
der zweiundzwanzigste	

 6-30 Berühmte Leute. Work with a partner to identify each person's historic achievement.

S1: Was hat Neil Armstrong gemacht?   **S2:** Er war der erste Mann auf dem Mond.

Name	Was sie/er gemacht hat
Neil Armstrong	1. Frau mit Nobelpreis
Angela Merkel	1. Frau im Kongress in den USA
Marie Curie	2. Mann auf dem Mond
Jeannette Rankin	1. Mann auf dem Mond
Viola Desmond	1. Kanadierin auf einer Banknote
John Adams	2. Präsident der USA
Buzz Aldrin	1. deutsche Bundeskanzlerin

> **Ach so!**
> When written as a numeral, an ordinal number is indicated by a period. It is never read as **eins** or **zwei**. Instead, it's **erst-** or **zweit-**.

Dates

6.8 State the date

To ask for and give the date, you use the following expressions.

Der Wievielte ist heute?	*What's the date today?*
Heute ist der Fünfzehnte.	*Today is the fifteenth.*
Den Wievielten haben wir heute?	*What's the date today?*
Heute haben wir den Fünfzehnten.	*Today is the fifteenth.*

Note that **Wievielt-** and ordinal numbers are capitalized unless they are followed by a noun.

WRITTEN: Heute ist der 23. Mai.

SPOKEN: Heute ist der dreiundzwanzigste Mai.

> **Der Wievielte ist heute?** and **Den Wievielten haben wir heute?** and their respective responses are synonymous.

> Dates are always masculine because they refer to the day: **der 23. [Tag].**

> **Achtung!**
> In giving the date in German, the day always precedes the month.

6-31 Wann ist dein Geburtstag? Draw a grid showing the months of the year. In a group of four, tell your classmates when your birthday is, ask for theirs, and record them on the grid.

S1: Mein Geburtstag ist der 5. November. Wann ist dein Geburtstag?   **S2:** Mein Geburtstag ist der 13. April. ...

Deutsche Einheit
der 3. Oktober

6-32 Daten. Take turns with a partner asking and responding to the following questions.

S1:
1. Den Wievielten haben wir heute?
2. Der Wievielte ist morgen?
3. Der Wievielte ist Sonntag?
4. Den Wievielten hatten wir letzten Sonntag?
5. Wann ist Valentinstag?
6. Wann ist Halloween?
7. Wann ist Neujahr?
8. Wann ist der amerikanische Unabhängigkeitstag?

S2:
Heute haben wir den _____.
Morgen ist der _____.
Sonntag ist der _____.
Letzten Sonntag hatten wir den _____.
Valentinstag ist der _____ _____.
Halloween ist der _____ _____.
Neujahr ist der _____ _____.
Das ist der _____ _____.

6.8 Video-Treff

Mein erster Job

6.9 Understand authentic video of German speakers talking about their first job

Susann, Thomas, Stefan Meister, and Stefan Kuhlmann talk about their first jobs. Be sure to complete the **Was ist das auf Englisch?** exercise before watching the video.

6-33 Was ist das auf Englisch?

1. Ich habe in einem Restaurant **gekellnert.**
2. **Während** der Schulzeit habe ich oft dort gearbeitet.
3. Ich habe 10 Mark **pro Stunde** verdient.
4. Das war **damals** noch die D-Mark-Zeit.
5. Ich habe den Job durch eine **Empfehlung** von Freunden bekommen.
6. Die Nachbarn wollten, dass es im Garten kein **Unkraut** gibt.
7. Als Kellner kann man viel **Trinkgeld** verdienen.
8. Ich musste im Supermarkt die **Regale** mit Hundefutter auffüllen.
9. Das war eine Menge Geld für einen **Zwölfjährigen.**

a. recommendation

b. waited tables

c. 12-year-old

d. shelves

e. weeds

f. back then

g. during

h. tips

i. per hour

> **Kellner:** Originally, each **Gasthaus** had its own **Weinkeller.** Among his other duties, the **Kellner** had to go to the **Keller** to get wine for his guests. Hence his name.

6-34 Wer sagt das? The following statements fit what Susann or Thomas said about their first job. Some of their first jobs happened a while ago, before the euro! Identify the person who best matches each statement.

	Susann	Thomas
1. Mein erster Job war im Supermarkt.	☐	☐
2. Ich habe in einem Restaurant für Touristen gekellnert.	☐	☐
3. Ich habe den Job durch Freunde bekommen.	☐	☐
4. Ich habe 10 Mark pro Stunde und dazu auch Trinkgeld verdient.	☐	☐
5. Ich habe zwei- bis dreimal in der Woche dort gearbeitet.	☐	☐
6. Ich habe die Regale mit Hunde- und Katzenfutter aufgefüllt.	☐	☐
7. Ich habe viel Geld für CDs ausgegeben.	☐	☐

6-35 Was passt? Complete the sentences with the appropriate information according to what you heard from Stefan Meister and Stefan Kuhlmann.

1. Stefan Meisters erster Job war _____.
   ☐ im Garten   ☐ im Supermarkt

2. Er war damals _____ Jahre alt.
   ☐ 16   ☐ 12

3. Er hat _____ gearbeitet.
   ☐ fünf Stunden pro Tag   ☐ fünf Stunden pro Woche

4. Er hat _____ im Monat verdient.
   ☐ 200 Mark   ☐ 20 Mark

5. Stefan Kuhlmanns erster Job war _____.
   ☐ im Supermarkt   ☐ im Restaurant

6. Er war damals _____ Jahre alt.
   ☐ 17   ☐ 16

7. Stefan Kuhlmann hat in der _____ gearbeitet.
   ☐ Kneipe   ☐ Getränkeabteilung

examples 8. Stefan gibt sehr viele Beispiele° von _____.
   ☐ nichtalkoholischen Getränken   ☐ alkoholischen Getränken

9. Er musste _____ acht Stunden arbeiten.
   ☐ jeden Tag   ☐ jede Woche

))) 6.9 Wortschatz 2

Wichtige Vokabeln

6.10 Learn vocabulary to talk about more everyday activities

Nomen

das Krankenhaus, ¨er	hospital
die Blume, -n	flower
der Geburtstag, -e	birthday
der Kellner, -	waiter
die Kellnerin, -nen	waitress
der Koffer, -	suitcase

Verben

ab·reisen	to depart
aus·geben (gibt aus), ausgegeben	to spend (*money*)
bezahlen	to pay
bedeuten	to mean
bringen, gebracht	to bring
füttern	to feed
gießen, gegossen	to water
liegen, gelegen	to lie; to be situated
passieren, ist passiert	to happen
putzen	to clean
recherchieren	to do research
rennen, ist gerannt	to run
rum·hängen, rumgehangen	to hang out
stehen, gestanden	to stand; to say
sterben (stirbt), ist gestorben	to die
üben	to practice
warten	to wait

Andere Wörter

begeistert	excited, thrilled
hoffentlich	hopefully, I hope (so)
müde	tired
plötzlich	suddenly
wahr	true
zweimal	twice

Ausdrücke

Das (Es) stimmt.	That's true (right).
in letzter Zeit	recently
die Wäsche waschen	to do the laundry
Den Wievielten haben wir heute? Der Wievielte ist heute?	What's the date today?
Heute haben wir den zweiten Mai. Heute ist der zweite Mai.	Today is May 2nd.
pro Stunde	per hour

Das Gegenteil

schwer ≠ leicht	difficult; heavy ≠ easy; light
packen ≠ aus·packen	to pack ≠ to unpack

Leicht zu verstehen

das Album, Alben	
der Song, -s	
warnen	
die Warnung, -en	

> Past participles are listed in vocabularies only for irregular and mixed verbs. The auxiliary verb is provided only when it is **sein**.

> **Recherchieren** derives from French, so **ch** is pronounced **sch**.

> **Stehen** means *to say* in expressions like **Im Pass steht …**, etc.

Wörter im Kontext

6-36 Was passt zusammen?

1. Hast du die Zimmerpflanzen
2. Hast du Klavier
3. Hast du die Wäsche
4. Hast du den Fisch
5. Hast du für dein Referat

a. geübt?
b. recherchiert?
c. gefüttert?
d. gegossen?
e. gewaschen?

Allgemeiner Deutscher Automobil-Club (ADAC): North American equivalents are the *AAA* (U.S.) and the *CAA* (Canada).

6-37 Warum David so spät nach Hause gekommen ist.

gelegen / erklärt / gewartet / gerannt / warten / passiert

Gestern Nacht habe ich stundenlang auf David _____. Als ich dann schon im Bett _____ habe, ist er plötzlich zur Tür hereingerannt. „Was ist denn _____, David?" habe ich gefragt, und er hat _____, dass er seinen Wagen nicht starten konnte, dass er viel zu lange auf den ADAC _____ musste und dass er dann den ganzen langen Weg nach Hause _____ ist.

6-38 Was ist hier identisch? Read the following sets of sentences aloud and decide which two in each set convey approximately the same meaning.

1. Was bedeutet dieser Text?
   Ich verstehe diesen Text nicht.
   Hast du diesen Text verbessert?

2. Opa Ziegler ist im Krankenhaus.
   Opa Ziegler lebt nicht mehr.
   Opa Ziegler ist gestorben.

3. Das stimmt nicht.
   Das kann warten.
   Das ist nicht wahr.

4. Wie ist die Bezahlung?
   Wie viel musst du bezahlen?
   Wie viel verdienst du?

6-39 Der ideale Ferienjob.

schwer / bezahlen / Hoffentlich / Bezahlung

Mein idealer Ferienjob muss am ersten Ferientag beginnen und ich möchte bis zum letzten Ferientag arbeiten. Die _____ muss gut sein, am besten acht oder neun Euro pro Stunde, damit ich viel Geld verdienen kann und mein nächstes Studienjahr fast ganz selbst _____ kann. Die Arbeit soll interessant und nicht zu _____ sein. _____ kann ich bald so einen Job finden!

Wörter unter der Lupe

Predicting gender

All nouns with the suffix **-ung** are feminine. Like most English nouns with the suffix *-ing*, most of these nouns are derived from verbs. Note that the plural forms always end in **-en**.

warnen	*to warn*	**die** Warn**ung, -en**	*warning*
landen	*to land*	**die** Land**ung, -en**	*landing*

However, many English equivalents of German nouns with the suffix **-ung** do not have the suffix *-ing*.

üben	*to practice*	**die** Üb**ung, -en**	*exercise*
übernachten	*to stay overnight*	**die** Übernacht**ung, -en**	*overnight stay*
wohnen	*to live*	**die** Wohn**ung, -en**	*apartment*
erzählen	*to tell*	**die** Erzähl**ung, -en**	*story*
ausstellen	*to exhibit*	**die** Ausstell**ung, -en**	*exhibition*

6-40 **Was ist das?** Form nouns from the following verbs and give their English equivalents.

1. erklären — *to explain*
2. bestellen — *to order*
3. beschreiben — *to describe*
4. lösen — *to solve*
5. bezahlen — *to pay*
6. übersetzen — *to translate*
7. bedeuten — *to mean*
8. verbessern — *to correct, improve*
9. einladen — *to invite*
10. warnen — *to warn*

Giving language color

Like other languages, German uses the names of parts of the body in many colorful expressions.

Er ist nicht auf den Kopf gefallen.	*He's no fool.*
Ich habe die ganze Nacht kein Auge zugetan.	*I didn't sleep a wink all night.*
Er hat wieder mal die Nase zu tief ins Glas gesteckt.	*He drank too much again.*
Das hat Hand und Fuß.	*That makes sense.*
Nimm doch den Mund nicht immer so voll!	*Don't always talk so big!*
Hals- und Beinbruch!	*Good luck!*

Hals- und Beinbruch: This expression stems from Hebrew and entered the German language through Yiddish. After a successful business transaction, Yiddish-speaking Jews wished each other **hazloche und broche** *(success and blessings)*. Speakers of German understood this as **Hals- und Beinbruch.** The English equivalent *Break a leg!* is often used in theatrical circles to wish an actor luck. It entered the English language in the 1920s and some sources surmise that it also has its roots in Yiddish, since many German Jews worked in the theater at that time.

6-41 **Was passt zusammen?**

1. Warum magst du Sebastian nicht?
2. Warum lässt du mich denn nicht fahren?
3. Warum bist du denn so müde?
4. Warum bekommt Maria für ihre Referate immer so gute Noten?
5. Ich muss jetzt gehen. Wir schreiben gleich eine Klausur.
6. Ist es wahr, dass Paul die Lösung für dieses Problem gefunden hat?

a. Na, dann Hals- und Beinbruch!
b. Weil alles, was sie schreibt, Hand und Fuß hat.
c. Klar. Er ist doch nicht auf den Kopf gefallen.
d. Weil du wieder mal die Nase zu tief ins Glas gesteckt hast.
e. Weil er den Mund immer so voll nimmt.
f. Weil ich die ganze Nacht kein Auge zugetan habe.

6.10 Alles zusammen

Ein interessantes Experiment

In this section, you'll meet Firas Alshater, a YouTuber, actor, comedian, and writer with roots in Syria. You'll read an excerpt from his book, *Ich komm auf Deutschland zu. Ein Syrer über seine neue Heimat* (2016), which tells about his experiences as a refugee in Germany. You'll retell the story of an "experiment" he conducted in Berlin and come up with some questions you'd like to ask his about his life in Germany or with some comments on his video.

Name: Firas Alshater

Geburtsjahr: 1991

Geburtsort: Damaskus

Vorfahren: aus Syrien

Wohnort jetzt: Berlin

Beruf: Autor, Schauspieler, YouTuber

Originally from Syria, Alshater worked as a journalist to help document what was taking place there during the civil war. As a result, he was imprisoned and tortured, but in 2012 was able to flee via Turkey to Germany. In Berlin he partnered with Jan Heilig on a film project, set up as an experiment: He stood blindfolded on Alexanderplatz, a busy public square, with a sign next to him saying "Ich bin syrischer Flüchtling. Ich vertraue dir — vertraust du mir? Umarme mich!" After a long wait, people finally started hugging him. The resulting film of this experiment, along with his commentary about what the results said about the Germans, was posted on YouTube and immediately went viral.

Schritt 1: Zum Lesen

Plötzlich YouTube-Star

Plötzlich bin ich hellwach. Das sind ja schon 20 000 Klicks auf das Video. 20 000 Menschen haben unser Video angesehen! Ich lade es direkt auf meinen Facebook-Kanal hoch — und noch am selben Abend hat es dort über 100 000 Zuschauer. Es ist unfassbar. Und als ich in die Shisha-Bar komme, in der ich mit Freunden verabredet bin, fragt mich der libanesische Wirt: „Bist du der Typ von dem Video, dieser Firas?"

[…]

Und schon rufen sie: „Du bist unglaublich, dein Video ist so toll … Können wir dich umarmen?"

Ja, können sie, natürlich.

Es folgt das verrückteste Wochenende, das ich je erlebt habe. Bis Sonntagnachmittag sehen knapp eine halbe Million den kleinen Videoclip. Ich rufe Jan an. Der hat erstaunlicherweise noch nicht viel davon mitbekommen.

„Meine Güte, Firas, da kriegt man ja Angst!"

„Ja, aber ist doch auch cool, oder?"

Jan ist skeptisch, befürchtet einen Shitstorm an Hasskommentaren, wie so oft, wenn es um das Flüchtlingsthema geht […] Doch unter unserem Video gibt es zwar Hunderte von Kommentaren, aber so gut wie keine negativen Sprüche oder gar Hass. Alle sind total begeistert. Jan ist immer noch skeptisch.

„Das ist nicht normal. Wo sind die ganzen Trolle?"

[…]

Jan wollte ja nur wissen, ob die Leute das mögen, und so ein Experiment sollte man nicht abbrechen. Wir verdienen sowieso nichts daran. Also geben wir es komplett frei – und das Video rauscht wie eine Lawine durch die Netzwerke. Die Leute teilen und teilen und teilen. Warum denn bloß? Haben die all noch nie einen Flüchtling gesehen, der witzig ist?

[…]

„Sie, Herr Alshater, sind eine Bereicherung für unser Land."

„Habe dein Video jetzt siebenmal angesehen, und lache immer wieder!"

Ein Kommentar berührt Jan besonders.

„Endlich mal kein Hass!"

6-42 Das Video ist viral gegangen. Am ersten Abend haben über 120 000 Menschen das Video angesehen. Sein Freund Jan ist skeptisch. Er erwartet …

☐ viele negative Sprüche.   ☐ viele virtuelle Umarmungen.
☐ nicht viel Geld für das Video.   ☐ mehr Hasskommentare.

Die Kommentare zeigen, dass die Leute …

☐ Firas sympathisch finden.   ☐ das Video nicht witzig finden.
☐ mit Hass reagieren.   ☐ begeistert sind.

Schritt 2: Zum Spielen

 6-43 Firas Alshaters Experiment. Spielen Sie Firas Alshaters Experiment in Berlin als Theater! Hier ist ein Skript.

> Das ist Firas Alshater. Er kommt aus Syrien, aber er lebt jetzt in Berlin.
>
> Firas hat in Berlin ein Experiment gemacht.
>
> Er hat ein Schild geschrieben: „Ich bin syrischer Flüchtling. Ich vertraue dir – vertraust du mir? Umarme mich!"
>
> Er hat auf dem Alexanderplatz in Berlin gestanden.
>
> Er hat lange gewartet. Und gewartet. Und gewartet.
>
> Viel später ist ein Mann gekommen. Er hat Firas interessant gefunden.
>
> Der Mann hat mit Firas ein Selfie gemacht.
>
> Dann sind viele Leute gekommen. Sie haben ihn angeschaut und haben sein Schild gelesen.
>
> Am Ende hat er viele Umarmungen bekommen!

Use the basic story provided here to prepare for your scene. Read it through once as a group and plan how you will act it out. You can add more information or even dialogue to bolster the story. Don't forget to use props for your performance!

Schritt 3: Zum Schreiben

6-44 Meine Fragen oder Kommentare an Firas Alshater:

_____

_____

_____

Kapitel 7
Feste und Feiertage

Perchtenlauf in Tirol, Österreich

Learning Objectives

7.1 Recognize key holidays and festivals celebrated in the German-speaking countries

7.2 Learn vocabulary to talk about holidays and gifts

7.3 Distinguish the German *r* sound from the English *r*

7.4 Indicate the person *to whom* or *for whom* something is done

7.5 Use expressions that require the dative case

7.6 Identify cultural practices for celebrating birthdays, giving presents, and congratulating people

7.7 Use various expressions for time, manner, and place with dative prepositions

7.8 Describe people, places, and things

7.9 Understand authentic video of German speakers talking about getting gifts

7.10 Learn vocabulary to talk about parties, presents, and everyday items

7.1 Vorschau

Eine Geburtstagskarte

7-1 **Ein Gutschein zum Geburtstag.** Schauen Sie die Geburtstagskarte an und beantworten Sie die Fragen.

1. Wer hat diese Geburtstagskarte geschrieben?
2. Wer hat Geburtstag?
3. Wann frühstücken Max und seine Mutter zusammen?
4. Wann hilft Max seiner Mutter?
5. Was tut er alles für sie?

> Beginning in this chapter, all directions for exercises are in German.

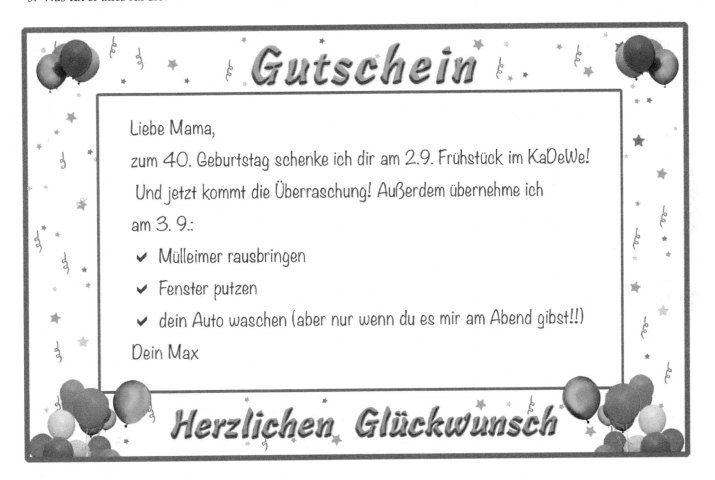

> **KaDeWe** stands for *Kaufhaus des Westens.* Situated in former West Berlin, this huge department store is the largest in continental Europe, drawing about 45,000 visitors a day. Its legendary gourmet food department, the so-called **Feinschmecker-Etage** on the 6th floor, features delicacies from around the world.

7-2 Was kann man dir zum Geburtstag schenken?

S1: Ich trinke viel Kaffee.   **S2:** Dann kann man dir eine Kaffeemaschine schenken.

1. Ich fahre immer mit dem Rad zur Uni.
2. Ich will mein Zimmer schöner machen.
3. Ich möchte nächsten Sommer durch den Schwarzwald wandern.
4. Ich komme morgens oft zu spät zur Vorlesung.
5. Ich kann nicht sehr gut kochen.
look 6. Ich möchte im Urlaub cool aussehen°.
7. Ich möchte mein Deutsch verbessern.
8. Ich möchte fit werden.
just 9. Meine Uhr ist gerade° kaputtgegangen.

fellow students **7-3 Geburtstagsgeschenke.** Sagen Sie, was Sie Ihren Mitstudenten° zum Geburtstag schenken wollen und warum.

S1: Ich schenke Daniel eine Lederjacke, weil er immer schicke Klamotten trägt.
S2: Ich schenke Julia eine Starbucks-Geschenkkarte, weil sie gern Kaffee trinkt.
S3: Ich schenke …, weil …

Geschenkidee: Ein Kinogutschein

7.2 Kultur 1

Feste und Feiertage

7.1 **Recognize key holidays and festivals celebrated in the German-speaking countries**

The German-speaking countries enjoy a wider array of public holidays than the United States or Canada. Many of these holidays have their roots in Christian traditions but frequently blend those with pre-Christian and folk traditions.

The Christmas season

As in North America, **Weihnachten** is still the biggest and most important holiday, and preparation begins four weeks in advance. Beginning on December 1, many children count down the 24 days to Christmas Eve **(der Heilige Abend)** with the help of an **Adventskalender.** Each day they open a door or window on the calendar and find motifs related to **Weihnachten** or a small gift. On the eve of **Nikolaustag** (December 6), children put their shoes outside their bedroom door for **Sankt Nikolaus** (the patron saint of children) to fill with candy, chocolate, fruit, and nuts. As in other countries, **Weihnachten** is associated with a Christmas tree **(der Weihnachtsbaum)** and gift-giving **(die Bescherung).** In the German-speaking countries the **Weihnachtsbaum** is frequently not put up and decorated until December 24, **am Heiligen Abend,** which is also when the **Bescherung** takes place. On December 25 **(der erste Weihnachtsfeiertag),** families gather for a traditional dinner. On December 26 **(der zweite Weihnachtsfeiertag),** it is customary to visit relatives and friends.

> The root of the word **Be<u>sch</u>erung** is related to English *share*.

Weihnachtsmarkt in Frankfurt

In the New Year

New Year's Eve **(Silvester)** is an evening of parties and revelry culminating at midnight with spectacular displays of fireworks.

In the time between New Year's and Lent, people in the German-speaking countries celebrate **Karneval** (as it is called in the **Rheinland**) or **Fastnacht/Fasching** (as it is called in Southern Germany, Austria, and Switzerland). **Karneval** celebrations include huge parades with marching bands, elaborate costumes, and floats. These floats often depict in satirical fashion scenes critical of politicians and unpopular government policies.

Muslim holidays

Islam is the largest non-Christian religion in the German-speaking countries. Its two most important holidays are **Fest des Fastenbrechens,** which marks the end of **Ramadan,** the holy month of fasting, and **Opferfest** (Festival of Sacrifice), which honors the willingness of Ibrahim to sacrifice his son.

Ein Osterlamm aus Schokolade

Easter holidays

Spring brings Easter **(Ostern).** Businesses are closed on Good Friday **(Karfreitag)** and on **Ostermontag.** On **Ostersonntag** children receive colored eggs and chocolate goodies from the **Osterhase.** The week before and after **Ostern** are school holidays. Pentecost or Whitsun **(Pfingsten)** is celebrated on the seventh Sunday and Monday after **Ostern** and brings with it another week of vacation from school.

Secular holidays

Secular holidays in the German-speaking countries include the **Tag der Arbeit** or **Maifeiertag** on May 1 as well as national holidays for each country. On October 3, Germany celebrates the **Tag der deutschen Einheit** to commemorate the reunification in 1990 of the **Bundesrepublik Deutschland (BRD)** and the former **Deutsche Demokratische Republik (DDR).** Austria has set aside October 26 **(Tag der Fahne)** to celebrate the day in 1955 when it declared its neutrality. On August 1, Switzerland celebrates the beginning of the Swiss confederation, which took place in 1291.

Regional, local, and seasonal festivals

Aside from celebrating the bigger holidays in their own traditional ways, individual regions also hold festivals to honor and celebrate their own local traditions and locally grown products, or to mark seasonal transitions. Today, many of these festivals have become tourist attractions and important events in the local economies. Some festivals have become world famous, like Munich's annual **Oktoberfest** and **Kieler Woche,** the world's largest sailing festival. Here are some others:

Fall and winter

- **Erntedankfest** *(harvest or thanksgiving festival)* is celebrated in many rural areas at the end of the summer harvest.

- The **Almabtrieb** is an annual event in the Alps, referring to cows being led into the valley from their **Alm** *(mountain pasture)* before the coming of winter. If no accidents occurred during the summer, the cows are decorated elaborately and the cow train accompanied by music and dance.

- People living in the Bavarian and Austrian Alps attempt to drive away the dark days of winter and the evil spirits by wearing ugly wooden masks. This ancient custom is called **Perchtenlauf** and takes place in the days after Christmas.

Almabtrieb in Pertisau (Österreich)

- Around Oldenburg **(Niedersachsen),** residents enjoy going on **Kohlfahrten,** boisterous excursions to country inns in wintertime to celebrate and enjoy the local winter harvest of kale.

Spring and summer

- In mid-April, the residents of Zurich celebrate **Sechseläuten** to mark the transition to spring. The festivities culminate with the burning of a giant snowman, the **Böögg,** on a pyre.
- The town of Beelitz **(Brandenburg)** celebrates its famous white asparagus with a **Spargelfest** in early June.
- In Mainburg **(Bayern),** the local hops production is celebrated at the annual **Hopfenfest** in July.
- In the wine-growing regions, **Weinfeste** are popular occasions throughout the summer for showcasing local wines and wineries. **Weinfeste** have a long history dating back to the fifteenth century. Often, a **Weinkönigin** is crowned at these events, who will act as the proud representative of each region.

7-4 Was sind Ihre Feste und Feiertage?

1. Feiern Sie Weihnachten? Wenn ja, wann ist die Bescherung? Wenn nein, wie heißt Ihr wichtigster Feiertag und wie feiern Sie ihn?
2. Wann ist der Tag der Arbeit in Ihrem Land?
3. Wie heißt Ihr Nationalfeiertag? Wann ist er und wie feiern Sie ihn?
4. Was für regionale Feste gibt es dort, wo Sie wohnen? Was und wie feiert man da?

7-5 Feste an der Mosel. Beantworten Sie die Fragen über die Mosel Weinfeste und Veranstaltungen.

1. Welche Spezialität hat diese Region?
2. Wann sind die meisten Feste hier? Warum, glauben Sie, ist das so?
3. Welches Fest hat nichts mit der regionalen Spezialität zu tun?
4. Zu welchem Fest möchten Sie gern gehen?

Locate the **Mosel** river on a map of Germany. What other countries does this river flow through?

))) 7.3 Wortschatz 1

Wichtige Vokabeln

7.2 Learn vocabulary to talk about holidays and gifts

Nomen

der Feiertag, -e	holiday
das Fest, -e	celebration; festival
Ostern	Easter
Silvester	New Year's Eve
Weihnachten	Christmas
der Weihnachtsbaum, ¨-e	Christmas tree

das Geschenk, -e	present; gift
die Geschenkkarte, -n	gift card
der Gutschein, -e	voucher
die Idee, -n	idea
die Überraschung, -en	surprise
der Fahrradhelm, -e	bicycle helmet
der Heimtrainer, -	exercise bike
der Wecker, -	alarm clock

Verben

aussehen (sieht aus), ausgesehen (wie)	to look (like), appear
fasten	to fast
feiern	to celebrate
schenken	to give (a gift)
schlürfen	to slurp; to sip

Andere Wörter

außerdem	besides; in addition
fröhlich	happy, merry
gerade	just, just now

Ausdrücke

den Mülleimer rausbringen	to take out the garbage
den Tisch decken	to set the table
Alles Gute zum Geburtstag!	Happy Birthday!
Herzliche Glückwünsche! **Herzlichen Glückwunsch!**	Best wishes!; Congratulations!
Frohe Weihnachten!	Merry Christmas!
Ein gutes neues Jahr! **Frohes neues Jahr!** **(Einen) guten Rutsch!**	Happy New Year!

HERZLICHEN GLÜCKWUNSCH

Das Gegenteil

leer ≠ voll	empty ≠ full
international ≠ regional	international ≠ regional

Leicht zu verstehen

das Wort, ̈er	**die Tour, -s**
das Wörterbuch, ̈er	**die Smartwatch, -es**
das Kochbuch, ̈er	**die Kaffeemaschine, -n**

> **Einen guten Rutsch:** Although most speakers of German understand **Rutsch** as coming from **rutschen** *(to slide)*, it probably stems from the Hebrew word **rosh** *(head, beginning)* as in Rosh Hashanah, the Jewish New Year. It is thought that the word came into German via Yiddish.

Wörter im Kontext

7-6 Was ist die richtige Reihenfolge°?   *sequence*

____ das Essen kochen   ____ essen
____ einkaufen   ____ den Tisch decken
____ Freunde einladen

7-7 Was passt zusammen?

1. Wenn man lieber Tee trinkt,   a. braucht man keinen Wecker.
2. Wenn man von selbst aufwacht,   b. braucht man keinen Fahrradhelm.
3. Wenn man fit ist,   c. braucht man kein Kochbuch.
4. Wenn man immer nur Auto fährt,   d. braucht man keine Kaffeemaschine.
5. Wenn man immer in der Mensa isst,   e. braucht man keine Smartwatch.
6. Wenn man immer pünktlich ist,   f. braucht man keinen Heimtrainer.

7-8 Was ich tue, wenn …

1. Wenn ich einen Gutschein bekomme,   a. muss ich ihn rausbringen.
2. Wenn der Mülleimer voll ist,   b. schenke ich ihr immer ein interessantes Kochbuch.
3. Wenn ich Geburtstag habe,   c. feiere ich mit meiner Familie.
4. Wenn meine Freundin Geburtstag hat, d. finde ich das toll.

Auf Tante Bettinas Geburtstagsfeier

7-9 Was brauche ich da? Beginnen Sie alle Antworten mit *Da brauche ich …*

1. Ich möchte fit werden.
2. Ich muss das Frühstück machen.
3. Ich suche ein Thema für mein Referat.
4. Ich weiß nicht, wie man Wiener Schnitzel macht.
5. Meine beste Freundin hat Geburtstag.
6. Ich weiß nicht, wie man auf Deutsch „Happy Birthday!" sagt.

a. ein Wörterbuch
b. ein Geschenk
c. eine gute Idee
d. eine Kaffeemaschine
e. ein Kochbuch
f. einen Heimtrainer

7-10 Tante Bettinas Geburtstag.

gerade / Überraschung / fröhlich / feiert / außerdem / Fest / geschenkt

Tante Bettina _____ heute ihren dreißigsten Geburtstag und hat zu diesem _____ die ganze Familie und alle ihre Freunde eingeladen. Sie haben _____ ein paar Flaschen Champagner getrunken und sind alle deshalb sehr _____. Als _____ haben Bettinas Freunde ihr eine Reise nach Kalifornien _____ und von ihrer Familie hat sie _____ einen neuen Koffer bekommen.

7.4 Zur Aussprache

German *r*

7.3 Distinguish the German r sound from the English *r*

Good pronunciation of the German **r** will go a long way toward making you sound like a native speaker. Don't let the tip of the tongue curl upward and backward as it does when pronouncing an English *r*, but keep it down behind the lower teeth. When followed by a vowel, the German **r** is much like the sound of **ch** in **auch.** When it is not followed by a vowel, the German **r** takes on a vowel-like quality.

 **7-11 Hören Sie gut zu und wiederholen Sie!**

1. Rita und Richard sitzen immer im Zimmer.
   Rita und Richard sehen gern fern.
2. Robert und Rosi spielen Karten im Garten.
   Robert und Rosi trinken Bier für vier.
3. Gestern war Ralf hier und dort,
   morgen fährt er wieder fort.
4. Horst ist hier,
   Horst will Wurst,
   Horst will Bier
   für seinen Durst.

Bier und Wurst für Horst

7.5 Kommunikation und Formen 1

The dative case

7.4 Indicate the person *to whom* or *for whom* something is done

The dative case: the indirect object

In *Kapitel 3* you learned that many verbs take direct objects and that the direct object is signaled by the accusative case.

Klaus möchte **einen iPad.**   *Klaus would like **an iPad.***

Some verbs, like **kaufen, schenken,** or **geben** take not only a direct object, but an *indirect object* as well. The indirect object indicates *to whom* or *for whom* something is done. It is almost always a *person*. In German the indirect object is signaled by the *dative case.*

Brigitte kauft **ihrem Mann** einen iPad.
Sie schenkt **ihrem Mann** den iPad zum Geburtstag.

*Brigitte buys **her husband** an iPad.*
*She gives **her husband** the iPad for his birthday.*

> In the dative plural, all nouns take the ending **-n** unless the plural form already ends in **-n (die Freundinnen, den Freundinnen)** or if it ends in **-s (die Chefs, den Chefs).**

	Masculine		Neuter		Feminine		Plural	
NOMINATIVE	der / mein	Vater	das / mein	Kind	die / meine	Mutter	die / meine	Kinder
ACCUSATIVE	den / meinen	Vater	das / mein	Kind	die / meine	Mutter	die / meine	Kinder
DATIVE	**dem / meinem**	Vater	**dem / meinem**	Kind	**der / meiner**	Mutter	**den / meinen**	Kinder**n**

All possessive adjectives **(dein, sein, ihr, unser, euer, ihr, Ihr)** and **ein** and **kein** have the same endings as **mein.**

7-12 Ein bisschen Grammatik. Finden Sie die indirekten Objekte!

▶ Brigitte Ziegler schenkt ihrem Mann einen iPod.

1. Stephanie feiert dieses Jahr Weihnachten nicht zu Hause in Chicago, sondern in München. Deshalb schickt sie ihrer Familie ein großes Paket. Sie schenkt ihrem Großvater ein gutes Buch, ihrem Vater ein schönes Bierglas und ihrer Mutter einen Kalender mit Bildern von München.

2. Und was schenkt Stephanie ihren Freunden in München? Sie schenkt ihrem Freund Peter ein Sweatshirt, ihrer Mitbewohnerin Claudia ein Paar Ohrringe und Claudias Freund Martin ein tolles Buch.

7-13 Geschenke. Patricias Familie feiert Weihnachten in Deutschland. Was schenkt sie ihrer Familie? Suchen Sie das beste Geschenk für jede Person.

S1: Patricias Bruder liebt Hip-Hop.

S2: Sie schenkt ihrem Bruder ein Album von Sido.

1. Patricias Opa trinkt gern Wein.
2. Ihre Mutter kocht gern italienisch.
3. Ihr Vater liest gern Romane.
4. Patricias Vetter ist Fitnessfreak.
5. Ihre Tante lebt in Amerika.
6. Ihr Onkel fotografiert gern.

Eine traditionelle Weihnachtspyramide

ein Kochbuch mit italienischen Rezepten	ein Fitnessarmband	einen Roman
eine Geschenkkarte für amazon.com	eine neue Digitalkamera	ein Album von Sido
eine Flasche Rotwein		

7-14 Ein Paket aus Deutschland. Drew studiert ein Jahr in Deutschland und schickt ein Paket nach Hause. Was schenkt er Freunden und Familie in Amerika? Bitte ergänzen° Sie den Text mit den passenden Endungen. *complete*

1. Drew schickt sein_____ Großeltern Schweizer Schokolade, sein_____ Vater ein Bilderbuch über Berlin, sein_____ Mutter ein schönes Notizbuch und sein_____ Bruder ein Fußballtrikot.
2. Sein_____ Freundin schenkt Drew einen schönen Kalender, sein_____ Mitbewohner schickt er eine Baseballkappe. Und sein_____ zwei Nachbarn kauft er kleine Flaschenöffner.

> **7-14, item 2:** Since you can tell who is receiving the gift by the dative endings on **sein-,** it's not necessary to have the subject (the gift-giver) at the beginning of the sentences here. See how "Drew" or **er** is still the subject throughout?

7-15 Was schenkst du …?

S1: Was schenkst du deiner Freundin zum Geburtstag?

S2: Ich schenke meiner Freundin ein gutes Buch zum Geburtstag.

Was schenkst du	deiner Schwester deinem Freund deiner Freundin unserem Deutschlehrer unserer Deutschlehrerin …	zum Geburtstag? zu Chanukka? zum Valentinstag? zu Halloween? …?

The interrogative pronoun in the dative case: *wem*

The dative form of the interrogative pronoun **wer** has the same ending as the dative form of the masculine definite article.

	Interrogative pronoun	Masculine definite article
NOMINATIVE	wer	der
ACCUSATIVE	wen	den
DATIVE	**wem**	**dem**

Wer ist der Mann dort?
Der Briefträger.

Who is that man there?
The letter carrier.

Wen hat Ihr Hund gebissen?
Den Briefträger.

Whom did your dog bite?
The mailman.

Wem schenken Sie den Wein?
Dem Briefträger.

*To **whom** are you giving the wine?*
*To **the** letter carrier.*

Ein Briefträger in Berlin

7-16 Wem schenkst du das alles? **S2** hat schon alle Weihnachtsgeschenke gekauft. Wem schenkt **S2** diese Sachen°?　　　　　　　　*things*

 ▶　　　　　　　　　　es mein_____ Mutter

S1: Wem schenkst du das Parfüm?　　**S2:** Ich schenke es meiner Mutter.

1. 　　　　　　　　　　　　sie mein_____ Vater

2. 　　　　　es mein_____ Schwester

3. 　　　　　ihn mein_____ Bruder

4. 　　　　　　　　　　　　sie mein_____ Großeltern

| das Armband | die Geldtasche | die Weingläser | der Pullover |

Personal pronouns in the dative case

In English, each personal pronoun has only one object form: *I* changes to *me* (he: *him*, she: *her*, we: *us*, they: *them*). In German, personal pronouns have two object forms. You are already familiar with the accusative form for direct objects. The dative form is used for indirect objects.

Kannst du **mir** eine Tasse Kaffee machen?　*Can you make **me** a cup of coffee?*
Wir servieren **Ihnen** hausgemachte Kuchen.　*We're serving (you) home-made cakes.*

Nominative	Accusative	Dative
ich	mich	**mir**
du	dich	**dir**
er	ihn	**ihm**
es	es	**ihm**
sie	sie	**ihr**
wir	uns	**uns**
ihr	euch	**euch**
sie	sie	**ihnen**
Sie	Sie	**Ihnen**

Ach so!

Ein Paar means *a pair*, i.e., *two* of something, like shoes or gloves. **Ein paar** means *a couple (of)* in the sense of *a few*.

7-17 Was soll ich diesen Leuten schenken? S1 ergänzt mit einer Dativendung. S2 ergänzt mit dem Pronomen **ihm, ihr,** oder **ihnen.**

► mein_____ Großmutter

S1: Was soll ich meiner Großmutter schenken?

S2: Schenk ihr doch ein Paar warme Hausschuhe.

1. mein_____ Vater

2. mein_____ besten Freundin

3. mein_____ Mutter

4. unser_____ neuen Nachbarn (pl)

einen Kugelschreiber	ein paar Flaschen Wein
ein Paar Handschuhe	einen Hockeyschläger

7-18 Vorschläge. Sagen Sie einander, was Ihre Freunde und Verwandten gern tun, und machen Sie einander dann Vorschläge° für passende° Geschenke.

suggestions / appropriate

S1: Meine Freundin spielt gern Tennis.

S2: Dann schenk ihr doch einen Tennisschläger.

Mein Freund (Mein Bruder, Meine Schwester, Meine Eltern, Meine Kusine, Mein Mitbewohner, …)

jewelry

candy

- hört gern Rapmusik (Country, Jazz, …)
- geht gern einkaufen
- spielt gern Computerspiele (Wii, …)
- liest gern Comics
- trinkt gern Bier (Kaffee, Wein, …)

- trägt gern Schmuck°
- reist gern
- liebt Süßigkeiten°
- spielt gern Golf (Baseball, Frisbee, …)
- hat keine Hobbys oder Interessen

Sprachnotiz   Word order: sequence of objects

The sequence of objects is very similar in English. Note that English often uses *to*, but in German you don't need a preposition because the dative already indicates *to* or *for* somebody.

Maria schenkt **ihrem Vater ein Buch**
   zum Vatertag.
Sie schenkt **ihm ein Kochbuch.**
Sie kann **es ihrem Vater** nicht persönlich geben.
Sie muss **es ihm** schicken.

*Maria is giving **her father a book**
   for Father's Day.*
*She's giving **him a cookbook.***
*She can't give **it to her father** personally.*
*She has to send **it to him.***

More on the dative case

7.5 Use expressions that require the dative case

Dative verbs

There are a few German verbs that take only a dative object.

antworten	Warum antwortest du **mir** nicht?	*Why don't you answer **me**?*
danken	Ich danke **dir** für deine Hilfe.	*I thank **you** for your help.*
gehören	Gehört dieser Wagen **dir**?	*Does this car belong **to you**?*
gratulieren	Ich gratuliere **Ihnen** zu Ihrem Erfolg!	*I congratulate **you** on your success!*
helfen	Kannst du **mir** bitte helfen?	*Can you help **me** please?*

> Note that **gratulieren** is also used to wish someone a happy birthday: **Ich möchte dir zum Geburtstag gratulieren.**

7-19 Kleine Gespräche. Ergänzen Sie die passenden Dativverben.

1. ALEXANDER: Wem _____ denn dieser tolle Wagen?
   SEBASTIAN: Meiner Freundin.

2. MARIA: Warum schreibst du denn deinem Bruder nie?
   NICOLE: Weil er mir auch nie _____.

3. STEFAN: Warum kommst du nicht zu unserer Party?
   ROBERT: Weil ich meinem Vater _____ muss.

4. HELGA: Warum rufst du Claudia an?
   SABINE: Sie hat heute Geburtstag und ich möchte ihr _____.

5. FRAU BACH: Aber Frau Kuhn! Warum bringen Sie mir denn Blumen?
   FRAU KUHN: Weil ich Ihnen für Ihre Hilfe _____ möchte.

7-20 Kleine Gespräche. Ergänzen Sie **mir, mich, dir** oder **dich.**

1. PAUL: Gehört _____ dieses tolle Fahrrad?

   SARA: Ja, meine Eltern haben es _____ gekauft.

2. BEATE: Heute früh hat mich Markus besucht! Er hat _____ zum Geburtstag gratuliert und hat _____ diese wunderschönen roten Rosen gebracht. Glaubst du, dass er _____ liebt?

   SOPHIA: Wenn er _____ rote Rosen bringt, liebt er _____ bestimmt.

3. STEFAN: Ich danke _____, dass du _____ bei meinem Referat so viel geholfen hast.

   MARIA: Wenn du _____ jetzt zum Essen einlädst, helfe ich _____ gern wieder.

4. LUKAS: Warum antwortest du _____ nicht?

   PAUL: Ich habe _____ nicht gehört.

The dative case with adjectives

The dative case is often used with adjectives to express a personal opinion, taste, or conviction.

Das ist **mir** sehr wichtig.	*That's very important* **to me.**
Rockmusik ist **meiner Oma** zu laut.	*Rock music is too loud* **for my grandma.**

> English uses the preposition *for* in sentences like *It's too loud for me.* But in German you only need the dative and no preposition: **Es ist *mir (ihm, ihnen)* zu laut.**

7-21 Warum? Ergänzen Sie die passenden Personalpronomen im Dativ.

▶ Sie ist _____ zu laut.

S1: Warum mögen deine Großeltern keine Rockmusik?

S2: Sie ist ihnen zu laut.

1. Warum kaufen Müllers das Haus nicht? — Es ist _____ zu klein.
2. Warum liest du den Roman nicht fertig? — Er ist _____ zu langweilig.
3. Warum trinkt Ingrid ihren Wein nicht? — Er ist _____ zu sauer.
4. Warum geht Robert nicht schwimmen? — Es ist _____ zu kalt.
5. Warum mag Maria diesen Film nicht? — Er ist _____ zu sentimental.
6. Warum nehmt ihr die Wohnung nicht? — Sie ist _____ zu dunkel.
7. Warum kauft Peter den Wagen nicht? — Er ist _____ zu teuer.

7-22 Die Geschmäcker sind verschieden.° Schauen Sie Ihre Mitstudenten an   *Tastes differ.*
und sagen Sie, was für ein Kleidungsstück Sie ihnen zum Geburtstag schenken
wollen, und warum.

S1: Ich schenke Anna ein Sweatshirt. Ihr Sweatshirt ist mir
       ein bisschen zu verrückt.

S2: Ich schenke Justin …

ein bisschen zu verrückt	nicht hip genug
viel zu konservativ	ein bisschen zu altmodisch
nicht sportlich genug	viel zu trendig

> You can also begin the
> sentence with the indirect
> object for emphasis:
> **Justin schenke ich …**

The dative case in idiomatic expressions

The dative case also appears in the following common expressions:

Wie geht es **Ihnen**?	*How are you?*
(Es) tut **mir** leid.	*I'm sorry.*
Das ist **mir** egal.	*I don't care.*
Wie gefällt **dir** mein Mantel?	*How do you like my coat?*
Diese Jacke steht **dir.**	*This jacket looks good on you.*

7-23 Was passt zusammen?

1. Mir geht es heute gar nicht gut.
2. Die Jacke steht dir. Warum nimmst du sie denn nicht?
3. Wie gefällt dir meine neue Jacke?
4. Weiß Jonas, dass du einen neuen Freund hast?
5. Ist Lisa immer noch so krank?

a. Nein, es geht ihr schon wieder viel besser.
b. Ja, aber ich glaube, es ist ihm egal.
c. Weil sie mir zu teuer ist.
d. Sie steht dir sehr gut.
e. Das tut mir aber leid.

> **Lerntipp!**
> To remember how to use
> the verb **gefallen,** think of
> the literal translation:
> **Das Geschenk gefällt mir.** =
> *The present is pleasing to me.*

7-24 Was gefällt Ihnen an Ihren Mitstudenten?

S1: An° Lana gefällt mir, dass sie so freundlich ist.   *about*
S2: An Thomas gefällt mir, dass er …

freundlich	pünktlich	sarkastisch	
lustig°	witzig°		*funny / witty*
natürlich optimistisch	ehrlich° ordentlich	sportlich	*honest*
höflich°			*polite*
cool	spontan praktisch	…	

7.6 Kultur 2

Parties and presents

7.6 Identify cultural practices for celebrating birthdays, giving presents, and congratulating people

Geburtstag feiern!

In the German-speaking countries, the person celebrating the birthday is often referred to as **das Geburtstagskind,** even if that person is an adult! It's the norm that **Geburtstagskinder** organize and host their own **Geburtstagsfeier.** The invited guests of course bring presents. The same tradition of **"einen ausgeben"** (*inviting* or *treating others*) is common at the workplace: You bring some birthday cake for your colleagues to celebrate your own birthday.

Geburtstagsgeschenke

If you're invited to a birthday party, especially to celebrate a **"runden Geburtstag"** (a birthday for any age that includes a zero, e.g., 20, 30, etc.), you can ask the person what they would like to receive. If the person is saving money for something big like a trip, guests contribute by giving money as a gift.

It's considered unlucky to celebrate a birthday—or even wish someone a happy birthday—before the actual date. A popular approach is **Reinfeiern:** You invite your guests to a party that begins late on the evening *before* your birthday; the partying starts before midnight, but friends are careful not to give birthday presents or wishes until the clock strikes 12.

Ein Mitbringsel

> **Achtung!**
> The German word for *present* is **das Geschenk.** The word **das Gift** is a "false friend": It sounds like English *gift,* but it means *poison!*

Einladung zum Essen

If you are invited for a meal **(zum Essen)** or **zu Kaffee und Kuchen** in a German-speaking country, it is customary to bring a small gift **(ein Mitbringsel)** for your hostess or host. The most common gifts are chocolates, a bottle of wine, or flowers. A small **Blumenstrauß** *(bouquet)* should contain an odd number of flowers because this is considered more pleasing to the eye. Only give red roses if you truly want to signal romantic affection!

Glückwünsche

To wish someone well on a special occasion, two common options are **Alles Gute** and **Herzlichen Glückwunsch.** You can then add **zu** or its contractions **zum** or **zur** to mention the occasion.

7-25 Alles Gute! Welcher Glückwunsch passt am besten zu jeder Situation?

Situation	Glückwunsch
Herr und Frau Niemeyer sind heute 50 Jahre verheiratet. Auf dem Kuchen stehen die Worte:	a. Alles Gute zum Uni-Abschluss!
Marlene bekommt heute ihren *Master in Politik*. Ihre Großmutter sagt ihr:	b. Herzlichen Glückwunsch zum Geburtstag!
Mattias schenkt seiner Freundin rote Rosen am 14. Februar und sagt ihr:	c. Ich gratuliere dir zum neuen Job!
Ahmet hat eine neue Arbeit bei Mercedes in Stuttgart. Du sagst ihm:	d. Die besten Glückwünsche zur goldenen Hochzeit!
Benjamin wird morgen 19 und lädt seine Freunde zur Party heute Abend ein. Um Mitternacht sagen ihm alle:	e. Alles Liebe zum Valentinstag!

7.7 Kommunikation und Formen 2

The dative prepositions

7.7 Use various expressions for time, manner, and place with dative prepositions

In *Kapitel 5* you learned the prepositions that are followed by an object in the accusative case: **durch, für, gegen, ohne, um.** The prepositions that are always followed by an object in the *dative case* are **aus, außer, bei, mit, nach, seit, von, zu.**

aus	out of	Nimm den Weißwein **aus dem Kühlschrank°!**	*refrigerator*
	from	Der Wein ist **aus dem Rheintal.**	
außer	except for	**Außer meinem Bruder** sind alle hier.	
bei	for, at	Mein Bruder arbeitet **bei der Bahn** und konnte nicht kommen.	
	at, at the home of	Diesmal feiern wir Muttis Geburtstag **bei meiner Schwester** in Potsdam.	
	near, close to	Potsdam ist **bei Berlin.**	
mit	with, by	Ich bin **mit dem Zug** nach Potsdam gekommen.	
nach	after	**Nach dem Geburtstagsessen** haben wir einen Spaziergang gemacht.	
	to	Ich fahre morgen **nach Bonn** zurück.	
seit	since	Ich lebe **seit dem letzten Sommer** in Bonn.	
	for	Meine Schwester lebt **seit zehn Jahren** in Potsdam.	
von	from	**Von meiner Schwester** hat Mutti ein schönes Bild bekommen.	
	of	Eine Freundin **von Mutti** hat ihr ein goldenes Armband geschickt.	
	about	Mutti hat uns oft **von dieser Freundin** erzählt.	
zu	to	Wir kommen alle sehr gern **zu meiner Schwester.**	
	for	**Zu ihrem 50. Geburtstag** hat Mutti von uns allen eine Reise nach Hawaii bekommen.	
	with	**Zu dem leckeren Geburtstagskuchen** haben wir Muttis Lieblingstee getrunken.	

is spending **7-26 Ein Brief aus Hamburg.** Stephanie, eine Studentin aus Amerika, verbringt°
Weihnachten bei Freunden in Deutschland. Ergänzen Sie **aus, außer, bei, mit** oder **nach**.

> Stephanie's letter to her family at Christmas shows some typical features of German snail-mail. What is different from the format of a letter in English? How does Stephanie wish her family a happy new year?

Hamburg, den 24. Dezember 2017

Liebe Eltern und lieber Opa,

herzliche Grüße _____ der Hansestadt Hamburg. Claudias Eltern wollten, dass ich
an Weihnachten _____ Hamburg komme, damit ich mal sehe, wie man _____ ihnen
Weihnachten feiert. Die ganze Familie ist hier _____ Claudias Schwester Maria. Sie studiert
in Berkeley und verbringt Weihnachten _____ Freunden in San Francisco. Heute Abend gibt
es _____ Bergers wie _____ den meisten deutschen Familien nur ein ganz normales, kleines
Essen, und _____ dem Essen ist dann gleich die Bescherung. Ich schenke Claudias Eltern einen
Kalender _____ vielen schönen Farbfotos von Amerika. Ich habe euch _____ München ein
Paket _____ ein paar Geschenken geschickt. Für Opa sind übrigens auch ein paar Münchener
Zeitungen im Paket.

Euch allen einen guten Rutsch ins neue Jahr!

   Stephanie

Sprachnotiz   Word order: time/manner/place

You have already learned that expressions of time precede expressions of place.

Claudia und Stephanie fahren **morgen nach Hamburg.**

When an expression of manner is added (i.e., when you want to say *how* something is done) the order is *time / **manner** / place.*

Claudia und Stephanie fahren **morgen *mit dem Zug* nach Hamburg.**

Der Hamburger Hauptbahnhof

7-27 Immer negativ. Ergänzen Sie mit Dativpräpositionen und Dativendungen.

S1:

S2:

1. Fährt dieser Zug _____ Bremen?

   Nein, er fährt _____ Hamburg.

2. Kommt Stephanie _____ Kanada?

   Nein, sie kommt _____ d_____ USA.

3. _____ wem hast du diese schönen Ohrringe? _____ deinem Freund?

   Nein, _____ mein_____ Eltern.

4. Wo verbringst du die Frühlingsferien? _____ deinen Eltern?

   Nein, _____ mein_____ Freund.

5. _____ wem gehst du heute Abend ins Kino? _____ deinem Bruder?

   Nein, _____ ein paar Freunden.

6. _____ wann hast du dieses schöne Fahrrad? _____ deinem Geburtstag?

   Nein, schon _____ ein_____ Jahr.

7. _____ welchem Zahnarzt gehst du? _____ Dr. Haag?

   Nein, ich gehe _____ Dr. Meyer.

8. Sind _____ David alle hier?

   Nein, alle _____ David und Florian!

7-28 Erzähl mir etwas von deinen Eltern! Stellen Sie einander Fragen zu Ihren Eltern. **S2** findet Tipps für die passenden Präpositionen.

S1: Woher ist deine Mutter/dein Vater?

S2: Aus …

Wo arbeitet sie/er?

Bei …

Seit wann arbeitet sie/er dort?

Seit …

Wie kommt sie/er zur Arbeit?

Mit …

Wohin fährt sie/er im nächsten Urlaub?

Nach …

…

7-29 Meine Winterferien. Stellen Sie einander die folgenden Fragen.

S1: Bei wem verbringst du die Winterferien?   **S2:** Bei …

S1: Was machst du da?   **S2:** Ich …

S2: Bei wem …   **S3:** Bei …

Contractions

The following contractions of dative prepositions and definite articles are commonly used.

bei + dem	=	**beim**	Brigitte ist heute Vormittag **beim** Zahnarzt.
von + dem	=	**vom**	Dieses Brot ist **vom** Öko-Bäcker.
zu + dem	=	**zum**	Fährt dieser Bus **zum** Bahnhof?
zu + der	=	**zur**	Seit wann fährst du denn mit dem Fahrrad **zur** Uni?

Sprachnotiz Wo, woher, and wohin and the dative prepositions

As you've seen, German makes a distinction between a fixed location (**wo?**) and movement away from or toward something (**wohin?, woher?**). This distinction affects the prepositions needed for sentences, too. It's easier to master several dative prepositions by connecting them to the notion of **wo, wohin,** or **woher:**

Wo ist Stephanie?   Sie ist **bei** ihrem Freund. *(at/with people)*
Wohin fährt sie?   Sie fährt **zum** Bahnhof. *(to a place, building)*
Woher kommt sie?   Sie kommt **aus** Amerika. *(as in to hail from a place)*

7-30: This exercise will be easier if you connect **wo** with **beim; wohin** with **zum/zur,** and **woher** with **vom,** as seen in the earlier *Sprachnotiz.*

7-30 Wo? Woher? Wohin? Ergänzen Sie die Antworten mit **beim, vom, zum** oder **zur.**

▶ Wo ist Brigitte?

S1: Wo ist Brigitte?   S2: Beim Friseur.

1. Wohin gehst du?

3. Wohin fährst du?

5. Wohin rennst du?

7. Wohin gehst du?

2. Woher kommst du?

4. Wo ist Silke?

6. Woher kommt ihr?

8. Wo sind Bernd und Sabine?

Lerntipp!
Nouns ending in **-ei,** like **die Bäckerei** and **Fleischerei** are always feminine and always stressed on the last syllable.

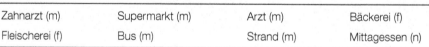

| Zahnarzt (m) | Supermarkt (m) | Arzt (m) | Bäckerei (f) |
| Fleischerei (f) | Bus (m) | Strand (m) | Mittagessen (n) |

Nach versus *zu*

When **nach** and **zu** indicate a point of destination, they both mean *to.* Which one you use depends on the type of destination.

nach		zu	
to a city	nach Leipzig	*to a building*	zum Bahnhof
to a state	nach Sachsen	*to an institution*	zur Uni
to a country	nach Luxemburg	*to a place of business*	zum Supermarkt
to a continent	nach Europa	*to someone's residence*	zu Zieglers

Zum Hotel
und zu den
Restaurants

Zum Parkplatz

7-31 Kleine Gespräche. Ergänzen Sie **nach, zu, zum** oder **zur.**

1. HERR BACH: Wie weit ist es von hier _____ Ihrem Ferienhaus bei
    Salzburg?

    FRAU KOCH: Von hier _____ Salzburg sind es etwa 500 Kilometer und von
    dort _____ Ferienhaus fährt man eine halbe Stunde.

2. FRAU WOLF: Warum fliegt Herr Meyer denn _____ Detroit?

    FRAU KUNZ: Ich glaube, er geht dort _____ Internationalen Auto-Show (f).

3. CLAUDIA: Fährst du in den Semesterferien wieder _____ Köln
    _____ deinem Onkel?

    SARA: Nein, diesmal fahre ich mit Peter _____ Berlin.

4. TOURIST: Wie weit ist es von hier _____ Hotel?

    TOURLEITER: Nicht weit! Und vom Hotel ist es nicht weit _____ den
    Restaurants.

Aus versus *von*

When **aus** and **von** indicate a point of origin, they both mean *from.*

aus		von	
from a city	aus Leipzig	*from a building*	vom Bahnhof
from a state	aus Sachsen	*from an institution*	von der Uni
from a country	aus Luxemburg	*from a person*	von meinem Freund
from a continent	aus Europa	*from a point of departure*	von Berlin nach Potsdam

7-32 Kleine Gespräche. Ergänzen Sie **aus** oder **von**.

1. SEBASTIAN: Weißt du vielleicht, wie lang der Bus _____ New York nach San Francisco braucht?

    PETER: Frag doch Stephanie. Sie ist _____ den USA und weiß es bestimmt.

2. CLAUDIA: Hier ist ein Brief _____ Chicago, Stephanie.

    STEPHANIE: _____ meinen Eltern?

    CLAUDIA: Nein, ich glaube, er ist _____ deiner Uni.

3. ANNETTE: _____ wem hast du diese Halskette?

    CHRISTINE: _____ meinem Freund. Er hat sie mir _____ der Schweiz mitgebracht.

7-33 Von wem hast du das? Schauen Sie, welche von Ihren Mitstudenten etwas besonders Schönes oder Wichtiges haben, und fragen Sie, von wem sie es haben.

S1: Von wem hast du den interessanten Ring, Andrea?

S2: Von wem hast du …?

S2: Von … / Ich habe ihn selbst gekauft.

S3: …

die coole Sonnenbrille   das Handy   deine Schuhe/Stiefel

…

die eleganten Ohrringe   die schicke Jacke   den neuen Rucksack

die lustigen Socken   das schöne Armband   die coole Wasserflasche

7-34 Eine Platzreservierung. Stephanie reserviert für eine Reise mit dem ICE einen Sitzplatz. Beantworten Sie mit Ihrer Partnerin/Ihrem Partner die Fragen zu dieser Reservierung.

1. Wohin reist Stephanie?
2. Von welchem Bahnhof fährt sie ab?
3. Wann fährt der ICE von München ab und wann kommt er in Hamburg an? (Datum und Uhrzeit)
4. Wie lange dauert die Fahrt?
5. Welche Zugnummer hat der ICE?
6. In welchem Wagen ist der reservierte Platz? Finden Sie die Wagennummer!
7. Welcher Sitzplatz ist für Stephanie reserviert?
8. Wie viel muss sie für diese Reservierung bezahlen?

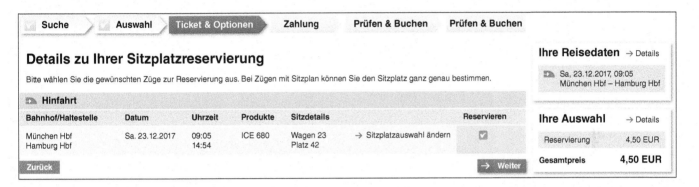

The preposition *seit*

When **seit** refers to a point in time, its English equivalent is usually *since*; when it refers to a *period of time*, its English equivalent is usually *for*. Note that German uses the present tense in such contexts, whereas English uses the perfect tense.

Mara lernt **seit** einem Jahr Deutsch.
Sie lebt **seit** Anfang Mai in Kiel.

*Mara has been learning German **for** a year.*
*She has been living in Kiel **since** the beginning of May.*

7-35 Kleines Interview. Seit wann? Interviewen Sie einander und ergänzen Sie die Dativendungen.

- Seit wann lernst du Deutsch?
- Seit wann studierst du an dieser Uni?
- Seit wann lebst du in ___?
- Seit wann hast du dein Handy?
- Seit wann kennst du deine Deutschprofessorin/deinen Deutschprofessor?
- Hast du einen Wagen? Seit wann?
- Hast du einen Hund/eine Katze? Seit wann? Wie heißt er/sie?
- Spielst du ein Instrument? Was für ein Instrument? Seit wann?

seit ein____ Monat   seit zwei Monat____   seit ein____ Semester
seit ein____ Jahr   seit zwei/drei/vier Jahr____   seit ein____ Woche

Lerntipp!
This exercise is easier if you review some simple genders in time expressions: **der Monat, das Semester, das Jahr,** and **die Woche.**

Dative endings of preceded adjectives

7.8 Describe people, places, and things

Adjectives that are preceded by a **der**-word or an **ein**-word in the dative case always take the ending **-en**.

Wer ist der Typ mit dem golden**en** Ohrring und den lang**en** Haaren?

Who's the guy with the gold earring and the long hair?

	Masculine		Neuter		Feminine		Plural	
DATIVE	dem / einem	jung**en** Mann	dem / einem	klein**en** Kind	der / einer	jung**en** Frau	den / meinen	klein**en** Kindern

7-36 Wer ist auf diesem Familienbild? Ergänzen Sie die passenden Endungen.

▶ die Frau mit dem grün___ Kleid und den braun___ Haaren

         Das ist …

S1: Wer ist die Frau mit dem grünen Kleid und den braunen Haaren?

S2: Das ist meine Mutter.

1. der Mann mit der blau_____ Jacke und der rot_____ Krawatte
2. der Junge mit den braun_____ Haaren und dem rot_____ Hemd
3. die Frau mit der weiß_____ Hose und der rosarot_____ Bluse
4. der Mann mit der schwarz_____ Brille und dem blau_____ Pullover
5. das Mädchen mit dem rosarot_____ Kleid und den weiß_____ Schuhen
6. die Frau mit dem grau_____ Hut und dem gelb_____ Kleid

7-37 Detektiv im Deutschunterricht. Wer ist das? Suchen Sie in Ihrer Deutschklasse 2–3 Studenten, aber sagen Sie ihre Namen nicht! Stellen Sie Fragen über diese Studenten. Der beste Detektiv identifiziert die richtigen Personen!

S1: Wer ist die Person mit der kleinen Brille und dem schwarzen T-Shirt?
S2: Das ist …
S3: Wer ist die Person mit dem schwarzen Rucksack und den braunen Schuhen?

Dative endings of unpreceded adjectives

You will remember that adjectives not preceded by a **der**-word or an **ein**-word show the gender, number, and case of the noun by taking the appropriate **der**-word ending. This also holds true for the dative case.

Zu französisch**em** Camembert trinkt Onkel Alfred immer kanadischen Eiswein.

With French camembert Uncle Alfred always drinks Canadian ice wine.

	Masculine	Neuter	Feminine	Plural
DATIVE	gut**em** Kaffee	gut**em** Bier	gut**er** Salami	gut**en** Äpfeln

7-38 Ein Gourmet. Onkel Alfred isst gern international. Ergänzen Sie die passenden Endungen.

1. Zu französisch_____ Weißbrot (n) isst er nur holländischen Käse.
2. Zu italienisch_____ Lasagne (f) trinkt er nur griechischen Wein.
3. Zu polnisch_____ Wurst (f) isst er nur französischen Senf°.   *mustard*
4. Zu englisch_____ Cheddar (m) isst er nur neuseeländische Äpfel.
5. Zu deutsch_____ Schwarzbrot (n) isst er nur irische Butter.
6. Zu italienisch_____ Eis (n) trinkt er nur türkischen Kaffee.
7. Zu belgisch_____ Schokolade (f) isst er nur israelische Mandarinen.
8. Zu amerikanisch_____ Kartoffelchips (pl) trinkt er nur deutsches Bier.

7.8 Video-Treff

Mein bestes Geschenk

7.9 Understand authentic video of German speakers talking about getting gifts

Stefan Kuhlmann, Stefan Meister, Ursula und André erzählen von ihrem besten Geschenk. Machen Sie die erste Aufgabe, **Was ist das auf Englisch?**, bevor Sie das Video anschauen.

7-39 Was ist das auf Englisch?

1. Das ist das Cover der Comic-**Ausgabe** von *Der kleine Hobbit*.
2. Das beste Geschenk ist ein **selbstgemachtes** T-Shirt.
3. Ich habe dieses Geschenk von meiner **damaligen** Freundin bekommen.
4. Termiten haben diesen Baum **ausgehöhlt.**
5. Ich habe dann selber **daran** gearbeitet.
6. Ich habe Inlineskates. Meine Freundin hat auch **welche.**
7. Sie sagte, dass ihre Familie diese Instrumente selber **herstellt.**
8. Madame Sec hat von **sich** erzählt.

a. herself
b. some
c. on it
d. at that time
e. hollowed out
f. produces
g. edition
h. homemade

7-40 Richtig oder falsch? Lesen Sie die Aussagen über Stefan Kuhlmann und Stefan Meister und ihre besten Geschenke. Sind diese Aussagen richtig oder falsch? Wenn eine Aussage falsch ist, korrigieren Sie sie!

	RICHTIG	FALSCH
1. Stefan Kuhlmann hat das T-Shirt von einer alten Freundin bekommen.	☐	☐
2. Das Bild auf dem T-Shirt ist von der Comic-Ausgabe von *Der kleine Hobbit*.	☐	☐
3. Stefan findet es nicht gut, dass das T-Shirt selbstgemacht ist.	☐	☐
4. Auf dem T-Shirt steht auch „Für Stefan".	☐	☐
5. Stefan Meister hat das Didgeridoo von einer australischen Freundin bekommen.	☐	☐
6. Das Instrument kommt aus einem teuren Souvenirgeschäft.	☐	☐
7. Das war ein besonderes Geschenk für ihn, weil es typisch australisch ist.	☐	☐

7-41 Was passt? Ergänzen Sie die Aussagen über Ursula and André.

1. Die Inlineskates hat Ursula ____ bekommen.
   ☐ zu Weihnachten   ☐ zum Geburtstag
2. Sie hat die Inlineskates ____ bekommen.
   ☐ vor zwei Wochen   ☐ vor zwei Tagen
3. Das war ein Geschenk von ____.
   ☐ ihrer Mutter   ☐ ihrer besten Freundin
4. Ursulas ____ hat auch Inlineskates und jetzt können sie zusammen fahren.
   ☐ Freundin Anke   ☐ Mutter Anke
5. André hat ____ zwei Geschenke bekommen: eine traditionelle afrikanische Trommel und ein Etui.
   ☐ vor fünf Jahren   ☐ vor vier Jahren
6. Das Etui ist für ____.
   ☐ Kleinigkeiten   ☐ die Djembe
7. André hat Madame Sec ____ kennengelernt.
   ☐ im Senegal   ☐ in seiner französischen Klasse
8. André findet die Djembe ein gutes Geschenk, ____.
   ☐ obwohl er selbst nicht spielen kann   ☐ weil er selbst gut spielen kann

))) 7.9 Wortschatz 2

Wichtige Vokabeln

7.10 Learn vocabulary to talk about parties, presents, and everyday items

Nomen

die Fete, -n	party
der Gast, ⁻e	guest
die Kerze, -n	candle
das Mitbringsel, -	small gift *(for a host)*
die Süßigkeiten *(pl)*	sweets; candy
die Geldtasche, -n	wallet
der Handschuh, -e	glove
der Hausschuh, -e	slipper
der Hut, ⁻e	hat
die Krawatte, -n	tie
der Schmuck	jewelry
der Hockeyschläger, -	hockey stick
der Tennisschläger, -	tennis racquet
das Stofftier, -e	stuffed animal
das Tier, -e	animal
der Briefträger, - **die Briefträgerin, -nen** }	letter carrier
der Kugelschreiber, -	ballpoint pen
das Paket, -e	package, parcel
der Zahnarzt, ⁻e **die Zahnärztin, -nen** }	dentist
die Zahnschmerzen *(pl)*	toothache
die Anzeige, -n	announcement; ad
der Führerschein, -e	driver's license
die Hilfe	help
die Sache, -n	thing
der Typ, -en	guy

Verben

antworten (+ *dat*)	to answer
danken (+ *dat*)	to thank
gehören (+ *dat*)	to belong to
gratulieren (+ *dat*)	to congratulate
helfen (hilft), geholfen (+ *dat*)	to help
wünschen	to wish
verbringen, verbracht	to spend *(time)*

Andere Wörter

einfach	simple; simply
einmal	once
noch einmal, noch mal	once more; (over) again
etwa	approximately
verschieden	different

witzig; lustig	witty; funny
wohl	probably; perhaps

Ausdrücke

eine Frage stellen	to ask a question
zum Geburtstag gratulieren	to wish a Happy Birthday
Zum Wohl!	To your health!
Prost!	Cheers!
Das ist mir egal.	I don't care.
Diese Jacke gefällt mir.	I like this jacket.

Diese Jacke gefällt mir.

Diese Jacke steht dir.	This jacket looks good on you.
Es tut mir leid.	I'm sorry.
Mir fällt nichts ein.	I can't think of anything.

Das Gegenteil

faul ≠ fleißig	lazy ≠ hard-working
glücklich ≠ unglücklich	happy ≠ unhappy
höflich ≠ unhöflich	polite ≠ impolite

Leicht zu verstehen

die Bäckerei, -en	**die Party, -s**
die Kartoffelchips *(pl)*	**der Ring, -e**
der Muttertag, -e	**die Rose, -n**
der Valentinstag, -e	**der Supermarkt, ⁻e**
das Parfüm, -s	

Wörter im Kontext

7-42 Was schenkst du diesen Leuten? Antworten Sie mit „Ich schenke ihr/ihm …"

1. Maria hat immer kalte Hände.
2. Stefan hat jetzt seinen Führerschein.
3. Mein Opa schreibt viele Briefe.
4. Paul trägt immer nur Anzüge.
5. Laura hat nur sehr wenig Schmuck.
6. Kurt macht viel Sport.
7. Meine Nichte Anna wird morgen ein Jahr alt.
8. Meine Oma hat immer kalte Füße.

a. eine schicke Krawatte
b. ein Paar warme Hausschuhe
c. ein goldenes Armband
d. ein süßes Stofftier
e. einen guten Kuli
f. ein Paar warme Handschuhe
g. meinen sehr alten Wagen
h. einen Tennisschläger und einen Hockeyschläger

> **Kugelschreiber:** This word is often shortened to **Kuli.**

> **Tennisschläger, Hockeyschläger:** These nouns are derived from the verb **schlagen** *to hit*.

> **-schmerzen** can be added to other body parts to indicate pain felt there: **Kopfschmerzen, Bauchschmerzen, Rückenschmerzen.**

7-43 Was ich für Leah alles tue.

1. Wenn Leah Geburtstag hat,
2. Wenn Leah zu viel zu tun hat,
3. Wenn Leah etwas für mich getan hat,
4. Wenn Leah Zahnschmerzen hat,
5. Wenn ich bei Leah eingeladen bin,

a. schicke ich sie zum Zahnarzt.
b. danke ich ihr.
c. kaufe ich ihr als Mitbringsel immer Blumen.
d. helfe ich ihr.
e. gratuliere ich ihr.

sentences **7-44 Mit anderen Worten.** Welche Sätze° bedeuten etwa dasselbe?

1. Diese Jacke gefällt mir.
2. Diese Jacke steht mir.
3. Sie wünschen?
4. Diese Jacke gehört mir nicht.
5. Sind Sie immer so faul?
6. Um wie viel Uhr beginnt eure Fete?

a. Wann ist eure Party?
b. Das ist nicht meine Jacke.
c. Ich finde diese Jacke schön.
d. Tun Sie immer so wenig?
e. In dieser Jacke sehe ich gut aus.
f. Was kann ich für Sie tun?

Sprachnotiz   Derselbe, dasselbe, dieselbe

The English equivalent of **derselbe, dasselbe,** and **dieselbe** is *the same*. Note that both parts of this German compound word take case endings.

Sag doch nicht immer **dasselbe!**
Hat Karin immer noch **denselben** Freund?

*Don't always say **the same** thing!*
*Does Karin still have **the same** boyfriend?*

Wörter unter der Lupe

Predicting gender

Infinitive forms of verbs are often used as nouns. Such nouns are always *neuter* and they are capitalized, of course. Their English equivalents usually end in *-ing*.

Wann gibst du endlich **das Rauchen** auf?   *When are you finally going to give up **smoking?***

When the contraction **beim** is followed by such a noun, it often means *while*.

Opa ist **beim Fernsehen** eingeschlafen.   *Grandpa fell asleep **while watching TV.***

7-45 Was passt?

Schwimmen / Wissen / Leben / Einkaufen / Trinken / Schreiben

1. _____ ist sehr gesund.
2. Gestern haben wir beim _____ fast zweihundert Euro ausgegeben.
3. Fang doch endlich mit deinem Referat an! Vielleicht fällt dir beim _____ etwas ein.
4. Das viele _____ hat diesen Mann krank gemacht.
5. Helga ist gestern Abend ohne Günters _____ mit Holger ausgegangen.
6. Dieses faule _____ gefällt mir.

7-46 Was ist das auf Englisch?

Giving language color

In *Kapitel 6* you saw how the names of body parts can be used metaphorically. As the expressions here show, the names of common food items can also be used in this way. The expressions with an asterisk are quite informal and should only be used with family or friends.

Es ist alles in Butter.*	*Everything's going smoothly.*
Das ist mir wurst.*	*I couldn't care less.*
Er will immer eine Extrawurst.*	*He always wants special treatment.*
Das ist doch alles Käse.*	*That's all bunk!*
Der Apfel fällt nicht weit vom Stamm.	*The apple doesn't fall far from the tree.*

Das ist mir wurst: In this expression **wurst** has an adverbial function and the initial letter is therefore lowercase.

7-47 Was passt zusammen?

1. Ralf ist wie sein Vater. Er fängt alles an und macht nichts fertig.
2. Hast du immer noch Probleme mit deinem Freund?
3. Deine neue Jacke gefällt mir gar nicht.
4. Günter sagt, dass du ihn liebst.
5. Alle anderen kommen zu Fuß, aber Lisa sollen wir mit dem Auto abholen.

a. Das ist doch alles Käse, was er sagt.
b. Das ist mir wurst.
c. Sie will doch immer eine Extrawurst.
d. Der Apfel fällt nicht weit vom Stamm.
e. Nein, jetzt ist alles wieder in Butter.

7.10 Alles zusammen

Herzlichen Glückwunsch!

In the German-speaking countries as in North America, significant life events and personal achievements are often celebrated through festive celebrations or parties. It's equally common to send personal congratulations in a **Grußkarte** (*greeting card*). Yet another option is to place a personalized announcement (**Anzeige**) in an online publication, usually a local newspaper.

Here you'll have the chance to read several small ads for a variety of occasions, decide on an appropriate present to give one of those people, and then create a **Grußkarte** of your own!

Schritt 1: Zum Lesen

7-48 **Glückwünsche!** Lesen Sie die vier Anzeigen. *Wer* feiert *was* hier?

	Wer hat die Glückwünsche geschrieben?	Was feiert man hier?
1.		
2.		
3.		
4.		

FÜHRERSCHEIN BUNDESREPUBLIK DEUTSCHLAND
D

Lieber Karl!

Endlich ist der Tag gekommen,
auf den Du schon so lange gewartet hast.
Herzlichen Glückwunsch zur bestandenen
Führerscheinprüfung. Wir wünschen Dir alles Gute
und einen großen Schutzengel für Deine Autofahrten!

Wir lieben Dich!

Opa und Oma

Liebe Marie,

Für deine Erstkommunion
am Sonntag, den 9. Mai
wünschen dir Mama und Papa alles Liebe.
Wir sind stolz auf dich, bleib so wie du bist!
Vielen Dank sagen wir auch allen,
die unserer Marie bei der
Vorbereitung zur Kommunion
geholfen haben.

Familie Meyer

Häppi Börsdee tu juhuhu!

Liebe Julia, 18 Jahre sind nun vergangen,
seit Dein Leben angefangen.
Sport und Spaß, das ist dein Motto,
besser als ein Gewinn im Lotto!
Wir gratulieren Dir zu Deinem Feste,
auch heute sind wir wieder Deine Gäste.
Seit dem 6. Lebensjahr feiern wir dieses
Fest gemeinsam,
deshalb sind wir auch nie einsam.
Deine Clique (Susi, Mel und Jen)

Hallo Welt, ich bin da!
Oskar
27. November 2017

Wir freuen uns über die Geburt unseres
Sohnes und Bruders. Die überglückliche Familie
Anna und Walter Leuschner mit Martin

Wir danken dem gesamten Team des Diakonie-Klinikums in Dissen.

Schritt 2: Zum Sprechen

 7-49 Geschenkideen. Planen Sie mit einem Partner ein schönes Geschenk. Sagen Sie auch, **warum** das ein gutes Geschenk ist!

S1: Was ist das perfekte Geschenk für Baby Leuschner?
S2: Was schenken wir Julia zum achtzehnten Geburtstag?

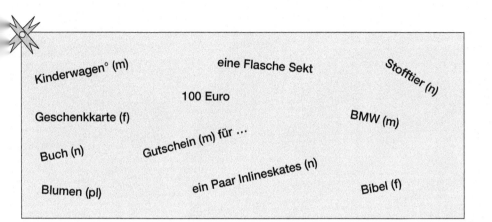

baby carriage

Schritt 3: Zum Schreiben

7-50 Die besten Glückwünsche. Schreiben Sie eine **Grußkarte** für eine Freundin, einen Freund oder für jemand aus Ihrer Familie. Weitere Beispiele finden Sie im Internet, wenn Sie „**Glückwunschkarten**" oder „**Glückwunschanzeigen**" googeln! Denken Sie zuerst an diese Fragen:

- Wem schreiben Sie diese Karte?
- Welcher Anlass ist das (zum Geburtstag, zum Valentinstag, …)?
- Was möchten Sie dieser Person wünschen? Ein paar Ideen: Herzlichen Glückwunsch, Alles Gute, Ich gratuliere dir zu/zum/zur…,

To compose your card, you can use ideas and phrases from the models here as well as **Glückwünsche** from **Wortschatz 1** and **Kultur 2!**

Kapitel 8
Wohnen

Ein Studentenheim in Nürnberg

Learning Objectives

8.1 Compare student housing options and amenities in North America and the German-speaking countries

8.2 Learn vocabulary to talk about where and how you live

8.3 Recognize and pronounce various sounds spelled with *s* in German

8.4 Distinguish between *wohin* and *wo* in questions and answers

8.5 Use two-way prepositions to distinguish between *movement toward a destination* and *being at a fixed location*

8.6 Describe moving things from one place to another

8.7 Describe where something is located

8.8 Identify important characteristics and accomplishments of the Bauhaus School

8.9 Say when something occurs

8.10 Create more complex sentences using infinitive phrases

8.11 Indicate possession or relationships

8.12 Understand authentic video of German speakers talking about their living situation

8.13 Learn vocabulary to talk about everyday things at home and in town

8.1 Vorschau

Mitbewohner gesucht!

Signs like this are commonly found around universities in German-speaking countries. This one from Berlin gives basic information about the room that's available and a sense of the people who'd be sharing the apartment.

A **Wohngemeinschaft (WG)** is one of the most popular housing choices of students in the German-speaking countries.

Andrea   Ben   Mia   ?

Richtig glücklich sind wir nur zu viert!

WG in **Kreuzberg** hat schönes **20m² großes Zimmer frei**

- vollständig möbliert (Bett, Schreibtisch, usw.)
- zentrale Lage - ca. 10 Min. zur Mitte
- großes, helles Wohnzimmer, Bad + zusätzliches Klo, Küche (mit Spülmaschine), Waschmaschine
- auch süße Hauskatze 🐱

Miete: nur 240 Euro kalt   Nebenk.: 30 Euro

Wir suchen einen supernetten, humorvollen, sauberen, nicht megalauten Mitbewohner. Bitte nur Nichtraucher!

8-1 Abkürzungen. Finden Sie die Abkürzungen in der Anzeige. Dann wählen Sie die passende Bedeutung auf Englisch.

Wort	Abkürzung	Bedeutung	Auf Englisch
Minuten	*Min.*	*e*	a. shared housing
Nebenkosten			b. toilet
und so weiter			c. square meters
Wohngemeinschaft			d. etc.
Quadratmeter			e. minutes
Wasserklosett			f. about
circa			g. additional costs

8-2 Was ist das auf Deutsch? Jetzt finden Sie in der Anzeige die deutschen Äquivalente für die folgenden Wörter und Ausdrücke: *living room, rent, dishwasher, location, furnished.*

8-3 Ist das Zimmer für mich?

Ja	Nein	
☐	☐	Ich rauche gern.
☐	☐	Ich habe keine Möbel.
☐	☐	Ich spiele Trompete und muss jeden Tag zwei Stunden üben.
☐	☐	Ich kann nicht mehr als 250 im Monat bezahlen.
☐	☐	Ich bin allergisch gegen alle Haustiere.
☐	☐	Ich bin Studentin, bin sehr nett und habe einen guten Humor.

Wo Studenten wohnen

 8-4 Wo und wie wohnen diese Studenten?

Magda = M　　　　　　　**Cindy = C**　　　　　　　**Kevin = K**

Wo wohnen alle?	Wie gefällt es ihnen dort?	Warum oder warum nicht?	Wie kommen sie zur Uni?
____ im Privathaus _M_ im Studentenheim ____ zu Hause ____ in einer WG	____ sehr gut ____ gut ____ nicht sehr gut ____ gar nicht	____ nette Mitbewohner ____ zu viel Arbeit ____ keine Küchenbenutzung ____ viele Partys	____ mit dem Wagen ____ mit dem Fahrrad ____ mit dem Bus ____ zu Fuß

Ein Zimmer mit Balkon im Privathaus

8-5 Wo und wie wohnst du? Stellen Sie einander die folgenden Fragen und berichten Sie, was Sie herausgefunden haben.

S1:

S2:

Wo wohnst du?　　Ich wohne
- ☐ im Studentenheim.
- ☐ noch zu Hause.
- ☐ mit ein paar anderen Studenten zusammen in einem Haus/einer WG.

　　　　　　　　Ich habe
- ☐ ein Zimmer in einem Privathaus.
- ☐ (mit einer Freundin/einem Freund zusammen) eine kleine Wohnung.

Gefällt es dir dort?　　Ja, weil
- ☐ meine Mitbewohner sehr nett sind.
- ☐ es dort sehr ruhig ist.
- ☐ das Zimmer (die Wohnung) groß und hell ist.
- ☐ ich dort kochen (backen, grillen) kann.
- ☐ …

　　　　　　　　Nein, weil
- ☐ ich keine Freunde einladen darf.
- ☐ ich keine laute Musik spielen darf.
- ☐ meine Mitbewohner so unordentlich sind.
- ☐ es mir dort zu laut ist.
- ☐ …

Wie kommst du zur Uni?　　Ich
- ☐ gehe zu Fuß.
- ☐ fahre mit dem Fahrrad (dem Wagen/dem Bus/…).

8.2 Kultur 1

Student housing

8.1 Compare student housing options and amenities in North America and the German-speaking countries

Finding a place to live in a **Universitätsstadt** in the German-speaking countries is often a challenge. Very few universities are situated on a campus. University buildings are scattered all over town, and the existing **Studentenwohnheime** don't come close to meeting the demand for student housing.

Privat wohnen

Many students choose to live at home or rent a room in a **Privathaus,** with or without **Küchenbenutzung** (*kitchen privileges*). But one of the most popular and economical living arrangements for students is the **Wohngemeinschaft (WG),** a group of students renting an apartment together and sharing responsibility for meals and household chores. It's typical to have three to four **Mitbewohner,** each of whom has a single room. Although they serve the practical purpose of providing a cheap place to live, **WGs** are also seen as a way to connect with a smaller **Gemeinschaft** (*community*), particularly in larger cities.

Beim Chillen in einer WG

Im Studentenheim

The most common living situation in dorms is a single room, typically furnished with a bed, shelves, a desk, and a sink. Residents on a hall usually share bathrooms as well as a kitchen. Kitchens are often supplied with necessities like pots, pans, and dishes, and in some dorms, residents pay a small fee each semester to keep the kitchen stocked with items that everyone can use, such as salt, pepper, oil, spices, coffee, etc. Some dorms are located close to university buildings, but others are in highrise buildings outside of town.

Even in dorms, everyone takes turns doing general chores, like taking out the recycling. A **Hausmeister** is available to handle problems like lockouts, broken toilets, and security issues. Dorms offer amenities such as a **Partykeller, Volleyballplatz,** and **Musikräume,** and events like a **Grillabend, Filme,** and organized **Radtouren.**

Ein typisches Zimmer im Studentenheim

The terms **Studentenwohnheim** and **Studentenheim** are interchangeable.

Auch im Studentenheim soll
man Energie sparen!

Nachhaltig leben

Sustainability **(Nachhaltigkeit)** is an integral part of dorm living in the German-speaking countries. Dorm residents must divide waste into compost and various recycling bins, and energy conservation (like turning off lights) is the norm. Thanks in part to student activism and innovation in places like Heidelberg, university buildings have even had solar panels installed on the roof, and new buildings are designed to meet high energy efficiency standards.

compare **8-6** **Studentenhaus Salzburg.** Schauen Sie die Webseite an und vergleichen° Sie ein paar Aspekte dieses Studentenheims mit einem typischen Studentenheim an Ihrer Uni.

Studentenhaus Salzburg

English Deutsch

Über uns / Zimmer / Virtuelle Tour / Uni Links / Kontakt | **Suche**

Online Reservierung
Familienname:
Vorname:
E-Mail:
Anfrage senden

Zimmerangebot:	Einzelzimmer und Doppelzimmer, pro Person monatlich € 217,– bis € 288,–
Lage:	Zentrumsnähe, 15 Gehminuten zum Bahnhof, sehr gute Einkaufsmöglichkeiten.
Ausstattung:	Alle Zimmer mit WC, Dusche, Telefon, u. Internet- Anschlüssen. Auch Zimmer mit Balkon.
Sonstiges:	TV-Räume mit Satelliten-TV, Studierraum, Musikzimmer, Clubraum, Sauna, Tischtennis, Tischfußball, großer Garten, Fahrradabstellplatz, Garagen. Abends Studentenkneipe.

Gefällt mir   +1

	Studentenhaus Salzburg	Ein Studentenheim an meiner Uni
Preis		
Lage		
Ausstattung		
Sonstiges		

))) 8.3 Wortschatz 1

Wichtige Vokabeln

8.2 Learn vocabulary to talk about where and how you live

Nomen

die Lage	location	**das Esszimmer, -**	dining room
die Miete	rent	**die Küche, -n**	kitchen
die Nebenkosten *(pl)*	additional costs; utilities	**der Herd, -e**	stove
die Wohngemeinschaft, -en		**der Kühlschrank, ¨e**	refrigerator
die WG, -s	} shared housing	**die Mikrowelle, -n**	microwave
		das Spülbecken, -	sink
der Flur, -e	hall	**die Spülmaschine, -n**	dishwasher
die Garderobe, -n	front hall closet	**der Stuhl, ¨e**	chair
die Möbel *(pl)*	furniture	**der Tisch, -e**	table
die Treppe, -n	staircase		
die Tür, -en	door	**das Schlafzimmer, -**	bedroom
		das Bett, -en	bed
das Bad, ¨er	bath; bathroom	**das Bild, -er**	picture; painting
das Badezimmer, -	bathroom	**die Kommode, -n**	dresser
die Badewanne, -n	bathtub	**der Nachttisch, -e**	bedside table
die Dusche, -n	shower	**der Schrank, ¨e**	wardrobe
das Klo, -s	toilet	**der Teppich, -e**	carpet, rug
die Toilette, -n	bathroom, restroom		
das Waschbecken, -	(bathroom) sink	**das Wohnzimmer, -**	living room
		das Bücherregal, -e	bookcase

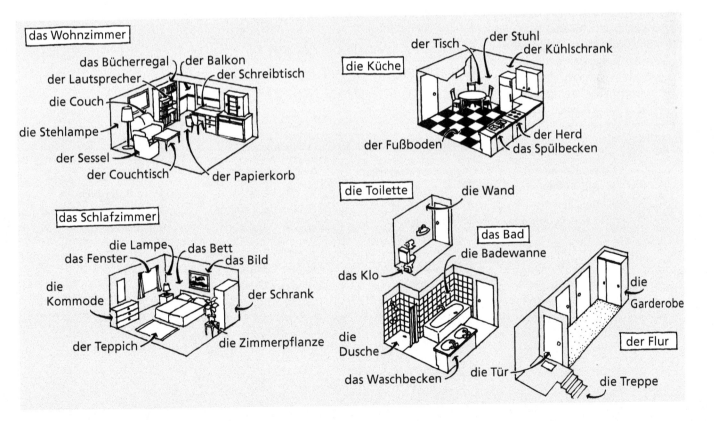

der Couchtisch, -e	coffee table
der Lautsprecher, -	speaker
der Papierkorb, ⸚e	wastepaper basket
der Schreibtisch, -e	desk
der Sessel, -	armchair
die Stehlampe, -n	floor lamp
der Fußboden, ⸚	floor
das Fenster, -	window
die Wand, ⸚e	wall

Verben

benutzen	to use
stören	to disturb
vergleichen, verglichen	to compare

Andere Wörter

gegenüber	across (the hall, the street, etc.)
möbliert	furnished
wirklich	really
zusätzlich	additional

Ausdrücke

| usw. (und so weiter) | etc. (et cetera, and so on) |
| zu viert | in a group of four |

Das Gegenteil

mieten ≠	to rent (from somebody) ≠
vermieten	to rent (to somebody)
ruhig ≠ laut	quiet ≠ loud
sauber ≠ schmutzig	clean ≠ dirty

Leicht zu verstehen

der Balkon, -s	grillen
die Couch, -s	zentral
die Lampe, -n	

Achtung!

In many homes in the German-speaking countries the tub, shower, and sink are in one room (**das Badezimmer**) and the toilet (with a very small sink) is in another (**die Toilette**). Also, the **Garderobe** in the entryway holds bulky coats and shoes. Inside a bedroom, the piece of furniture where clothing is hung is a **Schrank**.

Wörter im Kontext

8-7 Wo macht man das?

1. Hier duscht und badet man.
2. Hier kocht und bäckt man.
3. Hier sitzt man am Abend und sieht fern.
4. Hier schläft man.
5. Von hier geht man in alle Zimmer.
6. Hier isst man, wenn man Besuch hat.

8-8 Was passt in jeder Gruppe zusammen?

1. die Küche
2. die Toilette
3. der Flur
4. das Schlafzimmer

5. der Stuhl
6. das Bett
7. der Herd
8. die Zimmerpflanze

a. die Garderobe
b. die Kommode
c. der Herd
d. das Klo

e. gießen
f. kochen
g. liegen
h. sitzen

9. der Fußboden
10. die Wand
11. die Badewanne
12. die Garderobe

13. der Lautsprecher
14. die Lampe
15. der Kühlschrank
16. die Mikrowelle

i. das Bild
j. der Teppich
k. Jacken und Mäntel
l. das Wasser

m. schnell
n. kalt
o. laut
p. hell

8-9 Was passt wo?

Spülbecken / möblierte / ruhig / Nachttisch / Stört / Dusche / Spülmaschine

1. _____ es euch, wenn ich jetzt laute Musik spiele?
2. Eine Wohnung mit Möbeln ist eine _____ Wohnung.
3. Wenn man eine _____ hat, muss man den Abwasch° nicht   *dirty dishes*
   am _____ machen.
4. Neben meinem Bett steht ein _____.
5. Unsere neuen Nachbarn sind sehr nett und sehr _____.
6. Nach dem Joggen gehe ich gleich unter die _____.

8-10 Was ist das?

der Sessel ___   das Fenster ___
der Schrank ___   das Bild ___
der Teppich ___   das Klo ___
die Tür ___

> **Lerntipp!**
> Take an active approach to
> learning the many vocabulary
> items in this section: Use
> sticky notes to label furniture
> and other items in your room.

8.4 Zur Aussprache

German *s*-sounds when appearing as *st* and *sp*

8.3 Recognize and pronounce various sounds spelled with *s* in German

At the beginning of a word or word stem, **s** in the combinations **st** and **sp** is pronounced like English *sh*. Otherwise it is pronounced like English *s* in *list* and *lisp*.

👑 **Hier ist die Königin der Würste !**			
Bockwurst	1,80 €	Schaschlik	3,20 €
Bratwurst	2,30 €	Frikadelle 200g	1,80 €
Curry–Bratwurst	2,40 €	Pommes Frites	1,30 €
Schinkenwurst	2,30 €	Hamburger	2,50 €
Riesen–Hot Dog	3,70 €	La Flûte	3,40 €

))) **8-11** Hören Sie gut zu und wiederholen Sie!

1. **St**efan ist **St**udent.

   Stefan **st**udiert in **St**uttgart.

   Stefan findet das **St**udentenleben **st**ressig.

2. Ha**st** du Lu**st** auf eine Wur**st**

   cider   und auf Mo**st**° für deinen Dur**st**?

3. Herr **Sp**ielberg **sp**richt gut **Sp**anisch.

))) **8-12** Zur Aussprache: German *st* and *sp*. You will hear groups of three
German words. In each group there is one word in which the sound **st** or **sp** is
pronounced differently than in the other two. Listen closely and select this word.

1. ☐ Stuhl	☐ Liste	☐ Staubsauger
2. ☐ lispeln	☐ spielen	☐ versprechen
3. ☐ Lust	☐ Westen	☐ aufstehen
4. ☐ Spaß	☐ sparen	☐ Inspiration
5. ☐ kosten	☐ stellen	☐ Angst
6. ☐ Stiefvater	☐ Poster	☐ Künstler
7. ☐ Kaspar	☐ Spiegel	☐ lispeln
8. ☐ starten	☐ stören	☐ investieren

))) **8-13** Ein paar Zungenbrecher. Hören Sie die folgenden Zungenbrecher an und
lesen Sie sie dann laut vor. Achten Sie auf die Aussprache von **s**, **sp** und **st**!

Ein sehr schwer sehr schnell zu sprechender Spruch ist ein Schnellsprechspruch.

Ein Stachelschwein, ein Stachelschwein, das muss ein Schwein mit Stacheln sein,
doch hat es keine Stachelein, so ist es auch kein Stachelschwein.

8.5 Kommunikation und Formen 1

Wohin and *wo:* a review

8.4 Distinguish between **wohin** and **wo** in questions and answers.

In *Kapitel 1* you learned that the English question word *where* has three equivalents in
German: **wohin** (*to what place*), **wo** (*in/at what place*), and **woher** (*from what place*), and
you practiced this some in *Kapitel 7*. Since **wohin** and **wo** will play an important role in
this chapter, you will need to fine-tune your feeling for the difference between them.

The use of **wohin** or **wo** is obvious in the following questions.

Wohin gehst du?	*Where are you going? (**to** what place?)*
Wo ist mein Mantel?	*Where is my coat? (**in** what place?)*

For speakers of English it is less obvious whether to use **wohin** or **wo** in the following
example.

Where should I hang my jacket?   (*to* what place? or *in* what place?)

Here speakers of German think in terms of moving the coat from point A to point B
and would therefore use **wohin**.

Wohin soll ich meine Jacke hängen?	*Where (**to** what place) should I hang my jacket?*

Ach so!
The verb used in a question
gives you the clue in choosing
between **wo** and **wohin**. Verbs
of motion (moving toward
something) convey **wohin**
(*where to*); verbs of location
refer to **wo** (*where*) something
or someone is.

8-14 *Wohin* oder *wo?*

1. _____ gehst du?
2. _____ wohnst du?
3. _____ fährt dieser Bus?
4. _____ soll ich die E-Mail schicken?
5. _____ hast du dieses schöne Sweatshirt gekauft?
6. _____ fliegt ihr diesen Sommer?
7. _____ arbeitet Tina?
8. _____ soll ich meinen Mantel hängen?

Two-way prepositions

8.5 Use two-way prepositions to distinguish between *movement toward a destination* **and** *being at a fixed location*

Wohin fährt der Bus?

You have already learned that there is a group of prepositions followed by the accusative case and another group followed by the dative case.

A third group of prepositions may be followed by either the accusative case or the dative case, depending on the distinction just practiced:

- When the main verb signals *movement toward a destination*, the preposition answers the question **wohin?** and is followed by the **accusative** case.
- When the main verb signals a *fixed location*, the preposition answers the question **wo?** and is followed by the **dative** case.

		Wohin?	**Wo?**
		toward a **destination** + ACCUSATIVE	*at a* **fixed location** + DATIVE
an	on *(a vertical surface)*	Antje hängt das Poster **an die** Tür.	Das Poster hängt **an der** Tür.
	to	Kurt geht **an die** Tür.	
	at		Kurt steht **an der** Tür.
auf	on *(a horizontal surface)*	Antje legt das Buch **auf den** Tisch.	Das Buch liegt **auf dem** Tisch.
	to	Kurt geht **auf den** Markt.	
	at		Kurt ist **auf dem** Markt.
hinter	behind	Die Kinder laufen **hinter das** Haus.	Die Kinder sind **hinter dem** Haus.
in	in, into, to	Kurt geht **in die** Küche.	Kurt ist **in der** Küche.
neben	beside	Kurt stellt den Sessel **neben die** Couch.	Der Sessel steht **neben der** Couch.
über	over, above	Kurt hängt die Lampe **über den** Tisch.	Die Lampe hängt **über dem** Tisch.
unter	under, below	Antje stellt die Hausschuhe **unter das** Bett.	Die Hausschuhe stehen **unter dem** Bett.
vor	in front of	Kurt stellt den Wagen **vor die** Garage.	Der Wagen steht **vor der** Garage.
zwischen	between	Antje stellt die Stehlampe **zwischen die** Couch und **den** Sessel.	Die Stehlampe steht **zwischen der** Couch und **dem** Sessel.

Antje hängt das Poster an die Küchentür.

8-15 Wer macht was in der neuen Wohnung? Antworten Sie auf die Frage **wohin** und ergänzen Sie die Präpositionen.

unter / über / vor / an

1. Kurt legt den Teppich _____ die Couch.
2. Uli hängt das Landschaftsbild _____ den Schreibtisch.
3. Antje hängt das Poster _____ die Küchentür.
4. Das Baby will den Ball und krabbelt°_____ den Schreibtisch.

crawls

zwischen / hinter / auf / neben

5. Helga stellt den Papierkorb _____ den Schreibtisch.
6. Thomas stellt die Vase _____ das Radio und die Zimmerpflanze.
7. Die Maus läuft _____ die Couch.
8. Die kleine braune Katze springt _____ die Couch.

8-16 In der neuen Wohnung. Ergänzen Sie die Präpositionen.

hinter / über / vor / zwischen

1. Der Picasso hängt _____ der Couch.
2. Der Kalender hängt jetzt _____ dem Landschaftsbild und dem Picasso.
3. Die Stehlampe steht _____ dem Sessel.
4. Der Karton mit den Büchern steht _____ dem Bücherregal.

unter / vor / auf / in

5. Das Radio und die Zimmerpflanze stehen _____ dem Bücherregal.
6. Der Herd steht _____ der Küche.
7. Der Ball liegt _____ dem Schreibtisch.
8. Der Sessel steht _____ der Stehlampe.

The verbs *stellen*, *legen*, and *hängen*

8.6 Describe moving things from one place to another

In English, the verb *to put* can mean *to put something in a vertical, horizontal, or hanging position*.

> **Put** *the wine glasses on the table.*
> **Put** *your coats on the bed.*
> **Put** *your jacket in the closet.*

German uses three different verbs for the one verb *to put* in English. Because these verbs signal movement toward a destination *(to what place?)*, these verbs with two-way prepositions are followed by the *accusative case*.

stellen	*to put in an upright position*	**Stell** die Weingläser auf **den** Tisch!
legen	*to put in a horizontal position*	**Legt** eure Mäntel auf **das** Bett!
hängen	*to hang (up)*	**Häng** deine Jacke in **die** Garderobe!

 8-17 Wohin soll ich diese Sachen *stellen*, *legen* oder *hängen*?

► die Stehlampe   der Sessel

S1: Wohin soll ich die Stehlampe stellen?   **S2:** Hinter den Sessel.

1. der Kalender   der Schreibtisch

2. der Teppich   die Couch

3. der Papierkorb   der Schreibtisch

4. die Zimmerpflanze   die Ecke

5. das Landschaftsbild   die beiden Fenster

6. der Beistelltisch   der Sessel

7. der Fernseher   das Bücherregal

The verbs *stehen*, *liegen*, and *hängen*

8.7 Describe where something is located

German also tends to be more exact than English when describing the location of things.

stehen	*to be standing*	Die Weingläser **stehen** auf **dem** Tisch.
liegen	*to be lying*	Eure Mäntel **liegen** auf **dem** Bett.
hängen	*to be hanging*	Deine Jacke **hängt** in **der** Garderobe.

Since these verbs are describing location *(in what place?)*, a two-way preposition used with these verbs must be in the *dative case*.

Achtung!
The verb **hängen** has two meanings: *to put into a hanging position* (with accusative) or *to be hanging* (with dative).

 8-18 Wo *stehen*, *liegen* oder *hängen* diese Sachen?

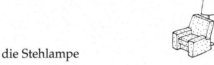

▶ die Stehlampe   der Sessel

S1: Wo steht die Stehlampe?   **S2:** Sie steht hinter dem Sessel.

1. der Kalender   der Schreibtisch

2. der Teppich   die Couch

3. der Papierkorb   der Schreibtisch

4. die Zimmerpflanze   die Ecke

5. das Landschaftsbild   die beiden Fenster

6. der Beistelltisch   der Sessel

7. der Fernseher   das Bücherregal

8-19 Mein Zimmer. Zeichnen Sie einen Plan von Ihrem Zimmer mit allen Möbeln, Türen und Fenstern. Beschreiben Sie dann, was Sie gezeichnet haben. Die Ausdrücke in Übung **8-18** und die folgenden Sätze können Ihnen dabei helfen.

- Mein Zimmer ist ziemlich groß (klein) …
- Die Möbel sind modern (alt, neu, vom Flohmarkt) …
- An der linken Wand/An der rechten Wand steht (hängt) …
- Neben dem Fenster/Unter dem Fenster steht (hängt) …
- Links (rechts) neben der Tür/dem Fenster … steht (hängt) …
- Zwischen … und … steht …

German *an*, *auf*, *in*, and English *to*

In *Kapitel 7* you learned that both **zu** and **nach** can mean *to*. The prepositions **an**, **auf**, and **in** can also mean *to* if they answer the question **wohin**.

- **An** indicates that your point of destination is *next to* something, such as a door, a telephone, or a body of water **(an die Tür, ans Telefon, ans Meer)**.
- **In** is generally used if your point of destination is *within* a place, such as a room, a theater, or even a mountain range **(ins Zimmer, ins Theater, in die Alpen)**.
- **In** is used instead of **nach** to express that you are going to a country if the name of the country is masculine, feminine, or plural **(in den Libanon, in die Schweiz, in die USA)**.
- **Auf** can be used instead of **zu** to express that you are going to a building or an institution, like the bank, the post office, or foreign student office, especially to do business **(auf die Bank, auf die Post, aufs Auslandsamt)**.

> When used to mean *to*, these prepositions can contract with the article **das (ans, ins, aufs)**.

> Other expressions where **auf** means *to*: **auf eine Party, auf die Toilette**.

8-20 Was passt in jeder Gruppe zusammen? S2 verwendet **ans, ins, auf** oder **in** in den Antworten.

▶ Man will Schwyzerdütsch hören.   die Schweiz

S1: Wohin fährt man, wenn man Schwyzerdütsch hören will?   **S2:** Man fährt in die Schweiz.

1. Man braucht Geld.
2. Man möchte schlafen.
3. Man will eine Sinfonie hören.
4. Man braucht Briefmarken.
5. Man schwimmt gern in Salzwasser.
6. Man will *Hamlet* sehen.
7. Man möchte *Carmen* sehen.
8. Man kocht nicht gern.
9. Man isst gern frisches Obst.
10. Man möchte Ski laufen.

- das Meer
- das Konzert
- die Bank
- das Bett
- die Post
- das Gasthaus
- der Wochenmarkt
- die Oper
- die Alpen
- das Theater

Gehst du heute auf den Wochenmarkt?

8-21 Eine Umfrage. Stellen Sie einander die folgenden Fragen. Machen Sie Notizen und berichten Sie dann, was Sie herausgefunden haben.

- Gehst du oft ins Theater (ins Konzert, in die Oper, ins Kino, ins Kunstmuseum, ins Gasthaus)?
- Was ist dein Lieblingstheaterstück (deine Lieblingsmusik, deine Lieblingsoper, dein Lieblingsfilm, dein Lieblingsbild, dein Lieblingsessen)?
- Fährst du lieber in die Berge, ans Meer oder an einen See? Warum?

8.6 Kultur 2

Das Bauhaus: Visionäre Kunsthochschule

8.8 Identify important characteristics and accomplishments of the Bauhaus School

buildings

8-22 Gebäude° und Architekten.

Meisterhaus in Dessau (1925)

> **Meisterhäuser:** Close to the Bauhaus campus, Walter Gropius built four houses for the Bauhaus professors, or "masters." These buildings were also intended to be **Musterhäuser,** model homes for modern living and for the Bauhaus aesthetic.

else

1. Welches Gebäude auf Ihrem Campus oder in Ihrer Stadt gefällt Ihnen am besten? Warum?

2. Gefallen Ihnen das Meisterhaus in Dessau und das Bauhaus in Dessau (siehe Fotos)? Warum oder warum nicht?

3. Kennen Sie den Namen eines berühmten Architekten/einer berühmten Architektin? Was hat er/sie gebaut und was wissen Sie sonst° von ihm/ihr?

8-23 Was ist das auf Englisch?

1. Der Architekt Walter Gropius **gründet** 1919 in Weimar das Bauhaus.

2. Ein **Lehrplan** beschreibt, was die Schüler lernen sollen.

3. Auf einer **Ausstellung** zeigt man Bilder, Skulpturen, Fotografien usw.

4. Gropius hat das Schulgebäude in Dessau selbst **entworfen.**

5. Die Ideen des Bauhauses hatten einen enormen **Einfluss** auf nordamerikanische Architekten und Designer.

6. Nach 1933 **verlassen** Gropius und viele andere Bauhauslehrer und -schüler das nationalsozialistische Deutschland.

7. Die meisten Bauhauslehrer finden in den USA eine neue **Heimat.**

a. leave

b. influence

c. founds

d. home

e. curriculum

f. exhibition

g. designed

Der Beginn des Bauhauses

Im Jahr 1919 gründet der Architekt Walter Gropius in Weimar das Bauhaus, eine Schule, wo Künstler, Architekten, Handwerker und Studenten zusammen leben und lernen und zusammen versuchen, für eine industrialisierte Welt neue Formen zu finden. Auf dem Lehrplan stehen Malerei, Skulptur, Architektur, Theater, Fotografie und das Design von Handwerks- und Industrieprodukten.

Klare geometrische Linien

Typisch für die neuen Formen – von der Teekanne bis zum größten Gebäude – sind klare, lineare geometrische Formen. Auf der großen Bauhaus-Ausstellung von 1923 charakterisiert Gropius den Bauhausstil mit den folgenden Worten: Kunst und Technik – eine neue Einheit.[1]

Das Bauhaus zieht nach Dessau

1925 zieht das Bauhaus von Weimar nach Dessau. Das Schulgebäude, das berühmte Dessauer Bauhaus, hat Walter Gropius selbst entworfen und seine Stahl- und Glasfassade wird zur Ikone der Architektur des 20. Jahrhunderts. In den Werkstätten des Bauhauses entwirft man funktionale und künstlerisch geformte Produkte und Gebäude für die Massenproduktion und für alle Menschen.

[1]**Kunst und Technik – eine neue Einheit:** *art and technology—a new unity*

Das Bauhaus in Dessau

Das Ende des Bauhauses

Aber schon 1933 kommt mit Adolf Hitler das Ende des Bauhauses, denn Gropius'
Ideen sind für die Nazis „undeutsch", zu modern und zu international. 1934
geht Gropius nach England und arbeitet dort als Architekt und Designer. 1937
emigriert er dann in die USA und wird dort an der Harvard-Universität *Chairman*
des *Department of Architecture*. Seine größten Projekte in den USA sind das Harvard
Graduate Center, das Pan Am Building (MetLife Building) in New York und das
John F. Kennedy Federal Building in Boston.

Der Einfluss des Bauhauses

Der enorme Einfluss des Bauhauses auf nordamerikanische Architekten und
Designer geht aber nicht nur auf Walter Gropius zurück, denn auch viele andere
Bauhauslehrer und -schüler verlassen damals[2] Hitler-Deutschland und finden in
den USA eine neue Heimat: László Moholy-Nagy gründet 1937 das *New Bauhaus*
in Chicago, Josef Albers lehrt am Black Mountain College in North Carolina und
später an der Yale-Universität, und Ludwig Mies van der Rohe lehrt am Illinois
Institute of Technology in Chicago.

Schönheit + Funktionalität: den Einfluss des Bauhauses sieht man heute noch.

[2] *at that time*

> **Das Bauhaus nach 100 Jahren**
>
> Seit 1996 sind die Bauhaus-Stätten in Weimar und Dessau Welterbe-Stätten[3]. Die Deutsche UNESCO-Kommission schreibt, dass das Bauhaus „zwischen 1919 und 1933 revolutionäre Ideen der Baugestaltung und Stadtplanung" etabliert hat. Viele sehen das Bauhaus als die einflussreichste Kunstschule des 20. Jahrhunderts. Es ist praktisch gleichbedeutend mit der Moderne in Architektur und Design. Die wichtigsten Prinzipien, die man in den Werken und Gebäuden des Bauhauses realisiert sieht, nämlich Demokratie, Humanität, Funtionalität, Ökonomie, sind auch in der heutigen Lebens- und Wohnsituation immer noch bedeutend und relevant.
>
> [3]**Welterbe-Stätten**: *world cultural heritage sites*

8-24 Wann war das? Finden Sie im Text die richtigen Jahreszahlen.

_____ Der Bauhauslehrer László Moholy-Nagy gründet in Chicago das *New Bauhaus*.

_____ Auf einer großen Ausstellung präsentiert das Weimarer Bauhaus seine Ideen und seine Produkte.

_____ Die UNESCO macht die deutschen Bauhaus-Stätten zu Welterbe-Stätten.

_____ Walter Gropius geht nach England und arbeitet dort als Architekt und Designer.

_____ Man gründet in Weimar eine Schule für Architektur, Kunst und Handwerk und nennt sie Bauhaus.

_____ Ende des Dessauer Bauhauses, weil die Nazis die Bauhausideen undeutsch und zu international finden.

_____ Das Bauhaus zieht von Weimar in das neue Schulgebäude in Dessau.

8.7 Kommunikation und Formen 2

The two-way prepositions *an, in, vor*, and *zwischen* in time phrases

8.9 Saying when something occurs

Phrases with the prepositions **an, in, vor**, and **zwischen** are often used to answer the question **wann**. In such time expressions, the objects of the prepositions are always in the dative case.

Ich bin **am** zehnten September in Salzburg angekommen.	*I arrived in Salzburg **on** September tenth.*
Das Wintersemester beginnt **im** Oktober.	*The winter semester begins **in** October.*
Vor dem Semesterbeginn muss ich aufs Auslandsamt gehen.	***Before** the start of the semester I have to go to the foreign students' office.*
Vor drei Jahren war ich zum ersten Mal in Österreich.	*Three years **ago** I was in Austria for the first time.*
Meine Eltern kommen **zwischen dem** ersten und **dem** zehnten Dezember zu Besuch.	*My parents are coming to visit **between** the first and the tenth of December.*

> Note that in time expressions, **an** and **in** can contract with the article **dem** *(am, im)*. These contractions can also be used for location expressions: *am* **Fenster**, *im* **Schlafzimmer**.

8-25 Wann …? Ergänzen Sie die Phrasen, die direkt gegenüber stehen!

▶ Wann fliegst du nach Europa?   In d__ Sommerferien (pl).

S1: Wann fliegst du nach Europa?   **S2:** In den Sommerferien.

1. Wann beginnt das Sommersemester
   in Deutschland?   I_____ April (m).

2. Wann besuchst du deine Eltern?   A_____ Wochenende (n).

3. Wann gehst du in die Bibliothek?   Zwischen d____ Mathevorlesung (f)
                                        und d_____ Mittagessen (n).

4. Wann gehst du auf den Markt?   Vor mein_____ ersten Vorlesung (f).

5. Wann hast du deinen Computer
   gekauft?   Vor ein_____ Woche (f).

> **Ach so!**
> In time expressions, **vor** can mean *before* or *ago*.

Linie Ziel   Abfahrt in

M85	S+U Hauptbahnhof	3 min
M48	S+U Alexanderplatz	3 min
200	Michelangelostr.	6 min
M41	Sonnenal./Baumschulenst	7 min
M85	S+U Hauptbahnhof	10 min

Varian-Fry-Straße

Der Bus zum Alexanderplatz fährt in drei Minuten ab.

> Even in cities much smaller than Berlin, signs like this make it easy to get around using public transportation, since you always know how long your wait will be.

8-26 Detektiv spielen. Jemand hat gestern zur Mittagszeit eine Riesenpackung Gummibärchen aus dem Büro vom Deutschprofessor gestohlen! Verhören° Sie Ihre Partnerin/Ihren Partner.   *interrogate*

- Wo waren Sie gestern in der Mittagspause?
- Waren Sie gestern in der Mensa? Wie lange waren Sie dort?
- Was haben Sie vor der Mittagspause gemacht? Und nach der Mittagspause?
- Haben Sie gestern Nachmittag Freunde getroffen? Wer kann uns sagen, wo Sie nach der Mittagspause waren?
- Was haben Sie gestern zwischen dem Mittagessen und dem Abendessen gemacht?

Word order

8.10 Create more complex sentences using infinitive phrases

Infinitive phrases

Infinitive phrases are phrases that contain an infinitive preceded by **zu.** Here are some verbs or expressions that may be followed by an infinitive phrase.

vergessen	**versuchen**	**Lust haben**	**Zeit haben**
versprechen	**vorhaben**	**Spaß machen**	

| Ich habe versprochen, **Tim zum Flughafen** *zu fahren.* | *I promised* **to drive** Tim to the airport. |
| Vergiss aber diesmal nicht, **einen Parkschein** *zu lösen.* | *But don't forget* **to buy** a parking **pass** *this time.* |

- In German, **zu** and the infinitive stand at the end of the phrase.
- The German infinitive phrase is often set off with a comma.

With separable-prefix verbs, **zu** is inserted between the prefix and the verb.

| Hast du wirklich vor, **bald** *umzuziehen?* | *Are you really planning* **to move** *soon?* |

If a phrase ends with more than one infinitive, **zu** precedes the last one.

| Hast du Zeit, **dieses Wochenende mit uns** *campen zu gehen?* | *Do you have time* **to go camping** *with* **us this weekend?** |

Some infinitive phrases are best translated into English using the *-ing* form of the verb.

| Hast du Lust, **einen Kuchen** *zu backen?* | *Do you feel like* **baking** a cake? |

8-27 Kleine Gespräche. Ergänzen Sie passende **zu**-Infinitive.

bleiben / joggen

1.   MIA: Macht es dir Spaß, jeden Morgen drei Kilometer _____?
      SYLVIA: Nicht immer, aber es hilft mir, fit _____.

kaufen / fahren

2.   LAURA: Hast du wirklich vor, einen Wagen _____?
      MARKUS: Klar! Ich habe keine Lust, immer mit dem Bus _____.

anrufen / sprechen

3.   JENS: Hast du vergessen, Moritz _____?
      JULIA: Nein, ich hatte heute keine Zeit, mit ihm _____.

tanzen gehen / gehen / anschauen

4.   LUKAS: Habt ihr Lust, heute Abend mit uns _____?
      BERND: Nein, wir haben vor, einen guten Film _____ und danach noch in die Kneipe _____.

8-28 Ein paar persönliche Fragen. Stellen Sie einander die folgenden Fragen. Berichten Sie, was Sie herausgefunden haben.

S1: Was hast du heute Abend vor?	**S2:** Heute Abend habe ich vor, ins Kino zu gehen.
Was hast du am Wochenende vor?	Am Wochenende habe ich vor, …
Was macht dir am meisten Spaß?	Am meisten Spaß macht mir, …
Was macht dir keinen Spaß?	Es macht mir keinen Spaß, …
Was möchtest du mal versuchen?	Ich möchte mal versuchen, …
Hast du mal vergessen, etwas Wichtiges zu tun?	Ich habe mal vergessen, …

8-29 Lust, aber keine Zeit! Was möchten Sie tun, was dann doch nicht geht? Diskutieren Sie mit einer Partnerin/einem Partner.

- Ich habe Lust, …. Aber ich habe keine Zeit, ….
- Ich habe Interesse, …. Aber ich habe nicht genug Geld, ….
- Es macht Spaß, …. Aber ich habe leider nie Zeit, …

Infinitive phrases introduced by *um*

To express the purpose of an action, you can use an infinitive phrase introduced with **um**. The English equivalent of **um … zu** is *in order to*. English often uses only *to* instead of *in order to*. In German the word **um** is rarely omitted.

Morgen früh kommt Pietro, **um** mir beim Umziehen **zu helfen.**
Tomorrow morning Pietro is coming (in order) to help me move.

Ich brauche ein paar Nägel, **um** meine Bilder **aufzuhängen.**
I need a few nails (in order) to hang up my pictures.

8-30 In der WG. Sie wohnen in einer WG und fragen einander, was Ihre Mitbewohner mit diesen Geräten° machen. Sabrina ist ein rationaler Mensch. Benedikt ist ein kreativer Mensch!

appliances

S1: Wozu° braucht Sabrina den Staubsauger?

S2: Um ihren Teppich sauberzumachen.   *what . . . for*

S1: Und Benedikt?

S2: Um ein großes Insekt in seinem Zimmer zu töten!

	Sabrina	Benedikt
der Staubsauger	ihren Teppich saubermachen	ein großes Insekt in seinem Zimmer töten
der Dosenöffner	eine Dose Suppe aufmachen	sein Fahrrad reparieren
das Bügeleisen	ihre Blusen bügeln	Quesadillas machen
die Kaffeemaschine	für ihre Freunde Kaffee kochen	ein paar chemische Experimente machen
der Korkenzieher	eine Flasche Wein aufmachen	Sabrinas Ring aus dem Klo holen
die Waschmaschine	ihre T-Shirts waschen	seine alten Jeans rot färben

The genitive case

8.11 Indicate possession or relationships

The genitive case is used to express the idea of possession or belonging together. You are already familiar with the **-s** genitive, which is used in German only with proper names. The ending **-s** is not preceded by an apostrophe.

Claudias Schreibtisch	*Claudia's desk*

For nouns other than proper names you must use a different form of the genitive. Note that this form of the genitive follows the noun it modifies.

das Büro **des** Professor**s**	*the professor's office*
das Zimmer mein**er** Schwester	*my sister's room*
der Teddybär dies**es** Kind**es**	*this child's teddy bear*
die Wohnung unser**er** Eltern	*our parents' apartment*

In German this form of the genitive is used for persons, animals, and things. In English it sometimes is expressed with *of*:

das Dach dies**es** Haus**es**	*the roof **of** this house*
die Wände unser**er** Wohnung	*the walls **of** our apartment*

	Masculine	Neuter	Feminine	Plural
GENITIVE	**des** Vater**s** **meines**	**des** Kind**es** **meines**	**der** Mutter **meiner**	**der** Freunde **meiner**

- Most one-syllable masculine and neuter nouns add **-es** in the genitive singular (**Kindes**), while masculine and neuter nouns with more than one syllable add **-s** in the genitive singular (**Vaters**).
- Feminine nouns and the plural forms of all nouns have no genitive ending.

The interrogative pronoun *wessen*

The genitive form of the interrogative pronoun is **wessen**.

Wessen Jacke ist das?	*Whose jacket is that?*

	Interrogative pronoun	Masculine definite article
NOMINATIVE	wer	der
ACCUSATIVE	wen	den
DATIVE	wem	dem
GENITIVE	**wessen**	**des + -s**

8-31 Wessen Sachen sind das?

► Handschuhe (pl)   mein__ Schwester

S1: Wessen Handschuhe sind das?   **S2:** Das sind die Handschuhe meiner Schwester.

Frau María Moser
Mariahilferstr. 52
1. A- 1070 Wien   mein_____ Tante in Österreich

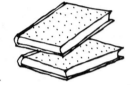

2.   Manfred____

3.   mein_____ Bruder____

4.   unser_____ Professor____

5.   Brigitte____

6.   mein_____ Eltern

Bücher (pl)	Adresse (f)	Schal (m)
Fahrrad (n)	Wagen (m)	Brille (f)

8-32 Genitiv im Alltag. Identifizieren Sie die Genitiv-Phrasen auf den Schildern und sagen Sie, was sie auf Englisch bedeuten.

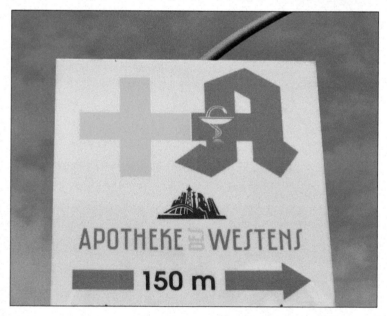

A typical timeframe for a **lange Nacht** in a museum is from 6 P.M. to midnight. Usually there are special events held during those hours to capitalize on the special atmosphere after dark.

Genitive endings of preceded adjectives

Adjectives that are preceded by a **der**-word or an **ein**-word in the genitive case always take the ending **-en**.

	Masculine	Neuter	Feminine	Plural
GENITIVE	des eines jung**en** Mannes	des eines klein**en** Kindes	der einer jung**en** Frau	der meiner klein**en** Kinder

8-33 Eine attraktive Lage. Am Beginn des nächsten Semesters ziehen Stephanie und Claudia in eine neue Wohnung. Ergänzen Sie mit Genitiv!

STEPHANIE: Schön, dass es in der Nähe° d____ neu____ Wohnung so viel gibt! **in der Nähe:** *in the vicinity of*

CLAUDIA: Ja, wir wohnen in der Nähe ein____ groß____ Supermarkt____ und ein____ toll____ Bäckerei.

STEPHANIE: Und auch in der Nähe ein____ cool____ Studentenkneipe!

CLAUDIA: Und unweit° ein____ spanisch____ Restaurant____. *not far from*

8-34 Und wo wohnst du? Diskutieren Sie die Lage Ihrer Wohnung und folgen Sie dem Beispiel.

▶ ein Supermarkt (m) / groß

S1: Liegt deine Wohnung in der Nähe eines Supermarkts?

S2: Ja, sie liegt in der Nähe eines großen Supermarkts!

Oder: Nein, aber sie liegt in der Nähe …

Universitätsbibliothek (f) / neu	Restaurant (n) / mexikanisch	Studentenkneipe (f) / cool
Supermarkt (m) / groß	Park (m) / grün	Buslinie (f) / günstig

Sprachnotiz   Using *von* + dative instead of the genitive

In colloquial German the idea of possession or of belonging together is often expressed by **von** with a dative object instead of the genitive case.

Ist das der neue Wagen **von** deinem Bruder?	=	Ist das der neue Wagen deines Bruders?
Herr Koch ist ein Freund **von** meinem Vater.	=	Herr Koch ist ein Freund meines Vaters.

Das ist die Wohnung von meiner Freundin.

8.8 Video-Treff

Mein Zuhause

8.12 Understand authentic video of German speakers talking about their living situation

Christoph und Christina Brieger, Ursula, Karen, André, Maiga, und Stefan Kuhlmann sprechen darüber, wo und wie sie wohnen. Machen Sie die erste Aufgabe, **Was ist das auf Englisch?,** bevor Sie das Video anschauen.

8-35 Was ist das auf Englisch?

1. Wir wohnen in einem sehr schönen **Wohnviertel.**	a. surrounding
2. Wir **wohnen** hier **zur Miete.**	b. in case
3. Es gibt viele Geschäfte in den **umliegenden** Straßen.	c. coal
4. Wir wohnen hier **zu fünft.**	d. really feel at home
5. Ich **fühle mich sehr wohl** hier.	e. tub
6. Ich muss immer **Kohlen** in den 4. Stock tragen.	f. rent
7. Ich habe keine **Wanne.**	g. residential area
8. Ich finde es sehr gut, wie die Wohnung **aufgeteilt** ist.	h. in a group of five
9. Man braucht eine große Couch, **falls** Freunde zu Besuch kommen.	i. divided up

8-36 Unser Zuhause. Ergänzen Sie die Aussagen über Christoph und Christina Brieger, Ursula und Karen.

1. Briegers wohnen in der Herderstraße 10 in ____.
   ☐ einem Einfamilienhaus   ☐ einer Wohnung

2. Christoph und Christina wohnen ____ von Wiesbaden.
   ☐ in der Nähe   ☐ praktisch im Zentrum

3. Von ihrer Wohnung ist es auch gar nicht weit zum ____.
   ☐ Bahnhof   ☐ Flughafen

4. Nicht weit von ihnen kann man gut ____.
   ☐ einkaufen gehen   ☐ schwimmen gehen

5. Außer dem Schlafzimmer, Wohnzimmer und Kinderzimmer haben Briegers ____.
   ☐ ein Esszimmer   ☐ ein Arbeitszimmer

6. Ursula wohnt in einer großen _____ in Berlin-Schöneberg.
   ☐ Wohngemeinschaft   ☐ Wohnung

7. Außer dem Wohnzimmer, Schlafzimmer und Arbeitszimmer hat Ursula in ihrer
   Wohnung _____.
   ☐ ein Gästezimmer   ☐ ein Kinderzimmer

8. Wenn Ursula abends Gäste hat, sind sie meistens _____.
   ☐ im Wohnzimmer   ☐ in der Küche

9. In ihrer Wohnung kann Karen _____.
   ☐ kein Bad nehmen   ☐ nur ein kaltes Bad nehmen

10. Karen findet ihre Wohnung _____.
   ☐ gar nicht schön   ☐ sehr schön

8-37 Richtig oder falsch? Lesen Sie die Aussagen über André, Maiga und Stefan
Kuhlmann. Sind diese Aussagen richtig oder falsch? Wenn eine Aussage falsch ist,
korrigieren Sie sie.

	RICHTIG	FALSCH
1. André wohnt allein in seiner Wohnung.	☐	☐
2. Auf dem Regal in Andrés Wohnzimmer stehen Bücher, CDs und Videos.	☐	☐
3. Außer der Küche und dem Badezimmer gibt es in seiner Wohnung drei weitere Zimmer.	☐	☐
4. Ihm gefällt an der Wohnung, dass die Zimmer nicht zu groß sind.	☐	☐
5. Maiga wohnt mit fünf anderen Leuten in einer Wohngemeinschaft.	☐	☐
6. In ihrer Wohngemeinschaft muss man das Bad und die Küche teilen.	☐	☐
7. Maiga hat das größte Zimmer in der WG.	☐	☐
8. Maigas Zimmer ist manchmal nicht so sauber.	☐	☐
9. Stefan Kuhlmann wohnt mit seiner Freundin zusammen.	☐	☐
10. In seiner Wohnung hat Stefan einen großen Fernseher, eine Couch, ein großes Bett und eine Waschmaschine.	☐	☐

))) 8.9 Wortschatz 2

Wichtige Vokabeln

8.12 Learn vocabulary to talk about everyday things at home and in town

Nomen

das Dach, ¨er	roof
der Flohmarkt, ¨e	flea market
die Fußgängerzone, -n	pedestrian zone
das Gebäude, -	building
das Hochhaus, ¨er	high-rise
der Keller, -	basement; cellar
die Küchenbenutzung	kitchen privileges
die Post	post office; mail
das Rathaus, ¨er	town hall; city hall
der Stadtplan, ¨e	map of the city/town
der Teil, -e	part
der Wochenmarkt, ¨e	open-air market

Ich gehe auf die Post.

das Bügeleisen, -	iron
die Dose, -n	can
der Dosenöffner, -	can opener
das Gerät, -e	appliance; utensil
das Haushaltsgerät, -e	household appliance
der Korkenzieher, -	corkscrew
der Staubsauger, -	vacuum cleaner
die Ausstellung, -en	exhibition
der Einfluss, ¨e	influence
der Künstler, - die Künstlerin, -nen }	artist

die Heimat	home (country)
die Mittagspause, -n	lunch break
der Schal, -s	scarf

Verben

auf·machen	to open
bügeln	to iron
legen	to lay (down); to put (in a horizontal position)
stellen	to put (in an upright position)
um·ziehen, ist umgezogen	to move (change residence)
versuchen	to try
wiederholen	to repeat

Andere Wörter

eigen	own
sicher	sure
wozu	what . . . for

Ausdrücke

Es macht mir Spaß, . . .	I enjoy . . .
Ich habe (keine) Lust, . . .	I (don't) feel like . . .
in der Nähe der Uni	near the university
zu Besuch kommen	to visit

Das Gegenteil

der Vorteil, -e ≠ der Nachteil, -e	advantage ≠ disadvantage
in der Nähe ≠ weit weg	in the vicinity of ≠ far away
zum ersten Mal ≠ zum letzten Mal	for the first time ≠ for the last time

Leicht zu verstehen

der Architekt, -en	das Poster, -
die Architektin, -nen	die Skulptur, -en
der Designer, -	die Technik
die Designerin, -nen	enorm
die Energie	recyceln

Wörter im Kontext

8-38 Was passt in jeder Gruppe zusammen?

1. die Post
2. die WG
3. der Keller
4. die Künstlerin

a. die Mitbewohner
b. der Brief
c. die Skulptur
d. der Wein

5. der Staubsauger
6. alte Zeitungen
7. die Tür
8. der Wochenmarkt

e. aufmachen
f. einkaufen
g. putzen
h. recyceln

8-39 Was ist die richtige Antwort?

1. Warum ziehst du aus dem Wohnheim?
2. Warum verkaufst du dein Auto?
3. Warum suchst du ein Zimmer mit Küchenbenutzung?
4. Warum gehst du heute Abend nicht mit uns tanzen?
5. Warum gehst du auf die Post?

a. Weil ich ein Paket abschicke.
b. Weil ich keine Lust mehr habe, immer in der Mensa zu essen.
c. Weil ich jetzt ein Zimmer in der Nähe der Uni habe.
d. Weil ich ein Zimmer in einer ganz tollen WG gefunden habe.
e. Weil es mir keinen Spaß macht, in die Disco zu gehen.

8-40 Wozu brauchst du das alles?

1. Wozu brauchst du einen Staubsauger?
2. Wozu brauchst du ein Poster?
3. Wozu brauchst du einen Korkenzieher?
4. Wozu brauchst du einen Dosenöffner?
5. Wozu brauchst du ein Bügeleisen?
6. Wozu brauchst du denn einen Stadtplan?

a. Um diese Weinflasche aufzumachen.
b. Um mein Kleid zu bügeln.
c. Um mein Zimmer sauber zu machen.
d. Um meine neue WG zu finden.
e. Um meine weiße Wand interessanter zu machen.
f. Um diese Sardinen essen zu können.

8-41 Was passt am besten zusammen?

1. Ich habe Lust, in ein Gasthaus zu gehen.
2. Frau Berg hat eine große Wohnung in einem Hochhaus.
3. Die Schweiz ist meine Heimat.
4. Im Keller von unserem Haus machen wir oft laute Musik.
5. Ich schaue gern Bilder und Skulpturen an.
6. Stefan gefällt es sehr gut in seiner WG.
7. Frau Otto ist Stadtarchitektin in Leipzig.

a. Meine Muttersprache ist Deutsch.
b. Ein Nachteil ist aber, dass seine Mitbewohner oft sehr laut sind.
c. So ein Glück, dass ich bald Mittagspause habe!
d. Ich gehe deshalb oft auf Kunstausstellungen.
e. Ihr Büro ist im Rathaus.
f. Sie vermietet zwei von ihren Zimmern an Studenten.
g. Ein großer Vorteil ist, dass wir dort niemanden stören.

Wörter unter der Lupe

Compound nouns

A compound noun can be a combination of:

- two or more nouns (**der Nachttisch, die Nachttischlampe**).
- an adjective and a noun (**der Kühlschrank**).
- a verb and a noun (**der Schreibtisch**).
- a preposition and a noun (**der Nachtisch**).

In German these combinations are almost always written as one word. The last element of a compound noun is the base word and determines the gender of the compound noun. All preceding elements are modifiers that define the base word more closely.

die Stadt + **der** Plan = **der** Stadtplan
der Fuß + der Ball + **das** Spiel = **das** Fußballspiel

Im Reformhaus kauft man gesundes Essen.

8-42 Was passt zusammen? Ergänzen Sie auch die bestimmten Artikel.

1. _das_ Wochenendhaus _c_
2. _____ Hausschuh ____
3. _____ Krankenhaus ____
4. _____ Haustier ____
5. _____ Hochhaus ____
6. _____ Hausarzt ____
7. _____ Reformhaus ____
8. _____ Kaffeehaus ____
9. _____ Einfamilienhaus ____
10. _____ Kaufhaus ____

a. family doctor
b. coffee house (café)
c. weekend cottage
d. single-family home
e. pet
f. department store
g. hospital
h. slipper
i. high-rise
j. health food store

Giving language color

In this chapter you have learned vocabulary that deals with housing and furnishings. This vocabulary is a source of many idiomatic expressions. The expressions marked with an asterisk are very informal and should only be used with family and friends.

Lena ist ganz aus dem Häuschen.	*Lena is all excited.*
Er hat wohl nicht alle Tassen im Schrank!*	*He must be crazy!*
Setz ihm doch den Stuhl vor die Tür!	*Throw him out!*
Mal den Teufel nicht an die Wand!	*Don't tempt fate!*
Lukas hat vom Chef eins aufs Dach gekriegt.*	*Lukas was bawled out by his boss.*
Auf Robert kannst du Häuser bauen.	*Robert is absolutely dependable.*

8-43 Was passt zusammen?

1. Unser Sohn will einfach keine Arbeit suchen.
2. Hat Anne eine Reise nach Hawaii gewonnen?

Thank God!   3. Gott sei Dank° hatten wir diesen Winter noch keinen Eisregen.
4. Warum ist Kurt denn plötzlich so fleißig?
5. Ist Sven ein guter Babysitter?
6. Ich habe mir gestern einen Porsche gekauft.

a. Ich glaube, er hat vom Chef eins aufs Dach gekriegt.
b. Aber natürlich. Auf ihn können Sie Häuser bauen.
c. Dann setzen Sie ihm doch den Stuhl vor die Tür!
d. Du hast wohl nicht alle Tassen im Schrank!
e. Ja, sie ist ganz aus dem Häuschen.
f. Mal bitte den Teufel nicht an die Wand!

8.10 Alles zusammen

Das ist mein Zuhause.

In this chapter, you've learned new words and tools to describe where and how people live. Now you get to create a short, guided video tour of your own room!

Schritt 1: Zum Hören und Sehen

8-44 Was hat Stefan in seiner Wohnung? Schauen Sie nochmal Stefan Kuhlmanns Wohnsituation im Video-Treff an (3:24). Was hat Stefan in seiner Wohnung? Listen Sie hier sechs Dinge auf (Möbel und Haushaltsgeräte):

_____ _____ _____

_____ _____ _____

Schritt 2: Zum Sprechen

 8-45 Wie ist deine Wohnsituation? Machen Sie zu zweit ein kurzes Interview!

Zur Wohnsituation
- ☐ Wo wohnst du: in einem Zimmer, in einer Wohnung, in einer Wohngemeinschaft?
- ☐ Wohnst du alleine oder mit anderen zusammen?
- ☐ Wie kommst du von dort zur Uni? Wohnst du in der Nähe der Uni?

Ein paar Details
- ☐ Was für Möbel hast du in deinem Schlafzimmer?
- ☐ Kannst du im Zimmer (oder in der Wohnung) kochen?
- ☐ Hast du ein eigenes Bad, oder musst du das Bad mit anderen teilen?

Positive und negative Aspekte
- ☐ Ist dein Zimmer groß oder klein? Dunkel oder hell? Alt oder modern?
- ☐ Was gefällt dir am besten?
- ☐ Was findest du nicht so toll?

Schritt 3: Zum Präsentieren

8-46 Das ist mein Zimmer. Präsentieren Sie Ihr Zimmer in einer Videotour!

Im Video müssen Sie:
- eine kurze Einleitung geben:
  Das ist mein Zimmer. Ich wohne hier mit meinem Freund Chris. Wir wohnen zusammen im Studentenheim …
- drei Möbelstücke im Zimmer zeigen
  Ich habe im Zimmer eine Couch …
- sagen, wo diese drei Möbelstücke *stehen, liegen* oder *hängen*:
  Meine Couch steht in der Ecke …
- am Ende sagen, wie Ihr Zimmer Ihnen gefällt:
  Ich finde mein Zimmer schön, weil …
  Oder: *Ich finde mein Zimmer nicht so schön, weil …*

> In your tour, you'll be describing where your furniture is located, thus using the dative case: **Auf meinem Schreibtisch steht eine Lampe.** You can use the structure from the interview you just completed to organize what you say.

Kapitel 9
Ich und meine Umwelt

Ein Gasthaus in München

Learning Objectives

9.1 Explore the variety of food in the German-speaking countries and learn eating customs

9.2 Learn vocabulary to talk about food and eating out

9.3 Distinguish between the pronunciation of German *s* and *z*

9.4 Talk about actions one does to or for oneself

9.5 Use idiomatic reflexive verbs

9.6 Discuss ways people in German-speaking countries lead healthy, sustainable lifestyles

9.7 Use relative clauses to describe people, places, and things

9.8 Understand authentic video of German speakers talking about what they like to eat and drink

9.9 Learn vocabulary to talk about your daily life and sustainable lifestyles

9.1 Vorschau

Im Restaurant

Hier sehen Sie eine Speisekarte aus einem gemütlichen Trierer Gasthaus, das auch bei Studenten sehr beliebt ist. Man findet es im historischen Zentrum Triers, ganz in der Nähe des Geburtshauses von Karl Marx.

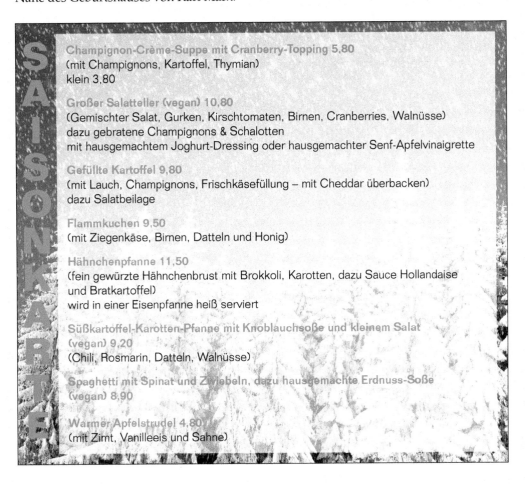

Champignon-Crème-Suppe mit Cranberry-Topping 5,80
(mit Champignons, Kartoffel, Thymian)
klein 3,80

Großer Salatteller (vegan) 10,80
(Gemischter Salat, Gurken, Kirschtomaten, Birnen, Cranberries, Walnüsse)
dazu gebratene Champignons & Schalotten
mit hausgemachtem Joghurt-Dressing oder hausgemachter Senf-Apfelvinaigrette

Gefüllte Kartoffel 9,80
(mit Lauch, Champignons, Frischkäsefüllung – mit Cheddar überbacken)
dazu Salatbeilage

Flammkuchen 9,50
(mit Ziegenkäse, Birnen, Datteln und Honig)

Hähnchenpfanne 11,50
(fein gewürzte Hähnchenbrust mit Brokkoli, Karotten, dazu Sauce Hollandaise und Bratkartoffel)
wird in einer Eisenpfanne heiß serviert

Süßkartoffel-Karotten-Pfanne mit Knoblauchsoße und kleinem Salat
(vegan) 9,20
(Chili, Rosmarin, Datteln, Walnüsse)

Spaghetti mit Spinat und Zwiebeln, dazu hausgemachte Erdnuss-Soße
(vegan) 8,90

Warmer Apfelstrudel 4,80
(mit Zimt, Vanilleeis und Sahne)

9-1 Ein leckeres Essen im Gasthaus. Schauen Sie die Speisekarte genau an und beantworten Sie die folgenden Fragen.

1. Lesen Sie zuerst die Namen und die Preise der Gerichte. Welche Gerichte auf der Speisekarte sind Vorspeisen, Hauptgerichte und Nachspeisen (Desserts)? Schreiben Sie sie auf.

Vorspeise	Hauptgericht	Nachspeise (Dessert)

It's typical to find restaurants with a **regionale Küche** as in this example of **Flammkuchen,** a recipe that stems from the **Elsass** *(French Alsace)* region. Why the name? A thin, bread-like dough is spread with sour cream, bacon, and onions, then put into the oven (earlier: **in die Flammen**).

2. Sprechen Sie die folgenden Wörter von der Speisekarte laut aus und versuchen Sie, die englische Bedeutung zu geben. Schreiben Sie dann die Wörter in eine der beiden Boxen: Leicht zu verstehen (fast wie Englisch) / Etwas schwieriger zu verstehen.

Thymian Walnuss Gurke Kirschtomate Schalotte Lauch Käsefüllung Dattel Honig Hähnchenbrust Karotte Eisenpfanne Süßkartoffel Knoblauch Rosmarin Soße Spinat Zimt Vanilleeis

Leicht zu verstehen (fast wie Englisch)	Etwas schwieriger zu verstehen

3. Das ist eine „Saisonkarte". Für welche Saison (Jahreszeit) ist diese Speisekarte?

4. Diane, Mark, Leonie und Thomas brauchen Ihre Hilfe. Welche Gerichte auf der Speisekarte sollten sie bestellen°? *order*

- Diane möchte ein Gericht mit wenig Kalorien essen.
- Mark ist Veganer, aber er hasst Spinat.
- Leonie möchte heute warm essen und sie hat Lust auf Fleisch.
- Thomas ist Vegetarier und isst gern Champignons und Käse.

9-2 Jetzt sind Sie im Restaurant. Sie gehen mit Ihrer Partnerin/Ihrem Partner in das gemütliche Gasthaus in Trier. Sagen Sie, was Sie bestellen wollen. Sagen Sie auch, was Sie nicht mögen. Was möchten Sie zu Ihrem Essen trinken? Wie viel geben Sie für Ihr Essen aus?

Ich bestelle …, weil ich … mag.

Ich hätte gern° …, weil ich … mag.   **hätte gern:** *would like (to have)*

Ich nehme …, weil ich … nicht mag.

Als Hauptspeise nehme ich …

Mein Essen kostet … Euro.

9-3 Wichtiges zum Essen im Restaurant. Was passt zusammen?

1. bestellen
2. getrennt bezahlen
3. die Rechnung
4. nachfüllen
5. das Trinkgeld
6. aufrunden

a. bill, check (in a restaurant)
b. tip
c. to round (an amount) up
d. to pay separately
e. to refill
f. to order

9.2 Kultur 1

Im Gasthaus

9.1 **Explore the variety of food in the German-speaking countries and learn eating customs**

Was ist „deutsches" Essen?

In den deutschsprachigen Ländern ist die Gastronomie oft sehr regional. Wer in Nordostdeutschland in ein Gasthaus geht, kann zum Beispiel Soljanka bestellen, eine würzige Suppe aus Osteuropa. In Österreich sieht man auf den Speisekarten oft Gulasch, das aus Ungarn stammt. Die Schweizer Küche verbindet Einflüsse aus der deutschen, französischen und norditalienischen Küche. Fondue und Raclette sind zwei weltbekannte Käsegerichte. In Nordamerika kennt man Spätzle (aus Süddeutschland und den Alpenländern) und einige Wurstsorten wie Bratwurst, Knackwurst oder Leberwurst.

Die internationale Gastronomie

Es gibt in den deutschsprachigen Ländern auch eine große internationale Präsenz. Viele Restaurants und Gasthäuser gehören Italienern, Griechen, Türken, Franzosen, Spaniern, Mexikanern oder Asiaten (Chinesen, Japanern, Vietnamesen, Thailändern). Viele dieser internationalen Köche und Köchinnen kombinieren die Spezialitäten aus ihren Ländern auch mit deutschen Küchentraditionen, um den deutschen Geschmack zu treffen[1]. Die Deutschen essen am liebsten deutsche Küche, gefolgt von Italienisch, Asiatisch und Griechisch. Diese Präferenzen haben mit der Geschichte der Migration nach Deutschland und mit den Reisezielen der Deutschen zu tun.

Schnellrestaurants

Diese Restaurants sind auch unter dem Namen Fast-Food-Restaurants bekannt und sind in den deutschsprachigen Ländern sehr erfolgreich. Neben den großen amerikanischen Ketten wie Starbucks, Burger King oder Subway sind auch andere Ketten etabliert, wie zum Beispiel die deutschen Ketten Nordsee (Fischspezialitäten) und

Currywurst: eine beliebte Berliner Spezialität

Tank @ Rast (Autobahnrestaurants) oder die schweizerische Kette Mövenpick Marché (frisches, lokales Essen). McDonald's ist das größte Gastronomieunternehmen in Deutschland. Die beliebtesten Fast-Food-Gerichte sind Pizza, belegte Brötchen, gegrillte Hähnchen und die Currywurst. In Berlin gibt es sogar ein Currywurst-Museum!

[1]**Geschmack treffen:** *to appeal to the taste*

9-4 Ein Restaurant kennen lernen.

Finden Sie (eins) im Internet ein …	… dann beantworten Sie diese Fragen!
☐ spanisches Restaurant in Bern ☐ griechisches Restaurant in Dortmund-Hörde ☐ vietnamesisches Restaurant in Graz ☐ türkisches Gasthaus in Düsseldorf	1. Wie heißt das Restaurant, das Sie besuchen? 2. Welche Gerichte auf der Speisekarte gefallen Ihnen? 3. Welche anderen interessanten Informationen finden Sie auf der Webseite des Restaurants?

Im Gasthaus

Eiswasser bekommt man im Gasthaus fast nie und auch Softdrinks trinkt man fast nie mit Eis. Wenn man Wasser trinken will, bestellt man Mineralwasser und bezahlt etwa € 1,80 für ein Glas oder ein kleines Fläschchen. Auch Brötchen und Butter muss man oft extra bestellen und bezahlen. Eine Tasse Kaffee kostet etwa € 2,00 und wenn sie leer ist, füllt der Kellner sie nicht nach. Wenn man mehr als nur eine Tasse Kaffee trinken will, bestellt man für etwa € 3,80 ein Kännchen (das sind zwei bis zweieinhalb Tassen). Wenn man die Rechnung bezahlt, rundet man die Summe auf und gibt etwa 10 Prozent Trinkgeld.

> **How to tip?** If your bill is €10.90, you might say **Zwölf Euro!** and the server will give you change as if the total bill were €12.

Wie man isst

Bevor man in den deutschsprachigen Ländern zu essen beginnt, sagt man meistens „Guten Appetit!" oder manchmal auch „Mahlzeit!" Beim Essen hat man das Messer immer in der rechten und die Gabel in der linken Hand und es gilt[2] als unkultiviert, das Messer auf den Tisch und eine Hand in den Schoß[3] zu legen. Wenn man gerade nicht isst, bleiben die Arme, aber nicht die Ellbogen, auf dem Tisch. Man sitzt gerade am Tisch, und die Arme bleiben eng[4] am Oberkörper.

> The photos show how people in the German-speaking countries hold silverware when eating. Between bites the lower arms (just above the wrist) rest on the table.

So hält man in Deutschland Messer und Gabel.

Der Arm ist eng am Oberkörper und bleibt auf dem Tisch.

9-5 Essen wie in Deutschland. Wenn Sie das nächste Mal essen gehen, zu Hause oder in der Mensa essen, versuchen Sie so zu essen, wie man das in den deutschsprachigen Ländern tut. Üben Sie, wie man das Messer und die Gabel hält, sitzen Sie gerade am Tisch und halten Sie die Arme korrekt.

[2]*is considered*   [3]*lap*   [4]*close*

))) 9.3 Wortschatz 1

Wichtige Vokabeln

9.2 Learn vocabulary to talk about food and eating out

Nomen

das Gasthaus, ̈-er	restaurant
die Bedienung (sing)	server, waiter, waitress
der Koch, ̈-e	
die Köchin, -nen	cook, chef
die Rechnung, -en	bill
die Speisekarte, -n	menu
das Trinkgeld, -er	tip
die Küche	cuisine
das Gericht, -e	dish (in a restaurant)
die Beilage, -n	side dish
die Vorspeise, -n	appetizer
das Hauptgericht, -e	main dish
die Nachspeise, -n	dessert
das Geschirr (sing)	dishes, tableware
der Teller, -	plate
das Besteck (sing)	cutlery, silverware
die Gabel, -n	fork

das Messer: Parents often admonish small children with the saying **Messer, Gabel, Schere** (scissors), **Licht** (i.e., matches), **sind für kleine Kinder nicht.**

das Messer, -	knife
der Löffel, -	spoon
der Esslöffel, -	tablespoon
der Teelöffel, -	teaspoon
die Pfanne, -n	pan
die Serviette, -n	napkin, serviette
das belegte Brötchen	sandwich (on a roll)
die Birne, -n	pear
der Champignon, -s	button mushroom
die Erdnuss, ̈-e	peanut
die Gurke, -n	gherkin; cucumber
das Hähnchen, -	chicken
der Knoblauch (sing)	garlic
die Sahne (sing)	cream
der Senf (sing)	mustard
die Soße, -n	sauce; gravy
der Spinat (sing)	spinach
die Zwiebel, -n	onion

Verben

aus·sprechen (spricht aus), ausgesprochen	to pronounce; say out loud
auf·runden	to round up (when tipping waitstaff)
bedienen	to serve (guests in a restaurant)
bestellen	to order
nach·füllen	to refill
getrennt bezahlen	to pay separately
zusammen bezahlen	to pay as a group

Ach so!
Bedienen means to serve guests in a restaurant; **servieren** means to serve a dish.

Andere Wörter

beliebt	popular; beloved
deutschsprachig	German-speaking
eng	close; tight
gebraten	roasted; pan-fried; sautéed
gefüllt	stuffed
gemischt	mixed
gewürzt	seasoned
hausgemacht	homemade
würzig	spicy; tangy

Ausdrücke

Ich bin Veganer/Veganerin.	I'm a vegan.
Ich bin Vegetarier/ Vegetarierin.	I'm a vegetarian.
als Hauptspeise	as a main dish (main course)
Ich hätte gern ...	I'd like (to have) …
eine Frage beantworten	to answer a question

Das Gegenteil

füllen ≠ leeren	to fill ≠ to empty
gerade sitzen ≠ krumm sitzen	to sit upright ≠ to slouch

Leicht zu verstehen

das Dressing, -s	**die Suppe, -n**
die Gastronomie (sing)	**servieren**
die Karotte, -n	**vegan**
der Pfeffer	**vegetarisch**
das Salz	

Wörter im Kontext

9-6 Was brauche ich? Beginnen Sie alle Antworten mit „Ich brauche …"

1. Ich habe die Speisekarte gelesen und möchte jetzt etwas zu essen bestellen.
2. Ich möchte jetzt die Suppe essen, die der Kellner mir gebracht hat.
3. Ich esse Spaghetti mit Tomatensauce.
4. Ich will Bratkartoffeln machen.
5. Ich bin jetzt fertig mit dem Essen.
6. Ich möchte Salat machen.
7. Ich möchte heute ein würziges Essen kochen.

eine Serviette	die Bedienung
eine Pfanne	Spinat und Gurken
die Rechnung	einen Löffel
Salz, Pfeffer und Knoblauch	

9-7 Was passt zusammen?

Other words for **Gasthaus** are **die Gaststätte, der Gasthof, das Wirtshaus, das Restaurant, die Raststätte** (on the **Autobahn**).

1. vegan   a. die Bedienung   5. gefüllt   e. servieren
2. die Pfanne   b. das Trinkgeld   6. die Nachspeise   f. die Kartoffel
3. das Gasthaus   c. der Salat   7. die Gäste   g. das Dressing
4. die Rechnung   d. die Hähnchenbrust   8. hausgemacht   h. bedienen

9-8 Mein Tisch im Restaurant. Was ist das?

a. _____
b. _____
c. _____
d. _____
e. _____
f. _____

9.4 Zur Aussprache

Pronouncing German *s* and *z*

9.3 Distinguish between the pronunciation of German *s* and *z*

Before vowels the sound represented by the letter **s** is *voiced*, i.e., it is pronounced like English *z* in **z**ip.

 9-9 Hören Sie gut zu und wiederholen Sie!

1. Wohin reisen Suse und Sabine? – Auf eine sonnige Südseeinsel.
2. So ein Sauwetter! Seit Sonntag keine Sonne!

Before consonants and at the end of a word, the sound represented by the letter **s** is *voiceless*, i.e., it is pronounced like English *s* in *sip*. The sounds represented by **ss** and **ß (Eszett)** are also *voiceless*.

1. Der Mensch **i**st, wa**s** er i**ss**t.

2. **I**st das alle**s**, wa**s** du wei**ß**t?

3. Wo **i**st hier da**s** beste Gasthau**s**?

The sound represented by the letter **z** is pronounced like English *ts* in *hits*.

1. Der **Z**ug nach **Z**ürich fährt um **z**ehn.

2. Wann kommt Hein**z** aus Gra**z** **z**urück?

3. **Z**ahnär**z**te **z**iehen **Z**ähne.

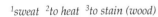

9-10 Aussprache von *s* versus *z*. Welches Wort hören Sie?

1. ☐ so	☐ Zoo	6. ☐ Gras	☐ Graz		
2. ☐ seit	☐ Zeit	7. ☐ Schweiß[1]	☐ Schweiz		
3. ☐ Saal	☐ Zahl	8. ☐ Kurs	☐ kurz		
4. ☐ selten	☐ zelten	9. ☐ heißen	☐ heizen[2]		
5. ☐ Sieh!	☐ Zieh!	10. ☐ beißen	☐ beizen[3]		

[1]*sweat* [2]*to heat* [3]*to stain (wood)*

Schloss Eggenberg in Graz, Österreich

Die U-Bahnstation Französische Straße in Berlin

9.5 Kommunikation und Formen 1

Reflexive pronouns

9.4 Talk about actions one does to or for oneself

To express the idea that one does an action *to oneself* or *for oneself*, English and German use reflexive pronouns. In German the reflexive pronoun can be in the accusative or the dative case, depending on its function.

ACCUSATIVE:	Ich habe **mich** geschnitten.	*I cut **myself**.*
DATIVE:	Ich hole **mir** ein Pflaster.	*I'm getting **myself** a bandage.*

When a sentence starts with the subject, the reflexive pronoun is placed directly after the verb, as in the examples above. When an element other than the subject stands at the beginning of the sentence, the reflexive pronoun usually follows the subject, which is placed after the verb, as in the examples below.

ACCUSATIVE:	Gerade habe ich **mich** geschnitten.	*I just cut **myself**.*
DATIVE:	Jetzt hole ich **mir** ein Pflaster.	*Now I'm getting **myself** a bandage.*

Volleyball, badminton, hiking, cycling, and Nordic Walking (pictured here) are popular in the German-speaking countries, even among those 60 and over. It's typical to join a club where you meet friends regularly and get some exercise. Posters like this are used by insurance companies to promote a healthy lifestyle for people of all ages.

Achtung!
The **-s** in **sich** for the **Sie**-form is not capitalized.

Reflexive pronouns in the accusative case

Ich wasche **mich.**	*I am washing **myself.***
Tina schminkt **sich.**	***Tina** is putting on makeup (= making **herself** up).*
Wann ziehen **Sie sich** um?	*When are **you** changing **(your clothes)?***

The above examples show there's not always a one-to-one correspondence in German and English. What's constant is that the person doing the action is doing it to himself or herself.

The accusative reflexive pronoun differs from the accusative personal pronoun only in the 3rd person singular and plural and in the **Sie**-form: **sich.**

Personal pronouns		Reflexive pronouns
NOMINATIVE	ACCUSATIVE	ACCUSATIVE
ich	mich	**mich**
du	dich	**dich**
er	ihn	
es	es	**sich**
sie	sie	
wir	uns	**uns**
ihr	euch	**euch**
sie	sie	**sich**
Sie	Sie	**sich**

Reflexive pronouns are used much more frequently in German than in English, for example with the following verbs.

Reflexive verbs	
sich waschen	*to get washed up*
sich baden	*to take a bath*
sich duschen	*to take a shower*
sich kämmen	*to comb one's hair*
sich rasieren	*to shave*
sich schminken	*to put on makeup*
sich anziehen	*to get dressed*
sich ausziehen	*to get undressed*
sich umziehen	*to change (one's clothes)*

Ach so!
You've already seen **baden** and **waschen.** When used without a reflexive pronoun, **baden** means *to go swimming*, and **waschen** means *to wash something*. The reflexive verbs **sich baden** and **sich waschen** mean *to bathe* or *wash (one's whole body).*

Achtung!
Umziehen without a reflexive means *to move*, as in *to change where you live*; **sich umziehen** means *to change clothes*. Based on this, what's the difference between **ausziehen** and **sich ausziehen**?

9-11 Was machen Otilia, Bernd, Moritz und Jens morgens und abends?

S1: Was macht Otilia um sieben Uhr zehn?   **S2:** Sie schminkt sich. Und Bernd?

	Otilia	Bernd	Moritz und Jens
7.10	Sie schminkt sich.	Er duscht sich.	Sie waschen sich.
7.25	Sie kämmt sich.	Er rasiert sich.	Sie ziehen sich an.
20.30	Sie zieht sich um.	Er badet sich.	Sie ziehen sich aus.

> Getting washed up in front of the sink instead of taking a shower or bath is a typical water-saving habit, especially common for young children. Try it out yourself sometime by renting a cost-saving hotel room without a shower, but with **Fließendwasser** *(running water)*.

9-12 Morgens vor der Uni.

►

S1: Was machst du morgens vor der Uni?

S2: Zuerst dusche ich mich.   Und dann rasiere ich mich.

1.

2.

3.

> **Ach so!**
> Word order with reflexive verbs is easy to handle. The reflexive pronoun comes as close to the conjugated verb as it can. **Ich will auf die Party gehen, aber ich muss *mich* noch schnell umziehen.** Notice that if something other than the subject starts the sentence, the subject comes just after the verb, but then the reflexive pronoun immediately follows. **Jetzt ziehe ich *mich* um!**

Registriere dich jetzt, um die Videos von deinen Freunden zu sehen!

use

news

9-13 Was ich alles mache, bevor ich zur Uni gehe. Schreiben Sie ein paar Sätze und verwenden° Sie so viele reflexive Verben wie möglich.

Ich stehe meistens um _____ auf.

Vor dem Frühstück …

Und nach dem Frühstück …

- ☐ joggen gehen
- ☐ sich duschen/baden
- ☐ sich anziehen
- ☐ frühstücken
- ☐ mein Bett machen
- ☐ schnell meine Hausaufgaben machen
- ☐ meine Facebook-Seite oder Instagram checken

- ☐ sich rasieren
- ☐ sich schminken
- ☐ sich kämmen
- ☐ Musik hören
- ☐ Nachrichten° anschauen
- ☐ mit meiner Freundin/meinem Freund chatten
- ☐ …

9-14 Bevor ich zur Uni gehe, … Erzählen Sie Ihren Mitstudenten, was Sie alles machen, bevor Sie zur Uni gehen.

9-15 Wir machen das gleich! S1 spielt die Mutter, S2 und S3 spielen die Kinder. Danach spielt S2 die Mutter, und S3 und S1 die Kinder, usw.

▶

MUTTER: Kinder, duscht ihr euch bald?   KINDER: Ja Mama, wir duschen uns gleich!

1.

2.

3.

4.

5.

6.

Reflexive pronouns in the dative case

In the examples below, the reflexive pronouns are indirect objects and are therefore in the dative case.

Ich kaufe **mir** ein neues Snowboard.   *I'm buying **myself** a new snowboard.*

Note the difference in the way German and English refer to actions that involve one's own body.

Oliver wäscht **sich** jeden Tag **die** Haare.   *Oliver washes **his** hair every day.*

Er putzt **sich** zweimal am Tag **die** Zähne.   *He brushes **his** teeth twice a day.*

Where English uses the possessive adjective (*his* hair, *his* teeth), German uses the dative reflexive pronoun and the *definite* article (*die* Haare, *die* Zähne).

Just like the accusative forms you've just learned, the dative reflexive pronoun differs from the dative personal pronoun only in the 3rd person singular and plural and in the **Sie**-form, where it is **sich.**

Personal pronouns		Reflexive pronouns
NOMINATIVE	DATIVE	DATIVE
ich	mir	**mir**
du	dir	**dir**
er	ihm	
es	ihm	**sich**
sie	ihr	
wir	uns	**uns**
ihr	euch	**euch**
sie	ihnen	**sich**
Sie	Ihnen	**sich**

9-16 Was machen diese Leute?

► Anita sich die Haare bürsten

Anita bürstet sich die Haare.

1. Peter

2. Stephanie

3. ich

4. wir

5. ich

6. Martin und Claudia

sich einen Film anschauen	sich die Hände waschen
sich die Haare waschen	sich ein Stück Kuchen nehmen
sich eine Tasse Kaffee machen	sich die Zähne putzen

Ach so!
Remember your 1st person reflexive pronouns: **ich → mir; wir → uns.**

9-17 Eine Umfrage: Wie oft machst du das? Stellen Sie Ihren Mitstudenten Fragen mit den folgenden reflexiven Verben. Markieren Sie die Namen Ihrer Mitstudenten in der Tabelle.

S1: Wie oft putzt du dir die Zähne?

S2: Ich putze mir zweimal am Tag die Zähne.

	nie	selten	jeden Tag	zweimal am Tag	zweimal die Woche	einmal im Monat
sich die Haare waschen						
sich die Hände waschen						
sich die Zähne putzen						
sich rasieren						
sich schminken						
sich die Haare färben						
sich die Haare stylen						

9-18 Was kaufst du dir mit diesem Geld? Sie haben 500 Euro gewonnen und sollen sich damit drei Dinge kaufen. Fragen Sie einander, wie Sie das Geld ausgeben. Berichten Sie, was Sie herausgefunden haben.

S1: Wow, 500 Euro! Was kaufst du dir?

S2: Ich kaufe mir zuerst …
Und dann kaufe ich mir …
Zuletzt kaufe ich mir …

S1: Lisa/David kauft sich zuerst mal …
Und dann kauft sie/er sich …
Zuletzt kauft sie/er sich …

Reflexive pronouns used to express *each other*

In German you can use the plural reflexive pronoun as a reciprocal pronoun meaning *each other*. Note that the pronoun is not always expressed in English.

Wie habt ihr **euch** kennengelernt?   *How did you get to know **each other**?*

Wo sollen wir **uns** treffen?   *Where should we meet?*

9-19 Was passt zusammen? Ergänzen Sie die Reflexivpronomen in den Fragen und beantworten Sie die Fragen. Ein paar Antworten passen mehr als einmal.

S1:

1. Seit wann kennen Claudia und Martin _____?

2. Wie haben sie _____ kennengelernt?

3. Wie oft rufen _____ die beiden an?

4. Wann trefft ihr _____ heute Abend?

5. Wie oft schreibt ihr _____?

6. Wann sehen wir _____ wieder?

7. Wo sollen wir _____ morgen Abend treffen?

S2:

Durch Freunde.

Hoffentlich sehr bald.

Um acht.

Am besten wieder bei mir.

Fast jeden Tag.

Seit einem halben Jahr.

9-20 Freundschaften. Stellen Sie einander die folgenden Fragen.

- Hast du eine gute Freundin/einen guten Freund?
- Seit wann kennt ihr euch?
- Wo und wie habt ihr euch kennengelernt?
- Wo trefft ihr euch am liebsten?
- Warum versteht ihr euch so gut?

Reflexive verbs

9.5 Use idiomatic reflexive verbs

Many German verbs are always or almost always accompanied by a reflexive pronoun even though their English equivalents are rarely reflexive. Here are some important ones. The reflexive pronoun for these verbs is in the accusative case.

Idiomatic reflexive verbs	
sich verspäten	*to be late*
sich beeilen	*to hurry (up)*
sich auf·regen	*to get worked up; to get upset*
sich benehmen	*to behave*
sich entschuldigen	*to apologize*
sich erkälten	*to catch a cold*
sich wohl fühlen	*to feel well*
sich bewegen	*to get some exercise, to move (your body)*
sich fit halten	*to keep yourself in good shape*
sich setzen	*to sit down*

> **Lerntipp!**
> To help you remember that these verbs are reflexive, you should always practice them together with the reflexive pronoun, e.g., *sich* **verspäten.**

9-21 Was passt zu jeder Situation? Finden Sie zu jeder Situation die passende Reaktion aus dem Kasten.

Situationen

1. Patrick ist gestern schwimmen gegangen, obwohl das Wasser noch eiskalt war. Heute Morgen fühlt er sich gar nicht wohl und denkt:

2. Holger ist mit Anna auf einer Party. Er isst und trinkt zu viel, steht dann plötzlich auf und will gehen. Anna fragt, warum er denn schon gehen will. Holger antwortet:

3. Günter ist mit Tina auf einer Party. Er trinkt zu viel und fängt an, ziemlich laut zu werden. Tina sagt:

4. Ralf bekommt bei einer wichtigen Prüfung in Deutsch eine schlechte Note. Er kommt zu seiner Deutschprofessorin in die Sprechstunde. Sie sagt:

Benimm dich doch nicht so schlecht!	Ich glaube, ich habe mich gestern erkältet!
Guten Tag! Bitte setzen Sie sich!	Ich fühle mich gar nicht wohl.

9-22 Was passt zusammen? Interpretieren Sie jedes Bild mit einem Partner.

1.   2.   3.

| Ich habe mich erkältet. | Reg dich nicht so auf! | Sie haben sich verspätet! |

4.   5.   6.

| Komm, setz dich zu mir! | Du benimmst dich schlecht. | Ich fühle mich nicht wohl. |

 9-23 Kleine Interviews. Stellen Sie einander die folgenden Fragen und notieren Sie die Antworten in Ihrer Gruppe. Finden Sie Gemeinsamkeiten° oder Unterschiede°?

similarities
differences

Thema 1: Wellness, Fitness

- Was machst du, wenn du dich erkältet hast?

  Wenn ich mich erkältet habe, …

- Bewegst du dich dreimal die Woche? Wie machst du das?

  Wenn ich Zeit habe, bewege ich mich …

- Was machst du sonst, um dich fit zu halten?

  Ich …, um mich fit zu halten.

Thema 2: Immer unter Zeitdruck°?

time pressure

- In welchen Situationen musst du dich beeilen?

  Ich muss mich oft beeilen, wenn ich …

- Verspätest du dich manchmal? Warum?

  Ich verspäte mich manchmal, weil …

- Regst du dich auf, wenn du dich verspätest, oder bleibst du cool?

  Ich rege mich auf, wenn … (oder)
  Ich bleibe meistens cool, wenn ich …

9-24 Was wir gemeinsam haben. Präsentieren Sie 1–2 Sachen, die für Ihre Gruppe typisch war(en). Hier sind ein paar Beispiele:

Alle in der Gruppe bewegen sich dreimal die Woche.
Wir bewegen uns jeden Tag. / Zwei von uns bewegen sich jeden Tag!

Wir müssen uns alle montags, mittwochs und freitags beeilen, weil wir schon um 9 Deutsch haben!
Einer von uns regt sich auf, wenn er sich verspätet. Die anderen regen sich aber nicht auf.

9.6 Kultur 2

))) Nachhaltig leben!

9.6 Discuss ways people in German-speaking countries lead healthy, sustainable lifestyles

Can you find multiple words for the typical motto heard in North America: *Reduce, reuse, recycle?*

Hier sprechen drei junge Leute über ihren Alltag. Finden Sie Gemeinsamkeiten oder Unterschiede zwischen ihrer Lebensweise und der Lebensweise in Nordamerika? Leben Sie persönlich so umweltbewusst wie diese Deutschen?

Ein Leben ohne Auto?

Karin: „Ich bin 24 und habe noch nie ein eigenes Auto gehabt. Ich leihe mir das Auto von meiner Mutter ab und zu, aber sonst komme ich wirklich ohne Auto ganz gut aus. Hier in Freiburg – das ist eine große Stadt mit über 200 000 Einwohnern, aber hier kann man wirklich alles mit dem Fahrrad oder mit dem Bus erreichen. Da braucht man kein Auto. Ich glaube, die Leute sagen sich, kann ich's ohne Auto machen, da mache ich es ohne Auto. Benzin ist sowieso sehr teuer hier in Deutschland, und das Parken kostet ja auch. Ein Auto ist eine feine Sache, aber das braucht man wirklich nicht."

Karin fährt zum Schwimmbad.

Einplanen, reduzieren, wiederverwerten

Florian: „In Deutschland plant man vor dem Einkaufen. Man bringt halt eine Einkaufstasche mit, und wenn nicht, da muss man eine Plastiktüte für 50 Cent kaufen, wenn man einkauft. Und ich verwende auch fast nie Einwegflaschen, die man einfach wegwirft. Ich nehme nur Mehrwegflaschen, weil das umweltfreundlicher ist. Und die Mülltrennung macht es eben auch ganz leicht, andere Sachen zu entsorgen, Altbatterien, Altpapier, und so. Es gibt an jeder Ecke Container für Altglas in verschiedenen Farben, und die blaue Tonne für Altpapier. Und den gelben Sack für Plastik. Zu Hause habe ich auch nur Energiesparlampen, weil das viel umweltfreundlicher ist. Die muss man zu einer Sammelstelle bringen, wenn sie nicht mehr funktionieren. Aber die kann man auch viel länger verwenden als Halogenlampen und sie sind besser für die Umwelt."

This reuseable **Einkaufstasche** is made of **Baumwolle** *(cotton)*. It's typical to stuff a few of these in your backpack in case you need to shop.

Germany, Austria, and Switzerland are consistently ranked among the countries that recycle the most. Households, businesses, and even factories recycle about half of their waste. Recycling is taken so seriously that private citizens can be fined by the **Abfallüberwachung** *(waste monitoring department)* for not complying with recycling regulations.

Achtung!
Exact measures for recycling differ from region to region. If you're a guest in a German household, a good first question for your hosts might be *Wie macht man das mit der Mülltrennung?*

Destiny recycelt Altpapier.

Und die Mülltrennung!

Destiny: „Ja, gelber Sack, blaue Tonne, Papier, Glasflaschen, Dosen. Man ist einfach daran gewöhnt, dass man Papier und Glas extra trennt. Und Dosen. Und dann in der Küche auch noch Kompost. Bei meinen Eltern zu Hause gibt es einen Riesenhaufen Kompost im Garten. Und seit 2015 gibt es überall die braune Tonne, wenn man nicht zu Hause kompostiert. Ich lebe in einer Wohnung ohne Garten und da sammle ich meinen Biomüll extra – Essensreste, Obst- und Kartoffelschalen, Brotreste und so weiter. Die kommen in die braune Tonne. Außerdem kann man viele Verpackungen recyceln. Das kommt in den gelben Sack. Und Restmüll ist alles, was man sonst nicht recyceln kann."

9-25 Wohin gehören diese Müllsorten?

1. Nicht recycelbare Marmeladengläser bringt man …
2. Zeitungen und Zeitschriften gehören …
3. Biomüll gehört …
4. Plastik und Aluminium kommen …
5. Alles, was man nicht recyceln kann, kommt …
6. Mehrwegflaschen bringt man …

a. in die blaue Tonne.
b. zum Altglascontainer.
c. in den gelben Sack.
d. wieder zum Supermarkt zum Recyceln.
e. in die braune Tonne oder auf den Komposthaufen.
f. in die Tonne für Restmüll.

9.7 Kommunikation und Formen 2

Relative Clauses

9.7 Use relative clauses to describe people, places, and things

Relative clauses and relative pronouns in English

Like adjectives, relative clauses are used to describe people, places, and things.

The beer _that was so cheap_ is very good.
(relative clause)

Relative clauses always start with a relative pronoun. The relative pronoun (*that, who,* or *which*) refers back to the noun it gives more information about, called its *antecedent.*

	RELATIVE CLAUSE		
ANTECEDENT	**RELATIVE PRONOUN**		
The beer	*that*	*was so cheap*	is very good.
Your friend	*who*	*likes to drink beer*	is coming to the party.
The party,	*which*	*starts at 9,*	will be great!

Relative clauses and relative pronouns in German: Subject forms

As in English, relative clauses in German always come after the noun they are describing and start with a relative pronoun. But in German the relative pronoun must have the same *gender* (masculine, neuter, or feminine) and *number* (singular or plural) as its antecedent. Its *case* (nominative, accusative, or dative) fits its function in the relative clause. When they are the subject of the clause, relative pronouns are in the nominative case:

	RELATIVE CLAUSE		
ANTECEDENT	**RELATIVE PRONOUN**		
Das Bier,	**das**	**so billig war,**	ist sehr gut.
Dein Freund,	**der**	**gern Bier trinkt,**	kommt zur Party.
Die Party,	**die**	**um 9 Uhr anfängt,**	wird ganz toll sein!

> **Achtung!**
> Relative clauses are dependent clauses. They are marked off by commas, and the conjugated verb appears at the end of the clause.

9-26 Wer sind diese Leute?

▶   Ein Psychiater ist ein Arzt, …

    der mir mit meinen Problemen hilft.
    Ein Psychiater ist ein Arzt, der mir mit meinen Problemen hilft.

1. Ein Kellner ist ein Mann, …   2. Eine Ärztin ist eine Frau, …

3. Ein Automechaniker ist ein Handwerker, …

                  4. Eine Marktfrau ist eine Frau, …

der kaputte Autos repariert.	die auf dem Wochenmarkt Obst und Gemüse verkauft.
der im Gasthaus das Essen serviert.	die kranke Menschen wieder gesund macht.

9-27 Kettenreaktion: Wie heißt …? Schreiben Sie zwei Fragen über eine Mitstudentin oder einen Mitstudenten. Eine Person beginnt dann eine Kettenreaktion und stellt der Klasse die erste Frage. Die Person, die korrekt antwortet, stellt dann die nächste Frage, und immer so weiter. Folgen Sie dem Beispiel.

▶ **S1:** Wie heißt der Student, der heute ein schickes, rotes T-Shirt trägt?

Maximilian

S2: Das ist Maximilian!

▶ **S2:** Wie heißt die Studentin, die schon viele Reisen gemacht hat?

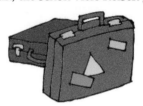

Anna

S3: Das ist Anna!

Relative clauses and relative pronouns: Object and indirect object forms

Sometimes the relative pronoun functions as the direct object or indirect object of the relative clause.

Der Wein, **den** du gekauft hast, schmeckt super!	*The wine **that** you bought tastes great*

Here the relative pronoun **den,** like its antecedent **Wein,** is masculine and singular. It is in the accusative case because it is the direct object of the verb.

In the example below, the relative pronoun **dem** refers back to **Freund** (masculine, singular) and is in the dative case because it is the indirect object:

Der Freund, **dem** du den Wein gibst, trinkt lieber Bier.	*The friend, **to whom** you're giving the wine, prefers to drink beer.*

In contrast to English, the German relative pronoun can never be omitted.

Der Wein, **den** du gekauft hast, schmeckt super!	*The wine you bought tastes great!*

> **Lerntipp!**
> To figure out the case of a relative pronoun, put the relative clause into sentence form: **"den du gekauft hast"** = Du hast <u>den</u> Wein gekauft.

Relative pronouns				
	MASCULINE	NEUTER	FEMININE	PLURAL
NOMINATIVE	der	das	die	die
ACCUSATIVE	den	das	die	die
DATIVE	dem	dem	der	**denen**

Note that except for **denen,** the forms in the chart are identical to those of the definite article.

9-28 Definitionen.

▶   Ein Beistelltisch ist ein Tisch (m), …

den man neben einen Sessel stellt.

Ein Beistelltisch ist ein Tisch, den man neben einen Sessel stellt.

1.   Italien ist ein Land (n), …   2.   Eine Schnecke ist ein Tier (n), …

3.   Ein Huhn ist ein Vogel° (m), …   4.   Eine Kaffeemaschine ist eine   *bird*
                                                Maschine, …

den wir für Eier und für Fleisch brauchen.   die man braucht, um Kaffee zu machen.
das die Deutschen gern im Sommer besuchen.   das man in Frankreich gern isst.

9-29 Der erste Tag. Heute ist Ihr erster Tag als Kellnerin/Kellner und Sie sind oft
noch ein bisschen verwirrt°. Ergänzen Sie die Relativpronomen …   *confused*

… im Nominativ:

1. Wo ist denn der Mann, d_____ dieses Bier bestellt hat?

2. Wo ist denn das Ehepaar, d_____ dieses Gulasch bestellt hat?

3. Wo ist denn die Frau, d_____ diese Tasse Kaffee bestellt hat?

4. Wo sind denn die Leute, d_____ diese Suppe bestellt haben?

… im Akkusativ:

5. Wo ist denn der Mann, d_____ ich so schnell bedienen soll?

6. Wo ist denn das Ehepaar, d_____ ich so schnell bedienen soll?

7. Wo ist denn die Frau, d_____ ich so schnell bedienen soll?

8. Wo sind denn die Leute, d_____ ich so schnell bedienen soll?

… im Dativ:

9. Wo ist denn der Mann, d_____ ich dieses Schnitzel bringen soll?

10. Wo ist denn das Ehepaar, d_____ ich diesen Rotwein bringen soll?

11. Wo ist denn die Frau, d_____ ich die Speisekarte bringen soll?

12. Wo sind denn die Leute, d_____ ich diesen Nachtisch bringen soll?

9-30 Weißt du das? S1 stellt die Fragen und ergänzt die Relativpronomen. S2 gibt die Antwort.

Geografie
Wie heißen die Berge, d_____ in der Schweiz liegen?
Wie heißt die österreichische Hauptstadt, d_____ an der Donau liegt?

Berühmte Personen
Wie heißt der schweizerische Tennisspieler, d_____ zwei olympische Medaillen gehören?
Wie heißt der Komponist, d_____ man in Salzburg liebt?
Wie heißt der syrische Immigrant, d_____ YouTube-Star geworden ist?

Architektur
Wie heißt die Brücke, d_____ der Ingenieur Johann August Röbling entworfen hat?
Wie heißt die berühmte Kunsthochschule, d_____ Walter Gropius 1919 gegründet hat?
Wie heißt das große Technikmuseum, d_____ man in München besuchen kann?

Sprachnotiz   The relative pronoun in the genitive case

You know that in German the interrogative pronoun *whose* is **wessen.**

Wessen Fahrrad ist das?   *Whose bicycle is this?*

Whose can also be a relative pronoun. In this function it has two German equivalents: **dessen** if the antecedent is masculine or neuter, and **deren** if it is feminine or plural.

Der Student, **dessen** Wagen ich kaufe, zieht in die USA.   *The [male] student **whose** car I'm buying is moving to the U.S.*

Die Studentin, **deren** Wagen ich kaufe, zieht in die USA.   *The [female] student **whose** car I'm buying is moving to the U.S.*

9.8 Video-Treff

Was ich gern esse und trinke

9.8 Understand authentic video of German speakers talking about what they like to eat and drink

Anja Szustak, Maiga, Thomas, Karen, Stefan Meister, Stefan Kuhlmann, Ursula und Öcsi erzählen, was sie gern essen und trinken. Machen Sie die erste Aufgabe **Was ist das auf Englisch?,** bevor Sie das Video ansehen.

9-31 Was ist das auf Englisch?

1. Mein Lieblingsgericht sind **Dampfnudeln**.
2. Am liebsten esse ich Salate mit **Putenfleisch**.
3. Ich esse lieber im Restaurant, weil ich da **bedient werde**.
4. Das ist eine **Frage des Geldes**.
5. Mir gefällt die italienische **Küche** so gut, weil sie so einfach ist.
6. Jetzt **schäle** ich die Karotten.
7. Ich werde das Gericht dann scharf **würzen**.

a. peel
b. turkey
c. dumplings
d. cuisine
e. get waited on
f. season
g. question of money

9-32 Richtig oder falsch? Lesen Sie die Aussagen über Anja, Maiga, Thomas und Karen. Sind diese Aussagen richtig oder falsch? Wenn eine Aussage falsch ist, korrigieren Sie sie.

	RICHTIG	FALSCH	
1. Anja mag sehr gern Sachen wie Kuchen, Torten und Schokolade.	☐	☐	
2. Anja kauft oft eine Waffel, weil sie nur drei Euro kostet.	☐	☐	
3. Statt zu Hause zu kochen, geht Maiga meistens ins Restaurant.	☐	☐	
4. Maigas Lieblingsgericht ist Dampfnudeln mit Vanillesoße.	☐	☐	
5. Thomas geht gern in „Die rote Harfe", ein Café und Restaurant in Kreuzberg.	☐	☐	
6. „Die rote Harfe" ist nur im Herbst und Winter geöffnet.	☐	☐	
7. Dort isst er am liebsten vegetarische Gerichte.	☐	☐	
8. Karen geht nicht oft ins Restaurant, und sie kocht auch nicht so oft.	☐	☐	
9. Am liebsten isst Karen eine Stulle°.	☐	☐	*sandwich*
10. Karen trinkt abends am liebsten Tee.	☐	☐	

9-33 Essen und Trinken. Welche der folgenden Aussagen passt zu den Aussagen, die Stefan Meister, Stefan Kuhlmann, Ursula oder Öcsi in dem Video machen?

	Stefan Meister	Stefan Kuhlmann	Ursula	Öcsi
1. Mein Lieblingsgericht ist ein sehr großer Hamburger.	☐	☐	☐	☐
2. Ich esse am liebsten alle Pastasorten.	☐	☐	☐	☐
3. Ich koche am liebsten für Freunde zu Hause.	☐	☐	☐	☐
4. Ich mag italienisches Essen, weil es nicht kompliziert ist.	☐	☐	☐	☐
5. Ich koche noch nicht sehr lange und deshalb brauche ich ein Kochbuch.	☐	☐	☐	☐
6. Was ich gern trinke, ist ein Bier aus Deutschland.	☐	☐	☐	☐
7. Mein Lieblingsrestaurant ist eine Rockkneipe.	☐	☐	☐	☐
8. Am liebsten esse ich Gerichte mit viel Gemüse drin.	☐	☐	☐	☐
9. Ich denke, ein Big Mac ist nicht so gesund.	☐	☐	☐	☐
10. Ich habe einen neuen Wok.	☐	☐	☐	☐

))) 9.9 Wortschatz 2

Wichtige Vokabeln

9.9 Learn vocabulary to talk about your daily life and sustainable lifestyles

Nomen

die Umwelt	environment
der Umweltschutz	environmental protection
die Nachhaltigkeit	sustainability
der Bürger, -	
die Bürgerin, -nen	citizen
die Handlung, -en	action
die Einkaufstasche, -n	reuseable shopping bag
die Plastiktüte, -n	plastic bag
der Müll	trash
die Tonne, -n	trash container, bin
der Föhn, -e	blow-dryer
die Haarbürste, -n	hairbrush
das Handtuch, ̈er	towel
der Kamm, ̈e	comb
der Lippenstift, -e	lipstick
der Rasierapparat, -e	shaver, electric razor
das Rasierwasser	aftershave
das Shampoo, -s	shampoo
die Seife, -n	soap
der Spiegel, -	mirror
der Waschlappen, -	washcloth
die Zahnbürste, -n	toothbrush
die Zahnpasta	toothpaste

Verben

sich an·ziehen, angezogen	to dress, to get dressed
sich aus·ziehen, ausgezogen	to undress, to get undressed
sich um·ziehen, umgezogen	to change one's clothes
sich baden	to take a bath
sich duschen	to take a shower
sich kämmen	to comb one's hair
sich rasieren	to shave
sich schminken	to put on makeup
sich setzen	to sit down
sich auf·regen	to get worked up; to get upset
sich beeilen	to hurry
sich benehmen (benimmt), benommen	to behave
sich bewegen	to get some exercise; to move about
sich erkälten	to catch a cold

sich entschuldigen	to apologize
sich fit halten (hält), gehalten	to stay in shape
sich verspäten	to be late
sich wohl fühlen	to feel well
sich (*dat*) die Haare färben	to color one's hair
sich (*dat*) die Haare föhnen/ trocknen	to blow-dry / dry one's hair
sich (*dat*) die Haare waschen (wäscht), gewaschen	to wash one's hair
sich (*dat*) die Zähne putzen	to brush one's teeth
handeln	to act (*behave*)
verwenden	to use
wählen	to choose, to select
treffen (trifft), getroffen	to meet
recyceln	
wiederverwerten	to recycle
weg·werfen (wirft weg), weggeworfen	to throw away

Andere Wörter

ähnlich	similar
sogar	even
nachhaltig	sustainable
umweltfreundlich	environmentally friendly

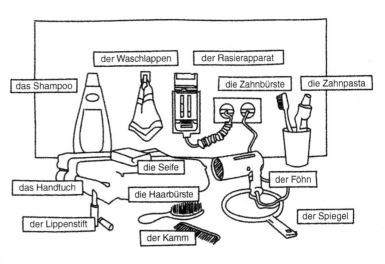

Ausdrücke

umweltbewusst leben	to live in an environmentally conscious way
nachhaltig leben	to live sustainably

Das Gegenteil

häufig ≠ selten	often, frequently ≠ seldom
die Gemeinsamkeit, -en ≠	similarity ≠
der Unterschied, -e	difference

Leicht zu verstehen

die Batterie, -n	**energieeffizient**
der Sack, ⸚e	**reduzieren**
die Tabelle, -n	**visuell**

Wörter im Kontext

9-34 Was passt zusammen? Beginnen Sie mit **Was brauche ich, …**

1. um mir die Haare zu waschen?
2. um mir die Haare zu trocknen?
3. um mir die Zähne zu putzen?
4. um mir die Hände zu waschen?
5. um mich zu kämmen?
6. um mich zu schminken?
7. um mich zu rasieren?

a. Einen Lippenstift.
b. Einen Kamm und einen Spiegel.
c. Einen Rasierapparat.
d. Wasser und Seife.
e. Ein Handtuch und einen Föhn.
f. Wasser und Shampoo.
g. Eine Zahnbürste und Zahnpasta.

9-35 Was passt?

sich umziehen / sich anziehen / sich ausziehen / sich beeilen
sich erkälten / sich wohl fühlen / sich entschuldigen

1. Bevor man sich duscht oder sich badet, _____ man _____ _____.
2. Nachdem man sich geduscht oder sich gebadet hat, _____ man _____ wieder _____.
3. Bevor man in die Oper geht, _____ man _____ _____.
4. Viele Menschen _____ _____ im Winter.
5. Wenn man morgens zu spät aufgestanden ist, sollte man _____ _____.
6. Wenn man sich verspätet hat oder wenn man sich schlecht benommen hat, sollte man _____ _____.
7. Wenn man _____ nicht _____ _____, sollte man zu Hause bleiben.

9-36 Was ist hier identisch? Welche zwei Sätze in jeder Gruppe bedeuten etwa dasselbe?

1. Ich fühle mich nicht wohl.
   Es tut mir leid.
   Mir geht es nicht gut.

2. Das mache ich nicht sehr häufig.
   Das mache ich selten.
   Das mache ich ähnlich.

3. Diese Plastiktüte soll man wiederverwerten.
   Man soll diese Plastiktüte recyceln.
   Diese Plastiktüte soll man wegwerfen.

4. Ich verwende nur Einwegflaschen.
   Ich lebe nachhaltig.
   Ich umweltbewusst.

5. Wir sind uns ähnlich.
   Zwischen uns gibt es viele Unterschiede.
   Zwischen uns gibt es viele Gemeinsamkeiten.

9-37 Nachhaltig leben. Was passt zusammen?

1. Eine Einkaufstasche ist eine Tasche,
2. Einwegflaschen sind Flaschen,
3. Mehrwegflaschen sind Flaschen,
4. Biomüll ist Müll,
5. Ein Ladegerät für Batterien ist ein Gerät,
6. In den Restmüll kommen nur Dinge,

a. die man immer zum Supermarkt mitbringt.
b. das Batterien wieder auflädt.
c. die man nicht nachfüllt.
d. die man nachfüllen kann.
e. den man kompostieren kann.
f. die man nicht recyceln kann.

> **Ach so!**
> A returnable glass bottle is a **Mehrwegflasche,** which is **umweltfreundlich** (good for the environment). Based on this, can you find the noun for a nonreturnable bottle?

Wörter unter der Lupe

Predicting gender

In German and in English the suffix **-er** is used to form *agent nouns*, i.e., nouns that show who or what does the action described by a given verb. Agent nouns with the suffix **-er** are always masculine and can refer to things as well as people. Some of these nouns take an umlaut.

| kaufen | to buy | **der** Käufer, - | buyer |
| wecken | to wake (someone) up | **der** Wecker, - | alarm clock |

If an agent noun refers to a female, the suffix **-in** is added to the masculine suffix **-er.**

| der Käufer | (male) buyer | **die** Käuferin, -nen | (female) buyer |

9-38 Was passt wo? Choosing appropriate infinitives, create German equivalents of the English nouns listed below. The articles indicate whether the nouns are to refer to a male or a thing **(der)** or to a female **(die)**. Note that there are three compound nouns.

vermieten / einwandern / verkaufen (Umlaut!) / übersetzen / Korken + ziehen / anfangen (Umlaut!) / kennen / besuchen / Arbeit + geben / Arbeit + nehmen

1. visitor   der _____
2. translator   die _____
3. sales clerk   der _____
4. immigrant   die _____
5. employer   der _____
6. beginner   der _____
7. connoisseur   der _____
8. employee   der _____
9. landlady   die _____
10. corkscrew   der _____

> **Achtung!**
> The feminine version of **Auswanderer** has only one **-er.** So it's not **Auswandererin,** but rather **Auswanderin.** The same is true for the feminine version of **Einwanderer.**

9-39 Nützliche Apps. *Wer* kann hier *was* lernen? Geben Sie ein englisches Äquivalent.

9.10 Alles zusammen

Leben Sie umweltfreundlich?

In *Kultur 2*, you learned how Germans often make everyday lifestyle choices based on the impact they'll have on the environment. Here you will read and interpret a visual diagram **(Grafik)** that displays statistics about those choices. Then you'll poll your class about environmentally conscious activities and create your own **Grafik** to show the poll results!

Schritt 1: Zum Lesen

9-40 Symbole für Umweltengagement. Verbinden Sie die Symbole in der Grafik mit der passenden umweltfreundlichen Handlung: **der Fisch, der Computer, der Apfel, die Einkaufstasche, die Baumwolle, die Waschmaschine, das Werkzeug, das Reinigungsmittel.**

▶ **Der Fisch** steht für die Handlung „Fisch / Meerestiere aus nachhaltiger Fischerei kaufen". **Der Computer** steht für …

Umweltschutz: So handeln die Bürger

Von je 100 Befragten sagen, dass sie …

	immer	sehr häufig
energieeffiziente Haushalts-geräte kaufen	46	25
beim Einkaufen auf Plastiktüten verzichten	27	35
energieeffiziente Fernseher und Computer kaufen	36	24
umweltschonende Reinigungsmittel kaufen	18	25
Fisch/Meerestiere aus nachhaltiger Fischerei kaufen	19	19
kaputte Gebrauchs-gegenstände reparieren lassen (wenn möglich)	13	23
Lebensmittel mit Bio-Siegel kaufen	3	17
als umweltschonend gekenn-zeichnete Kleidung (z. B. aus Bio-Baumwolle) kaufen	2	10

Repräsentative Onlinebefragung von 2 117 Personen ab 14 Jahren von Juli bis Aug. 2014   Quelle: BMU, UBA © Globus 10535

Achtung!
sehr häufig = sehr oft

Ach so!
Bio- or **Öko-** added to a word indicates that it is organic.

Schritt 2: Zum Sprechen

9-41 Eine Umfrage: Lebst du umweltbewusst? Wie viele aus Ihrer Klasse (oder Gruppe) handeln umweltfreundlich? Am Ende formulieren Sie selber eine Frage für Ihre Mitstudenten.

	immer	sehr häufig	häufig	nicht häufig	nie
Beim Einkaufen verzichte ich auf Plastiktüten.					
Ich gehe zu Fuß oder fahre mit dem Bus zur Uni.					
Ich kaufe energieeffiziente Fernseher und Computer.					
Ich verwende eine nachfüllbare Wasserflasche.					
Ich kaufe Lebensmittel mit Bio-Siegel.					
Ich recycele Altpapier, Pappe, Plastik und Glas.					
…					

Schritt 3: Zum Kreieren

9-42 Wie handelt der typische Student? Machen Sie eine interessante visuelle Grafik mit den Statistiken von Ihrem Deutschkurs. Verwenden Sie passende Farben und Symbole, so dass die Grafik visuell attraktiv aussieht!

For this activity, you're creating a graphic representation of you and your classmates' habits that protect the environment, parallel to the survey results you read in *Schritt 1.* Take a look at vocabulary in *Wortschatz 2* and exercise 9-41 for tips on how to characterize what you and your classmates do for the environment. What pictograms or graphics would best represent these to others?

Umweltschutz:
So handeln junge Menschen in Nordamerika

Kapitel 10
Lust auf Lesen

Büchermarkt in Freiburg

Learning Objectives

10.1 Identify several German contributions to communication technology

10.2 Learn words to talk about current media and technology

10.3 Distinguish between German *f*, *v*, and *w* sounds

10.4 Narrate past events

10.5 Distinguish between three ways to say *when* in German

10.6 Read and understand an authentic German fairy tale from the Brothers Grimm

10.7 Create detailed descriptions of people, places, and things

10.8 Use adjectives to describe people, places, and things

10.9 Understand authentic video of Germans talking about what they like to read

10.10 Learn vocabulary used in classic fairy tales and other types of writing

10.1 Vorschau

Historische Figuren

10-1 **Wie sagt man das auf Deutsch?** Finden Sie das deutsche Wort:

lived: _____ *wrote:* _____ *inventor:* _____

worked: _____ *master:* _____ *memorial plaque:* _____

> Historical markers like these are found on houses and buildings all over the German-speaking countries.

10-2 Was passt zu jeder Person?

Unruh: _____, _____, _____   Hoffmann: _____, _____, _____

Schiller: _____, _____, _____   Diesel: _____, _____, _____

a. schreiben	e. Brezeln	i. 20. Jahrhundert
b. erfinden	f. Lieder	j. 18. Jahrhundert
c. backen	g. Motoren	k. Anfang des 19. Jahrhunderts
d. komponieren	h. Gemälde	l. Ende des 19. Jahrhunderts

10-3 Jacob und Wilhelm Grimm. Sind die Aussagen richtig oder falsch?

	RICHTIG	FALSCH
Jacob und Wilhelm Grimm waren Geschwister.	☐	☐
Das Haus, in dem Jacob und Wilhelm Grimm in Berlin wohnten, war Linkstraße 1.	☐	☐
Jacob war jünger als Wilhelm.	☐	☐
Die zwei kämpften für eine geeinte deutsche Nation.	☐	☐
Zusammen gründeten sie die moderne Germanistik.	☐	☐

10-4 Nelly Sachs. Sie hören fünf Aussagen zu Nelly Sachs. Sind sie richtig oder falsch? Checken Sie die Infos auf der Gedenktafel.

	RICHTIG	FALSCH		RICHTIG	FALSCH
1.	☐	☐	4.	☐	☐
2.	☐	☐	5.	☐	☐
3.	☐	☐			

10.2 Kultur 1

Kommunikation und neue Technologien

10.1 Identify several German contributions to communication technology

Wenn man heute an neue Kommunikationstechnologien denkt, denkt man meistens an E-Mail, Instagram, Twitter, und wir vergessen, dass diese Entwicklung viel früher begann.

10-5 Schlüsselwörter. Finden Sie zuerst die andere Hälfte dieser Wörter, die im Text vorkommen.

- *invention* = die _____findung
- *daily newspaper* = die _____zeitung
- *ancient* = _____alt
- *printing* = der Buch_____
- *translation of the Bible* = die Bibel_____
- *to write down* = _____schreiben

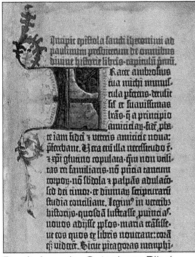

Der Anfang der Gutenberg-Bibel

1450

Die Erfindung des Buchdrucks

Johannes Gutenberg erfand den Buchdruck mit beweglichen Lettern. Vor Gutenberg brauchte ein Schreiber zwei volle Jahre, um eine einzige Bibel zu kopieren. Nach Gutenberg gab es bald Tausende von Druckereien in Europa, die Millionen von Büchern und andere Texte produzierten.

Die Entwicklung einer Sprache, die alle verstehen

Genauso wichtig wie die Erfindung des Buchdrucks war für die deutschsprachigen Länder Martin Luthers Bibelübersetzung. Die deutschen Dialekte waren so verschieden, dass die Menschen aus dem Norden ihre Nachbarn im Süden oft nicht verstanden. Luther übersetzte die Bibel in ein Deutsch, das auch einfache Menschen in allen deutschsprachigen Ländern verstehen konnten.

1534

Die Wartburg: Hier begann Luther seine Bibelübersetzung.

Eine Nachricht aus Wien im Sommer 1650

Veröffentlichung der ersten Tageszeitung

Der Drucker Timotheus Ritzsch veröffentlichte im Juli 1650 in Leipzig die erste Tageszeitung der Welt: *Einkommende Zeitungen*. Diese Zeitung erschien an sechs Tagen in der Woche.

1650

Sammlung deutscher Geschichten und Wörter

Im Jahr 1807 begannen die Brüder Jacob und Wilhelm Grimm, die uralten Volksgeschichten zu sammeln, die Leute einander erzählten. Sie wollten diese Geschichten aufschreiben und veröffentlichen, bevor sie für immer verloren gingen°.

Die Grimms waren auch Linguisten: Ihr zweites großes Projekt war das Deutsche Wörterbuch, das sich auf die Geschichte der Wörter konzentrierte.

1810

verloren gingen: *were lost*

It took generations of linguists to complete the monumental 32-volume dictionary, finally finished in 1960.

Die beliebte Märchensammlung der Brüder Grimm

10-6 Weitere Erfindungen in der Kommunikationstechnologie. Suchen Sie im Internet nach den fehlenden Informationen, um die Zeittafel zu vollenden.

1861 Philipp _____ erfand ein Telefongerät.

Konrad Zuse baute den ersten programmierbaren _____. **1941**

1963 Rudolf Hell erfand den ersten _____.

Ein Team des _____-Instituts entwickelte die Audiokompression MP3. **1995**

))) 10.3 Wortschatz 1

Wichtige Vokabeln

10.2 Learn words to talk about current media and technology

Nomen

der Dichter, -	
die Dichterin, -nen	writer; poet
die Entwicklung, -en	development
der Erfinder, -	
die Erfinderin, -nen	inventor
die Erfindung, -en	invention
das Jahrhundert, -e	century
die Medien (*pl*)	media
die Sammlung, -en	collection
die Übersetzung, -en	translation
die Veröffentlichung, -en	publication
der Zugang	access

Verben

auf·schreiben, schrieb auf, aufgeschrieben	to write down
bauen	to build
drucken	to print
entwickeln	to develop
erfinden, erfand, erfunden	to invent
erhalten (erhält), erhielt, erhalten	to receive
kämpfen	to fight
produzieren	to produce
sammeln	to collect
übersetzen	to translate
veröffentlichen	to publish
denken an (+ *acc*), dachte, gedacht	to think about
sich konzentrieren auf (+ *acc*)	to concentrate on

Andere Wörter

als	when (*conj*); as
damals	back then; at that time

Ausdrücke

gelten als (gilt), galt, gegolten	to be regarded as
den Nobelpreis erhalten	to receive the Nobel Prize

Das Gegenteil

uralt ≠ brandneu	ancient ≠ brand new

Leicht zu verstehen

die Bibel, -n	kopieren
der Dialekt, -e	das Projekt, -e
das Institut, -e	das Team, -s
der Linguist, -en	die Technologie, -n
die Linguistin, -nen	das Werk, -e
die Kommunikation	

> Starting in this chapter, irregular verbs are listed with all their principal parts. See p. 311 for more about principal parts.

Wörter im Kontext

10-7 Was passt in jeder Gruppe zusammen?

1. die Kirche	a. die Sprache
2. die Technologie	b. die Bibel
3. das Jahrhundert	c. die Zeit
4. der Dialekt	d. die E-Mail

5. drucken	e. das Projekt
6. entwickeln	f. der Text
7. das Team	g. Bücher, Radio, TV, Internet
8. die Medien	h. eine Idee

10-8 Was passt?

1. Dichter sind Leute, _____.	a. die literarische Werke schreiben
2. Ein Mensch, _____, ist ein Erfinder.	b. die Bücher veröffentlicht
3. Eine Firma, _____, ist eine Druckerei.	c. der sich etwas ganz Neues ausdenkt
4. Gutenberg ist der Mann, _____.	d. das Luther übersetzt hat
5. Ein Buch, _____, war die Bibel.	e. die Kinder gern lesen
6. Luther übersetzte die Bibel in ein Deutsch, _____.	f. das viele Leute verstehen konnten
7. Märchen sind Geschichten, _____.	g. die Märchen gesammelt haben
8. Jakob und Wilhelm Grimm waren zwei Brüder, _____.	h. der den Buchdruck erfunden hat

10-9 Was machten diese Leute?

baute / erhielt / veröffentlichte / erfand / entwickelte

1. Der Drucker Timotheus Ritzsch _____ die erste Tageszeitung der Welt.
2. Konrad Zuse _____ den ersten programmierbaren Computer.
3. Ein Team des Fraunhofer-Instituts _____ die Audiokompression MP3.
4. Nelly Sachs _____ den Nobelpreis für Literatur.
5. Rudolf Christian Karl Diesel _____ den Dieselmotor.

10-10 Hier ist … Antworten Sie auf die Aussagen mit: „Interessant! Zeigen Sie mal bitte Ihre …".

Übersetzung / Veröffentlichung / Sammlung / Erfindung

> Remember: Almost all nouns ending in **-ung** are feminine!

Ich habe einen deutschen Text ins Englische übersetzt.	*Interessant! Zeigen Sie mal bitte Ihre …*
Ich habe eine neue Technologie erfunden.	
Ich sammele gern alte Kameras.	
Letzte Woche habe ich einen Text veröffentlicht.	

10.4 Zur Aussprache

German *f*, *v*, and *w*

10.3 Distinguish between German *f*, *v*, and *w* sounds

In German the sound represented by the letter **f** is pronounced like English *f* and the sound represented by the letter **v** is generally also pronounced like English *f*.

10-11 Hören Sie gut zu und wiederholen Sie!

für	vier
Form	vor
folgen	Volk

Familie Feldmann fährt in den Ferien nach Finnland.

Volkmars Vorlesung ist um Viertel vor vier vorbei°.   *over*

Volker ist Verkäufer für Farbfernseher.

When the letter **v** appears in a word of foreign origin, it is pronounced like English *v:* **Vase, Video, Variation.**

In German the sound represented by the letter **w** is always pronounced like English *v:* **wann, wie, wo.**

10-12 Zur Aussprache: German *f*, *v*, and *w*. You will hear the speaker pronounce one of the two words in the word pairs you see. In each pair, decide which word you hear.

1. ☐ waren ☐ fahren
2. ☐ Welt ☐ Feld
3. ☐ wir ☐ vier
4. ☐ Wort ☐ fort
5. ☐ Wand ☐ fand
6. ☐ Wein ☐ fein
7. ☐ wer ☐ fair
8. ☐ Wetter ☐ Vetter
9. ☐ wie ☐ Vieh
10. ☐ was ☐ Fass
11. ☐ wählen ☐ fehlen
12. ☐ wischen ☐ fischen
13. ☐ wuchs ☐ Fuchs
14. ☐ warm ☐ Farm

Felder und Wälder

10.5 Kommunikation und Formen 1

The simple past tense

10.4 Narrate past events

The simple past tense is used mainly in written German to narrate a series of connected events in the past. Sometimes called the narrative past, it is usually found in texts that tell a story, like biographies, histories, police and news reports, and in literature.

Consider this simple description of Martin Luther's contribution to European history in the sixteenth century:

> Martin Luther **studierte** in Erfurt. Im Jahre 1510 **reiste** Luther nach Rom. Danach **kritisierte** er die Korruption in der katholischen Kirche. 1517 **nagelte** er seine 95 Thesen an die Tür der Schlosskirche in Wittenberg. 1521 **versteckte** sich Luther auf der Wartburg. Er **lebte** dort inkognito als „Junker Jörg" und **übersetzte** das Neue Testament der Bibel ins Deutsche.

You can see that many verbs in the German simple past tense closely resemble the past tense in English:

die Wartburg: The Wartburg castle is in Eisenach in the German state of Thuringia.

> *Martin Luther **studied** in Erfurt. In 1510 Luther **traveled** to Rome. After this he **criticized** the Catholic Church for corruption. In 1517 he **nailed** his 95 Theses to the door of the Schlosskirche in Wittenberg. In 1521 Luther **hid** out in the Wartburg castle. He **lived** there incognito as "Junker Jörg" and **translated** the New Testament of the Bible into German.*

The simple past of regular verbs

The simple past of regular verbs is formed by adding a past-tense marker to the verb stem (**-t-** in German and *-ed* in English). The **-t-** is inserted between the verb stem and the personal endings.

Regular verbs in the simple past use the same endings as **hatte,** which you learned in *Kapitel 5.*

Singular	Plural
ich lern**te**	wir lern**ten**
du lern**test**	ihr lern**tet**
er/es/sie lern**te**	sie lern**ten**
Sie lern**ten**	

The German simple past has more than one English equivalent.

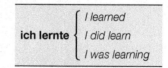

ich lernte	*I learned* *I did learn* *I was learning*

Just like in the present tense, verb stems that end in **-d, -t (land-en, arbeit-en)**, or certain consonant combinations **(regn-en)** add an **e** before the past-tense marker **-t-**. This makes it easier to hear the added **t** that signals the past tense:

Singular	Plural
ich arbeit**ete**	wir arbeit**eten**
du arbeit**etest**	ihr arbeit**etet**
er/es/sie arbeit**ete**	sie arbeit**eten**
Sie arbeit**eten**	

10-13 Die Geschichte einer deutschen Burg. Ergänzen Sie die passenden Verben
im Präteritum.

spielen / hängen / protestieren

> Die Wartburg _____ eine wichtige Rolle in der Reformation der
> katholischen Kirche in Deutschland.
> Martin Luther _____ gegen kirchliche Korruption, als er 95 Thesen an
> die Tür der Schlosskirche in Wittenberg _____.

übersetzen / verstecken / leben

> Drei Jahre später _____ sich Luther auf der Wartburg. Dort _____
> er inkognito als „Junker Jörg" und in nur elf Wochen _____ er das
> Neue Testament aus dem Griechischen ins Deutsche.

restaurieren / feiern / marschieren / demonstrieren

> Im Jahre 1817 _____ Tausende von Studenten auf die Burg
> und _____ für einen deutschen Nationalstaat. 1983 _____
> man die Burg und im selben Jahr _____ man die Neueröffnung der
> Burg zum 500. Geburtstag Luthers.

zelebrieren / reisen / nageln

> Und 2017 _____ man wieder ein sehr wichtiges Jubiläum von
> 500 Jahren: den Tag, an dem Martin Luther 1517 die 95 Thesen an die
> Schlosskirche _____! Und wieder _____ mehrere tausend
> Besucher nach Eisenach, um die Wartburg zu sehen.

Hier lebte Luther inkognito als „Junker Jörg".

The simple past of irregular verbs

Just as in English, the simple past of irregular verbs in German is signaled by a vowel change in the verb stem.

German		English	
sehen:	ich s**a**h	*to see:*	*I* **saw**
trinken:	ich tr**a**nk	*to drink:*	*I* **drank**
gehen:	ich g**ing**	*to go:*	*I* **went**
schlafen:	ich schl**ief**	*to sleep:*	*I* sl**ept**

The simple past of German irregular verbs has no ending in the 1st and 3rd person singular.

Singular		Plural	
ich	trank	wir	tranken
du	trankst	ihr	trankt
er/es/sie	trank	sie	tranken
	Sie tranken		

Some German past-tense verb forms have the same vowel change as in English (**trink, trank** = *drink, drank*), but many you will have to learn by heart. Irregular simple past tense forms are given in the *Wortschatz* lists and in the *Principal Parts of Irregular and Mixed Verbs* list on pp. A-17–A-19.

10-14 Präsens und Präteritum. Was passt zusammen?

kommt   spricht   fand   sprach   liest

schrieb   isst   las

half   findet   fuhr   schreibt   hilft

fährt   kam   aß

		Präsens	**Präteritum**
1. essen	er/sie	_____	_____
2. schreiben	er/sie	_____	_____
3. lesen	er/sie	_____	_____
4. kommen	er/sie	_____	_____
5. fahren	er/sie	_____	_____
6. helfen	er/sie	_____	_____
7. sprechen	er/sie	_____	_____
8. finden	er/sie	_____	_____

Sprachnotiz   Principal parts of verbs

Most verbs are *regular* verbs and their tenses derive from the stem of the infinitive. Their forms are completely predictable in German, just as in English.

lernen	er **lern**t	er **lern**te	er hat ge**lern**t
to learn	*he learns*	*he learned*	*he has learned*

In both German and English, all tenses of *irregular* and *mixed* verbs are derived from a set of *principal parts:* the infinitive, the simple past, and the past participle. If you know the principal parts of a verb, you can figure out any form of that verb.

Principal parts: **singen, sang, gesungen**   *to sing, sang, sung*
  schreiben, schrieb, geschrieben   *to write, wrote, written*
  bringen, brachte, gebracht   *to bring, brought, brought*

German verbs that are irregular in the present tense have an additional principal part that reflects this irregularity, e.g., **geben (*gibt*), gab, gegeben.**

10-15 Rotkäppchen. Kennen Sie die Geschichte mit dem bösen Wolf? Ergänzen Sie im Präteritum. Siehe Anhang S. A-17–A-19, *Principal Parts of Irregular and Mixed Verbs.*

tragen / bekommen / heißen / wohnen

Es _____ einmal ein Mädchen mit seiner Mutter. Das Mädchen _____ ein tolles Geschenk von seiner Großmutter: ein rotes Käppchen. Und weil das Mädchen immer das Käppchen _____, _____ es Rotkäppchen.

treffen / gehen / finden / laufen / fressen / sprechen

Das Mädchen _____ in den Wald, um ihre Großmutter zu besuchen. Sie _____ den Wolf, der sehr freundlich mit ihr _____. Rotkäppchen _____ schöne Blumen und wollte ihrer Großmutter einen Blumenstrauß bringen. Der Wolf aber _____ zum Haus der Großmutter und _____ sie auf! Dann kam Rotkäppchen an und der böse Wolf verschlang° auch das kleine, nette Mädchen!!!

devoured

10-16 Weitere Märchen von den Brüdern Grimm. Ergänzen Sie die ersten paar Zeilen von zwei weiteren Märchen. Benutzen Sie das Präterium. Siehe Anhang S. A-17–A-19, *Principal Parts of Irregular and Mixed Verbs.*

verlieren / sprechen / sein / kommen / helfen

Es _____ einmal eine Prinzessin, die gerne im Wald spielte. Eines Tages _____ sie ihren goldenen Ball und weinte bitterlich. Ein grüner Frosch _____ und _____ mit dem Mädchen. Der Frosch _____ dem Mädchen, seinen goldenen Ball wieder zu bekommen …

Can you give the English name of these two Grimm Brothers fairy tales?

geben / verlassen / werfen / heißen / finden

Es lebten einmal ein Junge und ein Mädchen mit ihrem Vater und ihrer Stiefmutter. Die Kinder _____ Hänsel und Gretel. Es _____ aber nicht genug Geld für Essen für die Kinder. Also brachten die Eltern die Kinder tief in den Wald und _____ sie dort. Die Kinder _____ kleine Steine auf den Weg und _____ den Weg zu ihrem Haus zurück …

Sprachnotiz   The simple past of separable-prefix verbs

In the simple past, the prefix of separable-prefix verbs is positioned just as it is in the present tense.

Rotkäppchen **ging** in den dunklen Wald **hinein.**

Als Rotkäppchen in den Wald **hineinging,** fand sie viele schöne Blumen für die Großmutter.

---

police report   **10-17 Aus dem Polizeibericht°.** Ergänzen Sie im Präteritum. Siehe Anhang S. A-17–A-19, *Principal Parts of Irregular and Mixed Verbs.*

laufen / geben / sterben / anrufen

Kollision: Am Samstag _____ es kurz vor 21 Uhr auf der Waldstraße eine Kollision zwischen einem Auto und einem Wolf, der über die Straße _____. Die 27-jährige Fahrerin _____ die Polizei sofort an. Das Tier_____.

einbrechen / kommen / stehlen

huge

Einbruch in Amerika: Ein 21-jähriger amerikanischer Student _____ am Freitag, 11. Mai, gegen 17 Uhr bei seiner Deutschprofessorin im Büro ein. Er _____ eine riesige° Packung Gummibärchen vom Schreibtisch seiner Professorin. Als er aus dem Büro _____, wartete schon ein Campuspolizist, der den jungen Studenten sofort schnappte. Grund für den Diebstahl: großer Stress am Tag seiner letzten Deutschprüfung!

German news reports often have a header such as **Einbruch.** To understand such one-word headers, connect the noun back to an infinitive form: **Einbruch → einbrechen** *(to break in).*

10-18 Zeittafel deutschsprachiger Erfinder und Entdecker, Dichter und Denker. Ergänzen Sie im Präteritum. Siehe Anhang S. A-17–A-19, *Principal Parts of Irregular and Mixed Verbs.*

Lerntipp!
Decide which verbs are irregular before doing this exercise. If you're not sure of a form, check the list in the *Anhang* on pp. A-17–A-19.

> entwickeln / erfinden / komponieren
>
> sammeln / schreiben (x2) / übersetzen

um 1150: Hildegard von Bingen _____ die Homöopathie der Pflanzen, _____ Gedichte und _____ Musik.

1440: Johannes Gutenberg _____ die Buchdruckerkunst in Europa.

1521: Martin Luther _____ das Neue Testament aus dem Griechischen ins Deutsche.

um 1700: Maria Sibylla Merian _____ wichtige Bücher über das Leben der Insekten.

1807: Die Brüder Grimm _____ Kinder- und Hausmärchen.

> bekommen / entdecken (x2) / erfinden (x2) /
> formulieren / erhalten

1859: Der Mathematik- und Physiklehrer Phillip Reis _____ das Telefongerät (aber 1875 _____ Alexander Graham Bell das Patent für die Weiterentwicklung des Telefons).

1876: Der Arzt Robert Koch _____ unter dem Mikroskop, dass Krankheiten von Bakterien kommen.

1905: Albert Einstein _____ die Relativitätstheorie.

1908: Melitta Bentz _____ den Kaffeefilter und gründete im selben Jahr eine kleine Firma, die sie mit Ehemann Hugo und den zwei Söhnen Willi und Horst führte.

1938: Die österreichische Physikerin Lise Meitner _____ mit Otto Hahn die Kernspaltung, aber im Jahre 1944 _____ Hahn allein den Nobelpreis dafür.

Die Metamorphose, eine Zeichnung aus einem Buch von Merian

The simple past of mixed verbs

In the simple past, mixed verbs have the stem change of the irregular verbs, but the past-tense marker **-t-** and personal endings of the regular verbs.

bringen	**brachte**	nennen	**nannte**
denken	**dachte**	rennen	**rannte**
kennen	**kannte**	wissen	**wusste**

The verb **werden** has some characteristics of a mixed verb: it has a stem change and the same personal endings as mixed verbs, but no **-t-** is added:

Tom **wird** morgen 21. ➜ Tom **wurde** gestern 21.

10-19 Mein erstes Semester. Ergänzen Sie im Präteritum. Siehe Anhang S. A-17–A-19, *Principal Parts of Irregular and Mixed Verbs.*

bringen / kennen

Anfang September _____ mein Vater mich zu meiner Uni. Obwohl ich dort keinen Menschen _____, fand ich bald viele Freunde.

denken / rennen

Wir _____ von einer Party zur anderen, hatten viel Spaß, aber _____ nur selten an unser Studium und unsere Noten.

nennen / werden / wissen

Natürlich _____ meine Noten immer schlechter. Mein Bruder _____ mich einen richtigen Loser. Im zweiten Semester _____ ich, dass ich viel mehr lernen musste!

10-20 Ich als Ersti! Schreiben Sie nun eine kurze Beschreibung von Ihren ersten 1–2 Wochen als Student/Studentin an Ihrer Uni.

- Wer brachte Sie zur Uni, und wer half Ihnen mit dem Umzug?
- Wo und mit wem wohnten Sie?
- Wen lernten Sie in den ersten Wochen kennen?
- Was wollten Sie studieren?
- Wie waren die ersten Vorlesungen?

Wann, als, and *wenn*

10.5 Distinguish between three ways to say *when* in German

Although **wann, als,** and **wenn** all correspond to English *when*, they are not interchangeable.

Wann introduces direct and indirect questions.

Wann macht man in Deutschland den Führerschein?	*When do people in Gemany get a driver's license?*
Ich weiß nicht, **wann** man das macht.	*I don't know **when** they do that.*

Als introduces dependent clauses referring to a single event in the past or a block of time in the past. Since **als** signals a dependent clause, the conjugated verb moves to the end of the clause.

Als ich **ankam,** klingelte das Telefon.	*When I **arrived,** the phone rang.*
Als wir in Bremen **lebten,** war ich sieben.	*When we **lived** in Bremen, I was seven.*

Wenn introduces dependent clauses referring to events in the present or future or to *repeated* events in any time frame. Since **wenn** also signals a dependent clause, the conjugated verb moves to the end of the clause as it does with **als.**

Ruf mich bitte gleich an, **wenn** du in Frankfurt **ankommst.**	*Please call me right away **when** you arrive in Frankfurt.*
Wenn Oma uns besuchte, brachte sie immer einen Kuchen mit.	*When (whenever) Grandma visited us, she always brought a cake.*

> Note that the verb in an **als**-clause is often in the simple past tense, even in conversation.

wann?	als	wenn
• questions	• single event in the past	• events in the present or future
	• block of time in the past	• repeated events (all time frames)

10-21 Fragen und Antworten. Ergänzen Sie **als** oder **wenn**.

1. Wann hat Stephanie Ali kennengelernt?

   _____ sie nach München kam, um dort ein Jahr lang zu studieren.

2. Wann macht Stephanie ihre tollen Pancakes?

   Immer _____ Ali zum Frühstück kommt.

3. Wann fährt Stephanie mit Ali zu seinen Eltern nach Berlin?

   _____ das Wintersemester zu Ende ist.

4. Wann fliegt Stephanie wieder nach Amerika zurück?

   _____ das Sommersemester zu Ende ist.

10-22 Ein toller Reiter. Ergänzen Sie **als** oder **wenn**.

_____ ich zwölf war, lebten wir in Berlin. Im Sommer 2017 besuchten wir meinen Großvater in Schleswig-Holstein. Er war Bauer und hatte ein wunderschönes Pferd. Jeden Morgen, _____ wir im Stall fertig waren, durfte ich auf diesem Pferd reiten. Mein kleiner Bruder hatte Angst vor° Pferden. Jedes Mal _____ Großvater das Pferd aus dem Stall holte, rannte er ins Haus. Aber _____ wir wieder in Berlin waren, sagte er zu seinen Freunden: „_____ ich bei meinem Opa in Schleswig-Holstein war, habe ich sogar reiten gelernt."

hatte Angst vor: *was afraid of*

> The verb for *to ride* depends on what you're riding. **Reiten** is used if you're riding a horse (**Pferd reiten**); but **fahren** is used whenever a vehicle is involved: **Fahrrad fahren, Bus fahren, Zug fahren,** etc.

10-23 Wann war das? Kettenfragen. Stellen Sie die folgenden Fragen in einer Gruppe von 3–4. **S1** stellt die erste Frage, **S2** antwortet auf die Frage und stellt die nächste. **S3** antwortet und stellt die nächste Frage, usw.

Tipp! Beginnen Sie jede Antwort mit „Als ich …" und verwenden Sie das Präteritum.

- Wann hast du Rad fahren gelernt? *Als ich …*
- Wann hast du schwimmen gelernt?
- Wann hast du deinen Führerschein gekriegt?
- Wann bist du zum ersten Mal zum Rockkonzert gegangen?
- Wann hast du zum ersten Mal Deutsch gesprochen?
- Wann bist du zum ersten Mal geflogen?
- …?

10-24 Eine Erinnerung°. Wählen Sie eine Frage von **10-23** und schreiben Sie kurz im Präteritum über diese Erinnerung: Wo war das? Mit wem waren Sie? War das eine schöne oder schlechte Zeit für Sie? usw.

memory

10.6 Kultur 2

Ein Märchen der Brüder Grimm

Kann der kleine Igel schneller
laufen als der Hase?

race

bet

10.6 **Read and understand an authentic German fairy tale from the Brothers Grimm**

10-25 Der Hase und der Igel.

1. Schauen Sie sich das Bild mit dem Hasen und dem Igel an. Wer, meinen Sie, kann schneller laufen, der Hase oder der Igel?

2. Kennen Sie aus Nordamerika ein Märchen mit einem Hasen und einem anderen Tier, das nicht so schnell läuft? Wie heißt dieses Märchen auf Englisch?

3. Normalerweise können Hasen relativ schnell laufen. Was kann der Igel vielleicht tun, um einen Wettlauf° gegen den Hasen zu gewinnen?

4. Wer, meinen Sie, gewinnt, wenn der Hase und der Igel um ein Goldstück und eine Flasche Schnaps wetten°?

10-26 **Was wissen Sie über Igel, Hasen und ihre Welt?** Was bedeuten die folgenden Wörter auf Englisch?

1. Ein Igel hat kurze, **krumme** Beine.
2. Auf dem Feld wachsen schöne **Rüben,** die der Igel gern frisst.
3. Zwischen den Reihen von Rüben findet man **Furchen.**
4. Man kann in den Furchen von der **oberen** Seite zur unteren Seite des Feldes laufen.

a. upper
b. beets, turnips
c. crooked
d. furrows (small ditches)

5. Wenn man dich nicht **grüßt,** ist das arrogant!
6. Wenn man über dich lacht, **ärgert** dich das!
7. Wenn man sich sehr ärgert, ist man **außer sich.**
8. Man ist **vergnügt,** wenn man einen Wettlauf gewinnt oder wenn man einen arroganten Gegner austrickst.

e. greets
f. amused, cheery
g. irritates
h. beside oneself

Lerntipp!

To get yourself ready to read a longer and less familiar fairy tale, take a minute to think a bit about fairy tales as a genre. Are the biggest and strongest usually the winners in the end? Ex. **10-26** will help you deal with some key words before reading, too.

Der Hase und der Igel

nach einem Märchen der Brüder Grimm

Es war an einem Sonntagmorgen zur Sommerzeit. Die Sonne schien hell vom blauen Himmel, der Morgenwind ging warm über die Felder und die Leute gingen in ihren Sonntagskleidern zur Kirche.

Der Igel aber stand vor seiner Tür und schaute in den schönen Morgen
5 hinaus. Als er so stand, dachte er: „Warum gehe ich nicht schnell aufs Feld und schaue meine Rüben an, solange meine Frau die Kinder anzieht und das Frühstück macht."

Als der Igel zum Rübenfeld kam, traf er dort seinen Nachbarn, den Hasen, der auch einen Spaziergang machte. Der Igel sagte freundlich: „Guten Morgen!"

10 Aber der Hase grüßte nicht zurück, sondern sagte: „Wie kommt es denn, dass du hier am frühen Morgen auf dem Feld herumläufst?" „Ich gehe spazieren", sagte der Igel. „Spazieren?" lachte der Hase, „Du, mit deinen kurzen, krummen Beinen?"

Diese Antwort ärgerte den Igel sehr, denn für einen Igel hatte er sehr schöne 15 Beine, obwohl sie von Natur kurz und krumm waren. „Denkst du vielleicht", sagte er zum Hasen, „dass du mit deinen langen, dünnen Beinen schneller laufen kannst als ich?" „Das denke ich wohl", lachte der Hase, „willst du wetten?" „Ja, ein Goldstück und eine Flasche Schnaps", antwortete der Igel. „Gut", rief der Hase, „fangen wir an!" „Nein, so große Eile hat es nicht", sagte 20 der Igel, „ich will erst noch nach Hause gehen und ein bisschen frühstücken. In einer halben Stunde bin ich wieder zurück."

Auf dem Heimweg dachte der Igel: „Diese Wette hast du verloren, lieber Hase, denn du hast zwar die langen Beine, aber ich habe den klugen Kopf." Als er zu Hause ankam, sagte er zu seiner Frau: „Frau, zieh schnell eine von 25 meinen Hosen an, du musst mit mir aufs Feld."

„Eine von deinen Hosen? Ja, was ist denn los?" fragte seine Frau. „Ich habe mit dem Hasen um ein Goldstück und eine Flasche Schnaps gewettet. Ich will mit ihm einen Wettlauf machen und da brauche ich dich." „Oh, Mann", rief da die Frau ganz aufgeregt, „bist du nicht ganz recht im Kopf? Wie kannst du mit 30 dem Hasen um die Wette laufen?" „Lass das mal meine Sache sein", sagte der Igel. „Zieh jetzt die Hose an und komm mit."

Unterwegs sagte der Igel zu seiner Frau. „Nun pass mal auf, was ich dir sage. Siehst du, auf dem langen Feld dort wollen wir unseren Wettlauf machen. Der Hase läuft in der einen Furche und ich in der anderen, und dort oben fangen 35 wir an. Du aber sitzt hier unten in meiner Furche, und wenn der Hase hier ankommt, springst du auf und rufst: ,Ich bin schon da.'"

Als der Igel am oberen Ende des Feldes ankam, wartete der Hase dort schon. „Können wir endlich anfangen?" fragte er. „Oder willst du nicht mehr?" „Doch", sagte der Igel. Dann ging jeder zu seiner Furche. Der Hase 40 zählte: „Eins, zwei, drei" und rannte wie ein Sturmwind über das Feld. Der Igel aber blieb ruhig auf seinem Platz.

Als der Hase am unteren Ende des Feldes ankam, sprang die Frau des Igels auf und rief: „Ich bin schon da!" Der Hase konnte es kaum glauben. Aber weil die Frau des Igels genauso aussah wie ihr Mann, rief er: „Einmal ist nicht 45 genug!" Und zurück raste er, dass ihm die Ohren am Kopf flogen. Die Frau des Igels aber blieb ruhig auf ihrem Platz. Als der Hase am oberen Ende des Feldes ankam, sprang der Igel auf und rief: „Ich bin schon da!" Der Hase war ganz außer sich und schrie „Noch einmal!" „Sooft du Lust hast", lachte der Igel. So lief der Hase noch dreiundsiebzigmal, und jedes Mal, wenn er oben 50 oder unten ankam, riefen der Igel oder seine Frau: „Ich bin schon da!"

Das letzte Mal aber kam der Hase nicht mehr bis zum Ende, sondern stürzte mitten auf dem Feld tot zur Erde. Der Igel aber nahm das Goldstück und die Schnapsflasche, rief seine Frau, und beide gingen vergnügt nach Hause. Und wenn sie nicht gestorben sind, so leben sie noch heute.

Achtung!
Use line numbers **(Zeile # bis #)** to help your partner locate the answers to each question below.

10-27 Märchenfiguren. Ein paar Fragen zur Interpretation. Wie gut verstehen Sie diese Geschichte? Beantworten Sie die Fragen mit einer Partnerin/einem Partner. Dann setzen Sie zwei Zweiergruppen zusammen und besprechen Sie Ihre Antworten.

1. Wie sind die typischen Rollen in diesem Märchen? Zum Beispiel, wer machte bei Familie Igel das Frühstück und zog die Kinder an? Wer hat morgens Zeit spazieren zu gehen?

2. Welche Figur war sehr unfreundlich und grüßte seinen Nachbarn nicht? Welche Figur regte sich darüber auf?

3. Wer wollte den Wettlauf machen? Und wer wollte *vor* dem Wettlauf schnell nach Hause laufen? Warum wollte er das machen, meinen Sie?

4. Warum musste sich die Igelfrau eine Hose anziehen? Meinen Sie, dass Igelfrauen normalerweise Hosen trugen? Warum machte sie das?

5. Wer saß am oberen und unteren Ende des Feldes, und wer rannte immer hin und her?

6. Mit anderen Worten, wer konnte schnell laufen? Und wer hatte den klügeren Kopf, der Hase oder der Igel?

7. Am Ende stirbt der Hase, und der Igel und seine Frau sind glücklich. Was, glauben Sie, soll man daraus lernen?

10.7 Kommunikation und Formen 2

The relative pronoun as object of a preposition

10.7 Create detailed descriptions of people, places, and things

In *Kapitel 9* you learned that except for the dative plural **(denen)**, the forms of the relative pronoun and the definite article are identical.

Forms of the relative pronoun			
	MASCULINE	NEUTER	FEMININE	PLURAL
NOMINATIVE	der	das	die	die
ACCUSATIVE	den	das	die	die
DATIVE	dem	dem	der	**denen**

You also learned that the relative pronoun has the same gender and number as its antecedent, but that its case is determined by its function within the relative clause.

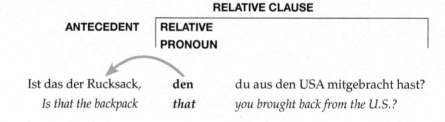

	RELATIVE CLAUSE	
ANTECEDENT	RELATIVE PRONOUN	
Ist das der Rucksack,	**den**	du aus den USA mitgebracht hast?
Is that the backpack	*that*	*you brought back from the U.S.?*

When a relative pronoun is the object of a preposition, the gender and number of the relative pronoun are still determined by the antecedent, but the case is determined by the preposition.

Shoppinghaus
Das Haus, in dem man gern shoppt

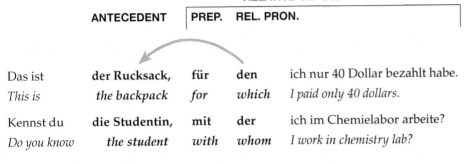

	RELATIVE CLAUSE	
ANTECEDENT	PREP.	REL. PRON.

Das ist **der Rucksack,** **für** **den** ich nur 40 Dollar bezahlt habe.
This is *the backpack* *for* *which* *I paid only 40 dollars.*

Kennst du **die Studentin,** **mit** **der** ich im Chemielabor arbeite?
Do you know *the student* *with* *whom* *I work in chemistry lab?*

Ach so!
In German, the preposition always *precedes* the relative pronoun (*in which, for whom, through which, by whom*, and so on) and the relative pronoun can't be omitted.

10-28 Wussten Sie das? Unterstreichen Sie das Antecedent und identifizieren Sie feminin, maskulin, neutrum, oder plural. Ergänzen Sie dann mit einem Relativpronomen im Dativ.

► München ist <u>die Stadt,</u>   in d_*er*_ das Oktoberfest stattfindet.

<u>fem.</u>/mask./neutr.   plural

1. Die Schweiz ist das deutschsprachige Land, in d_____ auch Italienisch eine offizielle Sprache ist.
   fem./mask./neutr.   plural

2. Die Donau ist der Fluss, an d_____ Wien liegt.
   fem./mask./neutr.   plural

3. Bienen sind Insekten, von d_____ wir Honig bekommen.
   fem./mask./neutr.   plural

10-29 Weißt du das? Stellen Sie drei Fragen und beantworten Sie dann drei Fragen, die Ihr Partner/Ihre Partnerin stellt. Die Antwort beginnt mit „Er/Es/Sie heißt …".

1. Wie heißt der Ozean, über den man von Amerika nach Europa fliegt?
2. Wie heißt das Land, in das man fahren muss, wenn man Sigmund Freuds Geburtshaus besuchen möchte?
3. Wie heißt das deutschsprachige Land, aus dem man Taschenmesser in die ganze Welt exportiert?
4. Wie heißt das Märchen, in dem es einen dramatischen Wettlauf gibt?
5. Wie heißt die Stadt, in der Walter Gropius 1919 das Bauhaus gründete?
6. Wie heißt die Burg, auf der Martin Luther inkognito lebte?

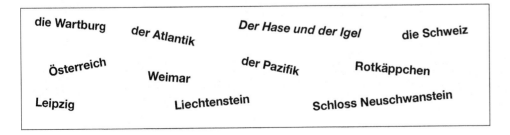

die Wartburg   der Atlantik   Der Hase und der Igel   die Schweiz
Österreich   Weimar   der Pazifik   Rotkäppchen
Leipzig   Liechtenstein   Schloss Neuschwanstein

10-30 Definitionen. Lesen Sie die gegebenen Relativsätze mir Ihrem Partner/ Ihrer Partnerin und formulieren Sie dann Relativsätze für die weiteren Fragen. Folgen Sie dem Beispiel.

▶ Was ist eine Kettensäge?

S1: Was ist eine Kettensäge?

S1: Eine Kettensäge ist ein Werkzeug, mit dem man Bäume fällen kann.

1. Was ist ein Lastwagen?

Ein Lastwagen ist ein Fahrzeug, …

2. Was ist eine Waschmaschine?

Eine Waschmaschine ist eine Maschine, …

3. Was ist ein Psychiater?

Ein Psychiater ist ein Mann, …

4. Was sind Weingläser?

Weingläser sind Gläser,

mit dem man über alles reden kann.	mit der man Klamotten wäscht.
aus denen man Wein trinkt.	mit dem man schwere Sachen transportiert.

A review of adjective endings

10.8 Use adjectives to describe people, places, and things

Adjectives preceded by *der*-words

Adjectives preceded by *der*-words take one of two endings: **-e** or **-en.**

	Masculine	Neuter	Feminine	Plural
NOMINATIVE	der jung**e** Mann	das klein**e** Kind	die jung**e** Frau	die klein**en** Kinder
ACCUSATIVE	den jung**en** Mann	das klein**e** Kind	die jung**e** Frau	die klein**en** Kinder
DATIVE	dem jung**en** Mann	dem klein**en** Kind	der jung**en** Frau	den klein**en** Kindern
GENITIVE	des jung**en** Mannes	des klein**en** Kindes	der jung**en** Frau	der klein**en** Kinder

> **Lerntipp!**
> To help remember the endings, think of the five places with the adjective ending **-e** as forming the shape of a frying pan. All other adjective endings are **-en.**

10-31 Der Hase und der Igel, ein bisschen anders. Ergänzen Sie die Adjektivendungen.

Es war an einem Sonntagmorgen zur Sommerzeit. Die warm____, hell____ Sonne schien vom blau____ Himmel, der Morgenwind ging warm über die grün____ Felder und die lieb____ Leute gingen in ihren Sonntagskleidern zu der schön____, alt____ Dorfkirche.

Der klug_____ Igel aber stand vor seiner Tür und schaute in den schön_____ Morgen hinaus. Dem fleißig_____ Igel gehörten mehrere Rübenfelder, die er jetzt anschauen wollte. Dort traf der Igel seinen Nachbarn, den elegant_____ Hasen, der auch über die Felder lief. Der Igel sagte freundlich: „Guten Morgen!" Aber der unfreundlich_____ Hase grüßte nicht zurück, sondern sagte: „Wie kommt es denn, dass du hier am frühen Morgen herumläufst?" „Ich gehe spazieren", sagte der Igel. „Spazieren?" lachte der Hase, „Du? Mit diesen kurz_____, krumm_____Beinen?"

Den dramatisch_____, schrecklich_____ Rest der berühmt_____ Geschichte kennen wir schon!

Ach so!

In the final sentence of this exercise, what is the subject? What is the direct object (accusative)? Are there other clues that can help you answer these questions?

Sprachnotiz   German *n*-nouns

There is a small group of masculine nouns in German that take the ending **-n** or **-en** in all cases except the nominative singular. This includes some common nouns identifying male persons and professional designations, such as **Nachbar, Student, Junge, Emigrant, Architekt, Pilot,** and **Polizist,** as well as some animals, like **Bär** and **Hase.**

NOMINATIVE	der / ein Nachbar
ACCUSATIVE	den / einen Nachbar**n**
DATIVE	dem / einem Nachbar**n**
GENITIVE	des / eines Nachbar**n*** (here the **-n** replaces the usual **-s**!)

Auf dem Feld traf der Igel seinen Nachbar**n**, den eleganten Has**en**.

The additional ending has no bearing on the word meaning.

Adjectives preceded by *ein*-words

Adjectives preceded by **ein**-words take endings identical to those after **der**-words, except in the three instances where the **ein**-word has no ending.

	Masculine	Neuter	Feminine	Plural
NOM.	ein jung**er** Mann	ein klein**es** Kind	eine jung**e** Frau	meine klein**en** Kinder
ACC.	einen jung**en** Mann	ein klein**es** Kind	eine jung**e** Frau	meine klein**en** Kinder
DAT.	einem jung**en** Mann	einem klein**en** Kind	einer jung**en** Frau	meinen klein**en** Kindern
GEN.	eines jung**en** Mannes	eines klein**en** Kindes	einer jung**en** Frau	meiner klein**en** Kinder

Lerntipp!

Again, it may help you to picture the five places where the adjective endings are *not* -en as having the shape of a frying pan.

10-32 Lieschen Maiers Hund. Ergänzen Sie!

Lieschen Maier hatte einmal einen klein_____, weiß_____ Hund. Er war ein sehr schön_____, weiß_____ Hund und Lieschen liebte ihn sehr. Jeden Morgen gab sie ihm eine klein_____ Dose Hundefutter und ging dann in die Schule. Wenn Lieschen nach der Schule mit ihrem klein_____, weiß_____ Hund im Park spazieren ging, hatte sie ihn immer an einer lang_____Leine°. Und in Lieschens Schlafzimmer stand neben ihrem eigen_____ Bett das Bettchen ihres klein_____, weiß_____ Hundes.

leash

10-33 Fritzchen Müllers Katze.

Fritzchen Müller hatte einmal eine groß_____, schwarz_____ Katze. Sie war eine sehr schön_____, schwarz_____ Katze und Fritzchen liebte sie sehr. Jeden Morgen gab er ihr eine groß_____ Dose Katzenfutter und ging dann in die Schule. Wenn Fritzchen nach der Schule mit seiner groß_____, schwarz_____ Katze im Park spazieren ging, hatte er sie immer an einer lang_____ Leine. Und in Fritzchens Schlafzimmer stand neben seinem eigen_____ Bett das Bettchen seiner groß_____, schwarz_____ Katze.

10-34 Unser Krokodil.

huge

Wir hatten einmal ein riesig_____°, grün_____ Krokodil. Es war ein sehr schön_____, grün_____ Krokodil und wir liebten es sehr. Jeden Morgen gaben wir ihm eine riesig_____ Dose Krokodilfutter und gingen dann in die Schule. Wenn wir nach der Schule mit unserem riesig_____, grün_____ Krokodil im Park spazieren gingen, hatten wir es immer an einer lang_____ Leine. Und in unserem Schlafzimmer stand neben unserem eigen_____ Bett das Bettchen unseres riesig_____, grün_____ Krokodils.

What do you feel like (having)?

10-35 Worauf hast du Lust?° Beschreiben Sie mit passenden Adjektiven, worauf Sie Lust haben.

S1: Worauf hast du Lust?　　　　　**S2:** Ich habe Lust auf einen großen, saftigen° Apfel. Und du?

juicy

deutsch / groß / riesig / frisch / fett / eiskalt / heiß / saftig / lecker / …

Wer hat jetzt Lust auf Popcorn?

	ZUM TRINKEN		ZUM ESSEN
ein _____ Glas Orangensaft		ein _____ Käsebrötchen	
ein _____ Mineralwasser		einen _____ Hamburger	
ein _____ Bier		ein _____ Eis	
eine _____ Tasse Kaffee / Tee		ein _____ Stück Apfelkuchen	
einen _____ Rotwein		einen _____ Salat	
…		…	

Unpreceded adjectives

When an adjective is not preceded by a **der**-word or an **ein**-word, the adjective shows the gender, number, and case of the noun by taking the appropriate **der**-word ending. The genitive forms are not listed here, because they are less common.

	Masculine	Neuter	Feminine	Plural
NOMINATIVE	gut**er** Kaffee	gut**es** Bier	gut**e** Salami	gut**e** Äpfel
ACCUSATIVE	gut**en** Kaffee	gut**es** Bier	gut**e** Salami	gut**e** Äpfel
DATIVE	gut**em** Kaffee	gut**em** Bier	gut**er** Salami	gut**en** Äpfel**n**

10-36 Mein persönlicher Geschmack. Erzählen Sie einander, was für Produkte Sie besonders gern haben.

amerikanisch	deutsch	holländisch	mexikanisch
japanisch	französisch	billig	dramatisch
teuer	schlecht	alt	neu
schnell	romantisch	komisch	spannend°

suspenseful

Ich trinke gern …　　　　　Bier (n), Wein (m)
Ich esse gern …　　　　　　Käse (m), Brot (n)
Ich lese gern …　　　　　　Bücher (pl), Krimis (pl)
Ich höre gern …　　　　　　Popmusik (f), Songs (pl)
Ich fahre gern …　　　　　　Autos (pl)
Ich gehe gern in …　　　　　Restaurants (pl)
　　…　　　　　　　　　　　…

Ich esse gern holländischen Käse.

10.8　Video-Treff

Meine Lieblingslektüre

10.9　Understand authentic video of Germans talking about what they like to read

Kristina, Anja Szustak, André, Stefan Meister, Maiga, Thomas und Stefan Kuhlmann erzählen, was sie gern lesen. Machen Sie die erste Aufgabe, **Was ist das auf Englisch?,** bevor Sie das Video anschauen.

10-37 Was ist das auf Englisch?

1. Ich lese englische Bücher, damit mein Englisch **am Leben bleibt.**
2. Das ist ein Mensch, der immer noch **auf der Suche** ist.
3. Ich lese Bücher, die mich **fesseln.**
4. Ich muss ja leider viel für die Uni lesen, und **das reicht mir.**
5. Hier geht es **größtenteils** um lokale Nachrichten.
6. Wenn ich **nicht gerade** Bücher lese, lese ich Zeitschriften.
7. Diese Zeitschrift gibt es **seit den 80er-Jahren.**

a. searching
b. largely
c. grab
d. not at the moment
e. since the eighties
f. stays alive
g. that's enough for me

Was liest du gern?

10-38 Richtig oder falsch? Lesen Sie die Aussagen über Kristina, Anja, André und Stefan Meister. Sind diese Aussagen richtig oder falsch? Wenn eine Aussage falsch ist, korrigieren Sie sie.

	RICHTIG	FALSCH
1. Kristina kauft sich jeden Monat eine Sportzeitschrift.	☐	☐
2. In der Zeitschrift gefallen ihr besonders die Informationen über Sport, Gesundheit und so weiter.	☐	☐
3. Anja isst kein Fleisch und kauft deshalb die Zeitschrift *Vegetarisch Fit*.	☐	☐
4. Sie kauft *Vegetarisch Fit*, weil sie die Leserbriefe so interessant findet.	☐	☐

	RICHTIG	FALSCH
5. André liest gern Krimis, Autobiografien und Fantasiegeschichten.	☐	☐
6. Er liest jetzt eine Autobiografie.	☐	☐
7. Das Buch, das André im Moment liest, ist sehr gut aber nicht sehr lang.	☐	☐
8. Stefan Meister mag Bücher mit Geschichten, mit denen er sich identifizieren kann.	☐	☐
9. Stefan liest manchmal Bücher auf Englisch.	☐	☐
10. Stefans Lieblingsbuch ist von einem deutschen Autor.	☐	☐

10-39 Was ich gern lese. Ergänzen Sie die Aussagen über Maiga, Thomas und Stefan Kuhlmann.

1. Maiga liest am liebsten Bücher _____.

   ☐ im Urlaub ☐ für die Uni

2. Maiga liest gern _____, die sie fesseln.

   ☐ Bücher ☐ Zeitschriften

3. Thomas sagt, die *Berliner Zeitung* ist eine _____.

   ☐ Wochenzeitung ☐ Tageszeitung

4. Im _____ der *Berliner Zeitung* liest Thomas zum Beispiel Berichte über die Berliner Oper.

   ☐ Wirtschaftsteil ☐ Kulturteil

5. In der *Berliner Zeitung* gibt es einen Teil über Berlin, in dem man sich gut über _____ Nachrichten informieren kann.

   ☐ lokale ☐ nationale

6. Stefan Kuhlmann sagt, _____ ist die beste Filmzeitschrift in Deutschland.

   ☐ *Empire* ☐ *Cinema*

7. Stefan meint, der deutsche *Rolling Stone* ist _____ der amerikanische *Rolling Stone*.

   ☐ sehr viel besser als ☐ nicht so gut wie

8. Stefan sagt, der *Musikexpress* existiert seit _____.

   ☐ den 60er-Jahren ☐ den 90er-Jahren

9. Die Zeitschrift, die ihm am wichtigsten ist, hat Information über _____.

   ☐ Fernsehprogramme ☐ Rockmusiker

10. Stefan Kuhlmann liest _____ Bücher.

   ☐ nie ☐ auch

Was war dein Lieblingsbuch, als du klein warst?

🔊 10.9 Wortschatz 2

Wichtige Vokabeln

10.10 Learn vocabulary used in classic fairy tales and other types of writing

Nomen

der Bericht, -e	report
der Diebstahl, ⸚e	theft; burglary
die Erinnerung, -en	memory
der Krimi, -s	mystery; crime story; thriller
die Krimiserie, -n	crime series
der Lastkraftwagen, - ⎫	truck
der Lastwagen, - ⎭	
die Nachrichten (*pl*)	news
das Werkzeug, -e	tool
die Erde	earth; ground
das Huhn, ⸚er	chicken
das Pferd, -e	horse
der Wettlauf, ⸚e	race (*contest*)

LKW Durchfahrt verboten

A typical abbreviation for **Lastkraftwagen (Lastwagen)** is **Lkw.** Similarly, **Pkw** stands for **Personenkraftwagen,** meaning a regular car that transports people.

Verben

ärgern	to make angry; annoy
ein·brechen (bricht ein), brach ein, eingebrochen	to break in
fressen (frisst), fraß, gefressen	to eat (*mostly for animals*)
schreien, schrie, geschrien	to scream; to shout
statt·finden, fand statt, stattgefunden	to take place
stehlen (stiehlt), stahl, gestohlen	to steal
verschlingen, verschlang, verschlungen	to devour
wetten	to bet

Andere Wörter

komisch	strange; funny
krumm	crooked
saftig	juicy
spannend	suspenseful; interesting
unterwegs	on the way
vergnügt	happy; merry

Ausdrücke

Angst haben vor (+ *dat*)	to be afraid of
jedes Mal	each time
das letzte Mal	the last time
einen Wettlauf machen	to run a race
Ich habe Lust auf ... (+ *acc*)	I feel like (*having or doing something*) ...

Das reicht (mir).	That's enough (for me).
Sie war außer sich.	She was beside herself.

Das Gegenteil

gewinnen, gewann, gewonnen ≠ verlieren, verlor, verloren	to win ≠ to lose
lokal ≠ national	local ≠ national
oben ≠ unten	above ≠ below
riesig ≠ winzig	huge ≠ tiny

Leicht zu verstehen

die Autobiografie, -n	**das Produkt, -e**
das Insekt, -en	**dramatisch**

Synonyme

kriegen = bekommen

klug = intelligent

Wörter im Kontext

10-40 Was passt zusammen?

1. Ein Lastwagen ist ein Fahrzeug,
2. Eine Autobiografie ist eine Geschichte,
3. Ein Krimi ist ein Buch,
4. Das Pferd ist ein Tier,
5. Ein Hammer ist ein Werkzeug,
6. Ein Marathonlauf ist ein Wettlauf,

a. auf dem man reiten kann.
b. mit dem man Nägel schlagen kann.
c. in der man von seinem Leben erzählt.
d. mit dem man schwere Sachen transportiert.
e. für den man lang trainieren muss.
f. in dem oft ein Detektiv eine wichtige Rolle spielt.

10-41 Was ist hier identisch? Welche zwei Sätze in jeder Gruppe bedeuten etwa dasselbe?

1. Stefan ist sehr klug.
   Stefan hat sich sehr aufgeregt.
   Stefan war außer sich.
2. Anna hat Lust auf Pizza.
   Anna kauft sich keine Pizza sondern einen Döner.
   Anna möchte sich eine Pizza bestellen.
3. Das Meeting fand gestern nicht statt.
   Das letzte Mal fand das Meeting in meinem Büro statt.
   Wir haben uns gestern gar nicht getroffen.

4. Ich bekomme bald einen neuen Computer.
   Bald kriege ich einen neuen Computer.
   Ich brauche bald einen neuen Computer.
5. Ich finde das spannend.
   Ich will nicht mehr.
   Das reicht mir.
6. Habt ihr nicht gewonnen?
   Habt ihr nicht gewettet?
   Habt ihr verloren?

10-42 Was passt wo?

riesiges / winziges / kluger / nationaler / vergnügte

1. Ein Feiertag, den das ganze Land feiert, ist ein _____ Feiertag.
2. Eine Studentin, die oft lacht, ist eine _____ Studentin.
3. Ein Insekt, das sehr klein ist, ist ein _____ Insekt.
4. Ein Mensch, der sehr intelligent ist, ist ein _____ Mensch.
5. Ein Gebäude, das so groß wie das Pentagon ist, ist ein _____ Gebäude.

Wörter unter der Lupe

Words as chameleons: als

You have learned that als has a variety of meanings. Here is a summary.

- *as*   in expressions like **als Kind**   **Als** Kind konnte ich sehr schnell laufen.
- *than*   after the comparative form of an adjective or adverb   Mit meinen langen Beinen konnte ich schneller laufen **als** alle meine Freunde.
- *when*   as a conjunction   **Als** ich mit meinen Freunden mal einen Wettlauf machen wollte, hatten sie keine Lust.
- *but*   after **nichts**   Ich hatte auch später nichts **als** Probleme mit meinen langen Beinen.

10-43 Was bedeutet *als* hier? *Than, when, as* oder *but?*

1. Als Mensch ist Professor Huber sehr nett.

2. Professor Huber ist viel netter als ich dachte.

3. Als Maria nach Hause kam, hatte ich das Buch gerade fertig gelesen.

4. Kathrin war schon als kleines Mädchen sehr sportlich.

5. In Hamburg hatten wir leider nichts als miserables Regenwetter.

6. Als wir in Hamburg waren, regnete es fast jeden Tag.

7. Diesen Juni hat es in Hamburg mehr geregnet als letztes Jahr im ganzen Sommer.

Giving language color

Hundreds of colorful expressions make use of the names of animals. Here is a small sampling.

Da hast du Schwein gehabt!	*You were lucky!*
Ich habe einen Bärenhunger.	*I'm hungry as a bear.*
Es ist alles für die Katz.	*It's all for nothing.*
Da bringen mich keine zehn Pferde hin!	*Wild horses couldn't drag me there!*
Du musst dir Eselsbrücken bauen.	*You'll have to find some mnemonic devices to help you remember.*
Mein Name ist Hase, ich weiß von nichts.	*Don't ask me. I don't know anything about it.*
Da lachen ja die Hühner!	*What a joke!*

10-44 Was passt zusammen?

1. Gehst du mit zum Fußballspiel?

2. Der Politiker sagt, dass alles besser wird.

3. Warum hörst du denn schon auf zu üben?

4. Wer hat denn das letzte Bier getrunken?

5. Wie soll ich denn alle diese Wörter lernen?

6. Sollen wir ins Gasthaus an der Ecke gehen?

7. Ich habe 10 Euro im Bus gefunden!

a. Du musst dir Eselsbrücken bauen.

b. Mein Name ist Hase. Ich weiß von nichts.

c. Da hast du aber Schwein gehabt!

d. Ja, sicher! Da lachen ja die Hühner!

e. Klar! Ich habe einen Bärenhunger.

f. Es ist ja doch alles für die Katz!

g. Bei dem Wetter bringen mich da keine zehn Pferde hin!

10.10 Alles zusammen

Nun eine Sage

You have already read a complete German **Märchen,** as recorded by Jacob and Wilhelm Grimm, in *Kultur 2*. In this section, you'll read a **Sage,** a German legend, also collected by the Grimm brothers in the early nineteenth century. In contrast to fairy tales, legends often construct a tale around historical events. Jacob Grimm described the difference between a **Märchen** and a **Sage** this way: "Das Märchen fliegt, während die Sage zu Fuß reist."

The version of *Rattenfänger* you'll read, however, is a more recent re-telling. You'll also have a chance to get creative by writing and sharing an alternative ending to the story, or a possible second chapter to add to the story.

Schritt 1: Zum Lesen und Sprechen

10-45 Fragen und Antworten. Lesen Sie den Text ein- oder zweimal. Dann suchen Sie im Text die Antwort auf diese Fragen. Identifizieren Sie zusammen die **Zeilen,** in denen die Antwort steht.

1. Welchen Beruf übte der Mann aus, der nach Hameln kam? Wie fanden andere Menschen diesen Beruf?
2. Was passierte, wenn er auf seiner Flöte spielte?
3. Warum hungerten die Bürger von Hameln in dieser Zeit?
4. Wie befreite der Rattenfänger die Bürger von der Ratten- und Mäuseplage?
5. Was bekam der Rattenfänger aber nicht von der Stadt? Wie reagierte er darauf?
6. Wohin führte der Rattenfänger die Kinder? Mit anderen Worten, wo waren die Kinder am Ende der Geschichte?

Die Geschichte vom Rattenfänger von Hameln
Eine Nacherzählung von Karin Gündisch

Es lebte früher einmal ein Mann, der einen unbeliebten Beruf hatte, den niemand mehr ausüben wollte. Er war Rattenfänger und trug einen auffälligen Flickenanzug, und die Leute drehten sich nach ihm um, wenn er durch die Straßen ging. Er konnte sehr gut Flöte spielen und verdiente sich mit seinem Spiel das tägliche Brot. Wenn er
5 auf seiner Flöte spielte, folgten ihm Ratten und Mäuse, wohin er sie führte.

Eines Tages kam der Rattenfänger nach Hameln. Den Bürgern der Stadt ging es damals sehr schlecht: Sie hatten kein Brot mehr, keine Butter, kein Maismehl, keine Kartoffeln. Alles hatten die Mäuse und Ratten verschlungen. Sie hatten sogar die Füße der Ferkel im Stall angefressen, und die Bürger fragten sich angstvoll, was die Ratten als Nächstes wohl fressen würden. Die Mäuse und Ratten vermehrten sich von Tag zu Tag.

10

Da war der Rattenfänger der Retter in der Not, denn er befreite die Bürger von der Plage. Ratten und Mäuse folgten ihm in den Fluss, wo sie ertranken. Danach wollte der Mann seinen Lohn von der Stadt. Die Bürger aber waren übermütig geworden, als die Gefahr vorbei war, und sie geizten mit dem Lohn. Der geprellte Rattenfänger rächte sich grausam. An einem Sonntag, als alle Einwohner der Stadt außer den Kindern in der Kirche waren, kehrte er als Jägersmann verkleidet nach Hameln zurück, spielte auf seiner Flöte wunderbare Lieder, lockte die Kinder auf die Straße und führte sie in eine Höhle in einen Berg hinein. Die Kinder kamen nie mehr nach Hameln zurück. Sie sind aus dem Berg in Siebenbürgen wieder ans Tageslicht gekommen.

15

20

Schritt 2: Zum Schreiben

10-46 Ein alternatives Ende für die Geschichte. Schreiben Sie ein neues Ende **oder** ein zweites Kapitel zu dem Märchen, das dann in Siebenbürgen stattfindet.

Option 1: Ein alternatives Ende: Beginnen Sie mit dem Satz (Zeile 18):

[Der Rattenfänger] lockte die Kinder auf die Straße und …

Option 2: Ein neues, zweites Kapitel für die Kinder in Siebenbürgen: Hier beginnt Ihre Geschichte am Ende der Sage (Zeile 20):

[Die Kinder] sind aus dem Berg in Siebenbürgen wieder ans Tageslicht gekommen. Dann …

Schritt 3: Zum Sprechen

10-47 Wir erzählen eine neue Geschichte. Bilden Sie Dreiergruppen und lesen Sie Ihr neues Ende für die Geschichte vor. Wenn Sie den neuen Versionen Ihrer Mitstudenten zuhören, versuchen Sie, die neue Moral zu identifizieren.

Need some ideas for how to start? For **Option 1:** What did the children do this time when the ratcatcher played his flute? For **Option 2:** What did the children do in Siebenbürgen without their parents? *(Or:)* What happened to the ratcatcher at the end?

Schreibtipp!
Be sure to use the simple past tense to write your new ending to the tale. But if you choose to have characters speak, use whatever tense suits what they are saying.

Kapitel 11
Geschichte und Gegenwart

Die Weltzeituhr, Berlin Alexanderplatz

Learning Objectives

11.1 Identify key features of the Berlin Wall before and after it fell

11.2 Learn vocabulary to talk about the Berlin Wall, past and present

11.3 Pronounce *pf* and *kn* in German

11.4 Describe processes using the passive voice

11.5 Describe people, places, and things using past participles

11.6 Identify and order important dates in German history since 1918

11.7 Expand the meaning of verbs with prepositions

11.8 Ask questions using prepositions: *wo*-compounds

11.9 Make statements using prepositions: *da*-compounds

11.10 Understand authentic video of German speakers talking about their experiences in the former East Germany (GDR)

11.11 Learn vocabulary to talk about German history and people's reactions to it

11.1 Vorschau

Extrablatt: Berliner Morgenpost

11-1 Extrablatt, 13. August 1961.
Was ist an diesem Tag passiert?

- ☐ Der Zweite Weltkrieg ist zu Ende.
- ☐ Man hat Deutschland in vier Zonen geteilt.
- ☐ Die Volksarmee hat Ost-Berlin blockiert.
- ☐ Ostdeutsche Soldaten haben eine Mauer durch Berlin gebaut.

Ostdeutsche Soldaten mit Stacheldraht

11-2 Schlagzeilen. Lesen Sie im Extrablatt die vier Schlagzeilen des Artikels. Was bedeutet jede Schlagzeile?

1. „Ost-Berlin ist abgeriegelt"

2. „S- und U-Bahn unterbrochen"

3. „An allen Sektorengrenzen Stacheldraht – Straßensperren"

4. „Volksarmee rund um Berlin"

a. Ostdeutsche Soldaten stehen um West-Berlin herum.

b. Der östliche Teil Berlins ist blockiert.

c. Die U- und S-Bahn-Linien fahren nicht mehr zwischen Ost und West.

d. Zwischen Ost- und West-Berlin sind die Straßen durch Stacheldraht gesperrt.

Between September 1949 and August 1961, more than 2.5 million people out of a population of approximately 17 million fled from East Germany into West Germany. The resulting hemorrhage of skilled workers became a significant threat to the East German government. In August 1961 it responded by building first barbed-wire barriers, and soon, a wall, to close off this **Fluchtweg** and stop the "brain drain." The communist government of the GDR called the Wall an **"antifaschistischer Schutzwall,"** designed to protect East German citizens from dangerous influences. The irony that this was a "protective wall" was not lost on East Germans, who made dark jokes and jabs at this until the **Wende** (*turning point*, i.e., the fall of the Wall) and even after the **Wiedervereinigung** (*reunification*).

11.2 Kultur 1

Die Berliner Mauer

11.1 Identify key features of the Berlin Wall before and after it fell

Herbst 1961: Ein Blick über die Mauer

1949 und der Kalte Krieg: Warum baute man die Mauer?

Von 1949 bis 1990 lag West-Berlin mitten in der DDR. Bis 1961 flohen 1,6 Millionen Ostdeutsche über West-Berlin in die BRD. Um diesen letzten Fluchtweg zu schließen, baute die DDR 1961 die Mauer. Der Teil der Mauer, der mitten durch Berlin ging, war 43 km lang und trennte Ost- und West-Berlin komplett. Die restlichen 112 km der Mauer trennten West-Berlin von der DDR. So war der westliche Teil Berlins eine „Insel" in Ostdeutschland.

1961–1975: Erst Stacheldraht, dann Beton

Die Mauer begann als eine einfache Sperre aus Stacheldraht. Sie wurde aber bald durch eine Mauer aus Betonklötzen ersetzt und immer weiter ausgebaut. Im Jahre 1975 gab es schon eine Mauer, die viel mehr als nur eine Mauer war. Bei der letzten Version der Mauer gab es nämlich einen 20-Meter-langen Einschnitt mit tödlichen Landminen zwischen Ost und West. Man nannte die Mauer deshalb den „**Todesstreifen**[1]". Wer fliehen wollte, bezahlte mit dem Leben.

Bis 1989: Der Todesstreifen. An der Mauer Schießbefehl!

Der Todesstreifen zwischen Ost und West hat für die DDR-Diktatur gut gewirkt. An der Mauer zwischen Ost und West haben in den 28 Jahren von 1961 bis 1989 über 160 Menschen ihr Leben verloren. Viele davon waren junge Männer unter 30 Jahre alt. Die Grenzpolizisten mussten auf jeden schießen[2], der versuchte, durch die Mauer zu fliehen. Erst am 9. November 1989 – nach 28 Jahren – wurde die Mauer, und damit der Weg zum Westen, geöffnet.

Die Mauer heute: Was bleibt?

Am 2. Oktober 1990, am Tag vor der offiziellen Wiedervereinigung Deutschlands, kam der historische Grenzabschnitt in der Bernauer Straße unter Denkmalschutz. Das Denkmal sollte an die Teilung Berlins und an die Todesopfer der Mauer erinnern. Zum 10. Jahrestag des Mauerfalls (1999) eröffnete man dort das Dokumentationszentrum. So können Besucher die historischen Reste der Mauer und die deutsch-deutsche Grenze durch Schaubilder, Fotos und Dokumentarfilme heute noch erleben.

Bei der East Side Gallery

Obwohl die eigentliche Mauer nicht mehr steht, bietet die **Gedenkstätte Berliner Mauer** in der Bernauer Straße allen Besuchern einen guten Einblick in die 20 Meter breite Zone des ehemaligen Todesstreifens. Jedes Jahr kommen Tausende Menschen aus aller Welt, um mehr über die Mauer und die deutsch-deutsche Grenze zu lernen. Bei der populären **East Side Gallery** kann man einen langen, neu bemalten Teil der Mauer besichtigen und sogar anfassen. Und der **Mauerpark** ist heute ein beliebter Ort, wo man Sport treibt, sich mit Freunden trifft, und Open-Air-Konzerte erlebt.

[1]*death strip*
[2]*to shoot*

Das Schaubild zeigt, warum nur wenige Ostdeutsche über West-Berlin in die BRD fliehen konnten.

- Zuerst musste der Flüchtling durch den **Kontaktzaun** (#1) kommen.

- Der Kontaktzaun aktivierte **Signalgeräte** (#2).

- Die Signalgeräte alarmierten die Grenzpolizisten in den **Beobachtungstürmen** (#3). Es war aber ein stiller Alarm, den der Flüchtling nicht hören konnte.

- Es gab eine **Beleuchtungsanlage** (#4), sodass die Grenzpolizisten bei Nacht alles genau sehen konnten.

- Unter den Beobachtungstürmen waren **Hunde** in **Laufanlagen** angeleint (#5).

- Der **Kfz-Graben** (#6) stoppte Fahrzeuge, die versuchten, durch die Mauer zu kommen.

- Zwischen dem Kfz-Graben und der eigentlichen Mauer gab es einen weiteren **Kontrollstreifen** (#7). Die Grenzpolizisten kontrollierten diesen Streifen Tag und Nacht.

- Nur wenn man durch diese vielen Hindernisse kommen konnte, erreichte man die **Betonplattenwand** (#8) oder den **Metallgitterzaun** (#9) der eigentlichen Mauer.

- Auf der anderen Seite dieser Mauer, die vier Meter hoch war, lag West-Berlin.

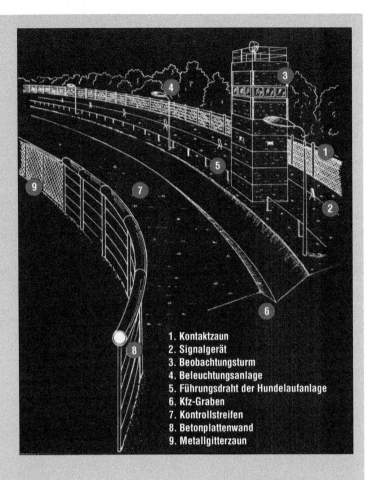

1. **Kontaktzaun**
2. **Signalgerät**
3. **Beobachtungsturm**
4. **Beleuchtungsanlage**
5. **Führungsdraht der Hundelaufanlage**
6. **Kfz-Graben**
7. **Kontrollstreifen**
8. **Betonplattenwand**
9. **Metallgitterzaun**

11-3 Wie erlebt man die Mauer heute?
Beschreiben Sie das Foto von der heutigen **Gedenkstätte Bernauer Straße.**

Beginnen Sie so:

    Auf diesem Foto sieht man …

    Links steht … , und im Hintergrund sieht man …

    In der Mitte steht …

    Im Vordergrund sieht man …

))) 11.3 Wortschatz 1

Wichtige Vokabeln

11.2 Learn vocabulary to talk about the Berlin Wall, past and present

Nomen

der stille Alarm	silent alarm
die Beobachtung, -en	observation
der Turm, ̈e	tower
der Beobachtungsturm, ̈e	(guards') observation tower
das Extrablatt, ̈er	special edition
der Flüchtling, -e	refugee
der Fluchtweg, -e	escape route
die Grenze, -n	border
die Mauer, -n	wall
der Ort, -e	place, location
die Sperre, -n	barrier
die Straßensperre, -n	barrier blocking off a street
der Stacheldraht	barbed wire
der Beton	concrete
der Befehl, -e	order, command
der Schießbefehl, -e	order to shoot
der Todesstreifen	death strip
die Wende	turn; change; *here*: turning point (at which the two Germanys reunited)
der Weg, -e	path, way
der westliche Teil	the western part
der östliche Teil	the eastern part
die Wiedervereinigung	reunification

Lerntipp!
Wiedervereinigung is easier to remember if you think of the familiar word **wieder** *(again)* and the German name for the United States. Since **Vereinigung** is feminine, so is the compound word.

Verben

fliehen, floh, ist geflohen	to flee
flüchten, ist geflüchtet	to flee; to seek refuge
schießen, schoss, geschossen	to shoot
schließen, schloss, geschlossen	to close
sperren	to close or block off
teilen	to divide
trennen	to separate

Lerntipp!
The principal parts of **fliehen, schießen,** and **schließen** have the same stem vowel changes in their past tense forms **(ie-o-o).** Learn these verbs in one group.

Andere Wörter

eigentlich	actually
überhaupt	at all
ehemalig	former

Das Gegenteil

die Demokratie ≠ die Diktatur	democracy ≠ dictatorship
der Krieg, -e ≠ der Frieden	war ≠ peace
schrecklich ≠ wunderbar	terrible ≠ wonderful

Synonyme

das Schaubild, -er = die Grafik, -en
öffnen = auf·machen

Leicht zu verstehen

die Blockade, -n	alarmieren
die Republik, -en	blockieren
der Soldat, -en	

Wörter im Kontext

11-4 Was passt wo?

geteilte / schießen / Diktatur / Demokratie / flohen / Fluchtweg / Mauer

1. Von 1961 bis 1989 war Berlin eine _____ Stadt. Das waren 28 lange Jahre!

2. Bis 1961 _____ 1,6 Millionen Ostdeutsche über West-Berlin in die BRD.

3. 1961 baute die DDR um ganz West-Berlin eine _____.

4. Die Mauer hat den _____ in den Westen geschlossen.

5. Die Grenzpolizisten mussten auf Menschen _____, die durch die Mauer nach West-Berlin flüchten wollten.

6. Die DDR war keine _____, sondern eine _____.

11-5 Wichtiges über die Mauer in Berlin.

Beton / stillen Alarm / gebaut / Todesstreifen / Stacheldraht / Schießbefehl

1. Die Mauer wurde im Jahre 1961 _____ und erst im Jahre 1989 geöffnet.

2. Sie begann als eine Sperre aus _____.

3. Bald hat man aber eine echte Mauer aus _____ gebaut.

4. Es gab eine 20 Meter breite Zone auf der östlichen Seite der Mauer, die man den _____ nannte. Denn viele, die über die Mauer fliehen wollten, bezahlten mit dem Tod.

5. An dem ersten Kontaktzaun gab es ein Signalgerät, der einen _____ auslöste. Das war also ein Alarm, den der Flüchtende nicht hören konnte.

6. An der Mauer mussten Grenzpolizisten auf Flüchtende schießen. Das heißt auf Deutsch _____.

11-6 Komposita zum Thema Mauer. Was passt zusammen?

1. die Flüchtlingszahlen	a.	Deutschland wurde wieder zu einem Land. Ost und West waren eins!
2. die Weltzeituhr	b.	ein historischer Treffpunkt in Ost-Berlin für Besucher aus dem Westen
3. der Beobachtungsturm	c.	die Anzahl von Menschen, die von Ost nach West flüchteten
4. die Grenzpolizisten	d.	ostdeutsche Polizisten, die an der Grenze zwischen Ost und West arbeiteten
5. die Wiedervereinigung	e.	ein Turm, in dem Grenzsoldaten standen, um alles im Todesstreifen besser zu sehen

The famous **Weltzeituhr** symbolizes the connectedness of today's Germany to the rest of the world. It is located in the largest open marketplace of the former East Berlin, **Alexanderplatz.** In the years of totalitarian rule, the clock was an equally good symbol of the irony that pervaded life in the GDR, since the citizens of East Germany were not permitted to travel to many of the cities depicted.

Sprachnotiz   Using *eigentlich* and *überhaupt* to intensify expressions

The German adverbs **eigentlich** and **überhaupt** intensify the meaning of the word or phrase directly following these words. Note how the bolded phrases below are best understood as a single unit. Each word of such phrases is stressed in spoken German.

Die Berliner Mauer war **eigentlich viel mehr** als nur eine Mauer.
*The Berlin Wall was **actually much more** than just a wall.*

Ich kenne Berlin **überhaupt nicht.**
*I do **not** know Berlin **at all.***

336 / dreihundertsechsunddreißig

11.4 Zur Aussprache

The consonant clusters *pf* and *kn*

11.3 Pronounce *pf* and *kn* in German

In the German consonant clusters **pf** and **kn**, both consonants are pronounced.

 11-7 Hören Sie gut zu und wiederholen Sie.

Pfanne	A**pf**el	Dam**pf**
Pfennig	im**pf**en°	Ko**pf**
Pfeffer	klo**pf**en	To**pf**
Pflaume	tro**pf**en°	Zo**pf**°
Pfund	Schnu**pf**en°	Strum**pf**°

to vaccinate — impfen°
to drip / braid — tropfen° / Zopf°
sniffles / stocking — Schnupfen° / Strumpf°

Nimm diese Tro**pf**en für deinen Schnu**pf**en.
A**pf**el**pf**annkuchen mit **Pf**efferminztee? **Pf**ui!

Knast°	**kn**abbern°	**Kn**äckebrot°
Kneipe	**kn**ipsen°	**Kn**oblauch°
Knödel	**kn**utschen°	**Kn**ackwurst

jail / to nibble / crispbread — Knast° / knabbern° / Knäckebrot°
to snap a photo / garlic — knipsen° / Knoblauch°
to smooch — knutschen°

Herr **Kn**opf sitzt im **Kn**ast und **kn**abbert **Kn**äckebrot.
Knusper, **Kn**usper, **Kn**äuschen. Wer **kn**uspert an meinem Häuschen?

Knusper, Knusper, Knäuschen: This rhyming phrase is said by the witch in the fairy tale *Hänsel und Gretel* when she finds the children munching on her house. Do you remember the rhyme from the English version?

11.5 Kommunikation und Formen 1

The passive voice

11.4 Describe processes using the passive voice

Distinguishing between active and passive voice

In grammatical terms, the doer of an action is usually the subject of the sentence. Such a sentence is said to be in the *active voice*.

Peter holt mich um sieben ab.   *Peter is picking me up at seven.*

However, when you find it unnecessary or unimportant to mention the doer of the action, you can make the *receiver* of the action the subject of the sentence. Such a sentence is said to be in the *passive voice*.

Ich *werde* um sieben *abgeholt*.   *I'm being picked up at seven.*

Note that in the passive voice

- the receiver of the action appears in the nominative case.
- the verb appears as a past participle with a form of **werden** as auxiliary.

The most commonly used tenses in the passive voice are the present and the simple past. The tense is indicated by the auxiliary **werden.**

| PRESENT | ich **werde** abgeholt | *I'm being picked up* |
| SIMPLE PAST | ich **wurde** abgeholt | *I was picked up* |

Use of the passive voice in present tense

In the passive voice, attention is focused on the receiver of the action and on the action itself. You may have been taught to avoid the passive in English, but in German it is used fairly frequently. In the example below, the active sentences give unnecessary information. Notice that the passive sentence is more natural and clear.

Passive (present tense)	Active (present tense)
Mein Nachbar **wird verhaftet!**	Die Polizei verhaftet meinen Nachbarn.
My neighbor is being arrested!	*The police are arresting my neighbor.*

 11-8 Was wird hier gemacht?

▶ **S1:** Was wird hier gemacht?   **S2:** Hier wird ein Haus gebaut.

> **Achtung!**
> Here all subjects are singular (including **Bier**), so all sentences will begin with **Hier wird …**

ein Haus / bauen

1. ein Auto / reparieren   2. Eis / verkaufen   3. im Garten / arbeiten   4. Bier / trinken

Due to environmental concerns, it's common that not all walkways are treated during the winter months. The passive makes sense here because what's done/not done is more important than the person who is doing it. **Note:** If you have ever eaten streusel cake you can guess the meaning of **streuen.**

An der Universität Trier

Use of the passive voice in the past tense

Just like the present-tense passive, the past-tense passive is built with the participle of the main verb at the end. But to form the past tense of the passive, you use the *past tense* of the auxiliary **werden → wurde.** Note that the passive sentences below focus on the Wall, and how it was built, opened, or torn down, and not on the people who did these things:

Die Mauer **wurde** 1961 **gebaut.**	*The Wall **was built** in 1961.*
Die Mauer **wurde** 1989 **geöffnet.**	*The Wall **was opened** in 1989.*
Die Mauer **wurde** danach **abgerissen.**	*The Wall **was torn down** after that.*

11-9 Was wurde hier gemacht?

► **S1:** Was wurde hier gemacht?   **S2:** Hier wurde ein Baum gefällt.

ein Baum / fällen

Achtung!

If the subject is singular, your (past tense) sentences will begin with **Hier wurde ... .** When the subject is plural, begin with **Hier wurden ... .** The (past tense) question for S1 will always be the same: **Was wurde hier gemacht?**

1. Bier / trinken   2. Brot / backen   3. Schnee / schaufeln

4. viele Äpfel / pflücken   5. 36 Fenster / putzen   6. zwei Hemden / waschen

11-10 Gute Vorsätze. Sie sind auf einer Neujahrsparty und es ist kurz vor Mitternacht. Schreiben Sie drei gute Vorsätze für das neue Jahr. Lesen Sie Ihre Vorsätze dann in Ihrer Kleingruppe vor.

	SINGULAR	
Von heute ab wird	jeden Tag Sport	
	viel mehr Gemüse	
	viel weniger Schokolade	gelernt.
	viel weniger Bier	ausgegeben.
	viel weniger Kaffee	gemacht.
	einmal täglich der Abwasch	erzählt.
	nicht mehr so viel Geld	gegessen.
	keine einzige Zigarette mehr	angeschaut.
	PLURAL	getrunken.
Von heute ab werden	keine blöden Witze° mehr	geraucht.
	keine doofen Seifenopern mehr	…
	jeden Tag ein paar deutsche Vokabeln	
	…	

> It's typical to make resolutions **(Vorsätze)** using the passive voice. Practice this carefully by focusing first on resolutions with singular subjects and then on resolutions with plural subjects.

blöde Witze: *stupid jokes*

Sprachnotiz   Using *von* to indicate the agent in a passive sentence

In most passive sentences, the agent (the doer of the action) is omitted, because it's already obvious or just not relevant. However, if it is relevant to mention this information, the agent appears in the dative case after the preposition **von.**

Mein Nachbar wurde **von der ostdeutschen Volkspolizei** verhaftet.
*My neighbor was arrested **by the East German police**.*

Describing people, places, and things

11.5 Describe people, places, and things using past participles

The past participle used as an adjective

In your reading you have frequently seen past participles used as adjectives. Before a noun, the past participle takes the same endings as other adjectives.

Er ist ein **gut bezahlter** Architekt.	*He is a **well-paid** architect.*
Der Spiegel ist ein **viel gelesenes** Magazin in Deutschland.	Der Spiegel *is a **much-read** magazine in Germany.*

11-11 Was ist das? Achten Sie dabei auf **Singular** oder **Plural** und **Adjektivendungen.**

▶ S1:

frisch / gepflückt

Das sind frisch gepflück**te** Äpfel.

▶ S2:

gut / gebaut

Und **das ist** ein gut gebaut**er** junger Mann!

1. **S1:** frisch _____ Hemden

S2: ein frisch _____ Brot (n)

2. **S1:** ein schlecht _____ Mann

S2: zwei _____ Koffer

3. **S1:** ein _____ Brief (m)

S2: vier _____ Bierkrüge

gebacken	gepackt	gewaschen	rasiert	ausgetrunken	angefangen

11-12 Modenschau im Deutschkurs. Beschreiben Sie, was Ihre Mitstudentinnen und Mitstudenten tragen.

S1: Lisa trägt einen langen, gestreiften Pullover. David trägt ein sportliches, blau und weiß gestreiftes Polohemd.

striped	interessant	braun	gestreift°	einen Pullover, einen Anzug, einen Rock
worn out (clothes)	cool	blau	abgetragen°	ein T-Shirt, ein Sweatshirt, ein Hemd
worn out (shoes)	sportlich	gelb	abgelaufen°	eine Bluse, eine Jacke, eine Hose, eine Sonnenbrille
ripped	praktisch	grün	zerrissen°	Schuhe, Stiefel, Sandalen
unironed	toll	rot	ungebügelt°	Jeans, Leggings, Shorts
	…	…	…	…

11.6 Kultur 2

Kleine deutsche Chronik: 1918 bis heute

11.6 Identify and order important dates in German history since 1918

Deutschland und Österreich-Ungarn verlieren den Ersten Weltkrieg. Der deutsche Kaiser geht ins Exil. Vom Reichstagsgebäude wird die neue Demokratie proklamiert. Später wird sie die Weimarer Republik genannt.

1918-1919

1933

Adolf Hitler wird zum Kanzler gewählt und macht Deutschland sofort zu einer Diktatur.

Am 12. März wird Österreich an Nazi-Deutschland angeschlossen.

In der „Kristallnacht", der Nacht vom 9. zum 10. November, werden tausende jüdische Geschäfte und Synagogen zerstört. Viele jüdische Deutsche werden ermordet. Tausende werden von der Polizei festgenommen und deportiert.

1938

Die deutsche Armee marschiert in Polen ein. Der Zweite Weltkrieg beginnt.

1939

Die Alliierten nehmen Berlin ein. Hitler nimmt sich das Leben. Ende der Nazidiktatur und des Zweiten Weltkriegs. In diesem Krieg sterben 55 Millionen Menschen. 6 Millionen von den Toten sind Juden, die im Holocaust sterben. Deutschland und Berlin werden in je vier Zonen geteilt: eine amerikanische, eine britische, eine französische und eine sowjetische.

1945

Der Kalte Krieg beginnt. Die Sowjetunion blockiert elf Monate lang alle Land- und Wasserwege nach West-Berlin. Präsident Truman startet die „Luftbrücke". Zehn Monate lang bringen Flugzeuge lebenswichtige Güter und Lebensmittel nach West-Berlin aus der Luft.

1948-1949

Deutschland wird in Ost und West geteilt. Aus den drei westlichen Zonen (von Großbritannien, Frankreich und den USA) wird am 23. Mai die Bundesrepublik Deutschland gegründet. Aus der sowjetischen Zone wird am 7. Oktober die Deutsche Demokratische Republik gegründet. Die Stadt Berlin bleibt in vier Zonen geteilt. Sie wird von den vier Alliierten gemeinsam verwaltet.

1949

1961

Tausende fliehen aus der DDR in den Westen. Am 13. August 1961 baut die Volksarmee der DDR eine Mauer mitten durch Berlin, um die Abwanderung der Ostdeutschen in die BRD zu stoppen.

Starker Ost-West-Konflikt. John F. Kennedy besucht West-Berlin. Er beendet seine Rede mit den berühmten Worten: „Ich bin ein Berliner."

1963

1989

Im Januar proklamiert Erich Honecker, der Staatschef der DDR, dass die Mauer in hundert Jahren noch steht. Aber am 9. November öffnet die DDR die Berliner Mauer und die Grenze zur BRD.

Ost- und Westdeutschland werden wieder ein Land.

1990

2005

Das neue Holocaust-Mahnmal in Berlin erinnert an die ermordeten Juden Europas während der Nazidiktatur. Das Denkmal steht in der Nähe des Reichstagsgebäudes und auf dem ehemaligen Todesstreifen.

Mehr als 60 Millionen Menschen weltweit suchen Schutz vor Kriegen und Konflikten. Deutschland nimmt mehr Flüchtlinge auf als die restlichen EU-Länder.

2015

11-13 Stationen der deutschen Geschichte. Lesen Sie die Informationen in der kleinen deutschen Chronik *(Kultur 2)*. Wann passierte was?

1918–1919	a. die Öffnung der Mauer
1938 (März)	b. die Blockade Berlins und die Luftbrücke
1938 (November)	c. die Eröffnung des Denkmals für die ermordeten Juden Europas in Berlin
1945	
1948–1949	d. die Gründung der Weimarer Republik
1949	e. die „Reichskristallnacht"
1989	f. die Wiedervereinigung
1990	g. der Anschluss Österreichs
2005	h. das Ende des 2. Weltkriegs
	i. die Gründung der DDR und der BRD

11.7 Kommunikation und Formen 2

Special verb-preposition combinations

11.7 Expand the meaning of verbs with prepositions

Many English and German verbs are used in combination with prepositions. In the examples below, the prepositions used in both languages have some parallels to English, but not all are direct equivalents.

Barbara studiert ein Semester **an** der Humboldt-Universität.
Sie arbeitet gerade **an** einem Referat über Berlin.

*Barbara is studying for a semester **at** the Humboldt University.*
*She's currently working **on** a report about Berlin.*

In most instances, however, the prepositions used in German verb-preposition combinations do not correspond directly to those used in English.

Barbara interessiert sich **für** europäische Politik.
Sie wartet **auf** die Chance, ein Praktikum im deutschen Bundestag zu machen.

*Barbara is interested **in** European politics.*
*She's waiting **for** the chance to do an internship at the German Bundestag.*

Below are two groups of commonly used verb-preposition combinations. The first four have prepositions with the accusative case; the second group of four uses the dative. Note that since these verbs are idiomatic expressions, all parts of the verb work as a unit. This means that the two-way prepositions appear only with the case listed below when used in these phrases. The test of **wohin/wo** is not relevant.

Das Reichstagsgebäude in Berlin

Verbs + Prepositions	
danken für	to thank for
denken an *(+ acc)*	to think of, about
sprechen über *(+ acc)*	to talk about
warten auf *(+ acc)*	to wait for
Angst haben vor *(+ dat)*	to be afraid of
arbeiten an *(+ dat)*	to work on
erzählen von	to tell about
wissen von	to know about

Ach so!
The **Bundestag** is Germany's national parliament. Its seat is the **Reichstag.** In the years of the Wall, the **Mauer** ran directly behind this building and in front of the historic **Brandenburger Tor,** cutting off West Berliners from passing through the city's iconic gate.

Lerntipp!
You already know the verbs in this list, so now you just need to memorize each one as a unit with its preposition and case.

11-14 Was passt zusammen? Ergänzen Sie die passenden Präpositionen. **S2** gibt eine sinnvolle Antwort.

S1:

1. Was weißt du _____ der ehemaligen DDR?
2. Wann erzählst du uns _____ deiner Reise nach Berlin?
3. Wie lange hast du _____ diesem Referat gearbeitet?

   a lot
4. Ich habe Angst _____ dieser Prüfung.
5. Wo soll ich _____ dich warten, Ali?
6. _____ wen denkst du, Martin?
7. Vielen Dank _____ deine Hilfe!

S2:

a. An Claudia.
b. Ich auch.
c. Bitte!
d. Eine ganze Woche.
e. Eine ganze Menge°.
f. Vor der Bibliothek.
g. Dieses Wochenende.

11-15 Was machen diese Leute? Ergänzen Sie zuerst die Präpositionen **an, auf, von** und **vor.** Dann ergänzen Sie die passenden Objekte.

1. Tanja hat Angst _____ _____.

2. Kevin wartet im Büro _____ _____ von seiner Ärztin.

3. Frau Kemp denkt oft _____ _____.

4. Bob weiß noch nichts _____ _____.

5. Nicole arbeitet _____ _____.

6. Holger erzählt _____ _____.

ihrem Referat	Mäusen	seiner Geburtstagsparty
seinem Autounfall°	ihren alten Vater	einen Anruf

automobile accident

Verbs that occur in verb-preposition combinations are often reflexive.

Reflexive verbs + Prepositions	
sich ärgern über (+ acc)	to be annoyed with, about
sich bewerben um	to apply for
sich erinnern an (+ acc)	to remember
sich entscheiden für	to decide on
sich freuen auf (+ acc)	to look forward to
sich informieren über (+ acc)	to find out about
sich interessieren für	to be interested in
sich verlieben in (+ acc)	to fall in love with

sich freuen: By changing the preposition to **über,** you change the meaning slightly: *to be happy about:* **Ich freue mich über meine guten Noten!**

Lerntipp!
Notice that this whole group of reflexive verbs and prepositions takes the accusative case. It's still a good study strategy to write in "+ acc" after any two-way preposition, though.

11-16 Was passt zusammen? Ergänzen Sie die passenden Präpositionen. **S2** gibt eine sinnvolle Antwort.

S1:

1. Warum interessiert sich Sabine so _____ die Geschichte der DDR?

2. Warum haben sich viele DDR-Bürger so sehr _____ ihren Staat geärgert?

3. Warum informierst du dich _____ Studentenheime in Berlin?

4. Warum hast du dich _____ ein Semester in Berlin entschieden?

5. Warum bewirbt dein Freund sich _____ den Job im Mauermuseum am Checkpoint Charlie?

S2:

a. Weil ich nächstes Semester dort studieren will.

b. Weil er deutsche Geschichte studiert hat.

c. Weil ich mich für die Geschichte des Kalten Krieges interessiere.

d. Weil ihre Familie aus der DDR kommt.

e. Weil sie nicht reisen und ihre eigene Meinung nicht sagen durften.

11-17 Was machen diese Leute? Ergänzen Sie zuerst die Präpositionen. Dann suchen Sie die passenden Objekte.

1. Ali hat sich _____ _____ verliebt.

2. Frau Klein ärgert sich _____ _____ .

3. Maria freut sich _____ _____ .

4. Rudi entscheidet sich _____ _____ .

5. Claudia findet alles in der Geschichte faszinierend. Sie interessiert sich _____ _____ .

ihren dickköpfigen° Sohn	einen verrückten Haarschnitt	Stephanie	*stubborn*
ihre Reise nach Italien	historische Maschinen		

Ach so!
A few *where*-compounds are still in general use in English, especially in legal terminology, e.g., *whereby*, *wherein*, and *whereupon*.

Asking questions about things or ideas using *wo*-compounds

11.8 Ask questions using prepositions: *wo*-compounds

Wo-compounds as question words

The question words **wem** and **wen** refer to persons. If a preposition is involved, it precedes the question word.

Vor wem hast du Angst?	*Who are you afraid of?*
An wen denkst du?	*Who are you thinking of?*

In contrast, the question word **was** refers to things or ideas. If a preposition is involved, a **wo**-compound (**wo-** plus the preposition) is used.

Wovor hast du Angst?	*What are you afraid of?*
Woran denkst du?	*What are you thinking of?*

Achtung!
Note that an *r* is added to **wo** if the preposition begins with a vowel: **woran, worauf, worüber,** etc.

Wo-compounds			
WO + PREPOSITION		WO + *R* + PREPOSITION	
Wobei?	Wonach?	Woran?	Worüber?
Wodurch?	Wovon?	Worauf?	Worum?
Wofür?	Wovor?	Woraus?	Worunter?
Wogegen?	Wozu?	Worin?	
Womit?			

11-18 Stress in der Beziehung. Wählen Sie die passende Frage.

KARIN: **Über wen / Worüber** ärgerst du dich denn so?
PAUL: Über meinen Freund, Alex. Er sagte, er will mit mir sprechen.

KARIN: **Über wen / Worüber** will er mit dir sprechen?
PAUL: Über unsere Zukunft. Ich habe ein bisschen Angst!

KARIN: **Vor wem / Wovor** hast du Angst?
PAUL: Vor seinen Eltern! Sie sind gegen unsere Beziehung.

KARIN: **Von wem / Wovon** weißt du das?
PAUL: Von seiner Mutter.

 11-19 Was für Leute sind Bernd und Karin?

S1: Wofür interessiert sich Bernd am meisten?

S2: Er interessiert sich für Politik und Geschichte. Und Karin? Wofür …

Ich heiße …	Bernd	Karin
Ich interessiere mich für …	Politik und Geschichte	Computer und das Internet
Im Moment arbeite ich an …	einem Projekt über deutsche Geschichte	einer Website für die Firma meines Vaters
Ich ärgere mich über …	Gruppenarbeit	konservative Politik
Ich habe Angst vor …	der Zeit nach dem Studium	Spinnen
Ich freue mich sehr auf …	die Sommerferien	ein Bier nach der Arbeit

11-20 Ärger oder Freude?

S1: Worüber ärgerst du dich oft?   S2: Ich ärgere mich oft über …

S2: Worauf freust du dich am meisten? S1: Im Moment freue ich mich auf …

Ich ärgere mich oft über …	**Ich freue mich im Moment auf …**
☐ unfreundliche Leute	☐ das kommende Wochenende
☐ schlechte Noten	☐ das Ende des Semesters
☐ Probleme mit meinem Computer	☐ ein A in Deutsch
☐ die Bürokratie an der Uni	☐ Besuch von meiner Familie
☐ unordentliche Mitbewohner	☐ meinen Geburtstag
☐ Geldprobleme	☐ nächsten Sommer
☐ die Politiker in meinem Bundesstaat	☐ die nächste Präsidentschaftswahl
☐ meine vielen Hausaufgaben in …	☐ mein Praktikum bei …
☐ …	☐ …

Use *da*-compounds to refer to things and ideas already mentioned

11.9 Make statements using prepositions: *da*-compounds

Da-compounds

Da-compounds combine **da** with prepositions to let you easily refer back to a thing or idea that has already been mentioned. Like **wo**-compounds, they can't be used to refer to people.

Arbeitet Jan noch an seinem Referat?   *Is Jan still working on his paper?*
Ja, er arbeitet schon zwei Monate **daran**!   *Yes, he's been working **on it** for two months!*

Interessiert er sich noch für das Thema?   *Is he still interested in the topic?*
Ja, er interessiert sich immer noch **dafür**! *Yes, he's still interested **in it**!*

If the preposition begins with a vowel, an **r** is added to **da**:

Da-compounds			
DA + PREPOSITION		DA + *R* + PREPOSITION	
dabei	danach	daran	darüber
dadurch	davon	darauf	darum
dafür	davor	daraus	darunter
dagegen	dazu	darin	
damit			

11-21 Onkel Max beschreibt sein Zimmer als Teenager in der DDR. Markieren Sie zuerst alle **da**-Verbindungen, die Sie finden, und schreiben Sie dann auf, welche Präpositionalphrasen durch die **da**-Verbindung beschrieben werden.

▶ <u>Davor</u> – vor dem Fenster

„Ich erinnere mich an mein Zimmer damals in der DDR – es war sehr klein aber ich hatte ein großes Fenster. Davor stand ein kleines Regal mit einem Fernseher darauf. Daneben stand eine Couch, und das war auch mein Bett. Tagsüber konnte ich darauf sitzen und lesen oder Musik hören. Am Bett gab es auch ein eingebautes Regal. Siehst du das Poster, das darüber hängt? Die Beatles waren auch bei uns im Osten sehr populär. Das war kein schönes Zimmer aber ich habe gute Erinnerungen daran."

Eine Zeitreise in die DDR

11-22 Ergänzen Sie mit einer *da*-Verbindung oder mit Präposition + Pronomen.

JAN: In ein paar Wochen ist das Semester schon zu Ende. Ich freue mich sehr auf den Sommer!

MARKUS: Ich freue mich auch _____! Hast du schon Pläne für den Sommer?

JAN: Ich wollte ein Praktikum bei Siemens machen, aber ich habe mich noch nicht _____ beworben. Und du?

MARKUS: Ich möchte wieder nach Berlin fahren. Da besuche ich meine Kusine Monika. Erinnerst du dich an sie?

JAN: Klar, ich erinnere mich sehr gut _____! Sie arbeitet dort an ihrer Magisterarbeit, oder?

MARKUS: Ja, sie arbeitet schon zwei Jahre _____. Sie interessiert sich sehr für die Geschichte der DDR.

JAN: Warum hat sie sich _____ entschieden?

MARKUS: Sie hat in Berlin ihren Mann kennengelernt und sich dort _____ verliebt.

11-23 Interessen und Ängste. Ergänzen Sie mit einer **da**-Verbindung oder mit Präposition + Pronomen.

S1: Ich interessiere mich für deutsches Essen. Du auch?

S2: Ja, ich interessiere mich auch dafür. Hast du Angst vor Hunden?

S1: Nein, ich habe keine Angst vor ihnen! Und du?

S2: …

> **Achtung!**
> Remember that animate objects (people and animals) aren't referred to with **da**-compounds. Instead, use a preposition + pronoun.

INTERESSEN	ÄNGSTE
☐ deutsches Essen	☐ dem Tod
☐ einen Sommerjob im Restaurant	☐ dem Fliegen
☐ ein Praktikum bei Google	☐ der Zukunft
☐ deutsche Geschichte	☐ Spinnen
☐ amerikanische Politiker	☐ Ratten
☐ lustige TV-Sendungen	☐ Schlangen
☐ alte Bücher	☐ Clowns
☐ Fantasiefilme	☐ Höhen
☐ Technologie	☐ Donner und Blitzen
☐ Kinder	☐ Hunden
…	…

11.8 Video-Treff

So war's in der DDR

11.10 Understand authentic video of German speakers talking about their experiences in the former East Germany (GDR)

Thomas, Ines und Susann erzählen von ihrem Leben in der DDR.

11-24 Was ist das auf Englisch?

1. Wo wir jetzt stehen war früher **Niemandsland.**
2. Die Mauer sieht erst seit **Anfang der 90er Jahre** so aus.
3. Früher war die Mauer nicht **bemalt.**
4. Auf der Mauer sind Bilder **zum Thema** Ost- und West-Berlin und zur Trennung der Stadt.
5. Für mich wurde die Mauer erst real nach der **Wende,** also Anfang der 90er Jahre.
6. Man konnte dann die Mauer **anfassen** und kleine Steine aus der Mauer nehmen.
7. Wir haben beide **Erinnerungen an** die DDR.
8. Meine Eltern haben dort **im Gefängnis** gesessen.
9. Sie **haben** die Meinung des DDR-Regimes **nicht vertreten.**

a. touch
b. in prison
c. painted
d. did not agree with
e. no man's land
f. on the topic of
g. memories of
h. turning point (i.e., the fall of the Wall)
i. beginning of the nineties

Die East Side Gallery

Die Mauer spricht!
In the days of the Berlin Wall, colorful graffiti created in protest completely covered the west side of the wall. The east side of the Berlin Wall was blank, because it was located within the **Todesstreifen** itself. After the Wall came down in 1989, artists from all over the world created the **East Side Gallery,** a huge outdoor gallery and memorial with over 100 paintings on a portion of its formerly inaccessible and untouchable east side. Although some of the paintings have deteriorated with time, it is the longest remaining section of the Wall.

11-25 Richtig oder falsch?

	RICHTIG	FALSCH
Die East Side Gallery		
1. Früher sah diese Seite der Mauer ganz anders aus: sie war nämlich nicht bemalt.	☐	☐
2. Die East Side Gallery ist ein Gebäude, in dem es Stücke der Berliner Mauer gibt.	☐	☐
3. Die Gallery ist jetzt ein Magnet für Touristen, die Fotos von der Mauer machen wollen.	☐	☐
4. Bei der East Side Gallery werden Andenken wie Fotos, Postkarten oder kleine Mauerstücke verkauft.	☐	☐
Familiengeschichten		
5. Wenn Ines in der DDR unter Freunden war, konnte sie endlich sagen, was sie denkt.	☐	☐
6. Susann hat länger in der DDR gelebt als Ines.	☐	☐
7. Susann ist mit ihren Eltern in den Westen geflohen.	☐	☐
8. Wenn Susann und Ines an die DDR denken, denken beide an Unfreiheit.	☐	☐

11-26 Das Leben in der DDR. Wer sagt was?

	Thomas	Ines	Susann
1. Ich habe 20 Jahre meines Lebens in der DDR verbracht.	☐	☐	☐
2. Ich habe acht Jahre in der DDR gelebt.	☐	☐	☐
3. Ich habe mein Abitur in der DDR gemacht.	☐	☐	☐
4. Anfang der 90er Jahre habe ich verstanden, was die Mauer für uns bedeutete.	☐	☐	☐
5. Meine Eltern sind aus der DDR in den Westen geflohen.	☐	☐	☐
6. Meine Eltern haben in der DDR im Gefängnis gesessen.	☐	☐	☐
7. In der DDR hatte ich immer das Gefühl, ich konnte nie sagen, was ich denke.	☐	☐	☐
8. Für mich wurde die Mauer erst dann real, als ich sie anfassen konnte.	☐	☐	☐

))) 11.9 Wortschatz 2

Wichtige Vokabeln

11.11 Learn vocabulary to talk about German history and people's reactions to it

Nomen

die Alliierten *(pl)*	the Allies
der Bundestag	German parliament
das Reichstagsgebäude	German parliament building (Berlin)
die Nachkriegszeit	post-war period
die Rede, -n	speech; talk
der Weltkrieg, -e	world war
die Erinnerung, -en	memory; remembrance
das Erlebnis, -se	experience
der Fehler, -	mistake; error
das Gefühl, -e	feeling
die Meinung, -en	opinion
der Witz, -e	joke
der Eiserne Vorhang	Iron Curtain
der Staat, -en	the state; government
die Zukunft	future

Hinter dem Reichstagsgebäude fließt die Spree.

Verben

erleben	to experience
ermorden	to murder
meinen	to mean; to think, voice an opinion
verhaften	to arrest
Angst haben vor *(+ dat)*	to be afraid of
arbeiten an *(+ dat)*	to work on
denken an *(+ acc)*	to think of, about
erzählen von	to tell about
sprechen über *(+ acc)*	to talk about

studieren an *(+ dat)*	to study at a college or university
warten auf *(+ acc)*	to wait for
wissen von	to know about
sich ärgern über *(+ acc)*	to be annoyed with, about
sich bewerben um	to apply for
sich entscheiden für	to decide on
sich erinnern an *(+ acc)*	to remember
sich freuen auf *(+ acc)*	to look forward to
sich freuen über *(+ acc)*	to be happy about; to be pleased with
sich informieren über *(+ acc)*	to find out about
sich interessieren für	to be interested in
sich verlieben in *(+ acc)*	to fall in love with

Andere Wörter

dickköpfig	stubborn
faszinierend	fascinating
jederzeit	(at) any time

Das Gegenteil

die Freiheit ≠	freedom ≠
die Unfreiheit	lack of freedom

Synonyme

zerstören = kaputt machen
das Souvenir = das Andenken
zu Beginn = am Anfang
eine Menge = viel
die Zone = der Sektor

Leicht zu verstehen

kommunistisch

Wörter im Kontext

11-27 Was passt zusammen?

1. Wenn jemand einen guten Witz erzählt,
2. Wenn man immer nur das macht, was man selbst will,
3. Wenn man einen neuen Job möchte,
4. Wenn man in einer Klausur eine Menge dumme Fehler gemacht hat,

a. ärgert man sich.
b. muss man sich darum bewerben.
c. lacht man.
d. ist man dickköpfig.

11-28 Meine Gefühle. Was passt zusammen?

1. Für die deutsche Geschichte
2. Vor den Klausuren in diesem Kurs
3. Über Fotos von meiner süßen Nichte
4. In meinen deutschen Freund
5. Auf den Besuch meiner deutschen Freunde

a. habe ich eigentlich nie Angst.
b. freue ich mich sehr.
c. interessiere ich mich sehr.
d. freue ich mich jederzeit.
e. habe ich mich beim Chatten im Internet verliebt.

11-29 Mein Leben an der Uni. Was passt zusammen?

1. An die Zeit nach der Uni
2. An einem Referat über die Berliner Mauer
3. Im nächsten Monat
4. Auf das Geld von meinen Eltern

a. muss ich mich für ein Hauptfach entscheiden.
b. habe ich noch nicht gedacht.
c. arbeite ich schon eine Woche.
d. muss ich oft viel zu lang warten.

11-30 Zusammengesetzte Nomen. Kombinieren Sie in jeder der zwei Gruppen die passenden Nomen.

▶ die Welt + der Krieg = **der** Weltkrieg

1. die Zeit
2. das Kristall
3. der Nazi
4. der Reichstag + **s**
5. das Volk + **s**
6. der Flüchtling + **s**

a. die Nacht
b. die Diktatur
c. die Reise
d. die Armee
e. die Frage
f. das Gebäude

Wörter unter der Lupe

Words as chameleons: *gleich*

As an adjective, **gleich** means *same*.

Monika und ich wurden im **gleichen** Jahr geboren.
*Monika and I were born in the **same** year.*

As an adverb, **gleich** has three meanings:

a. Expressing the idea of sameness, **gleich** means *equally*.

Monika und ich sind beide **gleich** intelligent.
*Monika and I are both **equally** intelligent.*

b. Expressing time, **gleich** means *right (away), immediately.*

Ich komme **gleich** nach dem Spiel.	*I'm coming **right** after the game.*
Ich komme **gleich**.	*I'm coming **right away (immediately)**.*
	*(OR:) I'll be **right** there.*

c. Expressing location, **gleich** means *right, directly.*

Die Bank ist **gleich** neben dem Postamt.	*The bank is **right** beside the post office.*

11-31 Was bedeutet *gleich*? *Same, equally, right (right away),* oder *right (directly)*?

1. Der Tennisplatz ist gleich hinter dem Studentenheim.
2. Die Jeans waren so billig, dass ich gleich zwei Paar gekauft habe.
3. Du hast ja genau das gleiche Kleid an wie ich!
4. Ich wohne gleich neben der Bäckerei Biehlmaier.
5. Steh gleich auf, Holger! Es ist schon zehn nach zehn.
6. Meine Schwester und ich spielen gleich gut Klavier.
7. Sind die beiden Hotels gleich teuer?

Predicting gender

All nouns with the suffixes **-heit** and **-keit** are *feminine* and most are derived from adjectives. The plural forms always end in **-en.** The suffix **-keit** is used whenever an adjective ends in **-lich** or **-ig.** Both suffixes frequently correspond to the English suffix *-ness.*

krank	*ill, sick*	**die Krankheit**	*illness, sickness*
freundlich	*friendly*	**die Freundlichkeit**	*friendliness*
richtig	*right, correct*	**die Richtigkeit**	*rightness, correctness*

Note that the German suffixes **-heit** and **-keit** do not always correspond to the English suffix *-ness.*

wichtig	*important*	**die Wichtigkeit**	*importance*
schön	*beautiful*	**die Schönheit**	*beauty*

Some adjectives are extended with **-ig** before the suffix **-keit** is added.

arbeitslos	*unemployed*	**die Arbeitslosigkeit**	*unemployment*

11-32 Was ist das? Form nouns from the following adjectives and give their English meanings. Adjectives marked with an asterisk must be extended with **-ig** before adding the suffix **-keit.**

1. dunkel
2. hell*
3. gesund
4. klar
5. frei

6. klug
7. dumm
8. schnell*
9. genau*

11.10 Alles zusammen

Zeitreise per Fahrrad (auf dem Mauerweg): ein Video

You have already listened to a group of Germans talk about life in the GDR and about the Berlin Wall in the **Video-Treff** of this chapter. In this section, you'll watch a short video produced by **Deutsche Welle**, Germany's public international broadcaster, about a bicycle tour of the places in Berlin where the Wall can still be seen and remembered. You'll also have a chance to find out more information about these sites and show the fruits of your research to your fellow students via a descriptive poster or PowerPoint slide **(PowerPoint-Seite)**.

Before you begin, consider the title of the video that follows the path of the former Berlin Wall: *Zeitreise per Fahrrad*. Why might this video be called a *Zeitreise?*

Schritt 1: Zum Ansehen

11-33 Zeitreise per Fahrrad (auf dem Mauerweg). Sehen Sie das Video einmal an. Welche wichtigen Orte auf dem Mauerweg hat Axel von Blomberg besucht? Wo war er zuerst, und wo zuletzt? Bringen Sie die folgenden Orte in die richtige Reihenfolge (1 = zuerst; 6 = zuletzt).

_____ das Brandenburger Tor, Symbol der Trennung – und der Einheit

_____ die East Side Gallery im Stadtteil Friedrichshain

_____ der Wachturm, ein Mahnmal im Berliner Stadtteil Alt-Treptow

_____ der Potsdamer Platz

_____ die Mauer-Gedenkstätte an der Bernauer Straße

_____ der ehemalige Grenzübergang Checkpoint Charlie

11-34 Schlüsselwörter. Sehen Sie das Video ein zweites Mal an. Dann schreiben Sie das passende Wort auf Englisch für die folgenden Schlüsselwörter.

1. Mauerweg
2. Wachturm
3. Grenzstreifen
4. Grenzübergang
5. grenzenlose Freiheit

Schritt 2: Zum Schreiben

11-35 Ein interessanter Ort in Berlin. Finden Sie im Internet weitere Informationen über einen Ort am Mauerweg oder anderswo° in Berlin, den Sie besonders   *elsewhere* interessant finden. Machen Sie dann ein Poster oder eine PowerPoint-Seite über diesen Ort, mit Bildern und mit Text. Beschreiben Sie den Ort und seine historische Bedeutung. Schreiben Sie auch, warum Sie diesen Ort gewählt haben.

Mögliche Orte:		
der Checkpoint Charlie	das Sony-Center	der Tempelhofer
die East Side Gallery	die Gedenkstätte Berliner	Flughafen / das
das Brandenburger Tor	Mauer in der Bernauer	Tempelhofer
die Museumsinsel	Straße	Feld
das Reichstagsgebäude	das Olympiastadion	der Fernsehturm auf
der Mauerpark	das Holocaust-	dem Alexanderplatz
der Berliner Zoo	Mahnmal	das Schloss Sanssouci

Schreibtipp!
Be sure to use the simple past tense when writing about events that happened at the Berlin site you chose and the present tense when describing the situation today. Use time indicators like **damals, im November 1989, heute,** or **ehemalig** to help make this distinction.

Pflastersteine markieren heute den Verlauf der Mauer am Potsdamer Platz.

Schritt 3: Zum Präsentieren

11-36 Mein Ort in Berlin. Präsentieren Sie Ihr Poster oder Ihre PowerPoint-Seite und beschreiben Sie für Ihre Kleingruppe Ihren Ort.

Hier sind ein paar mögliche Ausdrücke für Ihre Präsentation:
    Auf dem Mauerweg habe ich … gewählt. In der DDR-Zeit hat man hier …
    Mein Ort in Berlin ist … Das ist historisch interessant, weil …
    Ich finde es faszinierend, dass man hier …

Kapitel 12
So ist das Leben

Eve und Steve relaxen in einem Biergarten.

Learning Objectives

12.1 Discuss the status of women in Germany

12.2 Learn vocabulary to talk about future work, hopes, and dreams

12.3 Learn to pronounce glottal stops in German

12.4 Talk about contrary-to-fact situations

12.5 Express wishes and polite requests

12.6 Make polite requests

12.7 Explore opportunities for civic engagement using German

12.8 Talk about how things might have been

12.9 Use common genitive prepositions

12.10 Understand authentic video about how to spend a windfall fortune

12.11 Learn vocabulary used to apply for volunteer or work opportunities

12.1 Vorschau

Annett Louisan wurde 1977 in Havelberg im Bundesland Sachsen-Anhalt geboren.
„Eve" ist ein Lied von ihrem zweiten, sehr erfolgreichen Album Unausgesprochen.

Kennen Sie das Lied „Eve" von Annett Louisan? Suchen Sie es im Internet
und lesen Sie mit, während sie singt.

EVE
von Annett Louisan

meine Freundin Eve ist aktiv,
denkt immer positiv
kennt kein Stimmungstief
ihr Freund Steve
5 ist sportiv.

sie ist porentief rein und attraktiv
sie ist kreativ, dekorativ, sensitiv
sie lebt intensiv
für die Art wie mich das ankotzt gibt's kein Adjektiv
10 seh' ich Eve, sag' ich: „Na, Eve …"
treff' ich Eve, sag' ich: „Na, Eve …"

doch bei Eve geht nie 'was schief
sie ist sehr kommunikativ
überzeugt argumentativ
15 instinktiv
meistert Eve
spielend den Beruf
und den Alltagsmief

sie ist progressiv, alternativ
20 innovativ, sehr impulsiv
geschickt und effektiv
ich hasse sie abgrundtief
seh' ich Eve, sag' ich: „Na, Eve …"
treff' ich Eve, sag' ich: „Na, Eve …"

25 wär' ich Eve, hätt' ich Steve.
mein Leben wär' erfüllt
und nicht so primitiv
wäre, würde, rein fiktiv
was wär' wenn's für mich besser lief'
30 vollkommen bin ich leider nur
im Konjunktiv

seh' ich Eve, macht mich das aggressiv
treff' ich Eve, wechsle ich die Straßenseite
und zwar demonstrativ

12-1 Was ist das auf Englisch?

1. Eve ist sehr kommunikativ und **überzeugt** mich mit guten Argumenten.
2. Wenn ich Eve treffe, **wechsle** ich die Straßenseite.
3. Ich **hasse** sie, weil sie so schön ist.
4. Bei Eve **geht** nie was **schief.**
5. **Wenn ich** schön **wäre,** hätte ich auch einen tollen Freund.
6. Es **kotzt mich an,** dass sie in allem so talentiert ist!
7. Sie **ist porentief rein** und attraktiv.
8. **Na?** Wie geht's dir?

a. hate
b. makes me puke
c. has immaculate skin
d. what's up?
e. persuades
f. goes wrong
g. if I were
h. switch

12-2 Anders gesagt. Markieren Sie in Annett Louisans Lied die Aussagen, die etwa dasselbe bedeuten.

mood 1. Eve ist Optimistin und nie schlechter Laune°.

difficulties 2. Eve navigiert ohne Probleme durch alle Schwierigkeiten° bei der Arbeit oder zu Hause.

3. Ich kann nicht beschreiben, wie sehr ich sie hasse.

4. Weil sie so gut spricht, bringt Eve andere auf ihre Seite.

furious 5. Ich werde total wütend°, wenn ich Eve sehe.

6. Ich zeige Eve, dass ich sie nicht mag, wenn ich sie in der Stadt sehe.

7. Eves Freund macht viel Sport.

8. So perfekt wie Eve bin ich nur in meiner Imagination.

envious **12-3** Warum ist die Frau so neidisch° auf Eve? Markieren Sie die passenden Antworten.

☐ Weil Eve immer gut angezogen ist.

☐ Weil Eve einen attraktiven Freund hat.

☐ Weil Eves Eltern ihr immer Geld schicken.

constantly ☐ Weil Eve charismatisch ist.

☐ Weil das Leben von Eve perfekt ist.

☐ Weil Eve und Steve einen schnellen Sportwagen haben.

☐ Weil die Frau auch gern ein Fotomodell wäre.

☐ Weil das Leben der Frau nicht erfüllt ist.

☐ Weil Eve ständig° erzählt, wie gut ihr Freund küssen kann.

☐ Weil Eve auch im Beruf Erfolg hat.

12.2 Kultur 1

Frauen im 21. Jahrhundert

12.1 Discuss the status of women in Germany

12-4 Schlüsselwörter zur deutschen Demokratie. Lesen Sie die Definitionen und suchen Sie dazu das passende Wort auf Englisch.

1. Was sind **Grundrechte?** Das sind fundamentale Rechte, die alle Bürger haben.

2. Die **Verfassung** eines Landes ist ein Dokument, das die Grundrechte präsentiert.

3. Frauen **sind gleichberechtigt.** Das heißt, sie haben dieselben Rechte wie Männer.

4. Man bekommt in der Schule, an der Universität, in einem Praktikum oder in einem Jobtraining eine **Ausbildung.**

5. Wer gut ausgebildet ist, kommt in **höhere Positionen** und dann oft **in leitende Stellen.**

6. Die **Arbeitgeber** müssen Frauen gleich bezahlen, d. h. (das heißt) Frauen und Männer sollen dasselbe für die gleiche Arbeit verdienen.

7. Beide **Geschlechter,** Frauen und Männer, sollen dieselben Rechte haben.

employers	positions of leadership	have equal rights
more highly paid positions	constitution	basic rights
education	genders	

Die Verfassungen

In den Verfassungen der deutschsprachigen Länder steht, dass Frauen und Männer gleichberechtigt sind und dass Frauen deshalb auch die gleiche Bezahlung für gleichwertige Arbeit bekommen sollen. Auch für die Europäische Union hat die Gleichstellung der Geschlechter in allen Lebensbereichen[1] höchste Priorität (Artikel 3 der Europäischen Verfassung). Trotzdem gibt es immer noch einen großen Unterschied in der Bezahlung von Männern und Frauen.

Frauen zwischen Beruf und Familie

Ein Grund[2] dafür ist, dass viele ältere Frauen keine so gute Ausbildung haben und für besser bezahlte Berufe nicht qualifiziert sind. Aber auch jüngere und besser ausgebildete Frauen haben selten höhere Positionen. Wenn sie dann auch noch Mütter werden, wird ihre Karriere unterbrochen[3], und danach beginnen sie meist dort, wo sie aufgehört haben. Sie haben in den stressigen Jahren, in denen sie für Familie und Kinder sorgten[4], vieles gelernt, was in höheren Positionen oft wichtig ist, aber viele Arbeitgeber haben das noch nicht begriffen[5]. Viele Frauen möchten beides, Beruf und Familie, aber solange sie die meisten Aufgaben in Haushalt und Familie übernehmen[6], bleibt Gleichberechtigung im Beruf Utopie.

Angela Merkel, Deutschlands erste Bundeskanzlerin

Frauen in der Politik

Zum Glück[7] spielen Frauen in der Politik eine immer größere Rolle. Im November 2005 wurde Angela Merkel Deutschlands erste Bundeskanzlerin und sie

[1]*areas of life* [2]*reason* [3]*interrupted* [4]*cared*
[5]*grasped* [6]*take on* [7]*fortunately*

wurde 2009 und 2013 wiedergewählt. In der Schweiz wurde Doris Leuthard 2010 und 2017 zur Bundespräsidentin gewählt. So sah die Situation in der Politik 2017 aus:

Frauen im Kabinett ("Ministerinnen"):		Frauen im Parlament ("Abgeordnete"):	
Deutschland	6 Frauen (von 16)	Deutschland	37,1 % Frauen
Österreich	3 Frauen (von 13)	Österreich	30,6 % Frauen
die Schweiz	2 Frauen (von 7)	die Schweiz	33 % Frauen

Ach so!

Literally, **Abgeordnete** are persons who have been sent away to complete a professional task, in this case to represent the political interests of their constituents. Can you find out how many women are currently in the U.S. Congress or the Canadian Parliament, and in your state or provincial governments?

Aus den Verfassungen von drei deutschsprachigen Ländern:

All three constitutions guarantee gender equality. The Swiss constitution explicitly mentions equal pay for equal work by men and women. Can you find all the instances of the German word for *equal* in these excerpts?

Grundgesetz der Bundesrepublik Deutschland, Artikel 3

(1) Alle Menschen sind vor dem Gesetz gleich.
(2) Männer und Frauen sind gleichberechtigt. Der Staat fördert die tatsächliche Durchsetzung der

Verfassung der Republik Österreich, Artikel 7

(1) Alle Bundesbürger sind vor dem Gesetz gleich. Vorrechte der Geburt, des Geschlechtes, des Standes, der Klasse und des Bekenntnisses sind

Bundesverfassung der Schweiz, Artikel 8

(3) Mann und Frau sind gleichberechtigt. Das Gesetz sorgt für ihre rechtliche und tatsächliche Gleichstellung, vor allem in Familie, Ausbildung und Arbeit. Mann und Frau haben Anspruch auf gleichen Lohn für gleichwertige Arbeit.

12-5 Was ist wichtig für Frauen? Womit sind Frauen zufrieden? Dieses Schaubild zeigt, wie Frauen in Bayern in einer Studie diese Fragen beantwortet haben.

NEUE VOKABELN

nach Meinung der Frauen	*in the opinion of women*	**das Einkommen**	*income*
verfügbare Zeit	*time available*	**eine feste Beziehung**	*a stable relationship*
das Aussehen	*appearance, looks*	**die Zufriedenheit**	*satisfaction*
die Bildung	*education*	**die Wichtigkeit**	*importance*

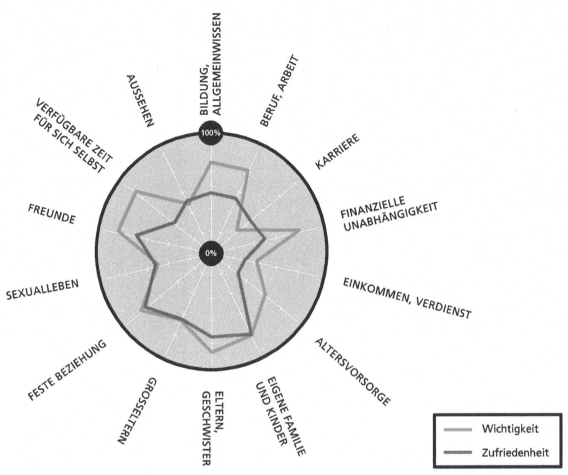

Lifestyles of young women and men in Bayern / Jutta Allmendinger, Sophie Krug von Nidda, Vanessa Wintermantel. Munich: Bayern Friedrich Ebert Foundation Forum, 2016. Page 29 Graph 3.3

1. Das Schaubild verstehen. Markieren Sie:

   a. Dieses Schaubild hat eine Kreisform. Auf der Außenseite des Kreises° gibt es _____ Lebensbereiche, über die Frauen gefragt wurden.   *circle*

      ☐ vierzehn   ☐ zwölf

   b. Im Kreis sieht man _____ Linien, die die Prozentzahl der Antworten zeigen.

      ☐ blaue   ☐ weiße

   c. Die Mitte des Kreises bedeutet _____ Prozent, und ein Punkt außen am Kreis bedeutet _____ Prozent.

      ☐ null ... einhundert   ☐ einhundert ... null

   d. Im Kreis zeigt die _____ Linie, wie wichtig etwas für Frauen ist.

      ☐ rote   ☐ blaue

   e. Im Kreis zeigt die _____ Linie, wie zufrieden Frauen mit etwas sind.

      ☐ rote   ☐ blaue

2. Was sind nach Meinung der Frauen die wichtigsten Lebensbereiche? Welche Bereiche finden Frauen nicht so wichtig? Mit welchen Lebensbereichen sind Frauen zufrieden?

3. Wo gibt es eine große Diskrepanz zwischen den roten und blauen Linien?

4. Welche Information aus dem Schaubild hat Sie überrascht?

5. **Meiner Meinung nach ...** Sprechen Sie mit Ihren Nachbarn. Welche Lebensbereiche sind Ihrer Meinung nach wichtig? Welche finden Sie nicht so wichtig? Haben Männer und Frauen in Ihrer Klasse unterschiedliche Meinungen zu diesen Fragen?

🔊 12.3 Wortschatz 1

Wichtige Vokabeln

12.2 Learn vocabulary to talk about future work, hopes, and dreams

Nomen

der Arbeitgeber, - die Arbeitgeberin, -nen	} employer
der Arbeitnehmer, - die Arbeitnehmerin, -nen	} employee
die Aufgabe, -n	assignment; task
die Ausbildung	education; job training
die Bezahlung	pay; salary
die Beziehung, -en	relationship
die Figur, -en	figure; physique
das Geschlecht, -er	gender
das Gesetz, -e	law
die Gleichberechtigung	equal rights; equality
der Grund, ̈e	reason; basis
der Haushalt, -e	household; housekeeping
der Kreis, -e	circle
die Laune, -n	mood
der Lebensbereich, -e	area of life; part of life
die Pore, -n	pore
die Schwierigkeit, -en	difficulty; trouble
die Verfassung, -en	constitution

> What are the literal meanings of **Arbeitgeber** and **Arbeitnehmer?**

Verben

begreifen, begriff, begriffen	to grasp; to comprehend
sorgen für	to take care of; to care for
übernehmen (übernimmt), übernahm, übernommen	to take on (a duty)
überzeugen	to persuade
unterbrechen (unterbricht), unterbrach, unterbrochen	to interrupt

> When **über-** and **unter-** are prefixed to verbs, they are usually inseparable.

Andere Wörter

eifersüchtig	jealous
fest	stable; firm
gleich	equal
ständig	constant(ly)
solange	as long as
unterschiedlich	varied

Ausdrücke

meiner Meinung nach	in my opinion
neidisch auf (+ acc)	envious of
gleichberechtigt sein	to have equal rights
gut ausgebildet sein	to be well-educated, to be well-trained
Karriere machen	to get ahead in one's career
den Haushalt machen	to do the housework
zum Glück	fortunately, luckily
wütend auf (+ acc)	furious at

Das Gegenteil

ich bin guter Laune ≠ ich bin schlechter Laune	I'm in a good mood ≠ I'm in a bad mood
positiv ≠ negativ	positive ≠ negative
unterschiedlich ≠ gleich	different ≠ same; equal(ly)
zufrieden (mit) ≠ unzufrieden (mit)	satisfied (with) ≠ unsatisfied (with)

Synonyme

das Einkommen = der Verdienst

Leicht zu verstehen

die Diskrepanz, -en	die Utopie, -n
das Kabinett, -e	
die Karriere, -n	aggressiv
das Parlament, -e	
die Position, -en	impulsiv
das Prozent, -e	instinktiv
	qualifiziert

> There are 25 members of Parliament **(Landtag)** in Liechtenstein. In 2017, five of them were women.

Parlament und Regierungsgebäude in Liechtenstein

Wörter im Kontext

12-6 Mit anderen Worten. Ergänzen Sie die Sätze in der rechten Spalte° so, dass sie   *column*
etwa dasselbe bedeuten wie die Sätze in der linken Spalte.

Aufgabe / gleichberechtigt / Karriere / unterbrichst / qualifiziert / Laune / ständig

1. Warum lässt du mich denn nie fertig   Warum _____ du mich denn
   reden?   immer?

2. Ich bin heute wütend und frustriert!   Ich bin heute schlechter _____!

3. Was soll ich tun?   Was ist meine _____?

4. Gina hat eine sehr gute Ausbildung.   Gina ist hoch _____.

5. Gina bekommt sicher mal eine hohe   Gina macht bestimmt mal _____.
   Position.

6. Im Grundgesetz der BRD steht, dass   Im Grundgesetz steht, dass Frauen und
   Frauen und Männer dieselben Rechte   Männer _____ sind.
   haben.

7. Sag doch nicht immer dasselbe!   Sag doch nicht _____ dasselbe!

Schrittgeschwindigkeit fahren

Fußgänger sind gleichberechtigt

Kinderspiele sind erlaubt

Ach so!
Schrittgeschwindigkeit =
walking speed.

12-7 Was passt zusammen?

1. Wenn Eves Freund eine bessere   a. muss Steve sie überzeugen.
   Bezahlung als Eve für die gleiche
   Arbeit bekommt,
                                          b. muss sie ein gutes Einkommen haben.
2. Wenn Eve nicht ins Kino gehen
   möchte,
                                          c. ist Eve nicht gleichberechtigt.
3. Wenn Eve und Steve eine feste
   Beziehung haben,
                                          d. ist sie guter Laune.
4. Wenn Eve ihre neue Position bei
   BMW anfängt,
                                          e. übernimmt sie sofort ein wichtiges Projekt.
5. Wenn Eves Mutter krank wird,

6. Wenn Eve zufrieden mit ihrem   f. dann bleiben sie lange zusammen.
   Leben ist,

7. Wenn Eve einen 5er BMW kaufen   g. muss sie für sie sorgen.
   möchte,

12-8 Mit anderen Worten. Ergänzen Sie die Sätze in der rechten Spalte so, dass sie
etwa dasselbe bedeuten wie die Sätze in der linken Spalte.

Schwierigkeiten / Haushalt / begriffen / unterschiedlich / Arbeitgeber / ausgebildet

1. Robert war auf einer sehr guten Uni.   Robert ist gut _____.

2. Anna weiß nicht, was sie tun soll.   Anna hat nicht _____, was sie
                                              tun soll.

3. Eve und Steve sind nicht einer   Ihre Meinungen sind _____.
   Meinung.

4. Paul ist nicht sehr gut in Physik.   Paul hat _____ in seinen
                                              Physikkursen.

5. Laura arbeitet bei BMW.   BMW ist Lauras _____.

6. Wer kocht und putzt bei euch?   Wer macht bei euch den _____?

12.4 Zur Aussprache

The glottal stop

12.3 Learn to pronounce glottal stops in German

In order to distinguish *an ice boat* from *a nice boat* in pronunciation, you use a glottal stop, i.e., you momentarily stop and then restart the flow of air to your voice box before saying the word *ice*. The glottal stop is much more frequent in German than in English. It occurs before words and syllables that begin with a vowel.

12-9 Hören Sie gut zu und wiederholen Sie!

1. Onkel __Alfred __ist __ein __alter __Esel!

enterben: *disinherit*

2. Tante __Emma will __uns __alle __ent__erben°!

3. Be__eilt __euch! __Esst __euer __Eis __auf!

4. Lebt __ihr __in __Ober__ammergau __oder __in __Unter__ammergau?

In Oberammergau (Bayern) gibt es außerordentliche Häuser.

Sprachnotiz   The future tense

You can use the present tense to express that something is going to happen in the future, as long as the context refers to future time.

Nächstes Jahr **studiere** ich im Ausland.	*Next year I'm going to study abroad.*
In zwei Jahren **bewerbe** ich **mich** um ein Praktikum in Deutschland.	*In two years I'm going to apply for an internship in Germany.*

You can also use the future tense to express the same idea. The future tense consists of the auxiliary verb **werden** and an infinitive:

Nächstes Jahr **werde** ich im Ausland **studieren.**	*Next year I'm going to study abroad.*
In zwei Jahren **werde** ich **mich** um ein Praktikum in Deutschland **bewerben.**	*In two years I'm going to apply for an internship in Germany.*

12.5 Kommunikation und Formen 1

The subjunctive in contrary-to-fact situations

12.4 Talk about contrary-to-fact situations

Present-time subjunctive

In English, when you talk about something that is contrary to the facts, you often use a different verb form than you do for factual statements.

FACT

*I **have** only fifty dollars.*

CONTRARY-TO-FACT

*If only I **had** a million dollars!*

The form *had* in the contrary-to-fact example is not the simple past and does not refer to past time. It is a subjunctive form of the verb *to have* and it refers to the present. By using subjunctive forms you indicate that what you are saying is contrary-to-fact.

I *don't* **have** a car.	If only I **had** a car!
David **isn't** here.	If only David **were** here!
David **has to** work and **can't** pick me up.	If David **didn't have to** work, he **could** pick me up.
I *don't* **know** where the nearest bus stop is.	If only I **knew** where the nearest bus stop was.

In German, you also use subjunctive forms to talk about contrary-to-fact situations. As in English, these subjunctive forms are very similar in form to the simple past, but they refer to present time.

Ich **habe** keinen Wagen.	Wenn ich nur einen Wagen **hätte!**
David **ist** nicht hier.	Wenn David nur hier **wäre!**
David **muss** arbeiten und **kann** mich nicht abholen.	Wenn David nicht arbeiten **müsste,** **könnte** er mich abholen.
Ich **weiß** nicht, wo die nächste Bushaltestelle ist.	Wenn ich nur **wüsste,** wo die nächste Bushaltestelle ist!

> **überlegen** means *to think about.* Are you familiar with the English parallel to this piece of wisdom? It starts with "Be careful what you ..."

The forms of the present-time subjunctive are derived from the simple past. Below are the subjunctive forms of **haben, sein, werden, wissen,** and the modals. Except for **sollte** and **wollte,** these forms are all umlauted.

Infinitive	Simple past	Subjunctive
haben	hatte	**hätte**
sein	war	**wäre**
werden	wurde	**würde**
wissen	wusste	**wüsste**
dürfen	durfte	**dürfte**
können	konnte	**könnte**
mögen	mochte	**möchte**
müssen	musste	**müsste**
sollen	sollte	**sollte**
wollen	wollte	**wollte**

In the subjunctive, all verbs have the following set of personal endings, which you learned earlier when learning **möchte** (also a subjunctive form, *would like to*).

Look how closely **hätte** resembles **hatte**, the simple past tense of **haben.** The addition of an umlaut changes the meaning completely: from *had* (past tense) to *would have* (subjunctive)!

Singular		Plural	
ich	hätt**e**	wir	hätt**en**
du	hätt**est**	ihr	hätt**et**
er/es/sie	hätt**e**	sie	hätt**en**
Sie hätt**en**			

Singular		Plural	
ich	wär**e**	wir	wär**en**
du	wär**est**	ihr	wär**et**
er/es/sie	wär**e**	sie	wär**en**
Sie wär**en**			

English equivalents for these forms often (but not always) include the auxiliary verb *would.*

Wenn du nicht so eifersüchtig **wärst,** **hätten** wir eine bessere Beziehung.

*If you **weren't** so jealous, we **would have** a better relationship.*

Du **könntest** doch versuchen, nicht immer so eifersüchtig zu sein.

*You **could** really try not to be so jealous all the time.*

When using the subjunctive of **sein,** the **-e-** in **du wärest** and **ihr wäret** is often omitted: **du wärst, ihr wärt.**

12-10 Was passt zusammen?

1. Wenn ich Pauls E-Mail-Adresse wüsste,
2. Wenn Moritz nicht so aggressiv wäre,
3. Wenn ich krank würde,
4. Wenn mein Deutsch sehr gut wäre,
5. Wenn ich mit 22 ein kleines Kind hätte und weiter arbeiten wollte,

child care

6. Wenn ich keine gute Kinderbetreuung finden könnte,

a. dürfte ich meine Klausur später schreiben.
b. hätte er bestimmt mehr Freunde.
c. könnte ich ihm schreiben.
d. müsste ich meine Karriere unterbrechen.
e. könnte ich in Deutschland ein Praktikum machen.
f. müsste ich eine gute Kinderbetreuung° finden.

12-11 Wenn das Leben nur nicht so kompliziert wäre! Ergänzen Sie Konjunktivformen.

1. Holger **hat** kein Fahrrad und **will** deshalb immer mein Fahrrad leihen. Ich mag das gar nicht, aber ich **kann** nicht nein sagen.

   Wenn Holger nur ein Fahrrad _____!

   Wenn Holger nur nicht immer mein Fahrrad leihen _____!

   Wenn ich nur „nein" sagen _____!

2. Es **ist** sehr heiß, aber weil ich erkältet **bin, darf** ich nicht schwimmen gehen.

   Wenn es nur nicht so heiß _____!

   Wenn ich nur nicht erkältet _____!

   Wenn ich nur schwimmen gehen _____!

12-12 Probleme mit der Liebe! Ergänzen Sie Konjunktivformen.

1. TILMANN DENKT: Schade°, dass ich Nicoles Telefonnummer nicht weiß!

   too bad

   Wenn ich ihre Nummer _____, _____ ich sie anrufen. (wissen / können)

   Wenn sie viele Hausaufgaben _____, _____ ich ihr helfen. (haben / können)

2. NICOLE DENKT: Gut, dass Tilmann meine Telefonnummer nicht weiß!

   Wenn er meine Nummer _____, _____ er mich anrufen. (wissen / können)

   Dann _____ ich sagen, ich _____ zu viele Hausaufgaben. (müssen / haben)

Würde + infinitive

To talk about a contrary-to-fact situation, you've learned how to use the subjunctive forms for **haben, sein, werden, wissen,** and the modals. For all other verbs, the German construction is parallel to English: You use *would + infinitive:* **würde** + *infinitive.*

Was **würdest** du **tun,** wenn dein Freund nie romantisch wäre?

*What **would** you **do** if your boyfriend were never romantic?*

Ich **würde** mir einen anderen Freund **suchen!**

*I **would look for** another boyfriend!*

Singular		Plural	
ich	würde suchen	wir	würden suchen
du	würdest suchen	ihr	würdet suchen
er/es/sie	würde suchen	sie	würden suchen
	Sie würden suchen		

Ach so!
These are the same endings as the ones for **wurde,** the simple past tense of **werden.** The umlaut changes this verb meaning completely: **würde** means *would!*

12-13 Ich brauche Hilfe! Was würdest du tun?

▶ Ich bin immer so müde.

   S1: Ich bin immer so müde. Was würdest du tun?

zum Arzt gehen

   S2: Ich würde zum Arzt gehen.

1. Ich kann nachts nicht schlafen.

2. Ich habe kein Geld mehr.

3. Ich habe Halsschmerzen.

mir einen Job suchen	weniger Kaffee trinken	ein langweiliges Buch lesen
mehr Sport machen		eine Schlaftablette nehmen
mit Salzwasser gurgeln	heißen Tee trinken	meine Eltern anrufen

4. Ich darf in meinem Zimmer keine laute Musik spielen.

5. Ich bin immer so nervös.

6. Mein Mitbewohner trinkt zu viel Alkohol.

Yoga machen	Kopfhörer kaufen	ihm sagen, dass das ungesund ist
mehr schlafen	mir ein neues Zimmer suchen	Kaffee aufgeben

12-14 Meine Wünsche und Träume für meine Karriere. Sprechen Sie mit einem Partner/einer Partnerin über Ihre Träume für den zukünftigen Beruf. Stellen Sie einander folgende Fragen:

- Was für Arbeit würdest du gern machen? *Ich würde gern …*
- Was wäre dein Traumberuf? *Mein Traumberuf wäre …*
- Für welche Firma möchtest du am liebsten arbeiten? *Ich würde am liebsten für …*
- Welche Fähigkeiten müsstest du für deinen Traumberuf haben? *Für meinen Traumberuf müsste ich …*
- Welche Fähigkeiten hast du schon, und welche müsstest du noch lernen? *Ich kann schon sehr gut … aber ich müsste besser …*

The subjunctive in wishes and polite requests

12.5 Express wishes and polite requests

In *Kapitel 4* you learned that **ich möchte** expresses wishes or requests more politely than **ich will,** and you have since used the **möchte-**forms without necessarily realizing that they are subjunctive forms.

Ich **will** ein Glas Bier.	I **want** a glass of beer.
Ich **möchte** ein Glas Bier.	I **would like** a glass of beer.

You can also express wishes or requests by using phrases like **hätte gern, wäre gern,** or **wüsste gern.**

Ich **hätte gern** Geld für einen Urlaub.	I **would like to have** money for a vacation.
Ich **wäre** jetzt **gern** in Hawaii.	I **would like to be** in Hawaii now.
Wir **wüssten gern,** was wir für dieses Quiz lernen müssen.	We **would like to know** what we have to study for this quiz.

wishes  **12-15 Wünsche°.**

S1: Was hätte Bernd gern?   **S2:** Er hätte gern ein Praktikum beim Bundestag.

Ich heiße …	Bernd	Karin
Ich hätte gern …	ein Prakikum beim Bundestag	einen Roboter
Ich wäre gern …	beim Skilaufen in den Alpen	zu Hause vor meinem Computer
Ich wüsste gern, …	was für eine Zensur ich für mein Referat bekomme	warum der Himmel blau ist

 12-16 Was sind deine Wünsche?

S1: Was hättest du gern?   **S2:** Ich hätte gern …
Wo wärst du jetzt gern?   Ich wäre jetzt gern …
Was wüsstest du gern?   Ich wüsste gern, …

12-17 Kurze Gedichte zum Thema: *ich.* Hier ist ein Gerüst° für ein *ich-Gedicht.* *framework*
Ergänzen Sie Zeile 1 mit drei Adjektiven. Dann schreiben Sie ein passendes Ende
zu den Sätzen.

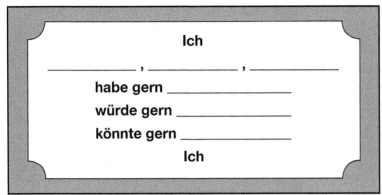

> **Achtung!**
>
> The first open-ended sentence
> is *not* subjunctive, so be sure
> you use this one to write about
> what you really do like to do or
> have: **... habe gern Freunde.**
> Vary the subjunctive if you
> like by using **müsste** or other
> modal verbs from this chapter.

The subjunctive in polite questions

12.6 Make polite requests

You can also formulate questions more politely by using **haben, sein, werden,
wissen,** and the modal verbs in present-time subjunctive.

Könnten Sie mir bitte sagen, wo die Apotheke ist?	*Could you please tell me where the pharmacy is?*
Wüssten Sie, wann der Bus kommt?	*Would you know when the bus will come?*

12-18 Höfliche Fragen. Sie sind neu an der Uni und brauchen Hilfe.
Formulieren Sie höfliche Fragen für die Mitarbeiter im Auslandsamt.

S1: Wo ist hier eine Apotheke?   **S2: Könnten** Sie mir bitte sagen, wo hier
                                                      eine Apotheke ist?

S2: Wo ist hier ein Supermarkt?   **S1: Wüssten** Sie vielleicht, wo hier
                                                      ein Supermarkt ist?

1. Wo ist hier eine gute Bäckerei?
2. Wo ist das Uni-Kino?
3. Wo ist die Universitätsbibliothek?
4. Wo ist die beste Mensa auf dem Campus?
5. Wo finde ich einen guten Supermarkt?
6. Wo sind die Tennisplätze?

Sprachnotiz   *Kommen* and *gehen* in present-time subjunctive

Instead of **würde** + infinitive you will also commonly read and hear present-
time subjunctive forms of verbs other than **haben, sein, werden, wissen,** and the
modals. The most frequent are:

ich **käme** = ich würde kommen   ich **ginge** = ich würde gehen

12.6 Kultur 2

Freiwilligendienst in Deutschland und Europa

12.7 Explore opportunities for civic engagement using German

> Freiwilligendienst leisten? Das heißt: ✓sich Zeit nehmen,
> ✓anderen helfen,
> ✓sich entwickeln,
> ✓den Horizont erweitern.
> Sagt JA zum Freiwilligendienst!

12-19 Schlüsselwörter zum Thema Freiwilligendienst. Lesen Sie die Definitionen und suchen Sie dazu das passende Wort auf Englisch.

Ach so!
A **gemeinnützige Organisation** is a not-for-profit entity designed to benefit a group of people in the community **(die Gemeinschaft)** with important needs they share. A **Gemeinde** is the word for a church or churches of the same faith working in a single area (i.e., a parish or congregation).

1. Eine Stelle, bei der man nichts verdient, ist eine **unbezahlte Stelle.**
2. Wenn man **ehrenamtlich aushilft,** bekommt man keine Bezahlung dafür. Das heißt, man arbeitet **freiwillig.**
3. Bei einem **bezahlten Freiwilligendienst** bekommt man ein wenig Geld, um einige Lebenskosten zu decken.
4. Manche **Freiwilligendienstler** arbeiten im Bereich der Kinderbetreuung.
5. In der **Kinderbetreuung** arbeitet man mit Kindern während oder nach der Schule. Man gibt Nachhilfe, spielt Spiele oder **beschäftigt** Kinder in der Freizeit.
6. Wenn man im **sozialen Bereich** dient, hilft man Menschen, die ärmer oder schwächer sind.
7. Man hilft zum Beispiel **alleinstehenden** Müttern oder älteren Menschen.
8. Bei einem Freiwilligendienst **im Ausland** lernt man eine neue Kultur kennen.

unpaid position	child care	volunteer workers	single, alone
paid volunteer position	abroad	works as a volunteer	social services field
occupies, does activities	voluntarily		

Ich arbeite gern mit Kleinkindern.

Was ist Freiwilligendienst?

In der Bundesrepublik Deutschland engagieren sich jährlich 30,9 Millionen Menschen freiwillig. Wer Zeit hat und helfen will, arbeitet meistens ohne Bezahlung bei verschiedenen gemeinnützigen Organisationen, Kirchen und Vereinen. In Schulen oder Seniorenheimen, bei Integrationsprojekten, in Theatern oder Museen, überall, wo Hilfe gebraucht wird, können Freiwillige dienen. Es gibt **geförderte** (d. h. bezahlte) und **nicht geförderte** (unbezahlte) Freiwilligendienste, sowie **Kurzzeit-** und **Langzeitdienste.**

Welche Bereiche gibt es beim Freiwilligendienst?

In Deutschland gibt es gemeinnützige Projekte in den folgenden Hauptbereichen:

- **Soziales (Bildung, Kinderbetreuung, Seniorenbetreuung, Hilfe für Obdachlose):** In diesem Bereich arbeitet man vor allem mit Menschen, die Anknüpfung an andere Menschen brauchen und schätzen. Man arbeitet in Schulen oder hilft Kindern nach der Schule, damit alle Kinder und Jugendliche einen guten Start in ihr Leben haben. Man kocht bei einer Kirche, die einen Mittagstisch (ein warmes Essen) für alleinstehende oder obdachlose Menschen vorbereitet, oder hilft älteren Menschen im Seniorenheim. Dort spielt man z.B. Gesellschafts- und Kartenspiele mit Senioren, die tagsüber eine sinnvolle Beschäftigung suchen.

- **Umweltschutz:** Wer sich für die Umwelt oder für Nachhaltigkeit interessiert, sucht sich im Bereich Umweltschutz eine passende Dienststelle. Man arbeitet bei gemeinnützigen Organisationen für den Umweltschutz oder bei einer Ökostation, in der man mit Kindern Projekte zum Thema Nachhaltigkeit macht. Einige Freiwilligendienstler bauen oder säubern Waldwege im Grünen.

- **Integration (Flüchtlingsbetreuung, Integrationshilfe):** In diesem Bereich hilft man Menschen aus anderen Ländern bei vielen Aspekten der Integration. Man kümmert sich um Essen, frisches Trinkwasser, oder Kleider für neu angekommene Flüchtlinge oder sucht für Flüchtlinge nach passenden Wohnungen. Freiwilligendienstler betreuen auch Kindergruppen, damit die Erwachsenen einen Deutschkurs machen können. Einige Freidienstleistende erteilen selber Deutschunterricht oder Nachhilfe für Kinder.

- **Kultur (Theater, Musik) oder Sport:** Wer musikalisch oder dramatisch begabt ist, kann sich um einen Einsatz im kulturellen Bereich bewerben. Freiwillige Helfer in diesem Bereich organisieren Theater-Workshops oder beschäftigen Jugendliche nach der Schule mit Musik- oder Puppentheater. Kunstfreudige Dienstler arbeiten ehrenamtlich in städtischen Museen. Sportler betreuen einen Klub oder Verein für Jugendliche oder für ältere Menschen.

Ich interessiere mich für Nachhaltigkeitsprojekte.

Kann man auch im Ausland dienen?

Wer zwischen 18–26 Jahren alt ist, etwas mehr Zeit hat, und Erfahrung im Ausland sucht, kann sich um einen Platz im Freiwilligendienst im Ausland bewerben. Meistens dient man 6–18 Monate. Der Auslandsdienst wird auch betreut: es gibt ca. zweimal im Monat Seminare, die man neben dem Dienst macht. So lernt man mehr über die Arbeit, Menschen und Kultur im Ausland. Im Normalfall wohnen und essen Freiwilligendienstler nicht weit von der Dienststelle auf Kosten der Organisation. Freiwilligendienstler bekommen auch ein kleines Taschengeld.

Wollt ihr mehr über den Freiwilligendienst lernen?

Das Bundesministerium für Familie, Senioren, Frauen und Jugend (BMFSFJ) verwaltet eine Zentrale für den Freiwilligendienst in Deutschland und im Ausland. Durch eine einfache Websuche im Internet findet ihr Weiteres über einen möglichen Einsatz.

12-20 Einen Freiwilligendienst finden. Was für ein Freiwilligendienst passt am besten zu Ihnen? Füllen Sie das Internetformular aus. Dann präsentieren Sie Ihre Interessen in einer Kleingruppe.

S1: Ich arbeite gern mit Kindern. Ich möchte einen bezahlten Dienst im Bereich Kinder- und Jugendbetreuung machen. Aber ich würde auch einen unbezahlten Dienst machen.

S2: Ich interessiere mich für die Umwelt. Ich würde am liebsten beim Umweltschutz dienen. Der Dienst könnte bezahlt oder unbezahlt sein.

Ich interessiere mich für einen Dienst in | Ort/Stadt:

Einsatzbereich(e)
- ☐ Kinder- und Jugendbetreuung
- ☐ Seniorenbetreuung
- ☐ Flüchtlingsbetreuung
- ☐ Kultur (Theater, Musik)
- ☐ Sport
- ☐ Umweltschutz, Nachhaltigkeit

Ich suche einen Freiwilligendienst, der …
- ☐ bezahlt ist.
- ☐ unbezahlt ist.
- ☐ bezahlt oder unbezahlt sein kann.
- ☐ im Ausland ist.

12.7 Kommunikation und Formen 2

The subjunctive in contrary-to-fact situations in the past

12.8 Talk about how things might have been

Past-time subjunctive

To talk about past-time contrary-to-fact situations, you use the past participle of the verb with the appropriate auxiliary in the subjunctive (i.e., a form of **wäre** or **hätte**).

FACT	CONTRARY-TO-FACT
Ich **bin** zu schnell **gefahren.**	Wenn ich nur nicht zu schnell **gefahren wäre!**
I was driving too fast.	*If only I hadn't been driving too fast!*
Ich **habe** einen Strafzettel **bekommen.**	Wenn ich nur keinen Strafzettel **bekommen hätte!**
I got a ticket.	*If only I hadn't gotten a ticket!*

Note that in past-time subjunctive, German never uses **würde**.

Meine Eltern **wären** nicht zu schnell **gefahren.**	*My parents wouldn't have driven too fast.*
Und sie **hätten** keinen Strafzettel **bekommen.**	*And they wouldn't have gotten a ticket.*

12-21 Wenn wir nur nicht so dumm gewesen wären! Ergänzen Sie die passenden Partizipien und **hätte(n)** oder **wäre(n).**

1. Gestern **sind** wir nicht in unsere Vorlesungen **gegangen,** sondern **haben** Günter **angerufen** und **haben** den ganzen Tag mit ihm Videospiele **gespielt.**

   Wenn wir nur in unsere Vorlesungen _____ _____!

   Wenn wir nur Günter nicht _____ _____!

   Wenn wir nur nicht den ganzen Tag mit Günter Videospiele _____ _____!

2. Gestern Nachmittag **habe** ich mich auf die Couch **gelegt** und **bin** gleich **eingeschlafen.** Deshalb **habe** ich mein Referat nicht fertig **geschrieben.**

   Wenn ich mich nur nicht auf die Couch _____ _____!

   Wenn ich nur nicht _____ _____!

   Wenn ich nur mein Referat fertig _____ _____!

regrets

12-22 Wenn ich das nur getan oder nicht getan hätte! Jeder Mensch tut manchmal Dinge, die er später bereut°. Erzählen Sie Ihren Mitstudenten ein paar Dinge, die Sie bereuen.

S1: Wenn ich nur meine Hausaufgaben gemacht hätte!

S2: Wenn ich nur gestern Nacht nicht so lange aufgeblieben wäre!

S3: …

12-23 Was hättest du getan, wenn …?

▶   Jemand hat meinen Wagen gestohlen.   … sofort zur Polizei gegangen.

S1: Was hättest du getan, wenn jemand   **S2:** Ich wäre sofort zur Polizei
deinen Wagen gestohlen hätte?   gegangen.

1. Ich habe eine Geldtasche mit 300 Dollar gefunden.
2. Meine Eltern haben mir verboten, in die Kneipe zu gehen.
3. Die Verkäuferin hat mir zehn Dollar zu viel herausgegeben.
4. Mir ist in Europa das Geld ausgegangen.
5. Ich habe in Europa meinen Pass verloren.

… mit ihr darüber gesprochen.	… meine Eltern angerufen.
… sofort zum nächsten Konsulat gegangen.	… ihr das Geld sofort zurückgegeben.
… damit zur Polizei gegangen.	

Wenn ich nur nicht so lange Beachvolleyball gespielt hätte! Dann hätte ich jetzt keinen Sonnenbrand!

Haben and *sein* in past-time subjunctive

In *Kapitel 5* you learned that most speakers of German use the simple past of **haben** and **sein** instead of the perfect tense to refer to past events.

Weil ich heute eine Klausur **hatte, war**   *Because I **had** a test today, I **wasn't** at Laura's*
ich gestern nicht auf Lauras Fete.   *party yesterday.*

However, when **haben** and **sein** are the main verbs in past-time contrary-to-fact situations, you need to use the past participles of these verbs.

Wenn ich heute keine Klausur **gehabt**   *If I **hadn't had** a test today, I **would have***
hätte, wäre ich gestern auf Lauras   ***been** at Laura's party yesterday.*
Fete **gewesen.**

12-24 Was hättest du gemacht, wenn …? Ergänzen Sie **wäre, hätte** oder **hättest.**

▶ …, wenn es gestern nicht so heiß gewesen _____?

Ich _____ Tennis gespielt.

S1: Was hättest du gemacht, wenn es gestern nicht so heiß gewesen wäre?

S2: Ich hätte Tennis gespielt.

1. …, wenn wir letzten Winter mehr Schnee gehabt _____?

2. …, wenn du letztes Wochenende mehr Geld gehabt _____?

3. …, wenn es letzten Sonntag nicht so kalt gewesen _____?

4. …, wenn dein Drucker gestern Nacht plötzlich nicht mehr genug Toner gehabt _____?

5. …, wenn das Konzert gestern Abend nicht gut gewesen _____?

6. …, wenn dein Fahrrad heute früh einen Platten° gehabt _____? *flat tire*

Ich _____ in einem teuren Restaurant gegessen.	Ich _____ den Bus genommen.
Ich _____ mein Referat von Hand fertig geschrieben.	Ich _____ Skilaufen gegangen.
Ich _____ aufgestanden und rausgegangen.	Ich _____ baden gegangen.

Expressing cause, opposition, alternatives, and simultaneity

12.9 Use common genitive prepositions

Genitive prepositions

The following prepositions require an object in the genitive case.

wegen	because of	**Wegen des Schneesturms** waren gestern keine Vorlesungen.
trotz	in spite of	Eve ist **trotz des Schneesturms** in die Bibliothek gegangen.
statt	instead of	Sie hat aber **statt einer Jacke** einen dicken Wintermantel angezogen.
während	during	Eve war **während des ganzen Schneesturms** in der Bibliothek.

Nur für Kunden während des Einkaufs.
Chip für die Ausfahrt an der Kasse.
◀ TICKET ZIEHEN **P**

Wann darf man hier parken?

12-25 *Wegen, trotz, statt* oder *während?*

1. Warum gehen wir nicht zu Bernd zum Kaffee trinken?

   Weil er _____ des Tages nicht zu Hause ist.

2. Warum war Sarah heute nicht in der Vorlesung?

   Weil sie _____ einer schweren Erkältung° im Bett bleiben musste.   *a bad cold*

3. Warum fühlt Laura sich denn nicht wohl?

   Weil sie _____ ihrer Erkältung tanzen gegangen ist.

4. Fährt Ralf immer noch seinen alten VW?

   Nein, er hat jetzt ein Motorrad _____ eines Wagens.

5. Warum spielst du dienstags nie mit uns Tennis?

   Weil ich _____ der Woche zu viel zu tun habe.

6. Isst du oft Fertiggerichte°?

   Nein, ich esse lieber Selbstgekochtes _____ Fertiggerichte.   *convenience foods*

7. Warum kaufst du deine Milch in Flaschen statt in Kartons?

   _____ der Umwelt.

8. Warum seid ihr denn so nass?

   Weil wir _____ des Regens zu Fuß zur Uni gegangen sind.

12-26 Aus der Verfassung der EU. Finden Sie drei Diskriminierungen, die von der EU-Verfassung verboten sind, die Sie ins Englische übersetzen können.

Artikel II-81: Nichtdiskriminierung

(1) Diskriminierungen insbesondere wegen des Geschlechts, der Rasse, der Hautfarbe, der ethnischen oder sozialen Herkunft, der genetischen Merkmale, der Sprache, der Religion oder der Weltanschauung, der politischen oder sonstigen Anschauung, der Zugehörigkeit zu einer nationalen Minderheit, des Vermögens, der Geburt, einer Behinderung, des Alters oder der sexuellen Ausrichtung sind verboten.

Deutsch	Englisch
wegen des Geschlechts	*because of /on the basis of gender*
wegen _____	_____
wegen _____	_____
wegen _____	_____

12.8 Video-Treff

Wenn ich im Lotto gewinnen würde, …

12.10 Understand authentic video about how to spend a windfall fortune

Anja Szustak und Kristina, Anja Peter, Öcsi, Stefan Meister und Stefan Kuhlmann
erzählen, was sie mit ihrem Lottogewinn tun würden. Machen Sie die erste Aufgabe,
Anders gesagt, bevor Sie das Video anschauen.

12-27 Anders gesagt.

1. Ich würde meinen Eltern einen Urlaub **spendieren.**
2. Ich würde einfach so **Kleinigkeiten** kaufen.
3. Ich würde einkaufen gehen, ohne aufs Geld zu **gucken.**
4. Ich würde 'n Job suchen, den ich **unbedingt** machen möchte.
5. Ich würde von den Zinsen leben, wenn es **richtig** viel Geld ist.
6. Dann würde ich beim nächsten Flug ins All **mitmachen.**

a. mitfliegen
b. sehen
c. absolut
d. bezahlen
e. kleine Sachen
f. sehr

12-28 Was passt? Ergänzen Sie die Aussagen mit der Information, die Sie im Video hören.

1. Mit so viel Geld würde Anja Szustak nach Australien oder ____ fliegen.

    ☐ Nordamerika ☐ Asien

2. Wenn sie im Lotto gewinnen würde, würde Kristina sich ____ kaufen.

    ☐ einen teuren Mantel ☐ ein teures Motorrad

3. Wenn sie reich wäre, würde Anja Peter ____ einen neuen Wagen kaufen.

    ☐ ihren Eltern ☐ ihrem Bruder

4. Mit 10 Millionen Euro würde Öcsi wahrscheinlich ____ kaufen.

    ☐ Land ☐ ein Haus

5. Öcsi möchte ____ in Dänemark verbringen.

    ☐ den Sommer ☐ den Winter

6. Wenn er so viel Geld hätte, würde Stefan Meister ____.

    ☐ nie wieder arbeiten ☐ einen interessanten Job finden

7. Stefan Kuhlmann möchte eine Wohnung in ____ verschiedenen Städten.

    ☐ drei ☐ zwei

12-29 Richtig oder falsch? Lesen Sie die Aussagen über Kristina, Anja Szustak, Anja Peter, Öcsi, Stefan Kuhlmann und Stefan Meister und ihre Pläne. Sind diese Aussagen richtig oder falsch? Wenn eine Aussage falsch ist, korrigieren Sie sie.

	RICHTIG	FALSCH
1. Hätte Kristina viel Geld, dann würde sie mit Freunden eine Reise machen.	☐	☐
2. Wenn Anja Szustak im Lotto gewinnen würde, dann würde sie sofort ins Reisebüro gehen.	☐	☐
3. Auch wenn sie im Lotto gewinnen würde, würde Anja Peter weiterstudieren.	☐	☐
4. Anja Peter würde auch eine Reise machen.	☐	☐
5. Öcsi hat sehr viele Ideen, wie er so viel Geld ausgeben könnte.	☐	☐
6. Wenn er richtig viel Geld hätte, würde Stefan Meister von den Zinsen leben.	☐	☐
7. Stefan Meister möchte mit dem Geld eine lange Reise machen.	☐	☐
8. Stefan Kuhlmann würde absolut nichts sparen.	☐	☐
9. Mit 10 Millionen Euro würde Stefan Kuhlmann als Allererstes überall hinreisen.	☐	☐
10. Stefan Kuhlmann hat schon seit langem den Traum, ins All zu fliegen.	☐	☐

))) 12.9 Wortschatz 2

Wichtige Vokabeln

12.11 Learn vocabulary used to apply for volunteer or work opportunities

Nomen

der Traum, ¨-e	dream
der Wunsch, ¨-e	wish
die Daten *(pl)*	data; information
der Dienst, -e	service
die Diskriminierung, -en	discrimination
die Erfahrung, -en	experience *(e.g., work)*
die Fähigkeit, -en	ability
das Interesse, -n	interest
die Kenntnis, -se	knowledge; skills
der Lebenslauf, ¨-e	résumé, CV
die Erkältung, -en	cold
der Strafzettel, -	(traffic) ticket
die Zinsen *(pl)*	(bank) interest

Verben

erfahren, erfuhr, erfahren	to learn of, come to know something
erledigen	to accomplish, take care of *(business)*
erwarten	to expect
herstellen	to produce
träumen	to dream
vollenden	to complete

Andere Wörter

stark	strong
statt *(+ gen)*	instead of
trotz *(+ gen)*	in spite of
während *(+ gen)*	during
wegen *(+ gen)*	because of

Ausdrücke

eifersüchtig auf *(+ acc)*	jealous of
einen Platten haben	to have a flat tire
eine schwere Erkältung	a bad cold
erkältet sein	to have a cold

Synonyme

freiwillig = ehrenamtlich

unbedingt = absolut

ein Haufen = eine Menge = viel

die Stelle, -n = die Position, -en = der Job, -s

Leicht zu verstehen

das Konsulat, -e	der Schneesturm, ¨-e
die Organisation, -en	die Tablette, -n

Wörter im Kontext

12-30 Was passt wo?

Konsulat / Stelle / Lebenslauf / Strafzettel / Zinsen

1. Wenn man zu schnell fährt, bekommt man einen _____.
2. Wenn man Geld auf der Bank spart, bekommt man _____.
3. Wenn man eine gute Ausbildung hat, bekommt man hoffentlich auch eine gute _____.
4. Wenn man ein Visum braucht, geht man zum _____.
5. Wenn man sich um einen Job bewerben möchte, schreibt man seinen _____.

12-31 Was sind die richtigen Antworten?

1. Warum bist du mit dem Bus gekommen?

2. Warum geht dein Bruder denn zum Arzt?

3. Wann gehst du einkaufen?

    a. Während der Mittagspause.

    b. Weil mein Fahrrad einen Platten hat.

    c. Wegen seiner Erkältung!

4. Warum war Sam gestern nicht in der Vorlesung?

5. Wie bist du so guter Laune?

6. Warum hat Frank die Stelle nicht bekommen?

    d. Wegen des Schneesturms.

    e. Weil BMW mir eine Stelle angeboten hat.

    f. Weil er noch keine Arbeitserfahrung hat.

12-32 Welche Antworten passen?

1. Hätten Sie lieber Tee statt Kaffee?

2. Warum lernt Doris jedes Wochenende, statt mit uns mal auszugehen?

3. Bist du wieder so oft aufgewacht?

4. Ich kann leider nicht zu deiner Fete kommen.

    a. Ja, aber bitte keinen so starken.

    b. Schade.

    c. Ja, trotz der Schlaftabletten.

    d. Weil ihre Lieblingsprofessorin ihr das geraten hat.

12-33 Was ist hier identisch? Welche zwei Fragen in jeder Gruppe bedeuten etwa dasselbe?

1. Wie viel Zinsen bezahlen Sie?
   Wie hoch ist Ihr Lohn?
   Wie viel verdienen Sie?

2. Was für Sprachkenntnisse haben Sie?
   Warum sprechen Sie nicht?
   Welche Sprachen können Sie?

3. Was für eine Position ist das?
   Könnten Sie mir etwas über die Stelle sagen?
   Was für Arbeitserfahrung haben Sie?

4. Was für eine Karriere möchten Sie?
   Was für einen Job haben Sie?
   Was ist Ihr Traumberuf?

Wörter unter der Lupe

The adjective suffix -los

Many German adjectives with the suffix **-los** have English equivalents ending in *-less*. With the knowledge of and feeling for the German language that you now have, you will have no trouble figuring out the English equivalents of the adjectives in the following activity.

12-34 Was ist das auf Englisch?

baumlos	fleischlos	hoffnungslos	selbstlos
bedeutungslos	geschmacklos	namenlos	schlaflos
obdachlos	harmlos	leblos	sprachlos
endlos	herzlos	kinderlos	taktlos
traumlos	hilflos	schamlos	humorlos

However, not all English equivalents of the suffix **-los** are *-less*. Sometimes the English equivalents end in *-free* or begin with *un-*, as in the words in the activity below.

12-35 Wie sagt man das auf English?

fehlerlos	arbeitslos	gefühllos
kostenlos	disziplinlos	interesselos
risikolos	erfolglos	skrupellos

The adjective suffix *-bar*

By attaching the suffix **-bar** to verb stems, German creates hundreds of adjectives. The English equivalents of **-bar** are often *-able* and *-ible*. These suffixes usually convey the idea that the action expressed by the verb can be done.

machen **machbar**   *to do*   *doable*

In contrast to German, English sometimes attaches the suffix *not* to the Germanic verb stem, but to its Latin-based counterpart.

hören **hörbar**   *to hear*   *audible*

To show that the action expressed by the verb can *not* be done, German attaches the prefix **un-** to the adjective. The English equivalents of this prefix are *un-* or *in-*.

bewohnen **unbewohnbar**   *to inhabit*   *uninhabitable*

12-36 Man kann es oder man kann es nicht. Write the German adjectives and their English equivalents.

	DEUTSCH	ENGLISCH
1. Man kann es trinken.	_____	_____
2. Man kann es essen.	_____	_____
3. Man kann es erklären.	_____	_____
4. Man kann es verwenden.	_____	_____
5. Man kann es waschen.	_____	_____
6. Man kann es nicht denken.	_____	_____
7. Man kann es nicht definieren.	_____	_____
8. Man kann es nicht kontrollieren.	_____	_____
9. Man kann es nicht übersetzen.	_____	_____

Achtung!

If you've written your résumé in English, you'll notice several significant differences between this one and the typical North American résumé, such as the inclusion of birth date and place. What other differences can you identify?

12.9 Alles zusammen

Mein Lebenslauf

In this chapter you've practiced expressing wishes, both in the present and in the past. In this final **Alles zusammen** section, you'll have the chance to think and talk about your own goals and wishes, as they relate to what you hope to do with your life. You'll first read a **Lebenslauf** *(résumé)* in German and you'll write your own résumé using the same format. Lastly, you'll talk with classmates about your wishes and dreams for the future.

Sara Murphy
301 East Street, Apt. 9
Washington, DC 20052
Tel: 202-555-0178
E-Mail: smurphy@wwumail.edu

LEBENSLAUF

Persönliche Daten: geboren am 16. Juni 1998 in Akron, OH; US-Amerikanerin; ledig

Ausbildung:

Seit 08/2015   **William Washington University**, Washington, DC
Studienfach: Germanistik
Studienschwerpunkte: Deutsche Literatur und Landeskunde
Durchschnittsnote: 3.5 (4.0 = sehr gut)
erwarteter Studienabschluss: *Bachelor of Arts* 2019

06-08/2017   **Heinrich-Heine Universität**, Düsseldorf
- Vollendung der europäischen Stufe B2 in Deutsch

Arbeitserfahrung:

Seit 09/2017   **Goethe Institut,** Washington, DC
Teilzeit-Praktikantin
- Veranstaltungsplanung durchführen
- administrative Aufgaben erledigen

09-12/2016   **Studienberatung,** William Washington University
Studentische Hilfskraft
- Briefe schreiben
- Internet Recherchen durchführen
- Arbeitsblätter herstellen

Besondere Kenntnisse und Interessen:

Computerkenntnisse: Microsoft Office, Webdesign

Sprachkenntnisse: Englisch: Muttersprache
Deutsch: sehr gut
Französisch: Grundkenntnisse

Sonstige Aktivitäten: Debattierklub, William Washington University
Deutschklub, William Washington University (Vizepräsidentin)
Help2Kids: Nachhilfeprogramm für Schüler (Tutorin)

Washington, DC 24.10.2017

Sara Murphy

12-37 Wo findet man diese Infos?

1. wo Sara geboren ist
2. welche Sprachen sie kann
3. was Sara für Freiwilligendienst gemacht hat
4. was für Computerprogramme sie verwenden kann
5. wo und was sie studiert hat

6. wo Sara schon gearbeitet hat

a. Persönliche Daten
b. Ausbildung
c. Arbeitserfahrung
d. Besondere Kenntnisse und Interessen: Computerkenntnisse
e. Besondere Kenntnisse und Interessen: Sprachkenntnisse
f. Besondere Kenntnisse und Interessen: Sonstige Aktivitäten

Schritt 2: Zum Schreiben

12-38 Mein Lebenslauf. Schreiben Sie Ihren Lebenslauf! Verwenden Sie dafür dieselben Kategorien wie bei Sara Murphys Lebenslauf.

Schritt 3: Zum Sprechen

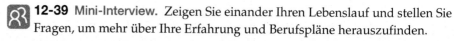 **12-39** Mini-Interview. Zeigen Sie einander Ihren Lebenslauf und stellen Sie Fragen, um mehr über Ihre Erfahrung und Berufspläne herauszufinden.

- Ich lese auf Ihrem Lebenslauf, dass Sie ___ studieren. Haben Sie auch ein Nebenfach?
- Wie lange lernen Sie schon Deutsch? Welche anderen Sprachkenntnisse haben Sie?
- Was für Computerkenntnisse haben Sie?
- Arbeiten Sie während des Semesters neben dem Studium? Was für ein Job ist das?
- Welchen Freiwilligendienst haben Sie schon gemacht?
- Was wäre Ihre Traumstelle?

Anhang

Expressions for the Classroom A-2

- What you might say or ask A-2
- What your instructor might say or ask A-2

German Grammatical Terms A-3

Useful Word Sets A-4

- Studienfächer A-4
- Jobs und Berufe A-4
- Hobbys und Sport A-5
- Musikinstrumente A-6
- Kleidungsstücke A-6
- Accessoires A-7
- Essen und Trinken A-7
- Länder A-8
- Sprachen A-9
- Persönliche Merkmale A-9
- Freundliche Ausdrücke A-10

Grammatical Tables A-11

Principal Parts of Irregular and Mixed Verbs A-17

Expressions for the Classroom

As you progress in this course, you will want to ask your instructor questions in German and understand and respond to your instructor's German instructions. The following expressions will help you.

What you might say or ask

I have a question. **Ich habe eine Frage.**

I don't understand that. **Ich verstehe das nicht.**

I don't know. **Ich weiß nicht.**

Pardon me? **Wie bitte?**

Could you speak more slowly, please? **Könnten Sie bitte langsamer sprechen?**

Could you please repeat that? **Könnten Sie das bitte wiederholen?**

What does . . . mean? **Was bedeutet . . .?**

How do you write (spell) . . .? **Wie schreibt (buchstabiert) man . . .?**

Is that correct? **Ist das richtig?**

What is . . . in German (in English)? **Was ist . . . auf Deutsch (auf Englisch)?**

What page is that on? **Auf welcher Seite ist das?**

Do we have to do that in writing? **Müssen wir das schriftlich machen?**

What homework do we have today? **Was haben wir heute für Hausaufgaben?**

When do we have to hand this in? **Wann müssen wir das abgeben?**

Will this be graded? **Wird das benotet?**

When are your office hours? **Wann sind Ihre Sprechstunden?**

What your instructor might say or ask

Auf Deutsch, bitte. In German, please.

Hören Sie bitte gut zu. Please listen carefully.

Wiederholen Sie das, bitte. Please repeat that.

Sprechen Sie das bitte nach. Please repeat after me.

Alle zusammen. All together.

Versuchen Sie es bitte noch einmal. Please try again.

Ausgezeichnet! Excellent!

Sprechen Sie bitte ein bisschen lauter (deutlicher). Please speak a bit louder (more clearly).

Schauen Sie bitte an die Tafel. Please look at the board.

Gehen Sie bitte an die Tafel. Please go to the board.

Bilden Sie bitte Zweiergruppen (Dreiergruppen, einen Kreis). Please form groups of two (groups of three, a circle).

Erzählen Sie einander (Ihren Mitstudenten), . . . Tell each other (your classmates) . . .

Fragen Sie einander, . . . Ask each other . . .

Stellen Sie einander die Fragen. Ask each other the questions.

Beschreiben Sie . . . Describe . . .

Berichten Sie . . . Report . . .

Machen Sie das bitte schriftlich (mündlich). Please do that in writing (orally).

Fangen Sie bitte an. Please begin.

Sind Sie fertig? Are you finished?

Schlagen Sie Ihre Bücher bitte auf Seite . . . auf. Please open your books to page . . .

Machen Sie Ihre Bücher bitte zu. Please close your books.

Finden Sie im Text . . . Find . . . in the text.

Wo steht das? Where does it say that?

Was fehlt hier? What is missing here?

Legen Sie bitte Ihre Handys weg. Please put away your cell phones.

Klappen Sie bitte Ihre Laptops zu. Please close your laptops.

Ergänzen Sie bitte die Endungen. Please supply the endings.

Ergänzen Sie bitte die Tabelle. Please complete the table.

Unterstreichen Sie bitte . . . Please underline . . .

Wer weiß die Antwort? Who knows the answer?

Lesen Sie den Satz vor. Read the sentence aloud.

Lesen Sie das bitte bis morgen. Please read that for tomorrow.

Legen Sie Ihre Hausaufgaben bitte auf meinen Schreibtisch. Please put your homework on my desk.

Wir schreiben (morgen) ein Quiz (eine Klausur). (Tomorrow) we're having a quiz (a test).

Hat jemand noch Fragen? Does anyone have any questions?

German Grammatical Terms

article — der Artikel, -
  definite article — der bestimmte Artikel
  indefinite article — der unbestimmte Artikel
  der-word — das der-Wort, ¨-er
  ein-word — das ein-Wort, ¨-er
noun — das Nomen, -
gender — das Genus, Genera
masculine, feminine, — maskulin, feminin,
  neuter — neutrum
singular — der Singular
plural — der Plural
case — der Fall, ¨-e; der Kasus, -
  nominative — der Nominativ
  accusative — der Akkusativ
  dative — der Dativ
  genitive — der Genitiv
subject — das Subjekt, -e
subject completion — der Prädikatsnominativ
object — das Objekt, -e
  direct object — das direkte Objekt
  indirect object — das indirekte Objekt
  object of the preposition — das Objekt der Präposition
pronoun — das Pronomen, -
  personal pronoun — das Personalpronomen
  interrogative pronoun — das Fragepronomen
  reflexive pronoun — das Reflexivpronomen
  relative pronoun — das Relativpronomen
possessive adjective — das Possessivpronomen
verb — das Verb, -en
  infinitive — der Infinitiv, -e
  principal part — die Grundform, -en
  regular verb — das regelmäßige Verb
  irregular verb — das unregelmäßige Verb
  mixed verb — das gemischte Verb
  prefix — das Präfix, -e
  separable-prefix verb — das trennbare Verb
  inseparable-prefix verb — das untrennbare Verb
  reflexive verb — das reflexive Verb
  modal verb — das Modalverb
tense — die Zeitform, -en; das Tempus, Tempora

present tense — das Präsens
simple past tense — das Präteritum
perfect tense — das Perfekt
past perfect tense — das Plusquamperfekt
future tense — das Futur
auxiliary verb — das Hilfsverb, -en
past participle — das Partizip Perfekt
imperative — der Imperativ
passive voice — das Passiv
  doer of the action — das Agens
  receiver of the action — das Patiens
subjunctive — der Konjunktiv
  subjunctive form — die Konjunktivform, -en
adjective — das Adjektiv, -e
  adjective ending — die Adjektivendung, -en
  comparative — der Komparativ
  superlative — der Superlativ
adverb — das Adverb, -ien
preposition — die Präposition, -en
  accusative preposition — die Akkusativpräposition
  dative preposition — die Dativpräposition
  two-way preposition — die Wechselpräposition
  genitive preposition — die Genitivpräposition
  contraction — die Kontraktion, -en
  da-compound — die da-Form, -en
  wo-compound — die wo-Form, -en
sentence — der Satz, ¨-e
  independent clause — der Hauptsatz
  dependent clause — der Nebensatz
  object clause — der Objektsatz
  infinitive phrase — der Infinitivsatz
  relative clause — der Relativsatz
conjunction — die Konjunktion, -en
  coordinating conjunction — die koordinierende Konjunktion
  subordinating conjunction — die subordinierende Konjunktion
flavoring particle — die Modalpartikel, -n
word order — die Wortstellung
  verb in second position — Verb an zweiter Stelle
  time / manner / place — Zeit / Art und Weise / Ort

Useful Word Sets

These word sets provide convenient groupings of active vocabulary from the **Wortschatz** sections of each chapter as well as supplementary vocabulary relating to each topic.

Studienfächer

I am studying / am majoring in . . .	**Ich studiere ...**
accounting	**Buchhaltung**
African studies	**Afrikanistik**
American studies	**Amerikanistik**
anthropology	**Anthropologie**
archaeology	**Archäologie**
architecture	**Architektur**
art	**Kunst**
art history	**Kunstgeschichte**
astronomy	**Astronomie**
biochemistry	**Biochemie**
biology	**Biologie**
botany	**Botanik**
business	**Betriebswirtschaftslehre (BWL)**
chemical engineering	**Chemotechnik**
chemistry	**Chemie**
Chinese language and literature	**Sinologie**
communications	**Kommunikationswissenschaft**
comparative literature	**Komparatistik**
computer science	**Informatik**
criminal justice	**Kriminologie**
East Asian studies	**Ostasienwissenschaften**
ecology	**Ökologie**
economics	**Volkswirtschaft**
education	**Erziehungswissenschaften**
electrical engineering	**Elektrotechnik**
English language and literature	**Anglistik**
environmental science sustainability	**Umweltstudien Nachhaltigkeitshuman-wissenschaft**
sustainable technologies	**Umwelttechnik**
exercise science	**Sportwissenschaft**
film studies	**Filmwissenschaft**
finance	**Finanzwirtschaft**
forestry	**Forstwissenschaft**
gender studies	**Geschlechterforschung, Gender Studies**
genetics	**Genetik**
geography	**Geografie**
geology	**Geologie**
German language and literature	**Germanistik**
graphic design	**Grafikdesign**
history	**Geschichtswissenschaft**
humanities	**Geisteswissenschaften**
interior design	**Innenarchitektur**
international affairs	**Internationale Beziehungen**
journalism	**Publizistik, Journalismus**
Latin American studies	**Lateinamerikastudien**
law	**Jura**
linguistics	**Linguistik**
marketing	**Marketing**
mathematics	**Mathematik**
mechanical engineering	**Maschinenbau**
media studies	**Medienkunde**
medicine	**Medizin**
microbiology	**Mikrobiologie**
Middle Eastern studies	**Mittelost-Studien**
music	**Musik**
nursing	**Krankenpflege**
nutritional science	**Ernährungswissenschaft**
philosophy	**Philosophie**
physical education	**Sport**
physics	**Physik**
political science	**Politikwissenschaft**
psychology	**Psychologie**
public health	**Gesundheitswesen**
religious studies	**Religionswissenschaft**
Romance languages and literatures	**Romanistik**
Slavic studies	**Slawistik**
sociology	**Soziologie**
theater	**Theaterwissenschaft**
women's studies	**Frauenstudien**
zoology	**Zoologie**

Jobs und Berufe

accountant	**Wirtschaftsprüfer/in**
actor	**Schauspieler/in**
archaeologist	**Archäologe/Archäologin**
architect	**Architekt/in**
artist	**Künstler/in**
athlete	**Athlet/in**
babysitter	**Babysitter/in**
baker	**Bäcker/in**
banker	**Bankkaufmann/ Bankkauffrau**

barber; hairdresser	**Friseur/in**
bookkeeper	**Buchhalter/in**
bus driver	**Busfahrer/in**
businessman/ businesswoman	**Kaufmann/ Kauffrau**
butcher	**Fleischer/in; Metzger/in**
chemist	**Chemiker/in**
computer programmer	**Programmierer/in**
computer specialist	**Informatiker/in**
construction worker	**Bauarbeiter/in**
cook; chef	**Koch/Köchin**
consultant	**Berater/in**
customer service	**Kundenbetreuer/in**
dancer	**Tänzer/in**
dentist	**Zahnarzt/Zahnärztin**
designer	**Designer/in**
detective	**Detektiv/in**
diplomat	**Diplomat/in**
DJ	**DJ**
doctor	**Arzt/Ärztin**
editor	**Lektor/in**
electrician	**Elektriker/in**
engineer	**Ingenieur/in**
event technician	**Veranstaltungstechniker/in**
factory worker	**Fabrikarbeiter/in**
farmer	**Bauer/Bäuerin**
fashion designer	**Modedesigner/in**
flight attendant	**Flugbegleiter/in**
gardener	**Gärtner/in**
homemaker	**Hausfrau/Hausmann**
interpreter	**Dolmetscher/in**
journalist	**Journalist/in**
lawyer	**Rechtsanwalt/ Rechtsanwältin**
letter carrier	**Briefträger/in**
librarian	**Bibliothekar/in**
lifeguard	**Rettungsschwimmer/in**
manager	**Manager/in**
mechanic	**Mechaniker/in**
model	**Dressman/das Model**
musician	**Musiker/in**
nurse	**Krankenpfleger/in**
occupational therapist	**Ergotherapeut/in**
office worker	**Büroarbeiter/in**
painter	**Maler/in**
pediatrician	**Kinderarzt/Kinderärztin**
pharmacist	**Apotheker/in**
physical therapist	**Physiotherapeut/in**
plumber	**Klempner/in**
police officer	**Polizist/in**
politician	**Politiker/in**
professor	**Professor/in**
psychiatrist	**Psychiater/in**
psychologist	**Psychologe/Psychologin**
real estate agent	**Immobilienmakler/in**
salesperson	**Verkäufer/in**
server (in a restaurant)	**Kellner/in**
scientist	**Wissenschaftler/in**
secretary	**Sekretär/in**
social worker	**Sozialarbeiter/in**
software developer	**Softwareentwickler/in**
stockbroker	**Börsenmakler/in**
tax consultant	**Steuerberater/in**
teacher	**Lehrer/in**
tour guide	**Fremdenführer/in**
translator	**Übersetzer/in**
trucker (long distance)	**Fernfahrer/in**
veterinarian	**Tierarzt/Tierärztin**
waiter/waitress	**Kellner/in**
writer	**Schriftsteller/in**

Hobbys und Sport

to bake	**backen**
to blog	**bloggen**
to collect stamps (old comics, beer bottles)	**Briefmarken (alte Comics, Bierflaschen) sammeln**
to cook	**kochen**
to draw or sketch	**zeichnen**
to garden	**im Garten arbeiten**
to go out with friends	**mit Freunden ausgehen**
to go shopping	**einkaufen gehen**
to go to a concert	**ins Konzert gehen**
to go to the museum	**ins Museum gehen**
to go to (the) movies	**ins Kino gehen**
to go to the theater	**ins Theater gehen**
to hang out	**rumhängen**
to knit	**stricken**
to listen to music	**Musik hören**
to make videos	**Videos machen**
to paint	**malen**
to play cards	**Karten spielen**
to play chess	**Schach spielen**
to play Scrabble	**Scrabble spielen**
to play computer games	**Computerspiele spielen**
to play video games	**Videospiele spielen**
to read	**lesen**
to sing	**singen**
to sew	**nähen**
to surf the Web	**im Internet surfen**
to take photos	**fotografieren**
to travel	**reisen**
to watch TV	**fernsehen**
to watch videos	**Videos anschauen**
to write (poetry, stories)	**(Gedichte, Geschichten) schreiben**

to do aerobics	**Aerobic machen**	to play football	**Football spielen**
to do archery	**Bogenschießen machen**	to play golf	**Golf spielen**
to do bodybuilding	**Bodybuilding machen**	to play ice hockey	**Eishockey spielen**
to do figure skating	**Eiskunstlauf machen**	to play pool	**Billard spielen**
to do gymnastics	**turnen**	to play racquetball	**Racquetball spielen**
to do martial arts	**Kampfsport machen**	to play rugby	**Rugby spielen**
to do sport climbing	**Sportklettern machen**	to play soccer	**Fußball spielen**
to do track and field	**Leichtathletik machen**	to play softball	**Softball spielen**
to do the triathlon	**Triathlon machen**	to play squash	**Squash spielen**
to do weight lifting	**Gewichtheben machen**	to play table tennis	**Tischtennis spielen**
to do weight training	**Krafttraining machen**	(Ping-Pong)	
to work out	**Fitnesstraining machen**	to play tennis	**Tennis spielen**
		to play volleyball	**Volleyball spielen**
to box	**boxen**	to play water polo	**Wasserball spielen**
to fence	**fechten**		
to run	**laufen**		
to wrestle	**ringen**		

Musikinstrumente

I play . . .	**Ich spiele …**
accordion	**Akkordeon**
(double) bass	**Bass, Kontrabass**
bassoon	**Fagott**
cello	**Cello**
clarinet	**Klarinette**
drums, percussion	**Schlagzeug**
flute	**Querflöte**
guitar	**Gitarre**
harmonica	**Mundharmonika**
harp	**Harfe**
harpsichord	**Cembalo**
keyboard	**Keyboard**
oboe	**Oboe**
organ	**Orgel**
piano	**Klavier**
recorder	**Blockflöte**
saxophone	**Saxofon**
trombone	**Posaune**
trumpet	**Trompete**
tuba	**Tuba**
viola	**Bratsche**
violin	**Geige, Violine**

to go biking	**Rad fahren**
to go bowling	**kegeln gehen**
to go camping	**campen gehen**
to go canoeing	**Kanu fahren**
to go dancing	**tanzen gehen**
to go fishing	**angeln gehen**
to go hang gliding	**Drachenfliegen gehen**
to go hiking	**wandern gehen**
to go horseback riding	**reiten gehen**
to go hunting	**jagen gehen**
to go ice skating	**Schlittschuhlaufen gehen**
to go in-line skating	**Inlineskaten gehen**
to go jogging	**joggen gehen**
to go kayaking	**Kajak fahren**
to go mountain biking	**mountainbiken gehen**
to go mountain climbing	**bergsteigen gehen**
(mountaineering)	
to go rowing	**rudern gehen**
to go sailing	**segeln gehen**
to go skateboarding	**skateboarden gehen**
to go sledding	**Schlittenfahren gehen**
to go skiing	**Skilaufen (Skifahren) gehen**
to do cross-country skiing	**Skilanglauf machen**
to do downhill skiing	**Abfahrtslauf machen**
to go snowboarding	**snowboarden gehen**
to go surfing	**surfen gehen**
to go swimming	**schwimmen gehen**
to go windsurfing	**windsurfen gehen**
to play badminton	**Federball (Badminton) spielen**
to play baseball	**Baseball spielen**
to play basketball	**Basketball spielen**
to play darts	**Dart spielen**
to play field hockey	**Hockey spielen**

Kleidungsstücke

I'm wearing . . .	**Ich trage …**
a baseball cap	**eine Baseballkappe**
a belt	**einen Gürtel**
a blazer	**einen Blazer**
a blouse	**eine Bluse**
boots	**Stiefel**
hiking boots	**Wanderstiefel**
clothes	**Kleider; Klamotten** (*colloq.*)
a coat	**einen Mantel**

a dress	ein Kleid
gloves	Handschuhe
a hat	einen Hut
a jacket	eine Jacke
a down jacket	eine Daunenjacke
a jeans jacket	eine Jeansjacke
a leather jacket	eine Lederjacke
jeans	Jeans
pants	eine Hose
a polo shirt	ein Polohemd
sandals	Sandalen
a scarf	einen Schal
a shirt	ein Hemd
shorts	Shorts
shoes	Schuhe
tennis shoes	Tennisschuhe
sneakers or running shoes	Turnschuhe
a skirt	einen Rock
slippers	Hausschuhe
socks	Socken
pantyhose	eine Strumpfhose
a suit (men's)	einen Anzug
a pantsuit (women's)	einen Hosenanzug
a sweater	einen Pullover
a light sweater	einen Pulli
sweatpants	eine Jogginghose
a sweatshirt	ein Sweatshirt
a sweatsuit	einen Jogginganzug
a tie	eine Krawatte, einen Schlips
tights	Leggings
a T-shirt	ein T-Shirt
a tuxedo	einen Smoking

Accessoires

I'm wearing . . .	Ich trage …
a bracelet	ein Armband
contact lenses	Kontaktlinsen
earrings	Ohrringe
an ear stud	einen Ohrstecker
glasses	eine Brille (sing)
sunglasses	eine Sonnenbrille (sing)
a nose stud	einen Nasenstecker
a necklace	eine Halskette
a ring	einen Ring
a wristwatch	eine Armbanduhr
I have . . .	Ich habe …
a beard	einen Bart
a goatee	einen Ziegenbart (Spitzbart)

a mustache	einen Schnurrbart
a tattoo	eine Tätowierung, ein Tattoo

Essen und Trinken

I eat . . .	Ich esse …
for breakfast	zum Frühstück
bacon	Speck
bacon and eggs	Eier mit Speck
a bagel	einen Bagel
with cream cheese	mit Frischkäse
(a bowl of) cornflakes	(eine Schüssel) Cornflakes
an egg	ein Ei
eggs, sunny-side up	Spiegeleier
scrambled eggs	Rührei
granola, muesli	Müsli
a granola bar	einen Müsliriegel
a muffin	einen Muffin
(a slice of) bread	(eine Scheibe) Brot
(a slice of) toast	(eine Scheibe) Toast
with butter	mit Butter
with honey	mit Honig
with jam	mit Marmelade
with peanut butter	mit Erdnussbutter
(a container of) yogurt	(einen Becher) Joghurt
with fruit	Fruchtjoghurt
a smoothie	einen Smoothie
for lunch	zum Mittagessen
for supper	zum Abendessen
a bowl of soup	einen Teller Suppe
bread	Brot
a burrito	einen Burrito
chicken	Huhn
chicken salad	Geflügelsalat
French fries	Pommes frites, Pommes
fish	Fisch
a hamburger	einen Hamburger
a hotdog	ein Hotdog
with ketchup	mit Ketchup
with mustard	mit Senf
with onions	mit Zwiebeln
with relish	mit Relish
meat	Fleisch
noodles	Nudeln
pickles	Essiggurken
a pizza	eine Pizza
porkchops	Schweineschnitzel
potatoes	Kartoffeln
potato salad	Kartoffelsalat
rice	Reis
rolls	Brötchen

a sandwich	ein belegtes Brot
a cheese sandwich	ein Käsebrot
a ham sandwich	ein Schinkenbrot
a sausage	eine Wurst
a steak	ein Steak
sushi	Sushi
a taco	einen Taco
tuna	Thunfisch
turkey	Pute

vegetables	Gemüse
asparagus	Spargel
beans	Bohnen
bell peppers	Paprika
broccoli	Brokkoli
carrots	Karotten
cauliflower	Blumenkohl
coleslaw	Krautsalat
corn	Mais
cucumbers	Gurken
eggplant	Aubergine
mushrooms	Champignons
peas	Erbsen
red cabbage	Rotkohl
salad	Salat
sauerkraut	Sauerkraut
spinach	Spinat
tomatoes	Tomaten

snacks	Snacks
nuts	Nüsse
potato chips	Kartoffelchips
popcorn	Popcorn
pretzels	Brezeln
tortilla chips	Tortillachips
for dessert	zum Nachtisch
(a piece of) cake	(ein Stück) Kuchen
(a piece of) layer cake	(ein Stück) Torte
with whipped cream	mit Schlagsahne
a chocolate bar	eine Tafel Schokolade
cookies	Kekse
(a dish of) ice cream	(einen Becher) Eis

fruit	Obst
an apple	einen Apfel
a banana	eine Banane
blackberries	Brombeeren
blueberries	Heidelbeeren
cherries	Kirschen
a grapefruit	eine Grapefruit
grapes	Trauben
melon	Melone
an orange	eine Orange
a peach	einen Pfirsich
a pear	eine Birne
pineapple	Ananas
a plum	eine Pflaume
raspberries	Himbeeren
strawberries	Erdbeeren

I drink . . .	Ich trinke …
(a bottle of) beer	(eine Flasche) Bier
(a can of) cola	(eine Dose) Cola
(a cup of) coffee	(eine Tasse) Kaffee
(a cup of) tea	(eine Tasse) Tee
(a cup of) cocoa	(eine Tasse) Kakao
(a glass of) milk	(ein Glas) Milch
(a glass of) sparkling wine	(ein Glas) Sekt
(a glass of) water	(ein Glas) Wasser
(a glass of) wine	(ein Glas) Wein
(a glass of) juice	(ein Glas) Saft
apple juice	Apfelsaft
grapefruit juice	Grapefruitsaft
orange juice	Orangensaft
tomato juice	Tomatensaft
a hot chocolate	eine heiße Schokolade
a soft drink	einen Softdrink

Länder

The names of most countries are neuter and are not preceded by an article. However, when the name of a country is masculine, feminine, or plural, the article must be used.

der Kontinent, -e / der Erdteil, -e

Asien

Afghanistan	die Malediven
Armenien	die Mongolei
Aserbaidschan	Myanmar
Bahrain	Nepal
Bangladesch	Nordkorea
Bhutan	der Oman
Brunei	Osttimor
China	Pakistan
Georgien	die Philippinen
Indien	Russland
Indonesien	Saudi-Arabien
der Irak	Singapur
der Iran	Sri Lanka
Israel	Südkorea
Japan	Syrien
der Jemen	Tadschikistan
Kambodscha	Taiwan (die Republik China)
Kasachstan	Thailand
Katar	die Türkei
Kirgisistan	Turkmenistan
Kuwait	Usbekistan
Laos	die Vereinigten Arabischen
der Libanon	Emirate
Malaysia	Vietnam

Europa
Albanien
Andorra
Belgien
Bosnien und Herzegowina
Bulgarien
Dänemark
Deutschland
England
Estland
Finnland
Frankreich
Griechenland
Irland
Island
Italien
Kroatien
Lettland
Liechtenstein
Litauen
Luxemburg
Malta
Mazedonien
Moldawien
Monaco
Montenegro
die Niederlande *(pl)*
Nordirland
Norwegen
Österreich
Polen
Portugal
Rumänien
Russland
San Marino
Schottland
Schweden
die Schweiz
Serbien
die Slowakei
Slowenien
Spanien
Tschechien
die Türkei
die Ukraine
Ungarn
Vatikanstadt
das Vereinigte Königreich
Wales
Weißrussland
Zypern

Afrika
Ägypten
Algerien
Angola
Äquatorialguinea
Benin
Botswana
Burkina Faso
Burundi
die Demokratische
  Republik Kongo
Dschibuti
die Elfenbeinküste
Eritrea
Gabun
Gambia
Ghana
Guinea
Guinea-Bissau
Kamerun
Kenia
Kongo
Lesotho
Liberia
Libyen
Madagaskar
Malawi
Mali
Marokko
Mauretanien
Mosambik
Namibia
Niger
Nigeria
Ruanda
Sambia
Senegal
Sierra Leone
Simbabwe
Somalia
Sudan
Südafrika
Südsudan
Swasiland
Tansania
Tschad
Togo
Tunesien
Uganda
Westsahara
die Zentralafrikanische
  Republik

Nordamerika
Belize
Costa Rica
die Dominikanische
  Republik
El Salvador
Guatemala
Haiti
Honduras
Jamaika
Kanada
Kuba
Mexiko
Nicaragua
Panama
die Vereinigten
  Staaten, die
  USA *(pl)*

Antarktika

Sprachen
Sie/Er spricht ...
Arabisch
Bengalisch
Chinesisch (Mandarin,
  Kantonesisch)
Dänisch
Deutsch
Englisch
Estnisch
Filipino
Finnisch
Französisch
Griechisch
Hebräisch
Hindi
Holländisch
Italienisch
Japanisch
Javanisch

Koreanisch
Kroatisch
Lettisch
Litauisch
Norwegisch
Persisch
Polnisch
Portugiesisch
Rumänisch
Russisch
Schwedisch
Serbisch
Slowakisch
Spanisch
Tschechisch
Türkisch
Ukrainisch
Ungarisch
Urdu

Südamerika
Argentinien
Bolivien
Brasilien
Chile
Ecuador
Französisch-Guayana
Guyana
Kolumbien
Paraguay
Peru
Suriname
Trinidad und Tobago
Uruguay
Venezuela

Australien/Ozeanien
Australien
Neuseeland
Papua-Neuguinea

Persönliche Merkmale
ambitious	ehrgeizig
angry	böse; verärgert
arrogant	arrogant
artistic	künstlerisch begabt
athletic	sportlich
attractive	attraktiv
(of) average height	mittelgroß
beautiful	schön
bilingual	zweisprachig

blond	**blond**	optimistic	**optimistisch**
brilliant	**genial**	outgoing	**aufgeschlossen**
brunette	**brünett**	pessimistic	**pessimistisch**
calm	**ruhig**	plump	**mollig**
chic	**schick**	polite	**höflich**
conservative	**konservativ**	popular	**populär; beliebt**
cool	**cool**	practical	**praktisch**
crazy	**verrückt**	pretty	**hübsch**
creative	**kreativ**	private	**introvertiert**
critical	**kritisch**	punctual	**pünktlich**
elegant	**elegant**	respectful	**respektvoll**
enchanting	**bezaubernd**	religious	**fromm**
envious	**neidisch**	romantic	**romantisch**
exotic	**exotisch**	selfless	**selbstlos**
extravagant	**extravagant**	sentimental	**sentimental**
fabulous	**fabelhaft**	serious	**ernst**
fair	**fair**	short	**klein**
famous	**berühmt**	silly	**albern**
fantastic	**fantastisch**	slim	**schlank**
fashionably dressed	**modisch gekleidet**	smart	**klug**
fit	**fit**	spontaneous	**spontan**
fun, funny	**lustig**	strong	**stark**
friendly	**freundlich**	stubborn	**dickköpfig**
furious	**wütend**	successful	**erfolgreich**
generous	**großzügig**	sweet	**süß**
great	**spitze** (colloq.)	tactful	**taktvoll**
happy	**glücklich; froh**	tall	**groß**
hard-working	**fleißig**	thrifty	**sparsam**
healthy	**gesund**	tidy	**ordentlich**
helpful	**hilfsbereit**	tired	**müde**
honest	**ehrlich**	tolerant	**tolerant**
humorous; having a sense of humor	**humorvoll**	witty	**witzig**
idealistic	**idealistisch**		
imaginative	**fantasievoll**		
impulsive	**impulsiv**		
informed	**informiert**		
in love	**verliebt**		
innovative	**innovativ**		
intelligent	**intelligent; klug**		
interesting	**interessant**		
jealous	**eifersüchtig**		
lazy	**faul**		
liberal	**liberal**		
messy	**unordentlich**		
modern	**modern**		
mood: (always) in a good mood	**(immer) guter Laune**		
moody	**launisch**		
musical	**musikalisch**		
nice	**nett**		
natural	**natürlich**		
nervous	**nervös**		

Freundliche Ausdrücke

All the best!	**Alles Gute!**
Bless you!	**Gesundheit!**
Get well soon!	**Gute Besserung!**
Good luck!	**Viel Glück!**
Thanks a lot!	**Vielen Dank!**
Thanks a million!	**Tausend Dank!**
You're welcome.	**Bitte schön.**
Don't mention it.	**Nichts zu danken.**
No problem.	**Kein Problem.**
That's too bad.	**Schade.**
Excuse me; I'm sorry.	**Entschuldigung; Es tut mir leid.**
Have fun!	**Viel Spaß!**
Have a good weekend!	**Schönes Wochenende!**
Have a nice day!	**Schönen Tag noch!**
Same to you!	**Gleichfalls!**
Take care! Be well!	**Mach's gut!**

Grammatical Tables

1. *Der*-words

Common **der**-words are **der, das, die** *(the)*; **dieser** *(this)*; **jeder** *(each, every)*; and **welcher** *(which)*.

	Masculine	Neuter	Feminine	Plural
NOMINATIVE	der dieser	das dieses	die diese	die diese
ACCUSATIVE	den diesen	das dieses	die diese	die diese
DATIVE	dem diesem	dem diesem	der dieser	den diesen
GENITIVE	des dieses	des dieses	der dieser	der dieser

2. *Ein*-words

The **ein**-words are **ein** *(a, an)*, **kein** *(not a, not any, no)*, and the possessive adjectives **mein** *(my)*, **dein** *(your)*, **sein** *(his, its)*, **ihr** *(her, its)*, **unser** *(our)*, **euer** *(your)*, **ihr** *(their)*, **Ihr** *(your)*.

	Masculine	Neuter	Feminine	Plural
NOMINATIVE	ein mein	ein mein	eine meine	— meine
ACCUSATIVE	einen meinen	ein mein	eine meine	— meine
DATIVE	einem meinem	einem meinem	einer meiner	— meinen
GENITIVE	eines meines	eines meines	einer meiner	— meiner

3. Pronouns
a. Personal pronouns

Nom.	Subj.	Acc.	Dir. obj.	Dat.	Ind. obj.
ich	*I*	mich	*me*	mir	*me*
du	*you*	dich	*you*	dir	*you*
er	*he, it*	ihn	*him, it*	ihm	*him, it*
es	*it*	es	*it*	ihm	*it*
sie	*she, it*	sie	*her, it*	ihr	*her, it*
wir	*we*	uns	*us*	uns	*us*
ihr	*you*	euch	*you*	euch	*you*
sie	*they*	sie	*them*	ihnen	*them*
Sie	*you*	Sie	*you*	Ihnen	*you*

b. Reflexive pronouns

	Accusative	Dative	Direct or indirect object
(ich)	mich	mir	*myself*
(du)	dich	dir	*yourself*
(er)	sich	sich	*himself, itself*
(es)	sich	sich	*itself*
(sie)	sich	sich	*herself, itself*
(wir)	uns	uns	*ourselves*
(ihr)	euch	euch	*yourselves*
(sie)	sich	sich	*themselves*
(Sie)	sich	sich	*yourself*
			yourselves

c. Interrogative pronouns

	For persons	For things
NOMINATIVE	wer	was
ACCUSATIVE	wen	was
DATIVE	wem	—
GENITIVE	wessen	—

d. Relative pronouns

	Masculine	Neuter	Feminine	Plural
NOMINATIVE	der	das	die	die
ACCUSATIVE	den	das	die	die
DATIVE	dem	dem	der	denen
GENITIVE	dessen	dessen	deren	deren

4. Adjective endings

a. After *der*-words

	Masculine	Neuter	Feminine	Plural
NOM.	der jung**e** Mann	das lieb**e** Kind	die jung**e** Frau	die lieb**en** Kinder
ACC.	den jung**en** Mann	das lieb**e** Kind	die jung**e** Frau	die lieb**en** Kinder
DAT.	dem jung**en** Mann	dem lieb**en** Kind	der jung**en** Frau	den lieb**en** Kindern
GEN.	des jung**en** Mannes	des lieb**en** Kindes	der jung**en** Frau	der lieb**en** Kinder

b. After *ein*-words

	Masculine	Neuter	Feminine	Plural
NOM.	ein jung**er** Mann	ein lieb**es** Kind	eine jung**e** Frau	keine lieb**en** Kinder
ACC.	einen jung**en** Mann	ein lieb**es** Kind	eine jung**e** Frau	keine lieb**en** Kinder
DAT.	einem jung**en** Mann	einem lieb**en** Kind	einer jung**en** Frau	keinen lieb**en** Kindern
GEN.	eines jung**en** Mannes	eines lieb**en** Kindes	einer jung**en** Frau	keiner lieb**en** Kinder

c. For unpreceded adjectives

	Masculine	Neuter	Feminine	Plural
NOM.	gut**er** Käse	gut**es** Brot	gut**e** Wurst	gut**e** Äpfel
ACC.	gut**en** Käse	gut**es** Brot	gut**e** Wurst	gut**e** Äpfel
DAT.	gut**em** Käse	gut**em** Brot	gut**er** Wurst	gut**en** Äpfeln

5. N-nouns

All **n**-nouns are masculine. They are listed in dictionaries as follows: **der Student, -en, -en**.

	Singular	Plural
NOMINATIVE	der Student	die Studenten
ACCUSATIVE	den Studenten	die Studenten
DATIVE	dem Studenten	den Studenten
GENITIVE	des Studenten	der Studenten

6. Prepositions

Accusative	Dative	Accusative or dative (two-way)	Genitive
durch	aus	an	statt
für	außer	auf	trotz
gegen	bei	hinter	während
ohne	mit	in	wegen
um	nach	neben	
	seit	über	
	von	unter	
	zu	vor	
		zwischen	

7. Irregular comparatives and superlatives

BASE FORM	gern	gut	groß	hoch	nah	viel
COMPARATIVE	lieber	besser	größer	höher	näher	mehr
SUPERLATIVE	liebst-	best-	größt-	höchst-	nächst-	meist-

8. Verbs

a. Indicative (to express facts)

Present tense

	lernen[1]	arbeiten[2]	reisen[3]	geben[4]	tragen[5]	laufen[6]	weg·gehen[7]
ich	lerne	arbeite	reise	gebe	trage	laufe	gehe … weg
du	lernst	arbeit**est**	reist	gibst	trägst	läufst	gehst … weg
er/es/sie	lernt	arbeit**et**	reist	gibt	trägt	läuft	geht … weg
wir	lernen	arbeiten	reisen	geben	tragen	laufen	gehen … weg
ihr	lernt	arbeit**et**	reist	gebt	tragt	lauft	geht … weg
sie	lernen	arbeiten	reisen	geben	tragen	laufen	gehen … weg
Sie	lernen	arbeiten	reisen	geben	tragen	laufen	gehen … weg

[1]Regular verbs
[2]Verbs with expanded endings (e.g., **arbeiten, finden, regnen, öffnen**)
[3]Verbs with contracted endings (e.g., **reisen, heißen, sitzen**)
[4]Irregular verbs with stem-vowel change **e** to **i (ie)**
[5]Irregular verbs with stem-vowel change **a** to **ä**
[6]Irregular verbs with stem-vowel change **au** to **äu**
[7]Separable-prefix verbs

Present tense of the auxiliaries *haben, sein, werden*

	haben	sein	werden
ich	habe	bin	werde
du	hast	bist	wirst
er/es/sie	hat	ist	wird
wir	haben	sind	werden
ihr	habt	seid	werdet
sie	haben	sind	werden
Sie	haben	sind	werden

Present tense of the modal verbs

	dürfen	können	mögen	(möcht-)	müssen	sollen	wollen
ich	darf	kann	mag	(möchte)	muss	soll	will
du	darfst	kannst	magst	(möchtest)	musst	sollst	willst
er/es/sie	darf	kann	mag	(möchte)	muss	soll	will
wir	dürfen	können	mögen	(möchten)	müssen	sollen	wollen
ihr	dürft	könnt	mögt	(möchtet)	müsst	sollt	wollt
sie	dürfen	können	mögen	(möchten)	müssen	sollen	wollen
Sie	dürfen	können	mögen	(möchten)	müssen	sollen	wollen

Simple past tense

	Regular verbs		Irregular verbs
ich	lernte	landete	ging
du	lerntest	landetest	gingst
er/es/sie	lernte	landete	ging
wir	lernten	landeten	gingen
ihr	lerntet	landetet	gingt
sie	lernten	landeten	gingen
Sie	lernten	landeten	gingen

You will find the principal parts of the irregular verbs used in this text on pp. A-17–A-19.

Simple past tense of the auxiliaries *haben, sein, werden*

	haben	sein	werden
ich	hatte	war	wurde
du	hattest	warst	wurdest
er/es/sie	hatte	war	wurde
wir	hatten	waren	wurden
ihr	hattet	wart	wurdet
sie	hatten	waren	wurden
Sie	hatten	waren	wurden

Simple past tense of mixed verbs

	bringen	denken	kennen	nennen	rennen	wissen
ich	brachte	dachte	kannte	nannte	rannte	wusste
du	brachtest	dachtest	kanntest	nanntest	ranntest	wusstest
er/es/sie	brachte	dachte	kannte	nannte	rannte	wusste
wir	brachten	dachten	kannten	nannten	rannten	wussten
ihr	brachtet	dachtet	kanntet	nanntet	ranntet	wusstet
sie	brachten	dachten	kannten	nannten	rannten	wussten
Sie	brachten	dachten	kannten	nannten	rannten	wussten

Simple past tense of the modal verbs

	dürfen	können	mögen	müssen	sollen	wollen
ich	durfte	konnte	mochte	musste	sollte	wollte
du	durftest	konntest	mochtest	musstest	solltest	wolltest
er/es/sie	durfte	konnte	mochte	musste	sollte	wollte
wir	durften	konnten	mochten	mussten	sollten	wollten
ihr	durftet	konntet	mochtet	musstet	solltet	wolltet
sie	durften	konnten	mochten	mussten	sollten	wollten
Sie	durften	konnten	mochten	mussten	sollten	wollten

Perfect tense

	Regular verbs		Irregular verbs	
ich	habe gelernt	bin gereist	habe gesungen	bin gegangen
du	hast gelernt	bist gereist	hast gesungen	bist gegangen
er/es/sie	hat gelernt	ist gereist	hat gesungen	ist gegangen
wir	haben gelernt	sind gereist	haben gesungen	sind gegangen
ihr	habt gelernt	seid gereist	habt gesungen	seid gegangen
sie	haben gelernt	sind gereist	haben gesungen	sind gegangen
Sie	haben gelernt	sind gereist	haben gesungen	sind gegangen

You will find the principal parts of the irregular verbs used in this text on pp. A-17–A-19.

b. Imperative (to express commands or requests)

FAMILIAR SINGULAR	Lern(e)!	Gib!	Sei!
FAMILIAR PLURAL	Lernt!	Gebt!	Seid!
FORMAL	Lernen Sie!	Geben Sie!	Seien Sie!

Examples: Lern(e) Deutsch!

Gib es hier!

Sei still!

c. Subjunctive (to express contrary-to-fact situations)

Present subjunctive

	haben	sein	können	wissen
ich	hätte	wäre	könnte	wüsste
du	hättest	wär(e)st	könntest	wüsstest
er/es/sie	hätte	wäre	könnte	wüsste
wir	hätten	wären	könnten	wüssten
ihr	hättet	wär(e)t	könntet	wüsstet
sie	hätten	wären	könnten	wüssten
Sie	hätten	wären	könnten	wüssten

For verbs other than **haben, sein, werden, wissen,** and the modals, use **würde** + infinitive.

ich	würde	lernen
du	würdest	lernen
er/es/sie	würde	lernen
wir	würden	lernen
ihr	würdet	lernen
sie	würden	lernen
Sie	würden	lernen

Past subjunctive

ich	hätte	gelernt	wäre	gegangen
du	hättest	gelernt	wär(e)st	gegangen
er/es/sie	hätte	gelernt	wäre	gegangen
wir	hätten	gelernt	wären	gegangen
ihr	hättet	gelernt	wär(e)t	gegangen
sie	hätten	gelernt	wären	gegangen
Sie	hätten	gelernt	wären	gegangen

d. Passive voice

	Present tense		Simple past tense	
ich	werde	abgeholt	wurde	abgeholt
du	wirst	abgeholt	wurdest	abgeholt
er/es/sie	wird	abgeholt	wurde	abgeholt
wir	werden	abgeholt	wurden	abgeholt
ihr	werdet	abgeholt	wurdet	abgeholt
sie	werden	abgeholt	wurden	abgeholt
Sie	werden	abgeholt	wurden	abgeholt

Principal Parts of Irregular and Mixed Verbs

The following list contains the principal parts of the irregular and mixed verbs in *Treffpunkt Deutsch*. With a few exceptions, the separable- and inseparable-prefix verbs are not included since the stem changes are the same as for the basic verb (e.g., **ausgeben–geben, mitbringen–bringen**).

Infinitive	Irr. present	Simple past	Past participle	
anfangen	(fängt an)	fing an	angefangen	*to begin*
backen	(bäckt)	backte	gebacken	*to bake*
beißen		biss	gebissen	*to bite*
beginnen		begann	begonnen	*to begin*
begreifen		begriff	begriffen	*to grasp; to comprehend*
bekommen		bekam	bekommen	*to get; to receive*
beweisen		bewies	bewiesen	*to prove*
bewerben	(bewirbt)	bewarb	beworben	*to apply (for a job)*
bieten		bot	geboten	*to offer*
bitten		bat	gebeten	*to ask*
bleiben		blieb	ist geblieben	*to stay; to remain*
bringen		brachte	gebracht	*to bring*
denken		dachte	gedacht	*to think*
einladen	(lädt ein)	lud ein	eingeladen	*to invite*
empfangen	(empfängt)	empfing	empfangen	*to welcome*
empfehlen	(empfiehlt)	empfahl	empfohlen	*to recommend*
entscheiden		entschied	entschieden	*to decide*
entwerfen	(entwirft)	entwarf	entworfen	*to design*
erfahren	(erfährt)	erfuhr	erfahren	*to learn of, come to know*
essen	(isst)	aß	gegessen	*to eat*
fahren	(fährt)	fuhr	ist gefahren	*to drive*
fallen	(fällt)	fiel	ist gefallen	*to fall*
fangen	(fängt)	fing	gefangen	*to catch*
finden		fand	gefunden	*to find*
fliegen		flog	ist geflogen	*to fly*
fliehen		floh	ist geflohen	*to flee*
fließen		floss	ist geflossen	*to flow*
fressen	(frisst)	fraß	gefressen	*to eat (of animals)*
frieren		fror	gefroren	*to be cold*
geben	(gibt)	gab	gegeben	*to give*
gehen		ging	ist gegangen	*to go; to walk*
gelten	(gilt)	galt	gegolten	*to be considered*
geschehen	(geschieht)	geschah	ist geschehen	*to happen*
gewinnen		gewann	gewonnen	*to win*
gießen		goss	gegossen	*to water*
haben	(hat)	hatte	gehabt	*to have*
halten	(hält)	hielt	gehalten	*to hold; to keep; to stop*

Infinitive	Irr. present	Simple past	Past participle	
hängen		hing	gehangen	*to be hanging*
heißen		hieß	geheißen	*to be called*
helfen	(hilft)	half	geholfen	*to help*
kennen		kannte	gekannt	*to know (be acquainted with)*
kommen		kam	ist gekommen	*to come*
laden	(lädt)	lud	geladen	*to load*
lassen	(lässt)	ließ	gelassen	*to let; to leave*
laufen	(läuft)	lief	ist gelaufen	*to run*
leihen		lieh	geliehen	*to lend*
lesen	(liest)	las	gelesen	*to read*
liegen		lag	gelegen	*to lie; to be situated*
lügen		log	gelogen	*to tell a lie*
nehmen	(nimmt)	nahm	genommen	*to take*
nennen		nannte	genannt	*to call; to name*
raten	(rät)	riet	geraten	*to guess; to advise*
reiten		ritt	ist geritten	*to ride*
rennen		rannte	ist gerannt	*to run*
riechen		roch	gerochen	*to smell*
rufen		rief	gerufen	*to call*
scheinen		schien	geschienen	*to shine; to seem*
schieben		schob	geschoben	*to push*
schießen		schoss	geschossen	*to shoot*
schlafen	(schläft)	schlief	geschlafen	*to sleep*
schließen		schloss	geschlossen	*to close*
schneiden		schnitt	geschnitten	*to cut*
schreiben		schrieb	geschrieben	*to write*
schreien		schrie	geschrien	*to shout*
schwimmen		schwamm	ist geschwommen	*to swim*
sehen	(sieht)	sah	gesehen	*to see*
sein	(ist)	war	ist gewesen	*to be*
singen		sang	gesungen	*to sing*
sinken		sank	ist gesunken	*to sink*
sitzen		saß	gesessen	*to sit*
spinnen		spann	gesponnen	*to spin; to be crazy*
sprechen	(spricht)	sprach	gesprochen	*to speak*
springen		sprang	ist gesprungen	*to jump*
stehen		stand	gestanden	*to stand*
stehlen	(stiehlt)	stahl	gestohlen	*to steal*
steigen		stieg	ist gestiegen	*to climb*
sterben	(stirbt)	starb	ist gestorben	*to die*
stinken		stank	gestunken	*to stink*
streichen		strich	gestrichen	*to paint*
tragen	(trägt)	trug	getragen	*to carry; to wear*
treffen	(trifft)	traf	getroffen	*to meet*

Infinitive	Irr. present	Simple past	Past participle	
trinken		trank	getrunken	*to drink*
tun		tat	getan	*to do*
übernehmen	(übernimmt)	übernahm	übernommen	*to take on*
unterbrechen	(unterbricht)	unterbrach	unterbrochen	*to interrupt*
verbieten		verbot	verboten	*to forbid*
verbinden		verband	verbunden	*to connect*
vergessen	(vergisst)	vergaß	vergessen	*to forget*
vergleichen		verglich	verglichen	*to compare*
verlieren		verlor	verloren	*to lose*
vermeiden		vermied	vermieden	*to avoid*
verstehen		verstand	verstanden	*to understand*
vorschlagen	(schlägt vor)	schlug vor	vorgeschlagen	*to suggest*
waschen	(wäscht)	wusch	gewaschen	*to wash*
werden	(wird)	wurde	ist geworden	*to become*
werfen	(wirft)	warf	geworfen	*to throw*
wissen	(weiß)	wusste	gewusst	*to know (a fact)*
ziehen		zog	gezogen	*to pull*

Modal verbs

dürfen	(darf)	durfte	gedurft	*to be allowed to*
können	(kann)	konnte	gekonnt	*to be able to*
mögen	(mag)	mochte	gemocht	*to like*
müssen	(muss)	musste	gemusst	*to have to*
sollen	(soll)	sollte	gesollt	*to be supposed to*
wollen	(will)	wollte	gewollt	*to want to*

German-English Vocabulary

This German-English vocabulary includes all the words and expressions used in *Treffpunkt Deutsch* except numbers and names of countries. The latter are listed in the *Useful Word Sets* on page A-8–A-9. Each item is followed by the number of the chapter (and E for *Erste Kontakte*) in which it first occurs. Chapter numbers followed by -1 or -2 (e.g., 1-1 or 1-2) refer to items listed in the first or second vocabulary list in each chapter (*Wortschatz 1* or *Wortschatz 2*). *Erste Kontakte* has only one *Wortschatz* list; words in that list are followed by E-1.

Nouns are listed with their plural forms: **die Studentin, -nen.** If no plural entry is given, the plural is rarely used or nonexistent. When two entries follow a noun, the first one indicates the genitive and the second the plural: **der Student, -en, -en.**

Irregular, mixed, and modal verbs are listed with their principal parts. Vowel changes in the present tense are noted in parentheses: **lesen (liest), las, gelesen.** Auxiliary verbs are given only for verbs conjugated with **sein: kommen, kam, ist gekommen; reisen, reiste, ist gereist.** Separable prefixes are indicated by a raised dot between the prefix and the verb stem: **an·fangen.** Reflexive pronouns are introduced with **sich.** Reflexive pronouns use the accusative case unless otherwise indicated as dative, i.e. (+ *dat*).

The following abbreviations are used:

abbr.	abbreviation	*dat*	dative
acc	accusative	*gen*	genitive
adj	adjective	*neg*	negative
adv	adverb	*pl*	plural
art	article	*prep*	preposition
conj	conjunction	*sing*	singular
coord	coordinating	*sub*	subordinating

A

ab: ab und zu from time to time (9)

ab·brechen (bricht ab), brach ab, abgebrochen to stop; to break off (6)

der Abend, -e evening (E)

Guten Abend! 'n Abend! Good evening! (E-1)

heute Abend this evening, tonight (1)

zu Abend essen to have supper (4-1)

das Abendbrot evening meal of bread and cold cuts (4)

das Abendessen supper; evening meal (4-1)

zum Abendessen for supper; for dinner (4-1)

abends in the evening (2)

aber *(coord conj)* but (1-2)

ab·fahren (fährt ab), fuhr ab, ist abgefahren to leave, to depart (4-2)

die Abfahrt, -en departure (8)

abgelaufen worn out *(shoes)* (11)

der/die Abgeordnete, -n representative (12)

abgetragen worn out *(clothes)* (11)

abgrundtief profound(ly)

Ich hasse sie abgrundtief. I hate her with a passion. (12)

abhängig dependent (6-1)

ab·holen to pick up (7)

das Abitur high school diploma (1)

die Abkürzung, -en abbreviation (E)

ab·reisen to leave, to depart (6-2)

ab·reißen, riss ab, abgerissen to demolish, tear down (11)

ab·riegeln to close off (11)

ab·schicken to send, mail *(a letter, package)* (8)

absolut absolutely (12-2)

der Abstieg, -e descent (2)

die Abwanderung moving away; migration (11)

der Abwasch dirty dishes (8)

den Abwasch machen to do the dishes (8)

abwischbar washable (12)

Ach so! I see! (E)

Achtung! Attention! Heads up! (3)

ADAC (Allgemeiner Deutscher Automobil-Club) German automobile club (E)

die Adresse, -n address (E)

der Adventskalender, - Advent calendar (7)

der Affe, -n, -n ape; monkey (2)

(das) Afrika Africa (6-1)

afrikanisch *(adj)* African (2)

der Agent, -en, -en/die Agentin, -nen agent (5)

aggressiv aggressive (12-1)

ähnlich similar (9-2)

akademisch academic (1)

die Aktivität, -en activity (12)

der Alarm: der stille Alarm silent alarm (11-1)

alarmieren to alarm (11)

das Album, Alben album (4, 6-2)

der Alkohol alcohol (2, 4-2)

alkoholisch *(adj)* alcoholic (6)

das All outer space (12)

alle all (the) (1); everybody (7)

allein alone (6-1)

alleinstehend single, alone (12)

allergisch (gegen) allergic (to) (8)

alles everything; all (1, 3-2)

Alles zusammen summary (*literally*: all together) (1)

Es ist alles für die Katz. It's all for nothing. (10)

das Allgemeinwissen general knowledge (12)

die Alliierten *(pl)* the Allies (11-2)

das Alltagsleben everyday life (4)

der **Alltagsmief** stale routine (12)

die **Alltagsszene, -n** everyday scene (4)

die **Alm, -en** alpine pasture

  der **Almabtrieb** *autumn cattle drive bringing the cows down from the alpine pastures* (7)

die **Alpen** *(pl)* Alps (1)

als as (1, 10-1); than (2); when *(conj)* (3, 10-1); but (10)

  als Hauptspeise as a main dish (main course) (9-1)

  als Kind as a child (5)

also so, thus (6)

alt old (1, 3-2, 5-1); used (9)

die **Altbatterie, -n** used battery (9)

die **Alte Pinakothek** *art gallery in Munich* (5)

das **Alter** age (1); old age (12)

die **Altersvorsorge** providing for one's old age, retirement provision (12)

das **Altfahrzeug, -e** scrapped car (9)

altmodisch old-fashioned (5-2)

das **Altöl, -e** used oil, waste oil (9)

das **Altpapier, -e** wastepaper (9)

(das) Amerika America (4)

der **Amerikaner, -** / die **Amerikanerin, -nen** American *(person)* (1-1)

amerikanisch *(adj)* American (2)

das **Amt, ̈er** office, department (8)

an *(prep + acc/dat)* about; at; to; on *(a vertical surface)* (2, 8)

an·bieten, bot an, angeboten to offer (12)

das **Andenken, -** souvenir (11-2)

ander- different, other (1)

ändern to change (4)

anders different(ly) (2)

der **Anfang, ̈e** beginning (4-2)

  am Anfang at the beginning (11-2)

  Anfang Juli (at) the beginning of July (5-1)

an·fangen (fängt an), fing an, angefangen to begin; to start (4-1, 4-2)

der **Anfänger, -** / die **Anfängerin, -nen** beginner (9)

an·fassen to touch (11)

an·fragen to inquire (5)

das **Angebot, -e** offering, choice (5-1)

angeln to fish (3, 5-1)

der **Angler, -** / die **Anglerin, -nen** fisher (5)

die **Angst, ̈e** fear (6)

  Angst haben vor *(+ dat)* to be afraid of (10-2, 11-2)

  Angst kriegen to get scared (6)

angstvoll fearful (10)

an·halten (hält an), hielt an, angehalten to stop (4-2, 10-1)

der **Anhang, ̈e** appendix

an·hören to listen to (4-2)

die **Anknüpfung, -en** connection (12)

an·kommen, kam an, ist angekommen to arrive (4-2)

an·kotzen: es kotzt mich an *(colloquial)* it makes me puke (12)

an·leinen to leash (a dog) (11)

an·locken to attract (5)

die **Anmeldung, -en** registration (2)

an·probieren to try on (4-2)

die **Anreise, -n** arrival (5)

an·rufen, rief an, angerufen to call *(on the telephone)* (4-2)

an·schauen to look at (5-2); to watch (9)

  sich *(dat)* **etwas an·schauen** to look at something; to watch something (9)

die **Anschauung, -en** view, opinion (12)

anschließen, schloss an, angeschlossen to annex (11)

der **Anschluss, ̈e** connection; access (8); annexation (11)

  der **Internetanschluss, ̈e** Internet access (8)

an·sehen (sieht an), sah an, angesehen to watch (6)

der **Anspruch, ̈e** right to (12)

antifaschistisch *(adj)* anti-fascist (11)

die **Antwort, -en** answer (E, 1-2)

antworten *(+ dat)* to answer (1, 7-2)

die **Anzeige, -n** ad; announcement (7-2)

sich **an·ziehen, zog an, angezogen** to dress, to get dressed (9-2)

der **Anzug, ̈e** *(men's)* suit (2-2)

der **Apfel, ̈** apple (1)

  Der Apfel fällt nicht weit vom Stamm. Like father, like son. (7)

der **Apfelkuchen, -** apple pie (10)

der **Apfelpfannkuchen, -** apple pancake (11)

der **Apfelsaft** *(sing)* apple juice (4)

der **Apfelstrudel, -** apple strudel (9)

die **Apotheke, -n** pharmacy (8, 9-2)

die / das **App, -s** app *(for mobile devices)* (2)

der **Apparat, -e** apparatus, appliance (9)

der **Appetit** appetite (4)

  Guten Appetit! Enjoy your meal! (4-1)

der **April** April (1-2)

das **Äquivalent, -e** equivalent (8)

die **Arbeit** work (2-2)

arbeiten to work (1-2)

  arbeiten an *(+ dat)* to work on (11-2)

der **Arbeiter, -** / die **Arbeiterin, -nen** worker (5)

der **Arbeitgeber, -** / die **Arbeitgeberin, -nen** employer (9, 12-1)

der **Arbeitnehmer, -** / die **Arbeitnehmerin, -nen** employee (9, 12-1)

das **Arbeitsblatt, ̈er** worksheet (12)

die **Arbeitserfahrung, -en** work experience (12)

arbeitslos unemployed (11)

die **Arbeitslosigkeit** unemployment (11)

das **Arbeitszimmer, -** study (8)

der **Architekt, -en, -en** / die **Architektin, -nen** architect (8-2)

die **Architektur** architecture (8)

der **Ärger** annoyance, trouble (11)

ärgern to make angry; annoy (10-2)

  sich **ärgern über** *(+ acc)* to be annoyed with, about (11-2)

das **Argument, -e** argument (5-2)

arm poor (5-2)

der **Arm, -e** arm (1, 6-1)

das **Armband, ̈er** bracelet (3, 5-2)

die **Armee, -n** army (4)

arrogant arrogant (10)

die **Art, -en** type; way; method (1, 12)

der **Artikel, -** article (4)

der **Arzt, ̈e** / die **Ärztin, -nen** physician (4, 5-2)

der **Asiat, -en, -en** / die **Asiatin, -nen** Asian *(person)* (9)

(das) Asien Asia (6-1)

der **Assistent, -en, -en** / die **Assistentin, -nen** assistant (2)

das **Asyl, -e** asylum (6)

die **ATM-Karte, -n** ATM card (5-2)

die **Attraktion, -en** attraction (3)

auch also (E, 1-1)

  Claudia kommt auch nicht. Claudia isn't coming either. (1-2)

der **Audi, -s** Audi *(car)* (5)

auf *(prep + acc/dat)* up (4); on, onto (6); to; on *(a horizontal surface)* (8)

auf·bauen to build something

  ein (neues) Leben aufbauen to build a (new) life (6-1)

das **Aufbaumodul, -e** preliminary course, module (1)

auf·bleiben, blieb auf, ist aufgeblieben to stay up (12)

der **Aufenthalt, -e** stay (5-1)

auffällig noticeable, recognizable (10)

auf·füllen to fill up (6)

die **Aufgabe, -n** assignment; task (7, 12-1)

auf·hängen to hang (*something*) up (8)

auf·hören to end; to stop (4-2)

auf·listen to list (7)

auf·machen to open (8-2, 11-1)

auf·passen to pay attention (4-2)

auf·räumen to clean up (4-2)

sich **auf·regen** to get worked up; to get upset (9-2)

auf·runden to round up (*when tipping waitstaff*) (9-1)

auf·schreiben, schrieb auf, aufgeschrieben to write down (4, 10-1)

auf·springen, sprang auf, ist aufgesprungen to jump out, up (10)

auf·stehen, stand auf, ist aufgestanden to stand up; to get up (4)

auf·teilen to divvy up (8)

auf·wachen to wake up (4-2)

das **Auge, -n** eye (2, 6-1)

kein Auge zutun to not sleep a wink (6)

der **August** August (1-2)

aus (*prep + dat*) from, out of (E-1)

aus·bauen to develop (11)

die **Ausbildung, -en** job training; education (12-1)

der **Ausdruck, ⸚e** expression (1)

die **Ausgabe, -n** edition (7)

aus·geben (gibt aus), gab aus, ausgegeben to spend (*money*) (6-2); to spend; to disburse (11)

ausgebildet: gut ausgebildet sein to be well-educated; to be well-trained (12-1)

aus·gehen, ging aus, ist ausgegangen to go out (4-2); to run out (*of something*) (12)

ausgezeichnet excellent (3-2)

aus·helfen (hilft aus), half aus, ausgeholfen to help out (12)

aus·höhlen to hollow out (7)

aus·kommen, kam aus, ist ausgekommen to get by (9); to get along

das **Ausland** foreign countries (5)

im Ausland abroad (5)

das **Auslandsamt** foreign students office (1-1)

aus·lösen to trigger (11)

aus·machen to represent, to constitute (6, 11)

aus·packen to unpack (6-2)

aus·probieren to try out (4-2)

die **Ausrichtung: die sexuelle Ausrichtung** sexual orientation (12)

die **Aussage, -n** statement (7)

das **Aussehen** (*sing*) looks, appearance (12)

aus·sehen (sieht aus), sah aus, ausgesehen (wie) to look (like), appear (7-1)

außen outside (12)

die **Außenpolitik, -en** foreign policy (1)

außer (*prep + dat*) except for (7)

Sie war außer sich. She was beside herself. (10-2)

außerdem besides; in addition (7-1)

außerhalb von (*+ dat*) outside of (3)

die **Aussage, -n** statement (7)

die **Aussprache** pronunciation (E)

aus·sprechen (spricht aus), sprach aus, ausgesprochen to pronounce; to say out loud (9-1)

die **Ausstattung** facilities (8)

aus·steigen, stieg aus, ist ausgestiegen to get off (*a train, bus, etc.*) (4-2)

aus·stellen to exhibit (6)

die **Ausstellung, -en** exhibition, exhibit (6, 8-2)

aus·tricksen (*colloquial*) to outfox, fool (10)

das **Austauschsemester, -** semester abroad (6)

(das) **Australien** Australia (*continent*) (6)

australisch Australian (7)

aus·üben to practice, perform (10)

die **Auswahl** selection, choice (7)

der **Auswanderer, -/die Auswanderin, -nen** emigrant (6-1)

aus·wandern, wanderte aus, ist ausgewandert to emigrate (6-1)

sich **aus·ziehen, zog aus, hat ausgezogen** to undress, to get undressed (9-2)

das **Auto, -s** car (1, 3-1)

Auto fahren (fährt Auto), fuhr Auto, ist Auto gefahren to drive (4)

die **Autobahn, -en** freeway, expressway (4-2)

die **Autobiografie, -n** autobiography (10-2)

die **Autofahrt, -en** drive, journey by car (7)

der **Automechaniker, -/die Automechanikerin, -nen** (car) mechanic (9)

der **Autor, -en/die Autorin, -nen** author (2)

der **Autounfall, ⸚e** car accident (11)

B

das **Baby, -s** baby (2)

der **Bachelor, -** Bachelor's degree (1)

backen (bäckt), backte, gebacken to bake (3-2)

der **Bäcker, -/die Bäckerin, -nen** baker (E)

die **Bäckerei, -en** bakery (7-2)

das **Bad, ⸚er** bath; bathroom (2, 8-1)

der **Badeanzug, ⸚e** bathing suit (4)

die **Bademöglichkeit, -en** (*place to go*) swimming; swimming facility (5-1)

baden to swim; to bathe (5-1)

baden gehen to go swimming (5)

sich **baden** to bathe (oneself), to take a bath (9-2)

die **Badewanne, -n** bathtub (8-1)

das **Badezimmer, -** bathroom (8-1)

der **Bagel, -s** bagel (4-1)

die **Bahn** (*sing*) railway (4)

der **Bahnhof, ⸚e** train station (4-2)

das **Bahnticket, -s** train ticket (5)

das **Bakterium, Bakterien** bacterium (10)

bald soon (1, 2-2)

so bald wie möglich as soon as possible (4)

der **Balkon, -s** balcony (8-1)

der **Ball, ⸚e** ball (1)

der **Balletttänzer, -/die Balletttänzerin, -nen** ballet dancer (2)

die **Banane, -n** banana (1, 4-1)

die **Band, -s** band (*music*) (1, 2-1)

die **Bank, -en** bank (5)

die **Banknote, -n** banknote (6)

der **Bär, -en, -en** bear (3)

einen Bärenhunger haben to be famished (10)

das **Barometer, -** barometer (2)

barrierefrei wheelchair accessible (5-1)

der **Bart, ⸚e** beard (5-2)

die **Baseballkappe, -n** baseball cap (1, 5-2)

der **Basketball, ⸚e** basketball (2)

Basketball spielen to play basketball (2-1)

der **Basketballspieler, -e/die Basketballspielerin, -nen** basketball player (2)

das **Basteln** (*sing*) crafts (4)

die **Batterie, -n** battery (9-2)

der **Bau** construction (10)

der **Bauch, ⸚e** stomach; belly (5)

die **Bauchschmerzen** (*pl*) stomachache (7)

bauen to build (5, 10-1)

Auf ihn kannst du Häuser bauen. He's absolutely dependable. (8)

der **Bauer, -n, -n/die Bäuerin, -nen** farmer (10)

die **Baugestaltung, -en** building design, layout (8)

der **Baum, ⸚e** tree (5-1)

baumlos treeless (12)

die **Baumwolle, -n** cotton (9)

bayerisch (*adj*) Bavarian (E)

(das) **Bayern** Bavaria (2)

der **Beachvolleyball** beach volleyball (E)

der **Beamer, -** LCD projector (E)

beantworten to answer (7, 9-1)

    eine Frage beantworten to answer a question (7, 9-1)

der **Becher, -** cup; container (4-1)

    ein Becher Joghurt a container of yogurt (4-1)

bedeckt cloudy (1)

bedeuten to mean (2-2, 6-2)

bedeutend important, prominent (6-1)

die **Bedeutung, -en** meaning (8)

bedeutungslos meaningless (12)

bedienen to serve (*guests in a restaurant*) (9-1)

die **Bedienung** (*sing*) waiter/ waitress, server (*in a restaurant*) (9-1)

sich **beeilen** to hurry (9-2)

beenden to end (11)

der **Befehl, -e** order, command (11-1)

der **Befragte, -n** interviewee (9)

befreien to rescue (10)

befreundet friendly, chummy (1)

befürchten to fear (6)

begabt endowed (6); talented

begeistert excited, thrilled (6-2)

der **Beginn** beginning (1)

    zu Beginn at the beginning (11-2)

beginnen, begann, begonnen to begin (1-1)

begreifen, begriff, begriffen to understand, to grasp, to comprehend (12-1)

der **Begründer, -** / die **Begründerin, -nen** orignator, founder (10)

beherrschen to know (5)

die **Behinderung, -en** disability, disablement (4)

bei (*prep + dat*) at (E); for; near, close to (7)

    bei uns, bei Zieglers at our house, at the Zieglers' (2-1)

beide both; two (2-2)

die **Beilage, -n** side dish (9-1)

das **Bein, -e** leg (6)

    Hals- und Beinbruch! Break a leg! Good luck! (6)

das **Beispiel, -e** example (6)

    zum Beispiel (z. B.) for example (e.g.) (3, 12)

beißen, biss, gebissen to bite (3)

der **Beistelltisch, -e** end table (8)

beizen to stain wood (9)

bekannt well-known (1, 4-2)

das **Bekenntnis, -se** religious affiliation (12)

bekommen, bekam, bekommen to get; to receive (1, 2-1, 10-2)

beleuchtet lit (3)

die **Beleuchtungsanlage, -n** illumination system (11)

belgisch (*adj*) Belgian (7)

beliebt popular, well-loved, beloved (1, 9-1)

bemalt painted (11)

sich **benehmen (benimmt), benahm, benommen** to behave (9-2)

benutzen to use (8-1)

das **Benzin, -e** gasoline (9)

die **Beobachtung, -en** observation (11-1)

der **Beobachtungsturm, ⸚e** (guards') observation tower (11-1)

die **Bereicherung, -en** enrichment (6)

bereuen to regret (12)

der **Berg, -e** mountain (5-1)

der **Bericht, -e** report (10-2)

berichten to report (8)

die **Bermudashorts** (*pl*) Bermuda shorts (3)

der **Beruf, -e** profession, occupation (3)

    Er ist Manager von Beruf. He's a manager by profession. (3)

    Was sind Sie von Beruf? What's your occupation? (3-2)

berühmt famous (3-2, 5-2)

berühren to touch (1)

beschäftigen to occupy, do activity (12)

die **Bescherung** gift-giving (*at Christmas*) (7)

beschreiben, beschrieb, beschrieben to describe (6)

die **Beschreibung, -en** description (11)

die **Beseitigung** elimination (12)

besondere(r, s) special

    besondere Kennzeichen distinguishing marks (6)

besonders particularly, especially (1-2)

besprechen to discuss (10)

besser better (1)

    besser als better than (3)

best- best (2)

das **Besteck, -e** silverware, cutlery (9-1)

bestellen to order (6, 9-1)

bestimmt definite(ly); for sure (4, 5-2)

das **Bestreben** effort; ambition (6)

der **Besuch, -e** visit (3)

    zu Besuch kommen to come to visit (8-2)

besuchen to visit (2-2)

der **Besucher, -** / die **Besucherin, -nen** visitor (5)

der **Beton** concrete (11-1)

der **Betonklotz, ⸚e** concrete block (11)

die **Betonplattenwand, ⸚e** wall made from concrete slabs (11)

betreuen to take care of (12)

die **Betreuung** care, assistance, support (12)

die **Betriebszeit, -en** business hours, hours of operation (3)

das **Bett, -en** bed (1, 8-1)

    ins Bett to bed (1-2)

das **Bettzeug** (*sing*) bedding, sheets, bedclothes (3)

bevor before (*sub conj*) (4-2)

sich **bewegen** to get some exercise, to move about (9-2)

beweglich movable (10)

sich **bewerben (bewirbt), bewarb, beworben** to apply (11-2)

    sich **bewerben um** to apply for (11-2)

bezahlen to pay (4, 6-2)

    getrennt bezahlen to pay separately (9-1)

    zusammen bezahlen to pay as a group (9-1)

die **Bezahlung** pay; wages (6, 12-1)

die **Beziehung, -en** relationship (12-1)

die **Bibel, -n** bible (10-1)

die **Bibliothek, -en** library (1)

    in die Bibliothek to the library (1-2)

die **Biene, -n** bee (10)

das **Bier** beer (1, 2-1)

    Das ist nicht mein Bier! That's not my problem! (1)

der **Bierbauch, ⸚e** beer belly (5)

der **Biergarten, ⸚** beer garden (5)

das **Bierglas, ⸚er** beer glass (1)

bieten, bot, geboten to offer (11)

das **Bild, -er** picture; painting (6, 8-2)

das **Bilderbuch, ⸚er** storybook; picture book (7)

die **Bildung** education (12)

das **Billard** (*sing*) billiards (2)

billig cheap (2-2)

der **Bioabfall, ⸚e** biowaste (9)

die **Biochemie** biochemistry (2)

biografisch biographical (3)

die **Biologie** biology (1)

der **Biologe, -n, -n**/die **Biologin, -nen** biologist (2)

das **Bio-Siegel** organic certification (9)

das **Birchermüsli, -s** muesli, cereal *(made from oats, milk, apple juice, lemon juice, apples, honey, yogurt, and nuts)* (4)

die **Birne, -n** pear (9-1)

bis until *(prep + acc)* (2-1); *(sub conj)* (6)

  Bis später! See you later! (1-1)

  von … bis from … to (1-2)

bisschen: ein bisschen a bit (1-2)

bitte please (E, 1-1)

  Bitte! You're welcome! (E-1)

  Wie bitte? Pardon? (E-1)

blau blue (1-1); drunk *(colloquial)* (3)

das **Blaukraut** red cabbage (3)

der **Blazer, -** blazer (E)

bleiben, blieb, ist geblieben to stay, to remain (3, 4-2)

der **Blick, -e** look (4)

blitzen: es blitzt it's lightning (1)

die **Blockade, -n** blockade (11-1)

blockieren to block (11-1)

blöd stupid; dumb (2-1)

der **Blog, -s** blog (3)

bloggen to blog (2-1)

blond blond (1, 3-2)

bloß *(flavoring particle)* **Warum denn bloß?** Why on earth is this happening? (6)

blühen to blossom; to flourish (5-1)

blühend blooming (5)

die **Blume, -n** flower (1, 6-2)

das **Blumengeschäft, -e** flower shop (6)

der **Blumenladen, ∵** flower shop (8)

der **Blumenstrauß, ∵e** flower bouquet (7)

die **Bluse, -n** blouse (1, 2-2)

das **Blut** blood (1)

die **Blüte, -n** blossom (5)

der **Bodensee** Lake Constance (4)

das **Boot, -e** boat (1)

die **Bootsfahrt, -en** boat ride (5)

der **Böögg, -e** *(Switzerland)* giant snowman (7)

der **Boss, -e** bossman, top dog (1)

die **Botanik** botany (2)

brandneu brand-new (10-1)

brasilianisch *(adj)* Brazilian (2)

die **Bratkartoffeln** *(pl)* fried potatoes (4-1)

die **Bratwurst, ∵e** sausage, bratwurst (9)

brauchen to need (3-2); to take *(of time)* (4)

das **Brauhaus, ∵er** brew house (3)

braun brown (1-1)

das **Brautkleid, -er** wedding dress (3)

der **Breitensport** recreational *(incl. intramural)* sport (2)

die **Brezel, -n** pretzel (10)

der **Brief, -e** letter (E)

die **Briefmarke, -n** stamp (8)

der **Briefträger, -**/die **Briefträgerin, -nen** letter carrier (7-2)

die **Brille, -n** (eye)glasses (3, 5-2)

bringen, brachte, gebracht to bring (4, 6-2)

britisch *(adj)* British

der **Brokkoli** broccoli (9)

die **Broschüre, -n** brochure (5-1)

das **Brot, -e** bread; sandwich (1, 4-1)

  belegte Brote open-faced sandwiches (4-1)

  das tägliche Brot daily sustenance (10)

das **Brötchen, -** roll (4-1)

  das belegte Brötchen sandwich (9-1)

die **Brücke, -n** bridge (3)

der **Bruder, ∵** brother (1, 3-1)

brünett brunette (3-2)

die **Brust, ∵e** breast; chest (6-1, 9)

das **Buch, ∵er** book (1-1)

der **Buchdruck** printing (10)

buchen to book *(travel accommodations)* (5-1)

die **Buchhandlung, -en** bookstore (1)

das **Bücherregal, -e** bookcase (8-1)

sich **buchstabieren: Das buchstabiert sich …** That's spelled … (1)

das **Buchungszeitraum, ∵e** booking period (5)

das **Bügeleisen, -** iron *(for clothes)* (8-2)

bügeln to iron (8-2)

der **Bulle, -n** bull (1)

der **Bund, ∵e** league (2)

der **Bundeskanzler, -**/die **Bundeskanzlerin, -nen** federal chancellor (6)

das **Bundesland, ∵er** German state (2)

die **Bundesliga, Bundesligen** premier league *(of sports)* (2)

der **Bundespräsident, -en, -en**/die **Bundespräsidentin, -nen** federal president (5)

das **Bundesministerium, Bundesministerien** federal ministry (12)

die **Bundesrepublik Deutschland (die BRD)** the Federal Republic of Germany (the FRG) (1-1)

der **Bundestag** German parliament (11-2)

bunt colorful (3)

die **Burg, -en** castle (10)

der **Bürger, -**/die **Bürgerin, -nen** citizen (9-2, 11-1)

das **Büro, -s** office (4)

die **Bürokratie, -n** bureaucracy (11)

bürsten to brush (9)

  sich *(dat)* **die Haare bürsten** to brush one's hair (9)

der **Bus, -se** bus (2, 3-1)

die **Bushaltestelle, -n** bus stop (12)

die **Buslinie, -n** bus route (5)

die **Butter** butter (1, 4-1)

  Es ist alles in Butter. Everything's going smoothly. (7)

C

der **Camembert** Camembert *(cheese)* (7)

campen to camp (4, 5-1)

  campen gehen to go camping (8)

das **Campen** camping (5-1)

der **Campingplatz, ∵e** campground; campsite (5-1)

der **Campus, -** campus (1)

die **CD, -s** compact disc, CD (8)

das **Celsius** celsius (1)

der **Cent, -** cent (9)

der **Champagner** champagne (7)

der **Champignon, -s** mushroom (9-1)

(die) **Chanukka** Hanukkah (7)

charakterisieren to characterize (8)

chatten to chat *(online)* (E)

das **Chatten** chatting *(online)* (2)

checken to check (9)

der **Cheddar** cheddar (cheese) (7)

der **Chef, -s**/die **Chefin, -nen** boss (5-2)

der **Chinese, -n, -n**/die **Chinesin, -nen** Chinese *(person)* (9)

chinesisch *(adj)* Chinese (4)

der **Chip, -s** potato chip (4); computer chip

der **Chor, ∵e** choir (5)

die **Chronik** chronicle (11)

Ciao! Bye! (E-1)

circa around, about, approximately (9)

der **Club, -s** club (2-1)

die **Cola, -s** cola (2-1)

das **College, -s** college (8)

die **Comics** *(pl)* comics (3)

der **Computer, -** computer (1)

das **Computerspiel, -e** computer game (1, 7-1)

der **Container, -** container (9)

cool cool (*excellent*) (E, 2-2)
  ziemlich cool kind of cool
    (*colloquial*) (5-2)
die **Cornflakes** (*pl*) cornflakes
  (*cereal*) (4)
die **Couch, -s** couch (8-1)
der **Couchtisch, -e** coffee table (8-1)
die **Currywurst** curry sausage (9)
das **Cyber-Mobbing** cyber-bullying (2)

D
da then (4)
das **Dach, ̈er** roof (8-2)
  eins aufs Dach kriegen to be
    bawled out (8)
dafür for it (6)
damalig at the time, former (7)
damals back then; at that time
  (6, 10-1)
die **Dame, -n** lady (1)
damit so that (*sub conj*) (6)
der **Dampf, ̈e** steam (11)
die **Dampfnudel, -n** dumpling (9)
danach accordingly (10)
der **Dank** thanks (2)
  Gott sei Dank! Thank God! (8,
    10-2)
  Tausend Dank! A thousand
    thanks! (2)
  Vielen Dank! Many thanks! (5)
danke thank you (E-1)
  Danke, gut. Fine, thanks. (E-1)
  Danke schön! Thank you!
danken (*+ dat*) to thank (2, 7-2)
  danken für to thank for (11)
dann then (E, 1-1)
darauf·streuen to sprinkle over (4)
das **Darts, -** darts (2)
das this; that (E, 1)
das heißt (d. h.) that means, that is
  (i.e.) (6-1, 12)
dass that (*sub conj*) (5)
dasselbe the same (7)
die **Dattel, -n** date (*fruit*) (9)
das **Datum, Daten** date (5); (*pl*) data
  (12)
die **Dauer** length, period, term (5)
die **Dauerhaftigkeit** durability (9)
dauern to last (7)
der **Debattierklub, -s** debate club (12)
decken: den Tisch decken to set the
  table (7-1)
dein, dein, deine your (2)
der **Delfin, -e** dolphin (2)
die **Demokratie, -n** democracy (1,
  11-1)
demonstrieren to demonstrate (10)
denken, dachte, gedacht to think (5)
  denken an (*+ acc*) to think, about,
    of (10-1, 11-2)

der **Denker, -**/die **Denkerin,**
  -nen philosopher (10)
das **Denkmal, ̈er** monument;
  memorial; statue (5)
  das **Völkerschlachtdenkmal** Battle
    of Leipzig monument (5)
der **Denkmalschutz** protection of
  historic sites (11)
denn because, for (*coord conj*) (1-2)
deportieren to deport (11)
derselbe, dasselbe, dieselbe the
  same (7, 9-2)
deshalb therefore; that's why (4-2)
der **Designer, -**/die **Designerin,**
  -nen designer (8-2)
das **Dessert, -s** dessert (9)
der **Detektiv, -e**/die **Detektivin,**
  -nen detective (7)
deutsch (*adj*) German (2)
das **Deutsch** German (*language*) (E)
  auf Deutsch in German (E)
der/die **Deutsche, -n** German
  (*person*) (1-1)
die **Deutsche Demokratische**
  Republik (DDR) German
  Democratic Republic (GDR) (7)
der **Deutschkurs, -e** German course;
  German class (4)
(das) **Deutschland** Germany (1)
deutschsprachig German-speaking
  (4, 9-1)
der **Deutschunterricht, -e** German
  class (5)
der **Dezember** December (1-2)
das **Dia, -s** slide, transparency (11)
der **Dialekt, -e** dialect (10-1)
der **Dichter, -**/die **Dichterin,**
  -nen writer; poet (10-1)
dick thick; fat (2-2)
dickköpfig stubborn (11-2)
der **Diebstahl, ̈e** theft; burglary (10-2)
der **Dienst, -e** service (12-2)
der **Dienstag** Tuesday (1-2)
  am Dienstag on Tuesday (2)
  am Dienstag früh early on
    Tuesday (6)
  am Dienstagabend on Tuesday
    evening (2)
  am Dienstagmorgen on Tuesday
    morning (2)
  am Dienstagnachmittag on
    Tuesday afternoon (2)
  dienstags Tuesdays, on Tuesdays (2)
dieselbe the same (7)
der **Dieselmotor, -en** diesel motor (10)
dieser, dieses, diese this (2)
diesmal this time (7)
die **Diktatur, -en** dictatorship (11-1)
das **Ding, -e** thing (2, 3-1)
direkt directly (5)

der **Direktor, -en**/die **Direktorin,**
  -nen director (*of a company*) (4)
die **Disco, -s** disco (1)
  in die Disco to the disco (1-2)
die **Diskrepanz, -en** discrepancy
  (12-1)
die **Diskriminierung,**
  -en discrimination (1, 12-2)
diskutieren to discuss (4)
disziplinlos undisciplined (12)
der **DJ, -s** DJ (E)
die **Djembe** African drum (7)
doch but; anyway (4); *used to
  contradict a negative statement or
  question* (10)
das **Dokument, -e** document (5)
der **Dokufilm, -e** (*short for* der
  Dokumentarfilm, -e)
  documentary film (3)
der **Dollar, -s** dollar (5)
  zehn Dollar ten dollars (5)
die **Donau** Danube (*river*) (1)
der **Döner, -** kebab (3)
der **Donner** thunder (1)
donnern: es donnert it's thundering (1)
der **Donnerstag** Thursday (1-2) (*see
  also* **Dienstag**)
doof stupid; dumb (2-1)
doppelt double (3)
das **Doppelzimmer, -** double
  room (5)
das **Dorf, ̈er** village (5-1)
dort there (1-2)
die **Dose, -n** can (8-2)
der **Dosenöffner, -** can opener (8-2)
downloaden to download (E, 2-1)
dramatisch dramatic (10)
die **Dreiergruppe, -n** group of
  three (10)
das **Dressing, -s** dressing (*for salad*)
  (9-1)
der **Dressman, Dressmen** male
  model (E)
drucken to print (10-1)
der **Drucker, -** printer (3)
die **Druckerei** print shop (10)
dumm stupid; dumb (2-1)
dunkel dark (1-2)
dünn thin; skinny (2-2)
durch (*prep + acc*) through (3)
durch·führen to execute; organize
  (12)
durch·lesen (liest durch), las durch,
  durchgelesen to read through
  (4-2)
durch·rauschen (*colloquial*) to sail
  through, to fly through, to rip
  through (6)
der **Durchschnitt, -e** average (12)
die **Durchsetzung** enforcement (12)

dürfen (darf), durfte, gedurft to be allowed to, be permitted to, may (4)

der Durst thirst (4)

   Ich habe Durst. I'm thirsty. (4-2)

die Dusche, -n shower (5, 8-1)

sich duschen to take a shower (9-2)

E

der E-Book-Reader e-book reader (3)

eben just (9)

echt real, really (2)

   echt schön really lovely 3)

   echt spitze really great (2-2)

die Ecke, -n corner (5-2)

egal: Das ist mir egal. I don't care. (7-2)

ehemalig former (10, 11-1)

der Ehemann, ̈er/die Ehefrau, -en husband/wife (10)

das Ehepaar, -e married couple (9)

ehrenamtlich on a voluntary basis (12-2)

ehrlich honest (4)

das Ei, -er egg (4-1)

eifersüchtig jealous (12)

   eifersüchtig auf (+ acc) jealous of (12-1, 12-2)

eigen own (3, 8-1)

eigentlich actually (11-1)

die Eile hurry (10)

   Es hat keine Eile. There's no rush. (10)

ein, ein, eine a; an; one (1)

einander each other, one another (E)

ein·brechen (bricht ein), brach ein, eingebrochen to break in (10-2)

eineinhalb one and a half (4)

einfach simple, simply (4-1, 7-2); ordinary (10-1)

ein·fallen (fällt ein), fiel ein, ist eingefallen to come to mind (7)

   Mir fällt nichts ein. I can't think of anything. (7-2)

das Einfamilienhaus, ̈er single-family home (8)

der Einfluss, ̈e influence (8-2, 10-2)

einflussreich influential (8)

das Einführungsmodul, -e introductory module (1)

der Eingang, ̈e entrance (1)

eingebaut built-in (11)

die Einheit, -en unity, whole (7)

das Einhorn, ̈er unicorn (1)

die Einkäufe (pl) shopping, purchases (9)

ein·kaufen to shop, (4, 5-2)

   einkaufen gehen to go shopping (5)

das Einkaufen shopping (7)

die Einkaufsmöglichkeit, -en shopping opportunity, facility (5)

die Einkaufstasche, -n reuseable shopping bag (9-2)

Einkommende Zeitungen Incoming News (name of a newspaper) (10)

ein·laden (lädt ein), lud ein, eingeladen to invite (4-2)

einmal once (7-2)

   noch (ein)mal once more; (over) again (7-2)

ein·marschieren to invade (11)

ein·packen to pack (4)

ein·planen to plan ahead (9)

einsam lonely (7)

der Einsatz, ̈e service, commitment, deployment (12)

ein·schlafen (schläft ein), schlief ein, ist eingeschlafen to fall asleep (4-2)

ein·steigen, stieg ein, ist eingestiegen to board, get on (a train, bus, etc.) (4-2)

der Eintritt admission (2)

der Einwanderer, -/die Einwanderin, -nen immigrant (6-1)

ein·wandern, wanderte ein, ist eingewandert to immigrate (6-1)

die Einwanderung immigration (6-1)

die Einwegflasche, -n nonreturnable, disposable bottle (9)

der Einwohner, -/die Einwohnerin, -nen inhabitant (9)

das Einzelkind, -er only child (3-1)

das Einzelzimmer, - single room (5)

der Einzelzimmerzuschlag, ̈e single room surcharge (5)

einzig single; only (7)

das Eis ice; ice cream (4-1)

das Eisen, - iron (9)

die Eisenpfanne, -n iron frying pan (9)

der Eiserne Vorhang Iron Curtain (11-2)

(das) Eishockey (ice) hockey (1)

   Eishockey spielen to play (ice) hockey (2-1)

eiskalt freezing, ice-cold (9)

der Eisregen, - freezing rain (8)

der Elefant, -en, -en elephant (2)

elegant elegant (2-2)

elektrisch electric(ally) (5)

das Elektronikgeschäft, -e electronics store (3)

das Element, -e element (5)

der Ellbogen, - elbow (1)

die Eltern (pl) parents (2, 3-1)

die E-Mail, -s e-mail (E)

die E-Mail-Adresse, -n e-mail address (E)

der Emigrant, -en, -en/die Emigrantin, -nen emigrant (6-1)

emigrieren to emigrate (8)

die Empfehlung, -en recommendation (6)

das Ende, -n end (1, 4-2)

   Ende Januar (at) the end of January (1-2, 5-1)

   zu Ende sein to be over (2-2)

enden to end (2)

endlich finally, at last (4-2)

endlos endless (12)

die Endung, -en ending (grammatical) (7)

die Energie, -n energy (4-1, 8-2)

energieeffizient energy efficient (9-2)

die Energiesparlampe, -n energy-saving lamp (9)

eng close; tight (9-1)

englisch (adj) English (2)

das Englisch English (language) (1)

   auf Englisch in English (1)

der Enkel, - grandson, grandchild (3-1)

die Enkelin, -nen granddaughter (3-1)

enorm enormous (8-2)

der Entdecker, -/die Entdeckerin, -nen discoverer (10)

enterben to disinherit (12)

der Entrepreneur, -e/die Entrepreneurin, -nen entrepreneur (3)

entscheiden, entschied, entschieden to decide (6-1)

   sich entscheiden für to decide on (11-2)

sich entschuldigen to apologize (9-2)

Entschuldigung! Excuse me! (E-1)

entweder ... oder either . . . or (4)

entwerfen (entwirft), entwarf, entworfen to design (8)

entwickeln to develop (4, 10-1)

die Entwicklung, -en development (10-1)

die Erde earth; ground (3, 10-2)

die Erdnuss, ̈e peanut (9-1)

erfahren (erfährt), erfuhr, erfahren to find out (12-2)

die Erfahrung, -en experience (12-2)

erfinden, erfand, erfunden to invent (10-1)

der Erfinder, -/die Erfinderin, -nen inventor (10-1)

die Erfindung, -en invention (10-1)

der Erfolg, -e success (7)

erfolglos unsuccessful(ly) (12)

erfolgreich successful(ly) (4-2)

erfüllt fulfilled (12)

ergänzen to complete (1); to supply (7)

erhalten (erhält), erhielt, erhalten to receive (10-1)

sich **erinnern an** (+ acc) to remember (11-2)

die **Erinnerung, -en** memory (10-2, 11-2)

sich **erkälten** to catch a cold (9-2)

erkältet sein to have a cold (12-2)

die **Erkältung, -en** cold (12-2)
  eine schwere Erkältung a bad cold (12-2)

erklärbar explicable (12)

erklären to explain; to declare (6-1)

die **Erklärung, -en** declaration; explanation (6-1)

erlaubt permitted (5-1)

erleben to experience (6, 11-2)

das **Erlebnis, -se** experience (11-2)

erledigen to accomplish, take care of (business) (12-2)

die **Ermäßigung, -en** discount (5)

ermäßigt reduced (in price) (5)

ermöglichen to make possible (4)

ermorden to murder (11-2)

das **Erntedankfest** harvest festival, Thanksgiving Day (7)

eröffnen to open up (shop) (11)

erreichen to reach (9)

erschaffen, erschuf, erschaffen to create (6)

erscheinen, erschien, ist erschienen to appear (10)

ersetzen (durch) to replace (with) (11)

erst (adv) not until (1-1)
  Die Vorlesungen beginnen erst morgen. (The) lectures don't begin until tomorrow. (1-1)

erst- first (1, 3-2)
  zum ersten Mal for the first time (8-2)

erstaunlicherweise astonishingly (6)

die **Erstkommunion** (sing) First Communion (7)

ertrinken, ertrank, ist ertrunken to drown (10)

der/die **Erwachsene, -n** adult (3)

erwarten to expect (6, 12-2)

erweitern to broaden (12)

erzählen to tell (a story) (6-1)
  erzählen von to tell about (11-2)

die **Erzählung, -en** story, narrative (6)

der **Erzbischof, -e** archbishop (3)

der **Esel, -** donkey (6)

die **Eselsbrücke, -n** mnemonic device (10)

essbar edible (12)

essen (isst), aß, gegessen to eat (3-2)
  zu Abend essen to have supper (4-1)
  zu Mittag essen to have lunch (4-1)

das **Essen** meal, food (7)

der **Esslöffel, -** tablespoon (4, 9-1)

das **Esszimmer, -** dining room (8-1)

die **Etage, -n** floor, story (7)

ethnisch ethnic (12)

das **Etui, -s** case (7)

etwa approximately (1, 7-2)

etwas something (4, 5-2)
  etwas knapp just barely in time (4)

euer, euer, eure your (2)

der **Euro, -s** euro (common European currency) (E, 2-2)

(das) **Europa** Europe (1, 6-1)

der **Europäer, -**/die **Europäerin, -nen** European (person) (6)

europäisch (adj) European (E)
  die **Europäische Union (die EU)** the European Union (the EU) (E, 3)

das **Examen, -** exam, test (1)

das **Exil, -e** exile (11)

das **Experiment, -e** experiment (5-2)

der **Export, -e** export (4)

exportieren to export (4)

extra (adv) separately (9)

das **Extrablatt, -er** special edition (11-1)

die **Extrawurst: eine Extrawurst wollen** to want special treatment (7)

extrovertiert extroverted (1)

F

fabelhaft fabulous (5)

der **Facebook-Kanal** Facebook page (6)

das **Fach, -er** field of study, subject (2-2)

die **Fähigkeit, -en** ability (12-2)

die **Fahne, -n** flag (7)

fahren (fährt), fuhr, ist gefahren to drive, to go (3-2)

das **Fahrenheit** Fahrenheit (1)

der **Fahrer, -**/die **Fahrerin, -nen** driver (5)

der **Fahrplan, -e** train or bus schedule (4-2)

das **Fahrrad, -er** bicycle (3-1)
  Fahrrad fahren to bicycle (5)

der **Fahrradabstellplatz, -e** bicycle parking area (8)

der **Fahrradhelm, -e** bicycle helmet (7-1)

der **Fahrradverleih, -e** bike rental (5-1)

die **Fahrt, -en** ride (7)

das **Fahrzeug, -e** vehicle (3-1)

fair fair (1)

der **Fakt, -en** (pl) fact (3)

der **Fall, -e** fall (11); case, circumstance (12)

fallen (fällt), fiel, ist gefallen to fall (6)
  Der Apfel fällt nicht weit vom Stamm. Like father, like son. (7)
  Er ist nicht auf den Kopf gefallen. He's no fool. (6)
  Mir fällt nichts ein. I can't think of anything. (7-2)

fällen to fell (6)

falls in case (8)

falsch wrong, incorrect, false (1-2)

die **Familie, -n** family (E, 3-1)

das **Familienauto, -s** family car (3)

der **Familienname, -ns, -n** last name, surname (E, 3-2)

die **Fantasie** imagination

fantasievoll imaginative (1)

fantastisch fantastic (E, 5-2)

die **Farbe, -n** color (1)
  Welche Farbe hat Lisas Bluse? What color is Lisa's blouse? (1)

färben to color, to dye (8)
  sich (dat) **die Haare färben** to color one's hair (9-2)

der **Farbfernseher, -** color TV (10)

das **Farbfoto, -s** color photo (7)

die **Farm, -en** farm (10)

der **Fasching, -s** (Southern Germany, Austria, Switzerland) Mardi Gras, carnival (7)

das **Fass, -er** barrel, drum (10)

die **Fassade, -n** façade (8)

fast almost (1-1)

fasten to fast (7-1)

die **Fastnacht, -en** (Rheinland) Mardi Gras, carnival (7)

faszinierend fascinating (11-2)

faul lazy (7-2)

der **Februar** February (1-2)

die **Feder, -n** feather (2)

fehlen to be missing (10)

der **Fehler, -** mistake; error (11-2)

fehlerlos error-free (12)

feiern to celebrate (7-1)

der **Feiertag, -e** holiday (7-1)

fein fine (1)

das **Feinkostgeschäft, -e** gourmet foods store (2)

der **Feinschmecker, -**/die **Feinschmeckerin, -nen** gourmet (7)

die **Feinschmecker-Etage** gourmet floor (6)

das **Feld, -er** field (5-1)

das **Fenster, -** window (7, 8-1)

die **Ferien** (*pl*) vacation (*generally of students*) (5-1)

> **Ferien machen** to go on vacation (5-1)

> **Wo machst du am liebsten Ferien?** Where's your favorite vacation spot? (5-1)

das **Ferienhaus, ̈er** vacation home (7)

der **Ferienjob, -s** summer job (6)

die **Ferienzeit** holiday time (5)

das **Ferkel, -** piglet (10)

der **Fernbus, -se** long-distance coach, bus (5-1)

das **Fernbusticket, -s** long-distance bus ticket (5)

fern·sehen (sieht fern), sah fern, ferngesehen to watch TV (4-2)

das **Fernsehen** TV (3)

der **Fernseher, -** television set (4-2)

> **vor dem Fernseher** in front of the TV (4-2)

das **Fernsehprogramm, -e** TV program (3, 10)

fertig ready; finished (4-1); (*with verbs*) finish (4)

das **Fertiggericht, -e** convenience food (12)

fertig lesen (liest fertig), las fertig, fertig gelesen to finish reading (5)

fertig schreiben, schrieb fertig, fertig geschrieben to finish writing (12)

fesseln to captivate, to grab (10)

fest stable (12)

das **Fest, -e** celebration; festival (2, 7-1, 12-1)

> **das Fest des Fastenbrechens** holiday marking the end of Ramadan (7)

fest·nehmen (nimmt fest), nahm fest, festgenommen to apprehend, arrest (11)

die **Fete, -n** party (7-2)

fett fat(ty) (10)

das **Fett** fat (10)

das **Fieber, -** fever (2)

die **Figur** (*sing*) figure; physique (10, 12-1)

der **Film, -e** film (1, 2-2)

der **Filmstar, -s** filmstar (*male or female*) (2)

die **Finanzwirtschaft** finance (1)

das **Finanzzentrum, Finanzzentren** financial center (4)

finden, fand, gefunden to find (1-2)

der **Finger, -** finger (1, 6-1)

der **Fingernagel, ̈** fingernail (1)

die **Firma, Firmen** business, company (2, 4-2)

der **Fisch, -e** fish (1, 4-1)

fischen to fish (2)

die **Fischerei** fish store; fishery (9)

fit fit (E)

sich **fit halten (hält), hielt, gehalten** to stay in shape (9-2)

das **Fitnessarmband, ̈er** fitness tracker (3)

das **Fitnesscenter, -** fitness center (5)

das **Fitnessstudio, -s** fitness studio (E, 12)

Fitnesstraining machen to work out (2-1)

der **Flammkuchen** tarte flambée (9)

die **Flasche, -n** bottle (5-1)

der **Flaschenöffner, -** bottle opener (7)

das **Fleisch** (*sing*) meat (4-1)

die **Fleischerei, -en** butcher shop (7)

fleischlos meatless (12)

fleißig hard-working (7-2)

der **Flickenanzug, ̈e** suit with patches (10)

fliegen, flog, ist geflogen to fly (1-2)

fliehen, floh, ist geflohen to flee (11-1)

fließen, floss, ist geflossen to flow (5-1)

Fließendwasser (*sing*) running water (*hotel*) (9)

das **Flirten** flirting (2)

der **Flohmarkt, ̈e** flea market (8-2)

die **Flöte, -n** flute (*musical instrument*) (4)

flüchten, flüchtete, ist geflüchtet to flee; to seek refuge (11-1)

der **Flüchtling, -e** refugee (6-2, 11-1)

die **Flüchtlingsbetreuung** refugee assistance (12)

der **Fluchtweg, -e** escape route (11-1)

der **Flug, ̈e** flight (5)

der **Flügel, -** wing (3-1)

der **Flughafen, ̈** airport (3)

das **Flugticket, -s** flight ticket (5)

das **Flugzeug, -e** airplane (3-1)

der **Flur, -e** hallway (8-1)

der **Fluss, ̈e** river (2, 5-1)

folgen, folgte, ist gefolgt (*+ dat*) to follow (6)

folgend following (5)

das **Folgende** following (4)

der **Föhn, -e** blow-dryer (9-2)

föhnen: sich (*dat*) **die Haare föhnen** to blow-dry one's hair (9-2)

das **Footballteam, -s** football team (1)

die **Form, -en** shape; form (4)

formulieren to formulate (10)

fort away (7)

das **Forum, Foren** forum (5)

das **Foto, -s** photo (1, 4-2)

das **Fotoalbum, -alben** photo album (2)

die **Fotografie, -n** photograph (8)

fotografieren to photograph, take a picture (2-1)

das **Fotomodell, -e** model (2)

die **Frage, -n** question (E, 1-2)

> **eine Frage beantworten** to answer a question (9-1)

> **eine Frage stellen** to ask a question (7-2)

> **Das kommt nicht in Frage!** That's out of the question! (9-2)

fragen to ask (1-2)

> **fragen nach** to ask about (10)

der **Franzose, -n, -n / die Französin, -nen** French (*person*) (9)

französisch (*adj*) French (1)

das **Französisch** French (*language*) (3)

Frau Mrs., Ms. (E-1)

die **Frau, -en** woman; wife (1, 2-2)

(das) **Fräulein, -** Miss (E)

frei free (*of time*) (2, 5-1); (*of space*) (4)

die **Freiheit** (*sing*) freedom (6-1, 11-2)

der **Freitag** Friday (1-2) (*see also* **Dienstag**)

freiwillig voluntarily (12-2)

die **Freizeit** free time; leisure time (5-1)

fressen (frisst), fraß, gefressen to eat (*of animals*) (10-2)

die **Freude, -n** joy, happiness (3)

sich **freuen auf** (*+ acc*) to look forward to (11-2)

sich **freuen über** (*+ acc*) to be happy about; to be pleased with (7, 11-2)

der **Freund, -e** (*male*) friend, boyfriend (1-2)

die **Freundin, -nen** (*female*) friend, girlfriend (1-2)

freundlich friendly (2-2, 3-1)

die **Freundlichkeit** friendliness (11)

die **Freundschaft, -en** friendship (2-2)

der **Frieden** peace (11-1)

das **Frisbee, -s** Frisbee (4)

frisch fresh (1)

der **Frischkäse** (*sing*) cream cheese (4)

die **Frisur, -en** hairdo; hair style (5-2)

froh happy (7)

fröhlich happy, merry (7-1)

die **Frucht, ̈e** fruit (4-1)

früh early (4-1)

> **morgen früh** tomorrow morning (7)

der **Frühling** spring (1-2)

das **Frühstück** breakfast (4-1)

> **zum Frühstück** for breakfast (4-1)

frühstücken to have breakfast (4-1)

das **Frühstücksbüffet, -s** breakfast buffet (5)

die **Frühstücksgewohnheit, -en** breakfast habit (4)

frustriert frustrated (12)

der Fuchs, ⸚e fox (1)

fühlen to feel (8)

    sich **wohl fühlen** to feel at home (8); to feel well (9-2)

führen to lead, guide (10)

der Führerschein, -e driver's license (7-2)

die Führerscheinprüfung, -en driver's test (7)

füllen to fill (9-1)

fünft: zu fünft in a group of five (8)

funktional functional (8)

die Funktionalität, -en functionality (8)

für *(prep + acc)* for (1)

die Furche, -n furrow (10)

der Fuß, ⸚e foot (1, 6-1)

    Hand und Fuß haben to make sense (6)

    zu Fuß gehen to go on foot, to walk (4-2)

der Fußball, ⸚e soccer; soccer ball (E, 1)

    Fußball spielen to play soccer (1)

der Fußballer, -/die Fußballerin, -nen soccer player (1)

der/die Fußballprofi, -s professional soccer player (4)

das Fußballspiel, -e soccer game (5)

der Fußballspieler, -/die Fußballspielerin, -nen soccer player (2-1)

das Fußballstadion, -stadien soccer stadium (5)

das Fußballteam, -s soccer team (2)

das Fußballtrikot, -s soccer jersey (7)

die Fußball-Weltmeisterschaft, -en soccer World Cup (E)

der Fußboden, ⸚ floor (8-1)

die Fußgängerzone, -n pedestrian zone (8-2)

füttern to feed (6-2)

G

die Gabel, -n fork (9-1)

ganz quite; very; all; whole (3); absolutely; completely (4)

    die ganze Familie the whole family (3-2)

gar even (6); tender *(in cooking)* (9)

    gar nicht not at all (1-1)

die Garage, -n garage (8)

die Garderobe, -n front hall closet (8-1)

der Garten, ⸚ garden (1)

der Gärtner, -/die Gärtnerin, -nen gardener (E)

die Gasse, -n small street (3)

der Gast, ⸚e guest; customer *(in a restaurant)* (3, 7-2)

der Gastarbeiter, -/die Gastarbeiterin, -nen guest worker (6)

das Gästezimmer, - guest room (8)

das Gasthaus, ⸚er restaurant (6, 9-1)

die Gaststätte, -n restaurant (9)

die Gastronomie *(sing)* gastronomy (9-1)

das Gebäude, - building (8-2)

geben (gibt), gab, gegeben to give (3-2)

    es gibt *(+ acc)* there is, there are (3-2)

das Gebirge mountain range (5-1)

geboren born (1)

    Wo bist du geboren? Where were you born? (6-1)

    Ich bin in Polen geboren. I was born in Poland. (6-1)

gebraten roasted; pan-fried; sautéed (9-1)

der Gebrauchsgegenstand, ⸚e regularly used object (9)

gebürtig native-born, native (of)

    gebürtige Amerikaner *(pl)* native-born Americans (6-1)

die Geburt, -en birth (7)

das Geburtshaus, ⸚er house in which one was born (9)

der Geburtsort, -e birthplace (1, 6-1)

der Geburtstag, -e birthday (1, 6-2)

    Alles Gute zum Geburtstag! Happy Birthday! (7-1)

    Herzliche Glückwünsche zum Geburtstag! Happy Birthday! (7-1)

    zum Geburtstag for one's birthday (6, 7-1)

    zum Geburtstag gratulieren to wish a Happy Birthday (7-2)

die Geburtstagsfeier, -n birthday celebration, party (7)

das Geburtstagsgeschenk, -e birthday present (7)

die Geburtstagskarte, -n birthday card (7)

die Geburtstagsparty, -s birthday party (11)

die Gedenktafel, -n commemorative plaque (10)

das Gedicht, -e poem (4, 10, 12-2)

geeint unified (10)

die Gefahr, -en danger (10)

gefallen (gefällt), gefiel, gefallen *(+ dat)* to like (7)

    gefallen an *(+ dat)* to like about (7)

    Diese Jacke gefällt mir. I like this jacket. (7-2)

das Gefängnis, -se prison (11)

das Gefühl, -e feeling (11-2)

gefühllos unfeeling(ly) (12)

gefüllt stuffed (9-1)

gegen *(prep + acc)* against; around *(time)* (5)

die Gegend, -en area (3, 11-2)

das Gegenteil, -e opposite (E)

die Gegenwart present *(time)* (11)

der Gegner, -/die Gegnerin, -nen adversary, opponent (10)

gegenüber across *(the hall, the street, etc.)* (8-1)

gehackt *(adj)* chopped, minced (4)

gehen, ging, ist gegangen to go (1-1)

    Wie geht es Ihnen?/Wie geht's? How are you? (E-1)

    zu Fuß gehen to go on foot, to walk (4-2)

gehören *(+ dat)* to belong to (7-2)

geizen to be stingy (10)

gelb yellow (1-1)

das Geld money (2-2)

    Mir ist das Geld ausgegangen. I ran out of money. (12)

die Geldtasche, -n wallet (7-2)

gelten (gilt), galt, gegolten to be considered (9)

    gelten als to be recognized as (10-1)

das Gemälde, - painting, picture (10)

gemein common (10)

gemeinnützig charitable, not-for-profit (12)

gemeinsam common (2-2)

die Gemeinsamkeit, -en similarity (9-2)

die Gemeinschaft, -en community (8)

gemischt mixed (9-1)

das Gemüse *(sing)* vegetables (4-1)

gemütlich cozy; comfortable (5-1)

genau exact(ly); careful(ly) (4-1)

genauso just as (10)

die Genetik genetics (2)

genetisch genetic (12)

genug enough (4-2)

die Geografie geography (1)

geometrisch geometric (8)

geprellt cheated (10)

gerade just, just now (6, 7-1); currently (10)

das Gerät, -e utensil; appliance (8-2)

das Gericht, -e dish *(in a restaurant)* (9-1)

gerieben *(adj)* grated, ground (4)

die Germanistik *(sing)* German Studies (1)

gern (lieber, am liebsten) gladly (2)

    Ich hätte gern … I'd like (to have) … (9-1)

    jemand *(acc)* **gern haben** to like somebody (2)

    Ich koche gern. I like to cook. (2-1)

das **Gerüst, -e** framework (12)
gesamt entire (7)
der **Gesamtpreis, -e** total price (7)
das **Geschäft, -e** business; store (2, 3-2)
die **Geschäftsfrau, -en** businesswoman (3-2)
der **Geschäftsmann, ̈er** businessman (3-2)
das **Geschenk, -e** present, gift (7-1)
die **Geschenkkarte, -n** gift card (7-1)
die **Geschichte, -n** history; story (6-1)
  die **neuzeitliche Geschichte** modern history (1)
geschickt clever; coordinated (12)
geschieden divorced (3-1)
das **Geschirr** (*sing*) dishes, tableware (9-1)
das **Geschlecht, -er** gender (2, 12-1)
der **Geschmack** (*sing*) taste (7)
  den Geschmack treffen to appeal to the taste (9)
geschmacklos tasteless (5-2)
geschmackvoll tasteful (5-2)
die **Geschwister** (*pl*) sisters and brothers, siblings (3-1)
die **Gesellschaft, -en** company (5); community, society (12)
das **Gesetz, -e** law (12)
das **Gesicht, -er** face (6-1)
das **Gespräch, -e** conversation (1)
die **Gestalt** stature, build (6)
gestern yesterday (1, 3-2)
gestreift striped (11)
gesund healthy (3-2, 4-2)
die **Gesundheit** health (10)
das **Getränk, -e** beverage, drink (2-1)
die **Getränkeabteilung, -en** beverage department (6)
das **Getreide, -** grain (3)
getrennt separate(ly); separated (2)
  getrennt bezahlen to pay separately (9-1)
  getrennt leben to be separated (3)
der **Gewinn** winnings (7)
gewinnen, gewann, gewonnen to win (1, 10-2)
gewiss certain (6)
die **Gewohnheit, -en** (4) habit
gewöhnt accustomed (9)
gewürzt seasoned (9-1)
gießen, goss, gegossen to water (6-2)
die **Giraffe, -n** giraffe (2)
die **Gitarre, -n** guitar (E)
  Gitarre spielen to play the guitar (2-1)
das **Glas, ̈er** glass (1, 4-1)
  die Nase zu tief ins Glas stecken to drink too much (6)

ein Glas Orangensaft a glass of orange juice (4-1)
glatt straight (*of hair*); smooth (3-2)
glauben to believe, to think (1-2)
gleich equal (6-1)
gleich right away (4-2); same; right, directly; equal(ly) (11, 12-1)
  gleich um die Ecke right around the corner (5)
gleichbedeutend synonymous (8)
gleichberechtigt sein to have equal rights (12-1)
die **Gleichberechtigung** equal rights; equality (12-1)
die **Gleichstellung, -en** equal treatment (12)
gleichwertig of equal value (12)
glitzern to glitter (3)
das **Glockenspiel, -e** chimes; musical clockwork (5)
das **Glück** luck (8)
  zum Glück fortunately, luckily (5, 12-1)
glücklich happy (7-2)
die **Glückseligkeit, -en** happiness (6)
der **Glückwunsch, ̈e** congratulations, best wishes (*pl*) (7)
  Herzliche Glückwünsche zum Geburtstag! Happy Birthday! (7-1)
die **Glückwunschanzeige, -n** congratulatory announcement (7)
die **Glückwunschkarte, -n** (congratulatory) card (7)
das **Gold** gold (2)
golden gold (3)
das **Goldstück, -e** gold coin (10)
(das) **Golf** golf (2)
  Golf spielen to play golf (2-1)
googeln to search the Internet using Google; to do research online (E)
(der) **Gott** God (10)
  Gott sei Dank! Thank God! (8)
der **Gourmet, -s** gourmet (3)
der **Graben, ̈** trench (11)
das **Grad, -e** degree (1)
die **Grafik, -en** chart, diagram (9, 11-1)
das **Gras, ̈er** grass (1)
gratulieren (*+ dat*) to congratulate (7-2)
  zum Geburtstag gratulieren to wish a Happy Birthday (7-2)
grau gray (1-1)
grausam (*adv*) horribly, cruelly (10)
die **Grenze, -n** border (1, 11-1)
grenzenlos boundless (11)
der **Grenzstreifen, -** border strip (11)
der **Grenzübergang, ̈e** border crossing (11)

der **Grieche, -n, -n / die Griechin, -nen** Greek (*person*) (9)
das **Griechisch** Greek (*language*) (10)
griechisch (*adj*) Greek (7)
grillen to grill (8-1)
groß large; big, tall (1, 2-1)
die **Größe, -n** height; size (1)
die **Großeltern** (*pl*) grandparents (3-1)
die **Großmutter, ̈** grandmother (2, 3-1)
größtenteils for the most part, largely (10)
der **Großvater, ̈** grandfather (3-1)
Grüezi! Hello! (*Swiss German*) (E)
grün green (E, 1-1)
  im Grünen in the outdoors (12)
der **Grund, ̈e** reason (4, 12-1)
gründen to found (4)
das **Grundgesetz** Basic Law (*constitution of Germany*) (12)
das **Grundrecht, -e** basic right (*legal*) (11)
die **Gründung, -en** founding (4)
grunzen to grunt (3)
die **Gruppe, -n** group (2)
die **Gruppenarbeit** group work (11)
der **Gruß, ̈e** greeting (7)
  Herzliche Grüße Kind regards (*closing in a letter*) (7)
grüßen to greet; to say hello (10)
  Grüß dich! Hello! Hi! (E-1)
  Grüß Gott! Hello! (*in Southern Germany and Austria*) (E)
die **Grußformel, -n** greeting (E)
die **Grußkarte, -n** greeting card (7)
gucken to look (12)
das **Gulasch** goulash (9)
gurgeln to gargle (12)
die **Gurke, -n** gherkin; cucumber (9-1)
der **Gürtel, -** belt (2-2)
gut fine, good, well (E)
  Guten Appetit! Enjoy your meal! (4)
  Guten Tag! Hello! Hi! (E-1)
die **Güter** (*pl*) goods (11)
der **Gutschein, -e** voucher (7-1)
das **Gymnasium, Gymnasien** (*academic*) high school (1, 6-2)

H

das **Haar, -e** hair (1, 6-1)
  sich (*dat*) **die Haare waschen (wäscht), wusch, gewaschen** to wash one's hair (9-2)
  sich (*dat*) **die Haare bürsten** to brush one's hair (9)
die **Haarbürste, -n** hairbrush (9-2)

der **Haarschnitt, -e** haircut (5-2)
haben (hat), hatte, gehabt to have
(1, 2-1)
Ich hätte gern … I'd like (to have)
… (9-1)
jemand *(acc)* **gern haben** to like
somebody (2)
die **Haferflocken** *(pl)* oats (oatmeal)
(4-1)
das **Hähnchen, -** chicken (9-1)
die **Hähnchenbrust, ̈e** chicken
breast (9)
halb half (2)
halb neun half past eight (2)
der **Halbbruder, ̈** half brother (3)
die **Halbgeschwister** *(pl)* half sisters
and brothers (3)
die **Hälfte, -n** half (10)
die **Halle, -n** hall (2)
Hallo! hello! Hi! (E-1)
(das) **Halloween** *(sing)* Halloween (4)
der **Hals, ̈e** neck; throat
Hals- und Beinbruch! Break a leg!
Good luck! (7)
die **Halskette, -n** necklace (5-2)
die **Halsschmerzen** *(pl)* sore
throat (12)
halten (hält), hielt, gehalten to hold;
to stop; to keep (3-2)
der **Hamburger, -** hamburger *(food)*
(10)
der **Hammer, ̈** hammer (1)
der **Hamster, -** hamster (10)
die **Hand, ̈e** hand (1, 6-1)
Hand und Fuß haben to make
sense (6)
handeln to act *(behave)* (9-2)
die **Handlung, -en** action (9-2)
der **Handschuh, -e** glove (7-2)
das **Handtuch, ̈er** towel (9-2)
das **Handwerk, -e** craft; artisanry (8)
der **Handwerker, -/** die
Handwerkerin, -nen
craftsperson, tradesperson (8)
das **Handy, -s** cell phone (E, 2-1)
das **Handy-Cover, -s** cell phone case
hängen to hang *(put in a hanging
position)* (8)
hängen, hing, gehangen to hang *(be
in a hanging position)* (8)
die **Harfe, -n** harp (2)
harmlos harmless (12)
hart hard (1)
der **Harz** Harz Mountains *(pl)* (1)
der **Hase, -n, -n** hare (10)
**Mein Name ist Hase, ich weiß von
nichts.** Don't ask me. I don't
know anything about it. (10)
der **Hass** hate (6)
der **Hasskommentar, -e** hate-filled
commentary (6)

hassen to hate (3)
der **Haufen, -** pile (9); a lot of (12-2)
häufig often, frequently (2, 9-2)
der **Hauptbahnhof, ̈e** main railway
station (6)
das **Hauptfach, ̈er** major *(field of
study)* (4)
das **Hauptgericht, -e** main course
(4, 9-1)
die **Hauptstadt, ̈e** capital city (1, 5-2)
das **Haus, ̈er** house (1, 2-2)
Auf ihn kannst du Häuser bauen.
He's absolutely dependable. (8)
nach Hause gehen to go home
(4-1)
zu Hause sein to be at home
(4-1)
der **Hausarzt, ̈e/** die **Hausärztin,
-nen** family doctor (8)
die **Hausaufgabe, -n** homework
(assignment) (4-2)
das **Häuschen: aus dem Häuschen
sein** to be all excited (8)
die **Hausfrau, -en** housewife (3-2)
hausgemacht homemade (7, 9-1)
der **Haushalt, -e** household;
housekeeping; budget (12-1)
den Haushalt machen to do
household chores (12-1)
das **Haushaltsgerät, -e** household
appliance (8-2)
der **Hausmann, ̈er** househusband
(3-2)
der **Hausmeister, -** janitor; building
caretaker (8)
die **Hausnummer, -n** house number
(E)
der **Hausschuh, -e** slipper (3, 7-2)
das **Haustier, -e** pet (3-1)
die **Haut, Häute** skin (5)
die **Hautfarbe, -n** skin color (12)
der **Heilige Abend** Christmas
Eve (7)
die **Heimat, -en** home (country)
(8-2)
das **Heimatland, ̈er** homeland (8)
**heim·gehen, ging heim, ist
heimgegangen** to go home (4)
**heim·kommen, kam heim, ist
heimgekommen** to come home
(4-2)
der **Heimtrainer, -** exercise bike (7-1)
der **Heimweg, -e** way home (10)
heiraten to marry (3-2)
heiß hot (E, 1-1)
heißen, hieß, geheißen to be called
(E); to mean (3)
das heißt (d. h.) that is (i.e.) (12)
Ich heiße … My name is … (E-1)
**Wie heißen Sie?/Wie heißt
du?** What's your name? (E-1)

heiter: es ist heiter it's mostly sunny
(1)
heizen to heat (9)
helfen (hilft), half, geholfen *(+ dat)*
to help (2, 7-2)
helfen bei to help with (7)
der **Helfer, -/** die **Helferin, -nen**
helper
hell light (1-2)
hellwach wide awake (6)
das **Hemd, -en** shirt (1, 2-2)
**heraus·finden, fand heraus,
herausgefunden** to find out (7)
die **Herausgabe, -n** publication (10)
**heraus·geben (gibt heraus), gab
heraus, herausgegeben** to give
(change) (12)
der **Herbst** fall, autumn (1-2)
der **Herd, -e** stove (8-1)
**herein·kommen, kam herein, ist
hereingekommen** to come
in (12)
**herein·rennen, rannte herein, ist
hereingerannt** to run into, to
rush into (6)
**her·fahren (fährt her), fuhr her, ist
hergefahren** to come here, to get
here; to drive here (6)
die **Herkunft, ̈e** origin (12)
Herr Mr. (E-1)
der **Herr, -n, -en** gentleman (E)
her·stellen to make, produce
(7, 12-2)
herum *(colloquial:* **'rum)** around (2)
**herum·hängen, hing herum, ist
herumgehangen** to hang out (4)
**herum·laufen (läuft herum), lief
herum, ist herumgelaufen** to run
around (10)
**herum·stehen, stand herum, ist
herumgestanden** to stand
around (12)
das **Herz, -en** heart (7)
herzlich warm, hearty (7)
**Herzliche Glückwünsche zum
Geburtstag!** Happy Birthday!
(7-1)
Herzlich willkommen! Welcome!
(greeting) (4)
herzlos heartless (12)
heute today (1-1)
heute Abend tonight (1)
heute Morgen this morning (1)
heute Nachmittag this afternoon
(1-1)
**Heute haben wir den zweiten
Mai.** Today is May 2nd. (6-2)
Heute ist der zweite Mai. Today is
May 2nd. (6-2)
hier here (1-2)
die **Hilfe** help (6, 7-2)

hilflos helpless (12)

die **Hilfskraft, ̈e** assistant (12)

der **Himmel** sky; heaven (1-1)

hinaus·schauen to look out (*of a window or door*) (10)

hin·bringen, brachte hin, hingebracht to bring there (10)

das **Hindernis, -se** barrier (11)

hinein·führen to lead, guide in (10)

hinein·gehen, ging hinein, ist hineingegangen to go in (10)

hinein·kommen, kam hinein, ist hineingekommen to come in (10)

sich **hin·setzen** to sit down (9)

hinter (*prep + acc/dat*) behind; (*as adj*) back (8)

der **Hintergrund, ̈e** background (6)

hinzu·mischen to add to the mixture (4)

hip hip (E, 2-2)

historiografisch historiographical (1)

historisch historical (9)

das **Hobby, -s** hobby (2-1)

hoch (hoh-) high (5-2)

das **Hochhaus, ̈er** high-rise (8-2)

hoch·laden (lädt hoch), lud hoch, hochgeladen to upload (6)

die **Hochschule, -n** university (1)

der **Hochschulsport** university sports (2)

die **Hochzeit, -en** wedding (3-2)

die **goldene Hochzeit** golden wedding anniversary (7)

der **Hockeyschläger, -** hockey stick (7-2)

hoffen to hope (2, 5-2)

hoffentlich hopefully, I hope (so) (6-2)

hoffnungslos hopeless (12)

höflich polite (5, 7-2)

die **Höhle, -n** cave; hole (10)

holen to get; to fetch (8)

holländisch (*adj*) Dutch (7)

der **Holocaust** holocaust (11)

die **Homöopathie** homeopathy (10)

die **Homepage, -s** home page (E)

der **Honig** honey (4-1)

das **Hopfenfest** hops festival (7)

hörbar audible (12)

hören to hear (2-2); to listen to (1)

der **Horizont, -e** horizon (12)

der **Horrorfilm, -e** horror film (3)

der **Hörsaal, Hörsäle** lecture hall (E)

die **Hose, -n** pants (1, 2-2)

das **Hotdog, -s** hotdog (3)

das **Hotel, -s** hotel (5-1)

hübsch pretty (2-2)

das **Huhn, ̈er** hen (9, 10-2)

Da lachen ja die Hühner! What a joke! (10)

die **Humanität** humanity; humanitarianism (8)

der **Humor** humor (8)

humorlos humorless (5)

humorvoll humorous (1)

der **Hund, -e** dog (1, 3-1)

das **Hundefutter** dog food (6)

der **Hunger** hunger (4-1, 5)

Ich habe Hunger. I'm hungry. (4-1, 5-2)

hungern to go hungry (10)

hungrig hungry (4, 10-1)

der **Hut, ̈e** hat (7-2)

I

der **ICE** InterCity Express (4)

ideal ideal (5-1)

die **Idee, -n** idea (E, 7-1)

identisch identical (6)

identifizieren to identify (7)

sich **identifizieren mit** to identify with (10)

der **Igel, -** hedgehog (10)

ihr, ihr, ihre her (1), their (2)

Ihr, Ihr, Ihre your (2)

die **Ikone, -n** icon (8)

die **Imitation, -en** imitation (4)

immer always (2-1)

immer mehr more and more (3-2)

immer noch still (3)

der **Immigrant, -en, -en**/die **Immigrantin, -nen** immigrant (6-1)

impfen to vaccinate (11)

impulsiv impulsive (12-1)

in (*prep + acc/dat*) in (E, 8), into; to (1, 8)

indisch (*adj*) Indian (*of India*)

das **Individuum, Individuen** individual (5)

industrialisiert industrialized (8)

die **Industrie, -n** industry (8)

industriell industrial (4)

der **Informatiker, -**/die **Informatikerin, -nen** computer specialist (12)

die **Information, -en** information (9)

sich **informieren über** (*+ acc*) to inform oneself about (10, 11-2)

der **Ingenieur, -e**/die **Ingenieurin, -nen** engineer (4, 6-1)

der **Inhalt, -e** content (4)

inklusive included (5)

inkognito incognito (10)

das **Inland** inland; home country (5)

die **Inlineskates** in-line skates (7)

die **Innovation, -en** innovation (4-2)

innovativ innovative (4-2)

insbesondere (*adv*) particularly (12)

das **Insekt, -en** insect (2, 10-2)

die **Insel, -n** island (5-1)

instinktiv instinctive (12-1)

das **Institut, -e** institute (10-1)

das **Instrument, -e** instrument (2)

die **Integrationshilfe** assistance with integration (12)

intelligent intelligent, smart (1, 2-1, 10-2)

interessant interesting (1-2)

das **Interesse, -n** interest (2, 12-2)

interesselos uninterested (12)

interessieren to interest (6)

sich **interessieren für** to be interested in (11-2)

international international(ly) (7-1)

das **Internationale Rote Kreuz** the International Red Cross (4)

das **Internet** Internet (2)

im Internet surfen to surf the Internet (6)

das **Interview, -s** interview (3-2)

interviewen to interview (7)

investieren to invest (4)

iPad, -s iPad (7)

der **iPod, -s** iPod (7)

irgendwann sometime or other (8)

irisch (*adj*) Irish (2)

israelisch (*adj*) Israeli (7)

der **Italiener, -**/die **Italienerin, -nen** Italian (*person*) (9)

italienisch (*adj*) Italian (2)

das **Italienisch** Italian (*language*) (10)

J

ja yes (E-1); (*flavoring particle*) indeed, of course (6)

die **Jacke, -n** jacket (1, 2-2)

der **Jägersmann, ̈er** huntsman (10)

das **Jahr, -e** year (1-2)

die 80er-Jahre the eighties (10)

Ein gutes neues Jahr! Happy New Year! (7-1)

Frohes neues Jahr! Happy New Year! (7-1)

letztes Jahr last year (5)

jahraus, jahrein year in, year out (1)

der **Jahrestag, -e** anniversary (11)

die **Jahreszeit, -en** season (1-2)

das **Jahrhundert, -e** century (1, 10-1)

jährlich yearly, annual(ly) (12)

der **Januar** January (1-2)

im Januar in January (1-2)

der **Japaner, -**/die **Japanerin, -nen** Japanese (*person*) (9)

(das) **Japanisch** Japanese (*language*) (1)

der **Jazz, -** jazz (*music*) (2)

je ever (6); every (9)

die **Jeans** (*pl*) jeans (1, 2-2)

jeder, jedes, jede each, every (2)

jederzeit (at) any time (11-2)
jemand somebody, someone (7)
jetzig present (4)
jetzt now (E, 1-1)
der **Job, -s** job (2-2)
der **Jockey, -s** jockey (2)
joggen to jog (2, 4-2)
   joggen gehen to go jogging
     (1, 2-1)
die **Jogginghose, -n** jogging pants (3)
der **Joghurt** yogurt (4-1)
das **Jonglieren** (*sing*) juggling (4)
der **Journalist, -en, -en**/die
   Journalistin, -nen journalist (4)
jubelnd jubilant (2)
das **Jubiläum, Jubiläen** anniversary
   (4)
der **Jude, -n, -n**/die **Jüdin, -nen** Jew
   (11)
jüdisch Jewish (11)
die **Jugend** (*sing*) youth (5-2)
die **Jugendherberge, -n** youth hostel
   (E, 5-1)
der/die **Jugendliche** youth (3)
der **Jugendstil** art nouveau (3)
der **Juli** July (1-2)
jung young (1, 5-1)
der **Junge, -n, -n** boy (5-2)
der **Juni** June (1-2)
das **Junkfood** junk food (4)
der **Juwelier, -e**/die **Juwelierin,**
   -nen jeweler (5)

K

das **Kabinett, -e** cabinet (12-1)
der **Kaffee** coffee (2-1)
das **Kaffeehaus, ̈er** coffee house
   (café) (8)
die **Kaffeemaschine, -n** coffee maker
   (7-1)
der **Kaiser, -**/die **Kaiserin,**
   -nen emperor/empress (3)
der **Kajak, -s** kayak (5)
der **Kajaker, -**/die **Kajakerin,**
   -nen kayaker (5)
der **Kakao, -s** cocoa (*plant and drink*)
   (4)
der **Kalender, -** calendar (2, 5-2)
(das) **Kalifornien** California (7)
die **Kalorie, -n** calorie (4)
kalt cold (1-1); not including heat (*of
   rent*) (8)
der **Kalte Krieg** Cold War (11)
die **Kamera, -s** camera (3-2)
der **Kamm, ̈e** comb (9-2)
sich **kämmen** to comb one's hair
   (9-2)
kämpfen to fight (10-1)
(das) **Kanada** Canada (1-1)
der **Kanadier, -**/die **Kanadierin,**
   -nen Canadian (*person*) (1-1)

kanadisch (*adj*) Canadian (2)
der **Kanal, ̈e** channel (6)
   der **Facebook-Kanal** Facebook
     page (6)
das **Kännchen, -** little pot (9)
die **Kantate, -n** cantata (3)
der **Kanton, -e** state (*in Switzerland*)
   (4)
der **Kantor, -en** cantor
der **Kanzler, -**/die **Kanzlerin,**
   -nen chancellor (11)
kaputt broken (1)
kaputt·gehen, ging kaputt, ist
   kaputtgegangen to break (7)
kaputt machen to break; to ruin
   (11-2)
der **Karfreitag** Good Friday (7)
der **Karneval** Mardi Gras (7)
die **Karotte, -n** carrot (1, 9-1)
die **Karriere, -n** career (12-1)
   Karriere machen to get ahead in
     one's career (12-1)
die **Karte, -n** card (*also* playing card);
   postcard; map (1-1, 5-2); ticket
   (3, 5-2)
das **Kartenspiel, -e** card game (5)
die **Kartoffel, -n** potato (4-1)
die **Kartoffelchips** potato chips (7-2)
der **Karton, -s** box, carton (8)
der **Käse, -** cheese (E, 4-1)
   Das ist alles Käse. That's all
     baloney. (7)
der **Käsekuchen, -** cheesecake (4)
der **Kasten, ̈** box (3, 9-1)
katholisch Catholic (3)
die **Katze, -n** cat (1, 3-1)
   Es ist alles für die Katz. It's all for
     nothing. (10)
das **Katzenfutter** cat food (6)
kaufen to buy (1-1)
der **Käufer, -**/die **Käuferin,**
   -nen buyer (9)
das **Kaufhaus, ̈er** department store
   (3-2)
der **Kaufmann, ̈er**/die **Kauffrau,**
   -en merchant (3)
kaum scarcely; hardly (10)
der **Kaviar** caviar (3)
kein, kein, keine not a, not any,
   no (1)
der **Keller, -** cellar, basement (6, 8-2)
der **Kellner, -**/die **Kellnerin, -nen**
   server, waiter/waitress (3, 6-2)
kellnern to work as a waiter/
   waitress (6)
kennen, kannte, gekannt to know;
   to be acquainted with (2, 3-1)
kennen·lernen to get to know
   (E, 4-2)
der **Kenner, -**/die **Kennerin,**
   -nen connoisseur (9)

die **Kenntnis, -se** knowledge; skills
   (12-2)
das **Kennzeichen, -** characteristic (6)
die **Kernspaltung, -en** nuclear
   fission (10)
die **Kerze, -n** candle (7-2)
der **Kessel, -** kettle (3)
die **Kette, -n** chain (*also of businesses*)
   (9)
das **Kfz, -** (das **Kraftfahrzeug, -e**)
   motor vehicle (10)
der **Kfz-Graben** (*ditch to stop motor
   vehicles crossing the Berlin Wall*)
   (11)
die **Kieler Woche** Kiel Week (*world's
   largest sailing festival*) (7)
der **Kilometer, -** kilometer (1)
das **Kind, -er** child (1, 3-1)
   als Kind as a child (5-2)
die **Kinderbetreuung** child care (12)
der **Kindergarten, ̈** kindergarten;
   nursery school (4)
kinderlos childless (12)
der **Kinderwagen, -** baby carriage (7)
das **Kinderzimmer, -** nursery (8)
das **Kino, -s** movies (1)
   ins Kino to the movies (1-2)
die **Kirche, -n** church (3)
die **Kirschtomate, -n** cherry tomato
   (9)
das **Kitesurfen** kite surfing (E)
die **Klamotten** (*pl*) clothes (3-2)
klar clear (8)
   Klar! Of course! (1-1)
die **Klarinette, -n** clarinet (3)
das **Klarinettenkonzert, -e** clarinet
   concerto (3)
die **Klasse, -n** class (3-2)
klasse (*adj*) great, terrific (1)
klassisch classical (2)
die **Klausur, -en** test (5-2)
   eine Klausur schreiben to take a
     test; to have a test (5)
das **Klavier** piano (2)
   Klavier spielen to play the piano
     (2-1)
das **Klavierkonzert, -e** piano
   concerto (3)
die **Klaviermusik** piano music (3)
das **Kleid, -er** dress; (*pl*) clothes
   (2-2)
das **Kleidergeschäft, -e** clothing
   store (3-2)
das **Kleidungsstück, -e** article of
   clothing (2-2)
klein little, small; short (1, 2-1)
der **Klick, -s** click (6)
klingeln to ring (10)
das **Klo, -s** toilet (8-1)
klopfen to knock (11)
der **Klub, -s** club (2-1)

klug smart, intelligent (10-2)
knabbern to nibble (11)
das **Knäckebrot** crispbread (11)
die **Knackwurst, ̈e** knockwurst (9)
knapp scant; just shy of (6)
der **Knast, -e** *(colloquial)* jail, prison (11)
die **Kneipe, -n** pub (1)
  in die Kneipe to a bar/pub (1-2)
das **Knie, -** knee (1, 6-1)
knipsen to snap a photo (11)
der **Knoblauch** *(sing)* garlic (9-1)
der **Knödel, -** dumpling (11)
knusprig crispy (4)
knutschen to smooch (11)
der **Koch, ̈e**/die **Köchin, -nen** cook; chef (2, 9-1)
das **Kochbuch, ̈er** cookbook (2, 7-1)
kochen to cook (2-1)
die **Kochmöglichkeit, -en** cooking facilities (5)
das **Koffein** caffeine (2)
der **Koffer, -** suitcase (5, 6-2)
die **Kohle, -n** coal (8)
die **Kohlfahrt, -en** *excursion in Lower Saxony to celebrate the kale harvest* (7)
der **Kollege, -n, -n**/die **Kollegin, -nen** colleague (4, 9-2)
die **Kollision, -en** collision (10)
(das) **Köln** Cologne (E)
kombinieren to combine (9)
komfortabel comfortable (5)
komisch funny; strange (4, 10-2)
kommen, kam, ist gekommen to come (E, 1-1)
  Ich komme aus ... I'm from . . . (E-1)
  kommend coming (11)
  Woher kommen Sie/kommst du? Where are you from? (E-1)
  zu Besuch kommen to visit (8-2)
der **Kommentar, -e** commentary (6)
die **Kommode, -n** dresser (8-1)
die **Kommunikation, -en** communication (1, 10-1)
kommunistisch communist (11-2)
die **Komödie, -n** comedy (2)
komplett complete(ly) (6)
komplex complex (4)
das **Kompliment, -e** compliment (2, 5-2)
kompliziert complicated (4-1)
komponieren to compose (10)
der **Komponist, -en, -en**/die **Komponistin, -nen** composer (2, 3-2)
die **Komposition, -en** composition (3)
der **Kompost, -e** compost (9)
kompostieren to compost (9)
der **Konflikt, -e** conflict (11)

der **Kongress, -e** congress; convention (6)
der **König, -e** king (1)
die **Konjunktion, -en** conjunction (1, 4)
können (kann), konnte, gekonnt to be able to, can (4)
konservativ conservative (1)
das **Konsulat, -e** consulate (12-2)
der **Kontakt, -e** contact (E)
die **Kontaktlinse, -n** contact lens (5-2)
der **Kontaktzaun, ̈e** electric fence (11)
der **Kontext, -e** context (E)
der **Kontinent, -e** continent (2, 6-1)
kontrollieren to monitor (11)
der **Kontrollstreifen, -** patrolled strip of land *(part of the Berlin Wall)* (11)
sich **konzentrieren auf** *(+ acc)* to concentrate on (10-1)
das **Konzert, -e** concert (1, 2-2); concerto (3)
  ins Konzert to a concert, to concerts (1-2)
die **Konzertkarte, -n** concert ticket (5)
der **Konzertmeister, -**/die **Konzertmeisterin, -nen** concertmaster (3)
die **Konzerthalle, -n** concert hall (3)
der **Kopf, ̈e** head (6)
  Er ist nicht auf den Kopf gefallen. He's no fool. (6)
die **Kopfhörer** *(pl)* headphones (3)
die **Kopfschmerzen** *(pl)* headache (7)
kopieren to copy (10-1)
der **Korken, -** cork (9)
der **Korkenzieher, -** corkscrew (8-2)
der **Körper, -** body (6-1)
korrekt correct(ly) (9)
korrigieren to correct (7)
die **Korruption** corruption (10)
kosten to cost (1-2)
die **Kosten** *(no sing)* cost (5)
kostenlos free of charge (12)
krabbeln to crawl (8)
das **Kraftfahrzeug, -e** *(abbr. Kfz)* motor vehicle (10)
der **Krampf, ̈e** cramp (3)
krank sick (3-2)
das **Krankenhaus, ̈er** hospital (6-2)
die **Krankheit, -en** illness, sickness (10)
die **Krawatte, -n** tie (7-2)
kreativ creative (2-1)
die **Kreativität, -en** creativity (4)
die **Kreditkarte, -n** credit card (5-2)
der **Kreis, -e** circle (12-1)
die **Kreislaufwirtschaft, -en** recycling-focussed economy (9)
das **Kreuz, -e** cross (1, 4)
das **Kreuzworträtsel, -** crossword puzzle (3)

der **Krieg, -e** war (6, 11-1)
  der **Kalte Krieg** Cold War (11)
kriegen to get, to receive (6, 10-2)
  Angst kriegen to get scared (6)
  eins aufs Dach kriegen to be bawled out (8)
der **Krimi, -s** mystery; crime story; thriller (10-2)
die **Krimiserie, -n** crime series (10-2)
die **Kristallnacht** Night of Broken Glass *(historical event)* (11)
kritisch critical (5)
kritisieren to criticize (10)
die **Krone, -n** crown (1)
krumm crooked, bent (10-2)
  krumm sitzen to slouch (9-1)
die **Küche, -n** kitchen (8-1); cuisine (9-1)
  die **Küchenbenutzung** *(sing)* kitchen privileges (8-2)
der **Kuchen, -** cake (4-1)
  ein Stück Kuchen a piece of cake (4)
die **Kuckucksuhr, -en** cuckoo clock (5)
die **Kugel, -n** ball (3)
  die **Mozartkugel, -n** ball-shaped chocolate confection (3)
der **Kugelschreiber, -** ballpoint pen (7-2)
die **Kuh, ̈e** cow (1)
der **Kühlschrank, ̈e** refrigerator (4, 8-1)
der **Kuli, -s** ballpoint pen (7)
das **Kulinarische** *(sing)* culinary offerings (2)
die **Kultur, -en** culture (E)
der **Kunde, -n, -n**/die **Kundin, -nen** customer (12)
die **Kunst, ̈e** art (5-2)
die **Kunstgeschichte** art history (1)
der **Künstler, -**/die **Künstlerin, -nen** artist (8-2)
künstlerisch artistic(ally) (8)
der **Kürbis, -se** pumpkin (4)
der **Kürbiskern, -e** pumpkin seed (4)
das **Kürbisschnitzen** *(sing)* pumpkin carving (4)
der **Kurs, -e** course; class (2, 5-2)
kurz short (2-2)
der **Kurzzeitdienst, -e** temporary service/job (12)
kuschelig cuddly (7)
die **Kusine, -n** *(female)* cousin (3-1)
küssen to kiss (12)
die **Küste, -n** coast (5)

L

das **Labor, -s** laboratory (2)
lachen to laugh (3-1)
  Da lachen ja die Hühner! What a joke! (10)

der **Lachs** salmon, lox (3)
laden (lädt), lud, geladen to load (6)
die **Lage, -n** location (8-1)
lahm lame (2)
das **Lama, -s** llama (2)
das **Lamm, ¨er** lamb (1)
die **Lampe, -n** lamp (E, 8-1)
das **Land, ¨er** country (E, 2-2); state (6-1)
landen, landete, ist gelandet to land *(of airplanes)* (3, 6)
die **Landmine, -n** land mine (11)
die **Landschaft, -en** landscape (5-1)
das **Landschaftsbild, -er** landscape painting (8)
die **Landung, -en** landing (6)
der **Landweg, -e** overland route (11)
lang long (1, 2-2)
langsam slow(ly) (3-1)
langweilig boring (3-1)
der **Langzeitdienst, -e** long-term service (12)
die **Lasagne** lasagna (7)
lassen (lässt), ließ, gelassen to let; to leave (3-2)
   Lass mich in Ruhe! Stop bothering me! (4-2)
der **Lastkraftwagen, -** *(abbr. Lkw)* truck (10-2)
der **Lastwagen, -** truck (10)
(das) **Latein** Latin *(language)* (6)
der **Lauch, -e** leek (9)
die **Laufanlage, -n** run *(e.g., for dogs)* (11)
laufen (läuft), lief, ist gelaufen to run (2, 3-2)
der **Läufer, -**/die **Läuferin, -nen** runner (9)
die **Laune, -n** mood (12-1)
   Ich bin guter/schlechter Laune. I'm in a good/bad mood. (12-1)
die **Laus, ¨e** louse (1)
laut loud (1, 3-2, 8-1)
der **Lautsprecher, -** loudspeaker (5, 8-1)
die **Lawine, -n** avalanche (6)
leben to live *(in a country or a city)* (1, 2-2)
das **Leben, -** life (2, 3-1, 6-1)
   ein neues Leben a new life (6-1)
   ein (neues) Leben auf·bauen to build a (new) life (6-1)
der **Lebensbereich, -e** area of life; part of life (12-1)
das **Lebensjahr** year of *(one's)* life (3)
der **Lebenslauf, ¨e** résumé, CV (12-2)
die **Lebensmittel** *(pl)* food; groceries (9)
die **Lebensweise, -n** way of life (9)
das **Lebenswerk, -e** life's work (10)
lebenswichtig essential (11)

die **Leberwurst, ¨e** liver sausage (9)
der **Lebkuchen, -** gingerbread (5)
leblos lifeless (12)
lecker delicious (5)
das **Leder** leather (2)
ledig single (3-1)
leer empty (7-1)
leeren to empty (9-1)
legen to lay *(down)*, to put *(in a horizontal position)* (8-2)
die **Legende, -n** legend (1)
die **Leggings** *(pl)* leggings (3)
lehren to teach (8)
der **Lehrer, -**/die **Lehrerin, -nen** teacher, instructor (1-2)
der **Lehrplan, ¨e** curriculum (8)
leicht easy; light (3, 6-2)
leid: Es tut mir leid. I'm sorry. (7-2)
leider unfortunately (5-2)
leihen, lieh, geliehen to lend (9)
die **Leine, -n** leash (10)
leisten to perform, carry out (12)
die **Leistung, -en** performance; benefit; service (5-1)
der **Leistungssport** competitive sport *(amateur or professional)* (2)
leiten to lead (4)
die **Lektüre** *(sing)* reading material (10)
lernen to learn; to study *(e.g. for a test)* (1-2)
lesen (liest), las, gelesen to read (1, 3-2)
letzt last (3-2)
   das letzte Mal the last time (10-2)
   in letzter Zeit recently (6-2)
   zum letzten Mal for the last time (8-2)
die **Leute** *(pl)* people (2-2)
libanesisch Lebanese (6)
liberal liberal (2)
das **Licht, -er** light (8); match (9)
lieb dear (6)
die **Liebe** love (2)
lieben to love (1, 5-2)
lieber rather (2)
liebevoll loving (5-2)
der **Liebling, -e** darling; favorite (3-1)
das **Lieblingsauto, -s** favorite car (3)
die **Lieblingsband, -s** favorite band (3)
das **Lieblingsbild, -er** favorite picture, painting (8)
das **Lieblingsbuch, ¨er** favorite book (2, 3-1)
das **Lieblingsessen, -** favorite meal, food (4)
die **Lieblingsfarbe, -n** favorite color (3)

der **Lieblingsfilm, -e** favorite film (2)
das **Lieblingsgedicht, -e** favorite poem (4)
das **Lieblingsgericht, -e** favorite dish (9)
das **Lieblingsgetränk, -e** favorite drink (3)
die **Lieblingsmusik** favorite music (2)
die **Lieblingsoper, -n** favorite opera (8)
das **Lieblingsrestaurant, -s** favorite restaurant (4)
die **Lieblingsshow, -s** favorite show (3)
der **Lieblingssport** favorite sport (3)
die **Lieblingstante, -n** favorite aunt (3)
die **Lieblingsvorlesung, -en** favorite lecture; class (3)
lieblos loveless (5-2)
liebst-: Wo machst du am liebsten Ferien? Where's your favorite vacation spot? (5)
das **Lied, -er** song (10)
liegen, lag, gelegen to lie, to be situated (6-2)
die **Liga, Ligen** league (2-1)
der **Likör, -e** liqueur (2)
die **Lilie, -n** lily (1)
der **Linguist, -en, -en**/die **Linguistin, -nen** linguist (10-1)
die **Linguistik** linguistics (1)
die **Linie, -n** line (8)
links left; to the left (4-2)
die **Lippe, -n** lip (1)
der **Lippenstift, -e** lipstick (3, 9-2)
lispeln to lisp (8)
die **Liste, -n** list (5)
die **Literatur, -en** literature (5-2)
der **Lkw, -s (**der **Lastkraftwagen, -)** truck (10-2)
locken to attract (10)
lockig curly (3-2)
der **Löffel, -** spoon (9-1)
der **Lohn, ¨e** wages, pay (10, 12)
lokal local (9, 10-2)
los: Was ist denn los? What's up? (10)
lösen to solve (6); to pay (8)
die **Lösung, -en** solution (6)
das **Lotto, -s** lottery (7)
der **Lottogewinn, -e** lottery winnings (12)
der **Löwe, -n, -n**/die **Löwin, -nen** lion/lioness (2)
die **Luft** air (12)
die **Luftbrücke, -n** airlift *(literally:* air bridge) (11)
lunchen to lunch (E)

die **Lüneburger Heide** Lüneburg Heath (1)

die **Lupe, -n** magnifying glass (1)

die **Lust** enjoyment (5)

  Ich habe (keine) Lust ... I (don't) feel like . . . (8-2)

  Ich habe Lust (auf) ... *(+ acc)* I feel like *(having or doing something)* . . . (10-2)

lustig funny, humorous; happy (7-2)

der **Lyriker, -**/die **Lyrikerin, -nen** lyric poet (10)

M

machbar doable (12)

machen to make; to do (1-1)

  Sport machen to do sports, to be active in sports (2-1)

das **Mädchen, -** girl (5-2)

das **Magazin, -e** magazine (2-2)

Mahlzeit! Enjoy the meal! (9)

das **Mahnmal, -e** memorial (11)

der **Mai** May (1-2)

das **Maismehl, -e** cornmeal (10)

die **Makkaroni** *(pl)* macaroni (3)

das **Mal, -e** *(occurrence)* time (8)

  das letzte Mal the last time (10-2)

  jedes Mal every time (10-2)

  zum ersten Mal for the first time (8-2)

  zum letzten Mal for the last time (8-2)

mal, einmal once; for a change (3)

  noch mal once more; (over) again (7-2)

malen to paint *(a picture)* (4)

das **Malen** *(sing)* drawing, painting *(as an activity)* (4)

der **Maler, -**/die **Malerin, -nen** painter; artist (10)

die **Malerei** painting *(as an activity)* (8)

die **Mall, -s** mall *(shopping)* (3)

man one, you (E, 4)

  Wie sagt man das? How does one say that? How do you say that? (4-1)

der **Manager, -**/die **Managerin, -nen** manager (3)

manche *(pl)* some (12)

manchmal sometimes (4-1)

die **Mandarine, -n** mandarin (orange) (7)

der **Mann, ̈er** man; husband (1, 2-2)

der **Mantel, ̈** coat (2-2)

das **Märchen, -** fairy tale (10)

  Kinder- und Hausmärchen fairy tales for children and families (1)

die **Märchensammlung, -en** collection of fairy tales (10)

der **Markt, ̈e** market (4)

das **Marketing** *(sing)* marketing (E)

die **Marmelade, -n** jam (4-1)

marschieren to march (10)

der **März** March (1-2)

die **Maschine, -n** machine (5-2)

der **Master, -** Master's degree (1)

die **Mathe** math (2)

die **Mathematik** mathematics (E)

die **Matheübung, -en** math class (2)

die **Mathevorlesung, -en** math lecture (8)

die **Mauer, -n** wall (11-1)

die **Maus, ̈e** mouse (1, 2-1)

die **Medien** *(pl)* media (10-1)

  soziale Medien social media (2)

das **Medikament, -e** medicine (5)

mediterran Mediterranean (2)

die **Medizin** medicine *(study or practice of)* (2)

das **Meer, -e** ocean, sea (2)

das **Meeting, -s** meeting (E)

mehr more (3-2)

  immer mehr more and more (3-2)

  nicht mehr no longer, not any more (3-2)

mehrere several (10)

die **Mehrwegflasche, -n** returnable bottle; deposit bottle (9)

mein, mein, meine my (E)

meinen to mean; to think, to be of or voice an opinion (3, 11-2)

die **Meinung, -en** opinion (11-2)

  meiner Meinung nach in my opinion (12-1)

meist most (4)

meistens most of the time, usually (4-1)

der **Meister, -**/die **Meisterin, -nen** master (10)

meistern to master (12)

die **Menge, -n** lot, great deal (6)

  eine Menge a lot (11-2, 12-2)

die **Mensa** university cafeteria (E, 1-1)

  in die Mensa to the cafeteria (1-2)

der **Mensch, -en, -en** human being; person; *(pl)* people (5-2, 6-1)

  Menschen mit Behinderung people with disabilities (4)

der **Mentor, -en**/die **Mentorin, -nen** mentor (5)

der **Mercedes** Mercedes (3)

das **Merkmal, -e** characteristic; trait (2)

das **Messer, -** knife (4-2, 9-1)

der **Messerschmied, -e**/die **Messerschmiedin, -nen** knifesmith (4)

der **Messerschmiedverband, ̈e** knifesmiths' association (4)

die **Messerwerkstatt, ̈en** knifesmith's shop (4)

das **Metall, -e** metal (4)

der **Metallgitterzaun, ̈e** metal mesh fence (11)

der **Meter, -** meter (1)

der **Mexikaner, -**/die **Mexikanerin, -nen** Mexican *(person)* (9)

der **Mief** *(sing)* smell; stench (12)

die **Miete, -n** rent (2, 8-1)

mieten to rent (6, 8-1)

der **Mietwagen, -** rental car (5)

die **Mikrobiologie** microbiology (2)

das **Mikroskop, -e** microscope (1)

die **Mikrowelle, -n** microwave (oven) (8-1)

die **Milch** milk (1, 2-1)

die **Milliarde, -n** billion (9)

die **Million, -en** million (6)

die **Minderheit, -en** minority (12)

das **Mineralwasser** mineral water (9)

der **Minister, -**/die **Ministerin, -nen** minister *(in government)* (12)

minus minus (1)

die **Minute, -n** minute (2-1)

die **Minze, -n** mint *(plant)* (3)

mischen to mix (4-1)

der **Mischmasch** mishmash (6-1)

die **Mischung, -en** mixture (4)

miserabel miserable (E)

mit *(prep + dat)* with (1, 5-2); *(as verb prefix)* along (4)

der **Mitarbeiter, -**/die **Mitarbeiterin, -nen** (fellow) employee (12)

mit·bekommen, bekam mit, mitbekommen to understand, get (6)

der **Mitbewohner, -**/die **Mitbewohnerin, -nen** housemate; roommate (1-2)

mit·bringen, brachte mit, mitgebracht to bring along (4)

das **Mitbringsel, -** small gift *(for a host)* (7-2)

miteinander with each other; together (2-1)

die **Mitfahrgelegenheit , -en** ride sharing opportunity (5-1)

mit·gehen, ging mit, ist mitgegangen to go along (4)

mit·kommen, kam mit, ist mitgekommen to come along (4-2)

mit·lesen (liest mit), las mit, mitgelesen to read along (4)

mit·machen to take part in (12)

mit·nehmen (nimmt mit), nahm mit, mitgenommen to take along (4)

mit·singen, sang mit, mitgesungen to sing along (4)

der **Mitstudent, -en, -en**/die **Mitstudentin, -nen** classmate; fellow student (7)

der **Mittag** noon; midday
  zu Mittag essen to have lunch
    (4-1)
das **Mittagessen** lunch; noon meal
    (4-1)
  zum Mittagessen for lunch (4-1)
die **Mittagspause, -n** lunch break
    (8-2)
die **Mitte, -n** middle (2)
  Mitte Juli (in) mid-July (5-1)
mittel average; medium
  mittelgroß of average size or
    height (3)
das **Mittelmeer** (*sing*) Mediterranean
    Sea (5)
mitten: mitten auf dem Feld in the
    middle of a field (10)
  mitten in der DDR in the middle
    of the GDR (11)
(die) **Mitternacht** midnight (2, 11-2)
  nach Mitternacht after midnight
    (4-2)
der **Mittwoch** Wednesday (1-2) (*see
    also* **Dienstag**)
mittwochs Wednesdays, on
    Wednesdays (2)
die **Möbel** (*pl*) furniture (8-1)
das **Möbelstück, -e** piece of
    furniture (8)
das **Mobiltelefon, -e** cell phone;
    mobile telephone (2)
möbliert furnished (8-1)
der **Modedesigner, -**/die
    Modedesignerin, -n fashion
    designer (2)
das **Modell, -e** model (6)
die **Modenschau** fashion show (11)
modern modern (1, 2-1, 5-2)
das **Modul, -e** thematic unit (1)
mögen (mag), mochte, gemocht to
    like (4)
  ich möchte I would like (3)
möglich possible (4-2)
  so bald wie möglich as soon as
    possible (4)
  so schnell wie möglich as quickly
    as possible (4)
die **Möglichkeit, -en** possibility (5)
Moin! Hello! Hi! (*Northern
    Germany*)
mollig plump (2-1)
der **Moment, -e** moment
  im Moment at the moment (1)
der **Monat, -e** month (1-2)
monatlich monthly (8)
der **Mond** moon (1)
der **Monitor, -e** (*pl also:* **-en**)
    (*computer*) monitor (3)
der **Montag** Monday (1-2) (*see also*
    Dienstag)
  am Montag on Monday (1-2)

das **Monument, -e** monument (3)
morgen tomorrow (1-1)
  morgen Abend tomorrow evening
    (1)
  morgen früh tomorrow morn-
    ing (7)
  morgen Nachmittag tomorrow
    afternoon (2)
der **Morgen, -** morning (E)
  Guten Morgen! Morgen! Good
    morning! (E-1)
  heute Morgen this morning (6)
morgens in the morning (2)
der **Morgenwind, -e** morning
    wind (10)
der **Moskito, -s** mosquito (2)
die **Mosel** Mosel (*river*) (1)
der **Most** cider (8)
der **Motor, -en** motor (3)
das **Motorrad, ¨er** motorcycle
    (2-1, 3-1)
das **Mountainbike, -s** mountain bike
    (3-2)
müde tired (3, 6-2)
der **Muffel, -** grump (2)
der **Muffin, -s** muffin (4)
der **Müll** garbage, trash (3, 9-2)
der **Mülleimer, -** garbage can (7-1)
  den Mülleimer rausbringen to
    take out the garbage (7-1)
die **Mülltrennung, -en** waste
    separation (9)
(das) **München** Munich (1)
der **Mund, ¨er** mouth (6-1)
  den Mund voll nehmen to talk
    big (6)
das **Museum, Museen** museum (2-2,
    5-2)
die **Musik** music (2)
musikalisch musical (2-1)
der **Musikdirektor, -en**/die
    Musikdirektorin, -nen musical
    director (5)
der **Musiker, -**/die **Musikerin,
    -nen** musician (3)
das **Müsli** (*sing*) muesli (*cold, whole-
    grain cereal with nuts and fruit*) (4-1)
  eine Schüssel Müsli a bowl of
    muesli (4-1)
  der **Müsliriegel, -** granola bar (4)
müssen (muss), musste, gemusst to
    have to, must (4)
das **Musterhaus, ¨er** model
    home (8)
die **Mutter, ¨** mother (E, 3-1)
mütterlicherseits maternal (6-1)
die **Muttersprache, -n** mother/first
    language (3)
der **Muttertag, -e** Mother's
    Day (7-2)
mysteriös mysterious (1)

N

na well (E); what's up (12)
nach (*prep + dat*) after; to (E);
    according to (10)
  meiner Meinung nach in my
    opinion (12-2)
  nach Claudias Vorlesung after
    Claudia's lecture (1-2)
  nach Florida to Florida (1-2)
  nach Hause gehen to go home
    (1, 4-1)
der **Nachbar, -n, -n**/die **Nachbarin,
    -nen** neighbor (5)
nachdem after (*sub conj*) (9)
die **Nacherzählung, -en** retelling of a
    story in one's own words (10)
nachfüllbar refillable (9)
nach·füllen to refill (9-1)
nachhaltig sustainable (9-2)
  nachhaltig leben to live sustaina-
    bly (9-2)
die **Nachhaltigkeit** sustainability
    (4, 9-2)
die **Nachhilfe** tutoring (6)
die **Nachkriegszeit** postwar period
    (11-2)
der **Nachmittag, -e** afternoon (1)
  heute Nachmittag this afternoon
    (1-1)
  morgen Nachmittag tomorrow
    afternoon (2)
nachmittags in the afternoon (2)
der **Nachmittagskaffee** afternoon
    coffee (4-1)
  zum Nachmittagskaffee for
    afternoon coffee (4-1)
die **Nachrichten** (*pl*) news (2, 10-2)
die **Nachspeise, -n** dessert (9)
nächst next (1)
  nächstes Jahr next year (1, 3-2)
die **Nacht, ¨e** night (2)
  bei Nacht at night (3)
  Gute Nacht! Good night! (E)
der **Nachteil, -e** disadvantage
    (8-2)
der **Nachtisch, -e** dessert (4-1)
  zum Nachtisch for dessert
    (4-1)
der **Nachtmensch, -en, -en** night
    person (4)
nachts at night (2)
der **Nachttisch, -e** bedside table (8-1)
die **Nachttischlampe, -n** bedside
    lamp (8)
der **Nagel, ¨** nail (10)
nageln to nail (10)
nah near (5-1)
die **Nähe** vicinity (8)
  in der Nähe in the vicinity of (8-2)
  in der Nähe der Uni near the
    university (8-2)

der **Name, -ns, -n** name (E)
  Mein Name ist … My name is … (E-1)
namenlos nameless (12)
nämlich namely; that is to say (11)
die **Narzisse, -n** daffodil (5)
die **Nase, -n** nose (1, 6-1)
  die Nase zu tief ins Glas stecken to drink too much (6)
der **Nasenstecker, -** nose stud (5-2)
nass wet (12)
die **Nation, -en** nation (10)
national national (3, 10-2)
der **Nationalfeiertag, -e** national holiday (7)
die **Nationalhymne, -n** national anthem (3)
die **Nationalität, -en** nationality (1)
nationalsozialistisch *(adj)* Nazi (8)
der **Nationalstaat** nation (10)
das **Nationalsymbol, -e** national symbol (4)
die **Natur** nature (5, 10)
  von Natur by nature (10)
natürlich of course (1, 2-2, 5-2); natural (2)
neben *(prep + acc/dat)* in addition to; beside, next to (8)
das **Nebenfach, ⸚er** minor *(field of study)* (12)
die **Nebenkosten** *(pl)* additional costs (8-1)
neblig foggy (1)
das **Neckholder, -** halter top (E)
der **Neffe, -n, -n** nephew (3-1)
negativ negative (4, 12-1)
nehmen (nimmt), nahm, genommen to take (3-2)
neidisch jealous, envious (12)
  neidisch auf *(+ acc)* envious of (12-1)
nein no (E-1)
nennen, nannte, genannt to call, to name (4)
nerven to get on one's nerves (4, 8-2)
nervös nervous, on edge (4-2)
nett nice; pleasant (2-1)
das **Netz, -e** net; Internet (2)
das **Netzwerk, -e** network (2)
  soziale Netzwerke social networks (2)
neu new (1, 3-2)
  Ein gutes neues Jahr! Happy New Year! (7-1)
die **Neue Pinakothek** *art gallery in Munich* (5)
die **Neueröffnung** reopening (10)
(das) **Neujahr** New Year (6)
neuseeländisch *(adj)* New Zealand (7)

die **Neuzeit, -en** modern age, modern era (1)
  Neuzeit – historiografische Perspektiven modern age – historical perspectives (1)
nice nice (2)
nicht not (E, 1-1)
  gar nicht not at all (1-1)
  nicht mehr no longer, not any more (3-2)
  nicht schlecht not bad (3)
  nicht so gut not so good, not so well (3)
  nicht so toll not great (3)
  noch nicht not yet (E)
  nicht X, sondern Y not X, but rather Y (3-2)
  überhaupt nicht not at all (11)
nichtalkoholisch nonalcoholic (6)
die **Nichte, -n** niece (3-1)
der **Nichtraucher, -** nonsmoker (8)
nichts nothing (1-2, 5-2)
  Ich weiß von nichts. I don't know anything about it. (10)
nie never (2-2)
niemand nobody, no one (3)
das **Niemandsland** no-man's-land (11)
nieseln: es nieselt it's drizzling (1)
der **Nobelpreis, -e** Nobel Prize (4)
  den Nobelpreis erhalten to receive the Nobel Prize (10-1)
noch still (1-1)
  immer noch still (3)
  noch einmal (over) again, once more (7-2)
  noch mal (over) again, once more (7-2)
  noch nicht not yet (E, 1-1)
das **Nomen, -** noun (1)
(das) **Nordamerika** North America (3, 6-1)
nordamerikanisch *(adj)* North American (8)
der **Norden** north (10)
der **Nordpol** North Pole (1)
die **Nordsee** North Sea (1)
normal normal (3)
normalerweise usually, normally (2, 4-1)
der **Normalfall, ⸚e** usual, normal case (12)
die **Not, ⸚e** emergency; hardship; poverty (10)
die **Note, -n** grade (1, 2-1)
das **Notebook, -s** notebook *(computer)* (E)
die **Notiz, -en** note (1)
der **November** November (1-2)
die **Nudel, -n** noodle (3, 4-1)

die **Nummer, -n** number (E)
nun now (4)
nur only (1-1)
die **Nuss, ⸚e** nut (3, 4-1)
nutzen: das Nachnutzen repurposing (9)
die **Nutzung** use (5)

O

ob whether *(sub conj)* (5)
obdachlos homeless
der/die **Obdachlose, -n** homeless person (12)
oben above (10-2)
ober upper (12)
das **Obst** *(sing)* fruit (4-1)
obwohl although, even though *(sub conj)* (4-2)
der **Ochse, -n, -n** ox (1)
oder *(coord conj)* or (E, 1-2)
offen open (2, 3-2)
öffentlich public (1)
der **Offizier, -e** officer (4)
öffnen to open (5, 11-1)
die **Öffnung, -en** opening (11)
die **Öffnungszeit, -en** hours of operation, business hours (5)
oft often (1-1, 3-1, 4-1, 4-2)
ohne *(prep + acc)* without (1, 5-2)
das **Ohr, -en** ear (10)
der **Ohrring, -e** earring (5-2)
O.K. okay (3)
der **Oktober** October (1-2)
das **Oktoberfest** Octoberfest (5)
ökologisch ecological (7)
die **Ökonomie, -n** economy (8)
der **Oldtimer, -** vintage car (E)
die **Olive, -n** olive (2-2)
das **Olivenöl** olive oil (2-2)
die **Oma, -s** grandma (3-1)
der **Onkel, -** uncle (2, 3-1)
die **Online-Zeitung, -en** (3) online newspaper (3)
der **Opa, -s** grandpa (3-1)
die **Oper, -n** opera (2-2)
das **Opferfest** Festival of Sacrifice (7)
optimal optimal(ly) (3)
der **Optiker, -/**die **Optikerin, -nen** optician (5)
optimistisch optimistic (1, 3-1)
die **Orange, -n** orange (4-1)
der **Orangensaft** *(sing)* orange juice (4-1)
das **Orchester, -** orchestra (3-2)
ordentlich neat, tidy (4-2)
die **Ordnung** order (4)
  in Ordnung bringen to tidy up (4)
die **Organisation, -en** organization
organisiert organized (1)
original original (4)

das **Ornament, -e** ornament (5)

der **Ort, -e** place, location (2, 11-1)
  vor Ort on-site (2)

die **Ortstaxe, -n** local tax (5)

der **Oscar, -s** Oscar (*film award*) (1)

der/die **Ostdeutsche, -n** citizen of East Germany (11)

(das) **Ostdeutschland** eastern Germany (5); East Germany (11)

der **Osten** east (1)

der **Osterhase, -n, -n** Easter bunny (7)

das **Osterlamm, ˝er** Easter lamb (7)

der **Ostermontag** Easter Monday (7)

Ostern Easter (7-1)

der **Ostersonntag** Easter Sunday (7)

(das) **Österreich** Austria (1-1)

der **Österreicher, -/die Österreicherin, -nen** Austrian (*person*) (1-1)

österreichisch (*adj*) Austrian (2)

(das) **Österreich-Ungarn** Austro-Hungarian Empire (11)

der **Ostersonntag** Easter Sunday (7)

östlich (*adj*) eastern (11)

die **Ostsee** Baltic Sea (1)

oval oval (6-1)

der **Ozean, -e** ocean (10)

P

das **Paar, -e** pair, couple (7)

paar: ein paar a couple of, a few (1-1)

packen to pack (4, 6-2)

die **Packung, -en** package (10)

paddeln to paddle (*row*) (E)

das **Paket, -e** parcel, package (7-2); package deal (*offer*) (5-1)

das **Papier, -e** paper (9)

der **Papierkorb, ˝e** wastepaper basket (8-1)

die **Pappe, -n** carboard (9)

das **Paradies** paradise (10)

das **Parfüm, -s** perfume (7-2)

der **Park, -s** park (3)

parken to park (4)

die **Parkmöglichkeit, -en** parking facility (5)

der **Parkschein, -e** parking pass (8)

das **Parlament, -e** parliament (3, 12-1)

die **Partei, -en** (*political*) party (E)

der **Partner, -/die Partnerin, -nen** partner (1, 3-1)

die **Party, -s** party (3, 7-2)
  auf eine Party gehen to go to a party (3)

der **Pass, ˝e** passport (5-2, 6-1)

passen to fit (E)

passend appropriate (7)

passieren, passierte, ist passiert to happen (6-2)

passioniert ardent (5-1)

das **Patent, -e** patent (*legal*) (10)

der **Patient, -en, -en/die Patientin, -nen** patient (5, 9-2)

der **Perchtenlauf** *festival in Bavaria and the Austrian Alps to drive away the dark days of winter* (7)

perfekt perfect (2)

die **Person, -en** person, individual (2, 3-2)

der **Personalausweis, -e** identity card (6)

das **Personalpronomen, -** personal pronoun (7)

die **Personenbeschreibung, -en** description of a person (6)

der **Personenkraftwagen, -** (*abbr.* **Pkw**) car (10)

persönlich personal(ly) (2)

die **Perspektive, -n** perspective (1, 2-1)

pessimistisch pessimistic (3-1)

der **Pfad, -e** path (3)

die **Pfanne, -n** pan (3, 9-1)

der **Pfeffer** pepper (1, 9-1)

der **Pfefferminztee** peppermint tea (11)

die **Pfeife, -n** pipe (3)

der **Pfennig, -e** penny (3)

das **Pferd, -e** horse (10-2)
  Da bringen mich keine zehn Pferde hin. Wild horses couldn't drag me there. (10)

(das) **Pfingsten, -** Pentecost (7)

die **Pflanze, -n** plant (3, 5-2)

das **Pflaster, -** Band-Aid, bandage (9)

der **Pflasterstein, -e** cobblestone (11)

die **Pflaume, -n** plum (11)

pflücken to pick (11)

der **Pfosten, -** post, stake, stanchion (3)

das **Pfund, -e** pound (3)

Pfui! Yuck! (11)

die **Philosophie, -n** philosophy (1)

die **Phrase, -n** phrase (3)

die **Physik** physics (3)

der **Physiker, -/die Physikerin, -nen** physicist (6)

der **Physiotherapeut, -en, -en/die Physiotherapeutin, -nen** physical therapist (3)

der **Pianist, -en, -en/die Pianistin, -nen** pianist (3)

das **Picknick, -s** picnic (4)

der **Pilot, -en, -en/die Pilotin, -nen** pilot (10)

die **Pistazie, -n** pistachio (2)

die **Piste, -n** ski slope (3)

die **Pizza, -s** pizza (3)

die **Pizzeria, -s** (*pl. also:* **-ien**) pizzeria (3)

der **Pkw, -s** (der **Personenkraftwagen, -**) car (10)

die **Plage, -n** plague; infestation (10)

der **Plan, ˝e** plan (2, 5-1)

planen to plan (5)

der **Planet, -en, -en** planet (8)

die **Plastiktüte, -n** plastic bag (9-2)

Platte: einen Platten haben to have a flat tire (12-2)

der **Platz, ˝e** place; space; room; seat (4, 5-1); city square (5)

die **Platzreservierung, -en** seat reservation (7)

plötzlich suddenly, all of a sudden (6-2)

die **Politik** politics (E)

der **Politiker, -/die Politikerin, -nen** politician (2, 6-1)

politisch political(ly) (2)

die **Polizei** police (E, 12-2)

der **Polizeibericht, -e** police report (10)

der **Polizist, -en, -en/die Polizistin, -nen** police officer (2, 10)

polnisch (*adj*) Polish (6)

das **Polohemd, -en** polo shirt (3)

die **Pommes/die Pommes frites** (*pl*) French fries (3, 4-1)

populär popular (1, 4, 10-2)

die **Pore, -n** pore (12-1)

die **Porzellantasse, -n** porcelain cup (5)

die **Position, -en** position (12-1)

positiv positive (12-1)

die **Post** post office; mail (8-2)
  auf die Post gehen to go to the post office (8)

das **Postamt, ˝er** post office (11)

der **Posten, -** position (*work*) (3)

posten to post (*computer*) (6)

das **Poster, -** poster (5, 8-2)

die **Postleitzahl, -en** zip code, postal code (E)

der **Praktikant, -en, -en/die Praktikantin, -nen** intern (12)

das **Praktikum, Praktika** internship (11)

praktisch practical (2-1)

die **Präsentation, -en** presentation (1)

die **Präsenz** presence (9)

der **Präsident, -en, -en/die Präsidentin, -nen** president (5)

die **Präsidentschaftswahl, -en** presidential election (11)

das **Präteritum** simple past tense (10)

der **Preis, -e** price (3-2); prize (4)

der **Preisvorteil, -e** price advantage (5)

preisgünstig inexpensive (3-2)

preußisch *(adj)* Prussian (5)

primitiv primitive (12)

der **Prinz, -en, -en**/die **Prinzessin, -nen** prince/princess (5)

das **Prinzip, -ien** principle (4)

die **Priorität, -en** priority (12)

privat private (2)

das **Privathaus, ̈er** private home (8)

pro per (5)

probieren to try out (4)

das **Problem, -e** problem (3-1)

das **Produkt, -e** product (4, 10-2)

die **Produktion** production (4)

produzieren to produce (4, 10-1)

professionell professional (1)

der **Professor, -en**/die **Professorin, -nen** professor (1)

der **Profi, -s** pro (1)

das **Profil, -e** profile (1)

das **Promi-Profil** celebrity profile (1)

das **Programm, -e** program (2)

programmierbar programmable (10)

progressiv progressive (1)

das **Projekt, -e** project (10-1)

der **Projektor, -en** projector (5)

proklamieren to proclaim (11)

der/die **Promi, -s** celebrity (1)

Prost! Prosit! Cheers! To your health! (7-2)

protestieren to protest (10)

das **Prozent, -e** percent (9, 12-1)

die **Prüfung, -en** test (7)

der **Psychiater, -**/die **Psychiaterin, -nen** psychiatrist (9)

der **Pudel, -** poodle (2)

der **Pulli, -s** sweater (2-2)

der **Pullover, -** sweater (1, 2-2)

der **Punkt, -e** dot; period (E)

Punkt acht at eight on the dot (5)

pünktlich punctual, on time (7)

das **Puppentheater, -** puppet theater (4)

das **Putenfleisch** *(sing)* turkey *(meat)* (9)

putzen to clean (4, 6-2)

sich *(dat)* **die Zähne putzen** to brush one's teeth (9-2)

der **Pyjama, -s** pyjama (2)

die **Pyramide, -n** pyramid (3)

Q

der **Quadratmeter, -** square meter (8)

qualifiziert qualified (12-1)

die **Quelle, -n** source (5)

quer *(adv)* across (4)

das **Quintett, -e** quintet (3)

das **Quiz, -** quiz (1, 5-2)

R

sich **rächen an** *(+ dat)* to take revenge on *(someone)* (10)

das **Rad, ̈er** bike; wheel (3-1)

Rad fahren (fährt Rad), fuhr Rad, ist Rad gefahren to ride a bike, to go cycling (4-2)

das **Radio, -s** radio (8)

der **Radiomoderator, -en, -en**/die **Radiomoderatorin, -nen** radio host (1)

die **Radtour, -en** bicycle trip (5)

eine Radtour machen to go on a bicycle trip (5)

der **Raketeningenieur, -e**/die **Raketeningenieurin, -nen** rocket engineer (6)

der **Ramadan** Ramadan (7)

rappen to rap (E)

der **Rasierapparat, -e** shaver, electric razor (9-2)

(sich) **rasieren** to shave (9-2)

das **Rasierwasser** *(sing)* aftershave (9-2)

die **Rasse, -n** *(biological)* race (12)

rasseln to rattle (3)

die **Raststätte, -n** restaurant *(on the freeway)* (9)

raten (rät), riet, geraten *(+ dat)* to advise (12)

das **Rathaus, ̈er** town hall; city hall (8-2)

das **Rätoromanisch** Romansch *(language)* (4)

der **Ratschlag, ̈e** piece of advice (5)

die **Ratte, -n** rat (1, 10)

der **Rattenfänger, -**/die **Rattenfängerin, -nen** rat catcher (10)

rauchen to smoke (4-2)

das **Rauchen** smoking (7)

der **Raum, ̈e** room (8)

rauschen to sweep; to whoosh

reagieren (auf + acc) to react (to) (10)

real real (11)

realisieren to put into effect, realize (8)

die **Recherche, -n** research (12)

recherchieren to do research (6-2)

die **Rechnung, -en** bill (9-1)

recht right *(adj)*

nicht ganz recht im Kopf sein not quite right in the head (10)

das **Recht, -e** right (6-1)

rechtlich legal (12)

rechts right; to the right (4-2)

recyceln to recycle (8-2, 9-2)

die **Rede, -n** speech; talk (11-2)

reden to speak, to talk (4-2)

reduzieren to reduce (9-2)

reduziert reduced (2)

das **Referat, -e** (oral) report; paper (4-2)

das **Reformhaus, ̈er** health food store (8, 9-2)

das **Regal, -e** shelf (6)

der **Regen** rain (2, 5-1)

der **Regenschirm, -e** umbrella (5)

das **Regenwetter** rainy weather (10)

das **Regierungsgebäude, -** government building (12)

die **Region, -en** region (7)

regional regional (7-1)

regnen to rain (1-1)

Es regnet. It's raining. (1)

Es regnet in Strömen. It's pouring. (1)

reich rich (1, 5-2)

reichen: Das reicht (mir). That's enough (for me). (10-2)

die **Reichskristallnacht** *(sing)* Night of Broken Glass *(historical event)* (11)

der **Reichstag** *(sing)* German parliament (11)

das **Reichstagsgebäude** German parliament building *(Berlin)* (11-2)

reif ripe (2)

die **Reihe, -n** row (10)

die **Reihenfolge** sequence (2)

rein pure(ly) (12)

das **Reinfeiern** *a party one gives that begins late on the evening before one's birthday* (7)

das **Reinigungsmittel, -** cleaning agent (9)

die **Reise, -n** trip (3-1)

eine Reise machen to go on a trip, to take a trip (5-1)

das **Reisebüro, -s** travel agency (5-2)

reisen, reiste, ist gereist to travel (1-2)

der **Reisetipp, -s** travel tip (5)

das **Reiseziel, -e** travel destination (5)

reiten, ritt, ist geritten to ride *(a horse)* (10)

der **Reiter, -**/die **Reiterin, -nen** horseback rider (10)

die **Relativitätstheorie** theory of relativity (6)

die **Religion, -en** religion (12)

rennen, rannte, ist gerannt to run (6-2)

reparieren to repair (4)

die **Republik, -en** republic (1, 11-1)

das **Requiem, Requien** requiem (3)

reservieren to reserve (7)

respektlos disrespectful (5)

respektvoll respectful (1)

das **Restaurant, -s** restaurant (1)

restaurieren to restore (10)

die **Reste** *(pl)* leftovers, scraps (9); remains (11)

restlich rest of the, remaining (11)

der **Retter, -**/die **Retterin, -nen** savior (10)

revolutionär *(adj)* revolutionary (8)

das **Rezept, -e** recipe (4)

der **Rhein** Rhine *(river)* (1)

das **Rheintal** Rhine valley (7)

richtig right; true (1-2)

die **Richtigkeit** rightness, correctness (11)

die **Richtung, -en** direction; orientation; tendency (2)

der **Riesenhaufen** huge pile (9)

die **Riesenpackung, -en** huge package (8)

riesig huge (10-2)

der **Ring, -e** ring (1, 5-2, 7-2)

der **Ringfinger, -** ring finger (6)

risikolos risk-free (12)

der **Risotto, -s** risotto (2)

der **Rock** *(sing)* rock music (2)

der **Rock, -̈e** skirt (1, 2-2)

das **Rockfest, -e** rock festival (1)

das **Rockkonzert, -e** rock concert (10)

der **Rockstar, -s** rock star (5)

die **Rolle, -n** role (10)

der **Roman, -e** novel (5-2)

romantisch romantic (10)

rosarot pink (1-1)

die **Rose, -n** rose (1, 7-2)

der **Rosmarin** rosemary (9)

die **Rostbratwurst, -̈e** grilled sausage (7)

rostfrei stainless (4)

rot red (1-1)

der **Rotwein, -e** red wine (2)

die **Rübe, -n** turnip (10)

die **Rückenschmerzen** *(pl)* backache (7)

der **Rucksack, -̈e** backpack (4)

rufen, rief, gerufen to call (6, 10-1)

die **Ruhe** peace and quiet (4)

  Lass mich in Ruhe! Stop bothering me! (4-2)

der **Ruhetag: Dienstag Ruhetag** closed all day Tuesday (1)

der **Ruhewagen, -** *train cars where speaking on a cell phone is discouraged* (5)

ruhig calm, quiet (8-1)

das **Rührei** *(sing)* scrambled eggs (4-1)

rum·hängen, hing rum, rumgehangen to hang out (6-2)

rund round (6)

  rund um around (11)

der **Russe, -n, -n**/die **Russin, -nen** Russian person

russisch *(adj)* Russian (2)

der **Rutsch: Einen guten Rutsch!** Happy New Year! (7-1)

S

der **Saal, Säle** hall (9)

die **Sache, -n** thing (7-2)

die **Sächsische Schweiz** Saxon Switzerland (E)

der **Sack, -̈e** sack (9-2)

der **Saft, -̈e** juice (4)

saftig juicy (10-2)

die **Sage, -n** legend *(story)* (10)

die **Säge, -n** saw *(tool)* (10)

sagen to say, to tell (2-1)

  sag mal say, tell me (1)

  Wie sagt man das auf Deutsch? How do you say that in German? (4-1)

die **Sahne** *(sing)* cream (9-1)

die **Saison, -en** season (9)

die **Saisonkarte, -n** seasonal menu (9)

die **Salami, -s** salami (2-2)

der **Salat, -e** salad (3, 4-1)

das **Salz** salt (1, 9-1)

sammeln to collect (9, 10-1)

die **Sammelstelle, -n** collection place (9)

die **Sammlung, -en** collection (10-1)

der **Samstag** Saturday (1-2) *(see also* **Dienstag***)*

die **Sandale, -n** sandal (3-2)

der **Sand, -̈e** sand (10)

der **Sandstrand, -̈e** sandy beach (E)

der **Sandstein** sandstone (E)

der **Sänger, -**/die **Sängerin, -nen** singer (2)

der **Sankt Nikolaus** Saint Nicholas (7)

die **Sardine, -n** sardine (8)

sarkastisch sarcastic (7)

der **Satellit, -en** satellite (10-1)

der **Satz, -̈e** sentence (3)

sauber clean (8-1)

säubern to clean (12)

sauer sour (1); annoyed (11)

das **Sauerkraut** sauerkraut (5)

die **Sauna, -s** sauna (5-1)

das **Sauwetter** rotten weather (1)

das **Saxofon, -e** saxophone (3)

die **S-Bahn** commuter train (5)

der **Scanner, -** scanner (10)

Schade! Too bad! (12)

der **Schal, -s** scarf (8-2)

die **Schalen** *(pl)* peelings (9)

schälen to peel (9)

die **Schalotte, -n** shallot (9)

schamlos shameless (12)

scharf sharp (2); spicy, hot (9)

schätzen to value, appreciate (12)

das **Schaubild, -er** diagram; graph (11-1)

schaufeln to shovel (11)

der **Schauspieler, -**/die **Schauspielerin, -nen** actor/actress (1)

die **Scheibe, -n** slice (4-1)

  eine Scheibe Brot a slice of bread (4-1)

der **Schein, -e** gift certificate (7); banknote, bill *(money)* (7); parking pass (8)

scheinen, schien, geschienen to shine (1-1)

schenken to give *(a gift)* (7-1)

schlürfen to slurp; to sip (7-1)

die **Schere, -n** scissors (9)

schick chic (2-2)

schicken to send (6-1)

schief crooked; leaning

  schief gehen to go wrong (12)

der **Schießbefehl, -e** order to shoot (11-1)

schießen, schoss, geschossen to shoot (11-1)

das **Schiff, -e** ship (2)

das **Schild, -er** sign (5)

der **Schimpanse, -n, -n** chimpanzee (2)

schlafen (schläft), schlief, geschlafen to sleep (3-2)

schlaflos sleepless (12)

die **Schlafmöglichkeit, -en** place to sleep (5)

die **Schlaftablette, -n** sleeping pill (12)

das **Schlafzimmer, -** bedroom (8-1)

schlagen (schlägt), schlug, geschlagen to hit; to beat (10)

die **Schlagzeile, -n** headline (11)

schlank slim (2-1)

schlecht bad (E-1)

  nicht schlecht not bad (3)

der **Schlepplift, -e** T-bar *(skiing)* (3)

schließen, schloss, geschlossen to close (11-1)

das **Schloss, -̈er** castle (5)

der **Schlosser, -** toolmaker (6)

das **Schlüsselwort, -̈er** key word (5)

schmecken to taste; to taste good (4-1)

der **Schmerz, -en** pain (7)

das **Schminken** face painting (4)

(sich) schminken to put on make-up (9-2)

der **Schmuck** jewelry (7-2)

schmutzig dirty (8-1)

schnappen to nab, to apprehend (10)

der **Schnaps, -̈e** schnapps; hard liquor (10)

schnarchen to snore (4)

die **Schnecke, -n** snail (9)

der **Schnee** snow (1)

der **Schneemann, ¨er** snowman (3)

das **Schneemännchen** little snow-man (3)

der **Schneesturm, ¨e** snowstorm (12)

schneiden, schnitt, geschnitten to cut (9)

schneien to snow (1)

Es schneit. It's snowing. (1)

schnell fast, quick (3-1)

der **Schnellimbiss, -e** fast-food stand (9)

das **Schnellrestaurant, -s** fast food restaurant (9)

der **Schnitt, -e** section (11)

das **Schnitzel, -** cutlet (7)

das **Wiener Schnitzel** breaded veal cutlet (7)

der **Schnupfen** the sniffles (11)

der **Schnurrbart, ¨e** mustache (5-2)

die **Schokolade** chocolate (1, 2-2)

schon already (1, 2-2)

schön nice; beautiful (E, 1-1)

die **Schönheit** beauty (8)

der **Schöpfer, -** Creator *(religious)* (6)

der **Schoß, ¨e** lap (9)

schottisch *(adj)* Scottish (3)

der **Schrank, ¨e** closet (8-1)

nicht alle Tassen im Schrank haben to be crazy (8)

schrecklich awful(ly), terrible; terribly (11-1)

schreiben, schrieb, geschrieben to write (E, 1-1)

der **Schreiber, -** scribe (10)

der **Schreibtisch, -e** desk (8-1)

das **Schreibzeug, -e** writing implement (3)

schreien, schrie, geschrien to scream; to shout (10-2)

die **Schrift, -en** writing (10)

schriftlich in writing; written (4-2)

die **Schrittgeschwindigkeit** *(sing)* walking speed (12)

der **Schuh, -e** shoe (1, 2-2)

die **Schule, -n** school (2)

der **Schüler, -/die Schülerin, -nen** pupil; student in a primary or secondary school (3)

das **Schulkind, -er** pupil (3)

die **Schulter, -n** shoulder (1)

die **Schulzeit** schooldays *(pl)* (6)

die **Schüssel, -n** bowl (4-1)

eine Schüssel Müsli a bowl of muesli (4-1)

der **Schutz** *(sing)* protection

der **Schutzengel, -** guardian angel (7)

schützen to protect (4)

der **Schutzwall, ¨e** protective wall, barrier

schwach weak (7)

der **Schwan, ¨e** swan (1)

schwanger pregnant (6-1)

schwarz black (1-1)

schwarzbraun dark brown (6)

das **Schwarzbrot** rye bread (7)

der **Schwarzwald** Black Forest (1)

die **Schwarzwälder Kirschtorte** Black Forest cake

schweigen, schwieg, geschwiegen to keep silent (4)

das **Schwein, -e** pig (8)

Du hast Schwein gehabt. You were lucky. (10)

der **Schweiß** sweat (9)

die **Schweiz** Switzerland (1-1)

der **Schweizer, -/die Schweizerin, -nen** Swiss *(person)* (1-1)

schweizerisch *(adj)* Swiss (4)

schwer hard; heavy; difficult (3, 6-2)

eine schwere Erkältung a bad cold (12-2)

die **Schwester, -n** sister (1, 3-1)

die **Schwierigkeit, -en** difficulty; trouble (12-1)

das **Schwimmbad, ¨er** swimming pool (5)

schwimmen, schwamm, ist geschwommen to swim (4)

schwimmen gehen to go swimming (1, 2-1)

schwül humid (1)

das **Schwyzerdütsch** Swiss German (4)

(die) **Science-Fiction** science fiction (3)

das **Scrabble** Scrabble (2)

das **Sechseläuten** *celebration on the third Monday in April in Zürich to welcome spring* (7)

der **See, -n** lake (5-1)

die **See, -n** sea (1)

die **Nordsee** North Sea (1)

die **Ostsee** Baltic Sea (1)

das **Segelboot, -e** sailboat (3)

segeln to sail (2)

sehen (sieht), sah, gesehen to see (3-2); to look (12-1)

sehr very (1-2)

sehr gut very well (E)

die **Seife, -n** soap (9-2)

die **Seifenoper, -n** soap opera (11)

sein, sein, seine his, its (1)

sein (ist), war, ist gewesen to be (E)

Ich bin … I'm … (E-1)

seit *(prep + dat)* since (2); for (7)

die **Seite, -n** page (5); side (10)

der **Sekt** sparkling wine (5-1)

eine Flasche Sekt a bottle of spar-kling wine (5-1)

der **Sektor, -en** sector (9-2)

die **Sekunde, -n** second (2-1)

selber myself; yourself; herself; *etc.* (3)

selbst myself, yourself, herself, *etc.* (4-2)

von selbst by oneself; on its own (7)

selbstgemacht homemade (7)

selbstlos selfless (12)

das **Selfie** selfie (6)

selten seldom, rarely (2, 3-1, 4-2, 9-2)

das **Semester, -** semester (1-1)

die **Semesterferien** *(pl)* vacation (7)

das **Semesterticket, -s** *low-cost student pass for public transportation* (E)

das **Seminar, -e** seminar (1, 4-2)

die **Sendung, -en** TV show (2-2)

der **Senf** mustard (7, 9-2)

der **Senior, -en** senior citizen (3)

die **Seniorenbetreuung** care for the elderly (12)

das **Seniorenheim, -e** home for the elderly (12)

die **Sensation, -en** sensation (3-2)

sentimental sentimental (5-2)

der **September** September (1-2)

die **Serie, -n** *(TV)* series (2)

der **Server, -** computer server (3)

servieren to serve *(a dish)* (7, 9-1)

die **Serviette, -n** napkin, serviette (9-1)

Servus! Hello! Hi! Good-bye! So long! *(Austrian)* (E)

der **Sessel, -** armchair (8-1)

der **Sessellift, -e** chairlift (3)

das **Set, -s** place mat (E)

setzen to set, place (3)

sich setzen to sit down (9-2)

sexuell: die sexuelle Ausrichtung sexual orientation (12)

das **Shampoo, -s** shampoo (9-2)

das **Shooting** filming (E)

der **Shootingstar, -s** *suddenly successful person* (E)

die **Shorts** *(pl)* shorts (2-2)

die **Show, -s** show (3)

sicher sure, certainly; probably (8-2)

das **Siegel, -** seal, mark of certification (9)

das **Silber** silver (7)

(der) **Silvester** New Year's Eve (7-1)

simpel simplistic (4)

die **Sinfonie, -n** symphony (8)

das **Sinfonieorchester, -** symphony orchestra (3)

singen, sang, gesungen to sing (2-1)

der **Sinn** meaning; sense (4)

sinnvoll meaningful (11)

die **Sinologie** Chinese Studies (4)

die **Sitte, -n** custom (9)

der **Sitz, -e** seat (3)

sitzen, saß, gesessen to sit (1-2)

gerade sitzen to sit upright (9-1)

krumm sitzen to slouch (9-1)

der **Sitzplatz, -̈e** seat (7)

skaten to skateboard (E)

Skateboard fahren (fährt Skateboard), fuhr Skateboard, ist Skateboard gefahren to skateboard (4)

skeptisch skeptical (6)

der **Ski, -er** ski (3)

das **Skigebiet, -e** ski area (3)

die **Skihütte, -n** ski hut (3)

Ski laufen (läuft Ski), lief Ski, ist Ski gelaufen to ski (3)

das **Skilaufen** *(sing)* skiing (3)

Skilaufen gehen to go skiing (8)

der **Skiläufer, -e**/die **Skiläuferin, -nen** skier (3)

der **Skiverleih** ski rentals (3)

skrupellos unscrupulous (12)

die **Skulptur, -en** sculpture (8-2)

die **Smartwatch, -es** smart watch (3, 7-1)

der **Smoking, -s** tuxedo (E)

der **Smoothie -s** smoothie *(beverage)* (3)

das **Snowboard, -s** snowboard (9)

snowboarden to snowboard (4)

snowboarden gehen to go snow-boarding (2-1)

so so, such (1)

so ein (ein, eine) such a (2)

so lang(e) *(adv)* so long (2)

so ... wie as . . . as (2-2)

Heute ist es (nicht) so kalt wie gestern. Today it's (not) as cold as yesterday. (2-2)

die **Social Media** *(pl)* social media (2)

die **Socke, -n** sock (2-2)

das **Sofa, -s** sofa (1)

sofort immediately, right away; in a minute (7)

das **Softdrink, -s** soft drink (E, 2-1)

sogar even (9-2)

der **Sohn, -̈e** son (1, 3-1)

solange *(sub conj)* as long as (10, 12-1)

solcher, solches, solche such (7)

der **Soldat, -en, -en**/die **Soldatin, -nen** soldier (4, 11-1)

der **Solist, -en, -en**/die **Solistin, -nen** soloist (5)

sollen (soll), sollte, gesollt to be supposed to, should (4)

der **Sommer, -** summer (1-2)

die **Sommerferien** *(pl)* summer holidays, summer vacation (5)

der **Sommerjob, -s** summer job (6)

das **Sommersemester, -** (mid-April through mid-July) summer semester (E)

sondern *(coord conj)* but; (3) (but) . . . instead; but rather (4-2)

der **Song, -s** song (3, 6-2)

die **Sonne** sun (1-1)

die **Sonnenbrille, -n** sunglasses (3-2)

die **Sonnencreme, -s** suntan lotion (4)

der **Sonnenschein** sunshine (E)

sonnig sunny (1)

der **Sonntag, -e** Sunday (1-2) *(see also Dienstag)*

sonst otherwise, or else (9)

was ... sonst what else (8)

sonstig *(adj)* other (12)

Sonstiges miscellaneous (8)

sooft *(sub conj)* as often as (10)

sorgen für to care for (12-1)

die **Soße, -n** sauce, gravy (9-1)

das **Souvenir, -s** souvenir (7, 11-2)

sowieso anyway (6)

sowjetisch *(adj)* Soviet (11)

die **Sowjetunion** Soviet Union (11)

der **Sozialarbeiter, -**/die **Sozialarbeiterin, -nen** social worker (2)

die **Spaghetti** *(pl)* spaghetti (2)

die **Spalte, -n** column (12)

der **Spanier, -**/die **Spanierin, -nen** Spaniard *(person)* (9)

(das) **Spanisch** Spanish *(language)* (1)

spanisch *(adj)* Spanish (9)

spannend suspenseful; interesting (10-2)

sparen to save (5,)

das **Spargelfest** white asparagus harvest festival (7)

der **Spaß** fun, enjoyment (3)

Es macht mir Spaß, ... I enjoy . . . (8-2)

Spaß machen to have fun (8)

Viel Spaß! Have fun! (7)

spät late (4-1)

Wie spät ist es? What time is it? (2-2)

später later (1)

Bis später! See you later! (1-1)

die **Spätzle** *(pl)* traditional Southern German egg pasta (9)

der **Spaziergang, -̈e** walk (7)

einen Spaziergang machen to go for a walk (7)

spazieren gehen, ging spazieren, ist spazieren gegangen to go for a walk (4-2)

der **Speck** *(sing)* bacon (4)

die **Speisekarte, -n** menu (9-1)

spenden to donate (4)

spendieren *(+ dat)* to buy *(for someone)* (12)

die **Sperre, -n** barrier; barricade (11-1)

sperren to close or block off (11-1)

der **Spezialist, -en, -en**/die **Spezialistin, -nen** specialist (E)

die **Spezialität, -en** specialty (3)

der **Spiegel, -** mirror (9-2)

das **Spiegelei, -er** fried egg (sunny-side up) (4-1)

das **Spiel, -e** game (2)

spielen to play (1-2)

spielerisch playful (4)

das **Spielzeug, -e** toy (3)

der **Spinat** spinach (9-1)

die **Spinne, -n** spider (11)

spitze great (2)

echt spitze really great (2-2)

spontan spontaneous(ly) (4)

der **Sport** sport(s), athletics (1)

Sport machen to do sports (4)

Was für Sport machst du? What sports do you do? (2)

das **Sportcoupé, -s** sport coupe (3)

das **Sportgeschäft, -e** sporting goods store (2)

der **Sportler, -**/die **Sportlerin, -nen** athlete (1)

sportlich athletic (1-2); sporty (2)

die **Sportreportage, -n** sports report (3)

das **Sportstadion, Sportstadien** sports stadium (3)

der **Sportverein, -e** sport club (2)

das **Sportzentrum, Sportzentren** sport center (1)

die **Sprache, -n** language (3-2)

die **Sprachkenntnisse** *(pl)* knowledge of languages (12)

sprachlos speechless (12)

die **Sprachnotiz, -en** note on language *(usage)* (E)

sprechen (spricht), sprach, gesprochen to speak, to talk (3-2)

sprechen über *(+ acc)* to talk about (11-2)

die **Sprechstunde, -n** office hour (9)

springen, sprang, ist gesprungen to jump (8)

der **Spruch, -̈e** saying (5)

das **Spülbecken, -** sink (8-1)

die **Spülmaschine, -n** dishwasher (8-1)

das **Squash** squash *(sport)* (2)

der **Staat, -en** state (11-2)

der **Staatschef, -s** head of state (11)

der **Stachel, -n** quill (8)

der **Stacheldraht** barbed wire (11-1)

das **Stachelschwein, -e** porcupine (8)

das **Stadion, Stadien** stadium (3)

die **Stadt, ̈-e** city, town (1, 2-2)

  in die Stadt to town

der **Stadtpark, -s** city park (2)

der **Stadtplan, ̈-e** map of the city/town (8-2)

der **Stahl** steel (4)

der **Stall, ̈-e** stable (10)

der **Stamm, ̈-e** tree trunk (7)

  Der Apfel fällt nicht weit vom Stamm. Like father, like son. (7)

der **Stammbaum, ̈-e** family tree (3, 6-1)

der **Stand** *(sing)* social status (12)

ständig constant(ly) (12-1)

stark strong (11, 12-2)

die **Stärke, -n** strength (6-2)

der **Start, -s** start, begin (2)

starten to start *(something, e.g., a motor)* (6)

die **Statistik, -en** statistic (9)

statt instead of (9) *(prep + gen)* (12-2)

statt·finden, fand statt, stattgefunden to take place (10-2)

staublos dust-free (10)

der **Staubsauger, -** vacuum cleaner (8-2)

stecken in *(+ acc)* to put in, to stick in (6)

  die Nase zu tief ins Glas stecken to drink too much (6)

stehen, stand, gestanden to stand; to be standing (1-2); to say (6-2)

  Diese Jacke steht dir. This jacket looks good on you. (7-2)

die **Stehlampe, -n** floor lamp (8-1)

stehlen (stiehlt), stahl, gestohlen to steal (10-2)

steigen, stieg, ist gestiegen to climb (10-1)

der **Stein, -e** stone (11)

die **Stelle, -n** job, position (12-2)

stellen to put *(in an upright position)* (4, 8-2)

  eine Frage stellen to ask a question (7-2)

sterben (stirbt), starb, ist gestorben to die (3-2, 6-2)

der **Stern, -e** star *(and name of a popular German magazine)* (2)

das **Sternzeichen, -** zodiac sign (1)

das **Steuer(rad)** steering wheel (11-2)

der **Stiefel, -** boot (2-2)

die **Stiefmutter, ̈-** stepmother (3-1)

der **Stiefvater, ̈-** stepfather (3-1)

die **Stiftung, -en** foundation, endowment, trust (4)

der **Stil, -e** style (4)

still still, quiet (4); silent (11)

stillen to satisfy *(hunger, thirst)* (4)

stimmen to be right (6)

  Das (Es) stimmt. That's true (right). (6-2)

das **Stimmrecht** right to vote (12)

die **Stimmung, -en** mood (12)

das **Stimmungstief, -** down mood (12)

stinklangweilig deadly boring (3)

der **Stocherkahn, ̈-e** punting boat (1)

der **Stock, Stockwerke** floor, story (8)

das **Stofftier, -e** stuffed animal (7-2)

stolz proud (7)

  stolz sein auf *(+ acc)* to be proud of (7)

stoppen to stop (11)

stören to disturb (8-1)

der **Strafzettel, -** *(traffic)* ticket (12-2)

der **Strand, ̈-e** beach (E, 5-1)

  am Strand at the beach (5-2)

  der **Sandstrand, ̈-e** sandy beach (E)

der **Strandkorb, ̈-e** *(literally)* beach basket (chair) (1)

die **Straße, -n** street (E, 2-2)

das **Straßenfest, -e** street festival (7)

die **Straßenseite, -n** side of the street (12)

die **Straßensperre, -n** barrier blocking off a street, barricade (11-1)

der **Strauß, ̈-e** bouquet of flowers (7)

der **Stress** stress (4-2)

stressig stressful (8)

streuen to sprinkle (4)

der **Strumpf, ̈-e** stocking (11)

das **Stück, -e** piece (3, 4-1)

  ein Stück Torte a piece of layer cake (3, 4-1)

  drei Stück Kuchen three pieces of cake (4)

der **Student, -en, -en**/die **Studentin, -nen** student (1-1)

der **Studentenausweis, -e** student ID (5-2)

der **Studentenchor, ̈-e** student choir (6)

die **Studentenermäßigung, -en** student discount (5)

das **Studentenheim, -e** dormitory, student residence (1, 2-2)

das **Studentenleben** student life (1)

das **Studentenwerk** student center (E)

der **Studienabschluss, ̈-e** graduation, formal university degree (12)

die **Studienberatung, -en** academic advising (12)

das **Studienfach, ̈-er** field of study; subject (2-2)

der **Studienschwerpunkt, -e** major course of study (12)

studieren to study *(i.e., to attend college or university)*, to major in (1-1)

  studieren an *(+ dat)* to study at a college or university (11-2)

das **Studium** *(sing)* studies (2)

der **Stuhl, ̈-e** chair (2, 8-1)

  jemand *(dat)* **den Stuhl vor die Tür setzen** to throw somebody out (8)

die **Stulle, -n** sandwich (9-2)

die **Stunde, -n** hour (2-1)

  pro Stunde per hour (6-2)

stundenlang for hours (2-1)

der **Stundenplan, ̈-e** schedule, timetable (2-2)

der **Sturm, ̈-e** storm (10)

der **Sturmwind, -e** gale wind (10)

stürzen to fall; to plunge (10)

stylen to style (E)

die **Suche** search (10)

  auf der Suche sein to be searching (10)

suchen to look for (4)

(das) **Südamerika** South America (6-1)

süddeutsch *(adj)* Southern German (2)

der **Süden** south (10)

der **Südpol** South Pole (1)

die **Südseeinsel, -n** South Sea island (9)

die **Summe, -n** sum, amount (9)

super super (E)

der **Superlativ, -e** superlative (5)

der **Supermarkt, ̈-e** supermarket (2, 5-1, 7-2)

supersüß very sweet (3)

die **Suppe, -n** soup (2, 9-1)

  ein Haar in der Suppe finden to find fault with something (9)

das **Surfbrett, -er** surfboard (4)

surfen to surf (4)

das **Sushi, -s** sushi (3)

süß sweet (3)

die **Süßigkeiten** *(pl)* candy; sweets (7-2)

die **Süßkartoffel, -n** yam, sweet potato (9)

das **Sweatshirt, -s** sweatshirt (E, 2-2)

der **Swing** swing *(music)* (1)

das **Symbol, -e** symbol (1)

sympathisch likeable; personable (6)

die **Synagoge, -n** synagogue (11)

das **Synonym, -e** synonym (10)

der **Syrer -**/die **Syrerin -nen** Syrian *(person)* (6)

syrisch *(adj)* Syrian (6)

T

die **Tabelle, -n** chart, table (9-2, 10-2)
der **Tabletcomputer, -** tablet (computer) (3)
die **Tablette, -n** pill, tablet (12-2)
der **Tag, -e** day (E, 1-2)
  Guten Tag! Tag! Hello! (E-1)
  Tag der Arbeit Labor Day (7)
  Tag der deutschen Einheit Day of German Unity (7)
  Tag der Fahne Flag Day (7)
  vierzehn Tage two weeks (5-1)
das **Tageslicht** daylight (10)
die **Tagesschau** *(TV)* news (2)
die **Tageszeitung, -en** daily newspaper (10)
täglich daily (2)
tagsüber during the day (11)
taktlos tactless (5)
taktvoll tactful (5)
das **Tal, ⸚er** valley (7)
talentiert talented (1)
der **Talkmaster, -**/die **Talkmasterin, -nen** talk show host (E)
die **Talkshow, -s** talk show (2)
der **Tango, -s** tango (2)
die **Tanne, -n** fir tree (5)
die **Tante, -n** aunt (3-1)
tanzen to dance (1-2)
  tanzen gehen to go dancing (8)
der **Tänzer, -**/die **Tänzerin, -nen** dancer (2)
der **Tanzrhythmus** dance rhythm (E)
die **Tasche, -n** bag; pocket (4-2)
das **Taschenmesser, -** pocket knife (4-2)
die **Tasse, -n** cup (4-1)
  eine Tasse Kaffee a cup of coffee (4-1)
  nicht alle Tassen im Schrank haben to be crazy (8)
die **Tätigkeit, -en** activity; employment (2)
die **Tätowierung, -en** tattoo (5-2)
tatsächlich actual(ly) (12-1)
tauchen to dive (5)
das **Taxi, -s** taxi (5)
das **Team, -s** team (2, 10-1)
die **Technik** technology (8-2)
die **Technologie, -n** technology (10-1)
der **Teddybär, -en, -en** teddy bear (E)
der **Tee** tea (2-1)
die **Teekanne, -n** teapot (8)
der **Teekessel, -** tea kettle (1)
der **Teelöffel, -** teaspoon (9-1)
der **Teenager, -** teenager (3)
der **Teil, -e** part, area (8-2)
  der **östliche Teil** the eastern part (11-1)
  der **westliche Teil** the western part (11-1)

teilen to share (6); to divide (11-1)
die **Teilung, -en** separation, division (11)
die **Teilzeit** part-time (12)
das **Telefon, -e** telephone (E)
telefonieren (mit) to talk on the phone (with) (2-1)
die **Telefonnummer, -n** telephone number (E)
das **Teleskop, -e** telescope (1)
der **Teller, -** plate (5, 9-1)
die **Temperatur, -en** temperature (5)
das **Tennis** tennis (1)
  Tennis spielen to play tennis (2-1)
der **Tennisball, ⸚e** tennis ball (1)
das **Tennismatch, -es** tennis match (10)
der **Tennisschläger, -** tennis racquet (7-2)
der **Teppich, -e** carpet, rug (8-1)
teuer expensive (2-2)
der **Teufel, -** devil (8)
  den Teufel an die Wand malen to tempt fate (8)
der **Text, -e** text (6)
  die **SMS-Text, -e** text message
der **Thailänder, -**/die **Thailänderin, -nen** Thai *(person)* (9)
das **Theater, -** theater (1)
  ins Theater to the theater (1-2)
das **Theaterstück, -e** play (8)
das **Thema, Themen** topic (4)
die **Theologie, -n** theology (3)
die **Theorie, -n** theory (6)
das **Thermometer, -** thermometer (1)
die **These, -n** thesis (10)
der **Thüringer Wald** Thuringian Forest (1)
der **Thymian, -e** thyme (9)
das **Ticket, -s** ticket (1)
das **Tief, s** low; low point (12)
tief deep; low (6)
  die Nase zu tief ins Glas stecken to drink too much (6)
das **Tier, -e** animal (2, 7-2)
der **Tipp, -s** tip, helpful hint (7)
der **Tisch, -e** table (7, 8-1)
  den Tisch decken to set the table (7-1)
das **Tischtennis** table tennis (ping-pong) (2)
der **Titel, -** title (1)
der **Toast** toast (4-1)
die **Tochter, ⸚** daughter (1, 3-1)
der **Tod, -e** death (3-2)
tödlich deadly (11)
das **Todesopfer, -** casualty (11)
der **Todesstreifen, -** death strip (11-1)
die **Toilette, -n** lavatory; bathroom; restroom (1, 8-1)
toll fantastic, neat (1-1)

  nicht so toll not great (3)
die **Tomate, -n** tomato (9)
der **Ton, ⸚e** tone; sound; note (2)
der **Toner** toner (12)
die **Tonne, -n** trash container, bin (9-2)
der **Topf, ⸚e** pot (11)
das **Tor, -e** gate (5)
die **Torte, -n** layer cake (3, 4-1)
  ein Stück Torte a piece of layer cake (4-1)
tot dead (3-2)
total completely (5)
die **Toten** *(pl)* dead people (11)
töten to kill (8)
die **Tour, -en** tour (7-1)
der **Tourismus** tourism (5)
der **Tourist, -en, -en**/die **Touristin, -nen** tourist (5-2)
die **Touristenattraktion, -en** tourist attraction (3)
die **Tournee, -n** tour (3-2)
die **Tradition, -en** tradition (5)
tragen (trägt), trug, getragen to wear (3-2); to carry (8)
trainieren to train (10)
der **Traum, ⸚e** dream (12-2)
der **Traumberuf, -e** job of one's dreams (12)
träumen to dream (12-2)
traumlos dreamless (12)
die **Traumstelle, -n** dream job (12)
traurig sad (4)
(sich) treffen (trifft), traf, getroffen to meet (3, 9-2)
das **Treffen, -** meeting; gathering (7)
trendig trendy (7)
trennen to separate (11-1)
die **Trennung, -en** separation (11)
die **Treppe, -n** staircase (8-1)
trinkbar drinkable (12)
trinken, trank, getrunken to drink (2-1)
das **Trinkgeld, -er** tip *(in a restaurant)* (6, 9-1)
sich *(dat)* **die Haare trocknen** to dry one's hair (9-2)
der **Troll, -e** *(computer)* troll (6)
die **Trommel, -n** drum *(musical)* (7)
die **Trompete, -n** trumpet (8)
die **Tropenhalle, -n** Tropics exhibit hall (5)
tropfen to drip (11)
tropisch tropical (5)
trotz *(prep + gen)* in spite of (12-2)
trotzdem anyway; nevertheless (5-2)
die **Truppe, -n** troop (5)
das **T-Shirt, -s** T-shirt (2-2)
Tschüss! Bye! So long! (E-1)
die **Tulpe, -n** tulip (1)

tun, tat, getan to do (1-2)
der **Tunnel, -** tunnel (4)
die **Tür, -en** door (8-1)
der **Türke, -n, -n**/die **Türkin,
-nen** Turk (*person*) (9)
das **Türkisch** Turkish (*language*) (4)
türkisch (*adj*) Turkish (7)
der **Turm, ⸚e** tower (3, 11-1)
das **Turnier, -e** tournament (2)
die **Tüte, -n** bag (9)
der **Typ, -en** guy (3, 7-2)
typisch typical(ly) (1, 4-2)

U

die **U-Bahn** subway (11)
üben to practice (6-2)
über (*prep + acc/dat*) about (1); across
(8); over (1), above (8); via (11)
überall everywhere (12)
der **Übergang, ⸚e** crossing; transition
(11)
überhaupt at all; anyway; absolutely
(11-1)
　überhaupt nicht not at all (11)
　überhaupt nichts nothing at all;
　　absolutely nothing
überkritisch overcritical (5)
überlegen to think about (12)
übermorgen the day after tomorrow
(3)
übermütig emboldened (10)
übernachten to spend the night; to
stay overnight (5-1)
die **Übernachtung, -en** overnight
accommodation (5)
**übernehmen (übernimmt),
übernahm, übernommen** to take
on (*a duty*) (7, 12-1)
überraschen to surprise (12)
die **Überraschung, -en** surprise (7-1)
übersetzen to translate (6, 10-1)
der **Übersetzer, -**/die **Übersetzerin,
-nen** translator (9)
die **Übersetzung, -en** translation
(10-1)
überzeugen to persuade (12-1)
übrigens by the way (2-1)
die **Übung, -en** exercise; seminar;
lab; discussion section (2-2)
der **Übungslift, -e** rope tow (*skiing*)
(3)
die **Uhr, -en** clock; watch (2-1)
　zehn Uhr ten o'clock (2-1)
　um zehn Uhr at ten o'clock (2-1)
　Um wie viel Uhr ...? (At) what
　　time . . . ? (2-2)
　Wie viel Uhr ist es? What time is
　　it? (2-2)
die **Uhrzeit, -en** time of day (7)
um (*prep + acc*) at (*time*) (2); around (5)

um die Ecke around the corner
(5-2)
um zehn Uhr at ten o'clock (2)
um ... zu in order to (8)
umarmen to embrace, hug (6)
die **Umarmung, -en** embrace, hug
(6)
sich **um·drehen** to turn
around (10)
die **Umfrage, -n** survey, poll (5)
umliegend surrounding (8)
**um·steigen, stieg um, ist
umgestiegen** to change trains
(4-2)
die **Umwelt** environment (9-2, 12-2)
umweltbewusst leben to live in an
environmentally conscious way
(9-2)
das **Umweltengagement,
-s** commitment to the
environment (9)
umweltfreundlich environmentally
friendly (9-2)
umweltschonend environmentally
friendly, environmentally
sound (9)
der **Umweltschutz** environmental
protection (9-2)
die **Umweltstiftung,
-en** environmental foundation (4)
**um·ziehen, zog um, ist
umgezogen** to move (*change
residence*) (8-2)
sich **um·ziehen, zog um, hat
umgezogen** to change (*one's
clothes*) (9-2)
der **Umzug, ⸚e** move (*housing*) (10)
unabhängig independent (6-1)
die **Unabhängigkeit** independence
(6-1)
　die **Unabhängigkeits-
　erklärung** the Declaration of
　Independence (6-1)
unbedingt really (12-2)
unbeliebt unpopular (10)
unbewohnbar uninhabitable (12)
unbezahlt unpaid (12)
und (*coord conj*) and (E, 1-2)
　und so weiter (*abbr. usw.*) and so
　forth (*abbr. etc.*) (8-1)
undankbar ungrateful (12)
undefinierbar indefinable (12)
der **Unfall, ⸚e** accident (11)
unfassbar unfathomable, surprising,
shocking (6)
die **Unfreiheit** lack of freedom
(11-2)
unfreundlich unfriendly (3-1)
ungebügelt unironed (11)
ungesund unhealthy (4-2)

unglaublich unbelievable (6)
unglücklich unhappy (7-2)
unhöflich impolite (7-2)
die **Uni, -s** university (1-1)
　an der Uni at the university (2-2)
　zur Uni to the university (2-2)
der **Uni-Abschluss** (*university*)
graduation (7)
die **Uniform, -en** uniform (3)
die **Universität, -en** university (1-1)
das **Universitätsleben** (*sing*)
university life (2-2)
die **Universitätsstadt, ⸚e** university
town (8)
unkontrollierbar uncontrollable
(12)
unkonventionell unconventional (4)
das **Unkraut** weeds (6)
unkultiviert uncultivated,
unrefined, uncultured (9)
unmöglich impossible (4-2)
unordentlich messy, sloppy (4-2)
unser, unser, unsere our (1)
unten under, below (8, 10-2)
　hier unten down here (10)
unter (*prep + acc/dat*) under, below
(3); beneath (8); among (11)
**unterbrechen (unterbricht),
unterbrach, unterbrochen**
to interrupt (12-1)
das **Unternehmen, -** company (9)
der **Unternehmer, -**/die
Unternehmerin, -nen
entrepreneur (6-1)
der **Unterschied, -e** difference
(9-2,12)
unterschiedlich different (3, 12-1)
unterwegs on the way (1, 10-2)
unübersetzbar untranslatable (12)
unveräußerlich inalienable (6)
unzufrieden (mit) dissatisfied (with)
(12-1)
up to date up-to-date (1)
uralt ancient (10-1)
die **Urgroßeltern** (*pl*) great-
grandparents (6-1)
die **Urgroßmutter, ⸚** great-
grandmother (6-1)
der **Urgroßvater, ⸚** great-grandfather
(6-1)
der **Urlaub** vacation (*generally of
people in the workforce*) (5-1)
　Urlaub machen to go on vacation
　(5-1)
der **USB-Stick, -s** USB stick, flash
drive (3)
usw. (und so weiter) etc. (et cetera,
and so on) (E, 8-1)
die **Utopie, -n** utopia (12-1)
die **UV-Strahlen** (*pl*) UV rays (7)

V

(der) **Valentinstag** Valentine's Day (6, 7-2)

das **Vanilleeis** vanilla ice cream (9)

die **Vanillesoße** vanilla sauce (9)

die **Vase, -n** vase (1)

der **Vater, ⁚** father (1, 3-1)

väterlicherseits paternal (6-1)

vegan (adj/adv) vegan (9-1)

der **Veganer, -**/die **Veganerin, -nen** vegan (9-1)

  Ich bin Veganer/Veganerin. I'm a vegan. (9-1)

der **Vegetarier, -**/die **Vegetarierin, -nen** vegetarian (9-1)

vegetarisch (adj/adv) vegetarian (9-1)

verabredet sein to have an appointment (6)

die **Veranstaltung, -en** event (2)

der **Veranstaltungsort, -e** event venue (2)

die **Veranstaltungsplanung** event planning (12)

der **Veranstaltungstechniker, -**/die **Veranstaltungstechnikerin, -nen** event technician (2)

das **Verb, -en** verb (1)

der **Verband, ⁚e** association (4)

verbessern to improve; to correct (6)

verbieten, verbot, verboten to forbid (E)

verbinden, verband, verbunden to connect (9)

verboten prohibited (5-1)

verbringen, verbrachte, verbracht to spend (time) (7-2)

verdienen to earn (3-2)

der **Verdienst, -e** earnings (pl) (12)

der **Verein, -e** club (2-1)

die **Vereinigten Staaten (die USA)** the United States (the U.S.) (E, 1-1)

die **Verfassung, -en** constitution (12-1)

verfügbar available (12)

verfügen über (+ acc) to have at one's disposal (5)

vergangen past (7)

vergessen (vergisst), vergaß, vergessen to forget (3, 4-2)

vergleichen, verglich, verglichen (8-1)

vergnügt happy, in a good mood (10-2)

die **Vergnügung, -en** pleasure (3)

verhaften to arrest (11-2)

verheiratet married (3-1)

verhören to interrogate (8)

verkaufen to sell (3-2)

der **Verkäufer, -**/die **Verkäuferin, -nen** sales clerk, salesman/saleswoman (3-2)

das **Verkehrszeichen, -** traffic sign (4)

verkleidet disguised (10)

verlassen (verlässt), verließ, verlassen to leave (8)

der **Verlauf, ⁚e** course (as in path) (11)

sich **verlieben in** (+ acc) to fall in love with (5, 11-2)

verliebt in love (2)

verlieren, verlor, verloren to lose (10-2)

sich **vermehren** to increase in number; to reproduce (10)

vermieten to rent (out) (8-1)

der **Vermieter, -**/die **Vermieterin, -nen** landlord/landlady (9)

das **Vermögen** wealth (12)

veröffentlichen to publish (10-1)

die **Veröffentlichung, -en** publication (10-1)

die **Verpackung, -en** packaging, wrapping (9)

verpassen to miss out on (5)

verringern to downsize; to reduce (9)

verrückt crazy; insane (4)

verschieden different (7-2); various (9)

verschlingen, verschlang, verschlungen to devour (10-2)

sich **verspäten** to be late (9-2)

versprechen (verspricht), versprach, versprochen to promise (8)

verstecken to hide (10)

verstehen, verstand, verstanden to understand (3-1)

verstümmelt mutilated, crippled (6)

versuchen to try (5, 8-2)

vertrauen (+ dat) to trust (6)

vertreten to represent (11)

verwalten to govern (11)

verwandt related (1)

der/die **Verwandte, -n** relative (3-1)

verwendbar usable (12)

verwenden to use (9-2)

verwirrt confused (9)

das **Verwöhnpaket, -e** "Let us spoil you" package (e.g., at a hotel) (5)

verzichten auf (+acc) to forgo (9)

der **Vetter, -n** (male) cousin (3-1)

das **Video, -s** video (3)

das **Videospiel, -e** video game (2)

viel much; a lot (E, 1-1)

  viel zu schnell much too fast (3-1)

  viel zu viel far too much (6)

viele many (1)

vielleicht maybe (1-2); perhaps (7)

vielseitig versatile, all-round, multifunctional (4)

viert: zu viert in a group of four (8-1)

das **Viertel** quarter (2)

  Viertel nach zehn quarter after ten (2)

  Viertel vor fünf quarter to five (2)

der **Vietnamese, -n, -n**/die **Vietnamesin, -nen** Vietnamese (person) (9)

vietnamesisch (adj) Vietnamese (9)

die **Villa, Villen** villa

violett purple (1-1)

die **Violine, -n** violin (3)

der **Violinist, -en, -en**/die **Violinistin, -nen** violinist (3)

viral viral (6-2)

virtuell virtual (6)

visuell visual (9-2)

das **Visum, Visa** visa (12)

der **Vizepräsident, -en, -en**/die **Vizepräsidentin, -nen** vice president (12)

der **Vogel, ⁚** bird (2)

die **Vokabeln** (pl) vocabulary (1)

das **Volk, ⁚er** people (5)

die **Völkerschlacht -en** battle (5)

die **Volksarmee** army of the former GDR (11)

die **Volksgeschichte, -n** folk tale (10)

voll full (1, 7-1)

  den Mund voll nehmen to talk big (6)

vollenden to complete (12-2)

die **Vollendung, -en** completion (12)

der **Volleyball, ⁚e** volleyball (2)

vollkommen perfect; immaculate (12)

vollständig complete(ly) (8)

von (prep + dat) from (E); of (E); about (7); by (11)

  von ... bis from . . . to (1-2)

  von heute ab from now on (11)

vor (prep + acc/dat) in front of; before (4, 8); ago (7)

  vor dem Fernseher in front of the TV (4-2)

vorbei sein to be over (10)

vor·bereiten to prepare (12)

die **Vorbereitung, -en** preparation (7)

die **Vorbestellung: auf Vorbestellung** by ordering in advance (9)

der **Vordergrund** foreground (11)

der **Vorfahr, -en, -en** ancestor (6-1)

vor·haben (hat vor), hatte vor, vorgehabt to plan, to have planned (4-2)

die **Vorhand** forehand (E)

der **Vorhang, ‥e** curtain (11)
  der **Eiserne Vorhang** the Iron
    Curtain (11-2)
der **Vorkämpfer, -**/die
  Vorkämpferin, -nen early
    champion (10)
die **Vorlesung, -en** lecture; class
    (1-1)
  in die Vorlesung (to go) to a
    lecture (1-2)
der **Vormittag, -e** morning (6)
vormittags in the morning (2)
der **Vorname, -ns, -n** first name
    (1, 3-2)
das **Vorrecht, -e** privilege (12)
der **Vorsatz, ‥e** resolution (11)
die **Vorschau** preview (1)
der **Vorschlag, ‥e** suggestion (7)
Vorsicht! Careful! (7)
vorsichtig careful(ly) (12)
die **Vorspeise, -n** hors d'œuvre
    (4, 9-1)
der **Vorteil, -e** advantage (8-2)
die **Vorwahl** area code (E)
der **Vulkan, -e** volcano (2)

W

das **Wachs** wax (5)
der **Wagen, -** car (3-1)
wählen to choose, select (8, 9-2)
das **Wahlmodul, -e** elective course
    (1)
wahr true (6-2)
während (prep + gen) during
    (6, 12-2)
die **Wahrheit, -en** truth (6)
wahrscheinlich probably (12)
der **Wald, ‥er** forest; woods
    (5-1)
der **Waldweg, -e** forest path,
    trail (12)
die **Walnuss, ‥e** walnut (9)
die **Wand, ‥e** wall (8-1)
**wandern, wanderte, ist
  gewandert** to hike (2)
  wandern gehen to go hiking
    (2-1)
der **Wanderschuh, -e** hiking boot (5)
die **Wanderung, -en** hike (5)
wann when (1-2)
die **Wanne, -n** bathtub (8)
warm warm (1-2)
warnen to warn (6-2)
die **Warnung, -en** warning (6-2)
warten to wait (6-2)
  warten auf (+ acc) to wait for
    (11-2)
die **Wartungsfreundlichkeit** ease of
    repairs (9)
warum why (1-2)
die **Warze, -n** wart (3)

was what (E, 1-2)
  Was für ein Sauwetter! What
    rotten weather! (1)
  Was für ein Superwetter! What
    great weather! (1)
  Was ist das auf English? What is
    that in English? (E-1)
  was … sonst what else (8)
waschbar washable (12)
das **Waschbecken, -** (bathroom) sink
    (8-1)
die **Wäsche** wash, laundry (6)
  die Wäsche waschen to do the
    laundry (6-2)
**waschen (wäscht), wusch,
  gewaschen** to wash (3-2)
  sich **waschen** to get washed up, to
    bathe or wash (9)
der **Waschlappen, -** washcloth (9-2)
die **Waschmaschine, -n** washer (4)
der **Waschsalon, -s** laundromat
    (6-2)
das **Wasser** water (1, 2-1)
die **Wasserflasche, -n** water bottle (4)
der **Wasserweg, -e** waterway (11)
das **WC, -s** (das **Wasserklosett**)
    toilet (8)
das **Web** World Wide Web
die **Webadresse, -n** Web address (E)
die **Website, -s** website (5)
wechseln to switch (12)
wecken to wake (someone) up (9)
der **Wecker, -** alarm clock (7-1)
weg away; gone (4)
der **Weg, -e** way, path (6, 11-1)
wegen (prep + gen) because of (12-2)
**weg·fahren (fährt weg), fuhr weg,
  ist weggefahren** to drive away
    (4-2)
**weg·fliegen, flog weg, ist
  weggeflogen** to fly away (4)
**weg·gehen, ging weg, ist
  weggegangen** to go away (4)
**weg·laufen (läuft weg), lief weg, ist
  weggelaufen** to run away (4)
**weg·nehmen (nimmt weg), nahm
  weg, weggenommen** to take
    away (4)
**weg·rennen, rannte weg, ist
  weggerannt** to run away (6)
**weg·sehen (sieht weg), sah weg,
  weggesehen** to look away (4)
**weg·werfen (wirft weg), warf weg,
  weggeworfen** to throw away (9-2)
weiblich feminine (2)
Weihnachten Christmas (7-1)
  Frohe Weihnachten! Merry Christ-
    mas! (7-1)
  **Herzlichen Glückwunsch zu
    Weihnachten!** Best wishes for
    Christmas! (7-1)

  zu Weihnachten at, for Christmas
    (7-1)
der **Weihnachtsbaum, ‥e** Christmas
    tree (7-1)
der **Weihnachtsfeiertag** Christmas
    holiday (7)
die **Weihnachtsferien** (pl) Christmas
    vacation (5)
das **Weihnachtsgeschenk,
  -e** Christmas present (7)
der **Weihnachtsmarkt, ‥e** Christmas
    market (7)
die **Weihnachtspyramide, -n**
    Christmas pyramid (traditional
    German decoration with candles and
    figures that turns with the heat of the
    lit candles) (7)
weil because (sub conj) (4-2)
die **Weimarer Republik** Weimar
    Republic (Germany 1919–1933) (1)
der **Wein, -e** wine (1, 2-1)
der **Weinberg, -e** vineyard (5)
weinen to cry (10)
das **Weinerntefest, -e** wine harvest
    festival (7)
das **Weinfest, -e** wine festival (7)
das **Weinglas, ‥er** wine glass (1)
der **Weinkeller, -** wine cellar (6)
die **Weinprobe, -n** wine tasting (7)
weiß white (1-1)
der **Weißwein, -e** white wine (7)
die **Weißwurst, ‥e** Bavarian veal
    sausage (5)
weit far (3, 5-1)
  weit weg far away (8-2)
weiter (as verb prefix) to continue (4)
weiter·arbeiten to keep on working
    (4)
die **Weiterentwicklung, -en** further
    development (10)
**weiter·essen (isst weiter), aß weiter,
  weitergegessen** to continue
    eating (4)
**weiter·fahren (fährt weiter), fuhr
  weiter, ist weitergefahren** to
    keep on driving (4-2)
**weiter·lesen (liest weiter), las
  weiter, weitergelesen** to continue
    reading (4-2)
**weiter·schlafen (schläft
  weiter), schlief weiter,
  weitergeschlafen** to continue
    sleeping (4)
**weiter·schreiben, schrieb weiter,
  weitergeschrieben** to continue
    writing (4)
weiter·studieren to continue
    studying (4)
welcher, welches, welche which (1);
    (pl) some (4)
wellig wavy (3)

der **Wellness-Bereich** spa (5)
die **Welt, -en** world (2, 5-2)
die **Weltanschauung, -en** world view, ideology (12)
weltbekannt world famous (6)
der **Weltkrieg, -e** world war (4, 11-1)
die **Weltreise, -n** trip around the world (5)
weltweit worldwide (4)
die **Wende** turn; change; turning point (*at which the two Germanys reunited*) (11-1)
wenig little (1-2)
wenn when (*sub conj*); if (*sub conj*) (4-2)
wer who (1-2)
werden (wird), wurde, ist geworden to become; to get; to be (3-2)
  Sie wird zwanzig. She's turning twenty. (3-2)
werfen (wirft), warf, geworfen to throw (10)
das **Werk, -e** work (10-1)
die **Werkstatt, ¨en** workshop (4)
das **Werkzeug, -e** tool (9, 10-2)
(das) **Westdeutschland** West Germany (11)
der **Westen** west (8)
westlich western (11)
  westlich (von) west (of) (11)
die **Wette, -n** bet (10)
  um die Wette laufen to run a race (*with someone*) (10)
wetten to bet (10-2)
das **Wetter** weather (1-1)
  Wie ist das Wetter? What's the weather like? (1)
die **Wetterkarte, -n** weather map (1)
der **Wettlauf, ¨e** race (*contest*) (10-2)
  einen Wettlauf machen to run a race (10-2)
die **WG, -s (die Wohngemeinschaft, -en)** shared housing (8-1)
wichtig important (4, 6-1)
die **Wichtigkeit** importance (11)
wie how (E, 1-2); like (3)
  so ... wie as . . . as (2-2)
  Wie bitte? Pardon? (E-1)
  wie ein König like a king (3)
  Wie geht es Ihnen? / Wie geht's? How are you? (E-1)
  Wie heißen Sie? / Wie heißt du? What's your name? (E-1)
  Wie ist das Wetter? What's the weather like? (1)
  Wie ist deine E-Mail-Adresse? What is your e-mail address? (E)

Wie schreibt man das? How do you write (spell) that? (E-1)
Wie spät ist es? What time is it? (2-2)
wie viel how much (E, 1-2)
  Wie viel ist ...? How much is . . . ? (E-1)
  Wie viel kostet das? How much does this cost? (E-1)
  Wie viel Uhr ist es? What time is it? (2-2)
wie viele how many (1-2)
wieder again (2-2)
  immer wieder again and again (6)
wiederholen to repeat (E, 8-2)
die **Wiederholung, -en** repetition (4)
wieder·sehen (sieht wieder), sah wieder, wiedergesehen to see again (E)
  Auf Wiedersehen! Wiedersehen! Good-bye! (E-1)
die **Wiedervereinigung** reunification (11-1)
wiederverwerten to recycle (9-2)
(das) **Wien** Vienna (1)
  das Wiener Schnitzel breaded veal cutlet (7)
die **Wiese, -n** meadow (5)
der **Wievielte**
  Den Wievielten haben wir heute? What's the date today? (6-2)
  Der Wievielte ist heute? What's the date today? (6-2)
Willkommen: Willkommen in Leipzig! Welcome to Leipzig! (5)
der **Wind, -e** wind
die **Windenergie** wind power (E)
windig windy (E, 1-1)
der **Windpark, -s** wind farm (E)
windstill windless, calm (1)
windsurfen to windsurf (E)
der **Winter, -** winter (1-2)
  im Winter in winter (1-2)
die **Winterjacke, -n** winter jacket (1)
der **Wintermantel, ¨** winter coat (12)
das **Wintersemester, -** (*mid-October through mid-February*) winter semester (E)
winzig tiny (10-2)
wirken to operate, function (11)
wirklich really (8-1)
die **Wirklichkeit** reality (11)
der **Wirt, -e** / die **Wirtin, -nen** pub manager; innkeeper (6)
die **Wirtschaft** economy (12)
das **Wirtschaftswunder** economic miracle (6)
das **Wirtshaus, ¨er** restaurant (9)

wischen to wipe (10)
wissen (weiß), wusste, gewusst to know (5-1)
  wissen von to know about (11-2)
der **Witz, -e** joke (11-2)
witzig witty; funny (6, 7-2)
wo where (*in what place*) (E, 1-2)
die **Woche, -n** week (1-2)
das **Wochenende, -n** weekend (1, 2-2)
das **Wochenendhaus, ¨er** weekend cottage (8)
der **Wochenmarkt, ¨e** open-air market (8-2)
der **Wochentag, -e** day of the week (1-2)
die **Wochenzeitung, -en** weekly newspaper (10)
woher where . . . from (*from what place*) (E, 1-2)
wohin where . . . to (*to what place*) (1-2)
Wohl: zum Wohl! Cheers! To your health! (7-2)
wohl probably; perhaps (7-2)
  sich wohl fühlen to feel well (9-2); to feel at home (8)
wohnen to live (*in a building or on a street*) (2-2)
  zur Miete wohnen to rent (8)
die **Wohngemeinschaft, -en (die WG, -s)** shared housing (2, 8-1)
das **Wohnheim, -e** dormitory (6)
der **Wohnort, -e** place of residence (1, 6-1)
die **Wohnung, -en** apartment (3)
das **Wohnviertel, -** residential area (8)
das **Wohnzimmer, -** living room (8-1)
der **Wok, -s** wok (9)
wollen (will), wollte, gewollt to want to (4)
wolkig partly cloudy (1)
das **Wort, -e** word (*in a meaningful context*) (6)
das **Wort, ¨er** word (*lexical item*) (1, 7-1)
das **Wörterbuch, ¨er** dictionary (7-1)
der **Wortschatz, ¨e** vocabulary (E)
wozu what . . . for (8-2)
wunderbar wonderful (3-2, 11-1)
das **Wunderkind, -er** child prodigy (3)
wunderschön very beautiful (3-2)
der **Wunsch, ¨e** wish (12-2)
wünschen to wish (7-2)
  Sie wünschen? May I help you? (7)
der **Wurm, ¨er** worm (1)

die **Wurst, ̈e** sausage; cold cuts (3, 4-1)

   Das ist mir wurst. I couldn't care less. (7)

die **Wurstsorte, -n** type of sausage (9)

würzen to season (9)

würzig spicy; tangy (9-1)

wütend furious (12)

   wütend auf *(+acc)* furious at (12-1)

Y

Yoga machen to do yoga (4-2)

Z

z. B.; zum Beispiel e.g., for example (3, 12)

die **Zahl, -en** number (9)

zählen to count (10)

der **Zahn, ̈e** tooth (5)

der **Zahnarzt, ̈e**/die **Zahnärztin, -nen** dentist (7-2)

die **Zahnbürste, -n** toothbrush (5, 9-2)

die **Zahnpasta** toothpaste (9-2)

die **Zahnschmerzen** *(pl)* toothache (7-2)

der **Zauber** magic

die **Zauberflöte** magic flute (3)

der **Zaun, ̈e** fence (11)

das **Zebra, -s** zebra (1)

zeichnen to draw *(a picture)*; to draft (8)

die **Zeichnung, -en** drawing (10)

zeigen to show (1-1, 8-2)

   Das Thermometer zeigt zehn Grad. The thermometer reads (shows) ten degrees. (1-1)

die **Zeile, -n** line *(of text on a page)* (10)

die **Zeit, -en** time (2-1)

   in letzter Zeit recently (6-2)

der **Zeitdruck** time pressure (9)

die **Zeitschrift, -en** magazine, periodical (10)

die **Zeittafel, -n** timeline *(graphic)* (10)

die **Zeitung, -en** newspaper (2, 3-2)

zelebrieren to celebrate (1)

zelten to camp *(in a tent)* (9)

die **Zensur, -en** grade (12)

der **Zentimeter, -** centimeter (5)

zentral central(ly) (8-1)

das **Zentrum, Zentren** center (1, 8)

zerrissen ripped (11)

zerstören to destroy (11-2)

das **Zeug** *(sing)* thing (3)

die **Ziege, -n** goat (9)

der **Ziegenkäse** goat cheese (9)

ziehen, zog, gezogen to move; to change residence (6-1)

   Meine Tante ist nach Chicago gezogen. My aunt moved to Chicago. (6-1)

das **Ziel, -e** goal, aim; destination (5, 10-2)

ziemlich quite; rather (4, 5)

   ziemlich cool kind of cool *(colloquial)* (5-2)

die **Zigarette, -n** cigarette (4-2)

die **Zigarre, -n** cigar (10)

das **Zimmer, -** room (2-2)

die **Zimmerpflanze, -n** house plant (5-2)

der **Zimt** cinnamon (9)

die **Zinsen** *(pl) (bank)* interest (12-2)

zirka approximately (2)

das **Zitronensaft** lemon juice (4)

die **Zone, -n** zone (11-2)

der **Zoo, -s** zoo (3)

die **Zoologie** zoology (2)

der **Zopf, ̈e** braid (11)

zu *(prep + dat)* to; too (1); for (7)

   zu Hause (at) home (4-1)

   zu viel too much (1)

   zu viert in a group of four (8-1)

der **Zucker** *(sing)* sugar (4-1)

zuerst first (1-1, 4-2)

zufrieden (mit) satisfied (with) (12-1)

der **Zug, ̈e** train (3-1)

der **Zugang** access (10-1)

die **Zugspitze** Zugspitze *(the highest mountain in Germany)* (1)

zu·hören to listen (E)

die **Zukunft** future (11-2)

zuletzt last (4-2); finally (6-1)

zum Beispiel (z. B.) for example (e.g.) (3, 12)

zum Glück fortunately, luckily (5, 12-1)

die **Zunge, -n** tongue (3)

zurück back (4)

zurück·bringen, brachte zurück, zurückgebracht to bring back (4)

zurück·fahren (fährt zurück), fuhr zurück, ist zurückgefahren to drive back (4)

zurück·geben (gibt zurück), gab zurück, zurückgegeben to give back (4)

zurück·gehen, ging zurück, ist zurückgegangen to go back (8)

zurück·kehren, kehrte zurück, ist zurückgekehrt to return (10)

zurück·kommen, kam zurück, ist zurückgekommen to come back (4-2)

zurück·nehmen (nimmt zurück), nahm zurück, zurückgenommen to take back (4)

zurück·rufen, rief zurück, zurückgerufen to call back (4)

zurück·ziehen, zog zurück, ist zurückgezogen to move back (6-1)

zusammen together (1-2)

zusammen·mischen to mix together (4)

zusammen·passen to go together; to match (1)

zusammen·wohnen to cohabitate, to live together (8)

zusätzlich additional (8-1)

der **Zuschauer, -**/die **Zuschauerin, -nen** viewers (6)

der **Zuschlag, ̈e** surcharge (5)

zwar indeed (6)

   und zwar *(for emphasis)* namely, in fact (12)

zweieinhalb two and a half (9)

zweimal twice (5, 6-2)

der **Zweite Weltkrieg** Second World War (4)

das **Zwergflusspferd, -e** pygmy hippopotamus (5)

die **Zwiebel, -n** onion (9-1)

zwischen *(prep + acc/dat)* between (8)

Index

A

das **Abendessen,** 120
abends, 66, 67
aber, 33, 138
das **Abitur,** 36
accusative case
  adjective endings in, 100, 101
  and dative object, 223
  der and **ein** in, 93–94
  der- and **ein-**words in, 95, 96
  personal pronouns in, 156
  possessive adjectives in, 96
  prepositions taking, 158
  reflexive pronouns in, 280
  in time expressions, 97
adjective(s)
  accusative endings of, when
    preceded by **der-**words, 100
  accusative endings of, when
    preceded by **ein-**words, 100
  accusative endings of
    unpreceded, 101
  comparative of, 160, 163
  dative case with, 224
  dative endings of, when preceded by
    der- and **ein-**words, 234
  dative endings of unpreceded, 235
  der words, preceded by, 320
  ein words, preceded by, 321
  genitive endings of, when preceded
    by **der-** and **ein-**words, 265
  nominative endings of, when
    preceded by **der-**words, 73
  nominative endings of, when
    preceded by **ein-**words, 76
  nominative endings of
    unpreceded, 77
  past participle as, 339
  possessive, 75, 96
  superlative of, 162–163
  unpreceded, 322
adverbs
  comparative of, 160
  superlative of, 162–163
agent (passive voice), 339
agent nouns, 297
Akademisches Auslandsamt, 36
Alexanderplatz (Berlin), 330, 335
die **Alpen,** 23, 24, 118
alphabet, 9
als, 314, 326
Alshater, Firas, 208–209
am _____ sten, 162–163
an, 251, 255, 258
Angles, 48
art and architecture, Austrian, 88
das **Asyl,** 196

au (diphthong), 92
auf, 251, 255
aus, 227
  von vs., 231
außer, 227
Austria, 87–89
die **Autobahn,** 143, 151
Autostadt Wolfsburg, 8
auxiliary verb
  position of, with past participle,
    187, 188
  sein as, in perfect tense, 192

B

die **Bahn,** 143, 151
-bar (suffix), 380
das **Bauhaus,** 256–258
bei, 227
Berlin, 8, 195, 211, 331–333
die **Berliner Luftbrücke,** 341
die **Berliner Mauer,** 331–333, 342,
  349
Bern, 119
beverages, 58
birthday parties, 226
der **Billigflieger,** 151
bitte, 135
der **Bodensee,** 128
body parts, 184
  in idiomatic expressions, 207
Bologna Process, 36
books, 303–304
die **Bundesliga,** 55
Bundesrepublik Deutschland (BRD),
  214, 331–332
der **Bundestag,** 7
Burgenland, 87

C

Celsius scale, 22
ch, pronunciation of, 10, 155
-chen (suffix), 122, 175
clothing, articles of, 39
cognates, 48, 81, 111
colloquial German
  accusative prepositions, 158
  flavoring particles, 168
  telling time, 63–64, 66, 67
colors, 25
comparative, 160, 163
compound nouns, 270
congratulations, expressing, 217, 237
conjunctions, 33
  coordinating, 138
  subordinating, 138, 165, 167
contractions, 229
  accusative prepositions in, 158
  dative prepositions in, 229

coordinating conjunctions, 138
country names, 26

D

da-compounds, 347, 348
dafür, 347
dagegen, 347
dann, denn vs., 145
das, 28
  accusative of, 94
dass, object clauses introduced by, 165
dates, 202
dative case, 218–222, 223, 224
  with adjectives, 224
  in idiomatic expressions, 225
  with indirect object, 218–219
  interrogative pronoun in, 220
  personal pronouns in, 221
  prepositions taking, 227, 229
  reflexive pronouns in, 282–283
  verbs taking, 223
  and word order, 223
days of the week, 46, 67
definite article
  in accusative case, 93–94
  gender of, 28
  plural forms, 29, 94
denn, 33, 54
  dann vs., 145
dependent clause(s)
  position of auxiliary verb and past
    participle in, 188
  verb position in, 138, 139
der, 28. *See also* **das**; **die**
  accusative of, 93–94
  as relative pronoun, 289
deren, 292
derselbe, dasselbe, dieselbe, 238
der-words
  in accusative case, 95
  accusative endings of adjectives
    preceded by, 100
  adjectives preceded by, 320
  dative endings of adjectives
    preceded by, 234
  genitive endings of adjectives
    preceded by, 265
  in nominative case, 72
  nominative endings of adjectives
    preceded by, 73
dessen, 292
die **Deutsche Bahn (DB),** 151
**Deutsche Demokratische Republik
  (DDR),** 214, 331–332, 342, 347
das **Deutsche Museum,** 165
Deutsche Welle, 354
die
  accusative of, 94

as feminine definite article, 28
as plural definite article, 29
dieser, dieses, diese, 72, 73, 95
diminutives, 122, 175
diphthongs, 92
direction, indicating, 32, 230, 250
direct object, 93, 290
disabilities, people with, 129
doch, 135, 166, 168
die Donau, 23
das Donauinselfest, 88
du, 5, 38
die Dufourspitze, 23
du-imperative, 136
Dunant, Henry, 119
durch, 158
dürfen
   present tense of, 124
   subjunctive of, 365

E
each other, 284
East Side Gallery (Berlin), 332, 349
ei
   as diphthong, 92
   ie vs., 27
eigentlich, 335
ein, eine, 30
   accusative of, 93–94
Einwanderer, 195–196
ein-words
   in accusative case, 96
   accusative endings of adjectives
     preceded by, 100
   adjectives preceded by, 321, 343
   dative endings of adjectives
     preceded by, 234
   genitive endings of adjectives
     preceded by, 265
   in nominative case, 75
   nominative endings of adjectives
     preceded by, 76
die Elbe, 7
Elsener, Karl, 133
e-mail addresses, 13
English
   German words used in, 16
   loan words in German, 16–17, 58
   similarities between German and, 48,
     81, 111
   verb forms in German vs., 31
der Englische Garten
   (München), 165
-ent (suffix), 175
er (pronoun), 38
-er (suffix), 160, 175, 297
es gibt, 104
Eszett (ß), 10, 11, 279
eu (diphthong), 92
euer, 96
der Euro, 88
die Europäische Union (EU), 88
"Eve" (Annett Louisan), 357

F
f, pronunciation of, 307
Fahrenheit scale, 22
Die Fälscher (film), 89
family members, 90
die Farben, 25
farewells, 4
Fasching, 213
fast food restaurants, 275
Fastnacht, 213
favorite, 86
Federal Republic of Germany. *See*
   Bundesrepublik Deutschland
   (BRD)
Federer, Roger, 8
Feiertage, 213–214
der Feldberg, 23
festivals, 213–214
der Fernbus, 151
Festspiele, 88
film, Austrian, 89
flavoring particles, 135, 168
food and drink, 58, 120, 275–276
"Frauen im 21. Jahrhundert,"
   359–361
Flüchtlinge, 196
Freiburg, 23
der Freiwilligendienst, 370–371
das Frühstück, 115–117
für, 158
furniture, 247–248
Fußball, 8, 49, 55–56
die Fußball-Weltmeisterschaft, 8
future tense, 364

G
Gastarbeiter, 195
das Gasthaus, 275–276
Geburtstagsgeschenke, 226
die Gedenkstätte Bernauer Straße,
   332–333
gegen, 158
gehen, in present-time
   subjunctive, 369
gender
   of agent nouns, 297
   and definite articles, 28
   grammatical, 38
   and noun suffixes, 175
   predicting, 175, 206, 238, 297, 353
Genf, 119
die Genfer Konvention, 119
genitive case, 262
   of interrogative pronoun **wer,** 262
   of preceded adjectives, 265
   prepositions taking, 374
   relative pronoun in, 292
   von + dative as alternative to, 265
German Democratic Republic.
   See **Deutsche Demokratische**
   Republik (DDR)
German language
   English loan words in, 16–17, 58

in North America, 182–183
   similarities with English, 48, 81, 111
Germany
   historical timeline (1918–present),
     341–342
   historical timeline
     (1949–present), 332
gern, 62
gern haben, 63
gleich, 352–353
glottal stop, 364
Glückwünsche, 226–227, 240–241
Gomringer, Eugen, 147
grading system, 37
grammatical gender, 38
greetings, 4, 18
Grimm, die Brüder, 305, 318–320, 330
grooming, 280
Gropius, Walter, 256, 257
das Grundgesetz, 360
Gutenberg, Johannes, 305
Gündisch, Karin, 330–331
das Gymnasium, 36

H
haben
   in past perfect tense, 373
   in past-time subjunctive, 373
   perfect tense of, 193
   perfect tense with, 186
   present tense of, 61
   simple past tense of, 168, 170
   subjunctive of, 365
hängen, 253, 254
der Harz, 23
die Heimat, 195
-heit (suffix), 353
hinter, 251
Hitler, Adolf, 252, 341
hobbies, 58
die Hochschule, 36
der Hochschulsport, 55
holidays, 213–214
der Holocaust, 341
Honecker, Erich, 342
house, rooms of a, 247, 248

I
ich, 38
idiomatic expressions
   animals in, 327
   body parts in, 207
   dative case in, 225
   food items in, 239
   housing/furnishing words in, 270
ie, ei vs., 27
-ig (suffix), 155
ihr, 5, 38
Ihr, 75
ihr-imperative, 135
imperatives, 134–136
in (preposition), 251, 255, 258
-in (suffix), 297

indefinite article, 30
 in accusative case, 93–94
 omission of, 72
independent clauses, verb position in, 138, 139
indirect object
 dative case with, 218–219
 in relative clauses, 290
infinitive phrases
 um, introduced by, 261
 and word order, 259–260
infinitive(s), 40–41
 with -n ending, 41
 as nouns, 238
 omission of, after modal verbs, 125
information questions
 as object clauses, 166
 verb position in, 31–32
inseparable-prefix verbs, past participle of, 198
das Internationale Rote Kreuz, 119
interrogative pronouns, 72
 in dative case, 220
 wen, 95
 wessen, 262
invitations, 226
irregular verbs, 102–104
 du-imperative with, 136
 past participle of, 188–189
 principle parts of, 334
 simple past of, 310
-ium (suffix), 175

J
ja, 33
jeder, jedes, jede, 72, 73, 95
jewelry, 157
Jugendherbergen, 152
Jugendstil, 88, 89

K
KaDeWe, 211
Kaffee und Kuchen, 226
der Kalte Krieg, 332–333, 341–342
Kantone, 118
Karneval, 213
Kärnten, 87
kein, keine, 30, 71
-keit (suffix), 353
Kennedy, John F., 342
kennen, wissen vs., 168
die Kieler Woche, 214
kitchen utensils, 276
Die Klavierspielerin (film), 89
Klubs, 55
kn (consonant cluster), 336
kommen, present-time subjunctive of, 369
Kommunikationstechnologien, 305–306
konkrete Poesie, 147
können
 present tense of, 122–123
 subjunctive of, 365

Krefeld, 182
Kristallnacht, 341

L
l, pronunciation of, 185
der Lebenslauf, 380–382
legen, 253
Lehnwörter, 57
-lein (suffix), 175
Leipzig, 176
letters, addressing of, 14
lieber, 63
Lieblings-, 86
Liechtenstein, 23
liegen, 254
likes, expressing, 62, 63
Linz, 23
literature, Austrian, 89
-los (suffix), 379–380
Louisan, Annett, 357
die Luftbrücke, 341
die Lüneburger Heide, 23
Luther, Martin, 305, 310–311

M
mal, 135, 166, 168
man, 116
der Mauerweg, 354–355
meals, 120
die Mensa, 36
Menschen mit Migrationshintergrund, 196
-ment (suffix), 175
Merkel, Angela, 7, 359–360
Meyer-Schurz, Margarethe, 183
die Migration, 195–196
mit, 227
das Mitbringsel, 226
die Mitfahrzentrale, 151
das Mittagessen, 120
Mittelland, 23
mixed verbs
 past participle of, 199
 principle parts of, 334
 simple past of, 313
möchte, 125
modal verbs (modals), 122–125
 meaning and position of, 122
 omission of infinitive after, 125
 position of nicht in sentences with, 125–126
 position of separable-prefix verbs with, 128
 simple past tense of, 168, 170
Module, 37
mögen
 möchte vs., 125
 present tense of, 124
 subjunctive of, 365
money, 316
months, 46
die Mosel, 23
Mozart, Wolfgang Amadeus, 98–99
die Mülltrennung, 288

München, 164–165
music, Austrian, 88
müssen
 present tense of, 122–123
 subjunctive of, 365

N
nach, 227
 zu vs., 230
nachhaltig, 287–288
die Nachhaltigkeit, 246
nachmittags, 66, 67
nachts, 66
narrative past. See simple past tense
nationalities, 26
neben, 251
nein, 33
nicht, position of, 34
 and direct object, 102
 in perfect tense, 188
 in sentences with modals, 125–126
 with separable-prefix verbs, 129
nicht . . . sondern, 138
n-nouns, 321
nominative case, 70
 adjective endings in, 73, 76, 77
 der-words in, 72
 ein-words in, 75
die Nordsee, 24
North America, German language in, 182–183
noun(s)
 adjective in comparative before a, 163
 adjective in superlative before a, 163
 agent, 297
 compound, 270
 n-, 321
 predicting gender of, 175, 206, 238, 297, 353
numbers
 cardinal, 12
 ordinal, 201

O
object clauses
 dass, introduced by, 165
 information questions as, 166
 yes/no questions as, 166
oder, 33
ohne, 158
Oktoberfest, 165, 214
-or (suffix), 175
ordinal numbers, 201
Ostern, 214
Österreich, 87–89
die Ostsee, 15, 24
Özoğuz, Aydan, 7

P
parties, 226
passive voice, 337–339
past participle
 as adjective, 339

in dependent clause, 188
of inseparable-prefix verbs, 198
of irregular verbs, 188–189
of mixed verbs, 199
position of, in perfect tense, 187, 188
of regular verbs, 186
of separable-prefix verbs, 197
past perfect tense, 373
past-time subjunctive
construction of, 372
haben and **sein** in, 373
perfect tense, 186–189. *See also* past
participle
formation of, 186
with **haben**, 186
position of **nicht** in, 188
of **sein** and **haben**, 193
sein as auxiliary in, 192
word order in, 187, 188
personal pronouns, 38
in accusative case, 156
in dative case, 221
pf (consonant cluster), 336
phone numbers, 13
place, word order with expressions
of, 35
plural forms
of definite articles and nouns, 29, 94
of personal pronouns, 38
polite questions, subjunctive in, 369
polite requests, subjunctive in, 368
possession, indicating, 262, 265
possessive adjectives
in accusative case, 96
in nominative case, 75
die Postleitzahl, 14
predicate, 70
preferences, expressing, 63
prefixes, separable. *See* separable-
prefix verbs
preposition(s)
accusative, 158
dative, 227, 229
preposition(s) (*continued*)
genitive, 374
relative pronoun as object of,
318–319
two-way, 251, 255, 258
verb-preposition combinations,
343–344
present tense, 33, 40–41
to express future time, 42
verbs with stem-vowel changes in,
102–104
present-time subjunctive, 364–369
construction of, 365–366
kommen and **gehen** in, 369
rom polite questions, 369
rom wishes and polite requests, 368
würde + infinitive, 367
Promi-Profile, 49–50
pronouns. *See also* personal pronouns
interrogative, 72, 95, 220

reflexive, 279–283, 284
relative, 288–290
pronunciation, 10–11
of alphabet, 9
of **ch**, 155
of **f, v,** and **w,** 307
of **-ig,** 155
of **l,** 185
of long vs. short vowels, 59–60
of **pf** and **kn,** 336
of **r,** 218
of **st** and **sp,** 249
of umlauted vowels, 121
of voiced and voiceless **s,** 278–279
of **z,** 11, 279

Q
questions
object clauses, information questions
as, 166
subjunctive in polite, 369
verb position in information
questions, 31–32
wo-compounds in, 346
question words, 32

R
r, pronunciation of, 218
Ramadan, 213
Recyceln, 287–288
reflexive pronouns, 279–283
in accusative case, 280
in dative case, 282–283
to express *each other,* 284
reflexive verbs, 285
Regensburg, 23
regular verbs
past particple of, 186
simple past of, 308
das Reichstagsgebäude, 341, 343
relative clauses, 288–290
relative pronoun(s), 288–290
in genitive case, 292
as object of preposition, 318–319
renewable energy, 7
resolutions, 339
résumé, 380–382
der Rhein, 23, 24
Roebling, John, 183
rooms of a house, 247, 248

S
s, voiced vs. voiceless, 278–279
die Sächsische Schweiz, 7
Salzburg, 98
Saxons, 48
Schnellrestaurants, 275
der Schwarzwald, 23
die Schweiz, 118–119
die Schweizer Alpen, 118
**die Schweizerische
Eidgenossenschaft,** 118
Schwyzerdütsch, 8
sein

as auxiliary verb in perfect tense, 192
in past perfect tense, 373
in past-time subjunctive, 373
perfect tense of, 193
present tense, 39
Sie-imperative form of, 134
simple past tense of, 168–169
subjunctive of, 365
seit, 227, 233
das Semester, 37
Semesterticket, 3, 36
separable-prefix verbs, 126–129
meaning of, 126–127
past participle of, 197
position of, with modals, 128
position of **nicht** with, 129
position of prefix in, 127
simple past of, 312
verb-noun and verb-verb
combinations behaving like, 130
sich, 280
sie, 38
Sie, 5, 38, 75
Sie-imperative, 134
silverware, 276
Silvester, 213
simple past tense, 308, 310–313
of **haben,** 168, 170
of irregular verbs, 310
of mixed verbs, 313
of modals, 168, 170
of regular verbs, 308
of **sein,** 168–169
of separable-prefix verbs, 312
social media, 69–70
sollen
present tense of, 124
subjunctive of, 365
sondern, 138
**Sozialdemokratische Partei
Deutschlands (SPD),** 7
soziale Medien, 69
soziale Netzwerke, 69
sp (consonant cluster), 249
sports, 55–56
st (consonant cluster), 249
-st (suffix), 162
statements, verb position in, 33
statt, 374
stehen, 254
Steiermark, 7, 87, 149
stellen, 253
Strauss, Levi, 183
das Studentenwerk, 36
das Studentenwohnheim, 245
student housing, 245
das Studienbuch, 37
subject, grammatical, 70
subject completion, 77
subjunctive
past-time, 372, 373
in polite questions, 369
present-time, 364–369

in wishes and polite requests, 368
subordinating conjunctions, 138, 165, 167
Südtirol, 164
suffixes, 175. *See also specific suffixes, e.g.:* **-keit**
superlative, 162–163
Swiss Confederation. *See* **die Schweizerische Eidgenossenschaft**
Switzerland, 118–119

T
der Tag der Arbeit, 214
der Tag der deutschen Einheit, 214
die Technomusik, 8
der Thüringer Wald, 23
time, telling, 58, 63–65, 66, 67
time expressions
 accusative case in, 97
 with present tense, 42
 referring to parts of the day, 66, 67
 two-case prepositions in, 258
 wann, als, and **wenn,** 314
 word order with, 35
time/manner/place, 228
Tirol, 88
to, 230, 255
toasts, 237
transportation, 90
travel, affordable, 151–152
der Todesstreifen, 332–333, 349
trotz, 374
24-hour clock, 65

U
über, 251
überhaupt, 335
um, 158
 infinitive phrases introduced by, 261
-um (suffix), 175
der Umlaut, 10, 11, 121
der Umweltschutz, 298–299
und, 33
-ung (suffix), 206
die Universität, 36
die Universitätsstadt, 245
universities, 3, 36, 37, 55, 245
unpreceded adjectives, 322
unter, 251
-ur (suffix), 175

V
v, pronunciation of, 11, 307
Vaduz, 23
verb(s). *See also specific headings, e.g.:* modal verbs; present tense

imperative form of, 134–136
infinitive of, 40–41
inseparable-prefix, 198
irregular, 102–104
mixed, 199
position of, in independent and dependent clauses, 138, 139
position of, in information questions, 31–32
position of, in statements, 33
principle parts of, 334
reflexive, 285
separable-prefix, 126–129, 197
with stem-vowel changes in present tense, 102–104
taking dative case, 223
verb-preposition combinations, 343–344
Vereine, 55
Verfassungen, 359–360
Victorinox (Firma), 132–133
von, 227
 aus vs., 231
 + dative (instead of genitive), 265
vor, 251, 258
vormittags, 66
die Vorwahl, 13
vowels
 pronunciation of, 59–60, 121
 umlauted, 10, 121

W
w, pronunciation of, 11, 307
während, 374
wann, 32, 258, 314
die Wartburg, 303, 309
warum, 32
was, as interrogative pronoun, 31–32, 72
Web addresses, 13w
wegen, 374
Weihnachten, 213
weil, 140
Das weiße Band (film), 89
welcher, welches, welche, 72, 73, 95
die Weltzeituhr (Berlin), 330, 335
wen, 95
die Wende, 330
wenn, 314
wer, 32, 72
werden
 in future tense, 364
 as mixed verb, 313
 in passive voice, 337–339
 subjunctive of, 365

wessen, 262, 292
die Wetterkarte, 21, 34
when, expressing, 314
wie, 31–32
Wien, 23, 87
wie viel?, wie viele?, 32
Windenergie, 7
wir, 38
das Wirtschaftswunder, 195
wishes, subjunctive in, 368
wissen
 conjugation of, 168
 kennen vs., 168
 subjunctive of, 365
wo, 32, 230, 250
wo-compounds, 346
woher, 32, 230
wohin, 32, 230, 250
die Wohngemeinschaft, 245
Wolfsburg, 8
wollen
 present tense of, 122–123
 subjunctive of, 365
women in the 21st century, 359–361
word order
 expressions of time and place, 35
 independent and dependent clauses, 138, 139
 with infinitive phrases, 259–260
 with **nicht,** 34, 102, 125–126, 129
 object clauses, 165–167, 166–168
 objects, sequence of, 223
 separable-prefix verbs, 127, 128
 of subject, 70
 time/manner/place, 228
würde + infinitive, 367

Y
yes/no questions
 as object clauses, 167
 verb position in, 31
you, 5
youth hostels, 152

Z
z, pronunciation of, 11, 279
zu, 227
 expressing congratulations with, 237
 with infinitive phrases, 259–260
 nach vs., 230
das Zuhause, 266, 271
Zürich, 119
zwischen 51, 258

Credits

Text Credits

p. 146: Gomringer, Eugen. Worte sind Schatten: Die Konstellationen 1951–1968. Edited by Helmut Heißenbüttel, Rowohlt Verlag GmbH, 1969, **pp. 27–75.** Print.

pp. 208–209: Alshater, Firas. Ich komm auf Deutschland zu. Ein Syrer über seine neue Heimat © 2016 Ullstein Buchverlage GmbH, Berlin

pp. 316–317: Grimm, Jacob and Grimm, Wilhelm. Kinder- und Hausmärchen, große Ausgabe, Band 2. Manesse-Verlag. Munich. 1857. Print.

pp. 328–239: Gündisch, Karin. Das Paradies liegt in Amerika. Eine Auswanderergeschichte. Weinheim, Verlagsgruppe Beltz Julius Beltz GmbH & Co. KG. 2000. Print.

p. 357: Annette Louisan. "Eve." Unausgesprochen, 2005. Peer Music.

Photo Credits

Cover: sborisov/123RF; **p. i:** michaeljung/Shutterstock; **p. i:** Duolingo; **p. ii:** Duolingo; **p. 2:** EQRoy/Shutterstock; **p. 3:** Andrew Dexter; **p. 4,** Beth A.V. Lewis; **p. 7, T:** honza28683/Shutterstock; **p. 7, M:** Ullstein Bild/Getty Images; **p. 7, B:** Konstantin Kalishko/123RF; **p. 8, T:** Cornelius Partsch; **p. 8, B:** Lasse Hendriks/Shutterstock; **p. 8, TM:** Thomas Quack/Shutterstock; **p. 8, BM:** Meng Yongmin/Xinhua/Alamy Live News; **p. 10:** Margaret Gonglewski; **p. 11:** Cornelius Partsch; **p. 14, T:** Margaret Gonglewski; **p. 14, B:** Cornelius Partsch; **p. 15:** msgrafixx/Shutterstock; **p. 16, B:** Widmaier, Fritz and Rosemarie; **p. 17, TL:** Margaret Gonglewski; **p. 17, TR:** Margaret Gonglewski; **p. 17, B:** Bess Gonglewski; **p. 17, M:** Margaret Gonglewski; **p. 18:** Beth A.V. Lewis; **p. 19, T:** Beth A.V. Lewis; **p. 19, B:** Beth A.V. Lewis; **p. 20:** Aylin Saglam/Alamy; **p. 23, L:** Kanuman/Shutterstock; **p. 23, BR:** Vichaya Kiatying-Angsulee/123RF; **p. 23, TR:** LaMiaFotografia/Shutterstock; **p. 24, L:** Julia Harris; **p. 24, R:** Julia Harris; **p. 25:** Margaret Gonglewski; **p. 26, L:** Widmaier, Fritz and Rosemarie; **p. 27, TL:** Cornelius Partsch; **p. 27, TR:** Beth A.V. Lewis; **p. 27, BL:** Beth A. V. Lewis; **p. 27, BR:** Beth A. V. Lewis; **p. 30:** Widmaier, Fritz and Rosemarie; **p. 31:** Cornelius Partsch; **p. 33:** Alice Gonglewski; **p. 36:** Andrew Dexter; **p. 37:** Margaret Gonglewski; **p. 38:** Widmaier, Fritz and Rosemarie; **p. 39, T:** Margaret Gonglewski; **p. 39, B:** Beth A.V. Lewis; **p. 42:** Cornelius Partsch; **p. 44:** Widmaier, Fritz and Rosemarie; **p. 45:** Margaret Gonglewski; **p. 46:** Cornelius Partsch; **p. 47:** Widmaier, Fritz and Rosemarie; **p. 48, TL:** Widmaier, Fritz and Rosemarie; **p. 48, TML:** Widmaier, Fritz and Rosemarie; **p. 48, TMR:** Widmaier, Fritz and Rosemarie; **p. 48, BL:** Widmaier, Fritz and Rosemarie; **p. 48, BML:** Widmaier, Fritz and Rosemarie; **p. 48, BMR:** Widmaier, Fritz and Rosemarie; **p. 48, BR:** Widmaier, Fritz and Rosemarie; **p. 49, T:** Sydney Alford/Alamy Stock Photo; **p. 49, B:** Xinhua/Alamy Stock Photo; **p. 50, T:** Everett Collection Inc/Alamy Stock Photo; **p. 50, B:** Tribune Content Agency LLC/Alamy Stock Photo; **p. 52:** Silvia Weko; **p. 55:** Courtesy König Ludwig Lauf; **p. 56:** German National Tourist Board; **p. 60, B:** Widmaier, Fritz and Rosemarie; **p. 60, T:** Cornelius Partsch; **p. 62:** Jrgen Schaetzke/123RF; **p. 66:** Widmaier, Fritz and Rosemarie; **p. 67, BL:** Cornelius Partsch; **p. 67, BR:** Cornelius Partsch; **p. 69:** Cornelius Partsch; **p. 70:** William Perugini/Shutterstock; **p. 72:** Widmaier, Fritz and Rosemarie; **p. 73, L:** Widmaier, Fritz and Rosemarie; **p. 73, R:** Cornelius Partsch; **p. 74, TL:** Beth A. V. Lewis; **p. 74, TR:** Beth A. V. Lewis; **p. 74, B:** Beth A.V. Lewis; **p. 77:** Widmaier, Fritz and Rosemarie; **p. 78, T:** Ulrich Mueller/Shutterstock; **p. 80:** Margaret Gonglewski; **p. 81, L:** Beth A. V. Lewis; **p. 81, R:** Beth A. V. Lewis; **p. 82:** Beth A. V. Lewis; **p. 84:** Austrian National Tourist Board; **p. 85, T:** Fingerhut/Shutterstock; **p. 85, B:** Thomas Quack/Shutterstock; **p. 86:** Bess Gonglewski; **p. 88, B:** Widmaier, Fritz and Rosemarie; **p. 88, T:** Cornelius Partsch; **p. 88, M:** Kanuman/Shutterstock; **p. 89, T:** Cornelius Partsch;

Rich Media Credits

Chapter 1: Courtesy Pittman Music

Chapter 2: mitja mithans/Getty Images

Chapter 3: Francesco Biondi/Getty Images

Chapter 4: softpiano/Getty Images

Chapter 5: softpiano/Getty Images

Chapter 6: Alandra/Getty Images

Chapter 7: Deep Blue Music/Getty Images

Chapter 8: The Sarasa Ensemble/Getty Images

Chapter 9: Shayan Mirza/Getty Images

Chapter 10: Fat Sams/Getty Images

Chapter 11: Oleg Gorbunov/Getty Images; "Zeitreise per Fahrrad" Deutsche Welle, 2 September 2015, http://p.dw.com/p/1GQME

Chapter 12: Oleg Gorbunov/Getty Images